The Mammoth Book of

Famous Trials

The Mammoth Book of

Famous Trials

Edited by
Roger Wilkes

CARROLL & GRAF PUBLISHERS
New York

Carroll & Graf Publishers
An imprint of Avalon Publishing Group, Inc.
245 W. 17th Street
11 th Floor
New York
NY 10011-5300
www.carrollandgraf.com

AVALON
publishing group incorporated

First published in the UK by Robinson,
an imprint of Constable & Robinson Ltd 2006

First Carroll & Graf edition 2006

ISBN 13-978-0-78671-725-5
ISBN-10-0-7867-1725-4

Printed and bound in the EU

CONTENTS

INTRODUCTION

Perhaps no drama seizes and rivets our interest more than a spectacular trial. It is the morality tale of our modern age, a showcase for every human emotion offering a grandstand view of human nature in the raw. A murder trial illuminates life and death with a merciless beam. For if crime is a snapshot of its time, the trial presents a forensic display of human nature tested to destruction – by the morals of an era, greed, jealousy, passions natural and perverse, even love. This book houses a collection of trials that often speak to history: such as the Edwardian case of Dr Crippen, henpecked and cuckolded in an age when divorce meant disgrace, and (from between the wars) that of Alma Rattenbury and George Stoner, two mismatched lovers from an era when love seldom if ever breached the class divide. But as we will see, the twentieth century also furnished trials of a deeper and darker dye, scenes from the theatre of the aberrant in which old-time killers without conscience such as George Joseph Smith with his wretched Brides in the Bath take centre stage with modern-day monsters like Charles Manson, driven by evil.

A classic trial is more than just a contrapuntal account of a crime. It is a psychological contest, a battle of wits fought for the highest stakes. Where there is doubt in a case – and in many of the cases that follow, there was indeed doubt – the adversarial nature of our judicial system often required a jury to decide whether a man should live or die. So it was, for example, in the case of Bruno Richard Hauptmann, tried in America in 1936 for the kidnap and murder of the Lindbergh baby. Who can read an account of Hauptmann on the witness-stand and be sure that he was not unjustly railroaded to his death? The same adversarial system demands that jurors read truth or falsehood in a face, observe mannerisms and judge demeanour as well as "to hearken to the evidence", and we can be certain that there were times when they got it wrong. In another case from the thirties featured here, this time in England, we can hear the inner voice of Wallace, the Liverpool insurance agent, whose ironclad Stoic bearing in the face of a capital charge was interpreted as callous indifference to his wife's brutal murder and reckoned against him as surely as any motive, real or imagined, might have been. In many cases – including the infamous Moors Murders, for example, or the killing of two-year-old James Bulger – the trial puts the killers firmly in their social context by fleshing out the unexpected details of their lives. So we learn, from Pamela Hansford Johnson's finely drawn vignette, that Myra Hindley was a lapsed Catholic who stuffed a left-luggage ticket – later a crucial piece of evidence – down the spine of the prayer-book given to mark her first Holy Communion. And, from the poet's pen of Blake Morrison, we catch a glimpse of the world of the truant ten-year-olds turned killers, their feral roaming miles from home unfettered by adult influence, the fractured families to which they returned, the inadequate parenting. Some of these trials are showcases for great forensic minds and feats of detection. They are also arenas in which advocates can perform so brilliantly they become the stuff of legend. Although my focus has been the twentieth century, I have included, from the Victorian sunset years, the catastrophic libel action brought against the Marquess of Queensberry by Oscar Wilde, in which Queensberry's counsel Edward Carson soared to stardom. In his deadly cross-examination, Carson cast Wilde as the defendant rather than the plaintiff and encapsulated the sexual restraint of his time by cross-questioning his quarry about a parade of rent boys without ever mentioning sex. Carson didn't need to: inference alone was damning enough.

There has always been an appetite for accounts of court cases. Trial literature is extensive – almost exhaustive – beginning with records of Old Bailey trials stretching back to 1678, through to the pamphlets sold at public hangings. Then came the penny dreadfuls of the Victorian era – cheap, lurid and often inaccurate accounts of crimes and criminals – and eventually, in our own time, the crime masterpieces of distinguished writers.

In the collection that follows I have sought to uncover writing of real power and insight, miniature masterpieces of observation on the human condition under stress. Masters of trial reportage can convey these elements with great skill, at the same time weaving around the inevitable *longueurs* of procedure that can and do afflict so many court cases. Many trials for murder lurch between the sickening and the somnambulant. "How can anybody be a journalist?" wailed the nauseated Nancy Mitford after filing 1,200 words to *Picture Post* on the sensational poisoning trial of Marie Besnard in 1950s France; just days into the gruesome Charles Manson trial at the end of the 1960s, one British correspondent found himself assailed by the narcotic torpor of boredom laced with dread. "It has moments of buffoonery, long periods of incompetence, episodes of sheer horror," he reported. "Sometimes it seems to be a circus."

Connoisseurs of true crime writing will be familiar with Britain's great scarlet monument to the nation's famous trials. Tapping into the traditional British appetite for murder, the Edinburgh publishing firm of William Hodge and Co. launched its unsurpassed *Notable British Trials* series in 1905. Plainly bound in cloth the colour of caked blood, and issued with flimsy paper jackets, each volume in the series contains the testimony of witnesses (a full transcript where available, a summary where it is not, as in some of the earliest cases), photographs of exhibits and the principal protagonists, the speeches of counsel, the judge's summing-up, and the jury's verdict. In each case, the crowning glory is the introduction, a lengthy exposition of the case, the background to the crime, a description of how the police or the authorities prosecuted the charge against the prisoner at the bar, and an account of the trial itself, its ebb and flow, its forensic triumphs and disasters. The series, which runs to 83 volumes appearing in the course of half a century, includes a smattering of actions for libel, mutiny and fraud, but most are concerned with homicide, and range across almost every great British murder case of the past 300 years. It is the great treasure-house of murder lore. Devotees scour second-hand bookshops and, more recently, the internet, for rare copies; as the owner of one of the few complete sets of *Notable*

British Trials in private hands, I consider myself a fully paid-up crackpot of crime. The veteran American murder-fancier Alexander Woollcott recognized the tendency many years ago when the series was in full spate, counting himself among the addicts of poison and throat-cutting, as enthralled as other madmen who collect coins, autographs or stamps. Another American, the crime writer Anthony Boucher, added his condolences. "Your monkey has swollen to a gorilla," he sighed, "and I have no further advice for you."[1] From the series I have chosen F(ryn) Tennyson Jesse's prelude to the case of Alma Rattenbury and her young lover George Stoner, probably the best single essay in the entire NBT canon. Combining a confident literary style with a firm grasp of what motivates people caught up in the messy business of murder, Miss Jesse's acute insights resulted in what the crime historian Jonathan Goodman regards as "a small masterpiece, perfectly conceived and composed, which engages the intellect and, at the end, touches the heart."[2] Watching the case unfold at the Old Bailey day by day, she recognized that Alma Rattenbury was a modern woman born out of her time. This trial too exposed the repressed sexuality of her age, when the judge, in tune with the morals and manners of inter-war bourgeois Britain, advised the jury that because Alma had committed adultery, they could only feel disgust for her. He was echoing the view of prosecuting counsel who suggested that regular sex between an older woman and a boy of eighteen would inevitably ruin the lad's health.

Sex has always drawn the British reading public to reports of court proceedings – and not just of criminal trials. When the Victorians established the Divorce Court in 1857, evidence in divorce cases was given in public, in open court, and reported, often at length. Half a century later, one sensational divorce generated unprecedented press coverage. Sex sold, but it also troubled the conscience of editors even of the tabloid press where one confessed shame at ventilating this "catalogue of evil passions and revolting vices".[3]

1 In *The Quality of Murder* (E. P. Dutton & Co., Inc., New York, 1962)
2 *Trials Series: Some Notable, Some Not* by Jonathan Goodman in *Medicine, Science, and the Law*, the official journal of the British Academy of Forensic Sciences, vol 13 no 1, January 1973 (Bristol: John Wright & Sons Ltd.)
3 Quoted by Thomas Boyle in *Black Swine in the Sewers of Hampstead* (Hodder and Stoughton, London 1990)

The question of what was appropriate for public consumption divided the popular press from the broadsheets until the 1960s. Before that, among the quality press, only the *Daily Telegraph* reserved its page 3 for any particularly juicy, salacious or scandalous trial and invariably reported it at length. By and large the big, broadsheet papers featured legal proceedings only in terms of questions of law. Back in 1952 for example, when the notorious child-killer John Straffen escaped from Broadmoor to kill again, papers including the *Daily Mail* and *Daily Express* (both at that time mid-market broadsheets) gave the case low-key treatment; domestic politics and even foreign affairs elbowed the Straffen story off the front page and on to the inside. Detailed press coverage of trials was mainly confined to the downmarket Sunday papers. The BBC, which had traditionally considered itself to be above crime and trials reportage, was forced to reconsider when commercial television started in 1955, but held out until the early 1960s before conceding that reports of criminal cases merited a place in its bulletins. In August 1961, BBC Television assigned a reporter to a murder case for the first time. This was the so-called A6 murder, for which James Hanratty was hanged the following year. The BBC justified its decision on the basis of the unprecedented hue and cry following the murder and the practical help it could give the police in the massive hunt for the man who had shot dead Michael Gregsten and raped, shot and paralysed his girlfriend Valerie Storie.

When crimes in which sex is a motive come to court there are fine judgments to make about how much should be reported and how much suppressed. Compared with the newspaper readers of the Victorian era, the modern mass media has brought with it a sense of public responsibility and a certain amount of self-censorship. Its advent can be seen as the nineteenth century drew to a close and the evidence in the trials of Oscar Wilde was judged so "extremely repulsive" by one editor that he banned the case from his pages altogether, announcing the fact in his contents bills. At some point thereafter the official records of the proceedings mysteriously disappeared, considered lost to posterity. But in 2000, an anonymous donor brought a transcript of Wilde's first trial to the British Library, where it was authenticated. It was an astonishing find. It provided the first complete, verbatim record of what occurred at the Old Bailey more than a century earlier.

In general the daily papers down played notorious crimes and coverage of criminal trials until the arrival of Rupert Murdoch's tabloid *Sun* in the late Sixties when everything changed. Under new ownership the *Sun* revived its flagging circulation by running lengthy, rehashed accounts of the Moors Murders case. The trial of Ian Brady and Myra Hindley in 1966 had attracted extensive coverage at the time, but its treatment (given the harrowing nature of the evidence) had been rather restrained. Now the *Sun* revisited the case with bells clanging and whistles blowing, signalling a new wave of crime coverage with almost no holds barred. Yet suspicions linger that some details in controversial cases are never released by the police, and that sometimes certain facts are glossed over if they are judged hurtful to the bereaved and irrelevant to the prosecution. As a journalist then working for the BBC, I learned that the prosecution in the James Bulger case had decided not to pursue in court the question of whether the crime had been sexually motivated, on the grounds that it would not affect the outcome. Forty years on, suspicion remains that the reported horrors of the Moors Murders, hideous as they were, did not amount to the full story as known to senior officers on the case.

As the *Sun* ushered crime and court reporting into every news outlet, the Sixties also saw another significant development in crime reportage, when the American writer Truman Capote published *In Cold Blood*, an account of a true-life crime that read like a novel. Giving crime a literary narrative was revolutionary. For Capote the stuff of horror was worthy of transformation into art. There was outrage that the perpetrators (a pair of "two-bit crooks" in the view of the investigating detective) had been dignified (some said glorified) by the power of Capote's prose when theirs was such a vicious, unprovoked and sordid crime. Many who snubbed the book also ignored the trial. Capote, in my extract, quotes the wife of one wealthy rancher, speaking for the local bourgeoisie. "It doesn't do," she explained, "to seem curious about that sort of thing." And yet Capote had opened up a new frontier by reconstructing the lives of the killers as meticulously as he had those of their victims, applying his human sympathies and formidable powers of description to a pair of antisocial misfits. It heralded a new age of psychological analysis in which writers (and by extension the public) sought to understand the perpetrators of even the most unfathomable evil, as though by understanding the criminal mind, wicked deeds could somehow be prevented. After Capote came a spate of books on true crime and crime history, many of which framed a trial as centrepiece, and I have chosen the stories that follow from this rich seam of material, as well as from earlier twentieth century writings by such practitioners as Damon Runyon, Edgar Lustgarten and the American-born Tom Cullen. I have discovered that women writers rank among the most acute observers of the courtroom scene, and there are contributions not just from criminologists such as Tennyson Jesse but also from the novelist and critic Rebecca West, whose memorable account of the trial of William Joyce (Lord Haw-Haw) first appeared in the *New Yorker* magazine ahead of the "minute shred of ceremony" she witnessed on a January morning in 1946 when a notice was pinned up at the gate of Wandsworth Prison stating that Joyce had been hanged. I am also delighted to include part of a trial narrative by another great woman novelist, Sybille Bedford, who, covering the case of Dr John Bodkin Adams in 1957, discovered an extraordinary talent for recording the proceedings from the point of view of an "alert spectator", a talent she would use again at the Lady Chatterley trial in 1960 and again in Dallas in 1964 when Jack Ruby was charged with the murder of Lee Harvey Oswald.

Among other first-rate writers to follow in Capote's footsteps is Brian Masters, whose unsparing study of Dennis Nilsen revealed a loner who killed young men for company. Many quality authors who are drawn to crime and its motives move easily between books, magazines and newspapers. Indeed, in the last few years, as newspapers have grown ever fatter, and added supplement to news review to colour section, coverage and analysis of celebrated trials has become so exhaustive that the market for true crime books has all but dried up. I include from Brian Masters his essay on the trial of O. J. Simpson in Los Angeles, in which he denounces the modern media and its pernicious influence on court proceedings. His analysis of how the judicial process is endlessly repackaged by the media for the entertainment of a global audience is typical of some of the best forensic reporting of our times.

For those of us who remain fascinated by crime and criminals, the best trial reporting carries us into court and brings us face to face with the often mundane perpetrators of extraordinary evils. Witness A. N. Wilson's musings on the deeds of Rosemary West, the Gloucester housewife and prostitute whose nondescript semi became a charnel house during a killing spree that spanned two decades and possibly longer. Through the pen of such writers we are invited to look into the eyes of the accused, to weigh their words, to judge for ourselves their innocence or guilt. Just like a real jury, we are obliged to muster all our experience of life, our powers of observation and deduction, to reach our own private verdicts. Sometimes the experience teaches us things about ourselves and our fellow men that we never knew before.

It's time for my collected cases to begin.

Silence in court!

All rise!

DR JOHN BODKIN ADAMS

(Old Bailey, 1957)

Sybille Bedford

The case of Dr John Bodkin Adams ranks among the most fascinating and controversial in modern legal history. The fate of an owlish general practitioner accused of murder in an English seaside town riveted international attention, so much so that the trial judge, Mr Justice Devlin, believed that press coverage might prejudice the outcome. The case raised crucial issues for the legal world about the admissibility of similar killings to prove guilty intent, and for the medical world through the court's efforts to define the boundary between what Dr Adams described as "easing the passing" and murder. His trial lasted longer than any previously heard at the Old Bailey. It revealed a curious provincial tale of an unattractive GP ("fat, ugly hands") rumoured to have killed off dozens of rich old ladies to benefit from their generous legacies. Adams dismissed local gossip as "the laughter of fools, the crackling of thorns under the pot." At his trial, he was said to have been the beneficiary in 132 wills, and to have amassed £45,000 in cash and trinkets, plus his Rolls-Royces. The judge believed Adams "thought lightly of the law", and one of his old partners likened Adams to Toad of Toad Hall, a disaster-prone fantasist incapable of believing that anything he thought reasonable might possibly be unlawful. In the wake of the trial, some blamed the worldwide publicity on Adams's fame as a sharpshooter (he was a crack shot); others believed it was really an attack on certain groups,

*the Masons, the Irish or homosexuals (Adams certainly belonged to at
least two of those minorities). Recounted by the novelist Sybille
Bedford (b. 1911), Bodkin Adams's trial becomes a drama, with a
beginning, middle and end, variations in pace and tone, different
voices asserting and contradicting. Born in Berlin of partly Jewish
descent, Sybille Bedford made her name as a writer in the 1950s, when
Evelyn Waugh enthusiastically reviewed her first novel. Sitting in
court day after day, she discovered that she was fascinated by the
panoply of justice, and could describe its complexities in pared-down
prose, taking the viewpoint of an "alert spectator". She sieved out any
gossip and rumour, and her understated reporter's style manages to
capture the trial's ebb and flow like a successful snapshot. In the 1960s,
Sybille Bedford covered the Lady Chatterley trial and that of Jack
Ruby for the murder of Lee Harvey Oswald in Dallas. This is her
beautifully observed account of the opening day of the Bodkin Adams
trial.*

> "The trial began at the Central
> Criminal Court yesterday. . . ."
> *The Times*

The Judge came on swiftly. Out of the side-door, an ermined
puppet progressing weightless along the bench, head held at an
angle, an arm swinging, the other crooked under cloth and gloves,
trailing a wake of subtlety, of secret powers, age: an Elizabethan
shadow gliding across the arras.

The high-backed chair has been pulled, helped forward, the
figure is seated, has bowed, and the hundred or so people who had
gathered themselves at split notice to their feet rustle and subside
into apportioned place. And now the prisoner, the accused himself
is here – how had he come, how had one missed the instant of that
other clockwork entry? – standing in the front of the dock,
spherical, adipose, upholstered in blue serge, red-faced, bald,
facing the Judge, facing this day. And already the clerk, risen
from below the Judge's seat, is addressing him by full name.

There cannot be a man or woman in this court who has not heard
it before

". . . You are charged with the murder . . ."

And that, too, is expected. It is what all is set for – nobody, today, is here by accident – yet, as they fall, the words in the colourless clerical voice consummate exposure.

"Do you plead Guilty or Not Guilty?"

There is the kind of pause that comes before a clock strikes, a nearly audible gathering of momentum, then, looking at the Judge who has not moved his eyes,

"I am not guilty, my Lord."

It did not come out loudly but it was heard, and it came out with a certain firmness and a certain dignity, and also possibly with a certain stubbornness, and it was said in a private, faintly non-conformist voice. It was also said in the greatest number of words anyone could manage to put into a plea of Not Guilty. A loquacious man, then, under evident pressure to make himself heard; and how many among those present who do not simply hope that the burden of his plea may be true.

Now what sounds like, but may not quite be, William Make-peace Leader, John Christian Henderson, James Frederick Wright, floats across the court. Men arise from back benches, scurry or shuffle into sight, get themselves into the jury box: two rows, one above the other, of six seated figures cheek by jowl and not a pin to drop between them. Two women are found to be there, side by side in the upper tier. One is in a red coat and hat, the other has jet black hair and a cast of features suggestive of having been reared perhaps under another law. Everybody in this box is, or appears to be, respectable, middle-aged.

The prisoner is still standing. His right to object to any member of his jury has been recited to him by the clerk and he has turned his large, blank, sagging face – a face designed to be jovial – to the jury-box and stares at them with round, sad, solemn eyes. The jurors, one by one, are reading out the oath. It is an old form of words, and it is not couched in everyday syntax. Some approach the printed text with circumspection, some rush it, most come several mild croppers, inexorably corrected – each time – by the usher.

All of this has taken no time at all. A routine dispatched without irrelevancy or hitch between clerk and usher in the well of the court like a practised sheep-herding, while bench and bar stayed aloof. Now counsel for the Crown is on his feet.

Outside in the street, the Old Bailey is sustaining a siege this morning. Police vans and press vans, cameras and cameramen, detective sergeants and C.I.D.s and hangers-on, comings and

goings in closed limousines, young men in bowler hats bent double
under the weight of papers nudging their way through the crowd, a
line of special constables at every door and thirty extra quarts of
milk left for the cafeteria. Here, inside the court, there is more than
silence, there is quiet.

A male voice droning: "May it please your Lordship –" and the
case is opened.

A trial is supposed to start from scratch, *ab ovo*. A tale is unfolded,
step by step, link by link. Nothing is left unturned and nothing is
taken for granted. The members of the jury listen. They hear the
tale corroborated, and they hear it denied; they hear it pulled to
pieces and they hear it put together again; they hear it puffed into
thin air and they hear it back as good as new. They hear it from the
middle, they hear it sideways and they hear it straight; they all but
hear it backward again through a fine toothcomb. *But they should
never have heard it before*. When they first walk into that court, sit
down in that box, they are like people before the curtain has gone
up. And this, one is conscious from the first, cannot be so in the
present case.

The accused, a doctor, in his fifties, is charged with the murder
of a patient six years ago. Leading counsel for the Crown is setting
out the prosecution's tale in manageable, spare, slow facts. It is the
Attorney-General in person. He is standing in his pew, sheaf of
foolscap in hand, a somewhat massive figure, addressing the jury in
a full voice. The beginning is a warning. They must try to dismiss
from their minds all they may have read or heard of this before.

"This is a very unusual case. It is not often that a charge of
murder is brought against a doctor . . ."

Above on the dais the Judge is listening. Full face and immobile,
the robed husk has taken on a measure of flesh and youth. The
black cloth and the delicate pair of gloves have been deposited. The
face is not the profile; gone is that hint of cunning. This is more
than a supremely intelligent face, it is a face marked with intellectual fineness. The Judge sits quite still, in easy absorption. Startling Mandarin hands flower from wide sleeves.

"A word about this doctor. You will hear that he is a doctor of
medicine and a bachelor of surgery, that he has a diploma in
anæsthetics, holds an appointment as anæsthetist to a hospital and
has practised anæsthetics for many years. With his qualifications
and experience, you may think perhaps it is safe to assume the

Doctor was not ignorant of the effects of drugs on human beings . . ."

It goes on in a sort of casual boom.

Now Mrs Morell was an old woman. A widow. A wealthy woman. She left £157,000. She was eighty-one years old when she died in November 1950 in her house at Eastbourne. In 1948, she had a stroke and her left side became paralysed. The Doctor was in charge. She was attended by four nurses; and these nurses will give evidence. They will say they never saw Mrs Morell in any serious pain. The Crown will also call a Harley Street authority. This medical man will tell them that he has formed the opinion that Mrs Morell was suffering from cerebral arterio-sclerosis, in ordinary language [here the Attorney-General lowers his voice a confidential shade], hardening of the arteries. They will hear that for pain to accompany such a condition is most unusual.

"You will hear of large quantities of drugs prescribed for her by the Doctor in the course of months, and supplied to her. One of the questions to be considered in this case will be: why were they given? It is one thing to give an old lady something to help her to sleep, but quite another to prescribe for her large quantities of morphia and heroin . . ."

Here come detailed figures. The listening mind is pulled up. Figures can be stumbling blocks. These are intended to sound large. They do sound large. Jotted down (roundly), they come to 1629 grains of barbiturates, 1928 grains of Sedormid, 164 grains of morphia and 139 grains of heroin, prescribed over a period of ten and a half months. One hundred and thirty-nine grains of heroin into ten months make how many grains, or what fraction of a grain, per day –? And how much is a grain of heroin in terms of what should or could be given –? To whom, and when, and for what –?

". . . You will hear that these drugs if administered over a period result in a serious degree of addiction to them, a craving for them, a dependence on them . . . [With weight] The Doctor was the source of supply. Did not Mrs Morell become dependent upon him? *Why* were these drugs prescribed to an old lady who was suffering from the effects of a stroke but who was not suffering from pain?"

Through all of this the Doctor has been sitting on his chair in the dock, warder on each side, like a contained explosive. He did not fidget and he did not move, but his face reflected that a remarkable degree of impassivity was maintained by will against an equally high degree of pressure from within. At certain assertions his mouth compressed slowly and hard, and he shook his head, to and fro, almost swinging it, as if prompted by an inner vision that did not correspond to what he had to hear. This head-shaking, which the Doctor repeated throughout his trial, seemed to express sorrow, anger, primness and exasperation all at once. It was oddly convincing.

"Perhaps," a hint of complacency in the delivery, "perhaps you may think that the answer lies in the changes made in her *will*." Mrs Morell's solicitor, Mr Sogno, will tell them that she made three wills in 1947 and that in none of these wills was there any mention of the Doctor. Then in April 1949 when she had been getting morphia and heroin for some months, the Doctor telephoned to her solicitor saying that she was extremely anxious about her will and wanted to see Mr Sogno that day. So Mr Sogno went to see her and eventually she made another will in which she bequeathed to the Doctor an oak chest containing silver.

"Nearly a year later the Doctor called on Mr Sogno without an appointment and a conversation took place," a sharp look over spectacles at the jury, "which you may think a very curious one. The Doctor told Mr Sogno that Mrs Morell had promised him her Rolls-Royce in her will and that she now remembered that she had forgotten this, and that she desired to leave him not only the Rolls-Royce car but also the contents of a locked box at the bank, a box which the Doctor said contained jewellery. The Doctor went on to say that though Mrs Morell was very ill, her mind was perfectly clear and she was in a fit condition to execute a codicil. Mr Sogno proposed that they might wait until Mrs Morell's son came at the week-end, but the Doctor suggested that Mr Sogno should prepare a codicil and that the codicil could be executed and later destroyed if it did not meet with Mrs Morell's son's approval. Was not that," another swift look at the jury, "rather an astonishing suggestion? It showed – did it not? – a certain *keenness*?"

The Attorney-General appears to be an earnest pleader. When he poses a rhetorical question, as he frequently does, it has a dutiful rather than dramatic sound.

Once more Mr Sogno went to see Mrs Morell, and Mrs Morell made another will leaving the Doctor the chest of silver and, if her son predeceased her, the Rolls-Royce and an Elizabethan cupboard. "Perhaps you might think it significant and sinister that during the period when he was prescribing for her these very substantial quantities of morphia and heroin the Doctor was concerning himself so much about her will and telephoning her solicitor."

In September of that year the Doctor went away on holiday and his partner looked after Mrs Morell in his absence. She was annoyed with the Doctor for leaving her and executed a codicil revoking her bequests to him.

Here there is one of those pauses which in court are filled not with coughs but an immense rustling of papers. The first exhibit in this case, a photostat of a graph, is being passed round, one up to the Judge, half a dozen to the jury, another copy or two for counsel of the defence. The graph demonstrates the alleged prescriptions by the Doctor.

". . . You will see how the prescriptions increased in quantity . . ." During the last thirteen days of Mrs Morell's life the rate of morphia was over three times higher than in any of the preceding months, and the rate of heroin seven and a half times. Why? What had happened to Mrs Morell necessitating these tremendous increases? If she had been in acute pain, heavy doses might have been justified, but she was *not* in acute pain. "The nurses will tell you that during her last days she was comatose or semi-conscious. And that brings us back to the question – why did the Doctor prescribe such quantities, such fatal quantities, for which there is no medical justification?" A pause. "The submission of the Crown is that he did so because he had decided that the time had come for her to die!

"He knew – did he not? – a lot about her will. Whether he knew of the codicil executed while he was on holiday and what happened to it, you may perhaps discover in the course of this trial. The Doctor may have thought she should have no further opportunity for altering her will!"

This leaves a sense of confusion. On the far back benches behind the dock, where the overflow of the irregular press sits squeezed, special correspondents scrawl on their pads and nudge their neighbours. "But he'd been *cut out* –?" "He didn't know." Someone says just under his breath, "Bet the old girl told him." "That wasn't what he said to the police at Eastbourne." "Shsh. . . ." "Shshsh . . ."

The Crown must come now to the night of her death. Mrs Morell was lying unconscious. "The night nurse will tell you she was very weak, except for occasional spasms. [Heavily] She was in

a coma. At 10 p.m. the Doctor came and himself filled a 5 c.c.
syringe with a preparation –"

The Attorney-General held up an object. It is always slightly
startling when an actual utensil of the outside world, not a chart or
a document or a photograph of one, appears in a court of law. It
does in fact quite often, yet it brings with it a hint of lurid
impropriety. It causes what is called a stir; people in the gallery
try to stand up and are instantly suppressed.

"The Doctor gave this syringe to the night nurse and told her to
inject it into the unconscious woman. [Tone of doom] She did so.
The Doctor took the empty syringe and refilled it with a similar
quantity – an unusually large quantity on each occasion – and told
the nurse to give the second injection to the patient if she did not
become quieter. The nurse did not like giving another large
injection from this unusually large syringe and later in the evening
she telephoned the Doctor. She received her instructions and it
was her duty to obey them. She gave the second injection. Mrs
Morell gradually became quiet, and at 2 a.m. she died.

"Why were those large injections given to an unconscious
woman on the Doctor's orders?

"The prosecution cannot tell you what they were. Mrs Morell
may indeed have been a dying woman when they were given. If she
was, then the prosecution submits that she was dying from over-
doses of morphia and heroin which the Doctor prescribed, and it
was murder by him. If, on the other hand, these two injections
accelerated her death, it was also murder. The prosecution will
submit that the only possible conclusion to which the jury can
come is that the Doctor killed her, deliberately and intentionally."

A slight pause; then before the court has been able to take stock.

"The case for the prosecution does not rest here. On the same
day, November 13th 1950, the Doctor filled in a form to secure
Mrs Morell's cremation. One question which he had to answer on
this form was, "Have you, as far as you are aware, any pecuniary
interest in the death of the deceased?" The Doctor's answer in his
own writing was, "Not as far as I am aware." Authority was given
for Mrs Morell to be cremated.

"Six years later when a detective superintendent from Scotland
Yard was making inquiries, he asked the Doctor about this cremation certificate. The Doctor said, 'Oh, that was not done wickedly.
God knows it wasn't. We always want cremations to go off
smoothly for the dear relatives. If I had said I knew I was getting

money under the will they might get suspicious, and I like cremations and burials to go off smoothly. There was nothing suspicious really. It was not deceitful.'

"But for this false answer on the form, there might not have been a cremation and the prosecution might have been in a position to say how much morphia and heroin there was in the body of Mrs Morell at the time of her death!

". . .In November 1950, Detective-Superintendent Hannam, with two other detectives, went to the Doctor's house. They went into the surgery and the Doctor was told they had a warrant for a search of the premises for dangerous drugs . . . The superintendent said, 'Doctor, look at this list of your prescriptions for Mrs Morell. There are a lot of dangerous drugs here.' Later he asked, 'Who administered them?' The Doctor answered, 'I did, nearly all. Perhaps the nurses gave some, but mostly me.' The superintendent asked, 'Were there any of them left over when she died?' and the Doctor replied, '*No, none. All was given to the patient*. Poor soul she was in terrible agony.'

"So there you have the Doctor saying that she was in terrible agony, when the nurses will tell you she was comatose and had been comatose for days and had not been suffering real pain."

And when this had sunk in:

"You will hear that the maximum quantity of heroin which should be prescribed in a period of twenty-four hours is a quarter of a grain. Yet no less than eight grains were prescribed by the Doctor on a single day. The maximum dose of morphia is half a grain. There were ten grains prescribed on the 8th of November, twelve on the 9th and eighteen on the 11th. The prosecution will call medical authority who will tell you that in their view Mrs Morell could not possibly have survived the administration of these drugs prescribed in her last five days."

From there the Attorney-General moves forward again to the near present, to 1956 and the inquiry six years after the death, a time-lag surely extraordinary in English justice, and about which we are told nothing.

". . . Last November the Doctor went to see Detective-Superintendent Hannam at police headquarters. He asked how the investigation was getting on. The superintendent said, 'I am still inquiring into the death of some of your patients, Doctor.' The Doctor said, 'Which?' and the superintendent answered, 'Mrs Morell is certainly one.' The Doctor said, 'Easing the passing of a dying person is not all that wicked. She wanted to die – that cannot be murder. It is impossible to accuse a doctor.' "

Half the court turned to look again at the accused.

"In December, the Doctor was arrested. He was told he would be taken to the police station and charged with the murder of Mrs Morell. He said, 'Murder – can you prove it was murder?' Superintendent Hannam said, 'You are now charged with murder.' And the Doctor said, 'I do not think you could prove it was murder – she was dying in any event.' As he left the house he gripped the hand of his receptionist and said to her, 'I will see you in heaven.' "

"*She was dying in any event!* [Decrescendo – businesslike] I submit to you that the evidence I and my learned friends will call before you will prove conclusively that this old lady was murdered." The Attorney-General sits down. The speech has lasted just under two hours.

Instantly a witness is on his way to the stand. A pharmaceutical chemist and what is called a formal witness. His name is given; his address. These will appear to-morrow in *The Times* and perhaps a half-dozen national and provincial newspapers. One of the three Crown counsel, a Q.C. swiftly extracts the relevant evidence – the drugs listed by the prosecution were in fact dispensed by Messrs Browne, the chemists, from prescriptions by the Doctor. We learn – if we care to listen – how chemists' books are kept and drugs recorded; we learn how the prosecution's list has been compiled. This witness is followed by another chemist; then a third. The Judge courteously puts a question. It is the first time that we hear him speak, and at once he reveals both grasp and charm. Could it not be stated, he asks, how many grains a 5 c.c. syringe would hold? 12.5 grains, witness replies; that is, if the syringe is quite full. And so, openly, honestly, humbly, the first bare facts are made secure beyond *unnecessary* doubt. It may be dull, it may seem redundant, it certainly is expensive and exacting; it is also gallant and essential, this toiling care to train the light of sequence, truth and reason on the obvious and minute – justice here is not only seen, it is understood being done. Rigged accusation, fake evidence? a demagogue would meet short shrift. It is thanks to the law's patient production – quixotic almost in its extreme sesquipedalian way – of these routine witnesses: George Albert Church of Greenover Road, Teddington, ironmonger's assistant, who has nothing to gain and nothing to lose and little to fear, that people can rest stolid in their trust that if a man be accused of poisoning or stabbing it must be shown where the poison or a knife came from. It has not always been like this, it may one day be so no longer; even at this time it is not so everywhere. But here and now, while the fourth pharmaceutical chemist is testifying to a preparation of eye-drops, we can allow our minds the luxury to stray.

Court No. 1 at the Old Bailey is a large court as English courts go. It is all the same no more than a large room, and it is packed to-day. As an auditorium it boasts some drawbacks. For one thing it is cram-ful of woodwork. Stained oak obstructs foot and eye. Boxes, desks, tables, benches, fitted ingeniously enough, jut at all angles; they hold about two hundred people, and some of them can hear nearly everything and see one thing very well. The witness-box, at conversational distance from the dais, stands in something like the relation of the lectern to the altar; other items bear the stamp of the committee-room, while the benches of the press-box might have come from a Victorian school. The shorthand writer has his own small pen. The dock is something else again. It is like a capacious loose-box, the only space in court that is not jammed, and it is set up plumb in the middle of everything, blocking every view. Yet the sum of these arrangements achieves a satisfying sense of unity. The prisoner can look across the well at the Judge; the Judge sees him. Between them, below, in the small square pit, furrowed by advocates' benches, munitioned from the solicitors' table, the fray takes place.

The jury have the ring-side view; but it is quite impossible for them to look a witness in the face. The public gallery proper is far and high beneath the roof. In court few members of the press or public can see the prisoner and none can see examining counsel *and* his witness at one time; and there are some low rows of seats behind the dock from which no one can see anything at all. All can see the Judge; which does not mean that he can be heard by everyone.

The purpose of a criminal trial is to determine whether a specific act, an event in time, took place or not, or took place in a certain way, to determine in short whether somebody has *done it*. The answer lies with the jury, twelve men and women selected at random within some, nowadays not very stringent, property qualifications. The facts connected with the alleged event are spread in open court by counsel and their witnesses, and re-assembled by the Judge; but it is the jury alone who must come to the conclusion,

Yes or No, it was like this or it cannot have been; without their verdict no man in England can be punished for any of the great offences, and their verdict, if it is acquittal, is irreversible.

We now have the bare bones of the prosecution's case. What do they amount to? A woman, eighty-one years old, half paralysed by a stroke, has died. The prosecution says she did not die of age or illness but of drugs. Large doses of drugs, not given at any one time – no poisoner's moment – but drugs prescribed during the last five days of her life without a medical reason. Three questions – at this stage – leap to the mind.

Was the quantity of drugs prescribed actually administered? ("All given to the patient," the Doctor himself had volunteered, though at a moment when perhaps he hardly had his wits about.)

Was the dosage of these drugs actually fatal, or was it merely – however incomprehensibly or dangerously – very large?

Was there in fact no medical or other reason short of murder for their administration?

On these points, so far, would seem to rest the weight of the whole case, and not on the weak motive or the answer given on a form, or the Doctor's utterances to the police, wild though they may be.

The motive, as presented by the prosecution, is bewilderingly inadequate. Can they be suggesting that a – sane? – man in the Doctor's circumstances would commit murder for the chance of inheriting some silver and an ancient motor-car ironically enough no longer mentioned in the will? Unless some sense or strength can be infused into the motive it must become the sagging point of this unequal web. Yet in way the motive has already drawn sustenance from an irregular but not secret source; it has waxed big by headlines, by printed innuendo, by items half remembered from the preliminary hearing. There have been published rumours of rich patients, mass poisonings, of legacy on legacy in solid sterling . . . Everybody knows a bit too much and no one knows quite enough; there is a most disturbing element in this case, extra-mural half-knowledge that cannot be admitted and cannot be kept out.

And so there is a sense of flatness after the prosecution's speech. Was that all? At the very least a tighter case has been expected. There are also some ill-fitted points. The back benches mutter.

"You believe in the unknown quantity in the *unusually large syringe*?"

"Pelion on Ossa."

"Cheap. Not what you'd expect to get in a British court."

"Chap's got to put *something* in his case."

"Shsh . . ."

"Wouldn't you think he could have taken his pick? Widows dying like flies, corpses dug up all over the country . . ."

"Why Mrs Morell?"

"No body."

"No reasonable gain."

"Stone cold."

"Shshsh."

"*We'll see.*"

The fifth witness for the prosecution – called after the short adjournment: one hour and five minutes for luncheon – is a woman, and a good deal less peripheral. Suddenly the case is under way. Nurse Stronach – stocky, a face of blurred features except for a narrow mouth and strong jaw. By question fitted after question, counsel gets her to put the court in the picture; we have returned to the tortoise from the spectator's hare.

Nurse Stronach was relief nurse to Mrs Morell (in Mrs Morell's own house). Three weeks of night duty in June 1950, one of day duty. Another three weeks of day duty in October. On the Doctor's instructions, she is prompted to tell, Mrs Morell was given a quarter of a grain of morphia every evening. The Doctor came every night.

Counsel [dead-pan, neutral voice] "Did you see him do anything with a syringe?"

Nurse Stronach [flatly] "He gave her injections."

"Did you see the Doctor give them?"

[Pursing her mouth] "We were not allowed in the room."

"Who forbade you to be in the room?"

"I think it was Mrs Morell's wish that we were not in the room."

[Making his point] "You personally did not see the actual injection given, but you did see the Doctor prepare the syringe?"

[Pleased to have this offering] "Yes, but I could not tell you what it was."

[Gravely] "You do not know what the injections which the Doctor gave her were?"

"No, sir, I have no idea."

"Did the Doctor ever say anything to you about them?"

"He did not tell us."

[In half tones from the Judge] "Mr Stevenson, is this perhaps a
convenient moment to adjourn?" The usher takes it up; we are on
our feet; the Judge has risen, he has his gloves, slides along the
bench, is gone. The prisoner has vanished. The pattern is broken
up, a crowd of people are making their way, talking, to the door.

Outside it is broad daylight. And one block away we are in London
on a warm afternoon in March at 5 p.m.

*The trial lasted another sixteen days. The case against him was strong,
but Adams was always convinced he'd be acquitted, and he was. "I'm
free," beamed Adams on his return to Eastbourne after the trial. "It's
thanks to God and British justice." But he remained shackled by
suspicion. He was struck off the medical register for some minor
infringements of the Forgery and Cremation Acts and, although
reinstated in 1961, he was dogged by notoriety thereafter. After
the trial he sold his life story to the* Daily Express *for £10,000, cash
that was found untouched in its envelope after his death in 1983.*

MAJOR ARMSTRONG

(Hereford, 1922)

Robin Odell

For such a little man, Major Herbert Rowse Armstrong, Master of Arts, had rather a lengthy style and title, but such was his vanity that he insisted on his name being bookended by rank and degree. At his trial for murder, he emerged as one of the most celebrated poisoners of the twentieth century. George Orwell squeezed Armstrong into "our great period in murder, our Elizabethan period, so to speak," ranking him alongside such titans as Jack the Ripper and Crippen. At Mayfield, his imposing house on the outskirts of Hay-on-Wye, Armstrong fitted Orwell's mould of the classic British murderer: a mild-mannered man of the professional class (he was a lawyer) living an intensely respectable life (Territorials, Church, Freemasonry), who poisoned in circumstances which, when unravelled in court, gave profound pleasure to readers of certain Sunday newspapers. On Derby Day in 1922, they hanged Major Armstrong in his best tweed suit at the age of 53, the only English solicitor ever to go to the gallows. Detectives had ransacked Mayfield, looking for the arsenic with which they were certain Armstrong had poisoned his wife Katharine, dead the previous winter but now exhumed from a snowy grave by the light of a hurricane lamp. What emerged was a tale of tea and telephones, scones and dandelions. The Armstrongs' life at Mayfield was rumoured to have been a ferment of wifely tyranny. Katharine Armstrong had forbidden her pint-sized hus-

*band to smoke in his own home, humiliated him on the tennis-court
by publicly calling him in for his bath, and at dinner had shooed
away the servants with the admonishment: "No wine for the
major!" No wonder Armstrong had taken up with another woman.
Then there was the business with Oswald Martin, Armstrong's rival
solicitor in Hay with offices directly opposite in Broad Street. Mired
in a professional dispute with Martin after his wife's death, Armstrong telephoned him daily with unwanted invitations to tea at
Mayfield. When Martin finally turned up, Armstrong handed him a
buttered scone with the apology "Excuse fingers". Returning home,
Martin was violently ill, poisoned – they said – like poor Mrs
Armstrong. Although physically slight, Armstrong was unflinching.
His experience as clerk to the Hay magistrates gave him confidence,
and when his trial opened at Hereford they were betting five to one
on his acquittal. Thriller writer Edgar Wallace reported the trial
and offered Armstrong £5,000 for a signed confession. He was
rebuffed. As was traditional in all high-profile poisoning cases
Armstrong was prosecuted by no less a figure than the Attorney-
General himself, in this case Sir Ernest Pollock, who painted the
little Major as an insidious poisoner, premeditating, callous and
cruel. Some of the greatest names in legal and forensic history
featured at Armstrong's trial. The judge was Lord Darling, and
the pathologist the legendary Dr (later Sir) Bernard Spilsbury.
Armstrong was defended by Sir Henry Curtis Bennett. While
working as an editor and publisher in an industrial research organization, Robin Odell (b. 1935) launched a parallel career writing
crime books and published* Jack the Ripper in Fact and Fiction *in
1965. This was followed by* Exhumation of a Murder, *the standard
study of the Armstrong case, and a number of books written with
crime historian Joe Gaute. Chief among these was the trilogy,* The
Murderers' Who's Who, Murder Whatdunit *and* Murder Whereabouts. *The first of these won an Edgar in 1980 from the Mystery
Writers of America. Robin Odell is currently working with Wilf
Gregg on a revision of the* Murderers' Who's Who *and his book*
Ripperology, *a study of the literature which has grown up around
the Jack the Ripper murders, is due to be published in America in
2006.*

*Do not be too hard on Major Armstrong because
he did not do what a wise man would have done.*
                              Sir Henry Curtis Bennett

Weeks before the trial began the police gathered opinions as to how Major Armstrong and the charge he faced were regarded in and around Hay. Sergeant Worthing of the Herefordshire Constabulary reported hearing a conversation about the case between two travellers at Hereford Railway Station. At the time, the Sergeant was escorting Armstrong to Worcester Gaol after one of the remands at the magistrates' hearing at Hay. The view expressed by both travellers, who failed to recognize the presence of the man they were discussing, was that the Major was guilty but would not be convicted because there was insufficient evidence.

The general opinion was that Armstrong was a much injured person and he was regarded by many local inhabitants as something of a martyr. Superintendent David Evans of the Breconshire Constabulary noted that ". . . many of his [Armstrong's] friends are betting upon the verdict of the trial, and are giving odds upon his being acquitted."

A similar view was reported by Superintendent Weaver who knew Armstrong personally. He said the majority of people had already made up their minds that the prosecution would fail to make a strong enough case to get a guilty verdict. There was a common feeling, too, that it was a flimsy case made up out of spite by Oswald Martin and his father-in-law.

Local feelings then were such that when Sir Henry Curtis Bennett rose to make his opening speech for the defence on Monday 10 April, he carried with him the support and hopes of many local people. He began by expressing something of the strain he himself was experiencing: ". . . I have never wondered more than during the last three days whether anybody realizes the terrible anxiety and responsibility which rests upon the shoulders of a member of the bar when he is defending a man for his life." With this reference to his own burdens Sir Henry quickly went into the attack.

The prosecution he contended had failed to show how or when Major Armstrong had administered the arsenic and no real motive had been put forward. He said he would attempt to show that Major Armstrong did not murder his wife and he made it clear that he did not consider it part of his task to prove who did.

He believed that the Attorney General had worked backwards from the post-mortem. "Everyone," he said, "has become extraordinarily wise." His view was that the history of Mrs Armstrong's illness showed her poor health was due to natural causes and in no way reflected suspicion on her husband. The facts showed a highly hysterical woman who had for years suffered from rheumatism and ill health and had finally reached a stage where a family friend thought she might commit suicide. Mrs Armstrong then went to Barnwood where, according to the prosecution, she developed multiple neuritis. It was Sir Henry's contention that she had multiple neuritis in 1918, months before the alleged poisoning began. Moreover, as a patient in hospital, Mrs Armstrong was given an arsenical tonic which the defence experts believed would have revived any symptoms of poisoning.

When Mrs Armstrong came home from Barnwood she had every hope of getting better but when this did not happen and her health deteriorated, she lapsed into a suicidal frame of mind. Defence counsel reminded the jury that Nurse Kinsey was so concerned that she left the Armstrong home saying that the patient needed a full-time mental nurse.

Sir Henry was scathing about the motives put forward by the prosecution; they were ludicrous, he said. He faulted the suggestion that Major Armstrong killed his wife in order to benefit from her will, on the grounds that Mrs Armstrong had told her sister she was thinking of altering the terms of the will in her husband's favour. In any event, when the will was proved and Major Armstrong inherited his wife's money he did not, "spend a farthing of it". The alternative suggestion, that Armstrong murdered his wife in order to leave him free to marry "that respectable lady" (Madame X), he described as "fantastic".

Defence counsel was inclined to dismiss the Martin incident; his opinion was that if Major Armstrong tried to poison Oswald Martin he must have been insane. It would have been more likely that Martin should have wanted to poison Major Armstrong; after all, Martin was the newcomer and Armstrong was the man with an established position. With regard to the tea party at Mayfield, Sir Henry said there was simply no evidence to show that Major Armstrong put any arsenic in the food. Moreover, the fact that Martin went home and was not sick for four hours suggested that the cause of his illness was something he had taken at dinner.

The one thirty-third of a grain of arsenic found in Martin's urine was quite possibly accounted for as an impurity in the hydrogen peroxide which the sample bottle had previously contained. "That sample," said Sir Henry, "was in my submission . . . in the highest degree unsatisfactory."

Finally, defence counsel said he would call medical witnesses whose opinion was that Mrs Armstrong died as the result of one large fatal dose of arsenic taken on 16 February. There was no evidence connecting anyone in the case with the administration of arsenic and there was certainly no evidence that Major Armstrong gave his wife poison.

Sir Henry's opening speech, in which he had made his strategy quite clear, lasted three hours. After a brief adjournment the prisoner was called and there was an eager, excited atmosphere as Major Armstrong stepped into the witness box. It is always an intense moment when the accused gives evidence, for it is then that he becomes to some extent master of his own fate. It is his chance to speak for himself instead of through others and an opportunity to tell his own story in his own way. There are also the pitfalls of cross-examination and the interpretation of his demeanour by judge and jury. Every reaction and reflex is observed and measured; arrogance, indignation, humility, innocence or self-pity are recorded in the minds of jurors and influence the final reckoning.

Throughout the trial, Armstrong had been attentive and unemotional as if he were detached from the proceedings rather than its central figure. When he was examined by Mr Bosanquet, he answered in a clear, firm voice that was audible right around the court. He gave an account of his business and domestic life and mentioned that his wife suffered from rheumatism when they were first engaged to be married. After that she had constantly recurring attacks of rheumatism and was also a "martyr to indigestion".

He first became aware that his wife was unwell in August 1920 when she indulged in self-recrimination about not looking after her children and of defrauding tradesmen. Referring to Mrs Armstrong's admission to the asylum, Bosanquet asked the witness, "Is there any truth in the suggestion that you administered arsenic to your wife prior to her removal to Barnwood?"

"Not the slightest," came the firm reply.

Counsel then led Armstrong on to the subject of Madame X: ". . . will you tell the jury your relations with her – what they have been?"

"Perfectly friendly relations. I used to visit at her house where her mother lived, and they were extremely hospitable and kind to me during the time while I was on service and quartered in their neighbourhood."

"Did you discuss the fact of your having a wife and children with her?"

"Yes, and I showed her a photograph both of my wife and my home and children."

These answers were well composed and no doubt Armstrong had thought them out in advance. Certainly his reply concerning his relationship with Madame X reflected his legal training.

Bosanquet then dealt with the tea party at Mayfield:

"You have heard Mr Martin's evidence with regard to your taking up a scone in your fingers and handing it to him, saying to Mr Martin 'Excuse fingers' or something of that kind. What do you say with regard to that?"

"Oh, that is incorrect."

"Do you remember using any expression of the kind?"

"I remember simply leaning across to help myself, and saying 'excuse me' but nothing further."

"To help yourself to what?" asked Mr Justice Darling.

"To a scone, my Lord. It was necessary for me to stretch in front of him to do so."

Armstrong was asked to give an account of his gardening activities and of his use of arsenic. He explained how he had put a packet containing white arsenic in a drawer of the bureau in the study at Mayfield. This now notorious piece of furniture was to feature in a little courtroom drama at the end of the trial's seventh day. The bureau which had been brought from Mayfield and locked up in the Hereford Under-Sheriff's Office was moved to an ante-room in the Shire Hall. Mr Justice Darling instructed that during the tea interval Armstrong should be escorted to the bureau and place in it the packet of arsenic in the manner which he had described in court. This was duly carried out in the presence of the jury, all the counsel engaged in the trial and the judge – all witnesses were excluded. After he had played his part, Armstrong was taken back to the witness box and Mr Matthews went out to show where he had found the packet of arsenic.

The story was that despite not having told the police specifically about the arsenic in the bureau, Armstrong was sure they would find it during their searches. When it did not feature in the police inventory, Armstrong told Matthews who went to Mayfield to make a search himself. He pulled open the central drawer of the bureau to its fullest extent of about four inches and ascertained that it was empty.

When it became clear that this arsenic was still not accounted for, Matthews went back to Mayfield, this time accompanied by his managing clerk. Again he pulled out the drawer to its fullest extent and this time decided to take it right out – but it was stuck. Feeling at the back of the drawer with his hand he found a piece of paper jammed there; on freeing it he revealed a folded paper packet and its removal allowed the drawer to be pulled right out. Matthews knew then that he had found the arsenic spoken of by Armstrong.

The packet was of white paper folded with a blue paper inside it; it was labelled, "Arsenic, poison: J.F. Davies". Matthews put the packet back as he had found it, closed the bureau and locked the room. A few days later he demonstrated his discovery in the presence of Dr Ainslie. The packet was then taken away and an analysis of its contents confirmed that the powder was indeed arsenic. This discovery was announced for the first time in court by Sir Henry Curtis Bennett.

Reporting on this courtroom incident to his chief, Crutchett wrote, ". . . I understand from one who was [present] that as soon as the drawer was opened the packet immediately caught one's eye." He went on, "The judge and jury then removed the drawer completely from its slide as they were anxious to know about the cavity at the back where Sir Henry Curtis Bennett had said the packet was found, but on investigation it was found that there was no cavity at the back at all, as the drawer just fitted the space, leaving no room for anything to have got behind or to lodge at the top or on either side."

After some more questions, Bosanquet sat down and Armstrong was then cross-examined. Sir Ernest Pollock went on the offensive immediately with questions about Mrs Armstrong's suicidal tendencies, recalling that Mr Chevalier had mentioned the possibility to the witness.

"Then it was that you put away your razors and your service revolver?"

"Yes."

"Did you think that was necessary?"

"It came as a shock to me to hear that from Mr Chevalier as I had never contemplated such a possibility."

"Mr Chevalier not being a doctor and being a solicitor might urge precautions that might be greater than necessary. I want to know what your view was."

"From the arguments that he put forward as to her then state of health it seemed to me that he was justified."

"You took a serious view of it?"

"I took a serious view of it then."

"You were afraid that there was a suicidal tendency?"

"At that moment."

Then came the moment that the Attorney General's questioning had been leading up to. Referring to the questionnaire on his wife's health which Armstrong completed and signed on 23 August 1920 as part of the procedure to admit her to the asylum, Sir Ernest read out a single question and answer.

"Question: Has she threatened or attempted self-destruction; if so, when, and by what means? Answer: No. Did you think it fair to the asylum not to make any disclosure of your anxiety as to this suicidal tendency?"

"I answered that question correctly; she had never made any attempt," replied Armstrong.

It must not be forgotten that Armstrong was a solicitor and consequently knew better than most men how to anticipate a question and have a ready answer. His reply on this occasion was clever but not very convincing; the prosecution had pointed a finger at a weakness in the prisoner's own testimony.

Explaining why he had been anxious for his wife to be completely released from Barnwood rather than to come home on leave, the Major said he thought that if she were given leave someone would have to come to examine her. He had since heard that would not have been necessary. He said that he had no further anxiety regarding her possible suicidal tendencies after she came out of the asylum.

Armstrong was questioned at great length about a supply of white arsenic, part of which he had used for weed killing. This was the four ounces of arsenic bought from Mr Davies, the Hay chemist, on 11 January 1921, which had not been coloured with charcoal in the normal fashion. The significance of this white arsenic was exploited by both sides. The prosecution contended that because it was the last arsenic to be bought and turned out not to have been coloured, there was every reason why Armstrong should have remembered all about it. The same reasons were used by the defence to reach a different conclusion: they argued that, as the prisoner could account for every scrap of arsenic in his possession, Mrs Armstrong must have taken a fatal dose from some other source, possibly weed killer, to which she had access.

Sitting in the study of Mayfield one June afternoon in 1921, Armstrong had divided up this four ounces of arsenic. He said he first roughly divided the bulk into two lots and then, taking one of these he sub-divided it with his penknife into twenty parts, each of which was wrapped in a piece of paper to make a little packet. These little packets were used that same evening to kill dandelions. His method was to make a hole next to the dandelion with a piece of metal and then to tip the contents of one little packet into it. Each weed was dosed separately but only nineteen packets of arsenic were used; the twentieth being found in the pocket of his jacket when he was arrested.

"Can you tell us how you came to use nineteen of the score and not the twenty?" asked the Attorney General.

"I do not know. I did not count the number that I was using."

That accounted for half of the original four ounces of arsenic but what of the second two ounces? In his statement to the police Armstrong said he had used some of that arsenic to make liquid weed killer by boiling it up with caustic soda. Now he said that was wrong – he had confused the 1921 arsenic with that bought in 1919.

It was only after he had been arrested and the twentieth little packet of arsenic was found among the things taken from his pockets, that he remembered where the other two ounces were – they were in the drawer of the bureau at Mayfield. "It all came back to my memory when I saw this little packet . . ." he said in reply to a question by Mr Justice Darling. The packet in question was entered as Exhibit 32 and lay on a table in the courtroom. It was a folded paper packet measuring about one and a half inches by three-quarters of an inch; the paper itself was similar to that used by chemists for putting up powders.

The Attorney General now proceeded to give the witness a gruelling time on this subject and he was assisted, if not actually outdone, by the judge. Sir Ernest read out part of the statement made by Armstrong to the police, "This arsenic I speak of is the only poison in my possession anywhere, excepting, of course, any contained in medicine." The Attorney General continued,

"Within an hour of signing that statement, by finding the little packet of white arsenic you knew that statement was all wrong?"

"Yes."

"And although you knew it was wrong, you took no steps with the police to correct it?"

"In the meantime I was arrested."

When the judge intervened, pressing home the same question, Armstrong explained, ". . . it was a very great shock, the arrest, naturally; and then I decided to say nothing further until I had seen my solicitor."

The prosecution had the bit between its teeth now and relentlessly pursued the same questions seeking to gain damaging admissions from the prisoner.

". . . to allow the police, to whom you had promised to render every assistance, to go away with a misleading statement in their possession. This statement is quite misleading, is it not?"

"When that statement was made, I did not know I was going to be arrested."

"We have passed that. You were allowing the police to go away with what you knew was a misleading statement in their possession?"

"I am afraid I did not think very much about it, about what the police were going to do. I was too much overcome by the position I had been placed in."

". . . you know these last three lines in your statement were untrue: 'This arsenic I speak of is the only poison in my possession anywhere excepting of course any contained in medicine.' You knew that to be untrue?"

"I do not think I had those particular words in my mind at the time."

Finally, the admission was clearly wrung from Armstrong:

"Then may I take it from you, first that the statement that you made to the police was before they left to your knowledge untrue?"

"The original statement that was made before arrest was incorrect."

But the most searching questions were put by the judge: "Why did you want to consult your solicitor before you should say anything further?"

"I was met with having found this little packet, and I was not at all sure how it would affect my defence."

The prisoner's long ordeal was nearly at an end. He was preparing to stand down from the witness box when Mr Justice

Darling motioned him to remain. Doubtless to Armstrong's utter dismay, the judge decided once again to go into the question of how he had used the arsenic.

He found it difficult to understand that Armstrong who had been so careful about other details in his police statement should have forgotten about the arsenic in the bureau.

"Do you tell the jury that you absolutely forgot about that white arsenic?"

"I do."

The judge thought this was remarkable and said, damagingly, "You are a solicitor. Does not it occur to you it would have been a very, very bad case for you if you had to tell the police that you had got not only weed-killing arsenic, but white arsenic in your possession?"

"But I did not remember it."

"That is not what I asked you," snapped Darling, and he repeated the question.

"It would have to be explained," admitted Armstrong.

His Lordship seemed to be enjoying the role of questioner, or perhaps he thought the prisoner was weakening. At any rate, the questions continued: ". . . did you realize that it was just a fatal dose of arsenic, not for dandelions only but for human beings?"

"No. I did not realize it at all."

Mr Justice Darling told the prisoner that it was suggested the moment he remembered there was arsenic in the little packet taken from his pocket when he was arrested that "you tried to get it back." Armstrong denied this. "You know now what you saw there [in the little packet] was a fatal dose of arsenic?"

"I know since the evidence in this case."

"And you realize what you had given the dandelions was a fatal dose of arsenic for a human being?"

"I have realized it since. I did not know it at the time."

"Why go to the trouble of making twenty little packets, one for each dandelion, instead of taking out the ounce you had got and making a hole and giving the dandelions something from the one ounce?"

"I do not really know."

"Why make up twenty little packets, each a fatal dose for a human being, and put it in your pocket?"

"At the time it seemed to me the most convenient way of doing it. I cannot give any other explanation."

Finally, as he had done throughout Armstrong's examination, the judge switched his questions. Referring to the arsenic found in the bureau, he asked, "You are a man accustomed to criminal procedure?"

"Yes."

"Would not it have been better to make a clean breast of it and say 'It is in the drawer of the bureau'?"

"It did not occur to me, my Lord."

Shattering as the judge's final onslaught of questions must have been, Armstrong nevertheless missed an opportunity to give a more convincing account of why he had divided up the arsenic into little packets. He could have said with irrefutable logic that the method he used ensured that every particle of arsenic powder was dosed directly onto the dandelions' roots and prevented the danger of the powder blowing away in the wind.

As it was, these last questions, put at the end of the prisoner's six-hour ordeal in the witness box, were probably the most destructive of the whole trial. The impression left with the jury was probably one of Armstrong struggling at the last fence to give a plausible reason for using arsenic innocently for weed killing in a manner which would also account for the packet found in his possession.

When Armstrong stepped down, the trial was as good as over in many people's eyes. He had not broken down; in fact he had conducted himself with considerable calm, but his replies had not convinced the sceptics. There was perhaps even a sneaking admiration for the little man whom the trial had cast as underdog; he had answered over two thousand questions and most of the judge's interventions, which had been frequent, had been against him.

While the conclusion of the prisoner's evidence seemed to make what followed an anticlimax, there was important testimony still to be heard. An early witness to follow Armstrong was his solicitor, Mr Matthews. He gave his account of the white arsenic found in the bureau at Mayfield. He expressed his surprise at finding it: ". . . it was the last thing in the world I expected to discover."

The prosecution was uneasy about this whole matter if only for the reason that the discovery had been made after the police searched the house. Consequently, Matthews was asked several questions about other persons who had been to the house. It seemed that two of Matthews's clerks and one of Armstrong's had been to Mayfield for various reasons after the police had completed their searches.

There was no direct imputation that the arsenic might have been planted, but Sir Henry Curtis Bennett intervened, as he put it, "to see that no attack was made". The Attorney General made it clear that no such suggestion was made and all agreed that Mr Matthews was a man of the highest reputation. So, the strange affair of the arsenic missed by the police, but discovered by the defence on the accused man's instructions, was accepted.

Then came the defence's medical witnesses. The first was Dr Frederick Sherman Toogood, a practitioner with varied experience in mental illness and pathology who had given evidence for the defence in the Greenwood trial. In answer to Mr Bosanquet's questions he gave it as his opinion that between 1915 and 1920 Mrs Armstrong was suffering from auto-intoxication caused by chronic indigestion. This was associated with the presence of gallstones which he thought indicated faulty digestion. She also suffered from neuritis which in his view was an effect of auto-intoxication.

Dr Toogood thought that Mrs Armstrong's condition when she went to the asylum was due to acute melancholia accompanied by the physical symptoms of vomiting and albuminuria. He did not think that she was suffering from any arsenical poisoning at that time. ". . . I say there was no evidence consistent only with arsenical poisoning up till the 16 February . . . in all probability the cause of her death was arsenical poisoning caused by arsenic taken about the 16 February, but none before. It must have been a large dose." Questioned about the size of the dose by Mr Justice Darling, the witness said he thought it must have been more than six grains because of the amount found after death. It was his opinion that a large portion of the arsenic became encysted in the stomach. Continuing his examination, defence counsel, asked, "Supposing that this large dose was given on the 16 February, would that, in your opinion account for what was found at the post-mortem?"

"Quite."

The 16 February was a date which repeatedly came up in the defence version of Mrs Armstrong's last illness. It was on that day that Dr Hincks was called to Mayfield to see Mrs Armstrong who was very ill and had been vomiting badly. Only the symptoms seen from that day until her death were recognized by the defence as indicating arsenical poisoning.

Dr Toogood was doubtful that the circumstances of Oswald Martin's illness added up to arsenical poisoning. He said, "Assuming a fatal dose of arsenic was taken at about five-thirty in the afternoon, I think it would be exceedingly unlikely that the person would be likely to be able to eat dinner at seven-thirty." He also thought that Martin's return to work was very quick for someone who had received a near fatal dose of arsenic. He described the sample of Martin's urine as not having been "taken in a scientific way" and he maintained that arsenic was a constant impurity of hydrogen peroxide. "By implication, therefore, the arsenic may not have been in the urine at all but in the sample bottle itself." He made the point that a sample of the washing water should also have been sent for analysis; no doubt that was also the private view of the prosecution.

The witness was cross-examined by the Attorney General and was taken through Mrs Armstrong's symptoms in detail. "With all these symptoms", asked Sir Ernest, "the heart, the albumen which cleared away, the subsequent peripheral neuritis, why do you prefer auto-intoxication to arsenical poisoning?"

"I prefer auto-intoxication, and the condition of acute melancholia. I never heard of arsenical poisoning emphasising melancholia."

A number of specialized medical matters were raised by the defence in an attempt to support their contention that Mrs Armstrong died of one fatal dose of arsenic taken six days before death. The analysis of the body organs pointed very strongly to poison being taken right up to the time of death. The jejunum (upper part of the small intestine) contained 1.6 milligrammes of arsenic; the ileum (lower part of the small intestine), 9.1 milligrammes, and the caecum and ascending colon (beginning of the large intestine), 37.6 milligrammes.

A possible explanation for this, although rated only a bare possibility by Spilsbury, was the encysted arsenic theory. The gradual release of arsenic from the stomach into the intestines days after the initial dose could explain the arsenic found in the alimentary canal after death. Another possibility was the migration of arsenic from one part of the body to another. Sir Henry Curtis Bennett had posed this idea to Spilsbury earlier on in the trial, suggesting migration of arsenic from the liver into the caecum after death; he supported the theory by quoting from Witthaus's work on toxicology. Spilsbury disagreed with the theory except where the organs had collapsed through putrefaction; then arsenic might pass in a fluid condition from one organ to another. He pointed out that in Mrs Armstrong's case the bowel was intact.

Dr Toogood, on the other hand, thought that encysted arsenic with subsequent migration of the poison was quite feasible. He was asked about this by Sir Henry Curtis Bennett; "If you found arsenic being encysted in the stomach, and gradually coming away, would you then find that arsenic going on down through the jejunum and the ileum into the caecum? Which is what was found in this case? Having heard the whole of the evidence . . ., having considered carefully the evidence which has been given by the other doctors, in your opinion was the arsenic from which Mrs Armstrong died given in one big dose on the 16th?"

Witness replied, "I believe it was given in one big dose."

Dr William Ainslie, who practised in Hereford and had represented Major Armstrong's interests at the post-mortem, gave evidence next. He concurred with Dr Toogood on all the major issues and was mildly critical of Spilsbury for not making a post-mortem examination for rheumatoid arthritis and for not opening any of the joints. He was closely questioned by the Attorney General about encysted arsenic.

". . . did you or did you not find any encysted arsenic in the stomach at the post-mortem examination?"

"I did not expect to."

"Perhaps you will answer the question . . . you did not?"

"No, I did not."

Several historical cases of arsenical poisoning were referred to including one in Blythe's *Poisons and their Detection*, where a suicide took a large dose of arsenic and lived for six days with symptoms of arsenical poisoning the whole time.

Counsel were by now used to Mr Justice Darling intervening with the last word before witnesses stepped down and he did so in this case. "How did you fix on six days before her death for the dose that killed her?" he asked. Ainslie replied, "Because, as I answered before, I did not think the symptoms occurring before the 16th were due to arsenical poisoning."

The last defence witness was John Steed, a doctor with a practice at Staunton-on-Wye. He added his opinion to those of his two predecessors: there was no evidence of arsenical poisoning before the morning of 16 February, when a large dose was taken.

★   ★   ★

The trial, now in its ninth day, was approaching its final phase: closing speeches by Counsel, the judge's summing up and the jury's verdict. Sir Henry Curtis Bennett took an hour and a half to make his final speech to the jury. He made his address a short one as he was aware that the proceedings had already been drawn out; he probably also realized that the jury were bored with expert witnesses. His contention was simply that Mrs Armstrong's illness up to the 16 February was due to natural causes. She was known to have suicide in mind and took a fatal dose of poison on that day. Addressing the jury, he asked, "Are you going to say in the face of that evidence that she did not take poison herself?" He said that the Prosecution had failed to establish a motive on Major Armstrong's part for murdering his wife.

The Martin incident was virtually brushed aside by the defence. It was not shown that Armstrong had the opportunity to put arsenic in the scones served to Martin, and in any event there was nothing to prove that Martin had suffered from arsenical poisoning. The symptoms of his illness were compatible with a natural complaint and the arsenic in the urine could have got there from other sources.

Sir Henry made a play on the fact that Armstrong went into the witness box even though he was not obliged to. "Did you not think," he asked the jury, "that Major Armstrong gave his evidence in the box like an honest man? Do you not think, and I put this before you as strongly as I can, that he emerged from four hours, I think it was, of cross-examination by the Attorney General, absolutely unscathed? . . . in my submission to you Major Armstrong was an excellent witness."

Knowing that the weak replies given by Armstrong to the judge's questions were likely to have made a firm impression on the jury, Sir Henry set about repairing the damage. He said that with hindsight it was easy to say that the prisoner should have told the police about the white arsenic in the bureau immediately he remembered it. But it was an understandable human reaction in someone who had been in the position of administering justice and is suddenly arrested and taken to the police station. ". . . I cannot see what the criticism of it is," said Sir Henry. "If Major Armstrong had been trying to deny that he had got arsenic upon his premises at all, then I could understand it. He knew they were inquiring about arsenic, and told them where they could find one packet . . . do not be too hard on Major Armstrong because he did not do what a wise man would have done."

Finally, there was the criticism of Armstrong's method of killing dandelions using his prepared packets of arsenic. Curtis Bennett suggested the method was quite sensible. "That is what he said he did; is there any reason to disbelieve him? There is no sort of evidence that he did not." Counsel thought the explanation of the packet of arsenic found in Armstrong's jacket was quite reasonable. "As I say, nobody is safe in possession of arsenic, because if you happen to be arrested, and you have some in your pocket, it is going to be said you are carrying it about for the purpose of poisoning somebody . . ."

Sir Henry said the jury's verdict would be read by many who were merely interested in sensations, "But for the friends of Major Armstrong it means, I hope, his freedom, for his children the restoration of their father to his home; and for Major Armstrong it means life," Sir Henry Curtis Bennett had done all he could for Armstrong and when he sat down the responsibility which he had carried – to argue for the prisoner's life – passed to the jury.

Thursday 13 April was the last day of the trial. As on the previous nine days, Armstrong was brought to the Shire Hall from Gloucester Gaol. Mr R.L. Ball, a Hereford resident, remembered seeing Armstrong's arrival: "I thought how intensely blue his eyes were and I saw no sign of foreboding in his face."

In his closing speech for the Crown, Sir Ernest Pollock said the prosecution's case had been strengthened during the trial. It was agreed by everyone that Mrs Armstrong died as the result of arsenical poisoning; what had to be decided was who administered that poison. The defence's thesis that there was no arsenical poisoning prior to 16 February and that her illness before then was due to natural causes, was not borne out in the document which described her condition on admission to Barnwood. This was the questionnaire completed and signed by Major Armstrong. Despite the contention that she was suffering from rheumatoid arthritis and auto-intoxication, Mrs Armstrong's health was described as "fairly good". And the question "Has she ever suffered from any serious disease, or is she subject to any particular constitutional or bodily ailment?" was answered with a "No."

The Attorney General criticized the defence for overlooking a good deal of evidence in maintaining that Mrs Armstrong took a fatal dose of arsenic on 16 February. Nurse Kinsey said she was told the patient had vomited on 27 January; and on 10 February, Mrs Armstrong herself complained of vomiting badly. Sir Ernest said this suggested that the prisoner had commenced once more to give his wife small doses of arsenic. As regards the suicide theory, both Dr Hincks and Nurse Allen had said that Mrs Armstrong was anxious to get better, and in his testimony Major Armstrong said he had ceased to be anxious that his wife might commit suicide.

Sir Ernest had no doubt about the prisoner's motive in wanting to be rid of his wife: ". . . it was abundantly clear on this evidence that the prisoner was minded to get for his advantage under the new will immediate possession of his wife's goods." The new will had one remarkable feature – everything went to the prisoner – whereas the previous will was drawn with particular regard to the children and provided an annuity for the faithful Miss Pearce.

There was a remarkable concurrence of testimony concerning the details of the tea party at Mayfield. Both Miss Pearce and Mrs Price said the scones provided from Mayfield's kitchen were uncut and unbuttered; Martin, however, said the scones were buttered and this was corroborated by Armstrong himself in his first statement; "The food consisted of buttered scones . . ." The implication was clearly that the scones were buttered at some stage after leaving the kitchen – that was the opportunity chosen by Armstrong to poison one of them.

Finally, there was the prosecution's interpretation of Armstrong's statement and the offending packet of arsenic. The Attorney General said there was "a meticulous particularity" about that statement and Armstrong knew that it was misleading as soon as the packet of arsenic was found on his person. The whole story of this busy solicitor making up a score of little packets of arsenic to dose individual weeds was merely to explain away that sinister discovery in his jacket pocket. "Gentlemen," said Sir Ernest Pollock, "If I am confident of one thing in this case, I am confident that no one will believe that story . . . I shall ask you to find a verdict that the prisoner is guilty."

Opposing Counsel had made their final assessments of the evidence, and who was to say which way the verdict would go? Was one set of experts more convincing than the other? Were there reasonable doubts about connecting Major Armstrong with the arsenic from which his wife died? These and other questions were not to be settled quickly. Above all else, the law takes its course and it now fell to the judge to make his charge to the jury.

Mr Justice Darling began his direction to the jury by saying, ". . . I doubt whether any of us engaged here today have in recollection so remarkable a case in its incidents." He dealt first with the Martin case, explaining that he believed it had a bearing on Mrs Armstrong's death: ". . . it is of value as showing that the defendant had arsenic in his possession, and that he would use it to poison a human being." When asking the jury to consider how Martin might have taken in the poison, the judge let it be known that they need not confine themselves to thinking only about scones, ". . . there were other victuals," he said. The defence doctors who believed that Martin's urine sample was not properly taken might be correct but, equally, Mr Davies, the chemist, was a man of experience who did not let his corks roll about in arsenic powder and he knew how to wash out bottles. "Therefore," Mr Justice Darling told the jury, "you try and come to a conclusion as to whether Martin really did suffer from arsenical poisoning. If he did, of course that does not prove that the defendant gave it to him." He added, however, that, according to his own evidence, Armstrong had arsenic in his possession at the time.

The judge permitted himself one indulgence in the kind of humour for which he was so well known. "Many, many people," he said, "have been poisoned and poisoned with arsenic . . . but, of course, these people did not see what was being done. No-one who had been asked to dine with Cesare Borgia would have eaten anything if they had seen him putting white powder on the victuals." This was an ace for the prosecution which, though suspecting the buttered scone, had been unable to prove exactly how Armstrong was supposed to have administered the poison to Martin.

In his summing up of Mrs Armstrong's death, the judge made a strong argument of the evidence which went against the idea of suicide. Referring to the dying woman's stated wish to live, he said, ". . . if you believe she said that (and it is not questioned that she said it) – do you believe that woman had already, with intent to kill herself, taken a fatal dose of arsenic?" Mr Justice Darling placed great emphasis on the testimony of Dr Hincks, "a perfectly competent doctor", who never heard a word spoken about a tendency on the part of his patient to commit suicide. Moreover,

on the 16 and 17 of February, when the defence said Mrs Armstrong took a fatal dose, Dr Hincks had testified "she could not
hold up a cup to her lips, and she could not use her arms, she could
not grip anything perfectly."

He referred to "the contest" between Dr Spilsbury and Sir
William Willcox on the one hand, and Dr Toogood and Dr Ainslie
and Dr Steed on the other. Speaking of Spilsbury's view that a
large dose of arsenic must have been taken twenty-four hours
before death, the judge appealed to the jury to consider Spilsbury's
manner as much as the evidence which he gave. "Do you remember Dr Spilsbury, do you remember how he stood and the way in
which he gave evidence? . . . Did you ever see a witness who more
thoroughly satisfied you that he was absolutely impartial, absolutely fair, absolutely indifferent as to whether his evidence told for
the one side or the other . . .?"

Such statements of confidence in the ability of the doctors were
not extended to the defence experts and Sir Henry Curtis Bennett
could have been forgiven for thinking that the summing-up was
becoming one-sided. The views of Dr Toogood and his colleagues
were given little more than a passing reference although the judge
missed an opportunity to point out their lack of experience in cases
of arsenical poisoning which had come out during cross-examination. Instead he chose to remark rather acidly that Dr Ainslie's
criticism of Hincks's vagueness about dates was, "a very confident
opinion, by one who never saw the deceased during her life, as
against Dr Hincks, who had seen her during life." He dwelled at
some length on the implications of the packet of arsenic in Armstrong's pocket: "He realized, the moment he saw the little packet
. . . it was a very awkward thing."

Finally, the judge crystallized the case for the jury: "He is
charged with murder by administering arsenic to his wife. She
had an administration of arsenic, and if you are satisfied beyond
doubt that he gave it to her intending to kill her, he is guilty. He
had the opportunity to give it to her, you can see on the evidence.
The question is whether he did give it . . . Take the whole case into
your consideration and say how you find it."

Mr Justice Darling's summing-up had lasted nearly four hours
and at eight minutes past five the jury filed into the assembly room
to consider their verdict. The judge retired to his private room and
the prisoner was taken down to the cells to await the decision which
would settle his destiny.

The courtroom, previously so silent when the judge had been speaking, now erupted with sound as everyone began talking at once. The corridors of the Shire Hall filled with court officials and pressmen avidly discussing the case and weighing up the prisoner's prospects for an acquittal. Sir Henry Curtis Bennett told a newspaper reporter: "I have been in forty-eight murder trials, for and against, and I have never known the verdict so open." People in the crowd gathered outside the court and in the streets of Hereford were quoting odds of five to one in favour of an acquittal.

In his book on the Armstrong trial in the Notable British Trials series, Filson Young wrote, "Sir Henry Curtis Bennett himself was so confident that he went for a walk, expecting to come back either to hear the verdict for acquittal or to meet Armstrong himself and find that he had already been released." Indeed, Curtis Bennett's optimism led him to sign a note to enable a photographer to take pictures of Major Armstrong when he was released:

After they had been out forty-eight minutes, the jury signalled that they had reached a decision. Armstrong was escorted back to the dock and was seated as the jurors walked to their places. The members of the jury seemed to show more signs of strain in their faces than the prisoner who eyed them keenly as if trying to elicit their secret in advance. Leaning over to one of his warders, the Major asked, "Shall I stand up while the jury give their verdict?".

The formalities were rigidly adhered to and for the last time the jury answered their names. Then, in a quavering voice the Deputy Clerk of Assize asked them, "Gentlemen of the jury, have you all agreed upon your verdict?"

The foreman replied, "Yes."

"Do you find the prisoner at the bar, Herbert Rowse Armstrong, guilty or not guilty of the wilful murder of Katharine Mary Armstrong?"

Whitefaced but with a controlled voice, the foreman answered, "Guilty."

"You say he is guilty and that is the verdict of you all?"

"Yes."

The only sounds were a few stifled gasps around the court. The Deputy Clerk of Assize now addressed the prisoner: "Herbert Rowse Armstrong, you stand convicted of the wilful murder of

Katharine Mary Armstrong. What have you to say why the Court should not now give you judgment to die according to law?"

Armstrong, standing to attention, answered quietly, "Nothing."

The court was absolutely silent and all eyes focussed on the judge as slowly, deliberately the black cap was placed on his head. He then passed sentence. Before uttering the final words that would decide the prisoner's fate, Mr Justice Darling announced that he concurred with the jury's verdict and considered as absurd and unsupported by any evidence the suggestion that Mrs Armstrong had committed suicide. He continued, "You have had a fair trial; and been brilliantly defended; and a jury of your countrymen have carefully considered their verdict. It is my duty now merely to pronounce the sentence of the Court. It is that you be taken hence to the place from whence you came; that you be taken thence to a place of lawful execution; and that you be there hanged by the neck until you be dead; that your body be buried within the precincts of the prison in which you shall last be confined; and may the Lord have mercy on your soul."

Throughout this final ordeal, Armstrong remained at attention, heels together and arms straight at his sides. He looked directly at the judge and the only hint of inner torment was the white knuckles of his tightly clenched hands. When sentence was passed, he turned about smartly at a nudge from one of his warders, and disappeared from public view down the steps to the cells.

The last act was complete. After the formality of excusing the jury members from further service for twelve years, the judge allowed the Martin indictment to stand over to the next assize in the event of a successful appeal against the verdict. The court then rose and Armstrong's trial was officially over.

Sir Henry Curtis Bennett's walk had taken him out along a country road and he stopped at a small village post office. The counter assistant told him that her husband who had been in Hereford had just telephoned to say the jury had found Armstrong "Guilty". Sir Henry was shattered. He later told his family, "I shall never do a case like that again. I know that I have never done a better case and never will do. It was unjust – a poor show."

A special edition of the *Hereford Times* was quickly on the streets proclaiming the verdict. The reaction among the several hundred people gathered outside the court was one of stunned silence. When Mr Justice Darling was driven from the court building many people respectfully raised their hats; then there was a great surge of spectators to the gaol gate of the Shire Hall to witness Armstrong's departure.

It was rumoured that Armstrong collapsed in his cell after sentence was passed, but within half an hour he was ready to be driven back to Gloucester Prison. He looked drawn as he walked the few steps across the inner yard to the waiting car. The double doors to the street opened and the car reversed out; press photographers were perched at every vantage point; they hung from pillars and windows and even from hastily procured ladders. The camera shutters clicked at the face in the back of the car as the vehicle sped away from the court. Like the other moments of drama that day, the departure of the man under sentence of death was witnessed in complete silence.

ELVIRA BARNEY

(Old Bailey, 1932)

Edgar Lustgarten

Why shouldn't I have fun? I died young, didn't I?
"Elvira" in Noel Coward's *Blithe Spirit*

*The trial of the socialite Elvira Barney ranks among the greatest
triumphs of the defender's art. She shot dead her lover, Michael
Stephen, during a brawl at her Knightsbridge mews flat. Elvira was
the daughter of a rich and influential father, one of the scandalous
Bright Young Things of the 1920s. Her trial was one of the most
sensational of the early 1930s, covering the front pages of the world's
press for weeks. It had many theatrical ingredients: a deadly crime of
passion, London society, wealth and the raffish world of the West End
stage all went into the mix. Even after Mrs Barney's acquittal – and
her exit from the court in a state of collapse – her notoriety continued;
next day she was photographed laughing and driving her car to the
hairdresser. Noel Coward reputedly named "Elvira" in his comedy*
Blithe Spirit *after her. At her trial, Elvira Barney was defended by
Sir Patrick Hastings KC, like his more flamboyant contemporary Sir
Edward Marshall Hall KC, one of the greatest jury advocates of his
age. It was his remarkable performance in court that impressed Edgar
Lustgarten (1907–78), a Manchester lawyer who became a popular
criminologist in post-war Britain through his books and broadcasts.*

1

Every outstandingly successful advocate is to some degree the creation of his age. By natural instinct or by conscious acquisition he reflects the temper and the ethos that prevails among the society in which his work is done. Failing this, no technical equipment will attain the topmost heights.

Patrick Hastings – who unquestionably takes rank among the greatest jury advocates who have ever adorned the Bar – is the supreme example of a forensic master precisely attuned to the requirements of the time. In any generation his exceptional talents would have won acknowledgment: his extraordinary acuteness as a cross-examiner; his agility and resourcefulness in argument; the vigour of his quick and lucid mind, keenly intelligent rather than deeply intellectual, which made him more at home – as befits a jury advocate – with people and affairs than with theories and ideas. But to these was added a decisive factor that served to set the lasting seal on his success and fame: a worldly knowledge that was rooted in the moment. This worldliness, this fund of contemporary sense, directed his approach to every case he undertook; to those for whom he fought, to those he fought against, to those upon whom rested the outcome of the fight. That approach can be defined in a single word, used in its best and most recent connotation. More than any other counsel of comparable eminence, Hastings was a *sophisticated* advocate – in fashionable practice when fashionable people were setting new standards in advanced sophistication.

Sophisticated people do not care for strident emphasis; they stand on guard against assaults on the emotions; they like effects to be subtle and power to be concealed. In the language of the theatre, they prefer to have their dramas underplayed.

Hastings introduced, or at any rate perfected, the art of under-playing in the English jury courts. He utterly discarded the barnstorming technique; nobody has ever been more unlike Marshall Hall – nor, one suspects, more pleased to be unlike him. Hastings never stormed nor shouted; never waved his arms about; never gave any sign that he felt at all excited nor that he wished to cause excitement among others. And yet, in the sphere of high life litigation, there has never been a more exciting advocate, nor one who could exert a more mesmerising spell. The personality, cool, self-contained, rather offhand, slightly cynical; the voice, no organ throb moving listeners to tears, but smooth and even purring with an undertone of sarcasm; the manner, informed with that assurance and that ease which, in a public performer, masks the highest art – they enthralled and fascinated London Special Juries, particularly in the years between the two world wars. Here was an advocate whose individual style accorded with current cultivated taste. Hastings was a portent and an influence at the Bar analogous with and parallel to du Maurier on the stage.

Like du Maurier, and for not dissimiliar reasons, Hastings' professional home was the West End – which includes, for these purposes, the east point of the Strand but does not extend as far as the Old Bailey. During his great years in the very highest flight, when he was seldom missing from a civil *cause célèbre*, Hastings engaged in little criminal work and hardly ever accepted a capital defence. "I have always hated trials for murder" – so he wrote after retirement; and one might well imagine that such trials would repel a genius of his type and temperament.

This did not mean, though, that were he once involved he would not defend a murder case with dazzling ability. Especially a murder case falling, however remotely, into his chosen province; a murder case with a sophisticated setting and, at least upon the surface, a sophisticated twist.

2

Murder is rarely a sophisticated act; and suspicion of murder is generally aroused by the presence of unsophisticated passions. Greed, hate, jealousy and lust – these are universal impulses to action; but in a highly civilised and sceptical community one expects them to remain under reasonable control. It is therefore not surprising that, in contrast to the Borgias of fourteenth-century Italy and to the Medicis of sixteenth-century France, the well-to-do classes of twentieth-century Britain did not go in for killing, except with motor cars. Their murder rate was low, their murder charges few, even in proportion to their restricted numbers. During the last two decades of their existence – for since 1940 they have been virtually wiped out in the redistribution of property and wealth – they found ample employment for their favoured advocates by libel, slander, probate squabbles, and divorce.

This had become such a convention of the epoch that its one

great murder trial which did involve the rich came to many as a
bolt out of the blue. It gave an entirely unexpected handle to those
who disliked and denounced sophistication, but had formerly had
no grounds for connecting it with violence. Even now, unless
qualified, the implication was unwarranted. For the tiny band
of debauchees and profligates that formed the human background
to the case of Mrs Barney was no more than a foul offshoot, a
leprous excrescence, of true sophistication. They enjoyed – either
at first or second hand – the wealth so helpful to sophisticated
living; they used what passed for sophisticated language; the
simple were deceived by their sophisticated front. But theirs
was sophistication that had run riot and turned rotten; sophistication that had gone into reverse. Idle, drunken, emotionally unstable, crude in conduct as they were coarse in spirit, they made a
natural forcing bed for frenzy and convulsion.

Out of the rank soil of this Mayfair saturnalia sprang the most
vivid murder trial of 1932. It gave the upper strata of society a
shaking, seized the undivided attention of the lower, and involved
all England in a passionate debate about the character and morals
of the woman they accused.

3

Life had showered many favours on Elvira Barney. She was well-
bred; her titled parents, with their house in Belgrave Square and
their country seat in Sussex, occupied a position of dignity and
respect. She was affluent; money raised no shadow of a problem
and her pleasures never had to be curtailed through lack of means.
She was attractive in the style her contemporaries preferred – a
face that was pleasing rather than beautiful; large grey eyes; a tip-
tilted nose; blonde and fluffy hair; a boyish figure (though by the
time of her trial, when she was only twenty-six, both figure and
face were paying for indulgence). She had animal energy and
natural intelligence. All these assets she threw heedlessly away.

From her very early womanhood the writing on the wall grew
steadily more visible. The existence she led, the diversions she
sought, the friends she cultivated – every one was trivial, rackety
and exhausting. For a period she did toy with the idea of being an
actress, and once even appeared on the stage of the Gaiety in some
tiny part in a musical play; but hard work enticed her less than

superficial glamour, and she did not press ahead with a theatrical career. She married, with characteristic levity and caprice, a cabaret singer who had performed at a function in her father's house and whom she decided she had fallen in love with at first sight; this marriage turned out badly – Mrs Barney later spoke of it as "hell" – and the couple separated, never to reunite. Mr Barney returned to the United States whence he had come, and contributes nothing to this story but his name.

The break-up of her marriage expedited Mrs Barney's downward course. London's Bright Young People claimed her for their own. You still sometimes meet survivors of this long extinguished set; they are mostly male and now almost invariably perverts. Gin-soaked, fish-eyed, tearful with self-pity, these middle-aged derelicts haunt the bars of Kensington and Chelsea, calling down curses on their present lot and feebly lamenting the gay days that are no more. It is hard to believe, looking at them now, that anyone could have ever found them tolerable. But youth, while it lasts, is a potent alchemist, and for Mrs Barney certainly they were not without appeal. Her home in Williams Mews, near Knightsbridge – a converted cottage – became one of their recognised resorts and her black and red two-seater an addition to their transport. There were many parties; there was much dashing to and fro; there was a brisk traffic in sexual partnerships, from which Mrs Barney did not hold herself aloof.

Her lover, who had no genuine occupation (he vaguely described himself as a dress designer), rented an apartment room on Brompton Road. Everyone called him Michael, although that was not his name. Like Mrs Barney herself, he was respectably derived; but his father, a prominent magistrate and banker, in disgust at his son's conduct, had cut off his allowance; Michael had lately kept himself supplied with cash by "borrowing" alternately from his mother and his brother. He was now apparently quite content to be kept by his new mistress.

There were several other things besides good family and a taste for dissipation that Mrs Barney had in common with this handsome wastrel. They were exactly the same age. They both drank far too much. And each was prone to sudden fits of jealousy, his petulant and sulky, hers unbridled and consuming.

As in all the circumstances could have been foreseen, their relationship was marked by wildly fluctuating phases. There were times of mutual rapture, all the more intense for being so perilously

poised; times when they made love with fierce abandonment or
wrote each other tender letters in the idiom affected by adults
when addressing infants. There were also times of mutual agony,
when they tore themselves and their shallow love to tatters; times
when they had painful and degrading scenes in public and quarrelled bitterly far into the night. Neighbours in the mews, mostly
chauffeurs and their wives, suffered whichever condition was
prevailing; the din of recrimination and dispute was matched by
the din of exultant celebration. Resentment aroused by these
continual disturbances was not without its bearing upon subsequent events.

   If that resentment fixed upon the woman, not the man, the
causes were manifest and comprehensible. She, not he, was the
tenant of the cottage. She, not he, was in constant residence, the
human storm spot of a peaceful neighbourhood. And she, not he,
was the dominating partner; even the least discerning could
perceive that at a glance. Hers was the more possessive and
explosive nature; the more self-willed; the more accustomed to
impose itself on others. Of Elvira Barney it might be said with
literal truth that she would rather die than be deprived of her own
way.

4

One has forgotten the smart jargon of 1932, so it is impossible to
say whether the party Mrs Barney gave on the 30th of May was
divine or marvellous or super or terrific. There were, however,
abundant indications that it gave great pleasure to the persons who
attended, and it presented the neighbours with a further opportunity of studying their social betters at close range. From shortly
after six the racing cars rattled and roared into the mews; their
occupants, loudly shouting to each other, vanished one by one
through Mrs Barney's door; the hubbub floating through the
windows steadily increased as the female voices grew more shrill,
the male more stentorian; sometimes a solitary guest, appearing
overtaxed, came out into the mews for a few minutes' fresh air; and
once or twice, keen-eyed observers noted, a couple would emerge,
drive off in one of the cars, and, half an hour later, return and go
inside again. Mrs Barney did nothing by half measures; she
entertained her friends in the style to which they were accustomed.

By half-past nine, though, all of them had gone. Michael – who had been handing drinks assiduously – and Mrs Barney – who had been assiduously taking them – now sat alone amid the residual débris. They drank some more – he faster, in order to catch up. When they had put themselves entirely in the mood they set off together on their usual nightly round.

Soon after ten o'clock they were seen having dinner in the Café de Paris. Soon after eleven they were seen at a well-known night resort in Dean Street – the management of which indignantly complained when the papers so described it in the days and weeks that followed. "We are a high-class social rendezvous and members' club." Soon after twelve they left this club and so far as is known went straight back to Williams Mews.

They were certainly there at three, when yet another of their quarrels broke the silence of the summer night. Sleepers in the mews reluctantly awakened; swore at the nuisance; prayed it would die down. But instead the uproar gathered force and swelled in volume. Woman's voice; man's voice; woman's voice; man's voice; separate and distinct at first, then jumbled together. The mews pulled its sheets round its infuriated head; but could not shut out this obliterating row. Groans, abuse, tears, entreaties – and was that the sound of a struggle, of a fight?

Somewhere about four there was a piercing crack. People sat up, startled. No, it couldn't be. Crazy as that woman was, it couldn't be . . .

Most of them had dropped off again to sleep before the doctor's telephone began to ring.

5

"I have been cautioned that I am not obliged to make this statement. I have known Michael for about a year. We were great friends, and he used to come and see me from time to time.

"He always used to see me home. He did so last night as usual. Immediately we got in we had a quarrel about a woman he was fond of.

"He knew I kept a revolver in the house. I have had it for years. It was kept in various places. Last night it was under the cushion of a chair in the bedroom, near the bed. I was afraid of it and used to hide it from time to time. He knew where it was last night.

"He took it, saying, 'I am going to take it away for fear you kill yourself.' He went into the room on the left. I ran after him and tried to get it back.

"There was no struggle in the bedroom. It was outside in the spare room, in the doorway. As we were struggling together – he wanted to take it away, and I wanted to get it back – it went off. Our hands were together – his hands and mine . . .

"I did not think anything had happened. He seemed quite all right. He went into the bathroom and half shut the door, and said, 'Fetch a doctor.'

"I asked, 'Do you really mean it?' I did not have the revolver then. I think it had fallen to the ground.

"I saw he looked ill, so I rang up a doctor, but no one answered. I went upstairs again and saw him sitting on the floor.

"I was upset and began to cry. I again rang up the doctor and he said he would come. I went upstairs again. Michael asked, 'Why doesn't the doctor come? I want to tell him what happened. It was not your fault.'

"He repeated that over and over again. I tried to cut his tie off, put a towel on his chest and got towels. I again rang up the doctor, and they said that he was leaving.

"I again went upstairs and saw he was dead and just waited. I don't remember what I did afterwards. I was so frantic. I am sure – as far as I know – there was only one shot fired.

"Michael and I have quarrelled on previous occasions, but not often."

Mrs Barney leaned back. Her face was ashen and her breath came heavily. While the Inspector read over her statement in official monotone, for the first time she allowed her eyes to wander over the bleak and bare police station room.

The foolscap sheets were put in front of her. Mechanically she signed.

It was morning, almost ten o'clock in the morning, after a night packed full with horror and distress. When the doctor arrived in response to Mrs Barney's summons ("There has been a terrible accident; for God's sake come at once!") he beheld a scene that might have been pleasing in a mystery novel, but was apt to harrow the steadiest nerves when encountered in real life. Michael sprawled at the top of the stairs, a bullet through his lung; it was obvious to the doctor that he was already dead. Close beside him lay a pistol; it contained five cartridges, two of which were spent. Mrs Barney herself was uncontrollably hysterical and only intermittently coherent. "He cannot be dead, he cannot be dead," she cried time and again. "I will die too; I want to die. I loved him so. I loved him so." As the doctor, stooping low over the corpse, confirmed his initial melancholy conclusion, she ran aimlessly to and fro, calling the dead man's name and trying to explain what had occurred in disconnected fragments.

The arrival of the police (whom the doctor as in duty bound immediately informed) seemed to drive the unhappy woman clean out of her mind. She said afterwards that she had no recollection of this episode, and quite conceivably she was in some sort of delirium; if not – whether innocent or guilty – her conduct would have surely been less hurtful to her cause. She cursed and fulmi-nated against the officers, calling them "vile swine" and ordering them to leave; when they used the telephone, she snatched it from their hands; when told that she must go to the police station for further questioning, she gave her interrogator a blow across the face. She shrieked, stamped, laughed and wept alternately. She was, said the doctor, absolutely frenzied . . .

No spark of frenzy lingered in Mrs Barney now. It had died when they took her away from the cottage that had been her home and where now her lover's body lay. Thenceforward she was calm but patently exhausted; what woman could be other-wise who in so few hours had passed through so many prostrating events? While she made her statement, under the horrified eyes of her distracted parents who had been apprised and had hurried to her side, Mrs Barney must have been close to collapse from sheer fatigue.

The clarity of her account thus becomes the more remarkable. Moreover, it entirely corresponded in essentials with all she had so far said and all she was yet to say. There were one or two omissions, probably deliberate. It would have been painful to reveal in the presence of her parents that she and Michael had been lovers many months; that the quarrel had developed after they had gone to bed; that Michael had threatened to leave her, got up again and dressed; that it was then she had talked of committing suicide. She hoped – no doubt expected – that the matter would soon drop without necessitating these intimate disclosures. But substantially the story that was outlined in her statement was the story that the doctor had already pieced together from her paroxysmal and confused ejacu-lations; nor was it changed in that excruciating hour when, with two prison wardresses beside her, she told it to a packed and palpitating court . . .

The police conferred together. Her own statement exculpated Mrs Barney, and they had no evidence yet to suggest it was untrue.

"Very well," said the Inspector, "we will not trouble you, madam, any more just now. You are free to go."

"She will come home with us, of course, Inspector," said her mother . . .

The respite was a short one. Only three days afterwards, as the troubled family prepared for dinner, the police came visiting the house in Belgrave Square. They had now been able to make a full investigation and, as a result, were no longer satisfied. Data in their possession could not be made to tally with the statement that the lady gave them earlier in the week.

That evening Mrs Barney, who had said she wished to die, stood in grave danger that this wish would be fulfilled.

6

From the moment of her arrest the popular press was in full cry; their headlines sometimes read like a satirical burlesque. "West End Flat Mystery," "Society Tragedy Sensation," "Mayfair Beauty in Shooting Drama," "Banker's Son Dead after Cocktail Party," "Knight's Daughter on Murder Charge"; variations revolved round these titillating words – save in one instance, where a banner frankly promised "Mrs Barney: The Biggest Thrills." The prisoner herself, on her first appearance at the preliminary proceedings in the police court, unintentionally added to the atmosphere of melodrama by falling to the floor of the dock in a dead faint.

Mrs Barney had good reason to feel deeply apprehensive. The police had not at all overstated their position; the new evidence – if accepted – made her story of an accident untenable. One female neighbour was fully prepared to swear she had heard Mrs Barney shout "I'll shoot you" just before the shot. Another female neighbour was equally prepared to swear that she had heard more than one shot being fired (an assertion that appeared to gain considerable force from the presence of a bullet mark on the cottage bedroom wall). Both women also spoke of an incident some days earlier when, as they declared, Mrs Barney from the window fired at Michael in the mews. And to all these presumed facts was added the opinion of two exceptionally influential experts, Churchill the gunsmith and Spilsbury the pathologist; each independently had come to the conclusion that Mrs Barney's version of the shooting was improbable. The former attached special significance to the type of pistol. "It requires both a long and heavy pull," he said.

The Crown thus had a formidable case and the prisoner sore need of a formidable defender. For once in a murder trial money was no object. The brief for Mrs Barney was offered to Patrick Hastings.

One may surmise that that distinguished advocate, then a little over fifty and at the very peak of his dazzling career, thought hard before he undertook this burden. It was in the middle of the summer term, and a dozen heavily marked briefs were on his desk. He was representing one of the great trusts in a claim for £60,000 from one of the great banks. He was retained by a leading theatre management in a suit for damages brought by a leading lady. He was concerned for the co-respondent in an aristocratic divorce with Eaton Square addresses and an adultery charge at Cannes. He was also concerned in a big probate action (disposed of four days before the Barney trial began), in a newspaper libel on a popular peeress (settled three days after the Barney trial concluded), and, as leader of a string of eminent counsel, in an appeal by the directors of a company against a verdict of £250,000 imposed upon them for conspiracy and fraud. (This last case actually started on the final morning of Mrs Barney's trial, and continued uninterruptedly thereafter for a fortnight.) There were certainly ample demands on Patrick Hastings – and there was, of course, his confessed dislike of capital defences.

Nevertheless, he did not decline the Barney brief, and this without doubt was artistically fitting. Here at last for the sophisticated advocate was a murder case that had at least grown out of his own world.

7

Any murder trial at any time tends to attract spectators if only because the stake is human life. A sensational Victorian trial like Mrs Bartlett's or a sensational Edwardian trial like Robert Wood's was not only sure of a continuously packed court, but also would draw and hold great multitudes in the adjoining streets. More recently this latter phenomenon had been rarely seen. It reappeared, however, at the trial of Mrs Barney, which, on 4th July and the two succeeding days, made the Central Criminal Court like a fortress under siege.

The military metaphor is far from inappropriate. For in one respect, at least, the crowds on this occasion easily surpassed all their predecessors. They were less demonstrative than some, partly because of the changed bent of the time, partly because at no point was there anything approaching unanimity of view upon the case's merits. But they were surely unique in ferocity and resolve. The waiting crowds of earlier years may have envied those within; they did not themselves seek entry by violence and brute force. But many of those who stood and stared at the walls of the Old Bailey, hour after hour while Mrs Barney was being tried, only accepted this second-best sensation after a pitched battle in which they were repelled.

The queue had begun to form on Sunday afternoon, more than twenty hours before the court was due to sit. Well before midnight it had grown so long and deep that the police decided it ought to be dispersed. Those who had already waited nearly half a day did not receive this decision with good humour. There were loud cries of protest; heated disputes developed; one poor old lady burst into bitter tears – she had been there since two o'clock and now her last train had gone.

The police, however, insisted on their orders being obeyed, and reluctantly the crowds withdrew from their vantage-ground. Some gave up altogether and went home. Some took refuge in the all-night cafés, where they debated plans for making a fresh attempt. But the majority merely split up into groups of two or three, who walked and stood and squatted in the neighbourhood all night and took up posts next morning within sight of the court door like so many beasts of prey around a water-hole.

These omens were not lost upon the police, and a strong protective cordon was established before giving the signal that the queue might be re-formed. Strong, but not strong enough to seize immediate control. From all directions men and women flew towards the spot with an impetus as if they had been shot from catapults. The cordon swayed, retreated and at one point final y broke; the mob hurled themselves madly at the gap; and that firs.

afternoon the newspapers had pictures of police and civilians struggling on the ground.

Only a handful of these warriors gained admission to the court, where most of the space had been allotted in advance by tickets bearing the full name of the successful applicant. But there, too, disorder threatened, though of a different kind. Many of the tickets had somehow been obtained by young, well-dressed and frivolous-minded women who regarded the trial as a theatrical first night and proceeded to behave like the audience at one. They giggled and chattered with indecent zest as they waited, all agog, for the performance to begin.

At any intimation of weakness on the Bench this animated bevy might have got right out of hand. There was no such intimation. "If there is any more of this," remarked his lordship coolly, when the female babble broke out for the first time in his presence, "the whole court shall be cleared."

Thenceforward silence reigned. Even the silliest could see that Mr Justice Travers Humphreys was a man who meant exactly what he said.

8

Hastings had come into court just before the appointed hour. After one contemptuous glance at the gay parade of fashion, he took his place without ostentatious fuss and sat there very straight and very quiet and very still. Those present who had witnessed Marshall Hall's volcanic entries on similar occasions, and the indisputable gallery play that followed them, could hardly fail to be struck by the sharp contrast. One thing only the two men had in common – a personality magnetic and commanding. Without the slightest effort – almost as though it were contrary to his wish – from the very moment when he first appeared Hastings dominated the entire Old Bailey scene. Long before he had said a single word, even during the opening statement for the Crown, the eyes of the jury were straying constantly to him . . .

A practised observer can usually detect when a prosecutor feels full confidence in his case. If he harbours any serious doubt himself, being imbued by his training with the salutary doctrine that the prisoner must receive the benefit of a doubt, this is almost sure to be reflected in his speech. He will pitch his argument in a lower key, sprinkle it with exceptions and provisos, leave the issue conspicuously open. In short, he becomes more narrator than accuser.

Nothing of this kind occurred at the trial of Mrs Barney. Percival Clarke, leading counsel for the Crown, gave the jury at the outset a strong and clear lead. His manifest integrity – befitting a son of Mrs Bartlett's great defender – lent his comments additional effect. Some of these consisted of direct denunciation. Of the prisoner's hysteria on the arrival of the doctor he said: "Perhaps she realised then what she had done." Of her assault upon the police: "You see what sort of temper this woman gives way to on slight provocation." And of the actual shooting he spoke in these uncompromising terms: "The medical evidence can definitely establish the direction in which the revolver was held when fired. You will learn from that that it is practically impossible for the man to have caused this injury to himself. If he did not, who did? There was only one other person there. If you are forced to the conclusion that she shot him, you will have to consider whether she did it by accident or design. In that connection you will bear in mind her admission of the quarrel. You will bear in mind what she shouted before the gun was fired. You will bear in mind that she had fired the gun during another quarrel on a previous occasion. Members of the jury, is there any explanation consistent with common sense which will enable you to understand how that man met his death unless this woman *deliberately* fired?"

To the lawyers in court – and there were a great number, some even disposing themselves upon the floor – it became more apparent as each minute passed that the prosecution were not pulling any punches. Obviously they believed in their case and they were both seeking and expecting a conviction.

9

The chief witnesses called on the first day of the trial were Mrs Barney's much-enduring neighbours from the mews.

There were three altogether; but the last, a chauffeur, was of little consequence. It was the two women who mattered – the women, each of them a decent chauffeur's wife, who had had their lives made wretched by Mrs Barney's escapades. The defence could not hope to find them favourably inclined, and their cross-examination needed infinite finesse.

One important gain, though, Hastings made without exertion; simply by watchfulness and tactical restraint. The first chauffeur's wife was being examined by the Crown. She had given her account of the earlier incident in the mews, describing how Mrs Barney leaned out of the window; how she was holding "something bright" in her *left* hand; how there was a report and witness saw "a puff of smoke." Now she had come to the night of Michael's death, and to the one real point at which she might have thrown some light upon it.

"So you heard the sounds of their quarrelling," Clarke said. "Were there any words – any *important* words – you could pick out?"

"Yes," she replied. "Just before the shot I heard Mrs Barney say, 'Get out. I'll shoot. I'll shoot.'"

Now "I'll shoot" is not at all the same thing as "I'll shoot *you*," which was what the woman had originally told the police; otherwise Clarke would not in turn have told the jury. "I'll shoot" is as consistent with a threat to commit suicide as a threat to commit murder. If the evidence stood thus – and no other witness claimed to have overheard this passage – it need no longer conflict with the prisoner's own story.

"You heard her say 'I'll shoot'?" Clarke repeated interrogatively.

The rules of British procedure do not permit counsel to put leading questions on matters in dispute to any witness that he himself has called. A leading question, one should point out, is not – as common usage would suggest – a question peculiarly probing or embarrassing; it is one so framed as to indicate the answer that the questioner desires or expects. It is not "leading" to ask "Where were you yesterday?"; it is "leading" to ask "Did you go yesterday to Brighton?" It would certainly have been "leading" had Clarke at this juncture asked the witness "Did you hear the prisoner call out, 'I'll shoot *you*,'" and Hastings, though he sat with folded arms, looking straight ahead, was poised to intervene with an immediate objection. But it did not prove necessary. Clarke bowed to the inevitable and passed to something else.

Hastings carefully refrained from mentioning the matter in cross-examination. Any attempt at that stage to emphasise the witness's cardinal omission ("So, after all, you only heard the prisoner say 'I'll shoot'?") might prompt her to reconsideration and retraction ("She *first* said 'I'll shoot,' and then after, 'I'll shoot *you'* "). There would be a later and a safer chance to enlarge on this discrepancy. Meanwhile prudence prescribed leaving well alone.

But there was still of course the earlier shooting to be dealt with, and the court now got its first glimpse of Hastings in full action.

10

He began in a tone so soft, so conversational, that spectators in the gallery held their breath for fear of missing a single word.

"This incident in the mews – it happened late one night?"

"Yes."

"About eleven o'clock next morning did you see the young man again?"

"Yes."

"Was he then leaving the cottage?"

"Yes."

"Was Mrs Barney with him?"

"Yes."

"Did they seem friendly?"

"Yes."

"On the best possible terms?"

"Yes."

Marshall Hall would have paused there and stared hard at the jury. Hastings would no more emphasise a point in such a fashion than Noel Coward would wink at the stalls to stress a witty line.

The questions continued; terse, pithy – and exact. They left no room for evasion or misunderstanding.

"You saw this earlier incident while standing at your window?"

"Yes."

"And the young man was below you in the mews?"

"Yes."

"Did you give evidence at the police court?"

"Yes."

"Did you say there that immediately after the shot was fired the young man spoke to you?"

"Yes."

"And in the police court there the matter ended?"

"Yes."

"But now," said Hastings, "I want you to tell us what he said."

That he had touched a highly sensitive spot was attested by the quickness of the Crown's reaction.

"My lord, I object." Percival Clarke had at once sprung to his feet. "I submit that what this witness and the young man may have said outside Mrs Barney's hearing cannot be admissible. That is why it was not tendered at the police court. And if it cannot be evidence for the Crown, equally it cannot be evidence for the defence."

He sat down. The judge cast an inquiring look at Hastings.

"In all my experience at the Bar," declared the latter, "I have never heard such an objection made before. The prosecution ask a question in the lower court and then they don't allow it to be answered." It was a perfect example of his gift for deadly ridicule, for deflating opposition in one swift, colloquial phrase. The jury, unversed in procedural technicalities, must have rejoiced in this attractive simplification – well calculated to excite their sympathy if the evidence should be ultimately excluded.

But the defence was very anxious that the evidence should be heard, and this depended not upon the jury but the judge.

Travers Humphreys listened attentively, impassively, as Hastings made his submission on the law. "Here the prosecution have proved a fact. They have proved there was the firing of a revolver from a window and that the deceased man *at that moment* made a statement to a witness. I submit it is always admissible to give evidence of any statement accompanying such an incident."

It was in fact a question involving much more doubt than might have been deduced from the defender's confident air. The judge, although an unsurpassed authority in this field, reflected deeply before giving a decision. "The matter is not free from difficulty," he said. "I think the objection was quite properly taken. But" – and the lawyers knew then the defence would get their way – "but . . . I do not think this evidence ought to be excluded."

The reason why both sides had treated this as a prime issue soon became apparent when Hastings, armed with sanction from the Bench, resumed.

"What conversation passed," he asked, "between you and the young man?"

"I told him to clear off," said the first chauffeur's wife, "as he was a perfect nuisance in the mews."

"What did he reply?"

"He said he didn't want to leave Mrs Barney because *he was afraid that she might kill herself*."

To the defence this admission was of immeasurable value. If Michael had previously confided to a stranger that he suspected Mrs Barney of suicidal tendencies, what was more likely than that, prior to going away, he would at least try to dispossess her of the pistol? And if he did, what more likely than that a woman of her temperament, whether genuinely contemplating suicide or not, should struggle fiercely to defeat him in this purpose lest her expressed intentions should appear frustrated? . . .

It was the beginning, this – the beginning of a long series of scores by Mrs Barney's advocate that gradually cemented what had seemed a flimsy case.

11

One such score was to be added before this witness left the box.

The defence were not going to disavow the earlier shooting, when Mrs Barney was upstairs and Michael in the mews. But they were going to deny that she had fired *out* of the window, maintaining she had fired, for effect, *inside* the room.

Others had seen Michael; others had heard the shot; but only this lady spoke of seeing Mrs Barney with the pistol in her hand at the moment it was fired.

There was ground for supposing an imaginative faculty occasionally influenced her powers of observation. Hastings brought this out into the light.

"When the shot was fired," he said, "you say you saw a puff of smoke?"

"I did."

"How big was it?"

The witness knitted her brows.

"Well –"

"As big as that?"

Counsel extended his hands about a foot apart.

"Oh no; not as big as that."

"How big, then?" Hastings asked encouragingly.

The witness spread her hands in turn.

"As big as that?"

"Yes."

Hastings nodded slightly. His next two questions seemed to come as afterthoughts.

"I suppose you didn't know that Mrs Barney's revolver contained cordite cartridges?"

"No." The witness answered with indifference.

"And I suppose you don't know either," Hastings added casually, "that cordite cartridges don't make any smoke?"

The ten men and two women on the jury may have known nothing of the properties of cordite; but they did know, by applying ordinary sense, that so shrewd a counsel would not make such an assertion if it were open to subsequent disproof by the Crown. The puff of smoke disappeared into thin air . . .

The second chauffeur's wife seemed to have seen a good deal less, but heard a good deal more. It was she who thought that on the night of Michael's death more than one shot had been fired, and that they came in quick succession. If the jury thought so too, the outlook for Mrs Barney would be bleak indeed.

Once again Hastings sought his ends without direct attack. Keenly aware of psychological resistances, he made no suggestion that the lady had been wrong. Instead of pressing her to cut down the number of the shots, he almost appeared to help her run them up. In no time at all she had sworn to hearing *five*.

"Quite a fusillade," observed defending counsel, absently fingering the barrel of the pistol, from which only two bullets had been fired in all . . .

Few yet realised exactly what had happened. They felt instinctively that this sardonic advocate, restrained but masterful, was having his own way and getting what he wanted; they did not at once perceive how much he had wanted nor how far he had gone. There had been none of the orthodox phenomena associated with a crisis in a murder trial; the rising voices, the deepening gravity, the open conflict between witnesses and Bar. All they had heard were some crisp and simple questions asked in the most natural and unpretentious style. But where now was the mews evidence – the shouting and the shots?

It was like a conjuring trick – but a conjuring trick performed without any drum rolls or spotlights or hey prestos. Nor did the conjurer bother to take a formal bow.

12

The witnesses from the mews, for all essential purposes, constituted the whole of the Crown's evidence of *fact*. But in a trial the emphasis may be more upon *opinion* – the opinion of experts formed after the event.

Many have gone to the gallows in consequence of these. Would Norman Thorne have been hanged but for Spilsbury's opinion that no cord was ever passed round Elsie Cameron's neck? Would Seddon have been hanged but for Willcox's opinion that Eliza Barrow died from acute, not chronic, poisoning? Would Rouse have been hanged but for Colonel Buckle's opinion that the nut in his carburettor pipe was purposely made loose?

This is not written in disparagement of experts – none will deny that Seddon and Rouse, at least, were rightly hanged – but simply to recall again their influence and power. A famous name, an authoritative style, the mystique of science and the glamour of detection – these may combine to produce such an effect that juries on occasion find it almost irresistible.

Unless, of course, the glamour can be stripped off and the mystique penetrated.

13

The experts in the Barney trial were called on the second morning, and Spilsbury was the first to go into the box. He made his usual excellent impression: suave, sure of himself, with every detail at his finger ends, he took great pains to make the jury understand that Michael could not possibly have committed suicide. He made play with the pistol. He explained the nature and direction of the wound. He told of experiments he had made upon a skeleton. It was all immensely neat and competent; it bore on every word and movement the authentic Spilsbury stamp.

As the pathologist went through this demonstration Hastings preserved an appearance of detachment. "A most interesting performance," his expression said; "remarkably learned, extraordinarily instructive; but, as the defence is not and never has been one of suicide, it has nothing whatever to do with Mrs Barney or with me." None the less, he was following most intently – waiting for any attempt on Spilsbury's part to dismiss as impossible the real defence of accident.

Although the point might not have struck the ordinary observer, no such attempt was ever made in positive terms. Whatever may have been the general tenor of his evidence, Spilsbury did not rule out accident in so many words. The omission, it seems certain, was one of policy. Both the Crown and their star witness doubtless expected events to trace a long familiar pattern; they thought defending counsel in cross-examination would try his utmost to get Spilsbury's blessing for his client's story. Better to hold direct comment on that story till then. Better leave the accident defence till it was raised.

But Hastings was a subtle and unorthodox tactician; he did not mind forgoing the slight chance of Spilsbury's blessing, provided he had not incurred his express condemnation.

The crowd was waiting eagerly for a titanic struggle between two such masters in their respective spheres. When Spilsbury's interrogation by the Crown was over, and Hastings was seen to be rising in his place, heads craned forward and hearts beat faster. People felt on the brink of an historical event.

Spilsbury watched Hastings narrowly as the first question was put.

"To qualify yourself to show how the bullet was fired into the body, you had to examine the skeleton of someone else?"

"I had to *confirm* it on the skeleton of someone else," said Spilsbury.

"Does each human body differ in formation?"

"Yes, in the formation of the bones."

"And the best way to see how a bullet is fired into a body . . . is to look at it, I suppose?"

"Yes," Spilsbury admitted.

They had quickly got to grips. The spectators resettled themselves for a long and thrilling tussle.

The next thing they knew was that, incredibly, unaccountably, Hastings had sat down.

"Sir Bernard Spilsbury," he observed later to the jury, "gave no shred of evidence to suggest that the young man's death could not have been caused in the way that Mrs Barney has always said it was . . . He did not affect my case. I had no questions to ask him."

This neutralising of the country's crack professional witness was ultimately justified by the strictest of all tests. Meanwhile those in court received a shock of non-fulfilment, the kind of shock you get when you put your foot on a step that isn't there.

14

A more spectacular battle, however, was to come – a battle fought out toe to toe with every move in view, a battle in which the art and flair of Hastings were displayed so that laymen no less than lawyers could admire . . .

Robert Churchill, who followed Spilsbury, was also a leading expert and a seasoned witness who had figured prominently in numerous murder trials. Whenever in a shooting case anything seemed to turn upon the bullets that were fired or the weapon that was used, more likely than not Churchill would be called on by the Crown. Level-headed, matter-of-fact, a savant in his sphere, he shared with Spilsbury an enviable legend of impregnability in cross-examination.

Upon that legend a chill wind was now about to blow.

Churchill had examined Mrs Barney's pistol and gave his views about it with definite conciseness. It was one of the safest revolvers ever made. It could only be fired by the exercise of considerable strength. Therefore the idea of it going off accidentally when no one wished to fire certainly did not commend itself to him.

The defence could not skirt gracefully round such evidence as this. It struck at the essentials of Mrs Barney's story. This time when Hastings rose it was no false alarm.

He placed the revolver on the flat of his hand and held it out before the witness and the jury.

"Do you seriously say," he asked, "that this is one of the safest weapons made?"

"I do," Churchill replied.

"Where is the safety device?"

"There isn't one."

"Isn't there one on most good hammerless revolvers?"

"Yes," said Churchill. "What I meant was that it's safer than a revolver with a hammer, safer than an automatic pistol."

"I see." Hastings suddenly grasped the pistol and held it up aloft. His finger pressed the trigger. Click-click, click-click, click-click it went continuously, with little more resistance than a child's cheap toy. ("It doesn't seem to require any terrific muscular strength?"

"It would require more," said Churchill, "if the weapon were held loosely."

"Would it?" Hastings promptly changed his grip and held the revolver as the expert had suggested. "Would it?"

Again he pressed the trigger, quickly and repeatedly, with disdainful ease. And again it was the only sound in the hushed and listening court: click-click, click-click, click-click, click-click, click-click.

"Well," said Churchill, speaking as best he could in competition with the pistol, "I still say it's safer than an automatic."

Hastings kept on pressing the trigger almost languidly. Churchill watched him, a shade uncomfortably. The incessant sound of clicking only ceased when it had imprinted itself on every mind.

The defender laid the pistol on the desk before him.

"You know the sequence of cartridges found in this revolver?"

"I do, yes."

"Did they go like this – discharged, live, discharged, live, live?"

"Yes."

"The two discharged cartridges represent shots fired?"

"Yes."

"Somehow one chamber in between had been passed over?"

"Yes."

"Have you noticed something peculiar about this revolver – that if you only half pull the trigger the pressure just rotates the cylinder?"

"Yes."

"Rotates it, without firing?"

"Yes."

"It looks, doesn't it, as though some time after the first shot had been fired *something* had happened to press the trigger, but not to the full degree?"

"The cylinder had certainly been moved," said Churchill guardedly.

Hastings took care not to press the point further, not to involve himself in argument as to what that "something" was. He relied upon the quicker-witted members of the jury; they would not fail to realise, in present circumstances, that a struggle for the weapon, with fingers clutching at it indiscriminately, was more likely to give rise to a half pull at the trigger than anybody's genuine attempt to fire a shot.

He again picked up the pistol and meditatively pressed the trigger once or twice.

"Supposing a person had got the revolver and another person came and there was a struggle, it is extremely likely that if they continued to struggle and the revolver was loaded it would go off?"

"Yes," said Churchill.

"And it is quite impossible for anyone who was not there to know exactly how the revolver in these circumstances would go off?"

"Yes," said Churchill.

"And if one person has the revolver in his hand and the other person seizes it and the revolver is pointing towards him, it is certain it will go off if it is pressed hard enough?"

"Yes," said Churchill.

"And if he happened to be there, opposite the revolver, he would be certain to be killed?"

"Yes," said Churchill. "Yes, he would; of course."

How exactly had they reached this situation? The witness himself might have found it hard to say. He had answered yes to a short series of questions, none of which sounded very deadly in itself and each of which hardly allowed of any other answer. And yet, at the end, he seemed to have agreed that no flaw could be pointed out in Mrs Barney's case. Or hadn't he?

Anyone who shares this slightly puzzled feeling should study those four questions phrase by phrase and word by word. Their deceptive facility masks perfect craftsmanship.

15

That afternoon Mrs Barney went into the box.

It is highly doubtful whether she had been able to form any clear impression of her trial or any distinct notion about how matters were going. In the first hour or so she had taken copious notes, but mainly with the object of occupying herself, and the effort of concentration soon became too great. Thereafter, most of the time, she had seemed pathetically remote. Now and again a sob, immediately stifled, had shown an awareness of what was being said; she could never hear, without betraying emotion, any direct allusion to her lover's death. For the rest she had sat back in her chair, her grey eyes fixed on some point above the bench, ceaselessly twisting a handkerchief through visibly trembling hands. She had been, as many prisoners mercifully are, partially numb from suffering and anguish.

But now, having taken the oath, as she turned to face the court she beheld her situation in cruelly sharpened outline. The judge, who seemed so frighteningly close; the rows of counsel in their austere black and white; her father's bowed head and her mother's piteous face upturned – all were assembled on her account. She, Elvira Barney, was being tried for murder, and the punishment for murderers was death. Her nerve momentarily snapped, and absolute breakdown threatened just when her life might turn upon her self-command.

Perhaps this challenge, dimly apprehended, lent her strength. Perhaps she drew comfort from her famous counsel, who spoke to her with reassuring informality, putting questions so specific yet so simply framed that she could easily follow them notwithstanding her distress. Perhaps the instincts of a quondam actress stood her in good stead during this critical performance. Certainly she fought and overcame her panic; only the first few answers came in choking whispers; soon she was pouring out the tale of her afflictions in a voice not less audible for being pleasantly low-pitched.

The order of her narrative – imposed, of course, by Hastings – was skilfully judged in its cumulative power. She began by describing the miseries of her marriage and the physical brutality exhibited by her husband; this might reasonably be expected to arouse – in all probability for the first time in the trial – a modest degree of compassion for the prisoner, and go a little way at least towards extenuation of the vicious and discreditable life she had led since. She went on to say that she had sought divorce, but she had been advised of legal difficulties,* and that she had earnestly desired to marry Michael; this put the liaison in a rather better light and made her appear less contemptuous of good morals. She explained her possession of the loaded pistol – not normally a young woman's dressing-table adjunct; it had been given her several years ago by an army friend she named, from whose country house they used to go out rabbit shooting; she had always kept it with her in the cottage, which was easy game for burglars and where she often was alone.

---

* Viz., that Barney being an American, she was a domiciled American herself.

Then Hastings guided her to the first mews episode. She told how she and Michael had quarrelled over money; how she had refused to finance his gambling; how he had walked out of the cottage but would not stay away, returning to create a scene in the middle of the night. "I was so unhappy," Mrs Barney said, "I thought I would make him think I was going to commit suicide. So, when he was outside, I fired the pistol at random in the room. Then I thought if he really believed I'd killed myself he'd go and fetch people, so I looked out of the window."

"When was the bullet mark made on the bedroom wall?" Hastings asked.

"On that occasion," answered Mrs Barney.

She maintained the mastery of her rebellious nerves even when asked about the night of Michael's death. Again she went through all the agonising details, from the start of the party early in the evening to the finish of it all in the shining summer dawn. Only when she spoke of Michael's last few living moments and of the last few words that she would ever hear him say, her will-power proved insufficient to the task and a storm of weeping broke upon her unrestrained . . .

She did not give way to the same extent again, but by the day's end, after being searchingly and closely cross-examined, Mrs Barney was not far from emotional exhaustion. But there was one more unexpected test for her to undergo.

"I want the revolver," said Hastings, "put on the ledge of the box exactly in front of the witness."

Everyone watched the usher carry out counsel's direction. Then their eyes moved back to Mrs Barney. She was gazing down wretchedly at the source of all her griefs.

Hastings faced the judge. He seemed about to address him. Suddenly, almost violently, he turned.

"Pick up that revolver, Mrs Barney!"

His voice rang out, deliberately harsh. That it gave Mrs Barney a surprise and shock was manifest to all; it was beyond her meagre acting skill to simulate such a jump. She picked the pistol up at once – picked it up with her right hand.

There was a mighty throb in court as people realised that the first chauffeur's wife had said she fired it with her left.

16

The Crown, though, were neither disconcerted nor deterred. Clarke, it is true, could hardly have foreseen the exact trend of events during the past two crowded days – otherwise so sound an advocate would have modified his opening – but he had patently not wavered in his own view of the case nor in his expectation of its outcome. All along he had shown unabated confidence, and now, winding up at the end of the second afternoon, he sounded like a man merely clinching a decision. He pointed to Mrs Barney's jealousy: "What was more likely to make her lose control?" He pointed to the peril in which she knew she stood: "What stronger motive could there be for colouring her story?" And that story itself? "It is incredible," he said. "If you can believe it – *if* you can believe it – of course, members of the jury, you will be happy to acquit. But" – and here the prosecutor spoke with solemn emphasis – "if you weigh the evidence carefully and dispassionately, I submit that you will find the accusation proved."

At this stage many, perhaps most, were ready to agree. I personally believe that if the verdict had been taken there and then Mrs Barney would not have been acquitted. The jury must have been keenly aware of the defence successes, so brilliantly accomplished and accented by her counsel, but the relation of these successes to each other and their implication when considered as a whole were as yet almost certainly beyond them. They could only be made plain by a feat of argument – not of eloquence, nor imagery, nor pathos – but sheer hard *argument*, explicit and translucent, which would convince the reason and satisfy the mind.

Such a performance was forthcoming on the morrow when Patrick Hastings made his closing speech.

17

That speech contains no quotable passages of rhetoric. It will never be a feature of collections or anthologies. For perfection of phrase and elegance of form it cannot compare with more sumptuous orations, such as that of J. P. Curran on behalf of Justice Johnson or that of John Inglis on behalf of Madeleine Smith. It was never designed nor intended so to do. It can only be judged within the context of the trial; by its aptness and response to the immediate demand; by its value in advancing the cause of the accused. The test of advocacy, in the last resort, is functional and empiric – and by that test Hastings' speech for the defence of Mrs Barney will hold its own in the most exalted sphere . . .

There were no eye-catching preliminaries; no pose adopted, no attitude struck, to mark the imminence of a big occasion. As soon as the court sat next morning he got up and began.

"Members of the jury, I shall not indulge in flights of oratory or dramatic surprises such as are supposed to be the attributes of an advocate. They may be amusing, but we are not in this court to amuse."

The note had been struck at once. As he stood facing them, almost motionless, hands clasped behind his back, he gave due notice that he meant to launch no emotional appeals. This was a serious matter, to be seriously considered, and not obscured by ill-timed histrionics. It was implied not more by his words than by his manner as he uttered a warning preface to his theme.

"I beg of you not to be unduly influenced by that first simple story that was put before you by the Crown two days ago. We know now that a great deal of it was . . . not absolutely accurate."

There was a sharp and icy edge to this restrained impeachment. It cut deep into the prosecution's case as Hastings backed it straight away by factual illustration.

"Do you remember how counsel for the Crown described Mrs Barney – took great trouble to describe her – as a lady who lived in an extravagantly furnished flat?" Percival Clarke searched among his notes; he had indeed made use of this expression, and many of the newspapers had found it to their liking. "An extravagantly furnished flat – I wondered at the time why it was necessary to discuss the furniture. I am still wondering. I also wondered what evidence would be produced to bear out this assertion. That point, at any rate, does not remain in doubt.

"We have now heard that evidence – evidence given by witnesses for the Crown. Downstairs there was a sitting-room with one or two armchairs. Upstairs there was a front room with a divan bed in it and a back room with practically nothing in it at all. That," remarked Hastings in cool, even tones, "was the extravagantly furnished flat in which Mrs Barney lived."

Needless to say, Clarke's blunder had been entirely innocent. He was probably misled at a much earlier stage when he learnt that the cottage had a fitted cocktail bar. This apparatus, though, must

have enjoyed priority in the eyes of Mrs Barney and did not typify
the rest of the appointments. Hastings was fully justified in
emphasising this, even if, as he said himself, the point was
secondary.

"But the next thing is rather more dangerous than that." He
recalled Clarke's reference to Mrs Barney's ugly behaviour with
the police, and the inference the jury had been desired to draw –
that such was the sort of temper she customarily exhibited upon
slight provocation. What was this "slight provocation"? Hastings
asked. "It was this: that she was a young woman, entirely by
herself, without the support and comfort of her parents or her
friends; that within a few yards of her lay a dead body – the body of
the man she obviously loved; that she was surrounded by a group
of officers who were proposing to remove her to the station. That,
says counsel for the Crown, is 'slight' provocation; a 'slight' strain
upon the temper and the nerves. I wonder," added Hastings,
looking gravely at the jury, "what provocation he would class as
serious."

The third and final thrust of this introductory phase had long
been deferred until the appropriate hour. The Crown knew it was
coming; its shadow had hung over them since early in the trial, but
there was nothing they could do to parry or prevent it. The
prosecution had to sit in silence while the wound was opened
with a surgeon's neatness and dispatch. "Three separate times
during the opening for the Crown you were told that Mrs Barney
had said 'I will shoot *you*.' People had heard her; they would say so
in the box . . . A good many people have been into the box, but not
a single one has said anything of the kind."

The prologue was over. The defender had made it clear that the
Crown had overcalled their hand. Now he was to bid upon the
merits of his own.

"There are cases," he said, "in which advocates feel in such
despair that they are driven to plead for mercy for their clients and
to urge that they are entitled to the benefit of the doubt."

It was rarely indeed that Patrick Hastings raised his voice. He
raised it now, and the effect was all the greater.

"I am going to do nothing of the sort. I am not going to ask you
for the benefit of the doubt. I am going to satisfy you that there is
no doubt. I am going to show you that there is no evidence at all."

18

As he set out to implement his pledge he held the jury in the hollow of his hand. Just as the supremely naturalistic actor makes his audience forget that they are looking at a stage, so this supremely naturalistic advocate almost made his audience forget they were in court. They were not conscious of listening to a speech, delivered upon a ceremonial occasion. They were engrossed in what was being said as people are engrossed in private conversation when matters of life and death are being decided. Their absorption was too complete for them to be aware of it.

The whole twelve followed in absolute surrender as Hastings came to deal with the earlier shooting in the mews. He first defined its precise relation to the case. "The prosecution ask you to believe that Mrs Barney tried to murder on this previous occasion; that she shot at Michael then and that her purpose was to kill." Three witnesses had said they *heard* the shot on this occasion; only one – the first chauffeur's wife – had said she *saw* it fired. Her evidence alone conflicted with Mrs Barney's description of the incident. And what exactly did her evidence amount to? How much confidence could be reposed in it? "She says she saw Mrs Barney holding something bright. You can see for yourselves – this is a perfectly black revolver. She says she saw a puff of smoke after hearing the report. This revolver does not make any smoke. She says Mrs Barney held whatever it was in her left hand. You will remember that I asked her to pick up the revolver at the conclusion of her terrible ordeal here in the box. She picked it up – like this – with her right hand." Displayed in counsel's grasp, the black lustreless pistol told its own tale to the jury. "It would be very odd indeed," Hastings quietly commented, "if the only time that Mrs Barney used her left hand was when it is alleged she tried to commit murder."

So swiftly and decisively was punctuated the direct, visual evidence relating to this matter – the evidence of what was supposed to have been seen and done. But Hastings had not yet finished with the subject. He turned now to the indirect evidence – the things that were not seen and the things that no one did.

"Supposing *you* had been shot at, what yould you have done? Wouldn't you have taken very quickly to your heels? Michael never budged. We have heard that he still stood about there in the mews, talking up at Mrs Barney in the window – this man who, according to the Crown, stood in great and imminent danger of his life.

"Supposing *you* had been a witness of the scene, and you had believed this woman was trying to murder the man below – what then would you have done? Something, I'll be bound. What did these people do? Nothing whatsoever. They all went back to bed, and – as the police told me when I asked them yesterday – not a living soul ever lodged any complaint. Can you imagine that any of them thought that the revolver had been fired *out* of the window?

"And if it had, wouldn't you expect to find some trace of the bullet in the mews? I asked the police about this too; you'll recollect the answer; they made a thorough search but not a sign of it was found.

"This is not surprising, for the mark of that bullet was on the bedroom wall; it showed that Mrs Barney had fired *inside* the room, to make this man whom she adored think she was so unhappy."

Any evidence there was against the prisoner on this incident had now been torn to shreds and irremediably scattered. The Crown indeed would have had a stronger-looking case without it. They would at least have been spared the scathing observation with which Hastings finally dismissed this episode. "If you think," he said, "that the prosecution have merely tried to bolster up their case by something of which there is no evidence at all – well, then, it may help you to see with some clarity what is the real position on the charge itself."

19

The real position on the charge itself – this Hastings now proceeded to size up. He had been speaking for an hour, and the utter silence waiting on his voice was the measure of the grip that he had gained upon the court. "Not a sound," said that evening's paper, "broke the steady stream of words, which seemed to hold everybody in a spell. The jury, it was noted, eagerly leaned forward."

In calmly level tones, sometimes faintly shot with irony, Hastings anatomised the night of Michael's death, scoring point after point in Mrs Barney's favour. The marks on the revolver had been too blurred for fingerprints to be deciphered, just as one would expect following a struggle; "if Mrs Barney's fingerprints *had* been detected on it, counsel for the Crown would have said it was conclusive – but is this tremendous artifice of science only to be used when it helps a prosecution?" Within a few hours of the tragedy Mrs Barney had made three separate statements – to the doctor, to the police at home, to the police at the station – but no question had been put to her in cross-examination suggesting that anything she had said in the statements was a lie; "I don't think counsel for the Crown has mentioned that, so I am venturing to supplement his speech." Everything denoted that Michael was the object of her passionate devotion; "in all her distress and anguish, she wanted to kiss the man who was dead."

Mrs Barney stared up at the high dome of the court. The reference had produced its invariable effect; her mouth trembled, and presently her face was stained with tears.

The compact argument flowed on uninterrupted. "Put yourself in her position. Put yourself in that box with the wardresses beside you. Suppose yourself under thorough questioning by the Crown, with the thought in your head of what each question might mean; not knowing what you were going to be asked, not knowing what construction might be placed upon your answers. Would you give your evidence like Mrs Barney did if what you were saying wasn't true? Was she caught out anywhere? Was there any discrepancy between what she told you and what she told the doctor and the police? Members of the jury, was that woman lying?"

Was that woman lying? The question was not posed in the traditional Old Bailey style of fierce defiance ("I dare you, I challenge you, to say this woman lies!"), but with the quiet assurance of one who has forged a solid chain of reasoning which will lose rather than gain from declamatory effects.

This was really the climax of the speech. It was the point at which the advocate would gather himself for his touching peroration, if touching peroration there was going to be. But Hastings remained faithful to the undertaking with which he had begun. Both temperament and technique caused him to recoil from anything remotely resembling a harangue. Nor was Mrs Barney's case one where sympathy, as such, could readily be roused; unlike that of Madame Fahmy, which had been heard in the selfsame court nearly nine years before, and was now being frequently recalled and quoted as a parallel. In each a young woman of good breeding and good station was charged with murdering the man whom she had loved. In each a revolver was the instrument of death. In each, oddly enough, Percival Clarke was prosecuting counsel. But Madame Fahmy, a Parisian lady of faultless morals and gentle disposition, had married a rich Egyptian prince whose suave drawing-room manner concealed a savage cruelty and perverted appetites; for several years before the shooting incident – in respect of which her successful plea fused self-defence and mishap – she had patiently borne great suffering at his hands. Mrs Barney, on the other hand, had engaged in an illicit and unsanctified relationship with the young man she was accused of having killed; her general standards of behaviour fell somewhat short of strict; her disposition was volatile if it was not violent; and any suffering there may have been she voluntarily endured, and in all likelihood commensurately repaid. With an English jury the differences were radical.

Notwithstanding, it is of interest to compare Hastings' conclusion to his speech for Mrs Barney with Marshall Hall's conclusion to his speech for Madame Fahmy, if only as an object lesson in contrasting advocates. "Members of the jury," Marshall Hall had said, after an address in which he imitated an oriental crouch, pointed the pistol at the faces of the jury, and threw it on the floor with a horrifying crash, "I want you to open the gates where this western woman can go out, not into the dark night of the desert, but back to her friends, who love her in spite of her weaknesses; back to her friends, who will be glad to receive her; back to her child, who will be waiting for her with open arms. You will open the gate, and" – here Marshall Hall pointed to the skylight – "you will let this woman go back into the light of God's great Western sun."

It was symbolical, romantic, picturesque – an unashamed and undiluted play upon the feelings. If Hastings had defended Madame Fahmy it is certain that he would have attempted nothing of the kind. It was doubly certain in the less propitious atmosphere of Mrs Barney's trial. Either the jury were won over by his reasoned argument or they would never be won over at all. Hence the simple finish to his magnificent defence. "I claim that on the evidence that has been put before you Mrs Barney is entitled as a right to a verdict in her favour. I ask of you, as a matter of justice, that you should set her free."

On the evidence. As a right. As a matter of justice. These – and not references to suns or gates or deserts – were the demands that Hastings formulated for his weeping client.

20

For a brief interval after he sat down there was no sound save that of Mrs Barney's anguish. Then, forthright in phrase and business-like in manner, the judge embarked upon his summing-up . . .

On Travers Humphreys the public and the legal profession could for once agree. Both rightly considered him the best British criminal judge of his generation. In this place of high regard he was succeeding Horace Avory, whose last years upon the Bench Humphreys overlapped. And, like Avory, Humphreys had assumed judicial office admirably equipped for the rôle he had to fill – equipped not merely with theoretical knowledge of criminal law, but by constant engagement at the Bar in criminal work. As Treasury counsel – an appointment that he held for more than twenty years – Humphreys had taken part on one side or the other in a high proportion of the epoch's best remembered cases. In his twenties he had been concerned with the defence of Oscar Wilde; in his thirties with the defence of Kitty Byron; in his forties with the prosecutions of Crippen, Seddon, Roger Casement and Brides-in-the-Bath Smith; in his fifties with those of Horatio Bottomley and Mrs Thompson, and with the defences of Colonel Rutherford and the financier Gerard Bevan. A remarkable catalogue of sensational cases, and it is only such cases that stand out, like the visible fragment of an iceberg, above the obliterating waters of remoteness. They act as indicator to several thousand more, now quite forgotten and sunk beneath the surface, that combined to produce the vast experience of the judge who, in his middle sixties, was to try Elvira Barney.

If Humphreys' career bore resemblance to Avory's, the men themselves were of very different mould. Avory was credited with a vein of callousness, a pitiless contempt for human frailty; Humphreys was never lacking in a disciplined compassion. Avory reasoned in the abstract as if all men were alike; Humphreys allied logic with imaginative insight. Avory forced life into the plaster cast of law; Humphreys made law serve the purposes of life. In a word, he had that precious attribute, humanity.

He was therefore merciful – but not indulgent; understanding – but not sentimental. He was invariably firm, and could be extremely stern once he had made his mind up that sternness was demanded. And in making up his mind he showed a penetrating shrewdness, bestowed on him by nature and sharpened to perfection by the manifold activities of his busy life.

Humphreys was the first man to appreciate a good point, but he was also the last to be hoodwinked by a bad one. Nor did he deal in compliments unless they were sincere. That being so, the first words he uttered to the jury paid Hastings a tribute that has seldom been surpassed. "You have just listened," he said, "to a great forensic effort. I am not paying compliments," went on this great veteran of so many famous trials, "when I say it is one of the finest speeches that I have ever heard delivered at the Bar."

21

The speech, deliberately aimed not at the heart but at the head, had indeed been of a kind to win the judge's admiration. It was, he went on to impress upon the jury, "free from anything like an appeal to sentiment and, one should add, of all the more assistance to you because it consisted of careful and accurate analysis." Moreover, before the summing-up had progressed very far it began to be apparent that in one vital respect Humphreys himself had been convinced by Hastings' argument – or had at least been thinking along very similar lines. He did not try to *impose* any opinion of his own, holding the balance with that scrupulous precision which is the mark of judges who believe in trial by jury. He warned them against shrinking from a disagreeable task. "If you are satisfied on the evidence as a whole that it is proved that she did intentionally fire the revolver, pointing it at the body of the man, and so caused the bullet wound from which he died, then she is guilty of the crime of murder, and no feeling of pity, no feeling of regret, should deter you from the duty you are called upon to do." But the judge gave an indication of his personal view in a form that almost echoed Hastings' chief contention. "What right have we to say her story is untrue?" he asked. "If it is not inconsistent with the facts that have been proved, a rejection of it would be simply and solely on the ground that it was told by a person under trial." He was judge, not jury, and took great care not to usurp the function of the latter. None now could doubt, though, that in Humphreys's judgment the prisoner's story was not demonstrably false – and unless that story was demonstrably false a conviction for murder could only be perverse.

There remained, however, another alternative to acquittal which had so far received no mention in the case. "Counsel," observed

Humphreys, "have said nothing about manslaughter; on the facts there was nothing that they could have said. It is for me to direct you on the law concerning this. Manslaughter is the *unlawful* killing of another without any *intention* of either killing or of causing serious injury." Having established the formal definition, he immediately applied it to the case that was before them. "It amounts to this," he said. "If the prisoner threatened to commit suicide – suicide, let me remind you, is a crime – and the deceased man removed the revolver in order to prevent it, and she, in order to carry out her intention, struggled with him and so caused the revolver to go off, she would then be guilty of manslaughter and answerable for that offence at law."

The sting in this passage was delayed until the end, when it suddenly dawned upon the judge's listeners that his manslaughter example exactly corresponded with Mrs Barney's own account of what had taken place . . .

When a judge, in the rightful discharge of his office, presents an assessment of the case for acceptance or rejection, he is sometimes said to be summing-up *for* a particular verdict. The expression is a loose one. But if one did venture to use it in respect of a well-nigh faultless jury charge, one would say that Humphreys summed-up for a manslaughter decision.

22

That the twelve men were not in any way obliged to follow suit had repeatedly been emphasised by the judge himself, and the outcome of the trial still appeared entirely open. No finding could be summarily ruled out. It was possible – some believed it probable – that they would convict the prisoner of murder; public disgust at the background of the case had been crystallised in a justifiable reference by the judge to Mrs Barney and her lover as "these rather worthless people" – and a jury's natural reluctance to destroy a useful life can sometimes tip level scales in a defendant's favour. It was possible that they would, by voluntary process, arrive at the manslaughter verdict which the judge had mooted. It was possible, after Hastings' great performance in the morning, that they would do neither and instead acquit outright . . .

The jury retired at five minutes to three. Judge and counsel also withdrew to their respective rooms. Mrs Barney left the dock like

some automaton; it required two pairs of hands to pilot her below.
The spectators remained in court, where long-pent-up excitement
at last found release in feverish discussion.

The sensation of suspense, greater than any crime reporters
present could remember, intensified as the jury's absence was
prolonged. Half-past three; quarter to four; four o'clock; a quarter
past – they had been conferring now for an hour and a half.
Everyone had his own views on the delay. They could not decide
between manslaughter and murder; they could not decide whether
to add a mercy rider; they could not decide about convicting her at
all. Some held that this length of time precluded an acquittal;
others that each added minute favoured the defence; yet others that
everything presaged a disagreement. Slowly moved the clock and
fast the ferment rose.

At a quarter to five the speculative tongues were stilled. The jury
had reappeared at the entrance to their box.

Officials hurried in. Counsel came back, the defending side with
deeply anxious faces; according to one observer, Hastings was
"almost haggard." The judge resumed his seat amid the crowded
bench; close to him his clerk held the dread black square in
readiness. Last of all, the wardresses brought up Mrs Barney;
her feet dragged so that the shuffling sounded oddly through the
court, and her white, manicured hands clutched the dock ledge for
support.

"Do you find the prisoner guilty or not guilty of wilful murder?"

"Not guilty," said the foreman of the jury.

"Do you find the prisoner guilty or not guilty of manslaughter?"

"Not guilty," said the foreman of the jury.

The crowd heaved a great sigh; someone laughed hysterically.
Mrs Barney cried out, "Oh!" and put her handkerchief to her
mouth. Just beside the dock her mother, who had sat there through
the trial, laid her head upon her arms and very quietly fainted.

23

It was a triumph, of course, but what was its especial nature? What
were the elements that made Hastings worth every penny of his fee
– which was certainly one of the largest ever marked upon a brief to
defend a charge of murder?

First, the rare capacity to judge a case's impact on contemporary life, and thus upon the jurors empanelled to decide it. Second, the requisite technique to act upon this judgment in setting the tempo and the key of his performance. Third, the delicate but devastating fashion in which he handled hostile witnesses. Fourth, the cool sense of his realistic plea.

These were the practical contributions of this fascinating advocate to a result that might have easily been different. For the student of forensic style, one point must be added. In the Barney trial the Bar's du Maurier tackled Sir Giles Overreach and, while strictly faithful to his own distinctive method, showed that he could play it as well as any Kean.

IAN BRADY AND MYRA HINDLEY

(Chester, 1966)

Pamela Hansford Johnson

The trial of Ian Brady and Myra Hindley, the Moors Murderers, sent a shock of horror through Britain and beyond. They were charged with the murders of two children, John Kilbride and Lesley Ann Downey, and a teenager called Edward Evans. The children's bodies were found buried in shallow graves on Saddleworth Moor above Manchester. Lesley Ann Downey had been snatched off the street, taken to Brady and Hindley's house, stripped, gagged, sexually violated, photographed in pornographic poses and then murdered. Her killing was recorded on a tape that was played in court; for over sixteen agonizing minutes, she was heard screaming, sobbing, pleading, begging for her life. Edward Evans had been battered to death by fourteen blows from an axe. To make doubly sure, Brady had strangled him with an electric flex. The murders were so horrible, so depraved, so disturbing, that the newspapers scarcely knew how to cover the trial, and coverage on radio and television was muted. Many people avoided reading about the case altogether. But the trial of the Moors Murderers marked the start of a modern populist bloodlust, driven by the tabloid press, that mixed an appetite for information about the intimate, preferably sexual, detail of crimes, with a craving for vengeance by the public on behalf of the victims (bulletproof screens

were erected around the dock). A Sunday newspaper sent the novelist
Pamela Hansford Johnson (1912–81) to watch the trial and write up
her impressions. "I intended to do no more than that," she recalled.
"But the effect of the trial upon me was so profound, and my
afterthoughts so nagging that I felt a subsequent need to write at
some length about the social implications I believed to exist, and to try
to explore whether there was not, in our increasingly permissive
society, some compost-heap of rottenness out of which such ugly weeds
could flourish and grow lush." The crimes of Brady and Hindley, she
argued, were the results of the total permissiveness of what became
known as the Swinging Sixties. Pamela Hansford Johnson travelled to
Chester to record her impressions of the trial's closing stages.

I arrived there, on a day which had turned from unnatural heat to
grey chilliness, with a threat of rain, on the twelfth day of the trial.
As it happened, my train was an hour and a half late, so I was
unable to see that night the journalist whose lot it was to act as my
bear-leader. After a lonely dinner, I went to inspect the town,
which I had never seen before.

It is one of the most beautiful cities in England, the only one
with its Roman walls intact. Within these walls are fine, half-
timbered buildings, some leaning forward, as if the centuries have
made them feel a little giddy. The "Rows", a double gallery of
shops, the upper level approached from the pavement by stone
stairways, are handy for strolling lovers or for getting out of the
rain, and at night they glitter like the arcades in Turin.

Yet there seemed to be a sort of infective madness in the air. I
climbed the narrow, dank stairs to the ramparts and walked some
way around the town. A light drizzle was falling now, bats were
flitting in the russet-coloured dusk. As I came to a bend in the
walls, I saw a couple closely embraced against the sweating stones.
Thinking it would be rough on them if I intruded, I began to walk
back the way I had come. Almost at once, they unlocked themselves and began to walk in my direction. As they passed by me, I
saw that both were men.

Then I strolled in the more populated Rows, but had not gone
far when I realized that I was being dogged by an elderly man,
wearing an old macintosh and a flat cloth cap of some gingery
material, whose aim was to keep as close as he could to my heels,

whispering dirt into my ears. I wasn't, of course, in any danger from this obsessed old person, yet when I found how hard it was to throw him off, I felt my flesh creep. He spoiled my walk. I had to retreat to my hotel: and even there, he parted from me only on the doorstep.

I am writing about these trivial experiences not because I have any hostile feeling towards the lovers on the walls or, indeed, much feeling, beyond that of irritation, about the aged whisperer. But it all seemed, in a way, indicative of the unrest, the fever, in the air. This harmless city had been forced to contain a horror: and I met nobody unaware that this was so.

Chester is a rich town, with a race-course. The Queen had just paid a visit to the Race Week, and Chester naturally preferred to keep its eyes upon her than upon what was happening in the Assize Court in the castle on the hill.

In the bar of the hotel, comforted by brightness and noise, I began to make some notes. A woman in a rose-petal hat got into conversation with me. "I saw you were writing away like anything. I've been to the races, I didn't like the Queen's clothes at all. She was wearing emerald, or you could have called it jade. It didn't suit her. Have you come for the trial?" Yes, I said, and waited for the dread-stricken, fascination-stricken, "*What are they like?*" But no. "I haven't read any of it," she said. "I can't bring myself to and I won't." Her shudder was real.

The mass of the public had, of course, been reading the Moors Case with avidity, but there was, and it is not without significance, a sizeable minority who refused to open their minds either to the facts or to the implications of this crime. I'm not blaming them.

Apart from what they were wearing, it would have been hard to distinguish, in the hotel crowd, the race-goers from the journalists. Both seemed excited, pepped-up. The pressmen, who had been supping with horror all day, felt the relief of getting out of "*that place*". They talked compulsively about the trial, because it was the only way of squeezing some of its abomination from their systems: they could not really bear to be alone. "I like being where the lights are," said one of them, "after all that."

Yet the Assize Court itself is oddly reassuring. It is clean, bright, has been newly decorated. Canopy and curtains of red velvet, braided with gold, frame the judge's seat. The benches of the public auditorium and of the Distinguished Visitors' gallery are upholstered in scarlet leather. Above the galleries are royal portraits: Charles II, crowned, sits with silken legs akimbo. It is a bizarre place to contain such monstrosity, even though the dock has been shut in, on three sides, with splinter-proof glass.

Well now: what are they like?

Let us look at the accused. Ian Brady's appearance would seem to call for some reassessment of Cesare Lombroso (1835–1909), whose theories concerning biological analyses of criminal behaviour have been under almost continuous attack since the time of formulation.

> The *habitual homicides* have cold, glassy eyes, immobile and sometimes sanguine and inflamed: the nose, always large, is frequently aquiline, or, rather, hooked; the jaws are strong, the cheek-bones large, the hair curly, dark and abundant; the beard is frequently thin, the canine teeth well-developed and the lips delicate; frequent nystagmus and unilateral facial contraction, with a baring of the teeth and a contraction of the jaws . . .

Brady is much taller than he seems. He is probably short-bodied, for when he sat beside Hindley in the dock, he seemed shorter than she. He is very thin, small-shouldered, his chest concave. His face is almost tragically gaunt. The bones of the large beaked nose, of the cheeks, of the strong, if narrow, jaw seem to shine through the flesh. If he shows emotion at all, it is in the contraction of the cheek-muscles, the tightening of the well-cut mouth.

He is a cross between Joseph Goebbels and a bird. His hair is medium brown, thick, wavy, lying back from his forehead like plumage; his entire colouring seems to be in various tones of that brown, which gives him a monochrome appearance. His eyes are cold and pale. He is dressed in a grey suit, a natty white handkerchief in his breast-pocket. On the whole, he looks ordinary.

Myra Hindley does not. Sturdy in build and broad-buttocked, though her face, hands and feet appear to be narrow and delicate, she could have served a nineteenth-century Academy painter as a model for Clytemnestra; but sometimes she looks more terrible, like one of Fuseli's nightmare women drawn giant-size, elaborately coiffed, with curled and plaited maid-servants reaching no higher than her knee. She wears a grey double-breasted suit with six buttons, a sky-blue shirt open at the neck, the cuffs neatly drawn down below the sleeves of her jacket. She was dark, once; now she is a Nordic blonde. Her hair is styled into a huge puff-ball, with a fringe across her brows. At the beginning of the trial it was rinsed to a lilac shade, now it is melon-yellow. The style is far too massive for the wedge-shaped face; in itself, it bears an uneasy suggestion of fetichism. But it is the lines of this porcelained face which are extraordinary. Brows, eyes, mouth are all quite straight, precisely parallel. The fine nose is straight, too, except for a very faint downward turn at the tip, just as the chin turns very faintly upward. She will have a nutcracker face one day.

How would she look if her hair were not dyed, if her face were unpainted? It is only fair to ask that question. Would she seem as ordinary as Brady, someone easy to pass by on the street? Now, in the dock, she has a great strangeness, and the kind of authority one might expect to find in a woman guard of a concentration camp.

In the witness-box, both were controlled and quiet; steadily and remorselessly, sometimes ingeniously, sometimes crassly, they lied and lied. Yet there was not always this quietude. Brady was twice in the box while the jury retired, since a legal submission was being debated. I was not there at the time, but I am told that he displayed a ferocity and arrogance terrifying in its intensity. Once he rounded upon the Attorney-General with dirty language that spouted from him like oil from a well. He must have been cautioned by his own Counsel not to repeat this performance when the jury came back into court.

He has a glottal Scots accent.

What were they both thinking? It is almost impossible to imagine. "Evil, be thou my good?" Or: "But this is *us*. You have no right to pass judgment upon us."

Novelists are conceited people; they tend to believe there is no mind into which they cannot imagine themselves, and here Dostoevski may have misled almost all writers who have tried to penetrate into the criminal consciousness. He has such demonic projective force that we tend to swallow whatever he tells us. He believes in the ultimate triumph of repentance in the murderer, that he *must* come to hate what he has done. He has given us Raskolnikov as a prototype. Yet the killer for gain or for personal gratification is almost always lacking in what the psychologists call *affect*, that is, any capacity for entering into the feelings of others. I believe very few of the guards in the concentration camps were true sadists: what had disappeared in them was the capacity to think of those they tortured as human beings at all. The prisoners were animals; they didn't have the same feelings as ourselves. There have been far more horrors committed in our time by the affectless than by the pathologically cruel.

We are living in a society which continuously encourages affectlessness, and we see its effects all round us; from the yobs who break into a children's playground and insert pieces of jagged glass through the planks in the slide, from the gangs who will beat up innocent people for "kicks" (that depraved word we have all lightly accepted), to the couple who buried Lesley Ann Downey and John Kilbride, making the moors an Abomination of Desolation in all the dreadful reality of that phrase.

In this court-room I learned a hard lesson: empathy in this case was impossible. I made a conscious effort to feel pity, but could do so for the flesh alone; the fatigue of the bone, the fallen cheek, the scoops of darkness under the eyes, the visible ravages of fear and hate. But one cannot imagine oneself into the situation of these two, far less into their heads. One cannot hear the tape-recorder that Brady carries in his skull: of this we shall never read the transcript.

It shook me that this was so, that I could not feel pity: but it would be sentimentalism if I pretended that I did. For this was something out of the human scale as we conceive it, even out of the common scale of murder. False empathy, in such circumstances, would have been dangerous simply because of its falsity.

Compassion is the greatest of the virtues, yet the mere word has been so debased that it may be used to cover a multitude of sentimentalities. There are times in this life when we *cannot* feel it, and are so alarmed because we cannot, that we tend to cook up a story, to make us appear better people and richer in human insight.

What I felt in Hindley's presence was terror. I asked others, pressmen, policemen, how they felt. They felt as I did, without a single exception.

As one detective said to me: "*You* were terrified? *I* was terrified!" He told me that in the prison where she was being held on remand, officers would take turns to go to her with meals, or on any other errand. "No, I went last time. It's your turn now." This was, of course, not a physical but a spiritual fear.

It was, however, possible to grasp that, dominant as Hindley might appear, she was not Lady Macbeth. She had no previous police record. She was once a Roman Catholic – indeed, a left-luggage ticket brought into evidence was discovered in the spine of the prayer-book given her on the occasion of her first Communion. She was a baby-sitter much sought after by mothers. Her mind seems to have been bigoted in the crudest sense: she would talk of "dirty niggers", "filthy coloureds".

Then she came under the thumb of Brady and was consistently depraved by him. Now she seems to carry the burden of this depravity almost contemptuously, except for her few admissions of shame at the sight of the photographs, her admissions that yes, she was cruel to Lesley Ann.

"Yes, I was cruel."
"And pitiless?"
"I was cruel."

The word "pitiless" she refused to admit.

She appeared to be devoted to Brady, who, during her evidence, did not once look at her. "I loved him . . . I love him still." "If he asked me to do something . . . I always went along with him eventually." It is probable that once she was not nearly so strong as he, though she has become so now.

When her grandmother, hearing the screams of Evans, asked what all the noise was about, Hindley shut her up promptly. "I told her it was the dogs barking."

I heard the owl scream and the crickets cry.

Still, she was no Lady Macbeth.

Each of the accused made some attempt to exculpate the other. Yet there is something baffling in this relationship. Was Brady homosexual? Bisexual? Women have been desperately in love with such men before, appetite growing not by what it feeds on, but by what it is denied. Was any sexual assault made by Brady on Evans? A dog's hairs found on the *inside* of his clothes indicate that at some time or other that evening Evans was naked. He seems to have been an invert; it was to him that Brady was referring when he spoke of planning to "roll a queer" (rob a homosexual). But was a sexual assault made on John Kilbride, and if so, did Hindley know it?

When the police, with understandable reluctance, took the clothes of the long-buried boy from their plastic containers, a stench of corruption rose which filled the entire court-room. One man whispered, "It takes me back to the trenches of Flanders in 1916." A French reporter said, "My God, have the English got no noses?"

Over the whole of this trial, and behind it, there was a psychic stench. There had been persistent rumours of the involvement of far more people than two in the hideous amusements enjoyed by Hindley and Brady, but I think these may be discounted. Certainly the police discount them, and they are as eager as all of us to see a total cleansing.

But nevertheless, during these hours in court, most of us felt we were seeing only the eighth of the iceberg.

The trial ended with Brady and Hindley being convicted of what the judge characterized as "calculated, cruel, cold-blooded" murders. Between them, they were sentenced to five terms of life imprisonment. Myra Hindley died in prison in November 2002, having served a sentence of more than 36 years; her lover Ian Brady, now a pensioner, has also been told he will die in jail.

AL CAPONE

(Chicago, 1931)

Damon Runyon

In 1920s America, Al Capone was Public Enemy Number One. Although accused of dozens of murders and other violent crimes, Capone enjoyed total immunity from prosecution under state laws. It was a Federal court that finally brought him to book, charged with income-tax evasion. When his trial began, huge crowds gathered at the Chicago courthouse, accompanied by a media circus. "I was willing to go to jail," he told reporters. "I could have taken my stretch, come back to my wife and child, and lived my own life. But I'm being hounded by a public that won't give me a fair chance. They want a full show, all the courtroom trappings, the hue and cry, and all the rest." He was right. But Capone's trial was all part of the myth-making, and served to cement his notoriety. Among the writers crammed into the court to cover the case was Damon Runyon (1880–1946) with whom Capone reputedly dined the night before the trial. Runyon was working for Hearst's American, *the New York paper he joined in 1911 as a sports-writer. During his heyday in the era of booze and bullets, Runyon was the world's highest-paid reporter, expanding his beat from sports to courts, and earning a reputation as a stylish chronicler of murder trials ("the main events", as he called them). A gourmet and a dandy, Runyon was hailed by one critic as "the prose laureate of the semi-literate American", although he also enjoyed great popularity in Britain in the 1940s. These off-the-notepad impressions offer a unique insider's view of Capone and his battle with Uncle Sam, the American taxman.*

Chicago, October 6, 1931

A fragrant whiff of green fields and growing rutabagas and parsnips along with echoes of good old Main Street, crept into the grime-stained Federal Building here today as your Uncle Sam took up the case of Al Capone and gathered a jury in what you might call jigtime.

It is a jury made up mainly of small towners and Michael J. Ahern, chief counsel for Al Capone, frankly admitted dissatisfaction to the Court about it.

He wanted all these persons dismissed but Judge Wilkerson overruled his motion. The jury was sworn in with nine veterans of court room juries among the twelve good men and true, and tomorrow morning at ten o'clock the Government of these United States starts work on Al Capone.

The truly rural atmosphere of the proceedings today was evidenced by horny-handed tillers of the fruitful soil, small town store-keepers, mechanics and clerks, who gazed frankly interested at the burly figure of the moon-faced fellow causing all this excitement and said,

"Why, no: we ain't got no prejudice again Al Capone."

At least most of them said that in effect, as Judge Wilkerson was expediting the business of getting a jury to try Capone on charges of income tax evasion.

Your Uncle Sam says Al Capone owes him $215,000 on an income of $1,038,000 in six years.

Your Uncle Sam hints that Al Capone derived this tidy income from such illegal didoes as bootlegging, gambling and the like.

"Do you hope the government proves the defendant guilty?" was one question asked a venireman at the request of counsel for the defense.

Apparently none cherished that hope.

"Have you any desire that the defendant be sent to jail?" was another question requested by the defense.

"Well no," was the general reply.

Al Capone sat up straight in his chair and smoothed his rumpled necktie. He felt better. The G-men – as the boys call 'em – want to put Al Capone in a Federal pokey, or jail, for anywhere from two to thirty-two years, to impress upon him the truth of the adage that honesty is the best policy.

As Al Capone sat there with the scent of the new-mown hay oozing at intervals from the jury box, he was a terrific disappointment to the strictly seeing-Chicago tourist who felt that Al should have been vested at least in some of the panoply of his reputed office as Maharajah of the Hoods. Perhaps a cartridge belt. Some strangers felt this Chicago has been misrepresented to them.

The jury as it now stands is as follows: Louis G. Wolfersheim, Chicago; Louis P. Weidling, painter, Wilmington, Ill.; Burr Dugan, farmer, DeKalb County; A. C. Smart, painter and decorator, Libertyville; W. J. Hendricks, lubricating engineer, Cook County; George M. Larsen, wood patenter; Dalton; W. F. McCormick, receiving shop, Maywood; A. G. Maegher, country store-keeper, Prairie View; Ambrose Merchant, real estate agent, Waukegan; Arthur O. Prochno, insurance agent, Edison Park; John A. Walker, abstractor, Yorkville, and Nate C. Brown, retired hardware dealer, St. Charles.

Selection of the jury in one day is regarded as amazingly quick work, and the trial may not be as long drawn out as expected.

Capone arrived for the opening session fifteen minutes ahead of time, which is said to be a record in punctuality for him.

A big crowd was gathered on the Clark Street side of the dingy old building waiting to see him, but Al popped out of an automobile and into the building like a fox going into a hole. Not many of the curiosity-seekers got a good peek at him.

He entered the court room alone and was quickly surrounded by a crowd of reporters, male and female, who began bouncing questions about his ears. They asked him if he was worried, and he replied, logically enough, "Who wouldn't be worried?"

He was scarcely the sartorial spectacle familiar to the winter inmates of Florida, where Al's sport apparel is one of the scenes of interest. In fact, he was quietly dressed this morning, bar a hat of pearly white, emblematic no doubt, of purity.

'Twas a warmish morning and Al, being stout, is susceptible to the heat. Then, too, he was in a hot spot. His soft collar was already crumpled. He frequently mopped his forehead with a white handkerchief. His swarthy jowls had been newly shaved. His black hair now getting quite sparse was plastered back on his skull.

Judge Wilkerson himself is a fine looking man with iron-gray hair. He is smooth shaven. His eyebrows are black and strong. He wore no flowing robe, like New York judges. He was dressed in a quiet business suit of dark color and wears horn-rimmed glasses.

His voice is clear and very decided. He sits far down in his chair while listening, but when he is doing the talking he leans far forward over his desk, his shoulders hunched up.

Wilkerson made it very clear to the men in the jury box that Capone is being tried on charges of violating the income tax law and nothing else.

Capone's chief counsel, Ahern, a tall, good looking chap of perhaps middle age, who wore a gray suit and tan shoes, approached the railing in front of the bench as court opened this morning, flanked by his associate in the defense, Albert Fink, a ruddy-faced, baldish man given to easy attitudes.

Ahern's first approach was with a mild protest against the arrangement of the court room by which the thirty or more representatives of the press were crowding defense attorneys out of house and home. He was satisfied when the scribes were shoved off a bit so their hot breath would not beat against the back of Al Capone's neck.

George E. Q. Johnson, the United States district attorney in charge of prosecution, is a forensic looking man. He has a pink complexion, a rather beaming countenance and a mop of gray hair, all mussed up.

At the request of Ahern, Wilkerson asked the veniremen:

"Do any of you belong to any law enforcement organization? Counsel asks specifically about the Anti-Saloon League?"

None did, it seemed.

"Have any of you ever contributed to a law enforcement organization?"

Well, one man had once chipped in ten dollars to the Crime Commission. His confession didn't seem important to the attorneys at the moment.

None of Capone's so-called bodyguards were in evidence anywhere around the court house, I am reliably informed. Naturally, I wouldn't know 'em myself. Al goes to his citadel, the Hotel Lexington, out south, as soon as he leaves the court. It used to be a noted hostelry. The President of the U.S.A. stopped there during the World's Fair. Now it is Capone's G.H.Q.

October 8, 1931

"What do you do with your money – carry it on your person?"

An income tax examiner asked this question of Al Capone in September, 1930, when Al was seeking a settlement with your Uncle Sam and could produce no books, bank accounts or anything else in writing bearing upon his financial transactions.

And, according to a transcript of the examination, Al replied: "Yes, I carry it on my person."

He must have had plenty of room on his person, judging from a letter his attorney at that time wrote to the Internal Revenue Bureau, for this letter, the basis of argument lasting most of the day's sessions, admitted Capone's income was nearly $300,000 in the years 1926 to 1929, inclusive.

Capone's lawyer at that time was Lawrence B. Mattingly, Washington income tax expert. In fighting the admission of the letter, one of Al's present lawyers, Albert Fink, characterized the letter as a confession by a lawyer in behalf of a client.

He argued that no lawyer has the right or authority to make a confession for a client.

Judge Wilkerson finally overruled objection to the admission of the letter, which was undoubtedly a big victory for the government. Capone seemed deeply concerned when he heard the Court's ruling.

Judge Wilkerson said he believed the weight of authority was in favor of the admissibility of the document.

The letter was read to Judge Wilkerson, but not to the jury, which was sent from the room while the lawyers argued. It was produced by Samuel Clawson, of Washington, one of the attorneys representing the government, as soon as court opened today.

The letter was written by Mattingly when he was endeavoring to adjust Al Capone's income tax troubles with the government, and traced Capone's financial rise from a modest $75 per week, prior to 1926, to an income of $26,000 in that year, $40,000 in 1927, "not to exceed $100,000" in 1928, and "not to exceed $100,000" in 1929.

The source of the income was mentioned as an organization, the nature of which was not described, in which a group of employes had a third interest, and Capone and three associates a fourth.

Mattingly wrote:

"Notwithstanding that two of the taxpayer's [Capone's] associates, insist that his income never exceeded $50,000 in any one year,

I am of the opinion his taxable income for the years 1926 and 1927 might be fairly fixed at not to exceed $26,000 and $40,000 respectively, and for the years 1928 and 1929, not to exceed $100,000."

Capone listened to the letter with keen interest. He seemed in great humor, although it was what you might call a tough day for his side. The letter went on:

"The so-called bodyguards with which he [Capone] is reputed to surround himself, were not as a general rule his personal employes, but were employes of the organization who participated in its profits."

Referring to Capone's assets, the letter said:

"The furniture in the home occupied by the taxpayer while he was in Florida was acquired at a cost not to exceed $20,000. The house and grounds have been thoroughly appraised, and the appraisal has been submitted to you. There is a mortgage against the house and grounds of $30,000. His indebtedness to his associates has rarely ever been less than $75,000 since 1927. It frequently has been much more."

The letter was produced by the government attorneys on the appearance of George E. Slentz, of Washington, D.C., first witness of the day. Slentz is chief of the power-of-attorney section of the Bureau of Internal Revenue, and Attorney Clawson wanted him to identify the letter written by Mattingly.

Helen Alexander, vault clerk at a state bank in Cicero, identified a contract for a vault signed in 1927 by Al Capone and Louis De Cava. She identified Capone's signature and pointed him out in the court room, but she did not recall seeing Capone at the bank in connection with her duties.

Louis H. Wilson, connected with the Internal Revenue Collector's office here, testified to a conference with Mattingly, who said Capone owed income tax, and was willing to pay.

There was another conference at which Capone was present in person, and also C. W. Herrick, Internal Revenue agent. Everything said at the conference was duly set down by a stenographer.

Judging from the transcript of that conference, read in court today, Capone's chief answer to questions about his income was: "I would rather have my lawyer answer that."

He denied having anything to do with a dog track, never owned a race horse and never had a bank account.

After Capone left the conference Mattingly told Wilson he would get some facts together as best he could and make a return.

He recommended, Wilson said, that the government get busy at once, as Capone had some money at the moment, and would pay up.

But apparently Mattingly's task was a little difficult. He reported he couldn't get definite records on Al Capone's income. Finally Mattingly produced the letter that caused the excitement today.

At the rate the trial is traveling now, it will take several weeks to conclude it. The defense attorneys are contesting every inch of legal ground. Al is getting a good run for his money, anyway. He came and went today mid the usual excitement outside the court house, but the crowds do not seem able to pick the hole he bobs out of with any degree of success.

Chicago, October 9, 1931

The soft murmur of the blue breakers caressing old Miami shore sort o' sneaked into Judge Wilkerson's court room this afternoon, between shrill snorts of the Chicago traffic coppers' whistles outside, as witnesses from the sunny Southland connected Al Capone up with $125,500 transmitted from Chicago to Miami by wire.

Having shown to the jury in the Federal Court where all those potatoes went, your Uncle Sam was going about the business of trying to prove whence they came when Judge Wilkerson adjourned to a half day session tomorrow.

The last witness of the day, one John Fotre, a sharp-featured citizen, wearing a slightly startled expression, who is manager of the Western Union branch office in the Lexington Hotel here, was identifying a money order showing some of the money went to Capone from Sam Gusick, when Wilkerson called a halt.

The Lexington Hotel is sometimes spoken of as "the Fort," and is said to be the citadel of the Capone forces. Sam Gusick is reputed to be one of Al Capone's business managers. Fotre said he couldn't say if it was Sam Gusick in person who sent the dough per the money order in question, because he didn't know him.

Much of the money was traced to the purchase and improvement of the celebrated winter seat of the Hidalgo of the Hoods on Palm Island, in Biscayne Bay, between Miami proper and Miami Beach.

It was traced through Parker Henderson, Jr., whose testimony indicated he was in Capone's confidence to an amazing degree. He was manager of the Ponce de Leon Hotel in Miami.

It was there Capone stopped when he first went to Florida in 1928, at which time, and later, according to the testimony today, the good burghers of Miami were so perturbed by his presence they held meetings.

How Henderson came to arrive on such terms with Capone did not appear, but it was Henderson who negotiated the purchase of the home, and who handled large sums of money for Capone in improving the place.

Henderson testified to signing numerous Western Union money transfers with the name of Al Costa, turning the money over to Nick Serritela, who worked for Capone, or to Capone himself.

They were generally for sums of $1,000 or $1,500. Other transfers were in the names of Peterson and Serritela. There were over twenty different transfers, amounting in all to $45,000, of which about $15,000 was transmitted to Henderson personally to be spent in improving the Palm Island property.

The rest was for Capone.

These transfers refer only to the telegraph office in Miami. Later witnesses added $30,300 as having gone through the Western Union branch in Miami Beach.

Capone listened with great interest as the witness testified.

Henderson narrated the detail of the purchase of the Palm Island property, which was made in his name. Later he transferred the property to Mrs May Capone, Al's wife.

Henderson came to Chicago, May, 1928, and saw Capone and got money to pay off the men working on the improvements.

He said Al invited him to stay at the Metropole Hotel, then the Capone G.H.Q., and while there he saw such celebrities as Ralph Capone, Jack Guisick, Charley Fuschetti, Jack McGurn, a party called "Mops" and others.

This was after Capone was living on Palm Island. The money came in batches of from anywhere from $600 to $5,000. Some of the transfers were to Albert Capone, a brother, but the witnesses said Alphonse Capone signed for many of them.

Vernon Hawthorn, a Miami attorney, told of a meeting at which Capone and a number of officials of Miami and Dade County, Florida, were present. It was in 1928; Capone had just appeared in Florida and the good citizens of Dade wanted to find out what the celebrated visitor intended in their startled midst. Al said he was there to rest.

The witness said Capone told him he was in the cleaning and pressing business in Chicago. Finally, the witness said, Al admitted his business was gambling and that he was interested in a Cicero dog track. Furthermore, that he had bought a home in Miami.

The question was asked him at that meeting, "What do you do?" and according to the transcript read this morning, Capone said, "I am a gambler. I bet on horses."

"Are you also a bootlegger?"

"No, I never was a bootlegger in my life."

He said the Palm Island home was in his wife's name. He denied he had received any sums of money from Charles Fuschetti under the name of Costa.

Morrisey Smith, day clerk and cashier at the Metropole Hotel, Chicago, where Capone used to have his headquarters in a suite of five rooms, was examined by Attorney Grossman, who asked, "Who paid for this suite of five rooms?"

"Mr Capone."

He did not know how much. Grossman handed him the cash sheets of the hotel and Smith picked out a payment of $1,500 for rooms in 1927. No period of time was stated. He was registered as Mr. Ross. The witness testified to numerous other payments, always in cash.

Counsel for the defense could not see what this was all about and spoke to the Court about it. The judge replied, "I presume it's to show he had money. If you pay out something you must have something coming in."

A party for Al's friends who came to the Dempsey–Tunney fight was listed. It cost $1,633. Al gave "small gratuities" to the hotel help now and then, Smith's idea of a "small" gratuity was something surprising. He explained, "He would give five dollars or something like that." Fred S. Avery was manager of the Hotel Metropole when Capone was there. He went to see Capone on one occasion and asked him about a little money and Capone personally paid him the next day. His bills ran around $1,200 to $1,500 a week. Avery said the Dempsey–Tunney entertainment ran two nights.

October 10, 1931

The life of Riley that Al Capone is supposed to live on Palm Island was reflected in testimony brought out by your Uncle Sam before Judge Wilkerson and the jury in the Federal Court this morning.

The butcher, the baker, and the landscape maker from Miami were among the witnesses, not to mention the real estate man, the dock builder, the telephone agent, and the chap who supplied the drapes for 93 Palm Island.

It came out that quite a batch of meat was gnawed up in Al's home in the course of several seasons – a matter of $6,500 worth. Also plenty of bread, and cake, and macaroni was consumed.

The telephoning was terrific. Someone must have been on Al's phone almost constantly. In the course of four Florida seasons there was gabbing, mainly at long distance, to the tune of over $8,000 not counting wrong numbers, but your Uncle Sam contented himself with standing on $4,097.05 in two years in his effort to prove Al must have had plenty of income because he spent plenty.

Your Uncle Sam argues that if a man spends a raft of money he must necessarily have a raft of money to spend, a theory that sounds logical enough unless your Uncle Sam is including horse players.

We had a slight diversion after Wilkerson adjourned court until Monday, with another warning to the jurors not to permit anyone to communicate with them.

The diversion consisted of the seizing of the mysterious Phillip D'Andrea, Capone's bodyguard who has been sitting behind Al since this trial started, by a United States deputy marshal, and the alleged discovery on his person of a .38-calibre John Roscoe, or pistol.

D'Andrea was ordered by Judge Wilkerson to stand trial for carrying a revolver in the court room, and was taken to jail.

D'Andrea is a short, stout bespectacled individual, who dresses well, and looks like a prosperous professional man.

He has been described as a friend of Capone's and Al seemed much perturbed by his seizure. He waited around while D'Andrea was in the marshal's office, with Capone's attorneys, Ahern and Fink, trying to get him out of his trouble.

Al said he didn't know D'Andrea carried a gun, and didn't believe he did.

*   *   *

The twelve men, most of them small towners, and of occupations that would argue a modest scale of living, listened intently to testimony that indicated Al's comparatively elaborate existence, although the reputed magnificence of Al's Palm Island estate dwindled somewhat in the imagination of the urban listeners when expenditures for improvements were related.

These expenditures were not unusually heavy. In fact, Al was depicted in some of the testimony as a householder with a repugnance for being "gypped" in small details.

This morning Capone had on fresh scenery in the form of a dark-colored double-breasted suit of greenish hue, white linen, a green tie and black shoes. He had gone back to his famous white hat.

The attendance at the session today was positively disappointing. Fewer than a dozen persons sat in the seats assigned to spectators when court opened. Can it be that Chicago is losing interest in Al Capone?

William Froelich, of government counsel, read a list of money transfers to the jury showing the transfer of a total of $77,500 to Capone in Florida.

W. C. Harris, office manager of the Southern Bell Telephone Company at Miami, was the first witness. He identified a contract for phone service between the company and Al Capone at 93 Palm Island.

Harris identified company bills for service to the Capone residence amounting to $955.55 in 1928 and $3,141.50 in 1929, a total of $4,097.05, mostly for long distance calls.

Richard Plummer, of Miami, testified to supplying the draperies for Capone's home in 1928 at a cost of $1,000. He said Capone paid him in cash.

George F. Geizer, night clerk at Capone's old G.H.Q., the Metropole Hotel, Chicago, testified to receiving payments in cash to the amount of $2,088.25 from Capone for hotel bills on August 4, 1921.

Louis Karlinch, of Miami, testified he sold meat to Capone to the amount of $6,500 over a period of three years, nearly always getting his money in cash. The bills amounted to around $200 a week. Albert Fink, attorney for Capone, asked, "Do you think Al ate all the meat himself?"

"No. One man couldn't eat it all."

H. F. Ryder, of Miami, built a dock for Capone on Palm Island

and worked around the place generally. Ryder, a small, dark-haired fellow, was inclined to be quite chatty about things. He spoke of seeing Capone with a roll of bills that would "choke an ox."

Fink wanted to know how big an ox. He also asked the witness if it couldn't have been a "Western roll," which the attorney explained is a roll of $1 bills with a big bill on top. Ryder said it might have been.

Ryder testified he still has $125 coming to him from Capone for work, but said he wasn't worried about that. He said he expected to get it when he ran into Capone. In fact, Ryder had a boost for Al.

When Ahern asked his opinion of Capone he answered, "A mighty fine man."

Curt Koenitzer, a chunky, red-faced builder and contractor in Miami, testified to building a garage and bathhouse on the Palm Island property. He was paid by one of Capone's brothers.

A swarthy, dapper chap with black hair and a black moustache was expected to turn out at least a duke, but is Al Capone's baker in Miami. His name is Milton Goldstron.

He delivered bakery supplies to Capone's house in 1929, 1930 and 1931 to a total of $1,130 and was paid by Frank Newton, caretaker of the Capone premises.

F. A. Whitehead, hardware merchant, testified to the building of iron gates for the Capone estate.

H. J. Etheritz, who is connected with Burdine's department store in Miami, testified to purchases by Capone of drapes amounting to $800.

Joseph A. Brower, landscape gardener, testified to doing some work on the Capone estate. He was paid $2,100 in checks signed by Jack Gusick. He said Capone described Gusick as his financial secretary.

Frank Gallatt, of Miami, said he was hired in 1929 to put up some buildings on Palm Island. Capone himself did the hiring, he said. Also Capone had paid him personally between $10,000 and $11,000 in cash.

October 12, 1931

A gleaming diamond belt buckle, one of a batch of thirty purchased by Al Capone at $277 apiece, or $8,310 for the lot, was flashed before the astonished eyes of the jury today.

Al bought these buckles for his friends. One of the buckles is said to have been worn by Alfred (Jake) Lingle, Chicago underworld reporter, who was assassinated in June of last year, for which crime Leo V. Brothers is now doing a stretch in the penitentiary.

The jurors peered at the buckle with interest. Each buckle is said to have been engraved with the initials of the recipient, but markings on the buckle displayed today were not revealed, a fact that is doubtless causing someone to heave big sighs of relief.

Judge Wilkerson seemed to think the exhibition of the buckle to the jurors might be with the idea of giving them a line on the quality of the gewgaw, and he remarked, "The quality of the goods makes no difference. It is immaterial whether the defendant got value received or not as long as he spent the money."

In other words, Al may have been "gypped," but that doesn't enter into the case.

Besides diamond buckles, Al passed suits of custom-made clothes around among his friends at $135 per copy, though not so many of these. He also had shirts made at from $22 to $30 apiece, with the monograms $1 each. His ties cost $4 each and handkerchiefs $2.75 apiece. He bought them by the "bunch."

We got right down to Al's skin today.

We found out Al wears silk union-suits at $12 a smash, and athletic "shorts" at $5 a clip. A Mr. J. Banken, of Marshall Field's and who evidently has an abiding artistic interest in his business, told us about that.

Albert Fink, Capone's attorney, who is a fellow you wouldn't think gave much thought to underwear, or other gents furnishings, perked up and interrogated Banken about those union-suits, especially after Banken had described them as a fine silk, "like a lady's glove." Fink leaning forward asked, "Warm?"

"No, not warm. Just a nice suit of underwear."

"How much are they now?"

"Ten dollars."

"Aha," said the attorney, reflectively, "they've gone down?"

"Yes, two dollars," replied Banken, and it looked for a moment as if he had a sale.

The testimony revealed Al as rather a busy and shrewd shopper. While he is usually pictured as a ruthless gang chieftain, he was today presented as a domesticated sort of a chap going around buying furniture, and silverware, and rugs, and knickknacks of one kind and another for his household.

He was shown buying linoleum for the kitchen, and superintending the interior decoration of his home on Palm Island, and personally attending to other details the average citizen is glad to turn over to friend wife.

Moreover Al appears to have been somewhat conservative in big household purchases, considering the amount of plunder he is supposed to have handled.

He spread out more when buying for his own personal adornment in the way of clothing, and neckties, and night shirts.

Oscar De Feo, of Marshall Field's, recalled making over twenty suits for Al and a few topcoats, along with suits for four or five of Al's friends at a total cost of around $3,600.

Samuel J. Steinberg, jeweler, who told of the diamond buckles, also said Al stepped into the store one day and bought twenty-two beaded bags at $22.50 apiece.

During the morning session we furnished Al's Palm Beach home from top to bottom, besides sending some furnishings out to a Prairie Avenue address, where his mother lives.

From Henry E. Keller, an elderly man from Miami, we had a clue to Al Capone's start in life.

Keller was dock foreman for Al on the Palm Island place, at a salary of $550 per month, and one day, when having lunch with Al, Al asked him where he was born. Keller replied, "In the old Tenth Ward, in New York."

"Is that so," said Al, according to the witness, "why, I came from New York. I got my start as a bartender on Long Island"

Al often grinned at the testimony, especially when we got down to his underwear.

October 13, 1931

Your Uncle Sam chucked a sort of Chicago pineapple of surprise under Alphonse Capone's lawyers this afternoon by suddenly announcing these United States of America rested its case against its most conspicuous income tax dodger of the hour.

"What?" ejaculated Mr Michael J. Ahearn, the urbane Irishman, who has been leading the defense.

"Huh," exclaimed Mr Albert Fink, his bluff and gruff associate.

Then their chairs rattled in chorus as they pushed them aside to step up to Judge Wilkerson's bench in the Federal Court.

Even Al Capone sensed something unusual and leaned forward to listen to the attorneys, his round features set in seriousness, a plump hand rigid before him.

Messrs. Ahern and Fink admitted their astonishment. You gathered they felt your Uncle Sam had sneaked up on them very suddenly from under cover of a day of dry proceedings all along the line of trying to connect Al Capone up with the gambling profits of the Cicero joints.

These profits, the government asserts, amounted to $177,500 in 1927 and $24,800 in 1928, a total for the two years of $202,300.

The startled attorneys argued desperately for the next half hour for a little delay to get their line of defense consolidated, and bring witnesses from New York and other points. But all their conversation did them no good.

It was 2:20 p.m. when the government lawyers concluded with the direct examination of a handwriting expert named Herbert Walters, only witness of the afternoon, who testified certain endorsements on a cashier's check bought with the profits of a Cicero gambling house were in the handwriting of Al Capone.

Indications are the defense will be comparatively brief. Capone's reputed huge gambling losses may be one line. That some of Al's lavish expenditures was on borrowed money may be another.

The government had a short, square-jibbed chap named Bobby Barton walking in and out of the court room every few minutes for identification by different witnesses as the man who handled a large sum of money for Jack Gusick, but Barton was never called to the stand.

The testimony throughout the trial has depicted Gusick as the money man of the Capone combination. He received the money, and apparently cut it up, too, and one witness testified Gusick told him on no occasion to give anyone else any of the money gathered in at Cicero, "not even Al."

Among the things presented by the government which the Capone attorneys say they never heard of before the case opened and against which they have had no time to prepare was the letter from Capone's income tax expert, Lawrence Mattingly, to C. W. Herrick, local revenue collector, offering to compromise Al's indebtedness to the government.

Fred Ries, the man whose testimony is said to have convicted Jack Gusick and Ralph Capone of income tax violations, was today's principal witness.

Ries was the cashier of the Radio and Subway gambling houses in Cicero in 1927 and had charge of all the finances. He identified a cashier's check for $2,500 made payable to J. C. Dunbar, which he cashed and turned over to Bobby Barton. Ries said he was J. C. Dunbar.

He said that as cashier he bought cashier's checks with the profits of the establishment, which he gave to Bobby Barton, who in turn gave them to Jack Guisck. He said he bought over $150,000 worth of checks in 1927. By profits he meant any surplus over the bankroll of $10,000.

There was a long discussion by the attorneys and the Court when Grossman offered the cashier's checks in evidence and Ahern objected.

The jury was sent from the room and Grossman questioned the witness further to show the Court he was going to connect Al up with the checks. Finally Judge Wilkerson decided to admit the checks.

Johnny Torrio, predecessor of Capone as Chicago's gang lord, and now living on Long Island, was not called upon to testify, although he was subpoenaed. The contempt case against Phil D'Andrea, Al's bodyguard, who has been in the coop since Saturday morning when he was grabbed with a pistol on his pudgy person, was postponed until Friday.

October 14, 1931

Your correspondent cheerfully yields the palm he has borne with such distinction for lo these many years as the world's worst horse player to Mr Alphonse Capone.

Yes sir, and ma'am, Al wins in a common gallop, if we are to believe the testimony brought up in his support today.

Up to closing time this afternoon Al had lost upwards of $217,000 of all that wrong money that your Uncle Sam has been trying to show went into the Capone pockets from gambling operations in Cicero, and what-not, and the end is not yet.

A string of bookmakers testified to clipping Al for his potatoes on the races. He was a high player, betting from $1,000 to $5,000 on a race, according to the testimony, and he must have picked out more lizards, beetles, armadillos, crocodiles, anteaters, polecats, penguins and polar bears than your correspondent on one of his best days.

Al never seemed to win. At least every bookmaker that went to the post today, testified to knocking him in for anywhere from $15,000 to $25,000. There were several other bookies in the paddock outside the court room when court adjourned.

Apparently Al didn't believe all horse players must die broke. He was belting away at 'em through 1924 down to 1927.

At the rate the bookies are going now, Al will not have any more of that $266,000 income that your Uncle Sam charges to him by the time court is over tomorrow.

Milton Held, a betting commissioner, testified Al lost between $8,000 and $10,000 at the Hawthorne track in 1924 and about $12,000 in the fall of 1925.

Oscar Gutter, a dark-complexioned little man with a low voice who also described himself as a betting commissioner, said Capone lost about $60,000 in 1927 on bets he handled.

Both Held and Gutter admitted on cross-examination that they had been summoned within the past few days to Capone's headquarters at the Lexington Hotel, where they conferred with Al and his lawyers.

Held said Capone would bet anywhere from $200 to $500 on a horse. Gutter told of bets from $1,000 to $3,000. Once Al bet $6,000 on a nag. He always paid off his losings in cash, either personally or through a "secretary."

The bookmakers say when they paid Capone off on rare occasions when he won they sent checks in the name of "Andy Doyle."

Then came a burly, fat-faced, black-haired chap who described himself as Peter Penovich, Jr. His name has often entered into the case as one of the partners and managers of a Cicero gambling house.

He said he had been subpoenaed by the government. Had appeared before the Federal Grand Jury and had been at the Federal Court House nearly every day for months. He was never called as a witness in this case by your Uncle Sam.

Penovich said he originally had twenty-five per cent of the Cicero place and later his "bit" was cut down to five per cent. Ralph Capone had told him he was to be chopped.

He said Ralph Capone had told him Frankie Pope was the boss of the place.

Ralph Capone is Al's older brother, and stands convicted of income tax violations along with Jack Gusick.

George Leidermann testified he was a café owner and is now a bookmaker. He said he had a book in 1924 with three other partners and that he often booked to Capone. Al would bet from $500 to $1,000 and would sometimes be betting on two or three horses to a race. Sometimes he would make as many as twenty bets a day. He figured Al lost $14,000 or $15,000 with him in 1924. In 1925 he beat Al for $10,000.

Leidermann admitted he now is running a gambling house under the direction of George "Bugs" Moran, seven of whose followers were massacred St. Valentine's Day in 1929.

Sam Rothschild, who said he was in the cigar business, with bookmaking on the side, said Capone had made perhaps ten bets with his books. These bets were all up in the thousands. He didn't recall Capone ever won.

A bald-headed chap named Samuel Gitelson testified he recorded bets for his brother, Ike, a bookmaker, and that Al had lost about $25,000 to the book.

Edward G. Robinson, the movie actor who has given movie characterizations that some believe are Al Capone to the life, was present in the court room peering at Al.

October 16, 1931

That Al Capone is the victim of a wicked plot, conceived in Washington and partly hatched in Miami, was the substance of an utterance by Michael J. Ahern, as he addressed those twelve tired good men and true in Judge Wilkerson's court this afternoon.*

Ahern was making the closing address on behalf of Al, whose trial on a charge of beating your Uncle Sam out of his income tax is nearing a close, and ought to be handed over to the jury about noon tomorrow.

* It became a legend that agents of the United States Treasury Department began looking into Capone's income tax record after President Hoover walked through a hotel lobby in Miami Beach, unnoticed, while Capone was being pleasantly mobbed by hero-worshippers. The implication was that the President, piqued, ordered the G-men into action. The truth appears to be that Chicago business men, despairing of Capone's arrogant depredations being checkmated by local police and prosecutors, besought intervention by Federal authorities.

Ahern went clear back to the Punic wars and the time of Cato, the censor, whose cry was "Carthage must be destroyed," and said there are a lot of Catos around nowadays, especially around Washington, whose cry is "Capone must be destroyed."

Several years ago when Al first lit in Miami he was summoned before what Mr Ahern spoke of as a "Spanish Inquisition" of officials and citizens of Miami, and interrogated closely as to his purpose there.

A stenographer took down the testimony at that time, during which Al is said to have admitted he was a gambler, and all this was introduced into the present case.

Ahern insinuated the inquiry was prompted from Washington just before an election and gave it as an idea the thing was the beginning of a plot to undo Al Capone.

Quite a gale of oratory zipped around the corridors of the old Federal Building before the day was done, what with Ahern's remarks, a lengthy outburst by his associate, Albert Fink, and a long lingual drive by Samuel G. Clawson, of your Uncle Sam's team of lawyers.

What Ahern and Fink said, when you boiled it down to a nubbin, was that your Uncle Sam hasn't proved all those things said about Al Capone in the indictments, and that he is entitled to his liberty forthwith.

What Clawson said, reduced to a mere hatful, is that Al had a lot of income and didn't pay tax on said income, and therefore ought to be put in the cooler.

Ahern who began the closing defense argument at 2:30, said the government had attempted to prove its case by circumstantial evidence. He declared the government was seeking on meager evidence to convict the defendant because his name is Al Capone, "a sort of a mythical Robin Hood."

It was his opinion Ahern said, that the government might better have diverted the money it has spent proving Al's profligacy to establish free soup kitchens.

October 17, 1931

Those twelve good men and true have gone into a big huddle on Al Capone.

Judge Wilkerson of the Federal Court handed the now famous

case over to them with a batch of instructions, which struck the listeners as very fair to Al, at 2:41 this afternoon.

Your Uncle Sam claims Al owes him $215,000 tax on an income of over $1,000,000 derived from illegalities such as Cicero gambling, and one thing and another, in the years 1924 to 1929 inclusive, and wants to clap him in the Leavenworth Penitentiary for anywhere from one to thirty-two years.

Al's claim is that Uncle Sam didn't prove the income alleged, although of course, he entered a plea of guilty last July to the very charges for which he has just been tried, under an arrangement with representatives of your Uncle Sam by which he was to take a jolt of two years and a half in prison.

It was Judge Wilkerson's declaration on hearing of this agreement, "You can't bargain with the Federal Court," that brought on the long trial. It closed with the solemn marching out of the twelve good men and true this afternoon.

Capone was certainly all sharpened up this morning. He has been gradually returning to his old sartorial glory the last few days, and he fairly bloomed today.

He wore a grass-green pinchback suit, reminiscent of Florida. He had on heliotrope socks and tan shoes. Al has meticulously refrained from jewelry during the trial, save for a thin, diamond-studded platinum watch chain.

The judge is rather a thick-set man, of medium height, with a thick shock of iron-gray hair. He told the jury:

"You are the sole judges of the facts of the case. The jury has nothing to do with the question of punishment. That rests with the Court.

"This is a criminal case and I shall give you some general rules applicable to criminal cases. The indictment is not to be considered evidence of the guilt. The defendant is presumed to be innocent until proven guilty beyond a reasonable doubt. He is entitled to the benefit of that presumption."

Judge Wilkerson explained the meaning of a reasonable doubt. If the jurors had a reasonable doubt it was their duty to acquit the defendant. If they believed the evidence proved him guilty beyond a reasonable doubt they should return a verdict accordingly.

In order to convict on circumstantial evidence the jury must be satisfied that the circumstances alleged are true.

Wilkerson told the jury to take up each count and return an opinion on each. He said it was not necessary for the government to show the exact amount of income alleged. The Court explained at length the meaning of income under the law. He quoted the provisions of the income tax law at length.

He said the jury might consider the evidence of the way the defendant had lived and the evidence of the money transmitted to him in determining if Capone had a taxable net income. He added:

"The expenditure of money alone isn't sufficient evidence of taxable income; the possession of money alone isn't sufficient evidence of taxable income. But the expenditure and possession of money may be considered in arriving at a conclusion as to whether the income existed.

"The charges of willful attempt to evade the tax couldn't be sustained unless there were some facts to show the attempt. The jury must first be convinced that the taxable net income of $5,000 existed. The mere failure to file an income tax return doesn't of itself prove an attempt to evade the tax but such failure must be considered with its relations to other actions."

The statement of a duly authorized agent may be considered against a principal, said Judge Wilkerson, dealing with the famous Mattingly letter to the revenue collector admitting Al had had an income of $266,000 for the years charged.

If the jury found that the statement of Mattingly were within the authority of the defendant, he continued, it might be considered in determining the guilt or innocence of the defendant. If they felt Mattingly had exceeded the scope of his authorization, then they should disregard the letter, he said.

On the subject of the corpus delicti or body of the crime, the court said that might be established by the circumstantial evidence. It is not incumbent on a defendant to testify in his own behalf, the judge said.

"This case will determine whether any man is above the law."

So said George E. Q. Johnson, United States attorney, in the final argument on behalf of your Uncle Sam this morning.

"Gentlemen, the United States Government has no more important laws to enforce than the revenue laws. Thousands upon thousands of persons go to work daily and all of them who earn more than $1,500 a year must pay income tax.

"If the time ever comes when it has to go out and force the collection of taxes, the Army and the Navy will disband, courts will be swept aside, civilization will revert to the jungle days when every man was for himself."

Pointing at Capone, Johnson demanded:

"Who is he, this man? Is he a mythical modern Robin Hood, as defense counsel has described him?

"The Robin Hood of history robbed the rich to give to the poor. Did Capone buy thousands of dollars worth of diamond belt buckles for the unemployed? Did the $6,500 worth of meat go to the unemployed? No, his purchases went to his mansion on Palm Island. Did he buy $27 shirts for the men who sleep under Wacker Drive? No, not he."

Johnson traced the early history of Capone, starting with the time when the defendant was a bartender at Coney Island. Then he said he was next heard of at Jim Colosimo's restaurant in Chicago. All the time, he said, the defendant was becoming more affluent. Johnson went on:

"Then we come to 1924, when this gambling establishment in Cicero was shown to have a profit of $300,000."

"Even if we take the defense statement that he had only an eight per cent share, his profits would have been $24,000. Let me remind you that the record shows profits of $215,000 in 1925.

"Then we come to 1926.

"Pete Penovich had a little gambling place of his own, which he gave up because of Capone's mob. In the parlance of the gentry, he was 'muscled' out. His successor, Mondi, was also muscled out, and after this there was no competition in the gambling business in Cicero."

Johnson drew attention to testimony, by Fred Ries, former associate manager of a Cicero gambling resort. Ries, he said, admitted that after taking out running expenses he bought cashier checks for Bobby Barton. Johnson went on:

"And Bobby Barton bought money orders transmitting $77,000 to Capone in Florida. Defense counsel was strangely silent about this. Even the master mind who plans the perfect crime – and this was intended to be the perfect tax crime – slips sometimes.

"Capone went to Florida, where he had occasion to spend a lot of money on his home in Palm Island. Again the master mind who attempted the perfect crime slipped when he gave his financial secretary, Jack Gusick, checks to pay his bills."

He scoffed at the testimony of defense witnesses that Capone lost $327,000 betting on the horses. He referred to them as "so shifty they couldn't look you in the eye."

Johnson reminded the jurors the defense lawyers had talked to them for four hours, but made no reference to the money orders sent from Capone's headquarters in the Lexington Hotel in Chicago to Capone in Florida.

He declared the records showed $77,000 was sent and received between Chicago and Florida.

Johnson warned the jury to remember the men and women who pay a tax on income over $1,500 a year. He contrasted them with Capone, whom he flayed for evading taxes during "this time of national deficit."

If members of the jury were fearful of what might happen to them in consequence of their upholding the law against the lawless and ruthless Capone, their verdict did not indicate it. They found Capone guilty on five charges. He was sentenced to eleven years imprisonment.

Reliable reporters said Capone had expected his political satraps to fix it for him to get off with a lighter sentence; they said he felt double-crossed. He actually served seven and a half years, in Federal prisons at Atlanta, Georgia; Alcatraz Island, California; and Lewisburg, Pennsylvania, which is considered the convicts' "country club." The "Big Guy" showed he had influence behind prison bars, and any punishment he suffered under man-made law was not rigorous. The punishment arranged by some other power was.

When he left Lewisburg, considerately protected by official secrecy, in November, 1939, it was to go to Johns Hopkins Hospital in Baltimore to be treated by an eminent syphilologist. He was not cured. The man who was the overlord of vice in Chicago suffered all his last years from the disease he had facilitated wholesale in its ravages upon others. Fittingly, it left him racked in body and – his doctors said – reduced to the mind of a child. Except for two or three brief intervals, he wasted the rest of his life within the walls of the home on Palm Island, at Miami Beach, that was among his ill-gotten gains.

It was asserted, by persons who claimed to know his affairs and doings, that he no longer had any say-so in gangdom in Chicago. The Federal Government, after having supposedly gone over his haunts with a divining rod, decided he couldn't dig up more than $30,000 and accepted that amount in 1942 as settlement for its claim for some $200,000 in unpaid income taxes.

Capone continued to live on in luxury, guarded like a tycoon, another five years and must have had means of support that weren't visible. In 1946, James M. Regan, Sr., elderly director of a horse-racing wire news service in Chicago, made a 98-page statement to police in which, among other things, he detailed how gangsters identified with Capone's career were endeavoring to seize control of Chicago's racetrack gambling rackets. A few weeks later Regan died of lead-poisoning – administered with a gun on a busy Chicago street in broad daylight, just as such things happened in the "old" days. A little later, it was intimated that a syndicate of Capone mobsters had cleaned up a sweet $3,000,000 in the sugar black market.

Whatever part Capone played in the machinations of Chicago's underworld definitely ended January 25, 1947. "I don't want to die in the street," he once said. He didn't. He died in bed, his boots off, of a complication of syphilis, pneumonia and apoplexy. There were some to grieve his death – he was surrounded at the end by his mother, Therese; his father, Ermio; a sister, Mrs Mafalda Mariote; two brothers, Ralph and Matthew; his wife, May; a son; and, of course, his bodyguards. He was forty-eight years and eight days old.

The man in whose outlaw empire an estimated 250 gangsters died violently between 1925 and 1930 alone, went for a last ride longer than most he had arranged. His body was carried in a hearse from Miami Beach to Chicago to rest, at last, in Mount Olivet Cemetery. Even in death, there was no Capone co-operation with society; the physician who tended him in his last days was refused permission to make an autopsy in the interest of science.

JOHN CHRISTIE

(Old Bailey, 1953)

Ronald Maxwell

The story of 10 Rillington Place, declared the criminologist Fryn Tennyson Jesse, is the most sordid in all English criminal trials. Her observation was made in pre-Cromwell Street days, but certainly the squalid sex murders committed at that most infamous west London address by the bespectacled little clerk John Reginald Halliday Christie still arouse controversy more than half a century later. Rillington Place, a grimy cul-de-sac in the then unfashionable area of North Kensington, first came to public attention in 1950 when an illiterate van-driver called Timothy Evans, lodging in the top-floor flat at Number 10, was hanged for the murder of his baby daughter Geraldine. Evans's wife Beryl was found strangled at the same time and it was generally assumed that he had murdered her as well, although he was not tried for this. At first Evans admitted both murders, but later accused Christie, who lived downstairs. Christie, teased for his sexual inadequacy as "Reggie-no-dick", testified at Evans's Old Bailey trial and denied any involvement. But three years later the bodies of six women were discovered at 10 Rillington Place. When arrested, Christie not only confessed to killing all six – his wife included – but to strangling Evans's wife as well. He told police how he trawled the pubs of Notting Hill and Paddington, luring women back to his flat where he staged a bizarre ritual, seating them in an old deckchair, offering them a rubber tube and persuading them to inhale what he claimed was merely aromatic Friar's Balsam to heighten their sexual pleasure. In fact Christie mixed the fumes with London coal gas, containing lethal carbon monoxide. As the woman passed out, Christie would whip out a rope and strangle her, sexually assaulting his victim for good measure. The question arose in the light of Christie's confession as to whether Timothy Evans had been hanged in error. Over the years this possibility has been the subject of two official inquiries, two Parliamentary debates, and a mountain of newspaper articles and books. Of these, the best-known is 10 Rillington Place, *published in 1961, in which Ludovic Kennedy argued the case for Evans's innocence. Even in June 1953, when Christie's trial opened on a sunny Monday morning, the case generated massive public clamour. The famous No 1 court at the Old Bailey, damaged by German bombs during the war, was newly refurbished. Spectators looking on from the gallery included an American playwright Robert Sherwood, who had made a special journey to England to be there, and a British one, Terence Rattigan, author of* The Deep Blue Sea *and* The Browning Version. *The vignette that follows is by Ronald Maxwell, one of the youngest journalists in court. He had followed the case from the discovery of the first bodies at Rillington Place, and won a seat at the Old Bailey in a lottery for press places. Christie was tried on a single charge of having murdered his wife Ethel, to which he pleaded not guilty. After a solemn opening speech by the Attorney-General, Sir Lionel Heald QC, the prosecution called psychiatric evidence from two doctors, Matheson and Curran, who both believed that Christie knew what he was doing, had planned it in advance, and knew that what he was doing was wrong. For the defence, Dr Jack Hobson took the opposite view. But before the medical evidence, Christie's counsel, Derek Curtis-Bennett QC – aiming for a verdict of guilty but insane – caused a sensation when he announced that he was going to call the accused man to testify himself.*

Christie walked jerkily from the dock to the witness-box, and stood there in silence for a full thirty seconds, looking at the wording of the oath. He appeared to be crying. He stood there in the panelled court, with the sounding board above his head, the jury on his right, the Judge on his left and the public and counsel facing him. The room was completely silent, as Christie fidgeted, and then mumbled the oath.

Mr Curtis-Bennett advised him to aim his voice towards the corner of the dock, as it had been found in that court that a voice aimed in such a way carried better. The accused man moved as directed, and leaned on the side of the box. There was a vague stare about his face, and his brow was furrowed. He was clasping and unclasping his hands, and he continued to do this for a large part of his time in the box. The rest of the time he was pulling at his ear, tugging his collar, stroking his cheek or rubbing his bald head. Occasionally it seemed to me as if the Judge's red robe was reflected in Christie's spectacles.

His evidence was given in a voice which was practically inaudible, and there were often long pauses before he answered the questions put to him. The story of his early life came out. He was born in 1898, and when he was eight years old he was invited by his parents to view his grandfather who was lying dead. He started working at a cinema at Halifax when he was fifteen, and joined the Army in 1916. He was invalided out in 1919, and married in 1920. Christie looked and sounded like a rather meek, henpecked husband when he said he had been very happy with his wife. In 1923 he lost the ability to speak. He had also been blind for six months some time before that.

In 1939 he enrolled as a special constable, serving for five years and being twice commended for distinguished service. He also obtained the first aid certificate. Then came the story of his meeting with Ruth Fuerst, who said she came from Vienna. Sometimes Christie's answers to questions seemed almost childish. He was asked how the woman felt towards him, and he replied, after a long pause: "She just said she was rather inclined to be affectionate towards me."

He told of killing her, and was asked: "Is that the first person you ever killed in your life?"

"I don't remember," he said.

"You don't even know that," said Mr Curtis-Bennett. Later he asked Christie: "May you have done more killings than you are going to tell us about?"

"I can't say exactly," came the reply. "I might have done." He added that there was something at the back of his mind sometimes, but he could not "get it out."

He went on to tell of people he killed – some of the seven mentioned in the statements. His story agreed roughly with the details in the statements. When he came to his wife, he wept openly in the box.

He was still giving his evidence when the day's hearing ended. He continued the next morning, and his voice sounded clearer because of the microphone which had been fitted into the witness-box. He continued his story about the women he strangled, and again he agreed approximately with his signed statements. This time, however, he added that he had no motives for his killings.

It never seemed clear in his evidence whether he had intercourse with the women while he was strangling them, or after they were dead.

He said that he "dismissed from his mind" the bodies in the cupboard after he put them there.

He told of the time after leaving his flat until he was arrested, and said that he had just wandered about. He could not remember details, but once he came to a cross roads and saw a sign saying Barking Road. He asked where he was and was told "East Ham".

Christie was asked again if he remembered whether he had killed anyone besides the seven women he had told about. He replied: "If you say I did, then I must have done."

When it was suggested that in the police van after he had been found at Putney he threw his wallet across to an officer, he replied quickly and resentfully: "I never threw anything. I passed it across."

Cross-examined by Sir Lionel, Christie was asked the reason for putting his wife under the floorboards. His answer was: "I did not want to be separated from her and lose her, and that is why I still had her in the house." He seemed a little pleased with himself as he said this.

"If there had been a policeman present when you killed your wife, would you have done it?" Sir Lionel asked.

"I do not suppose so," replied Christie.

After a total of nearly three hours in the box, Christie returned to the dock, and his place was taken by Dr John Abbott Hobson, consultant psychologist at Middlesex Hospital, who said he has seen Christie about ten or twelve times. He told the jury that Christie's was a very difficult history of a psychological illness called hysteria, a disease of the mind. He spoke to Christie about the killings, and they talked at great length about them.

"I felt throughout," said the doctor, "that when he has been unable to remember things, he has falsely remembered things. I believe that most of the time this falsification of memory or his forgetting resulted from his hysteria, or disease of the mind, and most of the time he did indeed forget and did not know that there was some purpose in this forgetting. At other times, of course, he also lied. At first he gave me a statement that was almost identical with the statement he gave the police. He remembered nothing of the murders in 1943, 1944 or 1949. He often makes statements one after the other which, to the listener seem self-contradictory, but he himself does not see the contradictions in these matters."

Dr Hobson said Christie was suffering from gross hysteria, particularly in the way it affected his reason, and that in his opinion Christie knew he was killing when he had killed, but did not know it was wrong. Hysteria could be a certifiable complaint. He could say less about Mrs Christie than about the others because Christie himself did not remember that incident so well. He was sure that some of Christie's statements about his wife were wrong. He thought Christie loved her as much as he was capable of loving anyone. Dr Hobson said he believed Christie's trouble partially dated back to his first sex experience.

Christie, with no experience, took an experienced girl in Halifax, and as a result she was disappointed. Christie, the doctor thought, had always been under sexed and unable to perform the sex act properly. It so happened that the evening after Christie was with this girl, she was picked up by his best friend, and she told him what had happened. As a result Christie was given a nickname "which implied that he was not quite a man."

Cross-examined by Sir Lionel, Dr Hobson said his belief was founded on concrete facts. One was that he could not speak for three and a half years. Dr Hobson added that he thought Christie himself believed what he had said about killing his wife, but that it was a false belief, in his opinion.

Dr Hobson was a witness for the defence. When he left the box, Sir Lionel called, for the prosecution, Dr John Cameron Matheson, principal medical officer at Brixton Prison. He had examined Christie on his admission to prison, and had kept him under observation while there. He understood that in his childhood Christie had been a good scholar, and this seemed correct as he was above average intelligence. He was fond of games, and a keen gardener as a child. He exhibited no signs of insanity.

"He is, in my opinion," continued the doctor, "a man of weak character. He is immature, certainly, in his sexual life. He is a man who, in difficult times and in face of problems, tends to exaggerate and act in an hysterical fashion. That is, he acts as people do who suffer from hysteria. He is not suffering from hysteria, but is a man with an hysterical personality who, in certain circumstances, behaves as a man suffering from hysteria would behave."

Dr Matheson was questioned by Mr Curtis-Bennett about whether Christie's actions – including the killing of seven people and having intercourse with them about the time of death, and collecting pubic hairs – brought him close to the McNaughten Rules. The doctor agreed that it did, but when further questioned, said it did not bring Christie "within the four walls" of the rules.

Dr Desmond Curran, psychiatrist at St George's Hospital, told the jury that he considered Christie to be an abnormal character rather than a victim of a disease. He did not believe that Christie's losses of memory were genuine. He was just like many other criminals and murderers – he had a remarkable capacity for dismissing the unpleasant from his mind. Dr Curran quoted from a report on Christie's conduct in Brixton Prison which said that he had mixed well with the other prisoners, but always led the conversation round to his own case. He seemed boastful about it, and compared himself with Haigh (the mass murderer who went so far as to bequeath his clothes to Madame Tussaud's with a long list of instructions about their care).

Christie was an egocentric, said the doctor, and even kept a picture of himself in his cell. He had often discussed his future with the doctor, and once said that, in principle, he had always been against capital punishment.

In his opinion Christie had no defect of reason or disease of his mind when he killed his wife. In reply to a question by the Judge about motive, Dr Curran replied that he thought it could only be that the accused man wanted to have intercourse with unconscious women.

Dr Curran's evidence concluded the day's hearing. Next day, Mr Curtis-Bennett addressed the jury for the last time. He spoke of Dr Hobson's statements in the witness-box, and said: "It is pretty evident from his evidence that he does not think much of Christie, and I do not suppose you do either. I won't ask you to say he is a nice man. What Dr Hobson does say, in my submission, is very important: that Christie was suffering from gross hysteria, and that is a disease of the mind that results in a defect of reason. He did know what he was doing, but very probably at the time he did this he did not know that what he was doing was wrong.

"If Dr Hobson is right, you can only find that special verdict of guilty but insane."

He spoke of the help which the defence had given in bringing to light the full details about Christie and the exhumation of Mrs Evans which they had asked for – all to see that the full truth was brought out at the trial. The murder of Mrs Christie, he continued, was motiveless. Nobody could suggest that the ten pounds taken from her savings was a motive. There was no sexual implication in this instance. Christie was an object of pity rather than horror, and he was a man who should be locked up for the rest of his life. This was murder of the most insane kind, and Christie could not have been telling the truth, because his barbiturate story had been "blown sky high." This was the best of the cases to show a motiveless, purposeless killing of the one person he liked.

He strangled two more women after killing his wife, and hid the bodies in the house. Then he had Miss MacLennan and Mr Baker there for three nights – sleeping there with three bodies in the house. "The man's crazy, isn't he?" asked Mr Curtis-Bennett.

Where did Christie go when he left his flat? he asked, and answered his own question. To Rowton House, and there he gave his correct name and address, and identity card number. This was the man supposed to be fleeing justice. In the case of Mrs Christie, contended counsel, there was no sign of premeditation.

"His wife was the person he loved best in the world. I suggest that this is maniacal behaviour this terrible sex indignity imposed by him on some of these women. You may think that a man who has intercourse with a dead or dying body is mad, and that I suggest is what has been proved here on one occasion at least. He is a man who keeps a collection of pubic hairs.

"We did not ask for the exhumation of Mrs Evans to amuse people or to give papers another headline. We asked for it to see if one of those sets of hairs could have been Mrs Evans's."

A doctor had said that one of the other sets of hairs could have been from Mrs Christie, and that, surely, indicated signs of sexual abnormality. The evidence of Dr Hobson – who said Christie suffered from gross hysteria – and that of Dr Matheson – who said Christie had an hysterical personality so that he behaved like a man with hysteria – showed great similarity. It was a question of diagnosis as to who was right and who was wrong.

The Attorney-General addressed the jury when Mr Curtis-Bennett had finished, and said that, if there was material there which clearly indicated that a verdict of guilty should be returned, then it was his duty to see that the jury understood the position, and was not influenced by any irrelevant considerations.

"We have to prove, and have very clearly proved, that Christie did deliberately and intentionally kill his wife on December 14. He killed her by strangling her with a stocking, and he knew perfectly well what he was doing."

Sir Lionel contended that Dr Hobson must be wrong, in the face of what other evidence there was. Dr Matheson and Dr Curran both said, and strongly maintained, that not only did Christie know what he was doing when he killed his wife, but that he knew he was doing something which was against the law.

He spoke of Christie in the witness-box, and mentioned the question which he (Sir Lionel) had asked about whether Christie would have killed his wife if there had been a policeman in the room.

"Christie said: 'I don't suppose I should.' There is no doubt about what he meant. He gave the matter thought. He looked round. He looked down. And then he said: 'I don't suppose I should.'"

Sir Lionel said that, as Dr Curran had said, sex perversion was not necessarily insanity. It was not a fact that a man who showed he suffered from violent sadistic impulses was justified in saying he was insane. He turned to motive.

"It is open to you to say that there may be all kinds of reasons why a man, unfortunately – according to our human nature – does kill his wife. It is certainly possible to think of a motive in a case like this where this man had associations with a lot of strange and not always very pleasant people. If his wife knew about that kind of thing, or if he thought she was getting to know too much about it, or might get to know too much, then that is ample reason why you might think that some murderous intention might arise in his mind, knowing what you do about human nature. Therefore it is not right to say there is no motive that might be suggested."

He dealt with the Evans case, and said there was not the slightest reason for anyone to think for a moment that Christie killed the child. There was enough on Christie without having that put on him as well.

The Judge began his summing up. The jury would decide when he finished.

"It is no misuse of words," he said, "to describe this case as a horrible one and a horrifying one. That will not cause you to shrink from examining the facts and coming to your conclusion. You are the judges of the facts in this case. My duty is to tell you what is the law. You and I are bound by the law as it is – not the way we might like it to be if we had our own view."

Mr Justice Finnemore spoke, in all, for nearly two and a half hours, sifting the evidence, and advising on its legal value. He went through the entire case on the evidence, and occasionally made comments.

"I do not know whether any jury in the country," he said at one stage, "or even in the world, has seen and heard a man on trial for one murder, go into the witness-box and say: 'Yes, I did kill this victim – and I killed six others as well over a period of ten years.' "

He also said that because "a man acted like a monster" that did not necessarily mean he was insane. He mentioned the question by Sir Lionel about whether Christie would have killed if there had been a policeman in the room, and said that in his opinion it was not sufficient to say merely: "This man said he would probably not have strangled his wife if a policeman had been there, therefore he is not insane."

The hands of the clock were already pointing to the hour at which the court had risen each day during the trial when the Judge finished his summing up, and the jury was asked to retire to consider the verdict. The court must wait for the answer, however long it should take. Three hundred years ago, things were faster, and more "organised". In fact, a jury which brought in an un-wanted verdict would be sent back to "reconsider" it. But justice is now more just.

The minutes dragged on as we waited. Christie, from the cell below the dock, asked for the score in the Test match.

An hour passed. An hour and a quarter. An hour and twenty minutes. Twenty-five minutes. The jury was returning!

The Judge took his seat. Christie came up the steps into the dock, and stood with one hand in his pocket, looking unconcerned. Mr Curtis-Bennett loosened his wig.

"Are you agreed on your verdict?" It was the voice of the Clerk of the Court.

"We are," came the reply.

"Do you find the prisoner guilty or not guilty?"

"We find him guilty." The verdict was in a clear voice, but the hand of the jury foreman shook, as he reached forward to the front of the box. Christie looked unmoved. He might not have heard. The Clerk addressed him.

"You stand convicted of murder. Have you anything to say why the court should not give judgment of death according to law?"

Christie made no reply. The black cap – a square of cloth – was placed on the Judge's head. His voice was sombre as he spoke: "You have been found guilty of murder by the jury and for that crime there is only one sentence known to our law and that is that you be taken from this place to a lawful prison and thence to a place of execution and there suffer death by hanging and that your body be buried in the precincts of the prison in which you shall have been last confined before execution."

The day sentence was passed was Thursday, 25 June 1953. By the following Monday it was known that there would be no appeal against the sentence. Only Royal intervention could save Christie from hanging.

But there was another aspect of the case which was riveting attention. It was Evans. Many people believed Christie had killed the child, in spite of the Attorney-General's assurance that no such suggestion had ever been made, and Christie's own denial.

But there was doubt – sufficient doubt to cause the belief that it was not for his own crimes that the name of Christie would appear most prominently in the annals of crime. It might be because his trial, casting doubt on an execution, might eventually end capital punishment in this country for ever.

DR CRIPPEN

(Old Bailey, 1910)

Tom Cullen

Dr Crippen's trial was an Edwardian spectacular, the first great twentieth-century murder trial to electrify the British public and an increasingly excitable popular press. Almost a century on, Crippen remains one of the best-known murderers in Britain, his name having passed into the language as a slightly quaint expletive. In fact he was an American, born in Coldwater, Michigan, who arrived in London as a travelling salesman in quack medical cures. A widower, he had married the daughter of a poor Polish grocer from Brooklyn who sought fame as an opera diva under the name Belle Elmore. But her meagre talent kept her confined to the Edwardian music-halls, and the marriage fell apart under the strains of Belle's drinking and infidelities. Crippen took his secretary Ethel le Neve as his mistress and murdered Belle, probably by poison, chopping up her remains and burying most of them (the head was never found) beneath the cellar of his house in Hilldrop Crescent, north London. He scarcely looked the murdering type. "There was something almost likeable about the mild little fellow who squinted through thick-lensed spectacles, and whose sandy moustache was out of all proportion to his build," reflected Chief Inspector Walter Dew, the Scotland Yard detective who pursued Crippen and le Neve (disguised as his son) across the Atlantic to arrest them and return them for trial. The case gripped the public for weeks. In the romantic twists and turns of the Crippen saga, millions discerned a fleeting counterpoint to their own drab, conventional lives. Crippen's trial was one of the most sensational on record. There were over 4,000 applications for seats, and such was the demand that a two-house system was instituted, with blue and red half-day tickets being issued to the public while friends and family of the lawyers, fashionable ladies and assorted bigwigs were allocated permanent seats. The Times *was outraged.* "A criminal court is not a showroom," *it thundered,* "nor is such a trial of the nature of a matinee." *Crippen condemned himself in the course of a deadly cross-examination by the leading Crown counsel, R. D. (later Sir Richard) Muir. Dozens of writers have described the Crippen trial; the case is one of the most picked-over of the twentieth century. This narrative is by Tom Cullen (1913–2001), an American who stayed in Britain when the US government confiscated his passport in the 1950s because of his Communist connections. Told to keep out of trouble, Cullen began work on a series of biographies of murderers, con-men and other reprobates, starting with a classic study of Jack the Ripper. Cullen's account of the Crippen case appeared in 1977.*

"Crippen crucified between two thieves . . ." Thus did a Garrick Club wit describe the scene which presented itself when, during a court recess, Hawley Harvey Crippen conferred briefly with his advisers. It was Tuesday, October 18, 1910, the opening day of Crippen's trial in the oak-panelled Court No. 1 of the Old Bailey with Lord Alverstone, the Lord Chief Justice, presiding.

As he leaned over the railing of the prisoner's dock to confer with his solicitor in the well of the court below Crippen easily dominated the tableau. Always the dandy, he wore a well-cut black coat with silk facings, a dove-coloured waistcoat showing a great deal of white shirt-front, and a neat black bow tie. His hair was carefully brushed to cover the bald spot on top. "His pink cheeks had a fresh, healthy look," notes a *Daily Mail* reporter. For one who was about to stand trial for his life Crippen bore the approaching ordeal lightly, betraying "not the slightest trace of care or emotion of any kind", according to this same *Daily Mail* reporter. He wrung no hands, mopped no perspiring brow, nor otherwise gave sign of anxiety as Day One of his trial unfolded.

Standing slightly apart from Crippen and his solicitor as they conferred was the lesser of the two thieves, Horatio Bottomley,

who had obtained a press ticket to the trial by virtue of the fact that
he was the proprietor and editor of *John Bull*, a muck-raking
weekly magazine. Swindler, demagogue and some-time Liberal
Member of Parliament for South Hackney, Bottomley, who himself looked like the John Bull of the newspaper cartoons, had a
vested interest in Crippen, for he had put up £50 for the latter's
defence (he was to put up another £150 later on for the appeal). A
quid pro quo was involved, to be sure: Bottomley's magazine was to
have exclusive rights to anything that could be wrung from
Crippen in the way of "copy". But that would come later, after
the trial: for the moment Bottomley was content to beam upon the
little man in the dock with a proprietorial air.

More in the guise of a jesting Pilate than that of the unrepentant
thief did Arthur John Edward Newton, solicitor, appear on the
opening day. Newton, however, did not hold with Pilate's hand-
washing routine, preferring instead to wear kid gloves of a dove-
grey colour (he ordered them by the gross from a glove-maker in
Jermyn Street) when he appeared in police court proceedings.
Once twitted about this sartorial foible Newton had protested,
"But in our profession it is so difficult to keep one's hands clean."
Arthur Newton found it more difficult than most.

A tall, heavy-set man of fifty with a pugnacious thrust of jaw,
Newton is shown wearing the tell-tale gloves with a morning coat
of matching grey in a *Vanity Fair* cartoon by Leslie Ward ("Spy").
Newton's speciality was "defending young men about town from
the consequences of youth and folly", in the words of one critic. In
1895 Newton had figured prominently in the two trials of Oscar
Wilde, when he was retained to represent Wilde's co-defendant,
Alfred Taylor. Five years earlier Newton had been retained to
represent the younger son of the Duke of Beaufort, Lord Arthur
Somerset, accused of patronising a male brothel in London's
Cleveland Street. As an aftermath of the so-called Cleveland Street
Scandal, Newton was gaoled for six weeks for having "conspired to
defeat the ends of justice" (he had attempted to spirit out of
England three telegraph boys who were prepared to testify that
Lord Arthur had committed acts of gross indecency with them).
Luckily for him, the Law Society did not strike his name from its
rolls.

Newton's mismanagement of Crippen's defence was on a par
with his involvement in the Cleveland Street Scandal. In fact, it
was so disgraceful that it was to result in the kid-gloved solicitor

being suspended from practice for twelve months in an action brought against him by the Law Society in the King's Bench Division of the High Court of Justice. In concurring with the suspension order, Mr Justice Darling held that, if anything, it erred on the side of leniency. "Crippen was not defended as he should have been," Mr Justice Darling observed, adding that Crippen's case "was conducted very largely for the purpose of making 'copy' for the newspapers." "Even the greatest criminal is entitled to have his case conducted from first to last with the sole view to his interest," the High Court Justice concluded.

Newton "captured" Crippen as a "professional speculation" in order to help pay off his racing debts, which ran into hundreds of pounds, according to W. E. Henchy, Newton's managing clerk. "I have known him to borrow from money-lenders at exorbitant interest merely to pay bookmakers," Henchy declares. This, however, was not the story Newton gave out to the press.

"I was on the eve of starting a short holiday," Newton told a *Daily Mail* reporter, "when an old business friend of Dr Crippen came to my office yesterday (August 2nd) and asked me if I would undertake his defence, saying he would do all he could to supply the necessary expenses for him." The business friend in question was that prince of quacks Eddie Marr, alias "Professor" Keith-Harvey, alias "Professor" Elmer Shirley, alias W. S. Hamilton, obesity specialist, who, when last seen was busy scraping Crippen's name off the office door in Craven House where the Aural Remedies Company did business.

It is doubtful, however, whether Marr came to Newton's office in Great Marlborough Street, whose fittings were in green leather, and whose cigar cabinets were stocked with the choicest Havanas. More likely the solicitor sought out Marr in a shake-down operation designed to persuade Crippen's shady friend to cough up money for the latter's defence. The upshot was that Marr agreed to advance £100, and on the strength of this Newton sent the following cablegram to Crippen, then under arrest and held in a Quebec prison: "Your friends desire me to defend you and will pay all necessary expenses. Will undertake your defence, but you must promise to keep absolute silence and answer no questions and do not resist extradition. Reply confirming. Arthur Newton."

Crippen, unaware of all of the backstage manoeuvres, was only too eager to avail himself of Newton's services, and cabled accordingly, agreeing to all the latter's stipulations. Commenting on his employer's offer, Newton's managing clerk writes, "It would have been worth taking on a case of this kind for its publicity value alone. Newton saw his way to get the publicity and the money, too."

Looking back it is evident that Crippen's only chance of escaping the gallows – and admittedly it was a slender one – lay in securing the services of the barrister who not only was recognised as the leading advocate in criminal cases of this kind, but who (inestimable advantage) actually believed in Crippen's innocence. He was Edward (later Sir Edward) Marshall Hall, KC. Three years earlier Newton had briefed Marshall Hall in the so-called Camden Town Murder in which a young artist was accused of murdering a prostitute by cutting her throat. Marshall Hall, against almost impossible odds, had secured the acquittal of this young man. The murder had excited much public interest.[1] It is not surprising therefore that Newton's first call in the process known as 'hawking the brief' should have been at Marshall Hall's chambers in the Temple Gardens.[2]

Unfortunately for all concerned, Marshall Hall was on holiday abroad. Almost certainly he would have intervened personally to secure the brief, instead of leaving the matter to the discretion of his managing clerk. For Marshall Hall, as has been said, strongly believed in Crippen's innocence. Moreover, the advocate, whom one of his friends described as "a walking chemist's shop", considered himself an expert on poisons in general, and on hyoscine in particular; and he had devised a defence which he felt sure would result in the charges against Crippen being reduced from murder to manslaughter.

1 It also inspired Walter Sickert to do an extraordinary series of paintings from his imagination picturing the murdered woman in her squalid surroundings.
2 In the episode that follows it is as well to bear in mind the division of labour that exists between the two branches of the British legal profession, barristers and solicitors. A barrister has the exclusive right to practise in the superior courts of England and Northern Ireland (in Scotland he is called an advocate). However a client cannot consult a barrister directly, but must do so through a solicitor, who instructs the barrister in a "brief". Barristers who are appointed King's Counsel have the letters "KC" after their names and are said "to take silk" – they wear gowns made of silk on ceremonial occasions to distinguish themselves from ordinary members of the Bar.

In Marshall Hall's absence, negotiations with Newton were conducted by the advocate's managing clerk, A. E. Bowker, and quickly foundered on the question of money. "We discussed terms," Bowker writes, "but when he [Newton] said that he was not prepared to pay any of the fees until the case was over, I became suspicious and insisted on a cheque with the brief. We haggled for a time, for I wanted the case badly," Bowker adds. "The defence of Crippen offered just the sort of challenge that would spur Marshall Hall to one of his great efforts of advocacy; but I continued to demand a cheque and would not budge."

In the long run it made little difference, for Crippen, determined upon martyrdom, would never have allowed Marshall Hall to put forward the defence which might have saved him from the gallows, and which incidentally the advocate believed to be the truth. By the time Marshall Hall returned from holidaying on the continent the committal proceedings at the Bow Street Police Court were already over, and, on Crippen's specific instructions, a line of defence had been adopted which the eminent barrister considered to be suicidal. As Marshall Hall expresses the dilemma: "Can counsel . . . take the responsibility of defending a man, of whose innocence he is convinced, if that man ties him down to a line of defence which that counsel knows to be a plea of 'guilty'? . . . I could not have defended Crippen on those lines."

Refusing to pay the barrister's fees in advance, Newton, a hot-tempered man, "banged out of the chambers, shouting," according to Bowker. "He walked up the Middle Temple Lane . . . furious at his failure to obtain the services of Marshall Hall. Three doors up the lane from Temple Gardens he saw the name of Alfred Tobin, and stopped. Newton knew quite well that Tobin . . . was not within miles of being a leading criminal 'silk'. Newton's temper, however, had got the better of his judgment, and ten minutes after leaving me he had arranged for Tobin to lead for the defence of Crippen."

Thus, as a result of Newton's personal pique, did Crippen get saddled with one of the dullest, the most plodding advocates in the business. Alfred (later Sir Alfred) Tobin may have built up a fair practice as a junior on the Northern Circuit, but, as Bowker points out, he could not touch the hem of Marshall Hall's robe when it came to criminal advocacy. He was strictly a bargain basement choice.

*　　*　　*

Any defending barrister, however, would have had his work cut out to ensure a fair trial, so great was the hostility that had been built up against Crippen by an unfriendly press. From the beginning the press had been at no pains to conceal its belief that Dr Crippen was guilty. Thus as far back as 17 July *Reynolds's Newspaper*, the London weekly, had described Crippen as a "degenerate". "One must search for a weakling," *Reynolds's Newspaper* advised, adding, "*Mens sans in corpore sano* is scarcely a description one would apply to the husband of a woman whose corpse lay mouldering for months under the floor almost over which the widower entertained and made high revel."

In the exciting sea chase which followed Captain Kendall's wireless message the big dailies vied with one another, their reporters going off into the realm of pure fantasy to scoop a rival. Thus while the *Montrose* was in mid-Atlantic the *Daily Express*'s omniscient correspondent was able to report that Dr Crippen had been arrested disguised as a clergyman and wearing false eyebrows ("Crippen was immediately searched and deprived of a revolver, a number of cartridges, and a pen-knife, while Miss LeNeve burst into tears.")

With Dr Crippen safely behind iron bars, press mendacity rose to new heights. The *Montreal Star* in a story datelined Quebec, Tuesday, 3 August, reported, "Crippen has made a full confession of the murder of his wife. This is an absolute fact." The same paper was back the following day with a direct quote from Inspector Dew, "Crippen will be a dead man in two months."

Inspector Dew, after the dust of the Crippen case had settled, was to reap a rich harvest from nine separate libel actions which he brought against newspapers for misquoting him to the detriment of his professional reputation.[3] "There is no longer any doubt that Crippen had made a confession to Inspector Dew," writes the *Daily Chronicle*'s reporter in Quebec, adding, "I not only have the very best authority for saying this, but I also have the admission of Inspector Dew." The *Daily Chronicle* then goes on to quote Dew as saying, "Yes, Crippen has now told me the complete story of the

3 Among the newspapers sued for libel by Dew were the *Montreal Star*, the *Daily Chronicle*, the *Evening Standard*, the *Pall Mall Gazette*, and the *Westminster Gazette*, the latter four being London dailies. Most of the actions were settled out of court for undisclosed sums, but Dew was awarded £400 damages plus costs from the *Daily Chronicle*.

crime and how her body was disposed of. He also related to me exactly how the murder occurred." The *Chronicle*'s "Special Correspondent" then declares "from a source which I know to be authoritative" that the confession was made Monday, 1 August, in the presence of Dew and three other police officers after the statutory caution had been given. Crippen is then quoted as saying, "It is true. I did kill my wife . . . I will say nothing until I return to England, and then I shall prove that I am not a murderer. I make this confession in order to free Miss LeNeve from suspicion."

The story of the alleged confession was picked up by Reuters and widely reprinted throughout the United Kingdom. "The papers," Crippen writes to Ethel from Pentonville prison, "have treated us so shamefully they all owe us a great reparation, which we shall never get. It is impossible to deny that everyone was prejudiced by the newspaper lies."

As if popular prejudice were not enough, defence counsel had Crippen himself to contend with in its efforts to make a good showing. For Crippen appeared to be bent upon self-destruction.

Most legal experts are agreed that Crippen's only hope of escaping the hangman's noose lay in entering a plea of guilty, making play of such mitigating circumstances as there were, then throwing himself upon the mercy of the court. Marshall Hall's biographer quotes him as saying "there was only one possible defence for Crippen, and that was to admit everything except the intent to murder." In so doing Crippen stood a chance of having the charge reduced from murder to manslaughter. As another distinguished jurist, Sir Travers Humphreys, points out, "In another country he [Crippen] would I feel sure have been given the benefit of 'extenuating circumstances'."

A guilty plea would have involved telling the truth and shaming the devil – that is, dragging into the open the whole sordid story of Crippen's married life with Belle, of her shrewishness, her addiction to alcohol, her infidelities. The risk, of course, was that the strategem might boomerang, and far from incurring their censure of Belle's behaviour, might have awakened the jurors' sympathy for the dead woman whose name was being blackened. Ethel would have to be called as a witness, and the story of Crippen's affair with Ethel – including her pregnancy and miscarriage – would have to be developed through her testimony in open court, and as a consequence, she would be exposed to the deadly crossfire of the prosecution. She would be lucky if there were even a fig-leaf to clothe her nakedness when she stepped down from the witness box.

Crippen of course would not for a single moment hear of calling Ethel in his defence. "Tell Ethel not to worry," were Crippen's instructions to Newton's managing clerk, when the latter came to see him in prison. "Tell her I will take all the blame. Give her my heart's love."

The decision to protect Ethel at all costs was not a hasty one. "I would have been ready any time and at all times to lay down my life and soul to make you happy," Crippen was to write to Ethel from his death cell. When had this determination formed in his mind? Was it in the early days of their "courtship", as he called it, when the two lovers sat in a corner at Frascati's listening to the palm court orchestra? Was it that rainy Sunday in the summer of 1903 of which Crippen recalled, "How happy we were together, with all sunshine in our hearts"?

Whenever it was, Crippen, once he had opted for martyrdom, was not to be cheated of it if he could possibly help it. He would plead not guilty, go into the witness box and lie. He would maintain under oath that Belle Elmore had left the domestic hearth to fulfill her oft-repeated threat of running away with another man. He would just as solemnly affirm that he knew nothing about the remains found in the cellar at No. 39 until told of their discovery by his solicitor. "Do you really ask the jury to understand," the Lord Chief Justice would ask somewhat incredulously, "that . . . without your knowledge or your wife's, at some time during the five years, those remains could have been put there?" Without blinking an eye, Crippen would reply, "It does not seem probable, but there is a possibility." The big lies would be bolstered by smaller lies, until in the end Crippen would be tangled up in a skein of lies from which it would be impossible to extricate himself.

Henchy, Newton's managing clerk, recalls Crippen's utter indifference to his fate during the numerous pre-trial consultations he had with the accused. "He couldn't seem to concentrate on his own case," Henchy writes. "He began to ask us about Ethel directly we arrived and he would still be talking about her when we left. Moreover what he did tell us was of little real use to the defence."

Unfortunately the Crippen trial was robbed of that dignity which usually accompanies justice. From the beginning it was treated more as a spectacle than as a judicial hearing where a man's life was at stake. This was evident in the boisterous, holiday mood of the crowd that queued for gallery seats on the opening day, "some begging, pleading wheedling, arguing, lying to gain admission", in the words of the *Daily Mail*, "others knowing the hopelessness of such endeavours, trying for no more than to catch sight of some of the people prominent in the case . . ." Inside, the confusion was no less marked. The demand for seats in the body of Court No. 1 had been so great that, in true music hall fashion, a two-house-a-day system had been inaugurated; thus in the corridor outside the courtroom there was much shouting of "Red tickets this way", and "Blue tickets over there", and one half-expected an usher to announce, "Ladies and gentlemen, will you kindly take your seats – the curtain rises in two minutes."

Whether or not it was out of respect for Belle Elmore's memory, the theatrical profession had turned out in force, headed by actor-managers Sir Herbert Beerbohm Tree and Sir John Hare. (At the earlier Bow Street committal proceedings W. S. Gilbert had been assiduous in his attendance. "Gilbert," as his biographer Hesketh Pearson points out, "always attuned to popular emotion, could not keep the subject out of his conversation and remained on tenter-hooks until Crippen was convicted.")[4]

No doubt members of the Music Hall Ladies' Guild too felt "attuned to popular emotion" as they chatted, exchanged smiles, even waved to one another across the crowded courtroom. Some of the guild ladies – notably Melinda May and Mesdames Martinetti and Smythson – were not in the courtroom, but awaited below in the witness room their turn to give evidence against Crippen. Now that Crippen had been brought to justice, they no longer thirsted for vengeance. They even found kind things to say of the doctor personally, though their cumulative evidence against him was damning. Thus Clara Martinetti declared, "He always appeared kind-hearted and exceedingly courteous towards his wife." Their only concern now was to see justice done.

4 The Crippen case was to inspire Gilbert to write *The Hooligan*, a one-acter about a condemned man awaiting execution in a prison cell. Nat Solly, the man in question, is a far cry from Crippen, however, as is made clear by his Cockney background ("My faver was a high toby cracksman, my muvver was a prig, and did two stretches, my bruvvers and sisters was all prigs . . .").

Not to see justice done, but to savour the full drama of it – this was the reason given by one pretty ingenue for being present in court. "This," she confided to the man sitting next to her, "is our real dramatic school."[5] By "this" the actress with a sweep of her hand indicated not only the prisoner in the dock, the row of bewigged counsel who sat facing one another with their law books piled beside them, but the Lord Chief Justice, Lord Alverstone, whose full-bottomed wig and scarlet and ermine robe she might have supposed had been rented from a costumier in Shaftesbury Avenue.[6]

The high point in theatricality was reached when actress Phyllis Dare, who not long previously had been toasted as "The Belle of Mayfair", was invited to share the Bench with his lordship, and accordingly took a seat to the left of the Lord Chief Justice and directly beneath the Sword of Justice whose gold-inlaid scabbard shimmered on the wall high above her head. This was too much for *The Times*. "A criminal court is not a showroom," *The Times* sternly reminded its readers; "nor is such a trial of the nature of a matinee; the Old Bailey is not a place to which fashionable ladies may fitly go in search of the latest sensation, where actors may hope to pick up suggestions as to a striking gesture or a novel expression, or where descriptive writers may look for good copy."

While actors and extras alike strutted and postured on the improvised stage of the courtroom, Hawley Crippen, in the prisoner's dock and screened from the public by a glass partition, contrived to remain aloof. "To all outward appearance he might have been a client slightly perturbed at the prospect of a summons for riding a bicycle without a light," in the words of Newton's managing clerk.

The trial quickly resolved itself into a forensic duel, with one set of medico-legal experts pitted against another. At issue was a piece of skin, eight inches long, horseshoe-shaped, and fringed by short,

5 The incident is reported in a letter to *The Times*, 28 October 1910.
6 In point of fact the actress would not have been far wrong. Lord Alverstone *was* a performer of sorts. His rich baritone had graced the choir of St Mary Abbot's, Kensington for forty years, and he was a shining light of the Old Madrigal Society. "I cannot speak too highly of the pleasure which I derived from the study of part music," his lordship writes in his memoirs, adding, "There is no more refining and interesting pursuit."

dark hairs. The Crown experts who examined the skin found that it had all the characteristics of a scar, namely no hair follicles or sebaceous glands, but only fibrous tissue. The fringe consisted of pubic hairs, indicating that the skin had come from a woman's abdomen, they would claim. The scar, the Crown would maintain, corresponded to that left on Belle's body after one of her ovaries had been removed. The defence, through the medical witnesses it would call, would contend just as vehemently that the so-called scar was no scar at all, but merely a mark made by a folding of the skin.

The horseshoe of skin was lifted from its formalin with pincers by pathologist Dr Augustus J. Pepper, a short, black-haired man with a heavy moustache, and gold pince-nez. It was then placed in a soup-plate, and passed along the jury-box, causing a *Daily Mail* reporter to have stomach twinges. None was more interested than Crippen who, as the dish was carried by an usher to the defence counsel's table, rose to his feet and leaned over the rail to look at its contents with the intelligent curiosity of a student of anatomy. Indeed, the Lord Chief Justice might almost have been rebuking a prankish member of such an anatomy class when he suddenly snapped at Mr Tobin, "You have taken an inky pen." In order to point to some detail of the skin fragment, Tobin in fact had snatched up the nib with which he had lately been making notes.

The Crippen case marked the public debut of Bernard (later Sir Bernard) Spilsbury, then 33, who was to become the most famous pathologist of his day. "To the man in the street he [Spilsbury] stood for pathology as Hobbs stood for cricket or Dempsey for boxing or Capablanca for chess," writes Edgar Lustgarten, adding, "His pronouncements were invested with the force of dogma, and it was blasphemy to hint that he might conceivably be wrong."

But in October, 1910, when he went into the witness-box the plump, pink-cheeked Spilsbury was unknown except to a re-stricted circle at St Mary's Hospital, Paddington, where he had done his work in pathology. In order to nail down the Crown's case for the piece of skin being scar tissue, Spilsbury invited the jurors to adjourn to an adjacent courtroom and there to peer through microscopes at slides he had prepared from the supposed scar. It was a theatrical *tour de force* which struck Coroner S. Ingleby Oddie as being "as futile as it was unusual". But it captured the imagination of reporters covering the trial. In the next quarter of a century Spilsbury would give evidence at nearly every important murder trial held in the south of England, including the celebrated "Brides in the Bath" case, in addition to conducting 25,000 post-mortems.

How Arthur Newton tricked two eminent pathologists into giving evidence for the defence forms one of the sorrier episodes of the trial. Newton was acquainted with Dr Gilbert Turnbull, director of the Pathological Institute of the London Hospital. Newton was also aware of a certain animosity which the London Hospital pathologist felt towards his more illustrious colleagues at St Mary's, Paddington. He was to use this knowledge with a skill born of low cunning. At a bridge party at which both Dr Turnbull and he were guests Newton suggested to the former that he might like to examine the disputed piece of skin "as a matter of interest". "Having done this, rather perfunctorily, Turnbull was so foolish as to sign a report to the effect that the skin came from the thigh, not the abdomen, and that the supposed scar was a fold," as Spilsbury's biographers point out. Turnbull also got the concurrence of his friend and colleague, Dr Reginald Wall. The understanding had been that neither man would be called as a witness, but the unsuspecting scientists little reckoned with the craftiness of the man with whom they were dealing.

Dr Turnbull in particular, was both stunned and angry when he was subpoenaed as a defence witness, for after a further examination of the skin and a study of the Pepper and Spilsbury depositions he had begun to entertain doubts about his first opinion. "Horrified to learn that he had been tricked into giving evidence at the trial, he [Turnbull] telephoned Spilsbury for advice. Spilsbury recommended him to withdraw the report. Finally, however, Turnbull determined to stand by it." Foolhardily Doctors Turnbull and Wall submitted to the Crown's devastating cross-examination, to emerge with their professional reputations badly dented. "To me at least it was a painful sight to see two men of undoubted probity and of considerable eminence in their profession one after the other having to admit that they had signed a statement . . . which they both had to admit was quite incorrect," writes Travers Humphreys, one of the Crown counsel at the trial.

For one other person it was a painful business. Crippen was to write to Ethel later, "Today at the appeal I realised more and more that the medical evidence for my defence was so mismanaged that it told against me rather than for me. This I saw at the Old Bailey in the judge's summing up and again today in the summing up of the Appeal. I am powerless now, and can do nothing more, but bow to the inevitable," he added.

Finally there remained only Crippen himself facing the Crown prosecution in the person of Scottish-born Richard (later Sir Richard) Muir. So formidable was Muir's reputation that Crippen is said to have muttered, upon learning that Muir was to lead for the Crown, "I wish it had been anybody else . . . I fear the worst." The son of a Clydeside shipbroker, Muir had come to London originally with the intention of going on the stage, but had been talked out of it by an older brother, who persuaded him that the law was more suitable to his talents. Traces of the would-be matinee idol were discernible in the profile, with its long, straight nose and prematurely silvered hair, which Muir now turned to the jurymen as he rested his arm on the jury box.

Faced with a defendant such as Crippen, who appeared determined to commit *felo-de-se* in the witness-box, Muir's present task was not such a difficult one, as is evident from Crippen's answers to the first six questions put to him in cross-examination.

> MUIR (to Crippen) – In the early morning of the 1st February you were left alone in your house with your wife? – Yes.
>
> She was alive? – Yes.
>
> And well? – She was.
>
> Do you know of any person in the world who has seen her alive since? – I do not.
>
> Do you know of any person in the world who can prove any fact showing that she ever left that house alive? – Absolutely not; I have told Mr Dew exactly all the facts.

And so it went on hour after hour, this relentless rebuttal, with Crippen being led over the minefield of his own lies, which were exploded, one by one, under his unwary feet. For Muir was a master of over-kill, as his notes on the Crippen case make evident.[7] "Muir's playing cards," they were called, these notes written in four or five different coloured pencils on small, numbered cards. Muir pored over his "playing cards" night after night until the

---

7 The notes are reproduced in their entirety in Sidney T. Felstead's biography of Muir.

case against Crippen was foolproof, and until "everybody connected with the prosecution of Crippen heartily cursed his [Muir's] name," according to his biographer.

Occasionally the Lord Chief Justice intervened to clarify a point. For example, Crippen testified that on Friday, 8 July, immediately after he had been questioned by Inspector Dew he contemplated fleeing London with Ethel LeNeve. His line of thinking he explained as follows: "If there is all this suspicion, and I am likely to have to stay in gaol for months and months and months, perhaps until this woman is found, I had better be out of it." (Note how he refers to his wife as "this woman".)

LORD CHIEF JUSTICE – Mr Crippen, do you really mean that you thought you would have to lie in gaol for months and months? Do you say that? – Quite so, yes.

MUIR – Upon what charge? – Suspicion.

Suspicion of what? – Suspicion of – Inspector Dew said, "This woman has disappeared, she must be found."

Suspicion of what? – Suspicion of being concerned in her disappearance.

What crime did you understand you might be kept in gaol upon suspicion of? – I do not understand the law enough to say. From what I have read it seems to me I have heard of people being arrested on suspicion of being concerned in the disappearance of other people.

The disappearance of other people? – Well, I am doing the best I can to explain it to you. I cannot put it for you in a legal phrase.

LORD CHIEF JUSTICE – Nobody wants you to put it in a legal phrase. The simple question is, What was the charge that you thought might be brought against you after you had seen Inspector Dew? – I could not define the charge, except that if I could not find the woman I was very likely to be held until she was found. That was my idea.

MUIR – Because of what? – I cannot say why. I can only say that no other idea than that entered my head. If I could not produce the woman –

Yes, what would be the inference? – Mr Dew told me that I should be in serious trouble. Well, I could not make out what the inference would be.

And that was why you contemplated on the afternoon of

8th July flying from the country? – Quite so; that, and the idea that I had said that Miss LeNeve was living with me, and she had told her people she was married to me, and it would put her in a terrible position. The only thing I could think of was to take her away out of the country where she would not have this scandal thrown upon her.

The cross-examination lasted for three hours, at the end of which Crippen, not visibly shaken, stepped down from the witness-box. To complete the illusion of the trial as a theatrical spectacle, the comments on Crippen's demeanour as a witness read like the notices of a stage performance. "Marvellous was the calm which he maintained throughout the trial . . . the demeanour of innocence so counterfeited as to deceive any one who forgot the evidence . . ." (*The Times*). "He had given a marvellous exhibition of nerve power under the strain of a terrible ordeal" (the *Daily Mail*). "He stood up to it . . . with wonderful composure and calmness" (S. Ingleby Oddie). "The most amazing feature of the trial was the absolute coolness and imperturbability of Crippen in the long and terrible cross-examination" (Filson Young).

The jury retired shortly after the lunch recess on Saturday 22 October, returning to the courtroom twenty-seven minutes later. A hush fell over the spectators as the jurors filed into the jury box. Then the Clerk of the Arraigns asked, "Gentlemen, have you agreed upon your verdict?" To which the jury foreman replied, "We have." At this point the mask of tragedy, insecurely held throughout the trial, slipped once again when it was discovered that the jury was about to discharge its office in the absence of the accused. "One moment," the Lord Chief Justice cried, holding up a hand to halt the proceedings. "The prisoner is not in the courtroom." At this signal Crippen suddenly appeared into view from up the stairs of the cell beneath the dock. It was as though he had been sprung through a trap-door. Crippen walked briskly towards the rail where he stood, wedged between two warders, facing the judge.

"Do you find the prisoner guilty or not guilty of wilful murder?" the clerk intoned.

"We find the prisoner guilty of wilful murder."

A *Daily Mail* reporter, whose eyes, like those of the other spectators, were fixed upon Crippen, describes the latter's reaction. "The little man's intertwined fingers tightened in the effort to preserve his self-command," the reporter observed. "A pallor spread over his forehead and cheeks. The bald patch at the back of his little, flat head became a dull white . . . The face showed no trace of emotion." The question whether the prisoner had anything to say before sentence was passed had to be repeated before Crippen replied in a firm voice, "I still protest my innocence."

The judge's marshal then placed the black cap on his lordship's wig; the usher with a loud "Oyez, oyez, oyez" commanded silence; and the Lord Chief Justice, declining to dwell upon the "ghastly and wicked nature of the crime", ordered Hawley Harvey Crippen to be "taken from hence to a lawful prison, and from thence to a place of execution, and that you be there hanged by the neck until you are dead". Then it was all over. The court rose, his lordship left the Bench, and the condemned man disappeared as suddenly as he had appeared.

HELEN DUNCAN

(Old Bailey, 1944)

Malcolm Gaskill

The last witchcraft trial in Britain, in March 1944, resulted in the conviction of Helen Duncan, a heavy-set Scotswoman of 45, and Britain's best-known psychic medium. She claimed to be able to materialize the actual physical form of a spirit, not in the flesh but in the strange semi-physical, semi-spiritual substance known as ecto-plasm. She was arrested at a séance in Portsmouth, where thousands who had lost loved ones in the war sought proof of their continued existence in the spirit world. At her trial, she was accused under the Witchcraft Act of 1735, the first – and last – such prosecution of modern times. Churchill himself wanted to know what on earth was going on. Why was a woman in England in 1944 being tried for witchcraft? The jury heard that once the audience was assembled in a flat above a shop, Mrs Duncan, dressed in black, vanished behind some curtains. The room was in darkness, save for the glow from a single red lamp. Albert, her spirit guide, would indicate he had a message for a person sitting in a particular chair. When the person concerned called out, a form would appear in the gloom. Sometimes this form was said to be that of an animal, such as a rabbit or cat. A parrot called Bronco materialized, squawking "Pretty Polly". Sometimes Albert invited the audience to sing a popular song of the day, such as "South of the Border", to produce "quick vibrations" said to encourage physical phenomena. Occasionally, Albert was replaced by another spirit guide, a child called Peggy, who spoke in a high-pitched Scots accent and led a rendition of "Loch Lomond" before vanishing behind the curtains saying "I'm gaun doon noo." The whole rigmarole, the jury heard, was a fraud, "a mere imposition" in the opinion of the Lord Chief Justice at the subsequent appeal "on human credulity." Unexpected seat swaps meant some messages went to the wrong recipients, there were messages from "passed-over" relatives still very much alive, and "ectoplasm" emanating from Mrs Duncan that felt suspiciously like cheesecloth. One night Mrs Duncan was discovered pushing a piece of flimsy white cloth "like butter muslin" down her front. When the lights went up, she was frantically putting on her shoes. At the Old Bailey, Mrs Duncan was charged with three others, but only one, Ernest Homer, gave evidence. No fewer than twenty-six further witnesses testified about Mrs Duncan's performances over many years, convinced that she was indeed genuine. Coarse-featured and plain spoken, Helen Duncan was raised in Scotland, a noisy, boisterous tomboy her friends called Hellish Nell. Mrs Duncan's biographer Malcolm Gaskill (b. 1967), a Cambridge historian, records that the wartime gaggle who queued for her trial were "curious citizens, successors to the Londoners of Hogarth's day who had gathered there to follow the condemned to Tyburn, jeering and sharing the latest from the Grub Street presses." Dr Gaskill, a fellow and director of studies at Churchill College, Cambridge, specializes in British social and cultural history, especially the history of witchcraft and popular beliefs. In his account of Helen Duncan's trial, he explains that her counsel Charles Loseby, an ardent spiritualist himself, embarked on a headstrong defence by seeking to demonstrate that the dead could, indeed, be brought back to life.

The trial began on the morning of Thursday, 23 March 1944 in Court No. 4 of the Blitz-damaged Old Bailey. The public gallery remained out of bounds, and eager spectators squeezed past each other in the precincts and corridors, hopeful of a downstairs seat or at least a place outside the door. It is possible to recover the court's experience a little too authentically, conveying the listlessness and ennui felt by all but a few as Loseby's twenty-fifth, thirty-fifth and, finally, his forty-fifth defence witness took the oath. More revealing are the emotions of that strange week in March, not least those of the quixotic, ill-starred Charles Loseby, the tragic figure fated to do right by no one.

Long before he was unnerved by stifled yawns and judicial obstruction, Loseby was troubled. After breakfast at his Kensington home he had paced the hallway in the manner which suggested to his wife and daughter that a great burden was weighing down on him. In court, once again he noted the impressive effect of John Maude's good looks and stature, his strong voice contrasting with Loseby's own softer, smoother drawl. Loseby was supported by Mr Simpson Pedler, a fellow member of Gray's Inn with two decades' experience at the Bar; but even as the junior he did not look up to Loseby the way Elam did to Maude, a figure whose self-assurance no amount of swotting, zeal, or casuistic ingenuity could assail. "He spoke," Loseby admitted, "with such adroitness, skill and economy of words that any ill-informed person might well imagine that there could be no effective answer to the case as he set it out." The judge, Recorder of London Sir Gerald Dodson, a practising Christian, was even-handed with his contempt, measuring out professional irritability to all and sundry without breaching the Old Bailey custom of humane treatment of prisoners in the dock. By the end, however, even Dodson could not conceal his desire to be elsewhere, perhaps back at the opening night of *The Rebel Maid*, the humorous musical he had part-authored, which may have caused him some wry amusement when he heard about the Duncans' rebellious servant, Mary McGinlay.

The witnesses were nervous, the exception being Stanley Worth whose testimony had become the vanguard of the Prosecution as the charge evolved from vagrancy to conspiracy to witchcraft. At the Portsmouth hearing, moreover, Cross had appeared uncomfortable whereas Worth, dapper in his lieutenant's uniform, Loseby noted, "gave his evidence with skill and a good eye to effect, being assisted in the latter by a flickering smile which seemed to be under command." And he could do all the voices, including Albert's. More worrying was Loseby's dilemma, one faced by all defending barristers: whether to let his clients testify and have them incriminate themselves under cross-examination; or deny them the privilege and make it seem they had something to hide. Daunted as they were, in the case of all but Mr Homer, Loseby chose the latter which, Elam remembered, looked very bad indeed. As for others present, the spectating public were boss-eyed and garrulous, the psychical researchers serious and studious, the Spiritualist women pious and lachrymose. W.A.E. Jones of the *Daily Herald*, who attended on all seven days, did not warm to

Helen the martyr and her disciples, many of whom had come up
from Portsmouth. "As she waddled her way to face the judge and
jury, women threw their arms around her, kissed her, sobbed over
her and blessed her in whispering voices."

The first, electrifying day was taken up by the opening speech
for the Prosecution and Worth's account of the seances of 14, 17
and 19 January. Maude's gentle but cruel mockery, deftly poised
ironies, learned perspectives and calm appeals to common sense
lowered the Defence into a slippery-sided pit from which it would
struggle to emerge. As Loseby cross-examined Worth, the formal
protocols of the exchange – begged pardons and craved indul-
gences – gave way to raised voices, the Recorder interjecting that
the court could hear them both perfectly well. They squabbled
over whether Worth thought himself to be a spy, and, indeed,
which of them had first used the word, Worth protesting that
Loseby had put it in his mouth so he had used it. To Loseby's
sarcastic parody of Mrs Duncan "playing bogey-bogey with a
sheet over her head," he needed to add nothing, acceding effort-
lessly to this interpretation. Worth was unshaken and Loseby
knew it. More than that, he was utterly persuasive, a seductive
quality which smoothed over the inconsistencies so hotly scorned
by the psychical researchers. The Recorder wound up proceedings
for the day by asking for a sketch plan of the seance room, and
releasing Mrs Duncan and her co-defendants on bail. Outside,
Frances Brown was not her usual talkative self and shielded her
face from the cameras.

The second day began with Worth, examined by Elam, defending his eyesight – he had a lazy eye – until the Recorder cut him off
before he started on his optician's opinion. Next Elijah Fowler, in
his diffident Scots voice, confirmed Worth's account of the first
seance; a police photographer amused the jury with his imitations
of spirit photographs seized from Frances Brown; Mr and Mrs
William Lock said their piece, which included the story of the
return of Pinky, an RAF pilot shot through the head; and Mr
Burrell likened Peggy to a fairy in a Christmas pantomime. Kitty
Jennings, an Air Raid Precautions supervisor, related how at an
afternoon seance on 19 January "this wretched Scotch child"
(Maude's words), jigging up and down, had confessed to using
Christine Homer's perfume and lipstick. When she hesitated
before describing Peggy, Maude raised a laugh by asking whether
she looked more like Helen of Troy or a pillowcase. A seasoned

actress before the war, Mrs Jennings agreed with Loseby that the
regional accents would be hard to mimic – unless, of course, one
were used to doing such a thing. Finally, after Rupert Cross had
corroborated the second part of Worth's testimony, Detective
Inspector Ford was brow-beaten by Loseby for failing to search
the sitters and his defence that it would have been pointless
without the presence of a doctor was received sceptically. Again
and again, Loseby asked for the significance of this until the
Recorder stopped him, as much from boredom as a desire to save
Ford's blushes, whereupon Maude stepped in: "It is obvious there
are certain places where things can be concealed?" "Yes, sir,"
replied Ford briskly. And with that, Maude rested the case for the
Crown.

That evening Loseby paced some more, while he rehearsed the
Defence's opening speech. In the morning he steeled himself and,
before another crowded court, did his level best to discredit the
Prosecution's witnesses, while steering towards the assertion that
Helen Duncan was a genuine materialization medium. The Recorder, for the time being, kept his feelings to himself, but they
resembled those expressed by the Lord Chief Justice in the mid-
1930s, namely that the validity of Spiritualism as a religion was a
topic "better discussed in the bracing air at a conference in
Blackpool". Loseby carried on obliviously, digging his hole deeper, making the sides ever more slippery. His attempt to call the
prisoners out of order was blocked, as was his proposal to present
Mrs Duncan for a test seance later on. He spoke of Mrs Duncan
having "gone down like a shot rabbit" when Worth shone his
torch, and referred to the burn on her cheek where ectoplasm had
re-entered her body; all eyes turned to the dock but no mark was
visible. The whey-faced, unassuming Mr Homer who followed,
did little to incriminate himself – describing a materialization of
Mrs Homer's grandmother joining her to sing a Welsh hymn – but
neither did he say anything to exculpate Mrs Duncan, still less to
substantiate Loseby's thesis that the bodies of gifted mediums
were portals through which the spirits of the dead revisited earth.
Pathos turned to bathos when, once more, Loseby sought approval
for Mrs Duncan to perform a private seance for the jury and this
time the Recorder explained his refusal. Like a medieval ordeal, he
argued, such a demonstration "might operate unfairly against this
woman because, supposing the spirit, if such a thing there be, was
not mindful to come to her assistance on this occasion, then the

verdict would have to be against her''. If Loseby quailed inside, he did his best not to show it as he called the first of his witnesses.

The twinkle in the eye of George Mackie, the RAF wing commander present on 19 January, did not alter the court's impression that, like Loseby's other "skilled investigators", he took himself too seriously. Of the fact that he had been reunited with his mother who had died in Australia in 1927 he was quite sure. "A man knows his mother," he observed. "I have the advantage also of knowing my father", to which the Recorder, eyebrows raised, responded politely: "Well, that's something", causing some spectators to rub their smiling faces. Harold Gill of Southsea followed, Maude talking him through his recollection of the ectoplasm by dangling a piece of butter muslin, much to the consternation of the Spiritualists. Mrs Gill knew about the belief that ectoplasm could rush back into the medium's body from a lantern lecture given by a Mr Lilley of the Portsmouth City Police finger-printing section in November 1943 – a curious detail not mentioned again.

The fourth day of the trial, Tuesday, 28 March, marked a watershed, the repetitiveness of the stories, however marvellous and poignant, eating away at the roots of the Recorder's tolerance. Proceedings resumed with some mild distraction in the form of documentary evidence: some receipts and letters of thanks for seance profits donated to the Wireless for the Blind Fund, the Two Worlds Publishing Company and the SNU Freedom Fund. The Homers claimed that all "surplus money" went to charities, receipts for £450 of which the police managed to trace, although less than £30 of that came from the Duncan seances. The first witness was a Mrs Cole who, speaking of the manifestation of her friend, complained that some people present in court were laughing at her trying to remember how long Albert's beard was and, from that point, for the Recorder all was sorrow tinged with desperation and anger, a darkening mood which Loseby at least pretended not to notice. Towards the end of the afternoon, having heard a Royal Marine speak fondly of the return of his grandparents and unable to bear another second, Dodson interrupted Elam cross-examining a witness about the kind of fairy light she had seen in Mrs Duncan's hand:

THE RECORDER: We will go into that tomorrow. Mr Loseby, can you give us any help at all with regard to the witnesses?

MR LOSEBY: My Lord, I shall call no more Portsmouth witnesses.

THE RECORDER: Any other sort of witnesses?

MR LOSEBY: Yes, my Lord.

THE RECORDER: How many more? I want to know, roughly.

MR LOSEBY: It is hard for me to estimate. I had in mind forty to fifty.

By way of reply, and yearning for his tea, the Recorder said nothing but merely scraped back his chair and made good his escape through the door behind the Bench.

Day five brought no relief to Sir Gerald Dodson. On top of his feelings of malaise, he became squeamish when Loseby, encouraged by the presence of Harry Price, speculated too long on the appearance of regurgitated cheesecloth. Basil Kirkby, a retired businessman, said he had spent twenty years researching "the stuff known as ectoplasm", behind which lay a power almost as amazing as radium had been to Marie Curie, and which he had observed alongside Sir Oliver Lodge and Sir Arthur Conan Doyle. Mention of a spirit budgerigar which, according to Kirkby, said "Pretty boy, pretty boy" (words a budgerigar of his acquaintance had used) led the Recorder to take over the questioning whereupon he learned that everyone has a spirit guide. "Have we?" Dodson asked incredulously. "Yes, every one of us," replied Kirkby, who had Chang, a Chinaman with an eighteen-inch moustache and a swinging pigtail. "Well, I don't seem to have one with regard to this evidence," said the Recorder. Next came an RAF officer who had seen Mrs Duncan at the Edinburgh Psychic College and Library in 1937 and again, since the outbreak of war, at Preston; Lilian Bailey, a medium employed by the IIPR; and Hannen Swaffer, the journalist who had trumpeted the British visit of American medium "Margery" in 1929, and the first defence witness to give Elam a run for his money.

After the wife of a Glasgow forgemaster had told of meeting her dead father in 1931 – complete, if that is the right word, with missing eye – it was the turn of B. Abdy Collins who earned the Recorder's respect by his having been a magistrate and sessions judge in India. Mrs Duncan's manifestations radiated an unearthly phosphorescence, he said, providing evidence of survival almost as

compelling as that offered by the ex-miner Jack Webber and quite
unlike a deception he himself had exposed at Reading. Testimony
for this, the fifth day, ended with a Battersea medium describing
the spirit of her husband Alf, and a man convinced by his wrinkly
old granny's Suffolk accent. The Recorder shaved off ten minutes'
free time and the court adjourned. Next morning the Recorder's
spirits were lifted a little by Loseby's announcement that this
would be the last day on which he would call witnesses. First up
was Alfred Dodd, the Shakespeare hobbyist (he believed that
Bacon wrote the sonnets) who had seen his first sweetheart Helen.
The Recorder's patience being fresh, Dodd was permitted to speak
at length, for instance, claiming that Mary, Queen of Scots, a
seance favourite, had struggled in vain to materialize at a seance in
1940 but had managed to pass on the message that she was a lady
attired in "an old-world dress" who spoke Scots tinged with
French and had lost her head on the block – the sort of historical
sketch one can imagine Mr Cumming having once made at Call-
ander Parish School.

Thus far Helen's 1933 conviction had been kept quiet, because
by the terms of the law of evidence it was no indication of guilt, and
but for Loseby's strategy it would not even have been mentioned.
Now, Dodd's allusion to 1933 prompted Elam to ask for the fact to
be disclosed in rebuttal of the Defence's continued claim that
Helen Duncan was a genuine medium. The jury retired, the story
was revealed through Dodd's cross-examination and the question
of whether the evidence would now be admissible was discussed.
Elam hesitated and asked that Maude be brought back (remember
he was simultaneously defending an accused murderer in Court
No. 1), whereupon the Recorder ruled that Loseby had chosen to
draw upon events pre-dating January 1944 and now the Prosecution should be allowed to do the same. Loseby's hopes were fading
and the failure of his case was etched into the faces of the newly
returned jurors, who remained unmoved even when Dodd, re-
telling the story of the Edinburgh trial, reduced a murmuring Mrs
Duncan to tears with his affirmation of her qualities. "She is a
genuine materialization medium," Dodd stated firmly, "and anything I can do to help that lady in her distress, I come here to do it,
because I owe her a debt."

Throughout the trial, Helen was surrounded by people who felt
similarly obliged, if not always for what she had done for them
personally, then at least for what she symbolized to the Spiritualist

movement. Released on bail, she stayed at SNU official Percy Wilson's house in Wimbledon, where she conducted six test seances, others having already been held before the start of proceedings, both there and at the Marylebone Spiritualist Association. At least one of these sessions was attended by Charles Loseby. As Percy Wilson recalled in the 1950s:

> After a day's hearing, we took her straight to Wimbledon, gave her some tea with good red jam – we were thinking, of course, of the regurgitation suggestion – and then upstairs to the seance room . . . I have never seen such a mass of ectoplasm. It bundled up on her bosom, dropped to the floor and then jumped up to her hand. It was as a result of this experience that we offered the court a sitting.

Wilson's son, Laurence, was almost knocked over by a tube of rubbery ectoplasm upon which a mischievous Albert had invited him to tread. Another son, Geoffrey, an undergraduate on vacation (later a scientific officer for the Admiralty), was appointed as a messenger for the Defence and was present throughout the trial, which bored him as much as it did anyone else. The seances at his home, however, were something quite different, with ribbons of wriggling grey ectoplasm and an abundance of apported flowers, Hylda Lewis-style. Loseby, too, was convinced and once he had agreed to suggest a test seance to judge and jury, Wilson and his wife hastily built a portable cabinet from copper gas piping, black cloth, curtain rings and an adapted standard lamp fitted with a rheostat.

Loseby made the most of his last day by calling another fourteen witnesses. Dr John Winning, Assistant Medical Officer for Glasgow and a committed psychical investigator, claimed to have seen over 400 of Mrs Duncan's manifestations, speaking not just in different accents, but in Gaelic, German and Hebrew. Relatives he had met in spirit were quite unlike the medium: his mother was slim, his brother quick in his movements, his grandmother eighty-four. Indeed, stretched over forty seances, Winning had attended the family reunion if not from hell, then from somewhere lighter and brighter. Aunt Elaine called by, as did several uncles including one whose features were entirely different from Mrs Duncan's, not least his beard and moustache. Winning was followed by a psychic healer from Baker Street, dewy-eyed veteran of 150 Duncan seances, who saw a child with withered arms; a Frenchwoman whose one-legged daughter sang *Au clair de la lune* and displayed dancing skills denied her in life; and a retired sanitary inspector from Kendal, slightly deaf, who received a message from his drowned daughter tapped out in Morse code. Vincent Woodcock, an electrical draftsman from Blackpool, identified first his wife from the spirit's palpitating heart, then his stepmother from a fatal wound sustained during the Manchester Blitz. The only witness who brought anything new to proceedings was Sir James Herries, an Edinburgh journalist and magistrate whose class and credibility were invaluable to Loseby. His friend Sir Arthur Conan Doyle had returned to him at a Duncan seance, if only to answer "yes" to a question before fading back, his legendary stamina for public engagements now sadly diminished. Herries had disagreed with the verdict in 1933 and, prompted by Loseby, pronounced Price's cheesecloth theory "perfectly absurd". For poor Sir Gerald Dodson the afternoon ended in an evidential blur – more glowing dogs and birds, another one-legged relative, boasts about spiritual healing, a doctor talking to his mother (in Swedish), the return of a French youth killed on the Maginot Line in 1940 and a South African called Gilbert who had perished in a plane crash. At last, Loseby said that he had called enough witnesses and the Recorder, in full agreement, asked that the case be concluded the next day. "One would like to reciprocate the patience the jury have shown," he remarked with an economical smile, "by not inflicting more upon them than we can help."

That evening, a dinner was held in Helen's honour at the Bonnington Hotel in Southampton Row. After they had finished eating, Loseby suggested she try to procure a spiritual message on a pad which he placed under the tablecloth, and which she held while she continued chatting and smoking. After a while, they were rewarded, but with scrawled words which made the dinner seem even more of a valedictory last supper: "Two will be convicted and two will go free." In the morning, judgement day found the court jaded, the defendants more alert now, fearing the worst. For simplicity's sake all the charges were dropped – including "effecting a public mischief" by exploiting the war bereaved – except that of conspiracy to contravene the Witchcraft Act. In Loseby's closing speech, the two hours and 11,000 words of which persuaded the Recorder that his optimism had been premature, the jury were asked whether they felt that the Prosecution had proved

beyond reasonable doubt that Helen Duncan had exercised or
pretended to exercise a kind of conjuration, and whether the 1735
Act was an appropriate statute upon which to try her and her co-
defendants. Perhaps this was the point when someone passed
Henry Elam a note reading: "The only evil spirit is now known
as Hooch; in 1735 all spirits were evil." If so, Loseby was too busy
with his own mockery to notice Elam smirk, so engrossed was he in
heaping derision upon the tribunal which had convicted Helen in
1933 and, indeed, upon the whole of Scotland, a country, he said,
which had objected to the introduction of the potato as an act of
impiety.

John Maude's cool-headed response was every bit as withering
as Loseby had feared, a rhetorical *coup de grâce*. The world beyond
the veil, he put it to the jury, was a dull and ridiculous world, not
awesome, merely awful:

> Let me ask you to imagine an afternoon in the Other World.
> They are sitting round Mary, Queen of Scots. Her head is on.
> St Sebastian, the pin-cushion saint, is there, perfectly nor-
> mal. There are various persons who have been mutilated,
> looking perfectly all right. No arm or leg cut off, no eyes out.
> Then suddenly someone says something that is sad. Off
> comes the Queen's head – under her arm, I suppose – St
> Sebastian begins to bleed, and unmutilated persons become
> mutilated.

The entire scenario was too fantastic. "If this is the sort of thing we
are coming to," advised Maude, "it is time we began to pull
ourselves together and exercise a little common sense." And
why did famous people so rarely return? Never did they see
Napoleon, Socrates, Shakespeare, Keats or Shelley, the last of
whom Maude quoted to address Bronco the parrot: "Hail to thee,
blithe Spirit! Bird thou never wert," adding: "For it was not a bird,
but a fraud." Like defending counsel in 1933, he also referred to
Browning's "Mr Sludge, the Medium," pointing out that dealing
with the occult had attracted charlatans for centuries.

After lunch, the Recorder delivered his summing-up, at two and
a quarter hours a masterpiece of compression, shaming Loseby
whose case, he suggested dispassionately, may well have defeated
itself "by being so prolix and multiplied". At 4.32 p.m. the jur –
the wartime variety of six men and one woman, all from th

surburb of Barnes – retired, returning twenty-four minutes later
with four guilty verdicts. Chief Constable West was then invited to
give an account of their records, calmly demolishing the ruins of
Mrs Brown's and Mrs Duncan's credit, referring to the former
helping herself in Selfridges (which had her shouting in denial)
and adding the following censure of the latter, who by now was
murmuring protests of her own. Paying little notice, West continued:

> This is a case where not only has she attempted and suc-
> ceeded in deluding confirmed believers in Spiritualism, but
> she has tricked, defrauded and preyed upon the minds of a
> certain credulous section of the public who have gone to these
> meetings in search of comfort of mind in their sorrow and
> grief, many of whom left with the firm conviction that the
> memory of the dead had been besmirched. She thought fit to
> come to Portsmouth, the first naval port of the world, where
> she would find many bereaved families, and there she prac-
> tised her trickery.

Interrupted by the Recorder, West expressed a wish to finish what
he had to say, which was granted. And then came the rub. West
made an unexplained fleeting reference to the darker danger Helen
Duncan had presented to public and nation in 1941, when a report
was filed about her "having transgressed the security laws, again in
a naval connection, when she foretold the loss of one of His
Majesty's ships long before the fact was made public."

The Recorder postponed sentencing until 10.30 a.m. on Monday 3 April, Loseby having requested a non-custodial sentence in
view of Helen's poor health; he was not optimistic, but at least this
way he had time to prepare his appeal application. While he paced
and scribbled, Helen and her dishevelled gang spent the weekend
in the cells, Albert having at last deserted her. When the Recorder
gaoled her for nine months, she shouted back: "I didn't do anything!" W. A. E. Jones described how "she sobbed. She moaned.
She groaned. And then she collapsed on the floor, hat off her head,
her fur coat flapping round her as prison matrons and the three
other defendants helped to raise her to her feet." Another reporter
affected surprise at her keening cry as to whether there was a God:
"For one professedly in touch with the world beyond this one, it
was a strange query." Frances Brown received four months for

aggravating Helen's offence, whereas the Homers were saved by their guilelessness, clean records and charity receipts, and were bound over. With the last of his strength, Loseby arranged for notice of appeal to be given on behalf of all four defendants and vainly attempted to have the case declared *sub judice,* again to restrain the press who were champing at the bit to get back down Ludgate Hill to Fleet Street in order to bash out their witch-trial stories. But the Recorder was in no mood to indulge Loseby and ended the trial with a sardonic remark indicating his view that it was rather rich for him to be resisting the press now when in the course of the previous week he had presented "rather a temptation to them".

"My Lord, I respectfully agree," said Loseby with a modest bow.

After a seven-day trial, the wartime jury of six men and a woman, having rejected the offer of a test demonstration of ectoplasm, convicted all four defendants. Helen Duncan was jailed for nine months. Despite the verdict, there were, and are, those who firmly believe in Mrs Duncan's powers. Lady Eleanor Smith, daughter of a former Lord Chancellor, condemned Mrs Duncan's conviction as "a disgrace to British justice, and another detestable attempt to interfere with our personal liberty. I'm only astounded," she added, "that she wasn't sentenced to be burned at the stake." In fact, Helen Duncan died in 1956, of natural causes. The Witchcraft Act has since been repealed, and campaigners for her rehabilitation want her conviction quashed and a posthumous pardon granted. Since the case, new evidence suggests that what worried the wartime authorities wasn't hocus-pocus. It was the fear that Mrs Duncan was revealing military secrets. In 1941, before official news had been released, Mrs Duncan told a séance that the British battleship HMS Hood had been sunk. At another, images of sailors with "HMS Barham" on their caps reportedly appeared. It transpired that a German U-boat had indeed sunk the battleship Barham, with heavy loss of life. But news of the disaster had been suppressed. Quite how Helen Duncan knew about the disaster remains a mystery.

MADAME FAHMY

(Old Bailey, 1923)

Nina Warner Hooke and Gil Thomas

In the torrid summer of 1923 a young Egyptian wastrel calling himself "Prince" Ali Fahmy and his French wife were staying at the Savoy Hotel in London. In the early hours of 10 July, Madame Fahmy, in her white evening gown, shot her husband dead in his pyjamas. In September of that year, she appeared at the Old Bailey charged with wilful murder. After just one hour's deliberation, the jury found her not guilty of murder or of manslaughter, despite clear evidence as to her culpability. The verdict was greeted with such applause that the judge couldn't make himself heard above the clapping and stamping, and he cleared the court. The jury appears to have exonerated Madame Fahmy on the grounds of her husband's racial "otherness", and his sexual perversity (it was implied that he buggered both his wife and his male secretary). Indeed, Ali Fahmy's murder was presented as explicable, even excusable. While the newspapers excitedly compared the case to popular fictional portrayals of the East ("desert romances"), the predominantly female audience at the Old Bailey treated the spectacle of the trial as sensationalist theatre. Much of the evidence breached contemporary taboos, because it dealt with Ali Fahmy's exotic sexual habits; one result of this was that accounts of the trial were bowdlerized to accommodate the conventions of the time. Madame Fahmy owed her deliverance to her barrister, the flamboyant, silver-tongued Edward Marshall Hall. "Of all Marshall Hall's

*great cases," wrote his young biographer, Edward Marjoribanks,
"this was perhaps the most dramatic. Even nature seemed in conspiracy to set for the tragedy a scene of gloom and splendour worthy of
any play of Aeschylus or Shakespeare." The trial of Madame Fahmy
– and her extraordinary acquittal – was one of Marshall Hall's
greatest triumphs, a forensic coup by a master at the pinnacle of
his powers – despite the ravages of phlebitis in his legs which made it
painful to stand in court to argue his case.*

In 1923 Marshall Hall was sixty-five. He had reached the age at
which many men are compulsorily retired from working life even
though their mental powers are unimpaired and they could still be
usefully employed. No such mandate applies in the case of the law.
Marshall had no intention of giving up the life he loved. As an
advocate he was in great demand and as a Bencher of the Inner
Temple he had great influence in his profession. He frequently
used this influence to help his younger colleagues, with whom he
was immensely popular. He enjoyed the company and admiration
of younger men, especially the very young ones, the fledglings who
had everything to learn and who benefited even from being seen
lunching with him at one of his clubs. No man ever relished the
fruits of success more than Marshall Hall. He liked to be liked and
he could show favour without condescension. Where other lumin-
aries of the Temple would give a newcomer a casual nod Marshall
would hail him with a cheery shout and cross the road to shake his
hand or thump him on the shoulder.

"How are you, my dear boy? Briefs coming in? Look me up.
Always glad to see you. Any time."

The effect was not calculated, as in the showmanship he used in
court. It was spontaneous and sincere. He was always ready to
welcome and to help, and he could make the sort of gesture that
explains why he was idolised by Marjoribanks and other young
men. He initiated a very pleasant custom that prevailed at 3
Temple Gardens: if a pupil was called to the Bar during his
pupillage Marshall pulled strings to get him a brief, usually
marked one guinea, to present to him when he walked into
chambers the morning after his call.

Among his older colleagues feelings about him were mixed. He
was not universally liked, but at least he had now no enemies. His

temper had not improved – it could be very testy, especially when aggravated by pain – nor had his intolerance of opposition. But he was less quick to take offence and readier to apologise when he had given it. Time had not subdued his personality but had mellowed it. He had reached that point in the life of every celebrity when he stands at the crossroads of assessment. If deficient in that elusive quality we call charm, he will take his place in the hall of fame but not in human hearts. Halls of fame are chilly places. Human hearts are warm. There is a world of difference between being "Old so-and-so" and "Dear old so-and-so." He was "dear old Marshall" now. His faults and foibles – the dragging in of personal experience, so frowned on by Bar etiquette, his over-hasty judgments, his way of distracting attention from opposing counsel by blowing his nose, spraying his throat, adjusting his wig or dropping a pencil – were not only affectionately tolerated but expected of him, like his spectacular entry into court. Edgar Bowker's memory of this performance is still vivid:

> He would come straight to the court by car, his robes and other paraphernalia being sent over. In the robing room he would proceed to gossip with all and sundry. Nothing would get him to hurry. As often as not he would be told that the judge was about to sit or the case about to begin. As a Bencher he invariably lunched in the Inner Temple and many a time did I have to get a judge's clerk to keep his judge back for a few minutes, as I knew M.H. would be coming over from the Hall arm in arm with one or other of the judges who had been lunching there.

Nothing pleased Marshall more than to throw open the court door as the jury was being sworn. On the threshold he would stand poised, his head upflung, sniffing the air as a warhorse smells the battle. His junior clerk would procede him into court with his medicaments – pills, smelling salts, nose and throat sprays – a shagreen instrument case containing compasses, rulers, magnifying glass, etc.; his air cushions and adjustable footstool.

> The throat spray must have been an instrument of torture to opposing counsel, for somehow – quite innocently and by coincidence, of course – it would happen just as counsel was making an impression on the jury in a closing speech or

asking a pertinent question of a witness, Marshall Hall's throat would become troublesome. Out would come the throat spray, and as he operated it there would be a disconcerting hissing of the spray, accompanied by a gargling sound from the sufferer, to the distraction of both counsel who was speaking and the jury who were listening. Often I've seen the fascinated eyes of the jury turn to watch the spray at work. And if it were not the throat spray, then there would be the adjustment of the footstool to give comfort to his painful leg, or else the blowing up of the air cushion.

Marshall's legs were permanently encased in bandages now. He could not stand for long at a time and was often in such agony that the sweat ran down his face. For all his aggravating mannerisms and the tricks he resorted to for the purpose of disconcerting counsel on the other side, there was something heroic in his ceaseless fight for the lives and rights of others while in such pain himself. His health generally troubled him a good deal and big cases took a lot out of him. Bowker had often to strip him and towel him down when he came back into the robing room.

He had never needed to muster his reserves of energy and strength more than in the case that was brought to him one morning in July 1923.

The protagonist was a beautiful Frenchwoman married to a brutal and fabulously wealthy Oriental. The setting was the Savoy, London's most luxurious hotel, and the charge was murder by shooting. Marguerite Fahmy, elegant, cultured and sophisticated, had been persuaded to marry a wealthy young Egyptian, the son of an industrialist whose lavish donations to charity had brought him his title. He was attached in a minor post to the Egyptian Legation in Paris where his work allowed him plenty of time for an extravagant courtship of Marguerite Laurient, to whom he appeared an attractive and eligible suitor. What she did not know until too late was that he was a psychopath of revolting depravity, a homosexual and a sadist.

His attitude to her before and after marriage is well illustrated by the contrast between the following letters. When begging her to marry him he wrote, "Your presence everywhere pursues me. Torch of my life, you appear to me surrounded by a halo. I saw your head encircled by a crown which I have reserved for you on your arrival in this beautiful country of my ancestors." The second, written to someone else shortly after the marriage, ran, "Just now I am engaged in training her. Yesterday I did not come in to lunch or dinner and I also left her at the theatre. This will teach her, I hope, to respect my wishes."

The marriage took place in Cairo, with festivities and feasting on a grand scale. Marguerite had adopted the Moslem faith, and immediately afterwards she bitterly regretted it. She found that her husband had struck out of the marriage contract a clause which would have allowed her to divorce him if she wished, and that she had no more rights than any other Moslem woman and could be divorced at any time. But this was not all. She was guarded by black servants, terrorized, beaten and forced to submit to perverted practices. The black guards were supposed to be indicative of Fahmy's jealous care of a beautiful wife, but in fact the poor young woman was a prisoner, perpetually spied on by her husband's secretary Said Enani. Though loaded with jewellery she was kept without money and had no chance to escape from an appalling situation. It had lasted for six months when in July 1923, Fahmy Bey brought his wife and secretary to London. They took a suite at the Savoy Hotel.

At lunch time on 9 July the leader of the orchestra went to Madame Fahmy's table to ask if she would like him to play any special piece of music. She said in French – for she could speak hardly any English – "My husband is going to kill me in twenty-four hours so I am not very anxious for music."

The orchestra leader, extremely startled by this strange reply, answered in the same language, "I hope you will still be here tomorrow, Madame."

The day was intensely hot and that night there developed one of those summer storms which frequently seem more terrifying in the city than in the country. There were crashing peals of thunder and almost continuous lightning for over two hours. At the height of the storm a servant on duty in one of the hotel corridors heard three pistol shots in rapid succession. Running down the corridor he turned a corner and saw a man in pyjamas lying near the lift with blood trickling out of his mouth. He recognized him as Fahmy. Madame Fahmy was kneeling by his side. She was wearing evening dress and magnificent jewels. On the floor lay a Browning automatic pistol and three empty shells.

The assistant manager was called at once. Knowing that she could not speak English he said to her in French, "Why have you done this terrible thing?" She replied, *"J'avais perdu la tête!"* To a doctor who was called to the scene accompanied by a police sergeant she said that she had "shot at her husband". When asked if she had shot him with the revolver she said, "Yes." Then she cried, "What have I done? What will they do to me? Oh, sir, I have been married six months and I have suffered dreadfully." She was arrested and charged with the murder of her husband.

The story had, of course, every ingredient to make it a crime reporter's dream. Madame Fahmy's foreign nationality added colour to it. Much was made of the fact that in her own country the killing would have been regarded as a *crime passionel* and the maltreated lady would have been released by an examining magistrate down whose cheeks trickled tears of sympathy. In England, however, life was sterner. A clear charge of murder, or manslaughter at the least, had to be answered.

Freke Palmer, one of the best known of criminal solicitors, who had briefed Marshall Hall many times before, telephoned Bowker in great excitement early one morning.

"Bowker, listen – I've got a very important job for M.H. It is one of the best things I have ever handled. I want to come over and see you right away."

Freke Palmer's recommendation was good enough for Bowker. He accepted the brief for the defence of Madame Fahmy at a fee of 650 guineas. Though Madame Fahmy herself had no money she had wealthy friends who came to her assistance and spent large sums on obtaining evidence of Fahmy's depravity, particularly in relation to other men. Marshall Hall had the advantage of being able to speak fluent French and thus could hear Madame Fahmy's story in her own words. But it seemed at first, on the known facts, that the defence had very little to offer except a plea in mitigation. Marshall was assisted by Sir Henry Curtis Bennett, K.C., and Roland Oliver, who subsequently became a judge. They made a powerful and costly team, out of whose intensive discussions there slowly began to emerge a possible answer to the charge.

Marshall borrowed a Browning automatic similar to the one used by Madame Fahmy and conducted various experiments with it, assited by Robert Churchill, the famous gunsmith. Madame Fahmy had said to the doctor in the hotel that after her husband had attacked her she was afraid he might be going to kill her as he said he would do. She had a pistol which he had given her himself for protection against jewel thieves. Wanting only to frighten him with it she first fired a shot out of the window to empty it, as she thought, but when she pointed it at her husband it somehow went off. This statement, coupled with Marshall's experiments, caused him to take the bold step of offering a complete and valid defence and trying for an outright acquittal. He knew that he could not be more fortunate in the judge who was to try the case. Mr Justice Rigby Swift, known as "*Rig*-ba" in legal circles because of his habit of lengthening a vowel and then snapping it off short, was one of the best liked and most humane judges on the Bench. He had once said, "I have been an associate of criminals all my life. I have defended them, prosecuted them and tried them. I know there is a very great deal of good in the worst of them." Madame Fahmy thus had every chance of a sympathetic hearing.

Percival Clarke who led for the prosecution opened by stressing the fact that she had admitted causing the death of her husband. He therefore felt justified in asking for a verdict of guilty. Marshall contended, and set out to prove, that Fahmy's death had not been caused intentionally but as the result of an accident. After subtly eliciting from Said Enani details of Fahmy's treatment of his wife he sensed the receptive mood of the court and proceeded to take the fullest advantage of it. He was in the position of an actor who knows the house is with him and can safely embark on his big scene. His case was that when Madame Fahmy pressed the trigger she had not known that the weapon was in a condition to be fired. Earlier she had tried to unload it by opening the breech cover but had not been able to pull it back. While she had struggled with it the gun had gone off, and in her total ignorance of firearms she had thought it was now unloaded. In fact by the discharge of the first bullet she had brought the second automatically into the firing position. The theory was fully corroborated by Robert Churchill.

The cause of the fatal quarrel was Fahmy's refusal to give his wife the money to go to Paris for a necessary operation unless she submitted to a painful and disgusting perversion. He brandished banknotes before her, struck and taunted her.

Through an interpreter she told the court in halting words the happenings of that terrible night. "I had taken the revolver in my hand. I thought it was empty. I went out into the corridor in front of the lift. He came after me. He seized me by the throat with his left hand. His fingers were pressing in my neck. I pushed him away, but he crouched to spring on me and said, 'I will kill you'. I lifted my arm in front of me and without looking pulled the trigger.

I do not know how many times the revolver went off. I saw Fahmy on the floor."

Marshall had already suggested that the translation of the phrase, "*J'avais perdu la tête*", which is a colloquialism, should be more accurately rendered "I was frightened out of my wits" instead of "I had lost my head", and this was agreed by the interpreter. He now handed her the pistol and asked her to pull back the breech cover. She tried hard but could not do it. It had been passed round among the jury for the same purpose and most of them had experienced difficulty – which corroborated her story.

But Marshall had not done yet. Before the trial was over he was to give one of the best pieces of dramatic acting ever seen in a court of law. It is still talked about even in an age when such tactics are outdated. It came during his closing speech. With all the eloquence of which he was capable he drew a picture of the dreadful life of his unhappy client. He described the thunderstorm and the super-charged atmosphere it created, and then Madame Fahmy's terror as her husband pursued her and seized her by the throat. He not only spoke his lines, he acted them, imitating the tigerish crouch of a man intent on violence.

"In desperation," he told the hushed court, "in sheer desperation as he crouched like an animal to make the last bound forward she put the pistol to his face and to her horror the thing went off." He had been holding the pistol in his hand and he now raised it, pointed it straight at the jury – and then let it fall. It sounds melodramatic to the point of absurdity by current standards. But it made its effect magnificently. Many people in court cried out as the weapon dropped to the floor, symbolizing the fall of a beastly and brutal tyrant.

Mr Justice Rigby Swift, completely won over, summed up patently in the prisoner's favour and the jury were not long in returning a verdict of "Not Guilty". It was followed by such a vociferous demonstration that the court had to be cleared before the accused could be acquitted on the secondary charge of man-slaughter. Marshall was so exhausted that when he entered the robing room he had to lie down to rest.

Whether the dropping of the pistol was an accident, as some say, or a calculated part of the performance is still debated. What is incontestable is that it helped to win Marshall's case for him and to save the life of a beautiful and much wronged woman.

Madame Fahmy was grateful. A few days after the trial she

called at Temple Gardens to express her thanks to her defender in person. Edgar Bowker gives a charming account of this meeting in his book of reminiscences, *A Lifetime with the Law*.

I was in my office when she arrived and I showed her into his room. The confrontation of counsel and client was almost as dramatic as the scene in court. Marshall was sitting with his back to the window, his face in shadow. As Madame Fahmy entered the sun shone full on her, lighting her vivacious features and gilding her dress. Whenever I think of the case I see her standing there, small and smiling, and Marshall rising from his chair to welcome her in French.

She stayed for tea. From time to time I heard laughter in the room and her rather shrill voice mingling with Marshall's vibrating and measured tones. He was obviously entertaining her with stories of his career.

THE GREAT TRAIN ROBBERS

(Aylesbury, Bucks., 1964)

Peta Fordham

In August 1963, a gang of fifteen masked men stopped the night mail train from Glasgow to London and robbed it of £2.5 million. By the end of the year, nine of them were in custody awaiting trial, while three were still on the run. The authorities decided to press ahead with what would inevitably be a show trial; the Great Train Robbery (as the press called it) had gripped the nation because of its sheer audacity and the amount of money stolen. The robbery had been committed in Buckinghamshire, and the trial would normally have taken place in the county town of Aylesbury. But the assize court there was too small for such a big case, so the trial was transferred to the newly built headquarters of the rural district council nearby. When the case opened on 20 January 1964, there were as many defendants as jurors. Among the ranks of journalists from the world's press sat Peta Fordham (1905–91), whose factual account of the crime and its aftermath, The Robbers' Tale, *became a best-selling book in 1965. Born Eugenie Freeman, Peta Fordham was the first editor of* Which?, *the Consumer Association's magazine launched in 1957. She wrote about the case with unique insight: she came from a family of lawyers and, as the wife of the barrister defending one of the accused, Ronnie Biggs, was the only member of the media to arrive each morning by Bentley. The novelist and critic Cyril Connolly was impressed with her style, declaring that Mrs Fordham had something of Rebecca West's gifts of characterization and reportage.*

There is always, at the beginning of a trial, the sensation of a curtain going up. The audience, seated, are waiting for the play to commence: meanwhile, they watch the stage being set. There is, also, quite plainly, a cruel element in their curiosity. This is the civilized equivalent of the gladiatorial combat. The contest is going to be fought out between Counsel and accused, with a colourful referee in the shape of the Judge, and with the jury as the representatives of the audience to express the verdict of the man in the street. One can be quite startled on occasion by the facial expressions of decent people in Court.

But this was not only a case: this was *the* case. There was an audible intake and let-out of breath as the accused took their places in the dock. The numbers had steadily grown: those who had followed the case through the Lower Court had seen them all: to some, all the faces were new.

The first reaction was one of surprise that they looked, on the whole, so ordinary; the second, that they looked so clean and well dressed. The old idea of the highwayman, in tattered finery, evidently dies hard. Only Hussey, perhaps, looked even remotely capable of violence: he was later to be described as a particularly good son! Welch, thin, nervous and silent, but with a misleadingly intellectual appearance and the amiable face of Charlie Wilson, ever ready to see the funny side of Bench, Bar, witness-box or dock, made up the front row, together with the small, redfaced Boal, who seemed remote from everything that was going on. Behind sat Biggs, large, amiable and smiling; James, unbelievably small and poker-faced; Goody, whose saturnine face stood out at once; Lennie Field, sullen and indignant, but with an attractive smile which could break through on occasion; and Brian Field, whose face looked, in repose, benign and rather pleasant. Wheater sat rigid. He appeared the caricature of respectability. There was the general tendency not to look at Wheater which betrayed a feeling of embarrassment. He ought not, one felt, to have been there, whatever the facts were going to disclose. So these were the desperate villains who had robbed Her Majesty's mail of a record amount. It seemed almost disappointing.

The trial began with a bang. It ended with a series of whimpers. It was all very, very English indeed. On the opening morning – and for several days – the crush was overwhelming. Everybody in Fleet Street had rubbered in somehow, on what was gleefully thought to be the trial to end all trials, speaking professionally. All the people one knew were there, together with all the ones one did not. The local sweet shops could not keep up with the demand for peppermints – the journalists' vice. Strange faces were accounted for knowingly, by those who did not know, as "foreign Press". A large number of these turned out to be local inhabitants who had somehow contrived to get passes. They soon disappeared. The heating of the Court was effected by means of night storage heaters round the room. The result was that the Press, who were obliged to sit immediately on top of them, were either cooked rather quickly (if the day were cold and they were opened) or frozen if they were shut. The ventilation seemed also specifically designed to blow straight down Press necks. No one who could possibly find a better hole stayed *there*. Nor was the rest of the court much better. The incidence of absenteeism, of mysterious "virus infections" was very high. Even the self-employed Bar, whose dependence upon "refreshers" keeps up the attendance rate remarkably, went sick more often than usual. Voices disappeared, coughs and colds abounded, to the accompaniment of innumerable remedies, exchanged during the luncheon adjournment. The Judge struggled gallantly with an obviously raised temperature and a cough. Only in the dock did health apparently abound. When the returning Council turned down, by eighteen soulless votes to ten, the suggestion that a plaque on the building should commemorate the trial, their spokesman gave as their reason that they "were not proud of having had to sit in a draughty Church Hall" during the trial. This, besides slightly eluding the point, seemed to those of us who had survived the ordeal by heat and cold in their R.D.C. offices, to bring a horse's laugh indeed.

The prosecution moved in, in force, to The Bell at Aston Clinton, where, in surroundings which could scarcely have been ordained by an all-wise Providence as more suitable for their spiritual and physical comfort, they spent the duration of the trial. The Bell is run by Gerard Harris, a retired solicitor, who has the enviable reputation of being about the best judge of wine in the business, of providing one of the best tables in the country and of being the least profit-making minded of men. He was, of course, intensely interested in this sudden reappearance of forensic intelligence into his life: provided a sitting room of great charm in which the team could work undisturbed all the evening and stayed them with flagons of both ponderable and imponderable nature.

With such a background a social life at once developed. The Bar is ever hospitable. The Midland Circuit were hosts: other members of the Bar were of guest status. So the Judge had a cocktail party for the Bar: the Bar had several dinners for him and for lesser mortals. The guests repaid the hospitality and there was an old boys' reunion after the case. All concerned settled down like boys at a public school, to an established ritual. Meanwhile, at Aylesbury, in the prison hospital, where accommodation was provided for the prisoners with maximum security in force, a not unpleasant halcyon period set in. Every privilege was in force and was used to the full. Food was sent in: drinks were ordered with reasonable lavishness. They were popular guests at the gaol! There was a certain atmosphere of "Two-way Stretch" apparent. Only little Boal, hard-up and out of it all, could not shake off his misery. Goody, with great kindliness, organized a whip-round and arranged that everything the rest of the gang enjoyed should be provided for the little man. In the yard of the Council offices, a number of new cars began to appear. The wages of sin, by the time they reach Counsel, are a most welcome little profit. It is generally assumed by the profession that you can seldom *afford* the things you want. If, however, you have the money at any one particular moment, you might as well buy them. This was put, with moving eloquence, by one "silk" who was a case in point, after an excellent lunch.

But, as the days wore on, the attendance dropped, and the excitement faded. The hopeful Pressmen, who had believed that drama would succeed drama, began to troop away. They were not lawyers: they had not realized the slow majesty of the Law, the long, tedious arguments about the admissibility or otherwise of evidence, the delays, the trivia which are of such great importance to justice and so unacceptable to news editors. Even the chase for the "story" – the background which nobody knew but everybody guessed at, began to pall. Boredom set in. A cloud of bank witnesses, proving the carriage of notes, was no reason for return. By the time the trial had been going for a month, only those Press who had to be there were still in attendance. By this time they were not as popular as they had been in the first careless rapture of the expense account. Their activities were mainly confined to the Bull's Head, a pleasant hostelry in the main square. Here lives a stalwart breed of waitresses, of mature years and outright speech. "You a journalist?" said one of them to me one day. I admitted the soft impeachment, as Sairey Gamp would have said. "Hm! You don't look like one," came the reply. I was uncertain whether to feel flattered or insulted, so stalled by asking for further and better particulars. "Well," she said. "Look at this lot!" (this embraced the representatives of most of our popular Press). "Call themselves *friends*!" she went on, warming to her work, "Why they won't even use the nice room they could – just sit here, glaring at one another and stealing each other's telephone calls. Disgusting, I call it!" How we deceive ourselves. There was many a brave reporter there who thought he was bringing glamour to Bucks.

The Judge's elegant little form seemed to sink into his small throne, as the days went on. His manners, always impeccable, held the tempo of the court together, as with the skill of a conductor, he would insert a gentle but deft witticism into a dull morning or afternoon and wake the proceedings up again. In the end, even he grew weary. His exhaustion was reflected in the summing-up, which began so brilliantly but, in the end, became the patently conscientious, weary work of a brilliant brain which had grown sick of the job.

It had been rumoured, just before the trial began, that the Judge was to be Mr Justice Hinchcliffe, noted for his heavy sentences on violence. This alarming news was discussed at length in Aylesbury Gaol and, on the suggestion of one of the defendants, it was seriously debated whether an attitude of passive resistance should, in these circumstances, be taken up. The prisoners, it was considered, might refuse to go to court: if lifted into the van, they should immediately lie down: and a similar attitude should be taken up in the dock where they were to remain mute. Considering the relative size of some of the prisoners this might well have resulted in the use of the old penalty of "*peine forte et dure*" to James and Boal. This was the application of heavy and increasing weights to prisoners who refused to speak or – in more picturesque language "remained mute of malice". The extraordinary thing is that adult and intelligent prisoners could imagine that such tactics would result in another judge being appointed to the trial! They need not have worried: in the event it would have been difficult to find any judge who sentenced them as fiercely as the kindly and courteous Mr Justice Edmund Davies. It really was hard luck: if they had known his previous reputation at the Bar, as a bonny fighter and quite a judge-baiter, they would have been even more surprised and hurt.

The trouble about being tried as a gang is that it is difficult to get a fair trial in the way that a single prisoner does. The statements made by the prisoners illustrate this point admirably. The people whose identifying marks were found at Leatherslade had all got splendid stories about themselves – the only trouble was that there were so many. One man alone, with a credible alibi or even a believable story, may well impress a jury to the extent that they feel it is unsafe to convict. Any one story might just possibly be true. But by the time that all the robbers' tales had been related to the Aylesbury jury ("Surely an Identikit jury?" murmured Ronnie Payne of the *Sunday Telegraph* to me, as we watched their anxious, dutiful faces) the picture built up was that an entirely different gang must have been at Leatherslade Farm, to whom some of these unfortunate, innocent gentlemen in the dock had merely supplied a little fruit and vegetables, in the days following the raid. This was more than any jury could reasonably have been expected to believe. Slowly, sadly, inexorably the collapse went on. Long before what was known as the "little conspiracy", (the one involving the two unrelated Fields and Wheater, in the obstruction of justice) was reached, it was clear that the jury did not place much credence on the hopeful state-ments given to the police. They were all good enough stories in their way. There were just too many of them.

The first drama of the trial came over the sudden release of Daly. This was on the 17th day and took everybody by surprise. Daly's finger-prints had been on the Monopoly cards, Daly had been in hiding and in fancy dress, and Daly had not used a Jaguar car for a long time, though paying at the rate of £39 a month for it one way and another. All in all things did not look good for Daly. However, like a doctor dealing with what he thinks to be an incurable illness, the good counsel never despairs, never gives up the fight. At the close of the case for the prosecution, submissions of "No case to answer" were made to the Judge by counsel on behalf of all the defendants. All, not unnaturally, were failing and the court was somewhat sleepily listening to the inevitable, when suddenly, on the day following the speeches, the Judge allowed the submission made on behalf of Daly, by Mr Walter Raeburn, Q.C. Raeburn argued that Daly's finger-prints, found on the Monopoly set at Leatherslade Farm, did not constitute a case against him, as there was no evidence as to when and where the prints got on to the set, or, for that matter, where the set was at the time that the prints were made. One is often asked how this differed from the case of the finger-prints that so firmly convicted others. The answer is that finger-prints found and identified as those of other defendants were discovered on articles either connected with the farm or connected with the crime. The Monopoly set did not belong to either class. It was not new and could have been used innocently before.

If I may digress for a moment, as far as I was concerned, the acquittal of Daly let loose all hell. I was sitting at home, having had a sharp attack of pink-eye, when the telephone rang and the Press of Fleet Street began to do what a sufferer had once described to me as "hook itself round my ear". The solicitor too had been caught out; it was the one day that he had not attended and he was in process of having an overdue hair-cut when the news broke. His one thought was to protect Daly from the Press and I was the only journalist he knew. He told the lot to ring me. I decided that the remedy was to tie up an "exclusive", as, when this is once done, all papers lose interest in another's scoop. After a little brisk haggling, during which a French farce was played out in my kitchen and drawing-room, as I hid the representatives of one paper from another, Daly was duly sold, for a decent sum, to the *Daily Sketch*. Then ensued one of the oddest days of my life. Shrouded behind dark glasses, to hide my weeping eyes, I roared, in a *Sketch* car, through the streets of London, as if in a chase from the Keystone Cops. If anyone got in front of us, all the reporters and photographers hung out of the window and yelled in a body. They were apparently looking forward to a rough house on arrival at Mrs Manson's flat, to which Daly and his wife were going on his release, and were inclined to be disappointed when I assured them that we should go through the waiting reporters like a knife through butter; which we did, my function in the matter being merely that of chaperon. The whole of the quiet little road was filled with Press cars and a disconsolate little group was waiting, in the vain hope that some crumb might be left from the "exclusive". One ran forward saying: "Is it really signed, sealed and delivered?" On my nod, he fell back and we passed on into the flat, into which Daly and wife had been easily inserted by use of a back door which had not been spotted by the Press. The rather sad business of getting a story out of a weary, wary man and an exhausted and half hysterical little wife took ages: we ate ham sandwiches and drank lukewarm champagne provided by the *Sketch*, whilst round us swarmed in *déshabillé* the children to whom Mrs Manson had given shelter. I never saw so many junior-cupid-bottoms in my life! We had to return the next day to complete it: my only enjoyment in the job was to watch the respectable neighbours in the block of flats, going in and out and pretending that there was absolutely nothing odd about the ground floor. Meanwhile, at Aylesbury, my husband was in a state of acute apprehension, the news having reached him that: "They're saying in Fleet Street Mrs Fordham is at Wimbledon selling Daly to the *Daily Sketch*." Not knowing of the chores sometimes attached to a dutiful wife, his past experience of odd happenings in the world of journalists had served to conjure up a vivid nightmare of possible breaches of etiquette. He was relieved to find that it was merely the protection of a client that had been effected. It is also rather nice to be able to record that the *Sketch* behaved with the utmost propriety, submitting to the solicitors the whole of the published material, in case any of the other accused should be in any way prejudiced.

There was, however, a grim little sequel to this. There were – and are – many nervous people about, to whom the finger could still point. Before Daly was torn away from the waiting Press, he made just one apparently harmless remark. Daly, as may be imagined, had some queer friends: he would not have been involved in this case if he had not. Two nights later, he had "visitors" who thought that the words pointed to them. It was exactly like blind Pugh and the black spot in *Treasure Island*. Apparently he satisfied them. But, as a friend of his said afterwards, "He wouldn't like to have visitors like that again!"

The particular "robbers tale" put forward by Hussey, Welch and Wisbey, though interesting and a happy little exercise of the "genius of the alibi", if I may adapt a phrase, came alas, to nought. A "fellow called Ronnie", a friend of Hussey's, had had to make a trip to deliver some foodstuffs. He had asked Hussey to go along with him, since they had had an appointment to meet that Saturday evening, 10th August and, by a strange coincidence, at the very moment that the lorry arrived at Hussey's door, with this invitation, Welch and Wisbey turned up. Hussey could not go out, as his mother was ill and he had to remain in to look after her, but he suggested that the other two, who had nothing particular to do (they had turned up on the off-chance that Hussey could go out with them) might like to make the trip. The reason for "Ronnie's" call was to explain that he might be late for the evening appointment. During this interesting conversation, said Hussey, he asked what was in the van and, told that it was fruit and vegetables, took an apple which he suddenly fancied out from under the tarpaulin, and, in so doing, left his finger-prints on the tailboard. He did a nice little charade of this in Court. Welch and Wisbey thereupon obligingly went with Ronnie, in order to bring him back for the evening appointment he had with Hussey.

Alas! for friendship. Ronnie, alluded to in court as "Dark Ronnie", could not be found to establish this interesting tale. Advertisements in the *Telegraph* and *Evening Standard* produced him, at length, just as they had found the witness over whose coat Goody had spilled that cup of coffee. A terrified little man, dark indeed, appeared in due course and tried manfully in the witness-box to stand up to the bowling of a formidable old hand Mr Arthur James, Q.C. Alas, again, for friendship! Mr Dark's talents were varied: they were not, however, such as to commend themselves to the jury. Graduate of an approved school, Ronnie had gone to Borstal for stealing some £50 from his brother. Then he broke and entered a Co-operative store, blowing open the safe and stealing over £2,000. He hid away after this for two years and was eventually caught and sentenced for another offence of breaking and entering and stealing £2,470. From this term of imprisonment he had emerged as recently as the 7th June before the mail robbery, and said that he had never been away from an address that Hussey knew. He could not think why Hussey did not know it without advertising. As to the country outing, he had been asked by another elusive gentleman, one Stanley Webb (not forthcoming) to do the lorry job. They had met at a dancing-club in Streatham "called, I think, the Bali-Hai, or some such name," said the Judge, a trifle shortly. Ronnie had no interest in the load. He had read about Leatherslade Farm but never thought that the place to which he went bore any resemblance to it. Arrived there (having picked up the elusive Mr Webb in a café outside High Wycombe) he and Wisbey went into the bathroom to wash their hands, and, in rather jerky pantomime, Ronnie gave another dumb charade of an opening door and the consequent sprawling over the bath which accounted for Wisbey's finger-prints on the rail. Welch, in his own story, had merely picked up a can of ale to look at it. He had, he said, been in the licensing trade in the past and had been interested in these new cans. All splendid detail – if believed.

Ronnie may have been accounted a brave man to support this tale. He was putting his head into the lion's mouth, so to speak. He certainly looked, throughout his evidence, as if he were aware that the jaws might close at any minute. He had, after all, only recently emerged from prison and was admitting, with understandable reluctance, a trip to that notorious farm. A bolder man than Ronnie might well feel uneasy: not all "persons of good character" would have cared to admit that they, too, had visited the fatal spot! But he stuck gamely to the story. He was sure of the date because it was after his birthday on 7th August. But it all led nowhere. Whatever the views of the court (and Mr Justice Edmund Davies said a few well-chosen and pithy words on the subject in summing-up) upon Mr Ronald Dark's veracity, his hard work did not disturb the general trend of the case against the three. He scuttled out of the witness-box at a reasonable speed, considering the circumstances, and disappeared from history.

Wisbey, incidentally, after a preliminary questioning by the police on 20th August, had gone on holiday to Spain. There he received a letter from home about police inquiries and decided to come back, whereupon he went voluntarily to Scotland Yard. His wife had told him that the police had taken some rubber boots of his. This conduct is also of interest for it shows that he too must have been confident that all finger-print evidence at Leatherslade had been destroyed.

There was found, in Roy James's possession, a document not in his handwriting, which is, in some ways, the most human little bit of evidence in the trial. This was a bit of paper, screwed up in the holdall in which was the money which was *not* identified directly with the robbery at all. There was a reckoning on it which went like this: "1st, 22,500 = 5. 2nd, 15,000 = 1. 3rd, 18,200 = 1. 4th, 6,800 = 1.5 (this number encircled) 14,000 = 5.", and some more. This little tally, which the Crown assumed to be the record of the count-out, so short and yet so eloquent of that night of fevered counting is the only piece of evidence surviving which bears witness to those hours in Leatherslade, when the world must have seemed within their grasp. There was very little to the case of Roy James: it was, however, from that strange sum of £109,500 found in his possession and from its resemblance to sums found in connection with the other accused, that the Judge (who, with the one exception of Boal, had the picture of guilt so accurately throughout) decided the probable cut that the thieves got. He was very nearly correct here too. The main four got a quarter of a million pounds each: the main "labourers" £100,000 and some expenses. Others got proportionately less and there were extra for "special services". The police are well alerted to watch for signs of spending in the right quarters – or the wrong ones, according to your point of view. The jackals are also out hunting in the underworld and wives and sweethearts are being threatened and blackmailed in the hope that they may pay up. "Protection" is muscling in.

Neither Wilson or James went into the witness-box, though James called some alibi evidence, including a taxi-driver fan, who said he had been playing cards with him at the time of the crime. The decision not to call a defendant is always a difficult one for Counsel to take: inevitably it tends to prejudice a jury, who think that there is something to hide, and who, of course, are generally right. In the case of Boal, things were worse. Cordrey had been prepared to give evidence on his behalf, but Cordrey had pleaded guilty to the conspiracy. Had Cordrey gone into the box, the inevitable first question would have been, "With whom did you conspire?" For the sake of all the defendants, this risk could not be taken. So the wretched Boal lost his one chance of direct evidence in his favour.

There were what might be called "unfortunate circumstances" during the trial of Wilson.

He had always strenuously denied that he had used the famous words about "the poppy"* – a piece of colourful English, which had caught the ear of the Press, made headlines on the front page of the *Evening Standard* when evidence of arrest was given at the Linslade court, been given in evidence to the magistrates, been used in opening at the trial and had received additional publicity from the Judge's inevitable remark, "What is poppy, Mr James?" and some subsequent joking about "lolly". Wilson's reasons for objecting have been mentioned elsewhere: his Counsel, however, realized that these were most damaging words and had wanted to

---

* "I do not see how you can make it stick without the poppy and you won't find that."

exclude them. This could not be done, since they appeared to have been made *after* Wilson had been cautioned.

The words were part of the deposition of Chief Superintendent Butler. Mr John Mathew, battling away hard, in the attempt to get them excluded, tried the argument, first, that although Charlie Wilson was not actually in custody at the time of the questioning, Butler had made up his mind to charge him, owing to the police information about finger-prints; and so the caution should have come at the beginning of the conversation. This, however, did not get him very far. He then suggested to Mr Butler that, in fact, Wilson was in custody all the time, and that, on these grounds, the caution should have been made right at the beginning of the conversation. This was denied.

The grounds for Mr Mathew's statement came from a notice of additional evidence he had received, that of Chief Inspector Baldock, who was with Butler at the time of the questioning. The evidence of Chief Superintendent Butler stated that Wilson was *in the charge-room* of Cannon Row Police Station when the conversation took place: that of Chief Inspector Baldock contained the words, "I saw the accused Charles Wilson detained *in the cells* at Cannon Row Police Station." Since this legal argument was going to be as to the admissibility of evidence, the jury were sent out, and, for this reason, the considerable sensation over this particular point did not get reported. Mr John Mathew continued to press the Chief Superintendent, whose reply eventually was that it must have been "some error of typing or something".

Chief Inspector Baldock, ignorant of the drama that had been going on, was then called. Mr Mathew, in a deceptively quiet voice, asked about the questioning. Then he whipped round, in a legal style rarely seen today, and one reminiscent of the fighting counsel of the past and called for the statement which had been put in late. He asked the Chief Inspector to begin reading it. The luckless policeman began "On the 22nd August, 1963, at 2.5 p.m. in company with Chief Superintendent Butler, I saw Charles Wilson detained in the cells." The Inspector almost choked with emotion. For the rest of his life, Mr Mathew will remember that moment of glory. It lasted only a split second, then the flat, police voice, finished the sentence "at Cannon Row Police Station." "You hesitated for a second, Chief Inspector Baldock," came the sharp, legal voice, "after the words, 'in the cells'." The answer was flat again, "Yes". "Did that come as a surprise to you?" "No." "Is it correct that you saw him detained in the cells?" "No. I did not. I saw him in the charge-room." "Will you explain that," went on the cruelly probing voice of Counsel. "It is just," was the reply, "I should imagine, a typing error."

At that point, the Judge intervened. At once one remembered what a formidable cross-examiner he had been in his Bar days. The questions rapped out like machine-gun fire. "Who typed that statement you signed?" "At your dictation?" "It could have been done on a dictaphone – what in fact happened?" "Now *how* could the typist make a typing error?" "You must have drafted out in longhand a statement, or you must have typed out a statement or you must have dictated a statement. Which was it?" The Chief Inspector hardly knew what had hit him. In answer to that last volley, he made his reply. "I cannot really remember." And, after a short display of the decencies which obtain between prosecution and defence, the battle was declared won. Mr Justice Edmund Davies struck out all the evidence that Mr Mathew had wanted excluded. But, unfortunately, the damage had been done. English Law is not perfect, though this exchange shows the care that can be taken to help accused person, in the face of police or other evidence which may be in any way improper. For ever after, Charlie will be known, as he was known then, as the "poppy boy".

There was a general stir in Court as Douglas Gordon Goody entered the box. He had, by this time, established himself as the outstanding character in the case. Now it was apparent why he made easy conquests of women: there was a subtle difference about him. Clearly, he had something they found different, a sort of general look above his class. The likeness to Macheath was at once apparent. I wondered whether this notion of mine as to the resemblance between the eighteenth-century *Beggar's Opera* and the modern train robbery was a piece of whimsy of my own. I soon had startling confirmation of its aptness. One of Goody's friends had taken her "Gran" to see the Shakespeare Company's revival at the Aldwych Theatre last year. Gran took no interest in the proceedings until Macheath entered. Whereupon she sat up and said, with great suddenness, "That's our Gordon to the life." After that she watched the whole opera with attention, matching friend after friend. Here was the swagger, the imitation of "his betters" – an outworn phrase which just happens to fit this occasion – the good clothes, the tendency to boast, the cool, fatalistic approach to what must have seemed, early on, to be inevitable, just as his prototype regarded the eventual journey in the cart to Tyburn. Goody would have made a brave exit this way – but he would have counted on a crowd.

By now, he was a favourite with the warders. A sense of humour is rather rare amongst prisoners. Goody was an exception. In Court, one day, evidence was given about a pair of knuckledusters found on Boal, frightened, bewildered, little man of minute size. "Who will protect me from this dangerous man?" cracked Goody to the warder sitting next to him. He had sent out the drawing of an Emmett-like train on his Christmas card: had joked with all the Counsel who had come into contact with him: had drawn remarkably good cartoons of many of those engaged in the case. To one Counsel, who, also an Irishman, passed over a sprig of shamrock on St Patrick's day, he sent the message, "Thank you very much, sir, but I'd rather have bail."

"Cheeky, cocky bastard," said the nice young policeman to me sourly. This was in reference to some of Goody's cartoons. The police do not like Goody: his sense of humour is interpreted as mickey-taking, as indeed it frequently may be. The trouble here, is, once more, that he is "different", an uncomfortable category for authority, which likes to be able to sew up a personality neatly into some familiar bag. But the old usher, who had once been a police officer in Linslade itself, had a wily peasant's eye for a novelty. As we sat at the back of the draughty Council Chamber, our mouths full of peppermints, he delighted in every moment of Goody in the box. Hoarse, inaudible chuckles, the lightning wink, both to me and to his friend the tipstaff, on his solemn pilgrimages in and out of Court, words of pungent wisdom, exchanged at suitable moments, all added up to the picture of someone whose retirement must have been a considerable loss to the Bucks Constabulary. We all missed him greatly when shingles, of all undignified complaints, took him from our midst towards the end of the trial.

Goody settled his long, loose limbs into the box, a high one, which had engulfed many of the previous witnesses. He appeared at ease but a tiny tic, apparent only from the right profile, betrayed the strain. He was neatly dressed, as were indeed the whole of the dock, in contrast to quite a number of Counsel. The Bar is not remarkable for natty dressing these days. Particularly, his linen was immaculate. Before the evidence had gone very far, the question of paint on the shoes brought up the question "Are you meticulous about your dress?" The answer, spoken quickly and rather softly, came, "I like to think so, my Lord." Here spoke the boy who had wanted to better himself, to escape into the world of purple and fine linen.

One could see, also, that he had once been a good steward on a ship. His movements were deft and easy. His manner to the Judge had just the right amount of deference, but without servility or the bouncy, all-chaps-together which we were later to see from Brian Field. Suddenly, one was bitterly sorry for all the women in his life. My grandfather, who used to breed horses, once told me that, if a young mare escaped and had a "love-foal" by the stallion of her choice, she was, ever afterwards, an unreliable breeder; for she was liable to throw back to the memory of that early mate. The women who drift into the world of the crook are accustomed to boredom in sexual relations, when the first thrill of what seems high adventure dies in the long years when husband or lover is in prison or on the run. But those who have been unlucky enough to have associated with Goody – and there are many – will find it difficult to discover another figure so colourful and, should they reach the haven of matrimony, will have their marriage-bed haunted by a demon-lover.

The decision to let in his bad record had been taken after long deliberation. It had been decided, in the end, by his insistence upon his version of the Irish trip which, he declared, had been a holiday with pay, in the shape of the profits of a smuggling racket, in which he had been intermittently engaged. (This was *not* where he had acquired the knowledge of smuggling of which he spoke glibly.) He had, I think, reckoned also without his country jury. Londoners seem to take a degree of smuggling for granted: there was no doubt as to the disapproving looks of those Buckinghamshire men. He had gone to Ireland, with his mother and one Jack Knowles, who turned up to give evidence at the Lower Court, but did not reappear, doubtless for reasons best known to himself. Mrs Goody, his mother, is a poor, nervous creature: one does not wonder at that! She had been in bad health and it was decided, said Goody, that a holiday with the O'Lone family, her brother-in-law and his daughters, might set her up. The holiday was to be for about ten days: Goody was to fish and shoot and then to return, with a load of smuggled watches, per favour of the Moylen gang. The trial of some of these last was going on at the Old Bailey at this moment.

According to Goody, the state of things at the O'Lone home, when they reached it, was indeed far from ideal. Mr O'Lone, who lived in a typical Irish cottage of the smallest possible kind in Lisburn, retained his own bedroom. The only other bedroom was occupied by Goody and Knowles. Mrs Goody slept on a mattress on the floor of the kitchen, together with the two girls.

The party arrived on Friday, 2nd August. On the Saturday, Knowles hired a vehicle and went, with Goody, into Belfast, which is about ten miles away. On the Sunday, they did some shooting. On the Monday, Goody went down to Dublin, picked up his load of watches and returned to the O'Lone home. By his time, he said, there was unpleasantness all round, as there might well have been. Mrs Goody was, not unnaturally, taking exception to her sleeping accommodation! Mr Knowles was grumbling about the quality of the hospitality provided and Goody, feeling fed-up generally, decided that he might as well return. He therefore went to Belfast. Airport on the Tuesday morning – the 6th August – and returned home, taking out a ticket in the name of McGonigil. It was very powerfully urged on his behalf by Mr Sebag Shaw, Q.C., that, had he wished the return ticket, bearing the name "Mr Goody and party" to establish an alibi, by a later return date than that of the robbery, he would have instructed his mother to delay returning, by every means, so as to ensure this. This he did not do. In fact, they returned on the succeeding day, the 7th August, in time, had they so desired, to be on the scene of the crime with something to spare. However, without entering into the extremely lengthy evidence about the exact wording on the tickets, or the exact arrangements between Goody and Knowles (who might have been considered to be a good friend indeed, if he was to be admitted to accommodation so intimate as that necessitated by the O'Lone close quarters), we can assume, with the information at our command, that this was to have been a good alibi. Had the raid taken place as planned, on the night of 6–7 August, the return ticket used by Mrs Goody and Knowles (a ticket which Mr Knowles had taken trouble to have altered to "Mr and Mrs Goody"), would have established Goody's whereabouts satisfactorily – to him. Knowles could, perhaps have been in the know; though if he was he was also rather dim to be in quite such a hurry: poor bewildered Mrs Goody clearly was not. I hear that Knowles is about again and is said to have got married. One can imagine a rather nervous home.

Mrs Goody was called by the defence mainly to establish this story and to confirm Goody's whereabouts at the time of the raid, which happened to be – never a dull moment – in bed with a pretty little fiancée, Pat Cooper. This game and faithful little girl has stuck by him in the most creditable way, and was able to support his story of The Windmill, in addition to more intimate details; and came through a very stiff cross-examination indeed at the hands of Mr MacDermot, without losing much face. But it is too much to expect that a jury will believe a girl-friend. Clearly, in the end, they did not.

Goody had given his evidence well and had even achieved a certain dignity considering that he was admitting to a pretty sordid record. Interminable evidence was yet to come over the paint: the point that had hit him most so far, and one which was to be raised on appeal, was the cross-examination, by Mr MacDermot, Q.C., as to his acquittal in the London Airport robbery. Until the very last moment, when the Court of Criminal Appeal came down in favour of the conviction, it looked as though this tough series of questions, with the inference that he had been lucky to escape as a free man, might well result in his conviction being quashed. The effect of such questioning at the moment of the jury's hearing, must, I think, have been to damage his image as a credible witness in their eyes. It was the association of just the same type of crime, the suggestion that he was lucky to get away at all, as summarized by one question. This related to the fact that the telephone number of his present solicitors, was found in a diary somewhat prior to the date for the robbery. It was suggested to him that it was ungrateful of him to wish to change his solicitor, after Brian Field had "brought off such a tremendous coup". The inference was plain. He ought not to have got away!

There then ensured the longest, dreariest and most baffling of all the arguments put forward in the case: the great paint controversy about specks found on a pair of shoes taken from Goody's bedroom at the Windmill public house. Lightened only, histrionically, by the fact that it was, eventually, what the Judge called "an ugly issue" (that is to say that the defence allegation was that the police had "mixed it", and this, naturally, has news value) the interminable evidence of experts went on. Even on the Judge's summing-up, the subject occupies a bewildering number of pages of the shorthand transcript. The evidence was unbelievably longer than this. I happen to know a little about paint, since it is a constant source of readers' complaints to newspapers and one with which I sometimes have to deal. By the end of this evidence, I was so confused that I did not know a spectrograph from a spectre. The jury must have been in a similar position. But there remains something very odd about it all.

Let us look at the thing in the worst possible light. We know that Goody was, in truth, deeply implicated in the crime. But he was also sensible enough to be extremely careful. He had had his alibi smashed, before the crime was committed, and he knew it. He had therefore every reason to be hypercareful – and he was. Alone of everybody charged, he seems to have observed the rules about wearing gloves at Leatherslade. This carefulness the police were in process of discovering. They were also, quite correctly, sure that he was in the raid and they had no intention of letting him slip through their fingers. It looked at first as though there was nothing to catch him on.

It was on 14th August that Detective Constable Milner first saw a squashed tin of paint at Leatherslade Farm. It was not until 28th August, when handed it by Rixon, that he took it away. That tin of paint was not handed over to Dr Holden until the next day. Milner was told to collect the squashed tin on the 28th. Was it coincidental, or was it that Goody's trip to Leicester had taken place on 22nd August and that there was *still* no evidence with which to pin him down? This, in effect, was the suggestion of the defence. It would undoubtedly have been happier for all concerned in the case if there had been a satisfactory answer to one question, pressed continually by Goody's Counsel. *Why*, suddenly, did the police send for a squashed tin that they had ignored before (though scrapings of yellow paint had been freely taken), just after shoes had been taken away? The explanation may well be that they had already found yellow paint and could not match it with the sample that they had, so they were tracking down all possibilities. If so, why not say so? It was quite evident, from his testimony, that, whoever knew the answer to this question, Milner genuinely did not.

But what is extremely worrying, if one can once get thinking about those interminable spectrographs, is a fact which is suitable for Maigret. The *khaki* paint was never proven to be identical, though it was certainly similar in some ways. Dr Holden thought it *was* the same. It was the *yellow* paint, of which so much was available, which coincided so nearly that it was virtually identical.

Now think yourself into the position of some person described by the Judge as "evil-minded". If you wanted to frame someone, who had used both yellow and khaki paint, and you had only dried samples of the khaki and no tin to guide you as to its origin, what would you do? Buy a near sample. But if, at hand, there was a *tin* which kindly gave you the name of the brand of the yellow paint, you would stand a chance, by buying the same, to be fairly close. I may have misread the evidence: but I do not think that a tin of khaki paint was ever found anywhere – only scrapings. Supposing then that the police or, for that matter anyone else had wanted to frame evidence. There had been a sample taken on the 19th from this very tin of yellow. Why, in heaven's name was the tin not taken away earlier? An open, squashed tin. Who can say what happens to the oozing paint? This point was very strongly made by Mr Sebag Shaw, Q.C., who also pointed out that on 19th August, both Chief Superintendent Butler and Chief Inspector Vibart were at Leatherslade Farm. They must have seen the tin: surely it was interesting to them? Or was it an incredible oversight on the part of experienced officers?

There is an even more disturbing possibility. The guard was taken off the farm at some date between the 19th and 26th August. Milner thinks it was on the 26th. At any rate, it was before the tin was handed over. That means that the tin was not under supervision at all for a period. If I had been on that jury, I should have longed to be able to answer "Not Proven" to that part of the evidence, whatever my views on eventual guilt. It is admittedly easy to make insinuations about people who cannot defend themselves. Here, there is absolutely no one at whom one can point a finger at all. The fact remains that Goody, to those to whom he does not bother to lie about his guilt, maintains with passion, that these shoes were never within fifty miles of Leatherslade. And since I must put the robbers' tale, this version must be recorded. In any case, the inference and all the facts are in the evidence, together with a cross-examination which should be read by any law-student as a model of clarity and persistence.

Meanwhile, Biggs had been removed from the main trial to await a separate one. Inspector Morris, of the Surrey Constabulary, giving evidence about the questioning of Biggs, let slip a most unfortunate remark to the effect that Biggs had said that he had met Reynolds in prison. The Judge's face twitched slightly, the only sign he gave of the deep anger that he felt. He had controlled the whole case calmly and efficiently, towards a tidy, orderly finish: this threw a spanner into the works. He let the Inspector finish, then he turned towards my husband, who was appearing for Biggs, and spoke in a voice so gentle, so controlled, that only someone who had followed his orderly conduct of the case could sense the effort that this calmness cost him and know the frightful possibilities of this blunder. In reply to the quick remark of Counsel unnoticed by the jury, "There is a matter which I think I ought to invite your Lordship to consider at some convenient moment, arising out of this witness's evidence," came from the Bench, "Perhaps it would be as convenient as any now. Probably it would be better to have the court a little differently constituted." The jury, wondering what had happened, filed out. There was a moment of extreme tension. This could mean the beginning of the trial all over again. As the exchanges took place in the absence of the jury, it could not be reported at the time as anything but a "slight irregularity". It is worth recording here as an instance of the protection afforded by English procedure to a defendant.

COUNSEL: My Lord, I am, of course, inviting your Lordship to consider the proper course to adopt in view of the officer's grossly improper – I think those are the proper words – observation upon a matter which, not only is not in issue but was not upon his deposition, about which he was not asked by myself or my friend, to the effect that the defendant Biggs was a man who had been serving a sentence of imprisonment.

MR JUSTICE DAVIES: That the Inspector who, of necessity, must be a man of great experience in his duties, should have so far forgotten his duties as to bring in a phrase of that kind quite gratuitously is grossly improper and cannot be too strongly condemned.

COUNSEL: I hoped my words were right.

MR JUSTICE DAVIES: Your words were not a bit too strong and I underlined them; quite gratuitously a stupid thing to do. What are you asking me to do? I am hoping, indeed I am doing more than hoping, I am almost praying, that the jury did not pick up the phrase. Are you making an application that this jury be discharged and we have to start again?

COUNSEL: I cannot make such an application as a reality.

I entirely leave the matter to your Lordship to take such course as your Lordship thinks proper.

MR JUSTICE DAVIES: I must ask you whether you are applying for that course to be adopted.

COUNSEL: It places me in an appalling difficulty, between the matter which is of very grave concern to everybody else, including all the accused and all those concerned and my client. I think before I answer your Lordship in the way that your Lordship said you almost prayed I should be able to answer – and I almost pray that I shall be able to answer it in that way – I ought to take instructions from my client.

MR JUSTICE DAVIES: I think you must. I do not desire to bring any kind of pressure upon you. I hope that I am doing that which is accurate. I hope, and think it is quite conceivably the case, that the jury did not pick up the phrase, but there it is.

COUNSEL: If it were an individual on trial I would have no hesitation as to the way my duty lay, but in a case like this with so many accused and a multiplicity of witnesses, I think I must take instructions.

MR JUSTICE DAVIES: We will adjourn for ten minutes. (*After adjournment*)

COUNSEL: At your Lordship's invitation, I have considered most carefully, with those instructing me and with my client, Mr Biggs, as to the right course to take in view of the gravely improper evidence that has been tendered. The view of it I have come to, and a view I have communicated to my learned friend Mr James, is to invite your Lordship to discharge the defendant Biggs without a verdict, of course, from this jury. I have no other course, in my opinion, that is open to me in his interests but to ask your Lordship to do that. I regret deeply having to make this application, but perhaps the defence are wholly blameless as far as the necessity for the application goes.

MR JUSTICE DAVIES: Wholly blameless. It is most regrettable because it does mean this, that Mr Biggs will have to remain in custody to await his trial.

So Biggs went back to the prison and the main trial did not have to re-start with a new jury. He was torn between the feeling that he might now stand a better chance, tried on his own, and the boredom of having nothing to do whilst the others were having their daily outing in Court. The prison authorities stretched a point and let him stay with his friends. He is an amiable soul and not without a sense of humour. To my husband who had an inability to turn up punctually after the luncheon adjournment, he said one day: "Twenty-five to three? You nearly made it today, sir!" My husband remarked that it was a very nice day and that he would like to be spending it elsewhere. "So would I, sir," answered Biggs, "only they would describe that as escaping."

The evidence about the purchase of Leatherslade Farm was long, complicated and tedious. It was a curiously assorted triangle that were involved in this fog of conveyancing and document, the solemn Wheater, with the small, surprising voice: the bouncy, self-assured Brian Field, his hands continually "washed" and rubbed, the smile always on the face; and the taciturn Lennie, who provided almost the only excitement by his sudden verbal attack in the witness-box upon Brian Field, when he realized that the drift of that gentleman's evidence was not giving him expected support. But the story of this particular aspect of the case is not part of the main story, which, so far as this lesser conspiracy to pervert the course of justice is concerned, became almost a "family" feud between the two unrelated Fields, who were at daggers drawn from this point. We can go back to the main case.

The summing-up lasted just about six full working days, and, whilst the case does not begin to rival the famous Tichborne matter in length, the immense complexity of issues, the number of accused, and the side-tracks which events had followed imposed a heavy burden on a single Judge. It was a summing-up which, in the end, the pundits criticized, saying that it became disappointing; to anyone who has struggled with the attempt to write a more or less connected narrative, the remarkable thing is that, with no interval to let evidence ripen in his mind, any man could do it at all. Re-reading it (and more particularly, with the findings of the Court of Criminal Appeal in mind) one can wish that, in a few places, what obviously seemed to him to be a clear issue had perhaps been strengthened a little: but, in his anxiety to give direction only in the most scrupulously proper manner, he forbore. One can also, on a re-reading, trace even more clearly than in Court, the growing exhaustion. It was too hard a task for one man. He had been intellectually lonely for so long: the casual social contacts had been of no relevance. There had been no one with whom he could discuss the case every evening and, as everyone else who had been connected with it had known, it was the cut and thrust of discussion, the arguments about the evidence, the putting forward and demolishing of theory after theory, that had really crystallized the facts in one's mind. I heard it said several times that it was a pity he had not had a young marshal with him, that charming, archaic survival of the young "squire", to help with all his intellectual needs – and to do some hard donkey work on the case. I have also thought, myself, that this long isolation may well have had an effect on sentencing. Alone, week after week, save at week-ends, he may have begun to get the thing out of proportion, to feel that the row of far from blameless records sitting in the dock were forces of evil, more potent even than they were. Many of us would have begun to see Apollyon before long; several unexpected people confessed to me that they were becoming obsessed by the case; and judges, though often – not always – wiser than other men, are but human after all. Let it be said, however, that no prisoner complained that any portion of this long arduous task had been unfair; and that is quite something. Only the unfortunate little Boal, his luck completely out over this trial, may have wished that he had not quite so often been used as the object of a sentence to demonstrate a possibility. The trouble was that Mr Boal was such a simple uncomplex human being to use.

At last it was over. I glanced down the dock. Boal's little red face was impassive: Wisbey looked his usual jovial self: Welch wore his usual worried frown. Hussey and Wheater were, as ever, blank of face: James looked happy. Goody was paler than he had been at the beginning, the red patches of nerves showing on his white cheeks; and Wilson looked nervous. Lennie Field, now separated from Brian, after his attack upon the clerk in the witness-box, wore a sullen, despairing look. Brian Field alone looked apprehensive. The wind had gone out of his sails and the bounce had gone out of his appearance. For a fleeting moment, one could not help feeling somewhat sorry for him.

The final speeches were made. The jury left the Court at 3.36 on Monday 23 March. It was the forty-ninth working day of the trial. There had been several alarms that jurymen were being interfered with: the gang were angered by this, saying that it was a put-up job, to turn public sympathy against them. It may just have been those lunatics who like this form of practical joking. Anyway, the result was to hide them like the Crown Jewels, though, as they went away

in a bus, clearly labelled "Friday's Child" and were at once trailed
by reporters, who wanly fancied they might get a story out of it, the
secret was fairly well-known at once. However, no one was cad
enough to reveal it to the public!

Then ensued one of the most painful waits in contemporary legal
memory. On the Tuesday, some people turned up. The Bar,
feeling fraternal – and also aware that this was reminiscent of
schooldays and of the sad end of the term when they were going to
leave – sought consolation at The Bell, where it was generally
agreed over mild potations that the whole case was a mighty
personal triumph for Mr Arthur James, Q.C., who had led the
prosecution and had borne the heat and burden of the day. At no
time had he shown any sign of impatience or irritation (and he had
had cause!) never had he fallen below the highest standards of
courtesy to everyone in the Court, prisoners included; and the *tour
de force* displayed in his lucid and unfailing grip of a mass of
documents that rose in Himalayan piles above the prosecution's
benches, was something all engaged in the case will remember. He
would tell me to strike this out, but he will not have the chance in
time. The Bar will support the pleasure of putting this particular
matter on record.

By Wednesday we were tired of waiting for the white smoke.
(This remark was made to a conscientious cub-reporter who took it
literally and subsequently asked me how they ensured that the
smoke would be white.) It was agreed that Desmond Fennell, the
junior of the prosecution team, would notify the London members
of the Bar and that they would check with each other. The police
also were kind enough to take responsibility for seeing that all was
well. We have never been more dutifully notified!

The calls came through on the Wednesday evening. The verdict
had been reached at 8.15. The Court would be convened for 10.30
the next morning.

By 10.30 there was really a crowd. Security was in full-swing.
The Bucks police, whom we all liked, have a curiously light opera
appearance: it is probably their look of robust health, which almost
suggests stage make-up against the pallor of their Metropolitan
brethren. If the whole backcloth of the scene had not been so
solemn, it would have looked, as the Court filled, rather as if a
scene from *Iolanthe* had got astray.

But it was real life. The Judge entered, brisk and serious. He
made an unusual announcement: "When the jury return, I want it

to be understood, quite clearly, that nobody is to enter or leave this Court until the proceedings are over. There is only one exception to this and that is this: if the prison officers would prefer to remove each individual accused as his case is dealt with, then that may most certainly be done; but apart from that, no one will leave the Court." I knew that Goody and Wilson had meditated a gaol-break but had decided against it, as the case seemed to be running their way at one stage. One Counsel had said to Wilson that the summing-up seemed to be a good one for him, to which Charlie Wilson, with his queer, brilliant smile, had replied, "Not so good as I am accustomed to, sir." Had there then been some rumour, some exceptional risk, something as dramatic as a helicopter, bogus policemen who would throw off their helmets to reveal gangsters, armed with sub-machine guns? No, nothing. Not even a city gentleman, in a bowler hat with a brief-case. The warning was simply the Judge's way of ensuring that this sombre moment would be marked by no demonstration, no scuffle and no loss of dignity. And no Pressmen trying to beat each other to the phone.

The jury came in. For the last time, the tipstaff, who looked on duty like a solemn whippet, but could, on occasion and when softened up by peppermints, flash a friendly wink so quickly you would think you had been deceived by it, led in his flock. They looked rather foolish: in fact, they were only acutely self-conscious and horribly embarrassed by the searchlight of fame trained upon them. There was no surprise in the first batch of verdicts, though it took a moment or two to get them going, for the procedure of counts was rather muddling.

Boal, guilty on counts 1 and 2. Wilson, guilty on counts 1 and 2. Wisbey, guilty on counts 1 and 2. Welch, guilty on counts 1 and 2. Hussey, guilty on counts 1 and 2. James, guilty on counts 1 and 2. Goody, guilty on counts 1 and 2. Brian Field, guilty on count 1. Not guilty of robbing or receiving. (This, unforeseen by the jury, was to let him out later in the Court of Criminal Appeal from the conspiracy charge itself.) Guilty of conspiracy to obstruct the course of justice. Leonard Field, guilty on count 1, not guilty of robbery or receiving, guilty of conspiracy to obstruct the course of justice. Wheater, guilty of conspiracy to obstruct the course of justice only.

There was no sign of flinching from the dock. There had been a final briefing the night before, as thorough as that which had preceded the robbery itself. Goody, a leader to the last, had drilled his troops like the Guards. They were, so to speak, to die with their boots clean.

As for Biggs, waiting anxiously in Aylesbury Gaol, he knew what to expect. He had worried a lot, with the result that, like some neurotic child, he had put on more than two stone in weight. He began to lose it again from now on: evidently, it was now the calm of despair.

The Judge paid tribute to the jury, seeming to find the release of tension in a carefully modulated lightness towards the end.

"Mr Foreman," he said, "that discharged at long last the almost intolerable burden you and your fellow jurors have carried over so many weeks; not only this County but the whole country is greatly in your debt. You can and never will be repaid, save by the assurance that your services are enormously appreciated. I recommend that you be exempted from jury service for the rest of your lives, so arduous and prolonged have been your present duties. I think you will find that you are never called upon to serve, though more worthy jurors I cannot imagine being found. You and I have been sitting in this Court for so long that, to quote another Judge on another occasion, 'Life will never seem quite the same without you.' On behalf of the County, and indeed the whole country, I thank you."

BRUNO HAUPTMANN

(Flemington, New Jersey, 1935)

George Waller

Bruno Richard Hauptmann's trial had all the ballyhoo of a sporting event. Hauptmann, a German immigrant carpenter, was accused of one of the most infamous crimes in American history, the kidnap and murder of the baby son of Charles Lindbergh, the great aviator and all-American hero. As a wave of anger and revulsion swept America, Lindbergh arranged for an intermediary, the garrulous old Dr John Condon, to hand over $50,000 in unmarked bills to the kidnap gang. Parked 100 yards away, Lindbergh heard the disembodied voice of one of them shout: "Hey, Doc!" Six weeks later the baby's body was found in a shallow grave in the woods near the Lindbergh mansion. For the critic Alexander Woollcott, the most unforgettable moment of the entire trial was when Anne Morrow Lindbergh, the child's mother, took the witness stand and identified the sleeping suit which her own hands had sewn for her little son. "In that hushed moment, the case, stripped to its essentials, was revealed for what it really was – evil incarnate standing accused by every American hearth." Woollcott shared none of the misgivings that some modern writers have expressed about the case. One of Britain's most distinguished crime historians, Sir Ludovic Kennedy, called the trial a travesty. Convinced of Hauptmann's guilt but unable to prove it, the police, he declared, invented evidence. Worst of all was Lindbergh's testimony, delivered two years later, when he swore that the man who shouted "Hey, Doc!"

*was Hauptmann. That clinched it for the jury. Journalist George
Waller, who wrote one of the first comprehensive accounts of the
Lindbergh baby kidnap, handles the case objectively, without raising
conspiracy theories. Although he spent many years researching the
case, he didn't have access to the files of the New Jersey State Police,
which were only opened in the 1970s.*

Flemington's town constable heard the news with mixed feelings:
the legal tussle to extradite Bruno Richard Hauptmann from New
York to New Jersey had been won and he would be tried in the
Hunterdon County Courthouse. It was gratifying to know that
Flemington would have its day in the sun, but its solitary police
officer would have his work more than cut out for him. Hundreds
of strangers would be in town. Hundreds? Thousands, maybe.

In normal times, the task of maintaining the peace in Flemington
was not arduous. New York City was only sixty miles away, but
Flemington was another world. Its citizens went to bed early, and
there weren't many more than twenty-seven hundred of them.
They lived in decent elderly houses with white walls and green
shutters and a good deal of ornamental woodwork, kept their
sidewalks clean and regarded the town constable mainly as a source
of reliable weather information.

Flemington had been settled by the Dutch in the seventeenth
century but took its name from Samuel Fleming, who set up as an
innkeeper in the peaceable hamlet in the 1750s. Some seventy years
later the courthouse, symbol of Flemington's eminence as the
Hunterdon County seat, was built on Main Street.

It was a handsome building, two and a half stories high, of native
stone with a white stucco façade and four Doric columns in the
Greek revival style, although the Colonial cupola reminded the
townspeople that this was, after all, America. The county jail,
small but quite modern, was directly behind the courthouse. The
town constable examined its appointments in preparation for the
new tenant, reflecting that an earlier one, also involved in the
Lindbergh case, had waited here to be tried: John Hughes Curtis,
the Norfolk boatbuilder.

The Union Hotel, the only hotel in Flemington, faced the
courthouse directly across Main Street. It was a lumbering affair
of nondescript vintage and architecture, four stories tall. A com-

modious porch ran across its front, with double-deck balconies above. Business was sparse inside, but the ground-floor front porch enjoyed sociable afternoons and evenings and heard much chat about affairs of the day as town gossips rocked in their chairs and inspected drowsy Main Street.

Then Main Street came to life.

Friday night, October 19, three sedans containing a dozen New Jersey detectives drove into town at about half-past ten. In a fourth car, which they escorted, Richard Hauptmann sat hand-cuffed between Captain John Lamb and Lieutenant Arthur Keaton of the State police. A thousand restless and inquisitive people (the town constable's estimate) had gathered around the entrance to the jail; some of them, not trusting Flemington's street lights and deter-mined to see all, had brought flares. In this garish light they watched Hauptmann's guards lead him from the car into the jail. The crowd was silent, staring. The prisoner was impassive.

Twelve State troopers stationed themselves outside.

The staff of the Union Hotel was still wondering how to cope with the huge problem the prisoner had brought to town with him. They had on hand messages from some nine hundred people – from all over the world, it seemed – requesting rooms for the duration of the trial. Many were sharply specific, stating that their rooms must be the best the hotel afforded; others, with wild incomprehension, spoke of suites; and at least one dwelt on a special diet which the hotel's kitchen must be prepared to dish up for him.

There were fifty rooms in the Union. The last few vacancies were taken by newspaper and radio reporters long before the great bulk of messages arrived; and even before that, six rooms on the top floor had been reserved for the trial jurors. Flemington house-wives, quickly learning about the problem and the opportunity it offered, began to make ready their spare rooms or, when there was none, double up the family's sleeping arrangements. It soon became apparent that even these emergency measures would not suffice. Flemington was booked solid. The overflow would have to be content with quarters in the Trenton hotels, twenty miles distant.

The front porch of the Union Hotel buzzed with interesting items. No less than three hundred reporters, many of them star reporters, some of them famous novelists turned reporter for the

trial – Walter Winchell, Edna Ferber, Arthur Brisbane, Fannie
Hurst, Damon Runyon, Kathleen Norris, Alexander Woollcott,
Adela Rogers St John – were coming to Flemington. Also, great
figures of the stage and screen, United States senators, crooners,
concert singers, social celebrities; and, of course, people who never
missed any important event – a World Series, a prize fight, a
murder trial – had announced that they would attend. An atmosphere of eager expectancy spread from the hotel porch through
the town. Faces never before seen by the townsfolk except in their
newspapers and magazines were glimpsed on Main Street, many, it
was true, behind dark glasses, but recognizable nevertheless.
Foreign accents were heard. Raoul de Roussy de Sales was in
Flemington, sent by *Paris-Soir*, and Lionel Shortt of the London
Daily Mail, and Dixie Tighe of the London *Daily Express*. A great
criminal lawyer, Samuel Leibowitz, had been engaged by a radio
network to comment on the progress of the trial, and professional
colleagues, no less familiar with the law's intricacies, were to
analyze the events in the courtroom for rival networks.

A phrase that hardly seemed inflated traveled from mouth to
mouth and back again: this was to be the trial of the century.

And the world was not to miss a word of it. Telephone and
telegraph technicians swarmed over the old, dignified courthouse,
trailing wires behind them. They stitched wires over the floors and
up the walls and into the garret, the center of their humming web.
Here, cramped places were made for forty telegraph and cable
operators, who would sit shoulder to shoulder and flash out each
word practically as it was uttered in the legal cockpit below. They
were prepared, the wireless companies stated, to transmit a million
words a day.

The weather sharpened; Christmas was in the air.

Some of the strangers in town were saying that because of the
crime's atrocious nature and the veneration in which the dead
child's father was held, the Lindbergh case couldn't possibly be
tried on its merits – Richard Hauptmann would never receive a fair
trial. *Wrong*, Flemington replied with a united voice, absolutely
wrong! No Hunterdon County jury would prejudge any defendant;
Hunterdon County people were fair-minded, you could count on
that.

Sounds of young voices floated through the crisp evening. The
fair-minded Hunterdon County people's children were chanting
carols outside Richard Hauptmann's cell.

But when was the trial to start? Flemington's constable understood that there had been something of a tussle over the date, too. The man who would prosecute, Attorney General Wilentz, had wanted it to begin on November 14, but the prisoner's counsel had said that wouldn't give him enough time and had proposed December 11; but *that* would run it through the Christmas holidays, not so good for the jurors; and, therefore, finally prosecution and defense had agreed to start the trial on the very first practical date after New Year's Day – Wednesday, 2 January, 1935.

Tuesday night, 1 January, was clear and cold; the rooftops were white under a lingering mantle of Christmas snow. Tomorrow promised to be a fine day.

Morning sunshine flowed over the white roofs. In nearby Trenton, Justice Thomas Whitaker Trenchard shaved, breakfasted and made ready for court. He thought it wise to slip a bottle of cough syrup into the pocket of his jacket, in case of any trouble with his throat. He did not expect any trouble – in fact, he had been resting in bed for the last two days, to make sure that he was fit for the sheer physical strain of the trial – but it was just as well to be prepared.

Judge Trenchard was seventy-one, a sedate, handsome, gray-haired man. His face, rather high-colored, customarily had a paternal look, and his manner in the courtroom had been described as one of sympathetic benevolence; for all that, he was a stickler for the proprieties. He had been sitting on the New Jersey Supreme Court bench for more than twenty-eight years and was starting his fifth consecutive seven-year term as a Supreme Court justice. His reputation throughout the state was second to none: Judge Trenchard's decisions were well known for the muscular thought behind them and their clarity of expression. To this refusal to countenance the slipshod in thought or word he owed his sterling record: he had never been reversed in a murder trial.

The judge waited in his chambers while the ten-o'clock bells were rung. The court crier pronounced the ancient words, "*Oyez! Oyez! Oyez!* All manner of persons having business with this Court . . . on this second day of January in the year of Our Lord One Thousand Nine Hundred and Thirty-five, let them draw nigh, give their attention, and they shall be heard."

Judge Trenchard entered the courtroom and took his place on the bench. The trial of Bruno Richard Hauptmann could begin.

Today, only a hundred or so spectators had been permitted to attend. The jury was to be selected, a delicate process that did not allow for the normal distractions of a trial audience. Those inside could hear the murmurs and occasional jeers of the crowd in the street; but by and by, under the indifferent stares of the guarding State troopers, the noise died down. Other troopers were posted throughout the building, keeping an eye on its furnishings, many of them valuable antiques.

The courtroom itself was a high-ceilinged hall with yellow walls, five large windows on either side and two more behind the judge's dais. The old benches, somewhat resembling church pews, could accommodate no more than five hundred spectators; to prepare for the weeks to come – the prosecution estimated the trial would last four weeks – folding chairs had been borrowed from the Flemington Fair and squeezed in wherever possible.

At the rear, a gallery looked down on the court, and here the press reigned, uncomfortably. Pine boards, squared off in eighteen-inch spaces, served as writing tables. One hundred fifty reporters – there was not conceivably room for a hundred-fifty-first – sat jammed at them.

Attorney General David T. Wilentz rose and moved the trial of the State of New Jersey against Bruno Richard Hauptmann; in his turn Chief Defense Counsel Edward J. Reilly announced that the defense was ready.

Maybe in the future, David Wilentz thought, he would find the questioning and cross-questioning of talesmen tedious or even downright boring; right now he didn't. It was fascinating. And grim, too, considering what might depend on each question, each answer: the life of that man over there, sitting behind his counselors.

This was David Wilentz's first murder case – his first criminal case of any kind, although he was Attorney General of New Jersey, chief prosecutor for the State, head of State's counsel. The grab bag of political circumstance had determined that. He was thirty-nine, very young for the office. Governor A. Harry Moore had appointed him attorney general last year after Wilentz, a vigorous and eloquent Democrat, had persuaded a majority of voters in traditionally Republican Middlesex County to switch over to the other side. He knew his law; a New York University Law School graduate, he had been admitted to the bar in 1919 after returning a lieutenant from the war; and although in this case he was up against one of the toughest, wiliest and most successful trial lawyers in the business, Wilentz was confident he was going to come out on top and put Richard Hauptmann in the electric chair.

As a private citizen, as a voter, if given the chance to vote for or against capital punishment, Wilentz would have voted whole-heartedly against. He thought the law barbaric. But it was New Jersey State law and he was the attorney general and if he did not fight tooth and nail to win the last full measure of the punishment the law decreed, he would be derelict, and that was one thing that would never be said of Attorney General David Wilentz.

He was all light and shadow, swift as mercury, with a rapier wit and tongue and a d'Artagnan poise to go with them, and more than a little of a d'Artagnan face, thin and dark under a magnificent head of black hair. That intrepid swordsman would have approved of his taste in clothes: away from the court's majesty, David Wilentz liked to wear an off-white felt hat, brim snapped down in front and on one side, a velvet-collar Chesterfield and a flashing white silk scarf. He cut a dash. His bright eyes regarded the world with humor and tolerance and unfailing interest. He was married and the father of three children, who liked him very much.

His eyes were studying Richard Hauptmann and another man, who sat three chairs away from the accused, in the same row – Charles Lindbergh.

Hauptmann had been led into the courtroom between two State troopers, followed closely by a deputy sheriff in plain clothes. Lindbergh had come in not long afterward, striding through the hush left by the prisoner's appearance. In a light gray suit with no vest, his familiar, gangling, still-boyish figure had deepened the hush. Wilentz's bright eyes had watched carefully, had seen Hauptmann glance up as the father of the dead child took his seat and then quickly look away. Charles Lindbergh, Wilentz had noted, didn't look at Hauptmann at all. Wilentz had noted something else. As he sat, chin in hand, watching Hauck and Fisher, studying each prospective juror, Lindbergh would lean forward occasionally and his gray jacket would fall open a little, revealing beneath it a pistol in a shoulder holster.

Wilentz knew that Lindbergh had had an excellent chance to inspect the prisoner. A week after Hauptmann's arrest, he and Lindbergh had been in the same room, the large private office of Samuel J. Foley, District Attorney of the Bronx. Lindbergh, who had just flown east with Anne, had requested the meeting, a meeting only he, not Hauptmann, would be aware of. Long before, still striving to come to grips with the author of the ransom notes, the young father had disguised himself in cap and dark glasses; he had put on the same disguise before coming into Foley's office and seating himself with a group of detectives. Then Hauptmann had been brought in. District Attorney Foley had instructed the prisoner to walk around and sit down and get up and repeat, over and over, in different tones, now in a quiet voice, now shouting, the words "Hey, Doctor! Hey, Doctor, over here!" – words Lindbergh had heard when John had called out his directions to Dr Condon from the darkness of St Raymond's Cemetery.

For ten minutes Lindbergh had watched Hauptmann walking back and forth, obediently following instructions: "Hey, Doctor! Hey, Doctor, over here!" No, Wilentz thought, he hardly needed to look at him now.

Lindbergh was obviously very much caught up in the questioning of the talesmen. The accused man, Wilentz thought, made an absorbing sight. Asked for a word to describe his attitude, you would have to say *confident*. Even cheerful. Hauptmann glanced around a lot, often met Wilentz's eyes coolly. He chatted with his counselors as if he and they were a group of spectators who had dropped in to watch the trial rather than a man accused of kidnaping and murder sitting with the men who hoped to save him from the chair.

An absorbing sight; as an individual, an absorbing study – all that he had learned about Richard Hauptmann bore that out, Wilentz thought. The psychiatrist Dudley Shoenfeld held that the crime was compulsive and to bolster his arguments had cited examples of the defendant's behavior, taken from the composite portrait of Richard Hauptmann which had been painstakingly pieced together out of information obtained from the German province where he was born and brought up, from friends, neighbors, acquaintances, from his wife, Anna – and, of course, from Hauptmann himself.

Tuesday 29 January, twentieth day of the trial. The axis on which the State's case slowly swung was the date of the ransom payment, 2 April 1932; in the prosecution's view, that day – or night – divided Richard Hauptmann's life into a dramatically contrasting before and after. Wilentz had pinpointed the date time and again during the weeks of testimony; this morning, he took it up once more.

He reminded the defendant that he had accounted for the day of 2 April, a Saturday, by saying that he had worked at the Majestic Apartments and that he had quit at the end of the day because he had been promised a hundred dollars a month and found he was being paid only eighty. On the other hand, the Majestic's time-keeper, a man presumably in possession of the facts, had testified that Hauptmann hadn't worked that Saturday, hadn't quit until the following Monday, 4 April. The timekeeper had produced records to prove it.

But he had worked at the Majestic on 2 April, 1932, Hauptmann answered firmly, no matter what anyone said.

And he'd quit because he was to get eighty dollars a month, not a hundred as he'd thought?

Yes.

Wilentz turned to his associates at the prosecution table and was given a sheaf of photostats, copies of the Majestic's payroll during the period; he turned again to the witness and pointed out his name and his pay – $3.33 a day.

Didn't $3.33 a day mean that he was getting $100 a month?

Hauptmann was silent.

Didn't it mean, too, that he hadn't quit over a few dollars' difference in salary, as he had said, *but because he had come into a fortune?* – fifty thousand dollars in extortion money?

No; that was *not* the reason.

Wilentz developed the theme. Just look at the luxuries he and his wife had enjoyed after the ransom was paid! – a splendid new radio, purchased in May for $396; an expensive, high-powered pair of German field glasses, bought in July for $126; Anna's trip to Europe the same month, at a cost of $706; two hunting trips, one to Maine, the other to New Jersey, for which he had paid $150, plus $56 for a hunting rifle, a gift to Karl Henkel, who accompanied him; $100 for a motor trip to Florida; all those carefree week ends on Hunter Island – now and then footing the bill for his convivial friends, perhaps? – and a canoe for their greater pleasure, a matter of $109.

The prosecutor paused, then capped the recital: And all that time he had been unemployed!

Hauptmann denied it: he had been busy in the stock market and had made money; had made money from the furs, too.

Wilentz ignored the explanation. How much would he say he had earned as a *carpenter* after 2 April 1932?

A couple of hundred dollars.

Wilentz nodded, satisfied, then moved to a new vantage point, displaying deposit slips the defendant had filled out at one of his banks during the period in question, all showing large deposits of silver coins.

Previously, when the prosecutor had implied that the defendant had spent most of his time after the fifty thousand dollar payment converting the bills into small change, Hauptmann had listened stolidly from his seat between the two guards; now, in the witness chair, he purposefully addressed himself to setting the evidence into the correct perspective. He never paid attention to the entry lines on deposit slips, he told Wilentz, and so a sum of money he had jotted down after the word *Silver* might properly have belonged after the word *Bills*, and the other way around. Even now, looking at the slips, he recalled some of the deposits and saw they were listed in the wrong place.

Wilentz greeted this with a smile; he seemed confident that the answer exposed its own flaws to anyone who had ever filled out a deposit slip and submitted it for a bank teller's inspection.

But the witness would admit, wouldn't he, that he had circulated Lindbergh money?

Hauptmann stared at him. No.

Hadn't he said that he spent some of the gold notes he found in the shoe box?

Yes, but –

Ransom bills?

– but he hadn't known it was Lindbergh money; he'd learned that after he was arrested.

Driving over the reply, Wilentz asked it he hadn't been circulating gold notes for a couple of weeks before then – that was true, wasn't it?

Yes.

Because he needed money?

Oh, no.

Why, then?

Simply because the bills were handy – he'd used a few to pay expenses, instead of taking money from his brokerage or bank accounts.

This was in September 1934?

Yes.

And he wasn't trying to convert the ransom bills into small bills and coins –?

Absolutely not.

If this was so, and he needed cash for expenses, why had he deposited in one of his bank accounts a couple of hundred dollars in silver and bills at the same time he was spending the gold notes? Why hadn't he used the money he deposited to pay for his living costs?

Hauptmann frowned. He had already explained, he said: the gold notes were handy.

And he didn't think it strange that he was using ten- and twenty-dollar gold certificates to pay for ordinary expenses while at the same time he was putting small bills and coins in the bank?

Hauptmann's frown deepened as he considered the question. Wilentz didn't help him. He hoped, the prosecutor said solicitously, he wasn't *confused?* – surely not that!

No, Hauptmann snapped, why should he be? He hadn't used the bank money because it was in an account in Mount Vernon his wife didn't know about and he was saving the money bit by bit to pay for their long-hoped-for trip to Germany.

Oh? Wilentz's tone was arch. Still another secret he kept from his wife?

The accused evidently did not consider this worthy of remark; his expression, a reporter noted, was contemptuous. It did not dismay Wilentz, who returned to the cache in the garage. How many gold notes had Hauptmann spent?

Twelve, maybe fifteen.

"How many did you intend to spend?"

"All I did spend. I wouldn't have spent any more."

"You were going to stop – even if you hadn't been arrested?"

"Yes."

"What were you going to do with the balance?"

"The other certificates?"

Yes, Wilentz assured him, that was what he meant: the other certificates.

"Give them to Fisch's brother."

"Why did you take twelve or fifteen if you weren't going to touch the others?"

Hauptmann said truculently, "I tell you there is no special reason for it."

"And the rest you were going to give to Fisch's brother?"

"My intention was to give him twelve thousand dollars."

As he listened to the earlier explanations, Wilentz's face had been skeptical if not downright incredulous; but now he seemed to go along with the defendant, if with a touch of playfulness.

He was going to give Fisch's brother only $12,000 when his friend and partner had entrusted him with about $14,800?

Again Hauptmann explained. Fisch owed him money and he meant to settle the debt. There was some $2800 involved – the $2000 he gave Fisch when his friend left for Germany and the rest due him from stock investments – and when the gold notes were dry he wrapped $2000 separately and put it aside and tucked $800 more into the holes drilled in the board. In this way he would be in no danger of losing the money that belonged to him, as he might be if he turned the full amount over to Fisch's brother: there was nothing in writing to establish the debt; the brother might refuse to acknowledge it.

Yes, yes, Wilentz murmured, he quite understood the need for such common-sense precautions – but how would the brother know about the gold notes hidden in the garage?

The defendant said he would show him the money.

He hadn't said anything about it in his letters to Fisch's family? He intended to.

Why hide the money in the garage? He had bank accounts, a safe-deposit box –?

Yes.

And, above all, he had that trunk!

Yes.

When he hid money of his own – the money he kept from his wife – he put it into the trunk?

Yes.

Not the garage?

No.

Quite so; not the garage, the trunk. Wilentz paused. Well, now, for that matter, why hadn't he turned in the gold notes to the Federal Reserve Bank? He knew that it was against the law to hoard gold, didn't he?

Yes, he knew. But nearly a year had gone by since the government's final warning about keeping gold; he might be closely questioned and punished, especially if it was found out that he was in the United States illegally. Anyway, the gold wasn't his.

Hadn't he said to the police, after his arrest, "I was afraid they would hook me up if I turned it in"?

Hauptmann considered. He couldn't remember, he said; but if he had, it was in reference to the explanation he had just given.

The prosecutor went back to the object that had engaged so much of his attention, the trunk: despite all its virtues as a hiding place, hadn't Hauptmann been just a little bit uneasy when he made the California trip with Anna and friend Kloeppenburg – with over $4000 in cash lying at home?

He hadn't left the money at home, the witness promptly replied; he had packed it in a satchel and left the satchel with his uncle in Brooklyn, not telling him what it contained.

This seemed to astonish Wilentz. Wouldn't it have been safer to put it in a bank?

Yes – but then his wife would have found out about the money.

She didn't know about his account in Mount Vernon, did she?

Hauptmann hesitated. He wasn't altogether sure.

Well, then, Wilentz pointed out, he could have opened a new account in some bank in the city –

The witness shifted in the chair. No, she would find out about it.

How? If he didn't tell her, how would she know?

Well, she – Hauptmann paused. She would find the bankbook.

Wilentz smiled, an understanding smile, a sort of between-friends, man-to-man smile. He could have hidden the bankbook where he hid the money – in the trunk! Why not? They both knew how safe the trunk was!

Hauptmann shifted again; his hands clasped and unclasped. No, impossible – that is, it wouldn't have been the thing to do – he always kept his bankbooks in the writing table.

Honestly, now, wouldn't it have been safer – and just as much a secret from his wife – if he had put the $4000 in a bank and hidden the bankbook in the trunk?

No. No.

Wilentz threw off the tone of sweet reasonableness. The fact was, it didn't matter, did it? – because there was no money in the trunk?

There was.

When he was arrested, had the police found any money in the trunk?

No.

Wilentz echoed, emphasizing it: No.

Because, Hauptmann said, because he had removed the savings a long while before.

Wilentz briskly fetched Hauptmann's account books from the exhibit table and reminded him that he had acknowledged that the notations in them were in his handwriting and were correct. He had testified, too, that Fisch had given him some $15,000 to invest in stocks and that he had given Fisch $2000 just before his friend sailed.

Yes.

But the truth was, Wilentz said in a hard voice, that all the money he ever got from Fisch was $2000, and the $2000 he gave Fisch – if he ever had given it – was to square matters between them.

Hauptmann replied sharply that that was not true.

The prosecutor shoved the books into the witness' hands and pointed to an entry. There it was: $2000 received from Fisch – that and no more.

But there *was* more – much more!

Where was it written down?

He had explained before that the accounts were incomplete –

Wilentz flipped the pages, pointed again. The witness had testified that he made several profits from the furs; what did the books say?

Hauptmann read aloud: $1737.51.

And that was the total profit, wasn't it?

No; he had said in the beginning that Fisch kept the fur records –

Wilentz moved ahead, pressing his examination to a close, using the letter of sympathy Hauptmann had written to Fisch's family after his friend's death to point out that although he said he and Fisch became partners in the spring of 1932, the first transaction between them mentioned in his letter was in the spring of 1933, a full year after the ransom was paid.

The afternoon was wearing out. Reilly followed Wilentz, endeavoring to smooth over the furrows the attorney general had left; before long, court was adjourned.

Wednesday morning, Reilly took the witness back over the day of the crime and the day of the ransom payment, reaffirming his innocence and pointing out that when he circulated the twelve or fifteen gold notes during the two weeks before his arrest he showed that he was unaware of the deadly nature of the money by spending it openly – without disguising himself or changing his car's license plates. And while the attorney general had devoted much time to the letters Hauptmann had written to Fisch's family, where were the letters the family had written to Hauptmann? They had been in his apartment when it was searched by the police!

Reilly finished, surrendered the witness once more to Wilentz; again the exchange grew sharp. At last the prosecutor turned away. "That is all," he said.

Hauptmann got up, stretched a little; he had a rather relaxed look, not tired, not worried. Followed by the guard, he began to walk toward his regular seat in the courtroom. He had answered questions for a total of seventeen hours; Wilentz's duel with him had lasted for eleven of them.

After a few steps he paused. He turned and looked at the jury and slowly smiled.

Anne Lindbergh had preceded her husband on the witness stand; Anna Hauptmann followed hers.

For the first time it occurred to some spectators that there were several points of similarity between the two women. Their Christian names were almost identical. Each was the mother of a baby son, Anne Lindbergh's second child, Anna Hauptmann's first. Their husbands were world-famous.

The similarities ended there. Anne's family background was one of great wealth, Anna's of decent poverty. Anne was fragile and dark-haired; Anna had a buxom figure and rust-blonde hair. Anne had dressed for her appearance on the stand in a jacket and skirt of black silk and a blue fox fur. Anna wore a navy-blue dress, with a cowl neck from which pleats ran through the heavy crêpe blouse, and a small black felt hat that somewhat resembled a trench cap and left a fringe of curls exposed. A white medallion hung from her neck on a black ribbon. She wore two rings, the gold wedding ring and a white-gold engagement ring set with small stones.

Reilly helped the witness into the chair and began in a quiet voice to lead her through her arrival in America and friendship with Richard, but he had to raise his voice and ask Anna to raise hers. He looked around, annoyed. The courtroom was jammed with a crowd equal if not even superior in numbers to that which had struggled into the building to see Anne Lindbergh. Again, people were standing on tables, sitting on radiators, were wedged fast in the aisles and into the window recesses. Again, they whispered, coughed, sneezed, complained of the insufferable conditions. Judge Trenchard relieved them. Everyone who was standing, he announced, must leave. The guards enforced the order. The complainers regretted their complaints.

Reilly resumed his sympathetic questions; Anna's accented voice could be heard quite clearly in the new hush. She seemed composed, but her eyelids blinked rapidly half a dozen times over the blue eyes as she began each answer. She watched Reilly devotedly, as if her life depended on him.

Yes, Richard and she met and were married and they worked hard and saved their money. She started to work at the Fredericksen bakery in June 1929. Mrs Fredericksen took two nights off a week, Tuesday and Fridays, and as a regular custom Anna worked until eight o'clock on those nights.

"Did the Fredericksens own a police dog?" Reilly asked.

Anna blinked her eyes. "Yes."

1 March 1932, was a Tuesday, Reilly went on; and on that night had her husband called for Anna at the bakery?

"Yes, he did."

"At what time?"

"Maybe it was seven o'clock, maybe quarter after, maybe quarter before. I don't know exactly the minutes."

"How long did he remain there before you and he left to go home?

"He was there until we went home together, about half-past nine, quarter to ten."

"You went right home?"

"We did."

"And after you arrived home did you remain there?"

Anna replied firmly, "Yes."

At a few minutes past nine on Tuesday night, 1 March 1932, Anne and Charles Lindbergh were chatting in front of their fireplace when Charles turned his head and, in answer to Anne's question, said he had heard a sound, a sound like breaking wood. They did not investigate.

Did Anna remember, in March 1932, about what time in the morning Richard went to work for the Majestic? She remembered that he would drive her to the bakery, where she started in the mornings at seven, and then go right to work. Now, Reilly continued, another date that had been spoken of a good deal, 2 April 1932, a Saturday – could she remember who was in her house that night? Hans Kloeppenburg was with her and Richard then, Anna told him, for a musical evening and a little card-playing.

She would remember her husband's birthday, wouldn't she? She would indeed. November 26. How about 26 November 1933? That was a Sunday, Anna said, and some friends were at their place for a birthday party, her niece and Paul Vetterle and Isidor Fisch and of course Richard and she.

Reilly asked about Gerta Henkel, and Anna replied that she had met Mrs Henkel through Richard.

"In connection with Mrs Henkel and your husband, have you ever entertained the slightest suspicion concerning his infidelity toward you?"

Anna flushed. "Mrs Henkel was not only a friend of my husband, she was my friend too."

"Did you ever entertain any thoughts or opinions that your husband was untrue to you?"

"Never."

As for Isidor Fisch – some information about him, please. Well, Anna had met him late in 1932 at the Henkels' house, where he lived. He and Richard were in business togeaher. The Hauptmanns had given a farewell party for him on a Saturday night, about four days before he sailed for Germany. Anna was in the baby's room when he arrived at the apartment that night and so she couldn't see if he brought any packages or bundles with him; but about a week before he sailed, or maybe a few weeks, he brought a suitcase with things he didn't want to take to Germany, and some boxes, like cardboard boxes, with furs, and a valise – "filled with books in," Isidor Fisch said.

Reilly nodded. "How tall are you, Mrs Hauptmann?"

Anna said she believed she was five feet four inches tall.

Then could she reach the top shelf in the broom closet next to the sink in the apartment?

Well, she would have to stretch herself.

"Did you know anything about any box, shoe box, cardboard box, on the top shelf?"

"No, I never used that shelf."

Reilly wished to know more about the closet, anything in connection with any water Anna may have found there and where the water came from. Anna began with the shelves. There were three, on the right side. On the first she kept a box with shoe polish and brushes, and soap and powder. On the second, an electric iron, and bottles of polish, and cleaning rags. And on the third, the top shelf –

"I believe I put up some few bundles of shelf trimming there, what I didn't use. There is a pipe, I don't know what for, and this goes through the ceiling, and the water came down on the pipe and on the top of the ceiling, and I noticed a few times that even my mop was hanging on the left side in the closet sometimes was very damp. The water came through the closet, through the ceiling, and many times the shelves were wet, and even down on the floor I had to put a pot."

Reilly's expression was that of a man ordinarily little interested in closets, mops, brooms, shoe polish, shelf trimming. He moved on to Anna's earnings; had she kept a record?

"Yes, we put it down in a book."

How much had she earned altogether since she came to America?

"Well, I would say around seven thousand dollars, a little over seven thousand dollars."

She saved most of it?

"Oh, yes!"

She and her husband had a joint bank account where they put all the family funds?

"Not all."

But all her savings were put there?

"Yes."

"You trusted your husband and he trusted you?"

"Sure."

Wilentz objected. "I move the part about the husband trusting her be stricken."

Agreeably, Reilly cut his question in half. "You trusted your husband, didn't you?"

Anna's blue eyes gave him a long look. "Who shouldn't trust a husband?"

"I don't know," Reilly said. Then this much-married man paused and added, in a tone the courtroom had not heard him use before, a little sad, altogether human, "That speaks well for some of us."

He glanced at Wilentz. "The witness is yours."

There was a ground swell of sympathy from the crowd for the woman on the stand as the attorney general approached her. He was swift, adroit, intelligent, and, as he had proved, capable of a battering-ram attack; she was a rather plain, rather dumpy housewife, capable of – what? Hard work, and, as she had proved, immense loyalty. Now the two were opponents. He would tear into her account of the three significant dates, the night of the kidnapping, the night of the ransom-money exchange, the night when a movie-theater patron had tossed an oddly folded bill to the cashier. Surely Anna Hauptman was no match for David Wilentz.

Anna watched him with apprehension and dislike. His violent exchanges with Richard had hardly prepared her to regard him with favor. Far more than that, he was a man professionally committed to obtaining Richard's death. For him, the death of her child's father would mean victory. She mustered what resources she had to stand up to his onslaught.

But Wilentz had a surprise up his well-tailored sleeve for her, for the crowd, and for the defense. It soon became evident that he was ignoring the three dates. Instead he was asking – and in a quiet, respectful voice – about the furs and other things Isidor Fisch had left with the Hauptmanns: books, clothing, an electric lamp, some pictures. Anna and Richard looked them over together, she said, after they heard that Fisch was dead in Germany. Then Richard stored them in the garage, except for the furs, which they put in the closet in the baby's room.

Wilentz seemed to muse. Then:

"You worked very hard, Mrs Hauptmann, didn't you?"

"I did."

"And until 1932 your husband worked very hard too, didn't he – and saved money?"

"He did."

"And you and your husband were quite happy?"

Anna smiled. The crowd had not expected to see her smile during the cross-examination.

"We were, very."

Wilentz smiled, too. "And the money you saved as the result of your hard work," he said respectfully, "you put it in the bank, didn't you?"

"Yes, I did."

"And then finally your husband started to gamble in the stock market?" he asked, as if a little distressed. "Is that right?"

"Yes."

"And then he lost some money?"

"I guess so," Anna said reluctantly. But she had warmed under his sympathetic interest.

Almost as if he were a neighbor chatting over the back fence in the sun, Wilentz inquired about Anna's domestic arrangements – familiar, congenial territory for her; she prided herself on her exemplary housekeeping. The neighborly Wilentz seemed to be chiefly concerned with the interior economy of a closet, the same broom closet in the kitchen which Anna had described to Reilly. It was a closet to which she went every day? Yes. She went to the closet every day but she never saw a shoe box on the top shelf?

Anna said she didn't know what was on the top shelf.

"You never saw a shoe box there?"

"I didn't."

"From November or December 1933, the month and the day that Mr Fisch was last at your home, until September 1934, you never saw a strange shoe box on the top shelf of that closet?"

"I never had anything to do with the top shelf. I didn't use it for my –" she hesitated "– for myself."

Wilentz was less neighborly. He appeared to be reverting to the man she disliked: the prosecutor. He brought out a photograph of the broom closet and asked Anna if it correctly showed the position of the shelves. Yes, it did. And the apron hanging on the hook there, he continued – she used to take her apron and hang it up there? Yes. She had no trouble hanging it up there?

"Oh, I could hang it up," Anna said.

"Now see if that hook isn't above the top shelf."

She said guardedly, "I see that."

"And you know if you stood a few feet away from it you could see everything on that top shelf?"

"Why should I stay away a few feet and look up there?"

The friendly neighbor had vanished. Wilentz was altogether the prosecutor. He demanded, "Will you please tell me if it is not a fact that if you stepped away from the closet a few feet, if the door was open, you could see everything on the top shelf?"

"I don't think so."

He shook his head. "You did your own cleaning, Mrs Hauptmann?"

"I did."

"And of course you cleaned the closet once in a while?"

Anna said indignantly, "I *do* clean closets!"

"How often did you clean this closet?"

"Almost every week."

"Did you ever clean the shelves?"

"I did."

"Did you ever clean the top shelf?"

"I never use the shelf."

"*Did you ever clean the top shelf?* That is all I want to know! If you didn't, say so."

The good, faithful housekeeper stared at him. Her freckled skin was flushed. At last she pronounced three words that might have been acid in her mouth:

"No, I didn't."

He was relentless. "Never cleaned the top shelf? You cleaned the first shelf, didn't you?"

"I had to clean the first and the second because I had my stuff there."

"So you cleaned the first shelf, and you cleaned the second shelf, but you never cleaned the top shelf?"

"No, I didn't use it!"

Wilentz said quietly, "You don't really mean that, do you, Mrs Hauptmann?"

"No, I didn't use that!" the good housekeeper said again.

But she used to keep something up there, he pursued – what was it she had told Mr Reilly? Shelf trimming? Yes, Anna said, shelf trimming; her niece had given it to her and she couldn't use it in the house and so she put it on the top shelf.

"Of course it wasn't dirty up there, was it? You didn't let dirt and dust accumulate, did you?"

"What should I do up there?" Anna cried. "I put that stuff up there and I left it there!"

He became interested in another closet, right next to the broom closet; from November and December 1933 right up until September 1934 she kept groceries in this second closet? Yes. She had never had to move the groceries out because it was wet in there? No, there was no water in that closet.

Back to the broom closet. Besides the trimming material, hadn't she kept a tin box on the top shelf? Yes, Anna remembered, she had. She kept soap coupons in the tin box? Yes. How often would she put the coupons in the box? Once every three months, four months. Then from November and December 1933 until September 1934 she must have taken down the tin box at least two or three times? Maybe she did, Anna admitted.

"To take that tin box down, you had to reach into that closet?"

"Yes."

"And into that top shelf?"

"Yes."

"You didn't see any shoe box there?"

"No, I didn't."

"You did not?"

"I didn't look!"

Pausing, Wilentz glanced at the jury and then at the good housekeeper's husband, who had testified that he had put Isidor Fisch's shoe box – which later had proved, Hauptmann said, to contain almost $15,000 – on the top shelf. Anna had just said she didn't see it. She had quickly added that she didn't look.

Hadn't she also kept cleaning rags in the closet? Yes. Had she kept them on the first shelf, second shelf or top shelf? Anna said she had kept them on the top shelf.

The prosecutor observed sardonically, "It was a pretty busy closet, a pretty busy shelf, wasn't it? Shelf trimming – old rags – coupons, a tin box. Do you remember anything else that was up there?"

"I don't know."

Wilentz's glance lingered on the jury again, on the housewives who were among its members. His questioning gaze seemed to ask: This conscientious, thrifty housekeeper would never have looked on the top shelf of her cleaning-materials closet? No? But if she *had* looked and *had* seen the strange box her husband has testified was there during all those months, wouldn't she have wondered what it was and what was in it – and opened it?

It now appeared that Wilentz had not intended to ignore altogether the three dates, at least not the first date, the date of the kidnapping. "You remember, of course, Mrs Hauptmann, that you were a witness in the Bronx in the proceedings in which your husband opposed his return to New Jersey?"

No one caught up the words *his return*; certainly not Anna. "Yes, I do," she said.

"I want to read to you a question that was directed to you in the Bronx and your answer," he continued, and quoted, " 'When your husband was arrested recently, Inspector Bruckmann spoke to you about this case, did he not?' Answer: 'Somebody spoke to me.' Question: 'And did you not tell Inspector Bruckmann and others who were there present that you had no recollection at all of what happened March first, 1932, and that it was too far back, that you don't know whether your husband was with you or not?' And didn't you answer, 'I did tell him that'?"

Anna said nothing.

"Did you tell that to Inspector Bruckmann?"

Anna asked him to read it again, please. The prosecutor did so, slowly.

"Did you tell Inspector Bruckmann that?"

"I was asked," she began, and paused, her eyelids blinking. "Someone asked me if I remember that night of the kidnapping and I said I do."

"Yes, ma'am," Wilentz said politely.

"And then someone asked me about the first of March and I said I didn't know if this was the first of March. I couldn't remember that, and I said it was too far back. I couldn't remember the first of March."

"You didn't know at the time that March the first was the night of the kidnaping, is that what you mean?"

"I didn't know it was the first of March."

Wilentz moved in to end it. "And so when they asked you about March first, you said, 'That's too far back; I can't remember whether my husband was with me or not'?"

Her voice was slow and heavy. "When they asked me about the first of March I believe I said that."

The prosecutor turned away, turned back. "Whatever your husband did in the garage with reference to taking those pieces of board and putting money in them and hiding them, that was done without your knowledge, wasn't it?"

"I didn't know anything about that," Anna's slow voice replied.

"And when that money was found, it was a surprise to you, wasn't it?"

"It was."

Wilentz bowed his head a little, as if to thank her. Their chat was finished.

Reilly hurried forward. Yes, Anna told him in answer to his question, she could see no more than the edge of the broom closet's top shelf, from the floor. And she hadn't any doubt at all that Richard had been with her on the night of 1 March 1932.

RICHARD HICKOCK AND PERRY SMITH

(Garden City, Kansas, 1960)

Truman Capote

One Monday morning in November 1959, the American writer Truman Capote read a single-column story buried on page 39 of The New York Times *headed Wealthy Farmer, 3 of Family Slain. "A wealthy wheat farmer, his wife and their two young children were found shot to death today in their home," the story began. "They had been killed by shotgun blasts at close range after being bound and gagged." On this slender pretext, Capote persuaded the* New Yorker *magazine to send him to Kansas. His assignment was to write an article about the effects of the murders on the small community of Holcomb and neighbouring Garden City, where the Clutters – the murdered family – had lived. Taking with him his earliest childhood friend, the writer Harper Lee, and arming her with a gun, he headed for Kansas, "this little gnome in his checkered vest," as one onlooker recalled, "running around asking questions about who'd murdered whom." He didn't have to wait long to find out. Shortly after his arrival, police arrested Perry Smith and Richard Hickock, a pair of jailbirds whose trial opened the following March.*

Capote, openly gay in an era when it jarred, especially in the conservative Midwest, turned up at court wearing a small cap, a large sheepskin coat, and – as one of the detectives later related – "a very long, fairly narrow scarf that trailed plumb to the floor, and then some kind of moccasins." Grumbling that he'd been assigned a seat with the newspaper reporting riff-raff, Capote made notes the best he could, but subsequently bought the court's transcript of record, which gave him the whole story, and persuaded him that it had outgrown a single article and had become a book, his masterpiece In Cold Blood. *Capote became fond of Perry Smith (and saw something of himself reflected in him, being the same height and build) although he disliked Hickock. He was traumatized by the pair's execution. But the success of* In Cold Blood *turned Capote's life around. Novelist and neighbour John Knowles believed that while the book was an overwhelming success both critically and financially, "he lost his grip on himself after that . . . That's when he began to unravel." The trial of Smith and Hickock opened on Tuesday morning, 22 March 1960, Judge Roland Tate presiding. No one doubted the pair's guilt – both had confessed, and there was conclusive physical evidence – so the question was: would it be life or death?*

The aristocracy of Finney County had snubbed the trial. "It doesn't do," announced the wife of one rich rancher, "to seem curious about that sort of thing." Nevertheless, the trial's last session found a fair segment of the local Establishment seated alongside the plainer citizenry. Their presence was a courteous gesture towards Judge Tate and Logan Green, esteemed members of their own order. Also, a large contingent of out-of-town lawyers, many of whom had journeyed great distances, filled several benches; specifically, they were on hand to hear Green's final address to the jury. Green, a suavely tough little septuagenarian, has an imposing reputation among his peers, who admire his stagecraft – a repertoire of actorish gifts that includes a sense of timing acute as a night-club comedian's. An expert criminal lawyer, his usual role is that of defender, but in this instance the state had retained him as a special assistant to Duane West, for it was felt that the young county attorney was too unseasoned to prosecute the case without experienced support.

But like most star turns, Green was the last act on the programme. Judge Tate's level-headed instructions to the jury preceded him, as did the county attorney's summation: "Can there be a single doubt in your minds regarding the guilt of these defendants? No! Regardless of who pulled the trigger on Richard Eugene Hickock's shotgun, both men are equally guilty. There is only one way to assure that these men will never again roam the towns and cities of this land. We request the maximum penalty – death. This request is made not in vengeance, but in all humbleness . . ."

Then the pleas of the defence attorneys had to be heard. Fleming's speech, described by one journalist as "soft-sell", amounted to a mild churchly sermon: "Man is not an animal. He has a body, and he has a soul that lives for ever. I don't believe man has the right to destroy that house, a temple, in which the soul dwells . . ." Harrison Smith, though he too appealed to the jurors' presumed Christianity, took as his main theme the evils of capital punishment: "It is a relic of human barbarism. The law tells us that the taking of human life is wrong, then goes ahead and sets the example. Which is almost as wicked as the crime it punished. The state has no right to inflict it. It isn't effective. It doesn't deter crime, but merely cheapens human life and gives rise to more murders. All we ask is mercy. Surely life imprisonment is small mercy to ask . . ." Not everyone was attentive; one juror, as though poisoned by the numerous spring-fever yawns weighting the air, sat with drugged eyes and jaws so utterly ajar bees could have buzzed in and out.

Green woke them up. "Gentlemen," he said, speaking without notes, "you have just heard two energetic pleas for mercy in behalf of the defendants. It seems to me fortunate that these admirable attorneys, Mr Fleming and Mr Smith, were not at the Clutter house that fateful night – very fortunate for them that they were not present to plead mercy for the doomed family. Because had they been there – well, come next morning we would have had more than four corpses to count."

As a boy in his native Kentucky, Green was called Pinky, a nickname he owed to his freckled colouring; now, as he strutted before the jury, the stress of his assignment warmed his face and splotched it with patches of pink. "I have no intention of engaging in theological debate. But I anticipated that defence counsel would use the Holy Bible as an argument against the death penalty. You have heard the Bible quoted. But *I* can read, too." He slapped open a copy of the Old Testament. "And here are a few things the Good Book has to say on the subject. In Exodus Twenty, Verse Thirteen,

we have one of the Ten Commandments: 'Thou shalt not kill.'
This refers to *unlawful* killing. Of course it does, because in the
next chapter, Verse Twelve, the penalty for disobedience of that
Commandment reads: 'He that smiteth a man, so that he die, shall
be surely put to death.' Now, Mr Fleming would have you believe
that all this was changed by the coming of Christ. Not so. For
Christ says, 'Think not that I am come to destroy the law, or the
prophets: I am not come to destroy, but to fulfil.' And finally –"
Green fumbled, and seemed to accidentally shut the Bible, whereupon the visiting legal dignitaries grinned and nudged each other,
for this was a venerable courtroom ploy – the lawyer who while
reading from the Scriptures pretends to lose his place, and then
remarks, as Green now did, "Never mind. I think I can quote from
memory. Genesis Nine, Verse Six: 'Whoso sheddeth man's blood,
by man shall his blood be shed.'

"But," Green went on, "I see nothing to be gained by arguing
the Bible. Our state provides that the punishment for murder in
the first degree shall be imprisonment for life or death by
hanging. That is the law. You, gentlemen, are here to enforce
it. And if ever there was a case in which the maximum penalty
was justified, this is it. These were strange, ferocious murders.
Four of your fellow citizens were slaughtered like hogs in a pen.
And for what reason? Not out of vengeance or hatred. But for
money. *Money*. It was the cold and calculated weighing of so
many ounces of silver against so many ounces of blood. And how
cheaply those lives were bought! For forty dollars' worth of loot!
Ten dollars a life!" He whirled, and pointed a finger that moved
back and forth between Hickock and Smith. "They went armed
with a shotgun and a dagger. They went to rob and kill –" His
voice trembled, toppled, disappeared, as though strangled by the
intensity of his own loathing for the debonair, gum-chewing
defendants. Turning again to the jury, he hoarsely asked, "What
are you going to do? What are you going to do with these men
that bind a man hand and foot and cut his throat and blow out
his brains? Give them the *minimum* penalty? Yes, and that's only
one of four counts. What about Kenyon Clutter, a young boy
with his whole life before him, tied helplessly in sight of his
father's death struggle. Or young Nancy Clutter, hearing the
gunshots and knowing her time was next. Nancy, begging for her
life: 'Don't. Oh, please don't. Please. Please.' What agony! What
unspeakable torture! And there remains the mother, bound and

gagged and having to listen as her husband, her beloved children died one by one. Listen until at last the killers, these defendants before you, entered her room, focused a flashlight in her eyes, and let the blast of a shotgun end the existence of an entire household."

Pausing, Green gingerly touched a boil on the back of his neck, a mature inflammation that seemed, like its angry wearer, about to burst. "So, gentlemen, what are you going to do? Give them the minimum? Send them back to the penitentiary, and take the chance of their escaping or being paroled? The next time they go slaughtering it may be *your* family. I say to you," he solemnly said, staring at the panel in a manner that encompassed and challenged them all, "some of our enormous crimes only happen because once upon a time a pack of chicken-hearted jurors refused to do their duty. Now, gentlemen, I leave it to you and your consciences."

He sat down. West whispered to him, "That was masterly, sir."

But a few of Green's auditors were less enthusiastic; and after the jury retired to discuss the verdict, one of them, a young reporter from Oklahoma, exchanged sharp words with another newsman, Richard Parr of the Kansas City *Star*. To the Oklahoman, Green's address had seemed "rabble-rousing, brutal!"

"He was just telling the truth," Parr said. "The truth can be brutal. To coin a phrase."

"But he didn't have to hit that hard. It's unfair."

"What's unfair?"

"The whole trial. These guys don't stand a chance."

"Fat chance they gave Nancy Clutter."

"Perry Smith. My God. He's had such a rotten life –"

Parr said, "Many a man can match sob stories with that little bastard. Me included. Maybe I drink too much, but I sure as hell never killed four people in cold blood."

"Yeah, and how about hanging the bastard? That's pretty goddam cold-blooded too."

The Reverend Post, overhearing the conversation, joined in. "Well," he said, passing around a snapshot reproduction of Perry Smith's portrait of Jesus, "any man who could paint this picture can't be one hundred per cent bad. All the same it's hard to know what to do. Capital punishment is no answer: it doesn't give the sinner time enough to come to God. Sometimes I despair." A jovial fellow with gold-filled teeth and silvery widow's peak, he jovially repeated, "Sometimes I despair. Sometimes I think old Doc Savage had the right idea." The Doc Savage to whom he referred was a fictional hero popular among adolescent readers of pulp magazines a generation ago. "If you boys remember, Doc Savage was a kind of superman. He'd made himself proficient in every field – medicine, science, philosophy, art. There wasn't much old Doc didn't know or couldn't do. One of his projects was, he decided to rid the world of criminals. First he bought a big island out in the ocean. Then he and his assistants – he had an army of trained assistants – kidnapped all the world's criminals and brought them to the island. And Doc Savage operated on their brains. He removed the part that holds wicked thoughts. And when they recovered they were all decent citizens. They *couldn't* commit crimes because that part of their brain was out. Now it strikes me that surgery of this nature might really be the answer to –"

A bell, the signal that the jury was returning, interrupted him. The jury's deliberations had lasted forty minutes. Many spectators, anticipating a swift decision, had never left their seats. Judge Tate, however, had to be fetched from his farm, where he had gone to feed his horses. A hurriedly donned black robe billowed about him when at last he arrived, but it was with impressive sedateness and dignity that he asked, "Gentlemen of the jury, have you reached your verdicts?" Their foreman replied: "We have, Your Honour." The court bailiff carried the sealed verdicts to the bench.

Train whistles, the fanfare of an approaching Santa Fe express, penetrated the courtroom. Tate's bass voice interlaced with the locomotive's cries as he read: " 'Count One. We the jury find the defendant, Richard Eugene Hickock, guilty of murder in the first degree, and the punishment is death.' " Then, as though interested in their reaction, he looked down upon the prisoners, who stood before him handcuffed to guards; they stared back impassively until he resumed and read the seven counts that followed: three more convictions for Hickock, and four for Smith.

"– and the punishment is death"; each time he came to the sentence, Tate enunciated it with a dark-toned hollowness that seemed to echo the train's mournful, now fading call. Then he dismissed the jury ("You have performed a courageous service"),

and the condemned men were led away. At the door, Smith said to
Hickock, "No chicken-hearted jurors, they!" They both laughed
loudly, and a cameraman photographed them. The picture appeared in a Kansas paper above a caption entitled: "The Last
Laugh?"

*Hickock and Smith were granted a stay of execution while their
request for a new trial was considered and refused; finally, following
five years of appeal after appeal, they were hanged on 14 April 1965,
as Capote looked on.*

THE HOSEIN BROTHERS

(Old Bailey, 1970)

William Cooper

The first kidnapping trial in modern British history, described by a master writer. Covering the trial of Arthur and Nizamodeen Hosein for the murder of Mrs Muriel McKay, the novelist William Cooper (1910–2002) unfolded "a story fit for Dostoevsky." He found a riveting set of elements. "A kidnapping where the wrong person was taken. A ransom demand of a million pounds – who on earth could find that? And a prosecution for murder with no trace of the body. Fantasy – fantasy tethered to reality only by the hideous actuality of the McKay family's anguish . . ." The whole appalling affair began with a bungle. Muriel McKay was seized in mistake for Mrs Rupert Murdoch, wife of the then chairman of the News of the World *newspaper group, of which Mrs McKay's husband, Alick McKay, was deputy chairman. Her body was never found, although – as the Hoseins' testimony suggests – the possibility that it was fed to the animals at Rook's Farm was never far from the surface. William Cooper (real name Harry Huff) attended the Hosein brothers' trial every day. He was a career civil servant as well as a key figure in the development of post-war English writing. Cooper's fifth novel,* Scenes from Provincial Life *(1950) influenced Kingsley Amis, John Wain, John Braine and the other so-called Angry Young Men. His staccato account of the Hoseins' trial in 1970 appeared the following year.*

"Put up Arthur Hosein and Nizamodeen Hosein!" So runs the formula with which the ritual of an English trial begins. At those words, uttered by the Clerk of the Court, the accused make their first, fateful appearance in the dock. The date is 14 September 1970; the place, the Old Bailey.

They stand, awaiting the beginning of a process in which they are presumed innocent until such time as the Crown may have proved beyond all reasonable doubt to a jury of twelve men and women drawn from the common public that they are guilty.

So it is with the trial of the Hosein brothers, two dark-skinned men from Trinidad, well-dressed, speaking English perfectly well (accent apart), brought to trial in Court One, the "star" court of the Old Bailey.

The Press are fitted mainly into benches on either side of the dock – it is unobtrusively in the far corner of one of these benches that Mr McKay and his son frequently sit, listening, unable to tear themselves away from it all, no matter how unbearable, because they want to know what, what became of Mrs McKay.

The brothers Hosein look so different from each other that one would not guess at first sight that they are brothers. They come from a family of tailors at some remove from the lower classes. Their father is in court, a thin, spare, reflective-looking man, wearing a suit that looks too big for him. He is said to be very "holy".

The Clerk of the Court reads the charges and asks the brothers if they plead Guilty or Not Guilty. Arthur Hosein: "Not guilty." Nizamodeen Hosein (softly): "Not guilty, sir."

Arthur is the smaller, plumpish, with the beginnings of an embonpoint that curves over his waistbelt, immaculately suited according to his lights – after all, he is a tailor's cutter by profession. He has handsome large black eyes with dark circles round them, and full cheeks, beautiful bushy black wavy hair, well cut, and a black moustache.

The younger brother Hosein does not watch the jury being called: he quietly, motionlessly, looks straight ahead. He is taller and more athletic in physique, yet his features are softish, amorphous, distinctly Chinesey. He wears spectacles, and has a wad of dark hair combed across his forehead.

The jury are sworn in. With a nod, the Judge tells the accused men to sit down, and on the front bench of counsel the Attorney-General, Sir Peter Rawlinson, prepares to rise and open the case for the prosecution.

This is the first trial in modern British legal history for kidnapping for ransom. (Our nearest example would appear to be a case in Australia, R.*v.*Bradley, in 1960.) Furthermore, it is an offence under Common Law here, but not statutory – as it is, for example, in France and the USA – which means that there is no prescribed punishment laid down.

The front bench of leading counsel shows the newspapers to have been wrong. They gave correctly Mr Barry Hudson, QC, and Mr Hubert Dunn for Arthur Hosein; but in giving only Mr Leonard Woodley for Nizamodeen, they omitted Mr Douglas Draycott, QC. Each brother has a leading counsel. So each brother has a separate defence.

"On the evening of 29 December, last year," the Attorney-General begins, "Mrs McKay disappeared from her home at 20 Arthur Road, Wimbledon. She has never been seen again." It is a dramatic opening; but although his manner is admirably polished, it is not in the least showy or theatrical.

The Crown alleges: "This was a brutal and ruthless scheme to kidnap a wife, and by menaces to extort from her husband a vast sum of money."

(A million pounds – we know that already).

The Attorney-General speaks of days and weeks in which Mr McKay was subjected to a systematic series of threats by telephone and by letter, threats to execute his wife, threats to kill her. He leans forward a little towards the jury as he delivers straightaway what sounds as if it is going to be the essence of the Crown case for alleging murder:

"We may infer that those who threatened to kill did kill."

The Attorney-General then launches the statement that the real intention of the kidnappers was to take another woman! She was Mrs Rupert Murdoch, wife of the chairman of The News Of The World group of newspapers. Mrs McKay's husband, Mr Alick McKay, is deputy chairman.

Both Mr McKay and Mr Murdoch are Australian, and in the middle of December Mr Murdoch and his wife went to Australia for a visit. In his absence, Mr McKay was acting chairman, and as such had use of the chairman's Rolls-Royce, travelling to and fro in it between 20 Arthur Road and the newspaper offices. The kidnappers, tracing the car, thought they were going to take the wife of the chairman. Arthur Hosein, the Attorney-General now tells the jury, had spoken to neighbours, telling them of his desire to become a millionaire.

The story begins, the Attorney-General says, on 19 December – the date on which, unknown to the brothers, Mr and Mrs Rupert Murdoch left for Australia – when Mr McKay began to use the Rolls-Royce.

So we come to 29 December, the day of Mrs McKay's disappearance for ever. Mr McKay left for the office in the Rolls; Mrs McKay went in her own car to fetch the daily help, went shopping, visited her dentist, and then, at 5 p.m., drove the daily help home. The daily help was the last person ever to see Mrs McKay alive – or dead. At that time Mrs McKay was wearing a green jersey suit, a black-and-white check topcoat, and cream-coloured leather driving shoes.

At 7.45 p.m. Mr McKay came home, got no answer to his ring on the doorbell, found the outer door not on the chain, opened the inner door, and saw a desolating sight . . . Furniture disarranged; the telephone off the hook, the disc giving the number (ex-directory) having been removed; his wife's open handbag with its contents scattered; and some alien objects . . . The Attorney-General suggests their purpose:

A billhook, such as might have been used for intimidating;

A strip of 2½ in. adhesive tape, for gagging;

Some baling twine, for trussing . . .

Mrs McKay's jewellery was gone, together with a reversible fawn and black topcoat.

Mr McKay seized the billhook to arm himself, rushed through the house – Mrs McKay's dachshund was sitting by the fire, and the television was on – and through the outbuildings. His wife was gone. In minutes the Wimbledon police arrived and a search was begun with dogs.

One of Mr McKay's two married daughters, Diane Dyer, joined him at 11.15 p.m. with her husband David. Shortly afterwards, his other daughter, Jennifer Burgess, arrived with her husband Ian.

"At 1.15 in the morning of 30 December, five hours later, the first approach from the kidnappers reached the house."

The call was from a public box at Epping – and it was overheard by the operator!

"Tell Mr McKay it is the M3, the Mafia."

A detective, listening on an extension, the Attorney-General says, took the conversation down.

"This is the Mafia Group 3. We are from America. Mafia M3. We have your wife." And then: "You will need £1,000,000 by

Wednesday." Today was Tuesday. "We have your wife. You will need £1,000,000 to get her back. You had better get it. You have friends. Get it from them. Have £1,000,000 by Wednesday night or we will kill her."

There was a second telephone call from M3 on the 30th; and that evening Mrs Diane Dyer was interviewed on BBC television about her mother's disappearance.

On 31 December, there arrived at Arthur Road a letter, a heart-rending appeal in handwriting identified without doubt as Mrs McKay's: "Alick darling, I am blindfolded and cold. Please do something and get me home. Please co-operate or I cannot keep going. I think of you all constantly and have kept calm so far. What have I done to deserve this treatment?"

The letter had been posted in Tottenham, London N.17; and the sheet of paper bears two fingerprints – of, the Crown says, Arthur Hosein.

On 1 January, Mr McKay's son, Ian, arrived at Arthur Road from Australia. That evening there was the next call, ending at 7.45 p.m., in which the caller asked to speak to Diane – he took to using the family's Christian names, it seems, without the least inhibition.

The Attorney-General mentions several letters from Mrs McKay received at later dates; but, he suggests, they could have been written earlier and posted by degrees. During that period, he says, proofs repeatedly demanded by the family that Mrs McKay was alive were refused.

Turning to the situation at Rook's Farm, Stocking Pelham (about twenty miles north of the northern edge of London), where the Hoseins lived, the Attorney-General notes that Arthur Hosein's wife had taken the children on a visit to her relations in Germany on 13 December and did not return until 3 January. But on 31 December, only 48 hours after the kidnapping, a girl-friend of Nizam's came to stay overnight at the farm: in the Attorney-General's submission, Mrs McKay must even then already have been dead.

On 19 January came a call ending at 3 p.m. The Attorney-General deliberately reads extracts from the transcript in a moderate tone. It makes unbearable hearing, in the anguish of Mr McKay and the boasting of the blackmailer. He demands the first half, £500,000. Mr McKay cries: "Look, bring a gun here and shoot me rather than ask unreasonable situations!" (In his agonising emotion, grammar fails him.) Mr McKay suggests a reasonable sum – he can raise £20,000. "No use. Accept or reject. Half a million."

The Attorney-General goes on to the next call, on 21 January, taken by Ian McKay, who says his father is now ill. The first discussions of a rendezvous take place. The Attorney-General says Ian had a police officer beside him, helping to suggest probing questions and to keep M3 on the line.

Ian asks what his mother says that proves that she is alive, but all he gets is M3's ranting.

A few minutes later, another call, this time about the date of the rendezvous. Ian had said his father was too ill to come – the police were determined, in case an international gang was at work, to protect Mr McKay now. The date is to be 1 February. "We want a million, but the first delivery has got to be half a million!"

The first ransom note arrived on 22 January. It warned the family not to inform the police and reiterated the demand for £1,000,000. It then gave Mr McKay his instructions – on 1 February to place £½ million in a black suitcase, drive his wife's car along the North Circular Road to the A10 Cambridge road, where he would see a public telephone-box: to enter it and wait for a call at 10 p.m. The black suitcase is to be locked, as it will be collected by a stranger who is paid to do the job; if he is caught, he will not be able to help the police.

At 10.30 a.m. on 23 January, the telephone calls to Arthur Road resumed with growing agitation. On the McKay family side they were handled by Ian, demanding proof that his mother was still alive; M3 sounding pressed and relapsing into menaces. "We won't be needing the money and you won't be seeing your mum." Ian says they have a quarter of a million – but they need proof, another letter.

Fifteen minutes later, he is back on the line. Mrs McKay is saying, he says to Ian, "Why have they forsaken me?" On 26 January, a letter addressed to Mr McKay and posted in London, N.22, was received at 20 Arthur Road. It contained two letters written by Mrs McKay.

"Alick darling – If I could only be home. I can't believe this thing has happened to me. Tonight I thought I see you. But it seems hopeless. You betrayed me by going to Police, not co-operating with the M3 gang. Love Muriel."

The other: "Darling Alick – You don't seem to be helping me. Again I beg of you to co-operate with the M3 gang. You do understand that when the . . ." There is something cut from the letter.

At 9 p.m. on 1 February, the Rolls leaves Arthur Road, driven by Detective-Inspector John Minors dressed as the chauffeur and with Detective-Sergeant Street disguised as Ian McKay. In the car they have a black suitcase containing bundles of false banknotes, each bundle has a genuine banknote on the top – half a million pounds!

The Rolls drives to the telephone box on the A10. "Ian" duly receives the M3 call, which directs him to another box about forty minutes' drive down the Cambridge road. In the second box, a call comes through quite soon. "Look on the floor! You'll see a cigarette packet with your instructions."

They are to go to a place called Dane End – about fifteen miles further – in High Cross, Hertfordshire. There, at the road corner, they will see two paper flowers stuck in the bank as markers for the depositing of the suitcase.

The suitcase is deposited and the Rolls drives back to the first telephone box, following M3's instructions, to hear from Mrs McKay . . .

Further down the road from Dane End there is a café where police (presumably working on information steadily radioed from the Rolls) are watching. At 2.30 a.m. the suitcase is still there, and Mr Minors is instructed to collect it, together with the paper flowers.

In the meantime, a dark-coloured Volvo saloon has passed the café, where two police officers are watching from a taxi. In the Volvo are a driver and a passenger with bushy hair. The rear nearside light of the car is observed not to be working. The Hoseins' car, the Attorney-General reminds us, is a Volvo, and when it was examined by detectives ten days later, the nearside rear light was found not to be working.

The Attorney-General returns to 3 February. There were two calls from M3 to Ian McKay. In the first, M3 says he is going to a meeting of the bosses, "the semi-intellectuals", to settle the time at which "your Mum" should be executed. As for the suitcase: "You know why I didn't even touch it. My boss, the Head Boy, was there. All The Boys were there. We saw cars parked all round there. Did you know they were all police?"

Two hours later came the second call. Another attempt to collect the ransom is on the tapes. "The Boys" insist on delivery being made by Mr McKay and Diane. M3 proposes they should bring the money this time in two briefcases. They must go in the Rolls, driven by Mr McKay, first to a telephone kiosk in Church Street, Tottenham, at 4 p.m.

So, on February 6, Detective-Inspector Minors, made up as Mr McKay, and a woman police officer disguised as Diane set off in the Rolls. At the first kiosk "Mr McKay" is directed to a second kiosk at Bethnal Green – M3 demands to speak to "Diane" to make sure she is there. They are told to take the Tube to Epping, then go to a specified telephone kiosk there. They drive to Theydon Bois, park the Rolls and get in the Tube – a member of the Flying Squad is in the same compartment.

At Epping they are told by M3 to take a taxi to Bishop's Stortford, stopping at Gates Garage, where in the used-car lot they will see a Minivan, UMH 587F. They are to drop the suitcases beside it.

Five minutes after the two suitcases have been deposited, the watching police officers see a dark blue Volvo, XGO 994G, being driven slowly past the used-car lot; neither of the nearside obligatory lights is working. The driver is alone. He looks out and drives slowly on. The Attorney-General says he has subsequently been identified as Nizam.

At 10.47 p.m. the Volvo comes back, but now with a man in the passenger seat – a man who has been subsequently identified, according to the prosecution, as Arthur Hosein.

At 11 p.m. two well-meaning members of the public drive by. They see the apparently abandoned suitcases, and stop; one gets out to stand guard while the other telephones the local police, who immediately come and take the suitcases away!

On 7 February, having traced the owners of the Volvo, a party of police, led by Detective Chief Superintendent Wilfred Smith, who has been in charge of the investigation with Detective-Inspector Minors as his second-in command, went to Rook's Farm with a search warrant for stolen jewellery, Mrs McKay's jewellery.

During the search which followed, the police discovered:

An empty Elastoplast tin of the size to hold 2½ in. tape;

Six paper flowers in various places – home-made, like those used as markers;

An empty tipped-cigarette packet.

"On further search, six days later," the Attorney-General adds with devastating effect, "the police found a pair of trousers belonging to Nizam, in the left-hand pocket of which was a piece of paper giving the number of the Minivan UMH 587F at Gates Garage used-car lot." In the search of Arthur's workroom, Chief Superintendent Smith took possession of two pairs of tailor's shears; in the kitchen he found a billhook.

The brothers were taken in separate police cars to Kingston Police Station. On the way, Arthur pointed out Sleepy Hollow Farm, home of a farmer-friend who, he says, lent the billhook to chop up a calf that had died.

But there are two billhooks. The other one is the one left at 20 Arthur Road, and it has been traced, the Crown alleges, to Arthur's home.

The Attorney-General reports interrogations.

Nizam gives handwriting specimens. He is shown the billhook from Arthur Road, and starts to shake, closes his eyes; the baling twine – more shaking of the head; then the sticking plaster – he suddenly cries: "Let me die!"

On the night of 10 February there is a final confrontation between Arthur and Chief Superintendent Smith, in which Arthur furiously says: "If you've got anything on me, then book me!" A little later, the brothers Hosein are formally charged with the murder of Mrs McKay and with demanding a million pounds by menaces from Mr McKay.

The first witness to be called is Mr Alick McKay.

The Attorney-General examines him, bringing out more detail of the familiar story. His return home, on the evening of 20 December. Photographs of the scene in the hall, as he saw it, are passed round to the jury. The process of identifying the exhibits is begun concurrently with eliciting the story.

There is a moment at which the oppression is lifted from Mr McKay, as he identifies his wife's handbag. "It has a special catch." As he finds it and springs it open, he looks up with a triumphant smile, as if taken out of himself, perhaps taken back to the time when his wife first showed it to him. He identifies the baling twine, the billhook – he can hardly look at it in his hands, though he watches it being passed round the jury.

Mr McKay goes on with his story. The fire built up, the dog sleeping in front of it. Then his rush through the house: the missing jewellery, valued for insurance at £600. Mrs McKay had lost most of her jewellery in a burglary the previous September. That was why she was nervous and kept the chain on the front door always.

He describes calling the police, the arrival of his two daughters and their husbands, friends coming round to the house as the news spread . . . The first call, at 1.15 a.m., from M3.

More telephone-calls and the question of identifying the kind of voice, or voices. "Sometimes softer and deeper," says Mr. McKay, "with a stronger American accent." The conclusion: that they were West Indian.

And so on to the final questions. "Was there a great deal of publicity?" And, "All your children were very close to their mother?" Mr McKay nods. The Attorney-General sits down.

Mr Hudson, for Arthur Hosein, cross-examines.

We now hear of hoaxes, other police traps and all the rest of it, giving intimations of mountainous detail behind the scenes. Mr Hudson sits down. And solitarily, almost unceremoniously, Mr McKay leaves the witness-box.

The morning of 16 September, and the third day of the trial begins with the other members of the McKay family: the two daughters, Diane and Jennifer, with their respective husbands, David Dyer and Ian Burgess: and the son, Ian, who flew in from Australia on 31 January.

The young women have the well-dressed, affluent look one would expect. Their father has an Australian accent: they have not. Their husbands are apparently English. So far as physical resemblance goes, it is only strong between father and son – and there it is very strong. They both have the same heavy build, the same rather pale complexion and small light eyes, the same thinning dark hair.

David Dyer goes into the witness-box first. He took M3's first call: like Mr McKay, he has heard the tapes so often since that he has to pause and think which is which. Mr Hudson cross-examines him about whether he thinks call No.2 and call No. 3 from M3 were made by different voices from that of the call he took. "Similar," he says.

Diane Dyer, slender and nervous, with her hair drawn back into a high bunch of curls, has to identify her mother's clothes, the letters, the pieces of material. But the essential part of her evidence is about when she spoke on television, as well as being seen.

(It seems now that both prosecution and defence must believe that the last moment at which they can be certain Mrs McKay was still alive was shortly after her daughter spoke on TV.)

Ian McKay makes a brief appearance, alert and businesslike – he knows the telephone calls by their numbers and does not need to refer to the transcripts.

Jennifer Burgess, sun-tanned and subdued-looking under a big white felt safari hat, took one of M3's telephone calls. "I gave my sister's name because he usually spoke to her." Another vista into the repulsive Christian-name intimacy forced by the blackmailers on the family. "I wanted to negotiate as quickly as possible."

More prosecution witnesses followed. Among them, Detective Chief Superintendent Harvey, who led the police expedition to Rook's Farm at 1.45 p.m. on 7 February.

We get a description of the sitting-room at Rook's Farm – photographs are passed round the jury. A biggish room with beams across the ceiling, and a style of furnishing appropriate to what would be called a "lounge" – an open fireplace, a curved bar with a couple of stools, some sofas, a radiogram, a television set. Incidentally, there is nothing either cheap-looking or inappropriate looking to contemporary dormitory-belt society about Rook's Farm. It is pretty from the outside, eighteenth century, painted white.

Mr Hudson cross-examines about the extensive searches of Rook's Farm in February and March, also others in June, July, and as recently as 10 August. Police officers galore, police dogs galore.

Mr Draycott, for Nizam, rises. 'Is it right to say Rook's Farm has been searched as scrupulously as it is possible to search anything?" – "Yes."

"Every skill has been employed?" – "Yes."

"And there is no trace of Mrs McKay having been on that farm?" "No trace whatsoever."

No trace whatsoever.

The Attorney-General re-examines about the sheds, the dark outhouses with bales of straw, the calves and the pigs; the surface of the passage – hard – to where the rubbish was dumped by a stream.

There is an intermission in police evidence while Mrs McKay's doctor testifies to her having been in good health, cheerful, stable and strong-minded.

The police evidence now comes to the two chief men in the case,

Detective Chief Superintendent Smith, who led the whole investigation, and Detective-Inspector Minors, who assisted him – also chauffeuring the Rolls in the first ransom-delivering expedition and disguising himself as Mr Alick McKay in the second. It is mainly due to these two men that the brothers Hosein are now in the dock.

Detective-Inspector Minors comes first. He is a big chap, full cheeked, very fresh-complexioned and blue-eyed, with smooth darkish hair and a moustache. The Attorney-General takes him through what is now the familiar story.

We come to 7 February at Rook's Farm, the search and the findings. Then the drive to Kingston Police Station, Arthur continually discoursing on his universal popularity, his intention of standing for the local council, the influence "in high places" of his wealthy father. And at the police station the first questions about 29 December and Wimbledon.

The following day, Mr Minors's examination-in-chief continues. We hear again about the continuing interrogations at Kingston Police Station of Arthur and Nizam alternately about the events of 6 February.

Nizam refused, like Arthur, to sign his statements; and, furthermore, refused to speak into the telephone for recording tests. In the evening Arthur and Nizam were told they were going to be taken to Wimbledon Police Station, where they would be charged. Arthur: "I have nothing to say, Mr Smith. You have your job to do." Nizam made no reply at all.

Then there were the extraordinary scenes, we hear, resulting from Nizam's asking to see Mr Smith and Mr Minors without his legal representatives present.

At the second such meeting came Nizam's extraordinary statement: "I could get out of ninety per cent of this trouble if I put my cards on the table."

Mr Smith: "What do you want to tell us?" After a silence, Nizam replied: "I want to think . . . I'll leave it till another day."

Mr Hudson rises and points out that the brothers were held in custody from Saturday, 7 February, to Tuesday, 10 February, "assisting the police" without being charged with anything.

Mr Hudson gets Mr Minors's assent to Arthur's complete denial of all knowledge of the crime, and comes to the last of his questions raised by what Arthur may say in the witness-box – that Mr Smith slapped him across the face. Mr Minors: "No, sir. That's news to me."

Now Mr Draycott slides smoothly and sweetly into a quite different line. "I have no quarrel with your evidence," he says: "I want you to assist me about Nizam. At Wimbledon Police Station, when he was seen on 12 June, he was on the brink of telling you something. He wanted to, but something held him back." Mr Minors: "We felt it did."

Mr Draycott: "Would you agree with me that, having seen these two brothers over a long period, it is abundantly clear, abundantly plain, that Nizam's relationship with his brother is unusual, in that it is based not on brotherly affection but on fear?"

Mr Minors: "That would appear to be the case."

Mr Draycott, still with most amicable courtesy – why should they quarrel? – says: "Nizam's fingerprints have been taken. You agree with me, do you not, that there is no evidence of fingerprints to connect Nizamodeen Hosein with Mrs McKay's home at Arthur Road, Wimbledon?" He eyes the jury sagely. Mr Minors: "No, sir."

Detective Chief Superintendent Smith is called. He is shortish and very strongly built. The Attorney-General examines him on substantially the same points as he did Mr Minors, since the two men worked together all the time. Mr Hudson, addressing Mr Smith as the senior officer in charge of the case, establishes that Arthur Hosein has no previous convictions for violence or dishonesty. He has convictions for speeding offences and was court-martialled for desertion in 1960.

Mr Hudson points out that after the charges were made, there were seventeen remands until the hearings began at Wimbledon on 8 June. During that time there were further searches; if there was anything to be found, there was a better chance if the brothers were not in possession.

Mr Hudson goes through some of the details of the investigation for Mr Smith's agreement. The Aga heater was dismantled. An architect and a builder were consulted about possible secret compartments. Ponds were drained by the fire brigade. The hedges and ditches in surrounding fields were searched, Sleepy Hollow . . .

"Also Epping Forest," says Mr Smith wryly.

Finally: "I now put this to you, personally. I suggest that during some parts of the investigation at Kingston Police Station, you punched Arthur Hosein and slapped him across the face."

"That is not true."

Later, Mrs Liley Mohammed, Nizam's girl-friend, is called. We know already from the Attorney-General that she spent the night of 31 December at Rook's Farm. She is a hospital nurse, a bit short, dressed in a brown-and-white striped suit. She looks frightened. Her face is oval, her hair drawn back from it into a high double bunch of curls like a more African version of Mrs Diane Dyer's.

The Attorney-General examines. Mrs Mohammed – she soon becomes known as Liley – says she first spent the night at Rook's Farm on 26 December.

Liley visited the farm, just for the day, in the early part of January, and then about a week later. Mrs Hosein and the children were there. Liley is now shown a box of coloured tissues with some paper clips. "It belongs to me."

The Attorney-General asks about a visit when she took some paper flowers she had made and gave them to Nizam.

Mr Hudson then cross-examines, beginning with her visit on Boxing Day, when at first she did not want to go.

While she was at the farm she saw only Nizam and Arthur; she did not leave the farm. Mr Hudson: "You told us about several subsequent visits to the farm. Did you get the impression on any of those visits that there was anything there to hide?" – "No."

Mr Hudson pauses. "At the farm, did you sometimes go out with Nizam while he was looking after the animals?" – "Yes." – "You helped him to skin the calf?" – "Yes."

Then Mr Draycott gets a surprising revelation. Referring to Boxing Night, he says: "I believe there was some trouble between Arthur and Nizam that night. In the course of that trouble, did Nizam get very frightened?" – "He did." – "And run out?" – "Yes." – "And when he came back, did he say he'd made a complaint to the police?" – "He did."

Mr Draycott pauses. "Less than seventy-two hours before they were allegedly going to kidnap Mrs McKay, Nizam called in the police!"

The Attorney-General re-examines.

"Did you know about the workshop?" he asks. Liley did not – not until Mrs Hosein came back.

"What was the calf cut up with?" – "A long knife. It looked like a chopper."

"I don't suppose you went to the shed where the dogs were kept?" – "No, I did not."

The law seems to take a long time, and the impression is not mitigated by the order in which witnesses are called. As we begin the last day of witnesses for the prosecution (21 September), it is difficult to see what order there has been. No doubt they were in the first place put down in an order that matched the development of the prosecution case. But that, for one reason or another – we have been told from time to time that a witness was not available – is not the order in which they turned up.

However, there has been a weekend in which to freshen up.

What is the defence going to be? What on earth *can* it be?

The Attorney-General announces the end of the Crown case. But all is not finished. Mr Hudson has something more to say. He stands up and tells His Lordship that he wants to make a submission in the absence of the jury.

The jury are sent out. Then Mr Hudson, with Mr. Draycott associated with him, makes a submission:

That on Count 1, murder, in the circumstances of the evidence before the jury, the case should not proceed further.

Mr Hudson argues that what became of Mrs McKay is, on the evidence, the basis not for rational hypothesis but only for speculation.

"There is a prima-facie case, I agree, that she is dead. But I submit there is not one scintilla of evidence that she was at Rook's Farm or met her death at Rook's Farm."

Mr Draycott, who has been whispering to his junior, now joins in, to argue that Mrs McKay could not have been at Rook's Farm – meanwhile, Arthur and Nizam, according to the evidence of Liley, *were* for most of the time at Rook's Farm.

The Judge listens. He looks at them. There is no other rational hypothesis, he tells them, than that those who abducted Mrs McKay are responsible for the fact that she is not on this earth. There *is* cause for the jury to consider Count 1.

It is the morning of 23 September.

"Members of the jury, there is a great deal more evidence in this case than you have already heard."

So begins Mr Hudson in the defence of Arthur Hosein. He leans a little forward towards the jury: "Arthur Hosein's defence," he says, "is that he had nothing to do with this dreadful crime at all!"

Arthur Hosein denies his guilt. It is not enough to say that. In support of his protestation of innocence, he will go into the witness-box, though he is not compelled to.

We all look at the dock, where a warder is opening the side door. Arthur Hosein goes down the steps, walks past the long table in the well of the court, and ascends the steps into the witness-box. He is smaller than I thought, seeing him on high in the dock. And for the occasion he has selected a slightly peculiar garb – at first sight it looks as if he is in a dinner-suit. It is black, single-breasted, with a U-shaped waistcoat that displays a bulging white expanse of chest under a black bow-tie. But the collar and cuffs of the white shirt are black with white polka-dots. "Selected" is the correct word: he has appeared in a different suit every day, and is reported to own fifty suits. (How does he keep *that* up, as well as Rook's Farm, the Volvo, and all the rest?). We have already heard of his boastfulness; his appearance makes one suspect that he is vain.

In the witness-box he stands a moment under the shadow of the light-oak canopy and against the dreary background of light oak, his hand to his face, touching his moustache. The black and white collar makes it difficult to see which is his neck and which is his shirt. He gives his profession:

"Fashion designer, cutter, etc."

His counsel, Mr Hudson, asks: "Where did you spend Christmas Day?" – "At home in Hertfordshire." The details of Monday the 29th. "My usual, awake between 11 and 12. I had a terrible cold. There was a 'flu epidemic. Nizam was up; it was his duty to look after the animals." – "Did you go out?" "I buy milk by bulk, so I keep calves – to get rid of the milk. Nizam said we had too much milk, could we have more calves? I didn't mind, said the fresh air might do me good. So we went to Pateman's farm, between 2.30 and 3.30." Later: "After Nizam and Pateman put the calf in the boot of the car, we went back to Rook's Farm."

"What then?" Mr Hudson asks. Arthur: "I told Nizam to take care of the rest."

And then? "Mr Coote telephoned between 5.15 and 5.30. I advised Nizam to take any telephone calls about business. Nizam came in and told me it's Mr Coote, so I spoke to Mr Coote."

Mr Hudson: "What did you do for the rest of the evening?" Arthur: "I told him who David Coote was." – "Did your brother stay?" – "After making me something to eat, coffee and biscuits." – "Did your brother stay in the house?" – "I bid him goodnight at 7.30. I took up a bottle of scotch and ginger ale to my bedroom, closed the door. There was I."

"When you went to bed, did you do something with the telephone? Someone rang up?" Arthur: "Yes, yes, I knew who it was, at about eight o'clock. I pressed the bell-button to switch off the bell, for Nizam to answer downstairs."

Mr Hudson moves on to 30 December.

"Did anyone call at the Farm that day?"

Arthur thinks – he seems disturbed. "I can't remember!"

Mr Hudson reminds him of the 31st, when they collected Mrs Mohammed in the car to come to the Farm. On 1 January, she says he, Arthur, never left the Farm. Can he recall Nizam leaving the Farm? Arthur: "I think he mentioned a bit of fresh air. I can't give the precise time."

Mr Hudson comes back yet again to telephone calls. "I have two questions: Did you make any telephone calls to Wimbledon?" Arthur: "I made no telephone calls to anyone at any time." Mr Hudson, with his second question: "Did you hear anyone in your house telephoning?" Arthur: "Well, sometimes . . . I might be wrong about these telephone . . ."

The Judge asks him to take his hand down, and repeats the question.

Arthur (looking down): "I believe that during the absence of my wife . . . No, I never heard anyone using my telephone, or any voices."

Mr Hudson studies the details of the trip to the tailoring "finishers". The schedule is important because of the M3 calls directing the ransom-bringer ultimately to Dane End, calls at 9.55 p.m. and 10.45 p.m., and the Volvo was seen at Dane End at 11.45 p.m.

Arthur and Nizam left Rook's Farm soon after six. The Judge asks how long the journey took to the first finisher. Three-quarters of an hour. Arthur confirms that Nizam borrowed money to telephone. The last finisher they visited was at Hackney Wick, at 7.50 p.m. After that, Arthur sent Nizam into a pub to buy him some cigarettes. "What did he do?" – "I waited for ten minutes, circulated, assumed he'd gone to his girl-friend." Then: "I know my brother can find his way home, so I went home."

Mr Hudson: "What time did you go to bed?" Arthur: "I sat in the lounge, had a drink, I'm enthusiastic about news – saw the Ten O'clock News. Then we both went to bed."

Mrs Hosein was worried about Nizam, who returned at midnight, disturbing the house. "His clothing was wet. I said, 'Take off your clothes or you'll get pneumonia!' Later Nizam's story comes out: he telephoned Liley, who was not in, so he'd hitch-hiked home. "He is twelve years my junior, a stranger in a strange land. My duty is to protect him. I didn't want to provoke him. But all the while I had considerable concern about him in this country."

We pass on to 6 February. (M3 calls the telephone kiosk in Church Street, Tottenham, at 4.45 p.m., in Bethnal Green at 6 p.m., in Epping at 7.30 p.m. Nizam is at Gates Garage at 9.00 p.m.). Arthur and Nizam delivered goods to the tailors that afternoon. Arthur interrupts himself to say to the Judge: "I've said I made no telephone calls. I meant for the ransom. I made calls about business."

Then they made for home. Mr Hudson: "What time did you arrive at the Raven Pub?" "I shall remember to my dying day! It was very cold. I sat at the front of the taxi. Between seven o'clock and five past seven."

Mr Hudson: "What time, Mr Hosein, did you leave The Raven?" – "At 10.20." "What time did the pub close?" – "Eleven o'clock." "What happened then?" – "My brother drove me home. I said goodnight . . ."

Mr Hudson asks for Arthur to be handed Exhibit 5, a billhook. Arthur handles it possibly with interest, certainly not with revulsion: he touches the blade casually.

Mr Hudson now asks for him to be handed the other billhook (taken by the police from the Rook's Farm kitchen on 7 February). Arthur behaves in the same way with it. "Do you use a billhook?" Arthur begins: "A calf died through mishandling. We were going to bury it." The Judge: "Did you chop the calf up?" – "I instructed my brother to." The Judge: "Was it fed to the dogs?" Arthur: "I believe so."

(What everyone is thinking about cannot be uttered, because there is not the faintest trace of forensic evidence to justify it, not the faintest trace.)

Mr Hudson's examination-in-chief continues during the afternoon. He asks about Arthur's letter-writing habits, letters to his relations in the West Indies – airmail paper was found at Rook's Farm. "Did you write the ransom letters?" Arthur: "Good heavens – I'd be stark staring mad!" Mr Hudson: "Did you write the directions on the cigarette packet?" – "No." "Have you any knowledge at all about the despatch of these letters and the calls to this telephone?" Arthur: "I have absolutely no knowledge of these suggestions." Mr Hudson sits down. That is the end of that.

Mr Draycott turns to the album of photographs of Rook's Farm. The tumbledown building used as a dog kennel, the coalhouse with a piece of sacking in place of a door. The work-room, a big room at the front of the house, no curtains to the window so as to give as much light as possible. "Was Mrs McKay ever at the Farm?" Arthur: "I haven't met, seen, or heard of such a person."

The night of Sunday, 1 February, when Arthur and Nizam parted company. Mr Draycott persists in dealing with the circumstances in which they parted company. Nizam will say they both drove towards Dane End together. Arthur says he drove home on the A11, alone. (Dane End is on the A10.) Nizam will say Arthur told him to plant the paper flowers. Arthur says he was at home by 9.30. Then there was a quarrel, suggests Mr Draycott. "No." "Because you told Nizam to go back and pick up the suitcase, and he wanted to know what it was about?"

"There was a row, a fight," Mr Draycott goes on, with his quiet, formal intimacy. "Nizam was tipped out of the car and was on his own. That's why he arrived home soaking wet, after you?" – "I sent him to buy cigarettes and I didn't see him till midnight."

The Attorney-General turns to the letters and fingerprints. On the 30th, M3 said he had posted a letter to Mr McKay. "Were you in London on that day?" Arthur: "No." "The letter arrived. It is said to bear your thumbprint. Did you handle any such letter before it was posted?" Arthur: "No." He argues that it would have to be proved that it was his thumbprint and that it had been taken from his home. "It is possible that my home was used, unknown to me."

When Arthur realises his last moment in the witness-box has come, he addresses the court:

"Believe me, I have great sympathy for the McKay family. I have a mother myself. I am no murderer even if I am found guilty. These hands" – he holds them out – "are artistic, not destructive. I believe in the preservation of Man. That is what I am living for!"

As other defence witnesses are called, the tiny panorama of English society in the dormitory-belt resumes its unfolding.

Mrs Hosein makes her way through the court. She is a good-looking woman, bigger than her husband; blonde and blue-eyed. When she returned from Germany on 3 January did she see anything unusual about the Farm? asks Mr Dunn, Mr Hudson's junior. – "No."

Mr Dunn goes on to 6 February, the night of Arthur's coming home from The Raven. "He'd had a few. As usual he was very hungry. And then we went to bed."

Mrs Hosein now has to face the Attorney-General. He wants to know whether a calf had died while she was in Germany: "No." Any more when she got back? One more.

Now we see another Hosein brother: Adam. He is short, stronger and heavier than Arthur, and he has a deep strong voice. He is a businessman, an insurance-broker, living in Thornton Heath. Mr Hudson elicits that Nizam turned up at 11.30 p.m. on the night of 29 December in Arthur's Volvo, delivering some trousers and collecting some shirts. His behaviour was normal. He mentioned that some people were helping him to get a permanent visa, but did not say who. He said Arthur was in bed ill.

Locations and routes are checked. Thornton Heath is twenty minutes' drive from Wimbledon. Finally a note Nizam wrote to Adam from Brixton Prison is produced. "Did you read it?" – "Not really." – "Did you realise he was asking you not to tell anyone he had been to your home on Monday evening?" – "At the time I didn't understand."

Now we come to the defence forensic expert and prepare ourselves for an accumulation of minute detail over an inordinate length of time. The defence expert is Dr Julius Grant, Vice-President of the Forensic Society.

They go over the fingerprints. Then: "I find a number of similarities in the writing," says Dr Grant, "and I reached the conclusion that there is reasonable doubt that Arthur Hosein wrote the letters. But I cannot exclude the possibility that he did."

The evidence of Dr Grant concludes on 25 September. The court momentarily lapses into a short busy spell of re-sorting papers and documents. And then it becomes one hundred per cent attentive. Mr Draycott is going to call his client to the witness-box.

The warder opens the door of the dock, and Nizam does not glance at his brother as he passes him to go out.

He stands in the witness-box looking nervous, shy, slightly lost. His voice appears to be non-existent.

Finally, the judge suggests one of those small microphones you wear round your neck and Nizam agrees. It is produced from somewhere and he stands submissively while it is hung round his neck.

Mr Draycott begins with establishing the relationship between the two brothers. Fear . . . "I was afraid of him," Nizam whispers. Mr Draycott probes further. Nizam says in a soft, nearly non-existent voice: "Whenever I don't do something he tells me to do, he has a go at me."

We come to 28 December and the visits of the police officers. Two different lots, one about Nizam's complaint, the other about "another matter". "Did they come regularly?" Mr Draycott asks. "Yes, to check if everything is all right."

Then the 29th. Mr Draycott: "As far as you can say, the day began in the ordinary way?" – "Yes, sir." On the 29th Arthur left in the Volvo – whose lights Nizam knew to be defective – at about 3 p.m. for the finishers. Nizam fed the animals, as usual, at 4 p.m. He next saw Arthur at about 8.15, when Arthur complained of 'flu and went to bed.

When he thought Arthur was asleep, Nizam went to look and saw him under the feather quilt. He then borrowed the Volvo, to go and see first his relatives at Norbury Crescent, and then his brother Adam at Thornton Heath.

One of the next points is the death of the calf while Mrs Hosein was away and the decision about what to do with it.

Then Sunday, 1 February. Mr Draycott: "Did you drive to Dane End?" – "Yes, sir." – "What did Arthur say?" – "There were two paper flowers on the dashboard. He said I was to stick them in the ground on the corner of the road."

Instead of driving home, Arthur told him to drive back to London. "Did he make a further request?" asks Mr Draycott. "Yes. He said he would leave the car with me and I would be going back to pick up a black suitcase where I had put the flowers. And I asked him why." – "Did he make any reply?" – "He asked me if I was going to do as I was told."

Mr Draycott goes through the events of 6 February. Nizam had been in London with Arthur, and at Bishop's Stortford Arthur stopped the car and told Nizam to go back to Gates Garage's used-car lot, where he would see two black suitcases opposite a Minivan. He was to pick them up, not to open them, and come to The Raven.

Nizam is asked: "Did you try and think of an excuse for not picking them up?" – "Yes. I could tell him they were white, not black." – "Could you have picked them up?" – "Yes, sir." – "But you didn't." – "No, sir."

The suitcases were left there, and Nizam never got an explanation from Arthur of what it was all about. The next day, the police came with the search warrant for some stolen jewellery. Mr Draycott: "Had Arthur told you what to do?" Nizam: "Keep my mouth shut."

We go on to the police station. Nizam did not realise the situation till Chief Superintendent Smith showed him the paper flowers and the billhook from Arthur Road. Then he was very frightened.

The following day, Nizam is still in the witness-box. Mr Hudson stands: "Why didn't you agree to speak on the telephone at the police station, as your brother did?" "I didn't know what was happening. I was frightened . . ."

Mr Hudson: "I suggest what you've been telling us about fear is an invention. You've told us that when you were with the police under interrogation, you were afraid to tell them what you've been telling the court now." Pause. "You were brave enough to call in the police on 28 December when you made a complaint?" – "Yes, because Arthur was doing something wrong . . ."

Mr Hudson pounces: "What bigger incentive to tell the police than when you were held on a graver charge – why didn't you?" Nizam (cowering): "I couldn't get myself together . . ."

In time, Mr Hudson launches into the final gambit. "I suggest that you are quite capable of dealing with a situation involving violence." Nizam shakes his head.

"And that you are not afraid of people?" Nizam is soundless.

Now the final cross-examination by the Attorney-General.

He refers to the journey back, through Epping; the call at 1.15 a.m. Nizam: "I could have been in the area, but I didn't make the call." The Attorney-General has the transcript of the M3 call handed to Nizam. "Will you read it? "This is Mafia Group 3 and so on."

Nizam reads, just audibly, hesitating occasionally.

More questions. "Were you involved in the fact that Mrs McKay was missing?" Nizam: "I was involved with the paper flowers." Attorney-General: "Then why should you say 'let me die'?" Nizam (on the edge of breaking down): "Mr Smith said I'd murdered her. Mr Smith said it was not a calf I chopped up, it was a woman . . ."

The words are out! The words that have never, so far, been uttered in the court.

The Attorney-General moves to Tuesday, 30 December. After

six hours' driving in the early hours about Surrey and Hertfordshire, what else was he doing? Nizam says he didn't feel good. Was
he watching TV? He doesn't remember. Did he see Mrs Dyer?
"No." Does he know her Christian name? "Diane." The Attorney-General produces transcripts of the next M3 call at 4.30 p.m.,
and makes Nizam read them aloud. "Your wife just posted a letter
. . . Don't call the police! You have been followed . . . Did you get
the money . . .?"

On 29 September Nizam is still in the witness-box. The Attorney-General cross-examining. On Thursday, 1 January, Liley was
at the Farm; Liley had wanted to go to a party, but Nizam had to
look after the animals. She was scared of Arthur, but Arthur "had
promised not to interfere with her again". It was important, Nizam
agrees, not to leave her with Arthur. Yet he did.

The Attorney-General tries to make him fix the time. There
were two M3 calls before 8 p.m. Nizam says "evening, 3 p.m."
"You call that evening?" – "In Trinidad we call it evening." When
he left, Arthur and Liley were watching television. "In the *afternoon*?" (TV does not begin till later [at the time]. But if it were
what we in England call evening, television would have begun.)

Later comes the dreadful call to Ian about his mother being very
worried, offering herself to the doctor. Attorney-General: "Do you
realise what a terrible thing it was for a son to hear those words?" –
"Yes sir." – "Did you speak them?" – "I never did."

The Attorney-General has marshalled his next notes: he begins
the final assault. The second ransom-attempt.

The Attorney-General points out that he, Nizam, wrote the
name and number of the Minivan on the piece of paper which was
subsequently found in his pocket. Nizam says he wrote it down
while he was on the Bishop's Stortford road.

Isn't it more believable that he noted down the number much
earlier in order to give it over the telephone to Mr Alick McKay?
The Attorney-General hammers it in with one accusing question
after another. Nizam looks more frightened.

The Attorney-General moves on to the police arrival at Rook's
Farm on the following day, saying first that they were looking for
stolen jewellery, then for a missing woman, then for Mrs McKay.
"You remember being shown the paper flowers by the police? Did
you realise then that the suitcases and the paper flowers had
something to do with the kidnapping?" Nizam: "Yes, sir."
"Why didn't you tell the police?" – "I was scared . . ."

Shortly, tears are in Nizam's eyes.

"You said to Detective-Sergeant Parker, 'Oh my God, what have I done? Arthur always gets me into trouble.'"

"I didn't know what I'd done! . . ." He is breaking down. "Was it your desire to die because you knew you'd done something dreadful?" Nizam: "I'd rather die than be charged with murder . . ." He is unable to speak for weeping. The Attorney-General sits down. Nizam gets out his handkerchief, standing there helplessly.

Eventually the evidence of Nizam is over. He returns from the witness-box to the dock. His counsel calls no further witnesses. The whole case for the defence of both brothers is over.

The Attorney-General's closing speech, like his opening speech, is relatively short.

Standing up straight and tall, he tells the jury, in his untheatrical, man-to-man tone, that he will not be repeating what he has said before. The jury will accept what the Judge says is the law: they will decide what is fact.

Of the brothers, he says that each is trying to saddle the other with some or all of the guilt. "The crime," he says, "was committed by both."

What is suggested by the Crown, he says, is that those two, calling themselves M3, kidnapped that woman: seeking Mrs Murdoch, they found Mrs McKay. He emphasises the jury's role in considering the situation. It is not a matter of law; the Judge will direct them on that. "No," he says: "If you are satisfied there are such circumstances as render the committing of the crime certain, that there is no rational hypothesis except that the crime was committed, then you are entitled to conclude that she was murdered." He pauses, and then exhorts them to think of the threats to execute, the total silence after the brothers were arrested. There is no rational hypothesis but that she met her death at their hands.

He calls for a verdict of Guilty on all counts for both brothers.

We now come to the closing speeches for the defence.

"This is the last time that I, who am charged with defending this man, Arthur Hosein, shall have the chance to speak to you on his behalf."

Mr Hudson has folded up his spectacles and put away his notes. He has begun a speech that will last for many hours.

Having dealt, often in detail, with just about every aspect of the evidence, he comes to "one last word, which may be of importance in the jury room". His tone is quieter now that he is on ground where there can be no possibility of anyone being against him. "All human beings are vulnerable. Don't allow your anger at an ordinary woman being brutally kidnapped, at the anguish of those near and dear to her . . . don't let it affect your reason! Because it has taken place, we all want the people responsible to be brought to justice. But only if you are sure . . . It must be something of which you are sure."

Finally: "On all the charges, I submit, there is reasonable doubt. Arthur Hosein has never given any indication, he has emphatically denied, knowing anything about the crime. If there's just a possibility that what he's said so often may be true, just a possibility that what he's said so often may be true, you must find him Not Guilty."

Mr Draycott, Nizam's counsel, is on his feet, looking small and sturdy, strong-nosed and bright-eyed, ready as ever with lively terrier-like energy to address the jury in his own, special, examining manner.

He exhorts the jury to be careful to consider each man separately, and each count against each one. "Don't approach it as 'the Hoseins', 'the brothers', unless the evidence compels you to it. It is a very, very easy mistake to make."

It is only a few moments before he has his finger on the essential fantasy of the case, the demand for a million pounds; and he is fixing it directly on Arthur. Grandiose ideas, lack of grasp of reality. . . . He quotes Arthur: "I am very sorry for you, Mr Smith. You have a very difficult case to solve."

"The whole thing," says Mr Draycott, "is the plan of a mind that has no understanding or grasp of reality." Having established Arthur's being thus off his rocker, he goes on: "So that when Nizam gives you to understand, and the police give you grounds to understand, that the relationship between these two was not a normal one, there was no affection but only fear, that point has been established time and time again."

Mr Draycott reiterates some of the most cogent of the defence arguments, linking them with the idea that somebody else must be concerned in the case.

Then he invites the jury to consider Arthur's attitude to Nizam. "Isn't it a waste of time to say Nizam was not afraid of Arthur, when domination and fear is everybody's evidence?"

Mr Draycott asks the jury to look at Nizam's attitude to Arthur. "Put yourselves in his position, with a brother who held him in terror and domination! If Nizam were a party to the kidnapping, is it conceivable that he would do the series of things he is known to have done – ring up the police just before the plan was put into operation, hang about at Gates Garage and so on?"

His Lordship, he says, will tell them about the necessity for considering each case separately, each defence differently; he gives them a final reminder that Nizam was under no obligation to go into the witness-box. Then he sits down.

It is time for the judge to sum up.

His Lordship, Mr Justice Sebag Shaw, addresses the jury on their duties and their attitude: they have to decide what facts are proved, what inferences they are entitled to draw, applying the same tests to witnesses from whichever direction they come. If in doubt, they must resolve in favour of the accused.

"If you think a view falls from me," he says, "you are entitled to disregard it if it's not consonant with your own."

His Lordship begins with two statements.

(i) Nobody could doubt that Mrs McKay was abducted – no one has sought to suggest otherwise. There is evidence of false imprisonment, blackmail and threat to murder.

(ii) The charge of murder is on a different footing. Unless and until they come to the conclusion, if they do, that it's proved that one or two of the defendants was party to the kidnapping, no charge of murder can be brought. Only if one or the other is concluded to be party must they begin to consider the charge of murder.

He touches on the event of one of two defendants giving evidence which supports the prosecution case against his co-defendant: they should not act on the evidence of one to the detriment of the other unless they are assured that it comes from a reliable source. And the evidence as it affects each of them is not the same. This makes it imperative to consider each separately and independently of the other.

The judge starts to go through the case detail by detail. He tells the jury he expects to complete his summing up the next morning (6 October).

This, one imagines, is the last day. Three and a half weeks – fourteen and a half working days!

The brothers are put up and the judge continues his summation.

Eventually, he comes to Count 1. "Unless and until you find either or both of the defendants guilty of kidnapping Mrs McKay, there is no vestige of a case against them for murder." He pauses. "If, however – in order to say what I have to say, I have to make an assumption – if you find one or other guilty of kidnapping, what are the indications that she is dead?" One indication is what the kidnappers were saying, but it doesn't follow that each is guilty of killing her.

His Lordship tells the jury what murder is, narrowing the definition for the purposes of this case: "Murder means doing an act which causes death when that act is done with intention to kill."

It is 12.35 p.m., and the jury retires to consider its verdict.

Something after half past four, the jury are rumoured to have sent for their tea and are consequently thought – don't ask me why! – to be nearing a decision.

In fact they are. So, after just over four hours, we all troop back into the court for the last time.

The accused men are put up. The jury file in, their foreman leading. Suddenly there is silence.

"Are you unanimous?" asks the Clerk of the Court.

"Yes," says the foreman. He stands, healthy-looking, spectacled, thoroughly in command of himself.

And then the Clerk of the Court reads out again, like a litany, the charges for each defendant, count by count. And count by count comes the answer, each time, for each count, the same answer. "Guilty." "Guilty." "Guilty." "Guilty."

It is over. But the foreman remains standing. He wishes to say something more. The Judge nods permission. He says the jury unanimously recommend leniency towards Nizamodeen Hosein.

Everyone is expecting an explosion from Arthur. The warders surrounding him must be at the ready. He wants to make a speech, of course. But it begins both bitterly and wittily.

"Injustice has not only been done. It has also been seen and heard by the public gallery" – he waves an arm towards us all – "to be done."

He addresses himself to the Judge:

"The provocation of your Lordship has shown immense partiality. To his Lordship I would say that from the moment I mentioned Robert Maxwell, I knew you were a Jew."

He is beginning to work himself up. "Not that I am anti-Jewish myself," he adds, thus showing his own absence of partiality. "You have shown throughout this case," he tells the Judge, "that you have directed the jury on only one side, to the Crown . . . I have produced thirty witnesses, and not once . . ."

His Lordship watches him steadily on the same level over the well of the court. Arthur goes on:

"You have denied me justice!"

Arthur is now raising his voice in sarcasm to the jury. "Thank you, members of the jury! It is a grave injustice!" The warders show signs of crowding in on him, and he becomes incoherent and stops.

The sentences are to be passed. Nizam has said not a word.

"On the conviction of murder, the sentence is life imprisonment." This is for Arthur. For Nizam the same, with a recommendation of leniency "from another quarter".

Now the kidnapping. His Lordship makes a short introductory speech to impart that every right-minded person will expect the punishment to be salutary. "The kidnapping and confinement of Mrs McKay was cold-blooded and abominable. She was snatched from the security of her home, and so long as she remained alive she was reduced to terrified distress. This crime will shock and revolt every right-minded person. The punishment must be such that law-abiding citizens may feel safe in their homes."

On the count of kidnapping, he sentences Arthur Hosein to twenty-five years. To Nizam he says: "I am not sure whether you are in any degree less culpable, but the jury's view is that you were under the influence of your brother and I have to regard the possibility that this was so." He sentences him to fifteen years.

Coming to the next count, he says: "There could not be a worse case of blackmail. You put that family on the rack for weeks and months in an attempt to extort money by your monstrous demands." For this both brothers receive the maximum sentence of fourteen years. For sending threatening letters, each gets the maximum of ten years. The sentences are to run concurrently.

Since the abolition of the death penalty, a Judge has power to recommend to the Home Secretary that the prisoner should not be released for a specified length of time. No such recommendation to the Home Secretary was made by Mr Justice Sebag Shaw – so it looks as if his Lordship is sending Arthur down for a certain twenty-five years, and Nizam for a certain fifteen years under the kidnapping conviction.

As it is the usual practice to remit one-third of a fixed sentence, provided the prisoner behaves himself, general opinion among the army of reporters seems to be that Arthur will serve just under seventeen years and Nizam ten years if they get their remission.

His Lordship has ordered the two brothers to be removed from the dock. For the last time we hear the cry which begins, "Be upstanding!" and ends – "God Save The Queen!"

Both brothers put in applications for leave to appeal, Arthur against the verdict and the sentence, Nizam against the verdict.

The applications are heard by Lord Justice Davies, Lord Justice Karminski and Mr Justice Melford Stevenson.

The brothers are brought in, now handcuffed to warders. There is a marked change in Arthur – he looks terrified, the whites of his eyes showing all round the irises as he glances at the people in the court. Has a short time in prison deflated him so far? And Nizam – he looks just as composed as ever.

Leave to appeal is refused; and refusing Arthur's application to appeal against the sentence, Lord Justice Davies says the maximum sentences were right, "for no more terrible crime could be conjured up." Then he says sharply: "Take them away!"

Editor's Note. In February 1990, Nizamodeen Hosein, who had been a well-behaved convict, was released from Verne Prison, Dorset, and immediately deported to Trinidad. His brother Arthur, who is considered to be mentally unstable, remains in a top-security hospital at Liverpool.

JANIE JONES

(Old Bailey, 1973)

Alan King-Hamilton

*A rare judge's-eye view of one of his many celebrated trials, deploying
a beady judicial glare and peppery wit in a case of sexual shenanigans
that cheered Britain up no end in the miserable strike-torn winter of
1973. In the dock sat Janie Jones, recording artiste and "high society
whore-house honey", who famously installed a two-way mirror at her
sumptuous Kensington town house for the titillation of her guests. The
case is redolent of every apocryphal encounter between bishop and
actress: High Court Judge (Cambridge, Middle Temple, wartime
Squadron-Leader) tries Celebrity Vice Queen (born Marion Mitchell, the daughter of a Durham miner). At the age of 16 she moved to
London, changed her name to Janie Jones and worked as a fan dancer
before launching herself on a singing career (her 1965 recording of
Witches' Brew climbed to number 37 in the hit parade). She made her
first court appearance the following year accused of blackmail.
Although acquitted, she was arrested again a month later and charged
with running a brothel. The case collapsed, but in 1971 the News of
the World splashed a story about a payola scandal at the BBC. Jones
was named as the head of a call-girl ring offering producers and disc-
jockeys girls for sex in return for parts on radio and television. Finally
in December 1973, Janie Jones found herself at the Old Bailey
charged on 21 counts. Although cleared of blackmail, she drew a
seven-year sentence for controlling prostitutes. In Holloway Gaol, she*

*befriended the notorious Moors murderess Myra Hindley. In 1977,
released on parole, she returned home to her infamous two-way mirror,
through which party-goers had been able to observe each other having
sex. Judge Alan King-Hamilton QC (b. 1904) branded Janie Jones
"the most evil woman I have ever met". In a long and eventful career,
he earned a reputation as a scourge of the liberal Left, having tried the
1960s insurance swindler Emil Savundra, a young Peter Hain (on a
charge of bank robbery) and presided at the* Gay News *trial for
blasphemy. In retirement, Judge King-Hamilton reflected on the
Janie Jones case in his memoirs.*

The first time I saw Janie Jones she was a witness for the Crown, as
was Eric Gilbert, the county court clerk. They were giving evidence against her ex-husband, John Christian-Dee, who was
charged with some offences arising out of his attempt to force
his way back into the matrimonial home against her will and with
intent to inflict grievous bodily harm. He was acquitted of those
charges. Little did I think that some ten months later I would see
all three of them again.

On this second occasion they were all in the dock together in a
much more serious case. Janie Jones was charged with ten counts
which, in effect, alleged that she compelled various women to be
prostitutes for her own financial gain. In four counts (two of them
jointly with John Christian-Dee) there were charges of attempting
to pervert the course of justice. The allegations were that attempts
had been made to interfere with prosecution witnesses by threats
or to get them to change the stories which they had already given to
the police. Jones alone was charged with five counts of blackmail
alleging demands on two of her "clients" for large sums of money,
on the threat of exposure of what they had been doing. There were
two counts of obtaining £4,000 by deception from one of the
alleged blackmail victims. Gilbert was charged with aiding and
abetting Jones in three of the prostitution offences, and jointly
with the other two defendants in one of the charges of attempting
to pervert the course of justice. A formidable indictment, containing twenty-one counts in all.

I severed the blackmail counts and those which alleged the
obtaining of £4,000 by deception. I thought the evidence on the
blackmail and two associated charges would seriously prejudice the

jury against Jones in the other charges, and vice versa. I tried the blackmail and other two charges about a month after the conclusion of the first part of the case.

All the offences were alleged to have taken place after Jones, in the summer of 1967, had bought and was living in a house in Campden Hill Road, W.8. It was a lavishly furnished Georgian-style terraced house. In September 1967, Gilbert went to live there as a lodger, but was treated more like a servant. A year later, Christian-Dee also went to live there. He married Jones in November of that year, but Gilbert continued to live there. He was much too useful to Jones, and knew too much. He wanted to leave but, according to him, she threatened to expose him to the Lord Chancellor's department if he did so. He stayed. It was a most extraordinary *ménage à trois*.

At the time of the trial Jones was thirty-seven years old. Her real name was Marion Mitchell and she was born in County Durham, the daughter of a miner. Her first job was a nanny, looking after a doctor's children. After three and a half years she left and came to London where she worked as "dancer and singer" at the Windmill Theatre. Leaving there after three years, she was employed as a singer in a night club in Soho. Three years later she toured England and parts of Europe in a double act with her sister. After a dispute with her sister they separated and she said she worked in television and did some recording and, from time to time, worked in cabaret at various night clubs. She claimed that her income had risen from £12 per week at the Windmill to about £200 per week by 1960, but declined to give details of her earnings since 1964. However, she owned the house in Campden Hill Road, valued in 1973 at £45,000, and she also had a Rolls-Royce. During the trial it emerged that she was prosecuted, in 1967, for running a brothel but had been acquitted. It was immediately after that acquittal that she started to run the call-girl service which gave rise to the charges in this first trial.

She was very strong-willed and determined, and quite ruthless in achieving her purpose. Woe betide anyone who attempted to defy her. And as events proved, she had little or no respect for the law. It is fair to say, however, that she had two redeeming features. She cured Christian-Dee from his addiction to drugs. And she seemed to have a sense of humour.

At the time of the trial Eric Gilbert was forty-two years old. His home was at Southport in Lancashire, where he normally lived

with his mother. He was a civil servant, being employed in the
Lord Chancellor's department as a county court clerk. He was
friendless, timid, shy and very weak-willed; almost the last person
one would expect to become associated with Janie Jones. But once
he was drawn into her web he was caught, trapped like a fly and
quite unable to break free. Throughout the six or seven days
during which he was giving evidence I was, by turns filled with
pity and contempt, nausea and anger that he should have been
treated as he was and put up with it as he did. His was the most
psychologically interesting character of the three.

John Christian-Dee was aged thirty-four. From 1954 to 1958 he
served in the Army and then worked for British Rail for about a
year. For the next nine years he earned a living by singing and
writing songs in Europe, but more particularly in Hamburg where
he had contacts. As I have already indicated, he became a drug
addict and when he met Jones and went to live with her, she
gradually cured him. He married Jones in November 1968 and
they were divorced in April 1973. It had been a very stormy union.
It was very noticeable that, despite giving evidence against Christian-Dee when he was tried alone for alleged offences in which she
was said to be the principal intended victim, and then divorcing
him two months later, Jones and he were on remarkably good
terms when they were in the dock together. But not a word passed
between either of them and Gilbert, who was as friendless in the
dock as he had been outside it.

The story which emerged in the trial provided yet one more
illustration of the aphorism that truth is stranger than fiction.
Leaving the blackmail charges till later, the story giving rise to the
call-girl offences is what I would imagine can be read in an old-
fashioned cheap French novelette, brought up to date.

She provided girls for sex of various kinds, both individually and
in orgies, which took place at fashionable hotels in the West End
(frequently with Arabs), in the flats of clients, or in her own home
in Campden Hill Road. Very recently, I have been shown a series
of articles, published in the *Sun* newspaper, under the title "Janie
Jones, Britain's ex-vice queen, tells her own story". One of the
articles, which referred to the parties which she regularly gave on
Friday nights, contained this paragraph: "Often I would go
upstairs and find full scale orgies going on. But what could I do?"

This suggested that she would have preferred that such things
did not occur but was powerless to prevent it. One may be forgiven

for regarding this as sheer hypocrisy, because a little further on in the same article is a description of the notorious two-way mirror and how it came about that she had it installed; her attitude to it is recorded as follows: ". . . I could see that the mirror could provide a lot of fun. I was right. It was a riotous success. Watching through it was better than any film."

In one of the bedrooms it appears to be an ordinary mirror, but from the adjoining bedroom it was possible to see through it into the first bedroom and observe whatever was going on in there. When giving evidence she first alleged that the mirror was already there when she bought the house, but later had to admit that she herself had had it installed.

It was in this first bedroom that there was a very large "King Size" bed. Very recently my attention was drawn to an advertisement in the columns of a very respectable Sunday paper which reads "Janie Jones's famous double 7 ft bed for sale. Divides into 2 × 3½ ft beds with gold velvet headboards to match. Offers invited". When one recalls all the orgies that were alleged to have taken place on those beds, many of which were viewed through the two-way mirror, one wonders who would be likely to make such an offer.

Sometimes Jones went with the girls to a hotel, to collect the money, and she then departed, leaving the girls there, although on some occasions she remained to supervise operations. Sometimes one of the girls was given the responsibility of collecting the money. On occasion, and according to him very much against his will, Gilbert was entrusted with that task, more of which later.

On her own admission Jones employed fifteen girls, one of whom was her seventeen-year-old niece, and not one of them was a prostitute before working for Jones. Seven were called as witnesses for the Crown. One of the girls said that Jones sometimes made her go with men every day, or at least several times a week and often two or three times a day. According to that girl's evidence (which generally was much the same as that given by the other six girl witnesses), the money which had to be collected was £25 or £30 per visit per girl, of which sum Jones gave each girl £5. If Jones employed all fifteen girls in the same way and as frequently, it may not be surprising that she was reluctant to give the police details of her earnings after 1964.

The girls said that they were recruited by Jones by her promising to introduce them to men who were influential in the entertainment world and who, if the girls had sex with them, would give them work in films or TV. It was the only way, they were told. Only one or two of the men were producers or directors and, save for one trifling exception, no girl got or was even offered film or TV work as a result of going to bed with the men, or at all.

The girls were not named in court. They were identified by letters of the alphabet. When each of them, apart from two, realised that there was to be no film or TV work, and that she was expected to be a prostitute working for Jones, they wanted to leave. Jones then threatened each of them that if they left, she would tell their parents or their employers what they had been doing. So they stayed, except for three who plucked up courage and broke away despite the threat of exposure. Two confessed to their parents what they had been doing. What none of them realised, doubtless due to their panic, was that if Jones did as they said she threatened to do, she would have exposed herself as running a call-girl service and living on immoral earnings.

The prosecution was in the hands of John Buzzard (then Senior Treasury Counsel at the Old Bailey and appointed as a judge there during this trial), Michael Worsley and Stephen Mitchell. At the conclusion of his opening speech, Buzzard asked Mitchell to call the first three girl witnesses. (Worsley was in another court at that time.) It was a wise move. Mitchell had taken them through their evidence at the committal proceedings in the magistrates' court and doubtless had, to some extent, gained their confidence. Nevertheless, they were most reluctant witnesses, not only because of the nature and details of the evidence which they were to give in a packed court with the public gallery also fully occupied but also because they said they had been threatened by Jones or Christian-Dee, or by both of them. It was necessary to take them through their evidence, which was very long and detailed, covering the events of several months, with the greatest care and tact. Mitchell did it superbly, with great finesse and delicacy. I have never heard a difficult examination-in-chief conducted with such skill. It all seemed so fresh, as though each girl was telling her story for the first time, easily and naturally. Those who have not had to do it will not be able to appreciate the long, arduous and meticulous preparation which is required to avoid the pitfalls and the irrelevancies and to keep it flowing smoothly. It was a masterly performance – and quite devastating.

Having given an indication of the general nature of the evidence given by the girls, there is no need to repeat it in all its sordid detail. Some matters, however, should be specifically dealt with.

Two of the girls became pregnant, Miss A and Miss F, and the evidence was that Jones insisted that they should each have abortions so that they could get back into the call-girl service as soon as possible. According to A, Jones herself tried to procure an abortion on her several times, but without success. She then told A to have a pregnancy test under the name of another girl, of whom one of the clients was very fond. By this means, she got the client to pay for the abortion and then used the money to pay for a private abortion for herself, leaving A to have hers under the National Health Service.

Something similar occurred with F. She was made to have a pregnancy test under another name, and money for an abortion was obtained from another client. According to F, Jones kept the money, and F also had the abortion under the National Health Service. F was one of the three who eventually could not stand that sort of life any longer and plucked up the courage to leave, and she herself told her parents what had been happening. The other two who broke their association with Jones were A and B, despite the threat of exposure.

Eventually, the *News of the World* came to hear about what had been happening, and began to investigate. Statements were taken from one or two of the girls and they were persuaded by the newspaper to go to the police. Jones was in the United States at this time, and when she heard about it she hurried back to London and consulted solicitors. In June 1971 a writ claiming damages for alleged libel and an injunction to restrain publication of further articles was served on the *News of the World*. The paper filed its defence to the effect that the contents of the articles were true in substance and in fact and that the paper would justify the words of which complaint had been made. The judge in Chambers refused to grant the injunction restraining further publication. Various further interlocutory steps were taken by each side, and by June 1972 it became apparent that the action was not going to be proceeded with. (It has probably long since been dismissed for want of prosecution.)

It is interesting to know that three or four years before this, Jones herself approached the *News of the World*. According to the evidence of the then Assistant Editor, he was told by Jones that she might have a story to sell concerning a high-class vice ring and a call-girl service which she ran and which involved top show-business personalities (in the world of 'pop' music) and other prominent people in public life. She outlined to the Assistant Editor details of her call-girl system in which she said she was personally involved, and she asked for several thousands of pounds for the story, offering to provide a written synopsis for examination. She pointed out that the synopsis would not reveal the names of the persons involved, who were highly placed in public life and public service, in the law and in show business, but she said the names would be supplied later if the story were accepted.

The synopsis was eventually supplied through a solicitor (who, doubtless, couldn't have read it, otherwise he must have advised his client against publishing what was obviously highly libellous material). When the Assistant Editor had read and discussed the synopsis with the Editor they decided not to buy the story and it was returned to her.

When he was cross-examined on behalf of Jones he said that the paper had innumerable offers from people with stories to sell. What Jones offered him was a story so bizarre that parts of it were etched on his memory for the rest of his life. It would be impossible to forget some of the incidents in the synopsis.

When Jones knew about stories being given to the *News of the World* and the police by some of the girls, she went to great lengths to try to get them to retract or change their stories. It is these incidents which gave rise to the charges of attempting to pervert the course of justice.

One Saturday in June 1971, after trying to get in touch with B at her home in the north of England, Jones went there with Gilbert. This was two days after B had given a voluntary statement to two detective sergeants (one of whom was Detective Sergeant Penrose from Scotland Yard) at her local police station.

According to B, Jones showed her copies of documents which she said were statements which she had obtained from some other girls. B said she did not read them and as she was handing them back Jones asked her how she would like to see her name emblazoned across the *News of the World* as a prostitute? She went on to say that it would ruin her life and she wanted B to return to London with her and make a statement to her solicitor.

B said she didn't want to go, but Jones insisted, implying that it would be the only way to prevent her parents and boyfriend seeing her name in the paper. B did all she could to resist the pressure.

She sat on the floor and said that she couldn't go because she had to be at work on Monday. Jones replied that it could be arranged because she would get her solicitor to call at the house on the Sunday and take her statement that day and B could return to the north by train on Sunday evening.

Eventually, B said, she realised that Jones wouldn't leave the flat unless she agreed to go and because of veiled threats of what might happen to her if she refused, with the utmost reluctance she left with Jones and Gilbert, who hadn't uttered a word.

At the station there was a considerable time to wait for the London train and whilst doing so, Jones telephoned to Christian-Dee in London and B phoned to her boyfriend. She told him where she was and with whom and why, adding that she was very frightened and asked him to phone Detective Sergeant Penrose at Scotland Yard. At that stage she had to break off the conversation because Jones went into the phone-box. At the trial the boyfriend confirmed that B had phoned him and that as a result of what she had said, he had phoned Mr Penrose.

In due course, the train arrived and B returned to London with Jones and Gilbert. On the train journey, during which they were the only three occupants of the compartment, Gilbert was as taciturn as ever, but Jones told B that two other girls, whom she named, would not be making statements to the police, implying, according to B, that she, Jones, had taken steps to ensure their silence. She added that she was trying to find A, who, Jones alleged, had started the trouble by going to the *News of the World*. B also said that Jones told her what to say to her solicitor, i.e. that when she had been interrogated by the police she was frightened of them and had therefore made a statement to them which was all lies. She was further told to inform the solicitor that when she had been to see Jones at her house, it was purely as a friend and that occasionally there was a party but nothing of a sexual nature had taken place.

On arrival at the house in Campden Hill Road they had a meal with Christian-Dee who was already there and both of them kept asking B what she had told the police. According to her, she only repeated parts of her statement to the police and she was told to tell the solicitor that it was all untrue.

Jones was unable to contact her solicitor that night, so B was allowed to go to bed. On Sunday morning they got up late. Jones tried again, unsuccessfully, to get through to her solicitor, but at about midday the front door bell rang. Two police officers were there, doubtless as a result of B's boyfriend having telephoned to Scotland Yard following her call to him before getting into the train. On discovering it was the police, Jones told B that if she had to speak to the officers she was to say that she was all right and was not being held against her will. At first Jones went upstairs and spoke to the officers and very soon afterwards she called B up. One of the officers asked her if she was all right and if she wanted to leave. By this time, B said, Christian-Dee was also at the door, and because she was frightened of what might happen to her, she repeated to the officers what Jones had told her to say. One of them asked to speak to B alone, but Jones refused to let them do so, and they left.

It is not difficult to imagine B's feelings at that time. Salvation, in the shape of two police officers, was only two or three feet away, but she was quite unable to do anything about it. It must have been like one of those nightmares when you are trying to run away from someone, but your legs and feet are like lead caught in a quagmire of liquid clay laced with glue and you can't move them. Not surprisingly, when the police officers left she completely broke down and Jones sent her to bed, but such was her condition that Christian-Dee sent for the doctor. Before the doctor arrived, Jones told her that when he came she was to try to appear to be even more upset than she was, and to keep on crying, the object being to persuade the doctor to send her to a mental hospital so that she would not be able to appear in court and give evidence.

When the doctor arrived, B did as she was told, which she didn't find difficult. She had, anyway, been sobbing ever since the police had left. At the back of her mind, B said in evidence, she thought that if she was sent to a hospital it would provide a means of escape. And so it proved, but not for some time.

The doctor arrived at about 2 p.m. and having examined B told Jones that she should go to hospital immediately because he thought B was suicidal. But the solicitor hadn't arrived and Jones and Christian-Dee were in a dilemma: if they took her to hospital immediately the opportunity for B to make her statement would be delayed and might even be lost for good. On the other hand, if they waited for the solicitor, who didn't in fact arrive until about 10.30 p.m., B might have become seriously ill and unable to make a statement.

When the solicitor arrived, B said he took a long statement from her (it extended to just over four pages of foolscap in manuscript, and was an exhibit in the case) by putting to her a series of questions which she answered on the lines indicated to her by Jones on their way back to London. It amounted to a repudiation of her statement to the police and alleged that the police kept her for five hours and wouldn't let her go until she had signed it, and that nothing of a sexual nature ever took place at Jones' home. Prior to making this statement to the solicitor, B said that although no direct threat was made to her, and Christian-Dee said she could leave whenever she wanted to, both Jones and he said what was going to happen to the other girls who "grassed" on Jones, and that someone's "heavies" would be dealing with them. It is a fact that one of the girls was so frightened of threats made to her that she went to live abroad and only returned for the trial under police protection.

After the solicitor had completed the statement which he got B to sign, Jones and Christian-Dee took her to St Mary Abbots Hospital nearby. She was then in a terrible state and it didn't help her condition when, according to her, she heard Jones telling the doctor that she should not be allowed to see any visitors nor to see the police. In fact, two days later, she left the hospital in the care of her parents, and the police. She did not see Jones again, until confronting her in court.

Other attempts of a similar nature were made to get two other girls to change their story. It is unnecessary to repeat the details. At the trial, one of them, H, first gave evidence more or less in accordance with her statements to the police, but somewhat hesitantly; as lawyers would put it, she "didn't quite come up to proof", which, in the circumstances I have described, is not very surprising.

When she was cross-examined on behalf of Jones she went back on what she had said and gave answers very much in accordance with a conflicting second statement which she said Christian-Dee had made her copy out. The original of this, according to her, had been written at her home by Christian-Dee, and had by now been somewhat expanded.

Very frequently when a witness goes back on what he or she has previously stated and signed, a judge will give counsel who called the witness permission to treat the witness as "hostile" and counsel can then, in effect, cross-examine his own witness, which cannot normally be done. If the witness is treated as "hostile" the original signed statement can be put to him or her, and will be at variance with the evidence which the witness has just been giving.

It was obvious that H's demeanour and evidence when cross-examined on behalf of Jones and Christian-Dee was largely, if not entirely, due to the pressure put upon her and threats made when Jones and Dee had gone to her place of work and then her home in July 1971. Although I have never heard of it being done before in re-examination of a witness, I suggested to Mr Buzzard, when he rose to re-examine H, that he might consider applying to treat her as "hostile". After some slight legal argument I gave him leave so to do. Reminding her that she was on oath, Buzzard then put to her the original statement which she had given to the police, almost line by line, and asked if it was true and she said "yes".

Some judges take the view, and direct juries accordingly, that "hostile" witnesses who have been contradictory in the witness-box can never be relied on and that their evidence should be ignored. I think that condemnation is much too sweeping. Each instance turns on its own facts. If an explanation for the contradiction is given by the witness and is convincing, I do not see why the original evidence should not be accepted. In fact, the reason for the retraction of the earlier evidence and then its subsequent reinstatement, sometimes enhances the validity of the earlier evidence, if the jury accepts it, after due warning of the dangers involved.

I duly warned the jury of the risks, emphasising that it was entirely a matter for them. In the result, they convicted Jones on Count 10 which charged her with attempting to pervert the course of justice by inducing H to make a false statement. So it follows that they accepted H's original evidence.

Jones' defence was a complete denial of the allegations. She said all the girls had lied to protect themselves, as had the men whom the Crown called as witnesses. She said, that no sexual activities had taken place at the parties at her home, and that girls were employed by her in an escort agency. In a masterly cross-examination by Worsley, Jones admitted that she had no letter-heads relating to an escort agency, no receipts and no diary for appointments; if any sexual activities occurred when the girls went to hotels or flats, it was entirely their own affair. She did not know of it, still less had she organised it.

However, she alleged that A, who lived with her at Campden Hill Road, was merely an *au pair* girl. She said the girl was too fond of brandy and, in her evidence, A admitted that on occasion she did have too much when it was given to her at parties before going upstairs for sex with one or more men. When I asked Jones if she usually gave her brandy to an *au pair* girl, she realised that she had fallen into a trap of her own making and tried to get out of it by saying that A brought her own brandy to the house. When I asked, flippantly as I admit, whether she charged A corkage, she had the grace to laugh.

Finally, before turning briefly to the blackmail case, I must refer to Eric Gilbert. I suppose those who are extremely lonely react to it in different ways. In the summer of 1963 he came to London for a holiday, stayed at a modest hotel near Paddington, and one night went, all alone, to a night club in the West End. Until then he had never had any friends, male or female. He said that before the cabaret began, Jones came to his table and started talking to him. The extrovert and the introvert. It must have been a somewhat one-sided encounter, but, according to Gilbert, a relationship began to build up because she was exceptionally easy to talk to. He went back to the same club a night or two later and she then invited him to visit her in the flat she was then occupying. She told him she was getting a new flat and, Gilbert said, asked if he would guarantee her mortgage. At the next meeting she said that wouldn't be necessary, but asked if he could help her with the deposit for the new flat. Such was his infatuation for her (and, probably, his gratitude for her friendship) that he gave, a gift, not a loan, of £800. At that time all he had was a deposit of £900 at the bank. In his evidence he said, "If I hadn't given it she would have found someone else to do so and I wouldn't have seen her again. I wanted to see her as much as I could, to be friendly." But that was only the beginning.

In the middle of 1964 there were two further gifts of £100 and £250. "If I didn't give it she wouldn't see me again; she said she would have to go to someone else."

Gilbert said that to raise one of those sums he had to borrow from the bank on the security of an insurance policy. He said he didn't want to keep on giving her money but he did want her friendship. There were several further payments, for which purpose he again borrowed from the bank. He said he phoned her once a week, and visited her in London once or twice, but he never had sexual intercourse with her. There was no reason to disbelieve that.

She had asked him for money to help her to move in to Campden

Hill Road. When she went there in April 1967 she asked for £50 but he could only afford £25. At that she shouted at him, very angrily, and it wasn't the first time. Later, he sent more money.

In September 1967, Gilbert was transferred to Croydon County Court and Jones suggested that he should lodge with her. He paid £28 per month rent; later it was raised to £50 per month. Gilbert said that, at first, he only intended to stay for a short time, because it was a long journey to Croydon and back, but she made him stay.

To begin with, he helped with the housework on Saturdays, but by 1973 he was doing the bulk of it. When, at first, he refused, she "flew off the handle and got in a rage", so he did it. He put it this way in his evidence: "After a time I noticed she was very domineering and expects people to obey."

He said that she asked for – and got – £300 towards doing up the kitchen, and further sums of £150 and £250 for making one of her records, and to raise these sums he had to surrender his life policy.

He was never invited to the parties; instead he had to help clear up afterwards. He couldn't even go to his room; Jones told him to sit in the kitchen and he presumed it was because his room was being used for sex. It was the one on the other side of the two-way mirror. On occasion he had to sit up in the kitchen until two or three in the morning.

Eventually Gilbert plucked up courage to tell Jones that he wanted to leave. According to him, she said that if he did, she could cause trouble by getting some of the girls to say that they had been to bed with him, and she would tell the Civil Service authorities.

Later, he was made to buy contraceptives in large quantities which Jones had ordered. Some were kept in the large bedroom used for orgies, and when the girls were sent out Jones supplied them with a contraceptive. On some occasions, he was made, under threats of violence, to accompany one or more girls so that he could bring back the money. "I thought I might get hurt," he said, if he didn't go.

There came a time when, using his home address at Southport, he wrote enquiring about flats, hoping his mother would send the replies to him. He never saw any replies. He gathered from what Jones said, that she opened the letters but didn't let him see them. Once he did leave for two or three days and stayed in a hotel. He then rang Jones to say that he had left and would call back for his things. She made some threats as before, to cause trouble with his employers. So he meekly returned.

He told the same story as B about the visit up north with Jones and taking her back to London, but added that Jones made him pay all the fares because she said she couldn't afford it.

Gilbert's defence to the charges against him (i.e. aiding and abetting Jones in three of the counts, by accompanying the girls and collecting the money, and the one charge of attempting to pervert the course of justice by going north with Jones and bringing B back to London) was that he was acting under duress, i.e. that he committed the offences under the threat of death or serious personal injury. It was not a defence that was really available to him in law because, even if there were threats of violence and he honestly believed them, he could have avoided it. There was nothing to prevent him from going to the police, or from seeking the advice of the County Court Judge at Croydon, or the Senior Clerk there. Moreover, in the course of his duties at the court he had come to know several solicitors whose advice he could have sought. And he could have left, as he did once for two or three days. The threats to expose him, falsely, to his employers did not amount to duress in law.

However, the jury obviously had great sympathy for him and, not surprisingly, he was acquitted on all three charges. He was most ably defended by Kenneth Machin, now a Queen's Counsel. In fact, it was partly on the strength of his advocacy in that case that when Machin, some time later, asked me to be one of his sponsors in his application for Silk, I was most happy to do so.

If Gilbert ever reads this he will doubtless be interested to know that even had he been convicted on all three counts, I would not have sent him to prison. Christian-Dee was also acquitted on all the charges against him. He was defended by a barrister named Bloomfield, who had also successfully defended him ten months previously when he was on trial alone.

At the end of the trial, when Jones was convicted, I said that I would not pass sentence until after the blackmail case, lest anything that I saw fit to say would prejudice her trial in that matter. And to that case I now turn.

Compared with the first trial, the blackmail case was much less exacting to deal with, though it had its own sensational moments and problems. It began about a month after the end of the first trial.

As I have already mentioned, there were five counts of blackmail and two (alternatives to two of the blackmail counts) of obtaining property by deception. The alleged victims were referred to in the trial as Mr Y and Mr Z. They were both particularly vulnerable for special, but different, reasons.

Mr Z was a man of no importance whatever. At all material times he was either an employee in business, or in business on his own account. He was not a wealthy man. He was only concerned in one of the blackmail counts. The sum was £40. It appears to have been a sample count because, he said, he parted with about £250 in all.

Mr Y was a bachelor. He was concerned in all the other counts, the sums demanded or obtained being £2,000, £3,000 and £4,000.

At the end of Michael Worsley's opening speech for the Crown, Peter Dow, QC, who led for the defence of Jones, made a formal admission in these terms:

> There is a formal admission I am instructed to make which I think will assist the Court and the jury and cut down the length of these proceedings. My Lord, it will be unrealistic to think that members of the jury are not aware that recently Miss Jones was tried in this Court on offences involving call-girls, and in the circumstances she thinks it right to admit, for the purpose of this trial, that she was running a call-girl service and was sending girls to Mr Y for money.

It was a sensible course to adopt in the circumstances, and saved a lot of time. What it meant, of course, was that whereas, in the first trial, Jones had accused the girl witnesses of perjury, she was now admitting that they had told the truth and it was she who had committed perjury.

Z was married. That, naturally, was the reason why he was vulnerable. The other reason was that he had met her, he said, at a "kinky and perverted" party. Two or three years later she telephoned him and said she wanted money to pay her solicitor for her forthcoming divorce. Thereafter, according to Z, she telephoned with ever increasing frequency, making bigger and bigger demands. In his evidence, he said that she knew that he liked to be whipped and to whip others. He said that was the hold she had over him. Moreover, according to him, she said she was writing a book and that people who helped her would not be in the book. But after it was published a lot of people would have red faces.

After trying to keep her at bay, he began to let her have small amounts which he passed to her surreptitiously at a prearranged

rendezvous in a multiple store. As an extra inducement to make
him part with the money, he said, she sent girls to meet him at a
friend's flat (L and G gave evidence to a similar effect) to satisfy his
perverted tastes. He said that he thought the girls were sent by way
of repayment of the loans, but he had to pay for their services. It
was mostly G who collected the money. One of the bizarre features
of the case was that whereas G was living with Jones during the
divorce proceedings, and the very first trial when Christian-Dee
was alone on trial, she (G) was living with him before and during
the blackmail trial.

Jones denied that she mentioned the book to bring pressure on
Z. She admitted receiving money from him on two occasions. It
had not been demanded, she said. She had written to ask him for
£150 for her divorce. He gave it to her in a coffee bar in the
multiple store, saying it was money he had stored away. There was
a second payment of £100, which he gave her at her house. She
said she was sitting at her desk going through some bills and
showed him one and he threw £100 over to her in notes, saying
"There you are". The smaller sums, she said, were payment for
the girls whom she sent to Z to whip him and be whipped.

Z was not an impressive witness. His evidence was equivocal; for
example he mentioned "loans". But in any event, it was perhaps
not surprising that Jones was acquitted of blackmailing Z.

Mr Y had first met Jones in about 1965 at a night club in the
West End. They became friendly and he called to see her both at
her flat and at Campden Hill Road. He was a peer and Jones knew
his position in public life. The other reason for his vulnerability
was that, as Jones well knew, he, too, was "kinky". His peculiarity
was that he liked to pretend that he was having sexual intercourse
with very young girls. For this reason A and C had to dress in
young girls' clothes, even to wearing a wig with long curls. These
incidents took place both at Y's flat and at Jones' house, she
making the arrangements and taking the money.

The money which Y passed to Jones was, according to him,
required by her to bring proceedings against the *News of the
World* and to prevent his name from being published. "I realised
that, bearing in mind my position in public life, I could not afford
the publicity." They were large sums, paid in cash, which he said
he had borrowed. He was recovering from a long and serious
illness and had not the strength to withstand her demands. He
said he asked for receipts but she never gave him one. Although,

he said, he asked Jones, from time to time, how the action against the *News of the World* was progressing, she never told him, other than to say the money was required to avoid publicity. By June 1971, he had given her £6,000, of which only £500 had been paid to her solicitor for the libel action. Y said that if he had known that, his attitude would have been different, and added, "until you have been in this position, you don't know what it is like. It is very difficult to bring yourself to the right frame of mind to go to the police. I suspected blackmail, but I had been a friend to her. But they were such big demands, I knew it couldn't have been spent on what she said . . . I should have gone to the police, but I had no guts to do so."

Y gave his evidence courageously and with dignity but he made many damaging admissions when cross-examined by Peter Dow. I quote three questions and answers:

"Weren't you terrified at the thought of publicity?" [in the *News of the World*] – "Yes."

"You were prepared to pay out large sums to avoid publicity?" – "Yes."

"You had something to hide and knew it?" – "Yes."

A little later on he said that he was ready and anxious to assist Jones in stifling publicity, that he knew it would be a very expensive business, and that Jones had said that she could not finance the action.

Jones, herself, was not a very good witness. Her explanation for having committed perjury in the first trial was far from convincing. When cross-examined by Worsley she said that she lied because she had promised Y she would deny having sent girls to him for prostitution. But long before she told that lie (among others), Y had himself given evidence at the magistrates' court in the committal proceedings to that very effect, his identity being protected by the anonymous letter Y. So there was no need for her to tell that lie – except, of course, because she was then denying running a call-girl service.

The final speeches of counsel were completed on the Thursday before Good Friday. The following week was the Easter vacation. I could not interrupt the trial for as long as that involved, and decided to resume on the Wednesday after Easter Monday, when I would begin to sum-up. On the Tuesday Rosalind and I went to the south coast to visit one of my sisters who was seriously ill. We went by train. As we arrived at the railway station for the journey back to

London I was horrified to see an evening newspaper placard which said (so far as I can now recall), "Identity of Mr Y revealed".

In blackmail cases it is customary for judges to order that the name of the alleged victim shall not be disclosed. Otherwise the victim would receive the very publicity with which he or she had been threatened in the first place. If their identity could not be protected in this way, victims would be too frightened to go to the police. They would probably go on paying the blackmailer until, as sometimes happens, in despair, they commit suicide. So it is very much in the public interest that such orders should be made, and the newspaper reporters almost invariably observe the judge's directions – certainly the "resident" journalists at the Old Bailey.

I bought the evening paper and it reported that both Mr Y's and Mr Z's names had been disclosed in a newspaper called "the *Socialist Worker*" The evening paper, to its great credit, did not repeat the disclosure.

I don't suppose the editor of the *Socialist Worker* was in court when I made the order. On the other hand, the trial was very widely reported in the national daily and evening papers, and as the alleged victims were referred to only as Mr Y and Mr Z it must have been obvious that I had made such an order. There had been rumours that Y was a peer and I can only think that, in naming him, the editor was giving vent to anti-establishment sentiments. He should have realised, however, that even he would be similarly protected were he to become the victim of a blackmailer.

As soon as we arrived home, Trixie, the indomitable senior telephonist at the Old Bailey, rang me. She warned me that the press had been trying to contact me all day, but (as is customary) all requests for my home address or telephone number had been refused. We are ex-directory. I then rang Carl Aarvold, who was at home in Surrey, to seek his advice. Whilst we were talking on the phone a car pulled up outside the house and the driver (a complete stranger) came to the front door and rang the bell. Fortunately I had alerted Rosalind. She opened the door and as the man began to say that he was a representative of (and he mentioned a national newspaper), Rosalind asked him if the car outside the house was his. When he said it was she told him to get back into it and drive away as fast as he could. He did just that. There are times when Rosalind has a very commanding look in her eye. I was able to give Carl a running commentary on it all. I can't begin to imagine how the man found my address. It passes understanding that editors or sub-editors get their staff to try to interview judges about cases they are currently trying. They must know that no judge would ever make any comment. However, I told Carl what I intended to do the following morning, which was to make a statement in court before beginning to sum-up. Carl made one or two shrewd amendments to the draft I had prepared on the train.

The following morning's *Times* and one or two other newspapers made rather a meal of it all, and even went on to say that I had ordered the Editor and Proprietor of the *Socialist Worker* to appear before me in court. This was wholly untrue. Nor could anyone at the Old Bailey have issued such an order. Leslie Boyd was on holiday in France at the time and his entire administrative staff were absent on the Tuesday; the office was closed.

On the Wednesday morning the Editor and another representative of the *Socialist Worker* came to court but I did not see them. Much more important, Carl also came up, although on holiday. He thought he should be on hand in case. I needed further help or guidance. I was greatly touched by this kind and considerate act. The statement I made was as follows:

Before I begin my summing-up in this case there is another matter with which I have to deal. My attention has been drawn to an article that has been published in a journal, which is, fortunately, obscure, which reveals the identities of the two victims of the alleged blackmail in the case which I am currently trying. Contrary to what has appeared in some newspaper articles this morning, let me say at once that neither I nor anyone on my behalf has asked that anyone should attend here this morning, but as my attention has been drawn to the article in question I feel it is my duty to deal with the matter at once.

A Judge has the inherent right to control the proceedings in his Court, and in accordance with the invariable practice in such cases I directed, as, indeed, did the learned Magistrate at the preliminary hearing, that the names of the alleged victims should not be disclosed. On the face of it, the publication in question, which not only reveals the names but a good deal else besides, would seem to constitute a deliberate contempt of Court. But it does not stop there. I understand – although I have not yet seen it – that recently another publication revealed the name of one of the alleged victims, linking it with this trial.

If alleged victims of blackmail fear that by going to the police their names will receive great publicity it must deter them from seeking the protection of the law, and that obviously would result in a serious interference with the administration of justice, and I am, therefore, bound to take a grave view of it. Accordingly, I have decided to refer the matter to the Director of Public Prosecutions with a recommendation that he takes appropriate action.

The papers were sent to the DPP and in due course the Director, Sir Norman Skelhorne, an old friend and fellow Bencher of the Middle Temple, sent me an opinion, written by one of his staff, to the effect that what the *Socialist Worker* had done did not amount to contempt of court. I did not agree. I looked up the law myself, wrote a short opinion, and asked Norman to come and see me. When he read my opinion, he agreed with me, and duly passed the matter on to Sam Silkin, the Attorney-General. Proceedings were taken in the Divisional Court. That court held that the conduct of persons who were parties to the publication of the victims' names during the course of the criminal proceedings, despite my direction, constituted contempt on two grounds: (a) in publishing the names they were committing a blatant affront to the authority of the court, and (b) if witnesses in blackmail proceedings were not adequately protected, potential victims in other such cases might be deterred from coming forward. Accordingly, by destroying the confidence of witnesses in future blackmail proceedings in the protection which they would get, there was an act calculated to interfere with the due course of justice. The newspaper company was fined. In giving the judgment of the Divisional Court, Lord Widgery, the Lord Chief Justice, said:

For more years than any of us can remember it has been commonplace in blackmail charges for the complainant to be allowed to give the evidence without disclosing his name. That is not out of any feelings of tenderness towards the victim of blackmail. . . . The reason why the Courts in the past have so often used this device in this type of blackmail case where the complainant has something to hide, is because there is a keen public interest in getting blackmailers convicted and sentenced, and experience shows that grave difficulty may be suffered in getting complainants to come forward unless they are given this kind of protection.

The Lord Chief Justice also referred, without disapproval, to the ruling I had made in the first trial whereby the girl witnesses were to be referred to by letters of the alphabet. Archbold's *Criminal Law and Practice*, the criminal lawyers' *vade-mecum*, put the matter this way:

> The judge permitted each of the seven girls called for the Crown to be referred to throughout the trial by a letter of the alphabet. Certain of the relevant considerations were (i) none of the girls had been engaged in prostitution prior to their association with Jones, (ii) all but one or two had not engaged in prostitution since terminating their relationship with Jones, and several had since either married or become engaged. In short, the rationale of this particular departure from the usual practice was that unless the anonymity of these former prostitutes was preserved, grave difficulty may be suffered in obtaining the necessary evidence in any future case of that nature.

To come back to the trial. After making the statement to which I have referred, I began to sum up, and sent the jury out the following morning. They came back with their verdicts that afternoon, acquitting Jones on all the charges in that part of the trial. The result was, perhaps, not surprising in the light of Y's admissions when cross-examined.

I then had to pass sentence on Jones in respect of the convictions in the first trial. When asked if she had anything to say before sentence was passed on her, she said that I had been unfair and prejudiced against her. I pointed out that it was to prevent any unfair prejudice that I had severed the blackmail charges, and postponed passing sentence until after the second trial.

In her recent series of newspaper articles, she describes gripping the rail of the dock whilst I was addressing her. She must have forgotten that, because I knew from medical reports from the prison doctor, that she was suffering from an internal complaint, I directed that she should remain seated, not only when the verdicts were being returned but also until after I had passed sentence.

On each of seven counts, which charged her with exercising control over prostitutes, I passed concurrent sentences of five years. The gravity of the offences was not in running the call-girl service but in the way she had lured the girls into the service by false promises and then pressured them into staying in it when they wanted to leave. In addition, on each of three counts charging her with attempting to pervert the course of justice, I sentenced her to concurrent terms of two years' imprisonment, but consecutive to the five years, making seven years in all. I also ordered Jones to pay £4,000 towards the costs of the prosecution of the first trial, within six months. In addition, I directed that she should pay the taxed legal aid costs of the defence in the first trial or £12,000, whichever was the lesser figure. In making those orders, I had regard to her valuable house and contents and car. In the course of passing sentence, I said:

> It is a thousand pities that you did not have the good sense, courage and honesty to plead guilty in the first trial and thereby save an immense amount of public time and expense and a good deal of expense to yourself. You would have saved yourself from going into the witness box and committing perjury in the most blatant way. You knew the risks you were running in operating a call-girl service, but such was your greed for money that you were prepared to take that risk. You lured these girls into your web of vice by false promises to get them work in television or films. Once they realised what they had let themselves in for, you prevented their escape by a form of blackmail by threatening to expose them either to their parents or employers. In this way you made sure that even your own niece kept on working in your loathsome trade which over the years must have made you many many thousands of pounds. In spite of the verdict of this jury, to which I will be completely loyal, I am bound to say that I regard you as using blackmail in one form or another as one of the tools of your trade. In my time I have come across many men whom it would be right to describe as evil but, in all my time at the Bar and on the Bench, I have only come across one woman, so far as I can recall, who merited such a description.

You are the second, and beside you, she was comparatively harmless . . .

Jones appealed against the sentences. In dismissing the appeal, Lord Widgery said "the seven years were not a day too long". In my long career I have tried only one woman who I believe more evil than Jones, but she did not even have the redeeming feature of a sense of humour.

LORD HAW-HAW (WILLIAM JOYCE)

(Old Bailey, 1945)

Rebecca West

Twentieth-century trials for treason are rare, but in the wake of the Second World War, they clogged the courts in London and Nuremberg. This is the case of William Joyce whose treachery, broadcast nightly from Nazi Germany, by turns terrified and amused his listeners in Britain. Nicknamed Lord Haw-Haw, his nasal tones drew a large and enthusiastic audience, mesmerized by his catchphrase "Jairmany calling" that promised as much comic relief as the antics of Tommy Handley and his zany ITMA crew. Joyce's brand of wireless propaganda, explains the trial historian C. E. Bechhofer Roberts, "provided a great deal of amusement for British listeners in the grim, blacked-out evenings: at its worst it was unconscious humour of the highest quality, while at its best – and William Joyce was undoubtedly the Germans' most outstanding broadcaster in English – it was entertaining but unimpressive." Arrested less than a month after the German surrender, he was repatriated to London where at his Old Bailey trial he was convicted of treason on a grand scale, the nearest thing to a major war criminal, in the opinion of one biographer, that Britain possessed. Joyce's trial turned on the question of his citizenship. He held a British passport, obtained in 1933, when he declared falsely on his application form that he had been born in

Galway. In fact he was born in the United States, in Brooklyn, New York, but the British post-war government tweaked the law to bring him to a traitor's death by dismissing the truth and accepting his lie. Rebecca West (1892–1983), who had listened to Joyce's broadcasts at home in Buckinghamshire, attended his trial in September 1945 and filed a 7,000-word article for the New Yorker, *the American journal for which she had been writing brilliantly since the outbreak of war. Her editor, Harold Ross, wired "Cover this trial" and she did so with intensity and at breakneck speed. In January 1946, she was among the gaggle of onlookers outside Wandsworth Gaol to witness the "minute shred of ceremony" that accompanied the official notification that Joyce had been hanged. (His execution was indecorous, Joyce's facial scar splitting open as the noose snapped his neck.) The author was born Cicely Fairfield, a name that she thought was too frilly for the kind of writer she wanted to be. So she took the name Rebecca West from a tough character in an Ibsen play. Although, as she confided to Cyril Connolly, she was "consumed with pity for Joyce", West had a horror for the crime of treason. She saw it as an issue in black and white, right and wrong. Yet she had been a rebel herself in her days as a young feminist and socialist. She notoriously had an affair with the (married) novelist H.G. Wells and bore him a son out of wedlock. Her observations on the trial of William Joyce, written with characteristic verve, slapped her portrait on the cover of* Time *magazine, which hailed her as "indisputably the world's No 1 woman writer." This extract ends with Joyce's Fascist friends dispersing at the end of his trial. Later West, with her gimlet eye for detail, reported how Joyce "halted on his way to the scaffold, looked down on the violent trembling of his knees, and calmly and cynically smiled."*

Everybody in London wanted to see William Joyce when he was brought to trial as a radio traitor, for he was something new in the history of the world. Not before have people known the voice of one they had never seen as well as if he had been a husband or a brother or a close friend; and if they had foreseen such a miracle they would not have imagined that the familiar unknown would speak to them only to prophesy their death and ruin. All of us in England had experienced that hideous novelty. It was difficult not to chance on Joyce's wavelength when one was tuning-in to the English stations, and there was an arresting quality about his voice which made it a sacrifice not to go on listening. It was a rasping yet rich voice, very like the voice of the American rabble-rouser, Father Coughlin, and it was convincing in its confidence. It seemed as if one had better hearken and take warning when he suggested that the destiny of the people he had left in England was death, and the destiny of his new masters in Germany life and conquest, and that, therefore, his listeners had better change sides and submit. This was often terrible to hear, for the news in the papers confirmed it. He was not only alarming, he was ugly; he opened a vista into a mean life; he always spoke as if he were better fed and better clothed than we were, and so, we now know, he was. He went further than that smug mockery of our plight. He sinned that sin which is the dark travesty of legitimate hatred because it is felt for kindred, just as incest is the dark travesty of legitimate love. When the U-boats were sinking so many of our ships that to open the newspapers was to see the faces of drowned sailors, he rolled the figures of our lost tonnage on his tongue. When we were facing the hazard of D-day, he rejoiced in the thought of the English dead that would soon lie under the West Wall.

So all the curious went off to the Central Criminal Court on 17 September 1945, when he came up for trial. It looked odd to those who had not seen it since the war. It had stood in a congestion of unlovely commercial buildings; the blitz had now converted it into a beautiful desert. Churches stood blackened but apparently intact; birds, however, flew through the empty sockets of the windows and long grass grew around their altars. A red-brick Georgian mansion, hidden for a century by sordid warehouses, looked at the great Renaissance dome of St Paul's across acres where willow-herb, its last purple flowers passing into silver clouds of seed dust, grew with the yellow ragwort from the ground plan of a lost city drawn in rubble. The courts themselves startled the eye that knew them as they were, housed in a solid building built of grey stone in the neo-classical style. Its solidarity had been sliced as if it were a cake, and the walls of the slice were raw, new red brick. At the time of the trial, because of the sealing-off of the bombed parts, and the heavy black-out, not yet removed owing to the lack of labour, all the halls and passages and stairs were in perpetual dusk. The courtroom – the Court No. 1 where all the most famous criminal trials of modern times have taken place – was lit by electric light, for the shattered glass dome had not yet been rebuilt. Bare boards filled it in, giving an odd-come-short look to what used to be an austerely fine room.

The strong electric light was merciless to William Joyce, whose appearance was a surprise to all of us who knew him only on the air. His voice had suggested a large and flashy handsomeness. But he was a tiny little creature and, though not very ugly, was exhaustively so. His hair was mouse-coloured and grew thinly, particularly above his ears. His nose was joined to his face at an odd angle, and its bridge and its point and its nostrils were all separately misshapen. Above his small dark-blue eyes, which were hard and shiny, like pebbles, his eyebrows were thick and pale and irregular. His neck was long and his shoulders were narrow and sloping. His arms were very short and very thick, so that his sleeves were like little bolsters. His body looked flimsy yet coarse. There was nothing individual about him except a deep scar running across his right cheek from his ear to the corner of his mouth. But this did not create the savage and marred distinction that it might suggest, for it gave a mincing immobility to his mouth, which was extremely small. His smile was pinched and governessy. He was dressed with an intent and ambitious spruceness which did not succeed in giving any impression of well-being, but rather recalled some Eastern European peasant, newly driven off the land by poverty into a factory town and wearing his first suit of Western clothes. He moved with a jerky formality which would have been thought strange in any society. When he bowed to the judge, his bow seemed sincerely respectful but entirely inappropriate to the occasion, and it was difficult to think of any occasion to which it would have been appropriate.

At right angles to the dock, against the wall of the court, sat the jury, none of its members greatly blessed by nature, though there was one woman, slender and high-nosed, of the colonel's-daughter kind, who had an irresistible charm. Day by day the journalists who watched the case became more and more convinced, for no reason at all, that she was a very good sort. But the members of the jury were all middle-aged, since the armies had not come home, and though they were drawn from different ranks of life, there was then no rank in which English people were other than puffy or haggard. But at that they were all more pleasant to look at and more obviously trustworthy than the homely and eccentric little man in the dock; and, compared with the judicial bench which he faced, he was of course at an immense disadvantage, as we all should be, for its dignity is authentic. Against oak panels, columns ran up to a pediment framing the carved royal standard and the sword of justice, which is affixed to the wall in its jewelled scabbard. At the foot of the wall, in a high-backed chair, sat the judge, dressed in his scarlet robe, with its neck-band of fine white linen and its deep cuffs and sash of purplish-black taffeta. Beside him, their chairs set further back as a sign of their inferiority to him, sat the Lord Mayor of London and two aldermen, wearing their antique robes of black silk with flowing white cravats and gold chains hung with chased badges of office worked in precious metals and enamel. These two sorts of pompous trapping are always given some real meaning by the faces of the men who support them. Judges are chosen for a combination of intellect and character, city honours are usually earned by competence and character and the patience to carry out a routine of tedious public duty over decades, and such qualities usually leave an imprint on the features.

Looking from the bench to the dock, it could be seen that not in any sane state would William Joyce have had the ghost of a chance of holding such offices as these. But when he was asked to plead he said, "Not guilty," and those two words were the most impressive uttered during the trial. The famous voice was let loose. For a fraction of a second we heard its familiar quality. It was as we had heard it for six years, it reverberated with the desire for power. Never was there a more perfect voice for a demagogue, for its reverberations were so strong that they were certain to awaken echoes in every heart that was tumid with the same appetite. What could the little man do – since he so passionately desired to exercise authority, and neither this nor any other state would give it to him – but use his trick of gathering together other luckless fellows, that they might overturn the sane state and substitute a mad one? That was the most profound cause which had brought him to the dock; but there was another which quickly became apparent.

This trial, like the great treason trial of the First World War, when Sir Roger Casement went to the gallows, was an Irish drama. From the first, rumours had been current that Joyce was Irish, but they had never been officially confirmed, and his accent was difficult to identify. But there was little doubt about it when one saw him in the dock. He had the real Donnybrook air. He was a not very fortunate example of the small, nippy, jig-dancing type of Irish peasant, and the appearance of his brother, who attended the court every day in a state of great suffering, was proof of the family's origin. Quentin Joyce, who was then twenty-eight, was eleven years William's junior. He was much better-looking, with a sturdy body, a fresh colour, thick and lustrous brown hair, and the soft eyes of a cow. Nobody in his senses could mistake him for anything but an Irishman from the provinces. There were also strong traces of Irish origin in the followers of Joyce who watched the trial. These were a singular crowd. There were also some women who especially attracted attention by an almost unearthly physical repulsiveness, notably an ageing and floozy blonde in a tight Air Force uniform, who sucked sweets and wept, as she swung an ankle creased with fat from crossed knees that pressed up against her drooping bosom. But she and her like, it seemed probable, had been merely on the fringe of the British Fascist movement and were sympathizers with Joyce rather than his associates.

These could be seen every day gathered round Joyce's brother, and his solicitor and his clerk. The solicitor was a fragile, even childish, figure with blond hair and a pale sensitive face who was acting for Joyce not because he wished to have him as a client or had any sympathy with British fascism, but because Joyce, being without means on his return from Germany to England, had had to apply for the services of a lawyer under the Poor Prisoners' Defence Act when he first came up before the minor judge we call a magistrate for the preliminary stages of his trial. This meant that the magistrate had had to select at random the names of certain lawyers from a rota, and call on them to perform the duty of defending Joyce, a summons which they were not allowed to refuse. The task must have been extremely onerous for this lawyer, who was a practitioner of high standing and had no need for notoriety. But he could not have behaved with more exquisite loyalty to his client, nor soothed more kindly the grief of the many persons associated with the case which he must heartily have wished he never had seen. Each day he bore himself amiably towards them, aided by his clerk, a girl in her twenties, with long and elaborately curled hair, bareheaded and dressed as if for the beach walk of a summer resort, with flowered frock, fleecy coat, and light shoes. There could not have been a figure more discordant with the peculiar dry decorum of the English courts. But she too was conscientiously gracious to Joyce's friends, the chief of whom was a thin man with fierce black eyes blazing behind thick glasses, a tiny fuzz of black hair fancifully arranged on his prematurely bald head, and wrists and ankles as straight as lead piping in their emaciation.

He was a Scotsman named Angus MacNab, the editor of a
Fascist paper and Joyce's best friend. He was plainly foredoomed
to follow odd by-paths, and a variation in circumstances might
have found him just as happily a spiritualist medium or a believer
in the lost ten tribes of Israel. As for the rest of the followers, men
of violent and unhappy appearance, with a look of animal shyness
and ferocity, and, in some cases, a measure of animal beauty, they
were for the most part darker in complexion than one would expect
in subscribers to the Aryan theory. One, especially, looked like a
true gipsy. Many of them had an Irish cast of feature and some
bore Irish names. It must be remembered that most of these men
were not followers of Sir Oswald Mosley, who picked a more
varied and more cheerfully brutal type. Joyce had seceded from
Mosley's movement some years before the war and started his
own. This was his private army, part of his individual hell.

The story developed during the first day and the morning of the
second, and it was certainly an Irish story. At first our attention
wandered from Joyce's personality because the lawyer for the
Crown was Sir Hartley Shawcross, the Attorney-General appointed by the new Labour Government. He was young for the
post, charming in manner and voice, and he set out a beautifully
lucid argument, and we were pleased, and pleased to be pleased.
For the English were eager to approve of whatever the new
government did; we were tired out by such excitements as had
produced this trial, and what we wanted was to hear the machine
ticking over. But the interest presently shifted to an ironical story
of a family who, for obscure reasons springing from one convulsion
of history, engaged in disingenuous conduct which, long after,
brought their dearest member a nonsensical doom in another
historical convulsion.

That the proceedings were to be odd was indicated by the three
counts of the indictment brought against him. He had offended, it
seemed, against the root of the law against treason: a Statute in
which Edward III, in the year 1351, "at the request of the lords
and commons" declared that "if a man do levy war against our
Lord the King in his realm or be adherent to the King's enemies in
his realm, giving them aid and comfort in the realm or elsewhere",
he was guilty of treason. So the Clerk of the Court, Sir Wilfrid
Knops, said: "William Joyce, you are charged in an indictment
containing three counts with high treason. The particulars in the
first count are that on the 18th September 1939, and on other days

between that day and the 29th May 1945, you, being a person owing allegiance to our lord the King, and when a war was being carried on by the German realm against our King, did traitorously adhere to the King's enemies, in parts beyond the seas, that is to say in Germany, by broadcasting propaganda. In a second count of the same indictment, it is charged that you, on the 26th September 1940, being a person owing allegiance as in the other count, adhered to the King's enemies by purporting to become naturalized as a subject of Germany. And in a third count, the particulars are the same as in the first count, that is to say, you are charged with broadcasting propaganda, but the dates are different, and the dates in this case are the 18th September 1939, and on days between that day and the 2nd July 1940." Later the first two counts were amended, for reasons emerging during the trial, and he was described in them as "a British subject", but, significantly, no such change was made in the third.

It seemed, in the early stages of the trial, as if William Joyce must be convicted on these two first indictments. He himself had again and again described himself as a British subject, and his father had done the same. The first evidence to this effect came from a comely and pleasant-voiced lady in early and spruce middle age with marcelled grey hair and a spirited red straw hat, the kind of lady who is photographed in women's magazines as having taken a prize for preserves at a Women's Institute fair, who, oddly enough, turned out to be the assistant secretary of the Committee for Military Education in the University of London. When one thought of the blond and boar-like young man or the Brünhilde-like young woman who would have held such a post in a German University, it became a better joke than ever that we had won the war. She was present because someone with a prodigious memory had recalled that in August 1922 William Joyce, then a boy of sixteen, had sent a letter of application for entrance to the London University Officers' Training Corps, in which he had described himself as a British subject, a description which was supported by his father, Michael Joyce. The boy's letter threw a light on the inner ferment that had brought him to the dock. In this letter he had said that he wanted to study with a view to being nominated by the University for a commission in the Regular Army; but it was obvious that he would find difficulty in following that road. His letter was a little too highfalutin, even for a boy of sixteen. Doubt would have crossed the mind of anybody who read it. And the letter from his father, the loving letter of a father eager to do his best for his son, was too illiterate. But they made themselves plain enough on the subject-matter of the correspondence.

"I must now," wrote the young Joyce, "mention a point which I hope will not give rise to difficulties. I was born in America, but of British parents. I left America when two years of age, have not returned since, and do not propose to return. I was informed, at the brigade headquarters of the district in which I was stationed in Ireland, that I possessed the same rights and privileges as I would if of natural British birth. I can obtain testimonials as to my loyalty to the Crown. I am in no way connected with the United States of America, against which, as against all other nations, I am prepared to draw the sword in British interests. As a young man of pure British descent, some of whose forefathers have held high position in the British army, I have always been desirous of devoting what little capability and energy I may possess to the country which I love so dearly. I ask that you may inform me if the accident of my birth, to which I refer above, will affect my position. I shall be in London for the September Matriculation Examination and I hope to commence studies at the London University at the beginning of the next academic year. I trust that you will reply as soon as possible, and that your reply will be favourable to my aspirations." At an interview with an official of the O.T.C. he conveyed that he was "in doubt as to whether he was a 'British subject of pure European descent'", a doubt which must have been honest if he expressed it at all in view of the ardent hope expressed in his letter; but he asserted that his father had never been naturalized. This the father confirmed when the official wrote to him for further particulars. "Dear Sir, your letter of 23rd October received. Would have replied sooner, but have been away from home. With regard to my son William. He was born in America, I was born in Ireland. His mother was born in England. We are all British and not American citizens."

But why, when William Joyce was making later declarations that he was a British subject, had he sometimes said that he was a British subject, and he sometimes said that he was born in Ireland and sometimes that he was born in America, when he had a birth certificate which gave his birthplace as Brooklyn? The answer is that he was probably never sure of the real facts regarding his own and his father's status till he learned them from his own defence lawyers just before the trial. In the statement he made to the

Intelligence officers on his arrest he expressed himself uncertainly. "I understand, though I have no documents to prove any statement, that my father was American by naturalization at the time of my birth, and I believe he lost his American citizenship later through failing to renew it, because we left America in 1909 when I was three years old. We were generally treated as British subjects during our stay in Ireland and England. I was in Ireland from 1909 till 1921 when I came to England. We were always treated as British during the period of my stay in England whether we were or not." But the truth was disclosed when Mr Gerald Slade, K.C.,[1] counsel for the defence, got going with the case for Joyce and told – with a curious dry and ascetic fervour which recalled that in his spare time he is a temperance advocate – a story which would have charmed a snake if read to it at dictation speed. For it turned out that William Joyce's father, Michael Joyce, had been a naturalized American long before William Joyce had been born at 1377 Herkimer Street, Brooklyn. Therefore William Joyce was by birth an American citizen and owed the King of England no allegiance arising out of British nationality. All his life he had described himself as a British subject, and his father had done the like; and they had been lying. There was no doubt about it. The documents of naturalization were present in good order, dated in 1894, and a torn certificate, printed in that early nineteenth-century type which we used to regard as hideous and now nostalgically think charming, proved that Michael Francis Joyce and Gertrude Emily Brooke had been married in All Saints Church, at 129th Street and Madison Avenue, New York, by Roman Catholic rites, on the 2nd of May 1902.

Then, to confirm all this, came Mr Frank Holland, who was a difficult witness. An old gentleman, white-haired and shrivelled and deaf and palsied and quavering, he stoutly gave evidence that he had been born in 1883; and there was apparently no mistake about it. Added to this, he was Irish beyond the normal provisions of nature, with the emphasis of art; he might have been one of the Dublin players taking part in a Sean O'Casey play. He also suffered from an eerie form of deafness, the inverse of a banshee's wail; one saw even the baritone of Sir Hartley Shawcross, which is as audible as an actor's voice, come to his ear and be attenuated and disappear into nothingness. Added to that, he had a mind which, in

1 Later Sir Gerald Slade, since June 1948 a judge of the High Court.

one sense fragile, was in another vigorous. He did not fly off at a
tangent – flying things can be brought down – but he crept off at
tangents, and not the entire forces of the Central Criminal Court
could bring him home. The defending counsel had announced that
he was calling Mr Holland to certify that when Michael Joyce was
leaving America for England, his passport had arrived after he had
left his home in Brooklyn to go down to the steamer, and that Mr
Holland had waited to take it from the postman and had carried it
down to his friend at a Hoboken pier, and that Mr Holland had
then seen it was an American passport. But when the relevant
questions were put to the old man, he bridled. They appeared to
him to cast aspersions on his gentlemanliness. Yes, he had helped
his friend by fetching him his passport, but how was he to know
what kind of passport? His attitude sharply indicated that other
people might know no better than to be inquisitive, but he had his
manners. As the examination went on, old age could be seen
shifting itself from the shoulders of Mr Holland to those of the
examining counsel; yet Mr Holland contributed enough.

Long ago he had known a girl named Gertrude Emily Brooke.
She was called Queenie, he told us, with a sudden affectionate
chuckle. She had married a man named Michael Joyce, who
worked in America. It was on Michael Joyce's advice that Mr
Holland himself had gone to America and followed his calling of
civil engineer under the employment of the Pennsylvania Railway
Company. He and his wife had seen much of the Joyces in
America; they had liked them, and even if they had not, would
have been inclined to visit them frequently for the simple reason
that they were the only people they knew anywhere near New
York. And indeed they were lucky to have friends with such a
pleasant home. For the Joyces' house, which has since been
reconstructed and is now an estate agent's office, stood on a corner
lot in a broad street planted with trees, which is now occupied at
one end by Negroes and at the other by Italians, but was then a
centre of the Irish community. The German quarter was not far
away. He went on to describe how Michael Joyce had told him that
he had become an American citizen and advised him to do the
same. He took the advice, but came home to England after the
outbreak of the First World War; he was greatly inconvenienced
by his American citizenship, for he had to register under the Aliens
Act which was passed in 1915 and report all his movements to the
police. At this time he had visited Queenie, then settled in Lanca-

shire, and had exchanged commiserations with her, because she was incommoded in the same way. His cracked old voice evoked two people grumbling together thirty years ago. That they had so grumbled could not be doubted.

This witness's evidence recalled the acting of Sir Henry Irving. It was impossible to hear a word of what Irving said for years before he left the stage, and as his memory had gone that was just as well; but the melodic line of his murmurs and the gesture of his gauntness never failed to evoke the truth concerning Shylock, because he knew that truth and charged such means of expression as still remained to him with instructions to transmit it. Mr Holland was as bewildering a witness as could be imagined. The name of Gertrude Emily Brooke's birthplace, the town of Shaw in Lancashire, inspired him to dazzling feats. Through his deafness he appeared to swear that he had been born there, that he had never been there, that he had seen the Joyces there, and that he had not seen them there, and that he had visited the Joyces in 1919 at a house in which they had in fact settled in 1923. But he had known the Joyces for fifty years; he did recognize the prisoner in the dock as the William Joyce who had been a baby in Herkimer Street, Brooklyn; he had heard Michael Joyce say he was an American and Gertrude Emily Joyce grumble about the necessity to register as an alien; and he was telling the truth. It showed in the irritable twitch of his eyebrows when he was asked to put what he said into a form more likely to convince the jury, the impatient wail of his voice as he made what seemed to him the superfluous repetition. The case against William Joyce, so far as it depended on his British nationality, lay dead on the courtroom floor when Mr Holland left the witness-box.

There came to confirm that evidence a police official named Woodmansey, who proved that in the last war Mr and Mrs Michael Joyce, oscillating between Galway and Lancashire with their children, had been registered as Americans. They had broken the rules by failing to report their movements and this had produced an illuminating correspondence between the police in Lancashire and the Royal Irish Constabulary in Galway. This revealed that both Michael Joyce and his wife had oddly met the situation with the nonsensical tale which we had heard before, that they were not really aliens, because Michael had failed to re-register as an American citizen within two years after leaving the United States. What was odder still was that the Galway constabulary – which must have known that it was nonsense, for there was nothing that an Irish policeman knew better than the American laws that affected Irish emigrants – recommended this preposterous story sympathetically to the Lancashire police, urging that Michael Joyce was "one of the most respectable, law-abiding, and loyal men in the locality, and one who has been consistently an advocate of the 'pro-Allied' cause since the beginning of the war", and expressing doubt "whether these people are aliens at all". The Lancashire police crisply resisted the suggestion, but dealt with the case by a caution. The Galway constable who had administered the admonition came to give evidence – a thin and aged giant, so disabled by blindness and partial paralysis that he had to be led to the witness-box and propped up in it, a tall blanched obelisk. It was odd to find that to this incident Mrs Joyce, who was by all accounts a person of scrupulous character, had contributed her own lie. She told the police that though her husband had been in the United States he was "only three or four years there altogether". It seems unlikely that she should not have known that he had lived there for eighteen years preceding their marriage.

The oddity of the situation was emphasized by the evidence of Quentin Joyce. There passed between him and the man in the dock a nod and a smile of pure love. One realized that life in this strange family must sometimes have been great fun. But it evidently had not been fun lately. Quentin told the court that his father had died in 1941, shortly after the house in which he had lived for eighteen years had been destroyed by a bomb, and his mother had died in 1944. Out of the wreckage of the house there had been recovered a few boxes full of papers, but none had any bearing on the question of the family's nationality, and there was a reason for that. Michael Joyce had told young Quentin, when he was ten years old, that he and all the family were American citizens but had bade him never speak of it, and had in later years often reiterated this warning. Finally, in 1934, the boy, who was then sixteen, had seen him burn a number of papers, including what appeared to be an American passport. He had given a reason for what he was doing, but the witness was not required to repeat it. The date suggested what that reason may have been. By that time the police knew William Joyce as a troublesome instigator of street-fighting and attacks on Communists and Jews, and in November 1934 Joyce was prosecuted, together with Sir Oswald Mosley and two other Fascists, on a charge of riotous assembly at Worthing; and though this prosecution failed, it indicated a serious attempt by the authorities to rid themselves of the nuisance of Fascist-planned disorder. Michael Joyce had every reason to fear that, if the police ever got an inkling of his secret, they would deport his son and not improbably the whole family.

The courtroom was by now in a state that would have puzzled those Americans who think of the British as a comfortably homogeneous people; for some of the spectators could not make head or tail of this old story, and some of them knew perfectly well where they were, even if they did not know exactly what was going on in that peculiar field. The people who knew where they were had two characteristics in common: they had Irish antecedents and they were not young. They knew what Ireland was before it was Eire, and the dreary round by which men, often brave and good men, kept in check, by a complicated mechanism of oppression and espionage, other men, also often brave and good, who retorted by shooting them from behind stone walls and burning down their houses. Because Michael Joyce had been married in a Roman Catholic church, and because of the surname he bore, which is extremely common in certain counties, it could be known that he was one of the native Irish, the mass of whom were against the English and on the side of the people who shot the English from behind stone walls. But when an officer of the Royal Irish Constabulary described him as one of the loyalest men in Galway, it meant that he was on the side of England. There were many such native Irish who turned against their own kind and worked with the alien oppressor, and we forget now how many of them were passionately sincere. Doubtless some were seduced by the bribery dispensed by Dublin Castle. But many, and among those we must include Michael Joyce, were people who honestly loved law and order and preferred the smart uniforms and the soldierly bearing of the English garrisons and the Royal Irish Constabulary to the furtive slouching of a peasantry distracted with poverty and revolutionary fever. The error of such people was insufficient inquiry into first causes, but for simple natures who went by surface indications their choice was very natural. It must have come very natural indeed to the Joyce family, who, as could be seen from the nervous neatness of both William and Quentin Joyce, and their bearing in court, had been reared to cultivate military smartness and to appreciate ceremonial to such a degree that their

appreciation did not entirely desert them even when the ceremonial belonged to a trial at which one of them stood charged with a
capital offence. These native Irish who had made that choice often
felt a love of England which struck English people as excessive and
theatrical: such a love as William Joyce had, at sixteen, expressed
in his letters to the secretary of the London University Committee
for Military Education, such a love as often led him in after-life to
make a demand – which struck many of his English acquaintances
as a sign of insanity – that any quiet social evening he spent with his
friends should end with the singing of the national anthem.

There was, in that letter he wrote when he was sixteen, an
astonishing sentence. "I have served with the irregular forces of
the Crown in an Intelligence capacity, against the Irish guerrillas",
wrote the boy. "In command of a squad of sub-agents I was
subordinate to the late Capt. P. W. Keating, 2nd R.U.R., who
was drowned in the *Egypt* accident. I have a knowledge of the
rudiments of Musketry, Bayonet Fighting, and Squad Drill." The
Egypt was sunk off Ushant in May 1922; which meant that if this
story were true the boy was engaged in guerrilla fighting with the
Black and Tans when he was fifteen years old. That story was true.
A photograph of him at this time shows him in battle-dress, and
many persons still living remember this phase of his life. He
repeated the statement later on an official form, giving the duration
of his service as four months, and the name of the regiment with
which he had been associated as the Worcestershires, and during
his trial at the Old Bailey an old man from County Galway stood in
the crowd outside and gave rambling confirmation to this claim.
He illustrated the Irish conception of consistency by expressing to
bystanders his hearty desire that William Joyce should be hanged
for treason against the King of England, on the ground that when
he was a boy he had worked with the Black and Tans in persecuting
the Irish when they were revolting against the English. The crowd,
with that tolerance which foreigners, possibly correctly, suspect of
being a form of smugness, was amused and sympathetic. It is
typical of the irony which determined William Joyce's life that not
only did that service he thought he rendered England mean
ultimately nothing, since now we see the severance of England
and Ireland as a historical necessity, but even at the time it can
have recommended him hardly at all to the Englishmen who read
his letter. The Black and Tans were terrified men, set down in a
country where it was impossible to tell friend and foe, and

assassination was the only art of the people; they burned and slew with the ferocity of fear. Even those who thought that England should not have relinquished Ireland were ashamed at this reminder of the inevitable impudicity of the conqueror's sword; and to all, a child who had partaken, even with gallantry, in such deeds, would have seemed to have had his childhood outraged.

To the end of his life this love of an obsolete England persisted in William Joyce, to be rebuffed by contemporary England. Its climax was related at the trial by an officer with the superb name of Alexander Adrian Lickorish, who described how it came about that William Joyce fell into the hands of justice at the end of the war. He might never have been arrested had it not been for his desire to do a service to two English officers whom he did not know, whose only value to him can have been that they were English officers. In November 1944 he had been given a fake passport, apparently for the purpose of enabling him to escape recognition if he fell into the hands of the British. The Germans provided these passports for all the traitors who had been broadcasters for them; but this one was not a very convincing document. It was made out to Wilhelm Hansen, but the holder was stated to have been born in Galway, Ireland, a detail which would have been likely to arouse the interest of any Intelligence officer. After William Joyce had made his last broadcast on 30 April 1945, a broadcast in which, not without dignity, he acknowledged the coming of the night, he took this false passport and with his wife went into hiding. On May 28, when evening was falling, Captain Lickorish and a Lieutenant Perry were walking in a wood near Flensburg, on the Danish frontier, looking for some branches to make a fire, when they came on a man who was wandering aimlessly among the trees. He watched them for a time, and then called to them in French, "Here are a few more pieces." Presently he said in English, "There are a few more pieces here." At once the voice betrayed him. The two officers conferred together, and then Lieutenant Perry said to him, "You wouldn't happen to be William Joyce, would you?" The man put his hand in his pocket, and Lieutenant Perry, thinking he was about to draw a revolver, shot him in the leg. He fell to the ground, saying, "My name is Fritz Hansen." Fritz is not an abbreviation of Wilhelm; but the slip did not matter, for when they searched him they found not only the civil passport (*Reisepass*) made out to Hansen but a military passport (*Wehrpass*) made out in the name of William Joyce.

*Once arrested, Joyce's sole answer to a charge of treason hinged on the
citizenship issue. If he could prove that he had never been a British
subject, even though he had lived on British soil for 30 years, he would
walk from court a free man. As long as he enjoyed the protection of
British law, he owed allegiance to the British state. But as soon as he
quit the country for Germany, such protection and allegiance ceased.
Long and detailed arguments over these crucial issues of residence and
allegiance were traded between the trial judge Mr Justice Tucker, the
Attorney-General and Joyce's counsel Gerald Slade KC, who made a
series of legal submissions quoting one legal authority after another.*

All this filigree work delighted the little man in the dock, who
watched his lawyers with a cynical brightness, as if he were
interested in seeing whether they could get away with all this
nonsense but had no warmer concern with the proceedings. He
showed no special excitement, only a continuance of amused
curiosity, when, on the third day of the trial, at the end of the
morning, the judge announced that he would give his ruling on
these legal submissions after the luncheon interval; and at two
o'clock returned to the dock still with his usual eccentric excess of
military smartness and this sustained tight-lipped derisiveness.
The judge announced that "beyond a shadow of doubt" William
Joyce had owed allegiance to the Crown of this country when he
applied for his passport, and that nothing had happened to put an
end to that allegiance during the period when the passport was
valid. In other words, he ruled that a person holding a British
passport owed allegiance to the Crown even when he was outside
the realm. This ruling made it quite certain that William Joyce was
going to be sentenced to death; and if the sentence were carried out
he would die the most completely unnecessary death that any
criminal has ever died on the gallows. He was the victim of his own
and his father's lifelong determination to lie about their nationality. For if he had not renewed his English passport, and had left
England for Germany on the American passport which was right-
fully his, no power on earth could have touched him. As he became
a German citizen by naturalization before America came into the
war, he could never have been the subject of prosecution under the
American laws of treason.

Now it was certain that the little man was to be sentenced to
death; and nobody in court felt any emotion whatsoever. That was
what made this case more terrible than any other case that any of us

could remember in which a death sentence was passed: it was not terrible at all. People wanted Joyce to pay the proper legal penalty for his treason, but not because they felt any personal hatred against him. They wanted to be sure that in any other war this peculiarly odious form of treachery, which climbed into the ears of frightened people, would be discouraged before it began, and that was about the limit of their interest in the matter. At no other such trial have the spectators, as soon as the jury went out to consider their verdict and the judge retired from the bench and the prisoner was taken down to the cells, got up from their seats and strolled about and chattered as if they were at a theatre between the acts. At no other such trial have the jury come back from considering their verdict looking as if they had been out for a cup of tea. At no other such trial has the judge assumed the black cap – which is not a cap at all but a piece of black cloth that an attendant lays across his wig – as if it were in fact just a piece of black cloth laid across his wig. He spoke the words of the sentence of death reverently, and they were awful, as they always must be: "William Joyce, the sentence of the Court upon you is, that you be taken from this place to a lawful prison, and thence to a place of execution, and that you be there hanged by the neck until you be dead; and that your body be afterwards buried within the precincts of the prison in which you shall have been confined before your execution. And may the Lord have mercy on your soul."

But the effect of these words was, on this uniquely shallow occasion, soon dispersed. It was indeed pitiful when Joyce was asked if he wanted to make a statement before sentence was passed on him, and he shook his head, the hungry and inordinate voice in him at last defeated. He had been even more pitiful earlier in the trial, when the judge had warned the jury to consider very carefully their verdict because a person found guilty must be sentenced to death, for he had put up his hand and touched his neck with a look of wonder. But that he deserved pity was noted by the intellect; pity was not felt. Nor was anybody in the court very much moved by the extreme courage with which he bore himself, though that was remarkable. He listened to the sentence with his head high, gave one of his absurd stiff bows, and ran down to the cells, smiling and waving to his brother and his friends, acting gaiety without a flaw. Such a performance would once have moved us, but not now. All has changed; and even a trial for a capital offence is quite different from what it was before the war. Then the spectators were living in a state of security, and the prisoner was an exceptionally unfortunate person who had strayed into a district not generally visited, perhaps for lack of boldness. But every man and woman who attended Joyce's trial had at some time during the past six years been in danger of undeserved death or pain, and had shown, or witnessed in others enduring such peril, great courage. These attributes in William Joyce made no claim on them, themselves pitiful and brave; and he could not arouse their interest by his exceptional destiny, since he was in the dock by reason of failure to acquit himself in their common destiny. So they turned away from him and left the court as if it had been a cinema or concert. But in the dark corridor a woman said: "I am glad his mother's dead. She lived near us in Dulwich. She was a sweet little lady, a tiny little woman. I often used to stand with her in the fish queue. In fact, that's how I met her. One day after the blitz had been very bad, I said something about that blasted Lord Haw–Haw, and someone said, 'Hush, that's his mother right beside you', and I felt dreadful. But she only said – but she was ever so Irish, and I can't speak like she did – 'Never mind, my dear, I'm sure you didn't mean it unkindly'." This story recalled the lilt of affection in the aged Mr Holland's voice when he had spoken of Queenie.

The dark corridor passed to a twilit landing. Down a shadowed staircase the band of Fascists were descending, tears shining on their astonished faces. Joyce's brother walked slowly, his eyes that were soft and brown like a cow's now narrowed and wet, and the slight blond solicitor just behind him. There was a block, and for a minute the crowd all stood still. The solicitor plucked at Quentin Joyce's jacket and said kindly, "This is just what he expected, you know". "Yes," said his brother, "I know it's just what he expected." The crowd moved on, but after it had gone down a few steps the solicitor plucked at the young man's jacket again and said, "It's the appeal that matters, you know," and Quentin said, "Yes, I know. The appeal's everything."

At the counter where the spectators had to collect their umbrellas and coats, the charming jurywoman was saying good-bye to one of her colleagues. They were shaking hands warmly and expressing hopes that they would meet again. They might have been people parting after a cruise. Jostling them were the Fascists, waiting for their raincoats, garments which those of their guild affect in all weathers, in imitation of Hitler. The young man who looked like a gipsy held his head down. Heavy tears were hanging on his long black lashes. He and his friends still looked amazed. They had wanted people to die by violence, but they had not expected the lot to fall on any of their own number. Another dark and passionate young man was accosted by a reporter, and he cried out in rage that he had been four years in Brixton Jail under Security Regulation 18B, all for patriotism, and he had come out to see the persecution of the finest patriot of all. His black eyes rolled and blazed about him. They fell on another bystander, who was not the best person to receive his complaint, for her name had been on the Gestapo list, recently discovered in Berlin, of persons who were to be arrested immediately after the Germans conquered England, and it was doubtful, had this happened, if it would have led to anything so comfortable as four years in Brixton Jail. But the bystander did not blaze back at him. Not possibly could she have achieved this force. There was this new universality of horrible experience, these vast common martyrdoms, that made these unhappy egotists, insisting on their own particular revolts and heroisms, seem so pathetically obsolete. Not with any degree of picturesque intensity could the bystander have struck an attitude on the ground that she was on that Gestapo list, because about twenty-three hundred other people had also been on it.

The little band of Fascists gathered together in a knot by the door, and after they had wiped their faces and composed themselves, they went out into the street. In the open space in front of the building was a line of parked cars, and behind them stood a crowd of silent people. The Fascists walked away from this crowd, down a street that narrowed and lost itself in a network of alleys. Nobody followed them, but they began to hurry. By the time they got into the shelter of the alleys, they were almost running.

LANDRU

(Versailles, 1919)

William Bolitho

Henri Desiré Landru achieved notoriety as the French Bluebeard. Short, balding and bearded, the ruthless Landru is thought to have murdered as many as thirteen unlucky women. The case – hailed as France's trial of the century – competed for column inches with the Versailles peace treaty negotiated at the end of the First World War. Landru began as a second-hand dealer and petty swindler, but transformed himself into a serial killer of lonely women, mainly widows, by advertising for brides. All but one ended up incinerated in the oven at his villa in Gambais, south-west of Paris. The sole survivor was his adoring mistress, Fernande Segret. Landru, fifty at the time of his trial, was a prolific philanderer, his notebooks showing that he had made the acquaintance of at least 283 women. Having slept with and swindled most of them, he discarded them alive, but eleven of them (including his final victim Marie-Therese Marcha-dier) never returned from Landru's villa. His trial in 1919 should have been a foregone conclusion but, as the prosecutor Maître Gode-froy realized, the authorities lacked clinching evidence in the shape of a body. Nevertheless the trial became a major public attraction; the most popular morning train from Paris to Versailles for the start of each day's hearing became known as the Landru Special. In court, Landru acted the great showman, playing to the gallery, mugging for the cameramen and court artists, and charming the crowds of admiring ladies with his wit. Watching it all was the writer William Bolitho (1891–1930). Although born and raised in South Africa, Bolitho achieved success in America and eventually settled in France. While still a student, he joined the British Army as a trooper and was wounded at the battle of the Somme. Bolitho covered Landru's trial while Paris correspondent of the Manchester Guardian. *He expanded his reports for the first of his two books,* Murder for Profit *(1926). Four years later, Bolitho died after an operation for appendicitis, aged only thirty-nine.*

At last the trial arrived, and we may turn our attention to Landru's great antagonist – Society. The daily badgering of the monster in his cage by the examining magistrate had lasted from 13 April 1919 to November 1921. His use to the Government had ended, for the dictatorship had fallen long ago, the people were restive for their final treat. But all this racking had not drawn out of the man a secret, the only one the examiners hoped for, how he had disposed of his corpses. The villa at Gambais had been excavated and sacked from rafters to cellar, without any results but a handful of charred bones which only cranks in the anatomy school could swear were not rabbits' bones. The kitchen stove, on which the spiritual eyes of 30,000,000 people were fixed ever since Salmon the reporter had playfully hinted that Landru might have used it as a private incinerator, had been dismounted and brought as a trophy; on Landru's own suggestion, the discomfited experts had scraped the soot out of the chimney for analysis, with no better result. Landru, like Smith, would have to be condemned only on coincidence.

This failure of the investigators undoubtedly worried the responsible minister, that is, a certain Monsieur Ignace, the chief tool of the dictatorship. Landru had been extremely useful, but it would never do to allow him to be acquitted, ridiculously, as was likely to happen in Paris, where criminal juries are always dramatic. As a terribly sure safeguard from this possibility, Ignace sent the trial to Versailles. The Versailles juries seldom err in mercy; they are drawn from a population of small farmers, rentiers, and master-workmen who believe in the law. From the moment of that decision Landru was as doomed as if infected with a cancer of the throat.

The selection of the law officers was as delicate as the partition of

rôles in an amateur theatrical society. Every judge on the list had
influence; everyone demanded the right of presiding over the most
famous case in French criminal history. The judging in such an
affair is not empty celebrity; during its course the judge is the most
esteemed figure in society, for he has the allotment of the court-
tickets, one of which every great lady in the city *must* secure. At last
the claims, political, social, of Mr Counsellor Gilbert prevailed for
the post of principal judge: a very social eminence, a man of the
world and fashion, whose tact and appearance – his magnificent
and well-groomed beard, his manicured gestures – hold some
reminiscence of the great magistrates of Balzac. The less but still
pretty office of Advocate-General, or prosecutor, was awarded to
Maître Godefroy, a bearish determined fellow who was evidently
making great progress in the "career". For Landru's defence the
prize had long been taken: Maître Moro-Giafferi, a risen Corsican,
with the largest and most profitable practice in France, as well as
the assured commencement of a remarkable political career on one
side or the other, had in the first month of Landru's success, seized
it for himself, and was, long before the trial, in enjoyment of its
luscious fruits of publicity.

So much preliminary drumming on the likelihood of enormous
crowds at the opening of the case had the contrary effect: on the
first day and until the truth was incautiously published by the
reporters, the court was only moderately full. It was a hall the size
of a meeting-house, distempered in a grim shade of green, whose
only ornament was a huge gas-chandelier, gummy and long un-
used. The weather was cold, the light hard. In front of the judge's
bench was a table covered with "material evidence", the heavier
parts of which were stacked far into the body of the court, so that
the witnesses on their way to the stand had to pick their way among
the burst mattresses, the dismounted iron bedsteads, past a rusty
stove, and look at the silky Gilbert across a square rod of false hair,
cardboard boxes of bones, jewellery that all looked sham, books
and iron bric-à-brac, the lesser spoils of Landru's victims. The
front of the court thus had the sordid and depressing air of a house-
removal. At the other end, there was a dock strongly barred off
where throughout the trial the ticketless public stood in a slab:
pale-faced rogues, gamboge-tressed women without hats, truant
workmen, and inquisitive middle-class women from Paris, all day
obsessed with the wish to gain a place nearer the front. In front of
them were twenty rows of school benches, where the reporters of

the world Press scribbled and quarrelled. On the third day the
court changed: the whole of leisured Paris came to fight for places;
a special train was run from the Gare d'Orsay in time for the
opening. Both the cavernous corridors and the wet street outside
were thick all day with a crowd that pushed like a panic in a theatre
to get in. Gilbert's careful plans to admit only the flower of his
friends were wrecked by force of numbers. The Sovereign People
itself had come to enjoy the function of judging. A place inside,
instead of being the present of a magistrate, was only to be won,
like all the other privileges of a democracy, by competition, and
became a trophy of ferocity in a woman, or cunning strength in a
man. The sucessful part of the nation, once inside, consolidated
positions, squeezed up beside the judge on his bench, forced its
way beside the jurymen, and occupied every window-ledge. The
principle of representation was abandoned; Society moved itself to
share in the condemnation and punishment of the offender. From
this confined rabble at every significant point of the trial rose
various sounds, ignoble roars of laughter, infamous grumblings,
and yells of delight and excitement. It was never quiet. The
ordinary machinery of justice clogged, only with the greatest
hardship managed to enter into action at all. The jurymen took
two hours and the assistance of a platoon of police to get to their
box. The judge, though he had a private entrance, was often late.
The reporters, unofficial delegates of our world civilization, abandoned their earlier composure in the crush and, fearing to be
excluded from the function by which they earned their living,
scuffled with the mob and fought their colleagues each for his own
hand with no less determination.

The French dock is a long bench, raised to the same level as the
judge's desk. In this, above the fleshly figure of his counsel, Moro-
Giafferi, was the profile of Landru, russet and bleached bone. The
horrible patina of the gaol was on his naked cranium, which
seemed to shine in the wintry light from a window behind. His
coat, which he never removed, was a mackintosh of the military cut
fashionable when he was arrested: a shade lighter than his beard,
which was trimmed in the shape of a fan. In the street he might
have passed as one of those innumerable petty speculators that
dealt in army stores. But on his dais framed by the broad blue
gendarmes, with the aura of his iniquity, he seemed unlike any
human seen before, as Napoleon might have appeared on the day of
his anointing. His skull was certainly strange with its dead colour

and incandescence. His nose was the greatest rarity, as thin and transparent at the bridge as a sheet of greased paper. When he sat and listened to the long requisitories, he could be taken for an actor in his carefully-attentive pose, but so thin and delicate that one could notice the outline of the small, sharp elbow through his sleeve. We saw his full-face but rarely: when he entered, stumbling and blinking through the side-door that ended the stone stairs from the prison-yard every morning; and sometimes when he turned to the roaring arena to protest. Then we caught a glimpse of his cavernous eyes, which never lost their abstraction even when he was shouting. Usually his manner was chosen and finicky, but after a few minutes in this style he would drop back into the Paris twang. When Fernande Segret was giving her evidence he closed his eyes; once when the rough Attorney-General, coming to the matter of Thérèse Marchadier's pet dogs which were found strangled with a waxed thread under an oleander clump at Gambais, rushed at him the question: "Is that how you killed all your victims, Landru?" – he seemed scared, and shook. Once, at eighth repetition of the question, "What became of this woman, Landru?" he lost his temper and stood up shaking his long, large hands with rage. He had many poses. He seemed sometimes like a fox, with his snout finding danger in the air; sometimes he seemed false, sometimes he seemed like a wood-insect, with undefined antennæ that felt their way along the board in front of him. Sometimes he would pause and slowly take out, wipe and don a pair of gilt spectacles before an answer; then he seemed simply a prematurely old man. Usually he was obviously immersed in a private dream; but he took great pleasure in the whirling combats between the hairy prosecutor and his sleek Corsican defender. He had a weakness for minor details, on which he extended himself, until he suddenly remembered some warning he had had of the danger of these tactics and sat down. The judge, after a few days' brow-beating, treated him with consideration. Both of them were interested in the crowd: the judge stroking his beard with his soft white hand, the accused sideways, without completely turning his head, as if he were eavesdropping. As in all multiple murder trials, the evidence was largely a repetition; each new victim had been met in the same way, traced in the same way, perhaps killed in the same way, it may be by this abominable new weapon of a waxed thread round the neck while asleep, which no agonizing effort could disengage. Probably, too, Landru disposed of their bodies in the same way; like Pel and Soleillant dissecting them minutely, then burning the pieces to ashes in a red-hot stove, then no doubt by the aid of his motor-car strewing their few pounds of relics in the hedges of distant lanes. The witnesses stepped after each other monotonously: concierges in Sunday clothes, little old women with dingy reticules, dry-eyed sisters, moustached detectives with long and precise records of their failures. The crowd, subtly changing every day, ceased to pay any attention to these. It fed its thousand eyes on the figure in the dock, which grew lighter and more transparent every day, like a discarded carapace. Landru fell into somnolences that lasted hours, during which the heaps of papers in front of him had obviously no part in the reverie. The classic attitude of the mass-murderer towards his punishment. Maître Moro-Giafferi, who at first had difficulty in inducing his client to resign the first rôle to him, composéd dramatic tantrums, revolved his black professional sleeves at the more honestly bad-tempered red advocate opposite, then, having had his effect, subsided, and put on pince-nez. The judge, badly handled by indignant reporters in the Press every morning, let an elegant melancholy creep over him, and little by little abandoned any effort to cow the crowd, which every day grew wilder and more primitive as the great moment of condemnation approached – and as the stage-element in its composition gradually gained the majority. Caricaturists, who in the first days had timidly made their sketches using their knees as easels, now boldly advanced among the undergrowth of *pièces de conviction*, blocking the defence's view of the witness-rail, and drew Landru to the life at three feet from his eyes. This seemed to please him and amuse him; at a sign from one of the artists he would turn his head at the angle they wanted. And a more encumbering breed, the Press photographers, doggedly impudent, lugged their ungainly apparatus into similar good positions and took time exposures of the court. To no avail – for the ration of winter light, already insufficient for their purpose, was now always barred off by the backs of those who had climbed into the window-ledges. Most photographers having failed, the camera-men took to the expedient of hanging incandescent lamps of great power over the prisoner's bench, when the court was not sitting, so that at any rate the great moment and the most interesting expression would not escape them and the millions for whom they deputized.

So the time arrived: the jury after all these days had nothing before them but a coincidence; but it was enough. Ten women (the prosecution fixed on this number somewhat arbitrarily) who had known, loved and followed Landru had vanished. In his possession were their papers, their birth certificates, their marriage papers, all the paraphernalia with which the human ant-hill tries to fix separate personality, without which there could be no emigration from France. Against this Moro-Giafferi could only weakly hint that possibly Landru had shipped them to the brothels of South America, where common superstition has it there come no newspapers. The man himself, in his extremity, had never dared to make such a defence. He relied on the weary romanticism of "an honourable man will never tell a woman's secret", which, carefully weighed by the stony jurymen, came to much the same thing. But to this the terrible quietus of the prosecution struck mortally: What? Women of over fifty? Women whose false hair, false teeth, false bosoms, as well as identity papers, you, Landru, have kept and we captured? The jury retired.

In these moments, while prisoner and judges were withdrawn, the court crowd, this assembly of a modern people which had just sacrificed 1,500,000 of its young men to preserve its institutions and its culture, was extraordinary. It had been waiting from an early hour to keep its place, and in its joy at success gave itself over to a debauch. These thousand compressed bodies were the elect of all Paris, all France, arrived by their abilities to the most coveted spectacle of the century: the sight of Landru's condemnation. They could not move, but within the inches of everyone's power, they rioted with abandon. The shrill cries of women at the daring contacts of their neighbours, the screams, the high giggles of chorus girls, the shouts of rage or pleasure of the men, combined in a chorus. It filled the street outside, and filtered no doubt to the ears of the man waiting in the cold cell somewhere beneath, wrapping himself close in the warm quilt of his sentimental day-dreams. It was not the cold formula of a delegated justice, but the voice of outraged society itself, doing its own justice. A thousand incidents kept the crowd alive while the tedious jury kept it in waiting. Girls pulled by the legs tumbled from their perch in the windows, strong men forced themselves from three places distant upon each other and revenged their dignity on some enemy with blows, which falling generously on the people between were returned, or saluted with bellows of pain. At last the jury, ill at ease and silent, filed back and the door opened for Landru. Immediately there was a frenzy. As the man stood half bowed forward to catch his fate and his sentence, at precisely the right moment the photographers fired their illumination. There was a great glare of light over him. From every part of the massed hall arms protruded upward with black boxes, cameras which aimed at him. And as though in the throes of an eruption, figures shot themselves out of the crowd-level with hands waving and their faces distorted with the effort of their struggle. One man (according to some it was the dean of the Comédie Francaise) actually succeeded in leaping to one of the advocate's benches, and stood there, hilarious, with opera-glasses to his eyes, greedily scanning the lost criminal's expression.

When the court was empty, the servants found the floor strewn like a holiday beach with bitten sandwiches, papers, bottles and other unmentionable, unmistakable traces of their presence which human beings, alas, must leave on a spot where they have been long hours kept immobile without privacy.

This immission of the sovereign people into judgment and punishment, or rather the disrespectful publicity given to it by the exasperated reporters, troubled the Government. They determined therefore that the final act, the execution of Landru, should be guarded, and only enjoyed by appointed proxies. Before dusk, troops took up their stations, and as soon as the trams stopped running, pickets enclosed the space of road outside the prison of Versailles, which is next door to the court. All the cafés and houses within this area were searched. Those numerous strangers, who, having shared or missed the condemnation, wished to witness the execution and had hidden themselves, sometimes in the most humble compartments of these places, were rigorously expelled beyond the barrier. Only the reporters were allowed to remain; these spent the night in billiards and dozing. Before dawn the guillotine was reared on the side-walk, before the principal door. At the appointed hour, before it was light, that door opened, and with tied feet, his chest bared by the executioner's shears, and ghastly rags of shirt hanging over his bound arms, Landru was jostled to the towering machine that in a flash ended him and all his secrets.

At that moment, by some error of the guards, a tram filled with workmen on their way to the yards was allowed to pass, and their curious crowded faces received the last sight of the living head of Desiré Landru.

TONY MANCINI

(Lewes, 1934)

Ronald Blythe

*The sweltering summer of 1934 produced two Brighton Trunk Crimes
– but only one trial, resulting in the sensational acquittal of a petty
crook calling himself Tony Mancini. The only Italian thing about
Mancini was his slick-sounding adopted name, his real one being the
more prosaic (albeit confusing) Cecil Lois England, with Jack Notyre,
Luigi Pirelli and Antoni Luigi comprising his other aliases. Mancini
stood trial for the second Brighton trunk murder; the first, a few weeks
earlier, is believed to have been the work of someone else. The
decapitated and dismembered remains of Mancini's sleazy girlfriend,
a prostitute called Violette Kaye, were discovered stuffed into a
travelling trunk at his basement flat in rundown Kemp Street. The
heavy trunk had been wheeled in a handcart from a similar flat in
Park Crescent where the couple had lived on Miss Kaye's immoral
earnings. When arrested, he told police he'd found her dead at Park
Crescent and supposed that one of her gentlemen clients had killed her.
Because of his criminal record, he'd panicked, bought a trunk and
trundled the body through the town to Kemp Street. His story turned
out to be a tissue of lies, but the trial was remarkable for the virtuoso
performance of Mancini's counsel, Norman Birkett KC, who was
persuaded to take on the defence brief in what was in every way a
grubby case. Mancini's low-life associates did not invite sympathy. "It
is an underworld," admitted Birkett, "that makes the mind reel."*

Nevertheless the judge summed up in Mancini's favour and the jury duly acquitted. "Not guilty, Mr Birkett? Not guilty, Mr Birkett?" was all that a bewildered Mancini could manage by way of post-verdict thanks. Three decades later, his trial was recalled by the novelist Ronald Blythe (b. 1922) in his classic social history of the interwar years, published before his novel Akenfield, *evoking the lost life of an English village, became a best-selling classic.*

Perhaps it was the classically Tussaud-like proportions of the Brighton Trunk Murders which so enraptured the public. Perhaps they fulfilled the British requirement of crime as a salutary entertainment, which was something which Fascist excesses consistently failed to do. The British are not, on the whole, sadistic, but they have always found much amusement in the processes of retribution. Sybil Marshall, in *An Experiment in Education*, tells how she once met an old woman who took her into her cottage to show her the shawl in which her great-grandmother had been married. "They were married at the church here in the morning," she said, "but after that they didn't know how to spend the rest of the day. So they walked into Cambridge to see a man hung."

In the last weeks of 1934, while civilization slithered, Mr and Mrs Everyman thronged to Lewes Assizes to see a little twenty-six-year-old waiter hanged. The material for Norman Birkett's legal homily was so seamy that no self-respecting Biff Boy would have been seen soiling his fist with it. The circumstances which gave rise to it were morbid and bizarre. In fact, the Trunk Murders were to have everything – except murderers.

On 18 June 1934, the left-luggage attendant at Brighton Station sensed that all was not well in his office. A large new brown canvas suitcase, left in his charge on Derby Day, was beginning to proclaim its uniqueness. For a 12s. 6d. suitcase "such as might be purchased anywhere", its eloquence was very terrible. The attendant wavered, stroked the plywood battens which held the case together and then called the station-master, who at once called the police. When the trunk was opened they saw a fat brown paper parcel tied up in yards and yards of new Venetian blind cord. Inside was what at first looked like the torso of a plump middle-aged woman, for such is the ungallantry of death.

That same evening, the attendant at the left-luggage office at

King's Cross Station found a suitcase containing two still very pretty legs. They had been deposited on 7 June, the day after Derby Day. At the time the King's Cross attendant found the legs he had not heard of what had happened at Brighton, but immediately afterwards there was tremendous activity throughout the left-luggage offices of England. But no head and no arms were discovered. Nor were they ever found. The effect of this crime on police and public alike was sensational, nor was the drama in any way lessened when Sir Bernard Spilsbury, seeing through the motley of corruption, pronounced the victim to be a meticulously well-cared-for girl of perhaps twenty, with light brown hair and long and beautiful toes, the latter having been pedicured only a few days before dismemberment.

The year 1934 was a great time for missing girls and the fate of this little *inconnue* of five-feet-two-inches – and five months gone with child – touched every imagination. A fate worse than death was expected for such girls. But this! The murder brought the speculative genius of the Press, the Newgate passions of the public and the full resources of Scotland Yard into a single concentrated obsession. The monster had to be found, if only because he alone was likely to produce the head, which was something everybody simply longed to see. But the girl's identity was never known and never will be. She had been dead for about three weeks. The brown paper shroud bore a single clue, the word "ford" in blue pencil. They thought it was the last syllable of a place-name, only which place? It was never discovered. The police worked hard for two or three days and then came up against a blank wall, after which they threw the whole affair open to the public. Anybody's guess was preferable to no guess at all. Such a death, it was maintained, could not be discreet. It prescribed mess, smell and noise. Brighton was asked to describe any strange occurrences during the past month which came into these categories and this had the result of Chief Inspector Donaldson of Scotland Yard receiving a dossier on the town which suggested that a massacre had taken place in it round about Whitsun. He put this wearily on one side. It was the first of an avalanche of "helpful" correspondence which was eventually to drive him from the uproar of Brighton police station to the rococo peace of Brighton Pavilion.

House agents and landlords handed in long lists of empty properties where such grim work might have been done without interruption, and these were all thoroughly searched. Scores of runaway girls were rounded up and returned to their provincial homes, much to their disgust. All day long, for weeks, people brought the Brighton police blunt instruments and bundles of women's clothes, until the police station began to look like a crook's jumble sale. On 26 June a young man found a human skull on the beach, drifting in a wash of cigarette cartons and scraps of bathing costume, but he did not retrieve it as he thought it had nothing to do with him. Epithets used for the murderer now changed from "brutal" to "cunning" and the ghastliest crime was now being called the perfect crime.

By the end of June they were digging up the race-course and examining all the jerry-built shacks which had spread like a pebble-dash pox round the coast of Britain since the war. Meanwhile, a report that the toenails had been painted was indignantly denied by the authorities, who were now assuming a very gentlemanly attitude towards their bits of girl. Similarly, when it was rumoured that the second toe on each foot was longer than the big toe, a statement was instantly issued to say that, far from being in any way abnormal, the toes were so perfectly formed that they gave the impression of being longer than usual. Hope was raised when it was thought the toes might have been part of a Miss Daisy Johnson from Cardiff, but were soon dashed when Miss Johnson appeared alive and well.

By the end of July the police had received 6,000 helpful letters, most of them prudently signed *Pro Bono Publico*, and the Detective-Inspector in charge of the case had collapsed with the worry of it all and had to be taken to hospital. It was shortly after this that the Chief Inspector fled to the comparative serenity of the Royal Pavilion. And on 12 August the officers from Scotland Yard put the whole affair back into the hands of the local police and went home. After all, it *was* 1934 and Trunk Murder Number One was not the only crime to be solved. The girl with the pretty toes had defeated them. She remained as she had been when the lid first rose on her in the baggage-room, headless, armless, nameless – a victim of what? Of whom? No one ever learned the answers. Moreover, the sad little victim was even to be denied the singularity of her fame, for on 15 July Trunk Murder Number Two came to light.

Some days before this happened, the police had checked up on the raffish human flotsam which eddied in and out of Brighton's crevices, and had interviewed a dark little man whom they knew as

Tony Mancini, but whom Brighton knew as Jack Notyre or Tony
English or Tony England or Mr Swinley or Antoni Luigi or Mr
Watson or, it seemed, as anything which happened to come into
the young man's head when somebody asked him his name. His
quite elegant real name was Cecil Lois England.

The police went to Mancini's basement flat in Kemp Street, a
dull little working-class thoroughfare conveniently near to Brighton Station, and there they found a trunk containing an entire
corpse. As in Trunk Murder Number One, the tray of the trunk
was missing. There was an immediate hunt for Mancini, who had
disappeared, and who was last seen carrying a portmanteau. A few
hours later he was picked up on a road near Blackheath, arrested
and charged with the murder of Violet Saunders, a dancer.

"All I can say, sir," said the nervous young man, "is that I am
not guilty."

And all the world could say, and did say long before he reached
the dock, was that he *was* guilty. His guilt was pronounced so
vehemently and so often that Mancini's forthcoming trial soon
took on the status of a formal legal convention, and although there
was nothing to connect him with the first Trunk Murder, the Press
and the public had made up its mind that he might as well be
hanged for both crimes and be done with it.

Cecil England, alias Mancini, was a flashily handsome youngster
of twenty-six who wore plenty of grease on his thick black hair and
whose chief delight was to dance. He was born in the East End and
had floundered through his teens and a few petty crimes before
meeting Violet Saunders, who was sixteen years his senior. He was
a good lover. His mixture of physical slightness, amorousness and
dependent affection brought out the protective side of otherwise
world-hardened older women, and they loved him. He had a
child's feckless gaiety which allowed him to dance nightly in cheap
cafés for hours at a time and with little thought for the morrow, and
when the terror caught up with him he was to show a child's fear.
The irony was, that the only breast to which he might have turned
in his extremity was that which lay unspeakably comfortless in the
big black trunk. Though who would believe this? Who would
believe anything Mancini said? In his mind, too, the verdict was
foregone. Guilty or Not Guilty were no more than words in his
experience of justice. They had got him; he would swing. It was
simple as that.

The trial opened nearly six months later, on December 10th, at

Sussex Assizes, by which time Mancini had been so besmirched and vilified in the Press that the scared Italian-looking youth in the dock and the monster in the newspapers who bore his name seemed to have no relationship. But the big legal guns which had been brought in to battle for his life – Quintin Hogg and J. D. Cassels for the prosecution; Norman Birkett and John Flowers for the defence – did much to reassure people that here was evil out of the ordinary. There was an all-male jury. Great crowds queued for the public seats. The few who reached them heard Mancini plead Not Guilty and saw him standing in the dock with a look of dull resignation on his white face.

They heard how he had come to Brighton the previous autumn with Mrs Saunders, who was known on the stage as Violet Kay and who was the other half of a dancing act called "Kay and Kay", her partner being a man named Kay Fredericks. When they reached Brighton, Mrs Saunders had shown signs of being in great fear and she was always packing her clothes and saying to her young lover, "Come on, we must move." So they moved many times. In March they came to rest in a basement flat in Park Crescent, where Mancini told his new landlord, Mr Snuggs, that he was a gentleman's clothes-presser. Mr Snuggs knew the couple as Mr and Mrs Watson, liked them and found them to be on entirely affectionate terms. In May, Mancini got himself a job as a waiter at the Skylark Café. It was the first job he had had since coming to Brighton in the autumn and all this time Violet had kept him and looked after him. On 7 May, two days after Mancini had begun work, Violet paid Mr Snuggs his rent, and that was the last time he saw her alive. That same afternoon a man had been seen driving the car belonging to an elderly man named Mr Moores, and this car had stopped at 44 Park Crescent and the driver had got out and spoken to Violet as she lounged in the doorway of the basement flat. This man was the very last person to see her alive.

A few days after this, Mancini gave a friend of his at the Skylark Café all Violet's clothes and told her that Violet had left him and gone to Paris. Also at this time, Mancini went to a dealer named Wood in Brighton Market and bought a big black trunk. He told the dealer that he needed the trunk because he had got himself a job in France. He continued to work at the Skylark Café and amongst his customers were a nice Mr and Mrs Barnard who lived in Kemp Street, near the railway station. On 14 May, just a week after Violet had been last seen, Mancini went to live at the Barnards' house in

Kemp Street. He arrived with another young man very early in the morning and between them they lugged a very heavy trunk into his new room. They had brought the trunk across Brighton on a hand-cart. He told the Barnards that his "wife" had gone away with his "uncle", meaning old Mr Moores. Once settled, he began to dance. He danced compulsively, excellently, ever-lastingly, in a jazz dive called Aladdin's Cave. He danced there sadly on the evening of the day he had spent at the police station, when he told his partner that he had only four more days of happiness left to him. Male gossips from the Cave were to describe how they had heard Mancini talking violently about his "wife", how he had "bashed her from pillar to post", etc., though, as it turned out, there wasn't a sign of a bruise on her body.

For two long months Mancini slept in a little bed by the side of Violet in her trunk. He even entertained his friends in the same room and blamed the smell on to the landlady "because she wouldn't let him open the window". The glassy-eyed court heard how Mrs Barnard had discovered fluid dripping from her lodger's luggage and hastened to the Skylark Café to tell him about it. "Don't worry," said Mancini, "it's only French polish," and he came home and mopped it up.

Mancini was on the early morning train to London when Chief Inspector Donaldson and Inspector Pelling entered 52 Kemp Street and opened the black trunk. There she was, no *inconnue*, no fair-footed waif but, on the contrary, an ageing creature all too well known, Violet Saunders, a woman who had abandoned her coal-miner husband for the bright lights and the wild freedom which had followed the Armistice. Kay of "Kay and Kay", where the world was concerned, but now nothing easily describable to the policemen staring down at her. Her brother, a meat-porter, iden-tified her. He said he knew her by her long thin hands. It was again a case of extremities.

Sir Bernard Spilsbury gave the cause of death as shock following a fracture of the skull. His presence was to spice the affair. He and Pierrepoint, the public hangman, were high on the list of those who diverted the age.

When Mancini was arrested on the main road from London to Maidstone, he said, "Yes, I am the man, but I did not murder her. I would not cut her hand. She has been keeping me for months."

They found blood on his clothes, blood in the cupboard of his previous lodgings. All this and more made up the case for the prosecution and the thoughts of everybody were on how the wretched young man in the dock would take the death sentence, when they heard a quiet, silvery, concise voice with an almost theatrical carrying-power asking questions. Norman Birkett said very little at first but even at his first sentence the helter-skelter self-assurance of the prosecution began to waver and lose its impetus. He forced Mr Snuggs to change his genteel tone, and did so without offending Mr Snuggs.

A man had been seen going down the basement flat. He was tall and he wore a trilby hat. This was about the end of April and the man stayed for about an hour. Mr Snuggs had also seen "uncle", who came to the flat in a chauffeur-driven car. "Uncle's" name was Charles Moores and he was an elderly bookie. But although Birkett could not get Mr Snuggs to say that a man called "Darky" and a man called "Hoppy" had visited Violet, he had proved his point. While Mancini was away, waiting or dancing, odd males drifted in and out of 44 Park Crescent. Kerslake, the chauffeur, added a strange new note. On 5 May, only a few days before Violet's disappearance, "Uncle" had been certified by the Brighton Relieving Officer and had entered a mental home. When he, Kerslake, had seen Violet on the day of her death, or the assumed day of her death, she had shaken so much and had looked so ill that he thought she had been drinking. As he came away he saw another man descend the basement steps.

The court was almost painfully still now. Everything was changing. The assumptions of the past five months lay in ruins. For all that, the white-faced prisoner continued to look like a cornered animal, though now not such an interesting animal. Birkett continued mellifluously to sow doubt, wreck assertions, challenge glibness. Then he began the super-human task of restoring to Mancini a few decent rags to cover his moral nudity. A five-month newspaper campaign had left him a monstrous scarecrow. Turning to Mr Barnard, the much-bothered landlord of the Kemp Street flat and someone who had every justification for being furious with Mancini for bringing all this trouble to his premises, Birkett asked softly, "You have no complaint to make about him?"

Mr Barnard then saw his ex-tenant as he was and replied, "No. All the time he was living with us he was a perfect gentleman."

A dancer came from Leicester Square to tell of her eleven-year friendship with Violet. She liked Violet's young friend and had often danced with him. She had always found them on the most affectionate terms. Kay Fredericks told of his and Violet's partnership, not only as "Kay and Kay", but as lovers. They had parted after three years and he had not seen her for a further two years. Since the break-up of their affair and their act he had lived at the Headquarters of the British Union of Fascists, where he was employed as a photographer.

A bombshell descended shortly after this evidence. Dr Roche Lynch, the pathologist, said that he had found no trace of blood on the hammer which the prosecution was assuming to be the murder instrument, that Violet had been dead too long for him to know her blood group and, most sensational of all, that her body contained morphine, which, after so long a time, could only indicate that she had taken a distinctly greater quantity of the drug than the normal safe dose.

Mancini's two statements were read out. The first was the lie about Violet going abroad with Moores. The second was without doubt the bleak and wretched truth.

"I got frightened. I knew they would blame me and I could not prove that I had not done it. I had not the courage to tell the police what I had found so I decided to take it with me. I bought a trunk. She was a prostitute. There were always men coming to the house all night. I did not kill her as God is my judge."

Chief Inspector Donaldson told the court why Mancini was frightened of the police. His convictions for petty theft sounded trifling in comparison with his present trouble, but he and Violet, who had been convicted for prostitution, were the sort of people who would never go to the police. The Chief Inspector added that most of the stories filling the Press were untrue.

Sir Bernard Spilsbury, always a star turn, revived flagging sensation by dramatically holding up a human skull. The court was dazzled by it. Mancini looked deeply shocked. It was, however, merely a skull from a medical school and Sir Bernard was demonstrating. Holding out a piece of bone he told the court that it was the exact piece which had formed the depressed area in Violet's fractured skull.

> *Birkett:* "How long have you been in possession of the small piece of bone which has been produced here *for the first time on the third day of the trial*?"
> *Sir Bernard:* "Since the first examination." [i.e. five months]

Birkett: "Did it not occur to you that the defence might have been informed?"

Sir Bernard: "I am afraid it did not occur to me."

Birkett: "Let me get this perfectly plain. You appreciate that *no doctor for the defence* was present at the post mortem?"

Sir Bernard: "I did not think anyone was in this case, certainly!"

Birkett: "For a piece of bone which has been in existence all this time to be produced on the third day of the trial does put the defence in some difficulty?"

Sir Bernard: (muddled and shaken) "I did not think it would take anyone long to examine it and come to conclusions . . ."

Birkett: (swiftly) "You will concede at once that there are many other possible theories available for the death of this woman?"

Sir Bernard: (very quietly) "Yes."

Birkett then began to make and substantiate a series of perfectly valid hypotheses for Violet's death. He made them with extreme courtesy, attacking no man's honour, merely proving to everybody present that a woman who drank, drugged and received, amongst other lovers, an elderly mental patient; who moved because she was scared and who, at the time of her death, was living at the bottom of a dangerously steep flight of area steps, could die from one of many reasons. He attacked the Press: "It is not merely unjust and un-English, it is a crime akin to murder that when a man is charged, and before he is charged, statements of that kind should be made."

When at last he questioned Mancini, the court was tense. Mancini, it was certain, would let his advocate down. How could he not? Then tension grew until it became well-nigh unbearable and when it was at bursting point, Birkett asked a question which took the prisoner by surprise, jolting from his lips the last thing people expected to hear.

"During the whole time you lived with her as man and wife, how did you get on together?"

"Strange as it may seem," said Mancini, "I used to love her. We were always on the most affectionate terms. There were no quarrels."

"Did that cover the whole time?"

"Yes, every second that she was alive."

The jury was out for two and a quarter hours. When the foreman announced the verdict, Not Guilty, the court looked stunned and Mancini put his hand to his pale face in an arrested, incomprehending manner and remained frozen in this attitude until the judge, Mr Justice Branson, said, "You are discharged." Mancini then bowed his head slightly, climbed from the dock and walked out of the court with his light dancer's step.

The verdict was received by the public with sullen incredulity. Its mood was not unlike that of a Colosseum mob on those sparse occasions when the emperor gave the thumb-up sign.

For once, the public had judged the mood correctly. More than 40 years on, in 1976, in an interview with the News of the World *headlined "I've Got Away With Murder" Tony Mancini confessed that he had indeed murdered Violette Kay. Brighton Trunk Crime No. 1, however, remains unsolved to this day.*

CHARLES MANSON

(Los Angeles, 1970–1)

George Bishop

Charles Manson took his place as one of the twentieth century's most notorious murderers when he and his hippie followers killed seven people in a two-day massacre in August 1969. Police called to a house in Los Angeles rented by the film director Roman Polanski found the body of his pregnant wife, actress Sharon Tate, and three house guests, Hollywood hairdresser and drug dealer Jay Sebring, the coffee fortune heiress Abigail Folger and her playboy boyfriend Voyteck Frykowski. They'd all been repeatedly stabbed. Outside, a chance visitor, Steven Parent, was found shot dead in his car. Next day, in another part of the city, a supermarket millionaire and his wife, Leno and Rosemary LaBianca, were discovered violently stabbed to death. Investigators interviewed members of a strange commune called The Family, based in the lonely California desert. Manson, an ex-convict, was their leader. One of his followers, Susan Atkins, described in horrifying detail how she and other cult members had carried out the killings, but withdrew her confession shortly before the case came to trial. She now claimed she'd invented the story implicating Manson and two other members of the commune, Patricia Krenwinkel and Leslie Van Houten. Another problem for the prosecution was that Manson himself had not been present at the Polanski house on the night of the murders. Deputy District Attorneys Aaron Stovitz and Vincent Bugliosi faced having to convict Manson on seven murder counts based on the theory that he'd ordered the killings. George Bishop was the only writer present in court at every session of the Tate/LaBianca trial. Here he describes the dramatic appearance of Linda Kasabian, a former member of The Family who was granted immunity in return for her testimony. Despite protests from Manson's lawyer Irving Kanarek and Krenwinkel's attorney Paul Fitzgerald that her recollection was worthless because she used LSD and other drugs, Kasabian took the stand on Day 41 of the trial.

The sight of Linda Kasabian, ex-Family member and now, in Vincent Bugliosi's words, the people's "star witness," stepping through the holding-room doors into the courtroom at 2:00 p.m. on Monday 27 July 1970 unleashed the agonizingly suppressed vigilantism of Irving Kanarek. Protestations on grounds of irrelevancy, immateriality and impropriety streamed from the stocky defense attorney's mouth in an unprecedented flow of legal flatulence.

He began in spectacular fashion, without waiting for the court clerk to finish his standard request of a witness: "Would you raise your right hand, please."

KANAREK: (On his feet and shouting) Object, your Honor, on the grounds this witness is not competent and she is insane!

Judge Older swivelled his chair around, frowning in astonishment.

BUGLIOSI: (On *his* feet and shouting) Wait a while, your Honor, move to strike that and I ask the court to find him in contempt of court for gross misconduct. This is unbelievable on his part.

OLDER: If you have anything to say, Mr Kanarek, come to the bench.

KANAREK: Very well, your Honor.

OLDER: The jury is admonished to disregard Mr Kanarek's comments.

Older, obviously restraining himself, faced the attorneys out of hearing of the jury and press.

FITZGERALD: I think I can more succinctly state the objection, if I might, with leave of the court.

It is our contention that this witness is incompetent to testify as the result of unsoundness, and we are willing to make an offer of proof in that respect.

OLDER: Make your offer.

FITZGERALD: Basically, our position is as follows: That Linda Kasabian – and we will offer to prove this by various witnesses, and I will state them separately at the conclusion – that Linda Kasabian, due to prolonged extensive illegal use of LSD is a person of unsound mind, is mentally ill, is insane, is unable to differentiate between truth and falsity, right or wrong, good or bad, fantasy and reality, and is incapable of expressing herself concerning the matter so as to be understood.

In connection with our offer of proof, we would like to incorporate by reference and resubmit to the court a motion, declaration and points and authorities filed on behalf of the defendants on 12 June 1970.

We would make a further offer of proof that Dr A. R. Tweed, whose declaration is attached to that motion, is an expert in the diagnosis and treatment of mental, emotional and psychiatric disorders, and he will testify as to the matter contained in his declaration.

Dr A. R. Tweed, a psychiatrist who identified himself as a medical examiner for the Superior Court, County of Los Angeles, declared:

"The statements ascribed to Mrs Kasabian of having supernatural powers while under the influence of LSD as well as her feelings of deep depersonalization when not directly under its influence is not only medically possible but highly probable with doses much smaller and with fewer times used than described.

"That further it is a confirmed fact that even one ingestion of LSD could cause an immediate bad reaction or return of what is called a flashback many times even several months later without further use.

"That the habitual long-term use of LSD for pleasure or escape produces the possibility for the impairment of good sense and maturation.

"That individuals so affected may become confused and dis-organized and are usually markedly suggestible."

At the time of Dr Tweed's original statement Fitzgerald also delivered an indictment of what, in his opinion, LSD could do to people who ingested it: "Lysergic acid is defined and classified as a hallucinogenic drug; a hallucinogenic drug itself it is my under-standing, artificially or chemically induces fantasy, and that is the crucial area of this motion, I think, that the chemical fact of lysergic acid is to distort reality and to blur distinctions between reality and fantasy.

"The drug itself induces mental states that are quite similar to psychoses, and some authorities feel the prolonged use of lysergic acid actually induces insanity, and results in organic brain disorder and disturbance.

"Certainly lysergic acid disturbs and distorts emotions. It dis-turbs and distorts organized thought processes. It disturbs and distorts memory, and disturbs and distorts recollections.

"It also disturbs and distorts the ability of a person to recollect and communicate about things they have perceived, and it is a drug that distorts perception itself.

"I think that when one is under the influence of lysergic acid diethylamide or the prolonged residual effect of LSD, that is in essence uncontrollable; that the person who has ingested the lysergic acid diethylamide presently is unable to control his mental or thought processes.

"There is substantial medical and scientific evidence to the effect that actual drug states are subject to recurrence without notice or warning. This is the so-called flashback effect of lysergic acid.

"It has been documented in several places that lysergic acid has residual effects to the organic brain processes. There has been a great deal of concern that at least in one mental area, at least in one physical-mental area it destroys the normal function of the chro-mosomes.

"It has led to permanent brain damage in large doses.

"It has led to permanent disturbances of motor functions, to permanent disturbances in intellectual functions. It also led to the disturbance of the so-called super-ego functions, which is the conscience or moral functioning area of the brain."

These statements are of considerable importance because at this time of the trial, with prosecution witness Linda Kasabian yet to take the stand, the defense is attempting to lay a foundation for its own case. This writer, anticipating the defense position, had done considerable research into the nature of the drug d-lysergic acid diethylamide tartrate and, as the trial progresses and the testimony warrants it, will intersperse facts impartially presented so that the reader may better understand the conflicting testimony.

Remember, Paul Fitzgerald referred to this in the beginning as, "The first of the acid murders." It is vital for our understanding of this case, and perhaps for our ultimate survival, to know all there is to know at present about LSD. As we shall see, defense or prosecution claims to the contrary, there is not all that much to know; what is very important is the unusual opportunity that Tate/La Bianca has presented: a chance to measure the observable effects of the drug in relation to a criminal act being debated in a public forum. [. . .] If we don't want carloads of people riding around in every city and town (as the prosecution will contend happened in Los Angeles), selecting you or me as random murder victims, we will do well to find out what role acid played in this landmark case.

Now we are back in Judge Older's court, at the bench, listening to Paul Fitzgerald continue to plead the defense case against the testimony of Linda Kasabian.

FITZGERALD: Two additional witnesses will testify as to their opinions concerning her sanity and/or mental illness.

OLDER: Who are these witnesses by whom you expect to prove matters stated in your offer?

STOVITZ: I'd like, at this time, to ask your Honor to remind counsel that it is quite unethical to take up a matter like this in the presence of the jury.

OLDER: There is no question about it, and your conduct is outrageous, Mr Kanarek.

KANAREK: If I may respond. Your Honor, it is a legal ground.

OLDER: That is not the point. You understand what the point is. It should have been done outside the presence of the jury.

FITZGERALD: I would offer for the court's consideration an additional declaration by June Emmer. This witness purports to be a close friend and personal acquaintance of Linda Kasabian, and spent the month of October, 1969, in her presence.

That Linda Kasabian made certain admissions and statements concerning her activities in California, and certain admissions and statements regarding the use of lysergic acid.

Also, in support of the motion I have a declaration under Florida law, an affidavit of Rosaire Drouin who purports to be the father of Linda Kasabian who in this affidavit sets out material indicating that his daughter the witness, Linda Kasabian, has extensively used the drug LSD.

OLDER: Do you expect to prove all of the facts of your offer of proof by these two witnesses?

FITZGERALD: We make an offer of proof as to a witness, Charles Melton, who is present in court and will testify as to personally taking LSD with Linda Kasabian on at least six occasions and will testify to her bizarre conduct under the influence of LSD.

We don't claim she is under the influence of LSD at this time, but if we could call Dr Tweed as a witness we would be able to demonstrate to the court the residual effects of LSD are such as to render someone incompetent as a witness, and Dr Tweed has so stated in his affidavit to the court.

OLDER: I have heard nothing so far that leads me to believe that there is anything in your offer of proof which has any connection with the competency of this witness to testify.

Mr Kanarek, if you do that once more in open court in front of this jury I am going to take action against you.

Is there any objection to the offer of proof?

BUGLIOSI: Yes, your Honor.

OLDER: The objection is sustained. You may proceed.

This private exchange at the bench is reported here to indicate how an attorney, without the public's knowledge, can delay the orderly procedure of a trial. As far as the jury and press knew, Mr Kanarek's objection was being given weighty consideration by the court when, in fact, it was Paul Fitzgerald's presentation that was being heard. Whether or not this constituted a deliberate defense strategy to make Kanarek the villain in open court and Fitzgerald the rational pleader at the bench or in chambers was not clear; what was clear was the emergence of Kanarek the obstructionist, the ogre paraded before us so unsuccessfully by the district attorney's office.

Linda Kasabian, her light brown hair trailing in two braids over her shoulders and wearing a blue and red peasant dress, was duly sworn. From the very first her eagerly awaited testimony was challenged by Manson's attorney. Vincent Bugliosi inquired:

Q: Linda, you realize that you are presently charged with seven counts of murder and one count of conspiracy to commit murder?

A: Yes.

KANAREK: Immaterial, your Honor, I object on the grounds I would like to approach the bench.

OLDER: Overruled, let's proceed.

KANAREK: I have a motion to make, if your Honor does not wish me to do it in the presence of the jury I will do it whichever way your Honor wishes.

OLDER: State your motion.

KANAREK: My motion is . . . your Honor wishes me to do it in the presence of the jury?

OLDER: State your motion.

KANAREK: The motion is for a mistrial.

OLDER: I did not want to hear your grounds, just the motion. The motion will be denied.

Let's proceed.

KANAREK: May I state the grounds at the bench?

OLDER: Is this something in addition to what you have already stated, Mr Kanarek?

KANAREK: Yes.

OLDER: All right, you may.

The following took place at the bench, outside of the hearing of the jury and press.

OLDER: Make your motion.

KANAREK: The motion, your Honor, is for a mistrial. I ask your Honor to consider the fact that she is named a defendant. It is reversible error for the district attorney to call a defendant to the witness stand.

OLDER: That is the ground? That is all?

KANAREK: This witness has not been granted immunity and I
   am sure the court agrees with me.
OLDER: Anything further?
KANAREK: No.
OLDER: All right. The motion is denied. Let's proceed.

Everyone back to open court. Bear in mind that Bugliosi had asked
only one question on direct examination. Kanarek's purpose, it would
seem, was twofold. First he was objecting for the record, for the
appeal; second he was objecting to rattle the witness, Linda Kasabian; although she appeared to be calm there was no question but
that the combination of being under the eyes of the international
community and, more immediately, of the Family, would take a toll.
Almost from the beginning the Family tried to catch her eye, to
communicate with her. Certain signs had meaning to the observer.
The girls would run their fingers rapidly over their lips in a
blabbering motion that, to Linda – in the words of her attorneys
Gary Fleischman and Robert Goldman – signified that she was a
blabbermouth. They would run their fingers straight up and down
their noses in a motion that meant lies were being told. On the second
day of her testimony Manson, during one session at the bench when
the attorneys were preoccupied, was heard to say "You're lying,
Linda. You lied three times." (About the Tate murders.)
   She was heard to answer clearly and with sincerity. "No, I'm
not, Charlie. And you know that."
   On another occasion Susan Atkins mouthed the words, "You're
killing us."
   To which Linda replied in a whisper quite audible to the jury:
"I'm not killing you. You've killed yourselves."
   The problem at the beginning was to get any testimony at all;
Bugliosi, after establishing that Linda Kasabian would be granted
immunity for testifying, asked her if she had any other reason for
being on the stand.

KANAREK: I object on the grounds, your Honor, that it is
   immaterial, conclusionary, calls for hearsay, assumes facts
   not in evidence. Clearly your Honor, her reasons are
   immaterial. She is called as a witness.
OLDER: I don't want to hear any arguments.
KANAREK: Those are the objections. May I approach the
   bench to make an argument?

OLDER: No.

KASABIAN: I strongly believe in truth, and I feel the truth should be spoken.

KANAREK: May I have that read back, your Honor?

OLDER: Read the answer.

KANAREK: Well, then, I ask that that be stricken. It is a self-serving declaration.

OLDER: Overruled.

After tortuously taking her through her background from the time she was born on 21 June 1949 in Biddeford, Maine through her on-again, off-again marriage to Robert Kasabian, Bugliosi got down to the business at hand. Here, with many of the repetitive objections and other matter extraneous to this narrative omitted, is how the testimony evolved:

Q: Did you ever go to live at the Spahn Movie Ranch in Chatsworth, California?

A: Yes, I did.

Q: I show you people's 28 for identification. Linda, do you know whose photograph that is?

A: Yes, I do.

Q: Who is shown in that photograph?

A: Gypsy.

Q: Do you know her by her real name?

A: Kathy.

Q: Does the name Katherine Share ring a bell?

A: Yes.

Q: You know her as Gypsy and Kathy?

A: Also she told me Minine or Minone.

Q: Did Gypsy have anything to do with your going to the Spahn Ranch?

A: Yes, she did.

Q: How was that?

A: She told me about a beautiful man that we had all been waiting for.

Q: Did you start to live at the Spahn ranch?

A: Yes, I did.

Q: When did you meet Charles Manson for the first time?

A: The next night.

Q: That would be July 5, then?

A: Right, and he was up and back at the ranch, in a cluster of trees, and he was working on a dune buggy.

Q: Did you have a conversation with Mr Manson on this first occasion?

A: Yes.

Q: What did he say to you?

A: He asked me why I had come. I had told him that my husband had rejected me and that Gypsy told me I was welcome here as part of the Family.

Q: After you told Mr Manson why you had come to the Spahn Ranch, did he do anything . . .

A: Yes, he felt my legs and seemed to think they were okay or whatever.

Q: Where did you stay that night?

A: In a cave up in back of the ranch.

Q: When was the next time you saw Mr Manson?

A: The next night or maybe the night after, I am not sure.

Q: Where did you meet Mr Manson on this following occasion?

A: Inside the cave.

Q: What took place at that time?

It must be remembered that all through this testimony Irving Kanarek is registering an objection after almost every question. He did so following the last question and it was sustained. But Kanarek was plainly getting on Judge Older's nerves, as this next exchange indicates. Again Bugliosi inquires:

Q: You mentioned earlier, Linda, about a Family. Is that what the people were called out at the Spahn Ranch?

A: Yes.

KANAREK: Objection on the grounds it is assuming facts not in evidence. There is no evidence of any Family. What they are called is hearsay, your Honor.

OLDER: Mr Kanarek, I told you before I just want the motion or the objection and grounds without the argument.

KANAREK: And I respectfully ask the court to ask the witness . . .

OLDER: Sit down, sir.

KANAREK: . . . not to respond . . .

OLDER: Sit down, sir.

All was not smooth sailing for the prosecution, either. After several questions by Bugliosi using the term "Family", trying to establish Manson's dominance over it, had been objected to and the objections sustained, the junior deputy district attorney asked to approach the bench.

The following discussion was held out of the hearing of the jury and press.

BUGLIOSI: Your Honor, with all . . .

HUGHES: I find it highly prejudicial, that we go to the bench whenever Mr Bugliosi wishes and not when Mr Kanarek asks.

OLDER: Don't interrupt. Mr Bugliosi was talking.

BUGLIOSI: With all deference to the court I don't understand why I cannot put in Manson directing . . .

HUGHES: I cannot hear this.

BUGLIOSI: I cannot understand, with all deference to the court how the court is not permitting me to put on evidence that Manson was in charge of the Family.

I have the highest regard for the court. I want the court to know that.

At this particular point, your Honor, I am shocked at the court's position. This is our case against Manson.

OLDER: That is not a legal argument, Mr Bugliosi, as you well know.

BUGLIOSI: I agree with the court on that.

OLDER: The questions called for hearsay. I find no exception under which it might come in. That is the reason I sustained the objection.

BUGLIOSI: The only way I can prove Manson was the head of the Family is that he directed everyone to do things. I am just at a loss for words.

OLDER: I think perhaps a good deal of it can be solved by phrasing your questions in some other manner.

As the court adjourned for the day some small in-fighting was taking place between defense and prosecution that escaped general notice. For several days members of the Family, long-haired, bearded and dressed in extremely casual fashion had been attempting to gain access to the courtroom. By order, the defense is allotted four precious permanent seats, as is the prosecution.

The prosecution, it can be assumed, did not want four bedraggled specimens giving Linda Kasabian a collective whammy while she was testifying. Accordingly, as each member applied for admission, he or she (or, as one bailiff suggested facetiously, it) was served with a subpoena as a witness for the prosecution. Since witnesses were automatically excluded from the courtroom if they were going to testify on evidence being heard, the ploy worked.

RATTENBURY AND STONER

(Old Bailey, 1935)

F. Tennyson Jesse

This controversial trial ended in topsy-turveydom. Of the two de-
fendants, one, the young, impressionable George Stoner, was convicted
of murder, sentenced to death but reprieved. The other, his older,
worldly mistress, Alma Rattenbury, was cleared of murder and
walked free from court but, a few days later, committed suicide.
The louche tale that had emerged in the course of their trial had
created an early example of media frenzy. The crime novelist Francis
Iles complained that "Mrs Rattenbury was, for all practical purposes,
hounded to her death by reporters." Stoner was still a teenager when
he was hired by Alma Rattenbury as a chauffeur-handyman. They
soon became embroiled in a passionate affair, Mrs Rattenbury's older
husband having told her she "could lead her own life." Shortly after
this, cuckolded Francis Rattenbury, a once distinguished architect now
sliding into a drunken dotage, was murdered with a mallet while
nursing his nightly whisky in his favourite chair. To try to save her
young lover, Mrs Rattenbury ardently confessed to a killing she had
known nothing about. Journalist James Agate, sent to write up his
impressions of the trial, thought it "pure Balzac . . . pure Flaubert
. . . pure Zola . . . The sordidness of the whole thing was relieved by
one thing and one thing only. This was when Counsel asked Mrs
Rattenbury what her first thought had been when her lover got into bed
that night and told her what he had done. She replied: 'My first

thought was to protect him.' This is the kind of thing that Balzac would have called sublime, and it is odd that, as far as I saw, not a single newspaper reported it." The trial showed the British legal system at its best and at its worst. While the hearing was admirably fair, the Old Bailey became a court of morals, condemning Mrs Rattenbury not for the crime for which she was arrested, but for offending against the conventions of her time. One of her staunchest defenders was the novelist F(ryn) Tennyson Jesse (1888–1958), great niece of Tennyson, the Victorian Poet Laureate, and a shrewd criminologist, who was present throughout the trial to edit an account for it in the Notable British Trials *series. Her introduction to the case impressed the influential critic Desmond MacCarthy, who considered it "as remarkable for legal analysis of evidence as for understanding and moral judgment."*

On 25 September 1934, the following advertisement appeared in *The Bournemouth Daily Echo*: "Daily willing lad, 14–18, for housework. Scout-trained preferred."

This advertisement had been inserted by a Mrs Rattenbury, of Villa Madeira, Manor Park Road, and was answered by a youth called George Percy Stoner. Since he was of an age to drive a car, and his previous employment had been in a garage, he was engaged as chauffeur-handyman.

On Monday, 27 May 1935, Alma Victoria Rattenbury and George Percy Stoner were charged at the Central Criminal Court, Old Bailey, with the murder of the woman's husband, Francis Mawson Rattenbury. Both the accused pleaded Not Guilty.

Mrs Rattenbury was thirty-eight years old, and Stoner had attained the age of eighteen in November of 1934. Mrs Rattenbury and Stoner had become lovers soon after Stoner was taken into Mr Rattenbury's employ in September of that year.

Both Mr and Mrs Rattenbury had been previously married; he once and she twice. Mr Rattenbury had a grown-up son; and Mrs Rattenbury, a little boy called Christopher, born in 1922. The marriage of Francis Rattenbury and Alma Victoria took place about 1928, and a boy, John, was born a year after. Since the birth of this child, Mr and Mrs Rattenbury had not lived together as husband and wife. Mr Rattenbury was sixty-seven years old and not a young man for his age. He was an architect of distinction, and had lived most of his working life in Canada, but when he retired in 1928, he and his wife came to live in Bournemouth.

Eventually, they took a little white house called Villa Madeira in a pleasant suburban road near the sea, shaded by pines. A companion-help, Miss Irene Riggs, came to live with them. Little John went to school but came home every week-end, and Christopher, the child of Mrs Rattenbury's second marriage, spent his holidays at Villa Madeira.

When Stoner was first employed at Villa Madeira, he lived at home and went to his work by day, but in November he took up residence in the house. He had become Mrs Rattenbury's lover before that.

On the night of Sunday, 24 March 1935, Mr Rattenbury was attacked from behind as he sat sleeping in an armchair in the drawing-room. It was never in dispute that the weapon employed was a carpenter's mallet which Stoner had fetched from his grandfather's house that afternoon.

The events that night, as they first were made known in the newspapers, were as follows:

Mrs Rattenbury declared that at about 10.30, after she had gone to bed, she heard a groan from the room below, and that she went downstairs and found her husband in the easy-chair, unconscious, with blood flowing from his head. She called Irene Riggs and told her to telephone for Dr O'Donnell, who was her doctor. He arrived and found Mrs Rattenbury very drunk, and Mr Rattenbury unconscious, with blood flowing from his head. Mrs Rattenbury said: "Look at him – look at the blood – someone has finished him."

Dr O'Donnell telephoned for Mr Rooke, a well-known surgeon. Mr Rooke arrived and found it impossible to examine the patient as Mrs Rattenbury was very drunk and excitable and kept getting in his way. The ambulance was sent for, and the patient removed to Strathallen Nursing Home. After his head had been shaved in the operating theatre, Mr Rooke and Dr O'Donnell saw three serious wounds that could not have been self-inflicted; accordingly, they communicated with the police.

Mr Rooke operated on Mr Rattenbury; and between 3.30 and 4 a.m., Dr O'Donnell returned to Madeira Villa. He found Mrs Rattenbury running about, extremely intoxicated, four or five police officers in the house (some of whom she was trying to kiss), the radio-gramophone playing, and all the lights on. He gave Mrs Rattenbury half a grain of morphia, and put her to bed. During the hours of progressive drunkeness, Mrs Rattenbury had kept on making statements to the effect that she had killed her husband. The next morning, she repeated her assertions in a slightly varied form, and she was taken to the Bournemouth Police Station and charged with doing grievous bodily harm with intent to murder. When she was charged, Mrs. Rattenbury said: "That is right – I did it deliberately, and would do it again."

Such was the terrible case for the prosecution against Alma Victoria Rattenbury. The picture that had inevitably formed itself before the public mind was revolting.

There was probably no one in England – and no one in Court when the trial opened, save Mrs Rattenbury, her solicitor and counsel, Stoner and his solicitor and counsel, and Irene Riggs – who did not think that Mrs Rattenbury was guilty of the crime of murder. In everyone's mind, including my own, there was a picture of Mrs Rattenbury as a coarse, brawling, drunken and callous woman.

But life is not as simple as that, and very often an accurate report fails to convey truth, because only certain things have been reported. The form of the English oath has been very wisely thought out – "the truth, the whole truth, and nothing but the truth". It is possible to give an erroneous impression by merely telling the truth and nothing but the truth. The "whole truth" is a very important factor. The whole truth about Mrs Rattenbury came out during the trial, and the woman, who at first seemed so guilty, was seen to be undoubtedly innocent. This was not merely because there proved to be no evidence beyond her own drunken utterances, but because of her own attitude in the witness-box. For there is no test of truth so relentless as the witness-box – it is deadly to the guilty, and it may save the innocent.

In most criminal trials, the pattern is set at the beginning and merely strengthens as the trial progresses. In the Rattenbury case, the evidence – which seemed so damning on the first day – completely altered in character; what had seemed to be undoubted fact proved to be an airy nothing, and the whole complex pattern shifted and changed much as the pattern of sand changes when it is shaken – and, like sand, it slipped away between the fingers, leaving a residue of grains of truth very different from the pile that the prosecution had originally built up. Even at the end of the trial, so rigid is the English fashion of thinking (or rather feeling, for it is not as careful or accurate a process as thought) on sexual

matters, that many people still considered Mrs Rattenbury morally
damned. That worst of all Anglo-Saxon attitudes, a contemptuous
condemnation of the man and woman – but more particularly the
woman – unfortunate enough to be found out in sexual delin-
quency, never had finer scope than was provided by the Rattenbury case.

Mrs Rattenbury was born Alma Victoria Clark, in Victoria, British
Columbia, and was the daughter of a printer in quite humble
circumstances. She was extremely talented musically. The cheap
strain in her came out in the lyrics of songs she wrote, but she was a
really fine pianist. She grew up to young womanhood just before
the Great War, already well known in Western Canada as a
musician, and, although not strictly speaking pretty, very attractive to men. In the witness-box she still showed as a very elegant
woman. She was well and quietly dressed in dark blue. She had a
pale face, with a beautiful egg-like line of the jaw, dark grey eyes,
and a mouth with a very full lower lip. She was undoubtedly, and
always must have been, a *femme aux hommes*. That is to say that,
although she had women friends and was a generous, easy, kindly,
sentimental creature, she was first and foremost a woman to attract
men and be attracted by them.

She first married a young Englishman called Caledon Dolly,
who joined the Canadian forces on the outbreak of war and was
transferred to England. She followed him and obtained employment in Whitehall. She was very devoted to her husband, but he
was killed in action. This was the only completely happy relationship with a man which Mrs Rattenbury was ever to know. She
joined a Scottish nursing unit, and then became a transport driver,
and worked hard throughout the war. After the Armistice, she
married a man whose wife had divorced him, citing Alma Victoria
Dolly. She married this second husband in 1921, and the child of
that union was born the following year. The marriage was unhappy, and she returned to the house of an aunt in Victoria, and
there met Mr Rattenbury. He, married at the time, fell very much
in love with Alma Victoria, and his wife divorced him, citing her.
At this time Mr Rattenbury was about sixty years of age, and Mrs
Rattenbury thirty-one. Life was not too easy for Mr Rattenbury
and his new wife in a country where everyone knew of the scandal
of the divorce, and this was the chief reason why the Rattenburys
came to England to settle in Bournemouth.

Mrs Rattenbury was a highly sexed woman, and six years of being deprived of sexual satisfaction had combined with the tuberculosis from which she suffered to bring her to the verge of nymphomania. Now, nymphomania is not admirable, but neither is it blameworthy. It is a disease. In spite of the urgency of her desires, which must have tormented her, Mrs Rattenbury had not, so far as is known, had a lover since the birth of little John. She certainly had had none during the four years she had lived in Bournemouth, and she had no abnormal tendencies. She was fond of her husband in a friendly fashion, and he was devoted to her, very interested in her song-writing and anxious for her to succeed. He would often talk to Irene Riggs about his wife, dwelling on the unhappy life she had led, and he never in these conversations said anything against her. Miss Riggs, one of my informants as to these matters, also said that Mrs Rattenbury was very kind to her husband – that she was, indeed, kind to everyone.

The household was not an unhappy one, but neither was it happy. For one thing, Mrs Rattenbury was a gregarious creature, and her husband was of an unsociable frame of mind. He knew hardly anyone of his own station in life, except Dr O'Donnell and Mr Jenks, a retired barrister who had an estate at Bridport. But Mrs Rattenbury was very different from her husband; she had that lavish, easy friendliness which one associates with music-hall artistes, and she could not live without affection. When she made a friend of Irene Riggs, she did so because it was her nature to be friendly with the people who surrounded her. She was fond of Irene Riggs, who, on her side, was devoted to her employer, in spite of the latter's impatient temper. Any little outing to London, any treat such as a visit to a theatre, Mrs Rattenbury shared with Irene Riggs, and the girl has remained attached to the memory of the kindest person she ever met, who helped anyone in need that she came across. But the chief devotion of Mrs Rattenbury's life was for her children. No one denies that she was a good and loving mother. Dr O'Donnell and Miss Riggs both say that Mrs Rattenbury thought nothing too good for her children, and that there was nothing she would not have done for them. She was forever thinking and talking about them, and occupying herself in practical ways for their welfare.

The Rattenburys lived peaceably as a rule, but sometimes they had quarrels – these were about money. Mr Rattenbury, like a great many men, was generous in big matters but difficult in small ones. He allowed his wife £1,000 a year, and many newspapers reported this fact in such a manner that the reading public might easily have imagined that this sum was hers for herself alone. As a matter of fact, out of it she paid for the food for herself, her husband, the domestics and the children when at home, and for one of the boys' schooling. She also paid for Mr Rattenbury's clothes and for her own, and she paid the servants' wages. Mr Rattenbury was a heavy drinker of whisky, and every few weeks Mrs Rattenbury would drink more cocktails than would be good for her, so that the bill for drinks alone must have amounted to a good deal. Mrs Rattenbury had very little money sense, and her husband had every reason to fear her lavish spending. About twice a year she would coax an extra sum out of him: a large sum, over £100, but this he parted with much more easily than he would have parted with small sums more often. Mrs Rattenbury did not pretend that she told her husband true stories to induce him to give her this extra money. She admitted that she invented whatever story would be the most likely to achieve the desired result. Mr Rattenbury was frequently very depressed about financial matters; like everyone else, he had suffered in the slump, and he was apt, during his moods of depression, to threaten suicide. One day in July 1934, he harped on this threat at greater length than usual, and his wife lost her temper and told him it was a pity that he did not do it instead of always talking about it. Mr Rattenbury in his turn then lost his temper and hit his wife, giving her a black eye. She sent for Dr O'Donnell, who found her very agitated and upset. Her husband had left the house, and she feared that he really had gone to kill himself. Mr Rattenbury did not return till about two in the morning, by which time Dr O'Donnell also was extremely anxious. Mrs Rattenbury was by then so ill that he injected a quarter of a grain of morphia, and she slept for twelve hours. After that, life went on as usual with the Rattenburys. She bore him no grudge for having struck her. She was a person of quick temper herself, but generous in what children call "making it up". This was the only serious quarrel between the Rattenburys that Dr O'Donnell or Irene Riggs knew of in four years. In the witness-box, Mrs Rattenbury was asked whether her married life was happy, and she answered: "Like that . . .!" with a gesture of her hand. A gesture that sketched the married life of the larger part of muddled humanity.

Life might have gone on in the usual pedestrian fashion at Villa
Madeira for ever; but George Percy Stoner joined the household,
and Mrs Rattenbury fell in love with him.

The expression "falling in love" is an attempt to define something which escapes definition. Mankind has a natural weakness
for labels, for they simplify life, and though this particular label is
one of the most pernicious which have been evolved, it must be
remembered that it covers not only a multitude of sins, but of
virtues. Perhaps no two people would give quite the same definition of its meaning. Very few people trouble to try.

Mrs Rattenbury herself was a woman who dealt in labels, and
she accepted the expression "falling in love". She was "in love"
with Stoner, who, except for his virility, was not a particularly
interesting or attractive person. Indeed, lack of taste is one of the
chief charges against Mrs Rattenbury, both in her work and in her
life. She was very uncontrolled emotionally. Her lyrics were
appalling. She was subject to drinking bouts, which added to
her natural excitability. She had not scrupled, twice, to take other
women's husbands away from them, and she seems to have been, to
use a slang phrase, a natural-born bad picker. When she took
Stoner as her lover, she said to Dr O'Donnell: "There is something
I want to tell you. I am afraid you will be shocked and never want
to speak to me again." Dr O'Donnell replied that there were very
few things he had not been told in the course of his life, and that he
was not easily shocked. She then told him the step she had taken,
and he spoke to her seriously, warning her that she was probably
being very unwise. But she was too far gone in love by then to heed
any advice he gave her. She merely reiterated that she was in love
with Stoner.

One of the things that told most strongly against Mrs Rattenbury's moral character was that, in the witness-box, she admitted
that she had had connexion with her lover when little John was
asleep in his bed in the same room. This was to many people in
Court, including myself, a very shocking statement. However, it
must be admitted in fairness that there are unfortunately thousands of families in England where the same thing goes on. I myself
have come across such families, and I consider the practice to be
nonetheless shocking because the parents happen to be married.
There is no doubt that an innocent child, awakening and seeing
what was going on, would get an impression of something ugly and
terrifying, even unnatural, which might do him harm for the rest of

his life. But it is only fair, also, to add that Dr O'Donnell has assured me that he never knew a child who slept as soundly as little John. If the Doctor and Irene Riggs were attending Mrs Rattenbury when she happened to be ill, John would sleep undisturbed throughout the visit. I should also add that relations of Mr Rattenbury, who took Mrs Rattenbury into their house after her acquittal, told me that she said: "I can't think what made me say that in the witness-box about Stoner making love to me when little John was in the room. He didn't. I got bewildered, and lost my head, and heard myself saying it." There is, of course, no means of knowing whether Mrs Rattenbury was speaking the truth when she made this remark. I can only say that I think it unlikely: she gave the impression throughout her evidence of being a witness of truth, of being so terrified of what might be the result if she diverted from the truth that she dared not do so, even when it told against her. It may be thought that the solution to the riddle is that, generally, she did go into Stoner's room when little John was at home, but that on some occasions connexion took place in the room where the child was. If so, Mrs Rattenbury's bad taste is again manifest.

The obvious answer to the question as to what love meant for her is that it meant physical satisfaction. Yet, if it had meant only this, it would have deserted her when she stood in peril of her life. It did not do so – and neither did Stoner's love for her. Stoner refused to go into the box, and told his counsel that he did not deny having attacked Mr Rattenbury. The woman for weeks insisted, to her solicitor and counsel, that she wished to take the blame, so as to save Stoner. Mr Lewis-Manning, her solicitor, made it clear to her that, if she lied, her story would not stand the test of the witness-box and that she would only hang herself without saving Stoner. But not till Christopher, the little boy of her second marriage, was sent to her in prison to plead with her to tell the truth did she give way. And afterwards, in the witness-box, she said as little against her lover as possible, making light of certain alleged attacks of violence towards herself, attacks which had frightened her so much that, long before the murder, she had consulted Dr O'Donnell about them.

One of the most interesting points in this case is that it is the only one, so far as I am aware, where two people have been charged together on the capital indictment when neither of the accused has abandoned the other in a scramble for safety. Milson and Fowler,

Field and Gray, Gabrielle Bompard and Eyrand, Mr and Mrs
Manning, Ruth Snyder and Judd Gray, to remember only a few at
random, all tried to throw the blame on the partner in crime. In
1922, Mrs Edith Thompson, terrified and conscious of her own
innocence of murder, never gave a thought to the safety of her
lover, Bywaters. But Mrs Rattenbury was willing and anxious to
take the whole blame if by so doing she could save her lover. It is
Mr Lewis Manning's considered opinion that she was not merely
in a condition of exaltation that would have failed her at the last
pass, but that she would have hanged without a tremor if by so
doing she could have saved Stoner.

The story of Mrs Rattenbury's life is a mingling of tragedy and
futility. It is easy to be sentimental and see only the tragedy. It is
easy to be stupid and see only the futility. The truth is that it is
always easy to label people – but because a thing is easy, it is not
necessarily accurate. No human being is simple. Stoner may have
seemed simple enough to his family; he had always been a quiet
boy who did not make friends, but his quiet appearance concealed
stormy adolescent yearnings. He had the dramatic instincts natural
to the young, and, unfortunately, circumstances thrust him into
real drama before he could tell the difference between what was
real and what was make-believe. Physically, he was very passionate, and nothing in his mental training had equipped him to cope
with the extraordinary life to which it had pleased Mrs Rattenbury
to call him.

Francis Rattenbury, that outwardly quiet man, is a pathetic
figure in retrospect. Mr Justice Humphreys referred to him as
being "that very unpleasant character for which, I think, we have
no suitable expression, but which the French call a *mari complaisant*. A man who knew that his wife was committing adultery, and
had no objection to it." Mrs Rattenbury said, in the box, that she
thought her husband knew because she had told him she was living
her own life. But she may well have told him that without his
taking in the meaning of her words. He was completely incurious,
and he lived not in the present but in regrets for the past and
anxieties for the future.

Irene Riggs, Dr O'Donnell, and, indeed, everyone acquainted
with the household to whom I have spoken, was of the opinion that
Mr Rattenbury was not aware that his wife and his chauffeur were
lovers. But when I saw Villa Madeira, I thought this difficult to
credit. It is so small as to be remarkable, small as the witch's

cottage in *Hansel and Gretel*. On the ground floor are the kitchen, drawing-room, dining-room, and a room that Mr Rattenbury used as a bedroom, and which opened off the drawing-room. Is it possible that a man, in a house as small as Villa Madeira would not hear the footsteps over his head whenever Stoner went into Mrs Rattenbury's room, and that he would not hear the occasionally loud quarrels which took place between them? Looking at Villa Madeira, the answer would seem to be that it would be quite impossible. And yet Mr Rattenbury's known character and habits supply a different answer. Every night, he drank the best part of a bottle of whisky. He was a man brilliant in his profession, with many excellent qualities, and he was not a drunkard; but he was not a young man, and he was very deaf. The alcohol which he consumed every night explains why he no longer lived with his wife, why he was completely incurious as to her doings, and why he heard nothing of what was going on over his head. He was not, in the opinion of all who knew him – the doctor, his own relations, and Irene Riggs, who lived in the house – the character stigmatised by Mr Justice Humphreys as a *"mari complaisant*, not a nice character". He was a quiet, pleasant man whose finances worried him, and whose emotional relationships had disappointed him.

A man in Mr Rattenbury's condition, and of his age, is apt to forget the power that the natural inclinations of the flesh had over him in youth and middle age, and he may fail to realise that it is still a factor in the life of anyone else. So far as he knew, he was a good husband to his wife. He admired her, was genuinely fond of her. There was nothing within his power that he would not have done for her, and Mrs Rattenbury was astute enough to take advantage of this whenever possible. In regard to his wife, his chief anxieties were financial, and after he had started to take his prolonged night-cap each evening, the rest of the world existed very little for him. The passions, the jealousies, of a decade earlier had ceased, not only in the present, but even as a memory of the past. The chief tragedy in life is not what we are but what we have ceased to be, and Mr Rattenbury was an example of this truth. It is easy to say that a man who knows that his wife is committing adultery and has no objection is not a nice character. But it is not necessarily the truth. It is possible that a man who no longer leads a normal life with his wife yet thinks of her, not as his property, but as a human being who belongs to herself, with a right to a normal life. I do not say that this was Mr Rattenbury's attitude (although Mrs Rattenbury said that it was): I merely say that it would not necessarily have been a despicable attitude. But, of course, the judgment of the man in the street is the same as that of Mr Justice Humphreys. It is an Anglo-Saxon attitude.

Another Anglo-Saxon attitude, accepted by the learned Judge, by counsel on both sides, and by the British public, was that, because of her greater age, Mrs Rattenbury dominated her young lover. It was this same assumption which hanged Edith Thompson. There has been a growing consensus of public opinion ever since the Bywaters–Thompson trial that the female prisoner was wrongly convicted; and the memory of the earlier trial haunted the courtroom like a ghost. The Rattenbury case seemed like an echo of that tragedy, and it is not fanciful to say that Mrs Thompson's fate did much to save Mrs Rattenbury. A judge who knew how to point out firmly and clearly to the jury that a woman must not, because of her moral character, be convicted of murder, and a jury who were determined that no confusion of thought or prejudice should lead them into giving a wrong verdict, were two great safeguards for Mrs Rattenbury, and the uneasy memory of Edith Thompson was yet a third. Nevertheless, the assumption of the Bywaters–Thompson case, that an elderly woman dominates her young lover, still obtained at the Rattenbury trial. The actual truth is that there is no woman so under the dominion of her lover as the elderly mistress of a very much younger man. The great Benjamin Franklin knew this, and there is extant a letter of advice written by him to a young man, which is a model of clear thinking. The original belongs to the US Government, and is in the custody of the Librarian of Congress at Washington, DC. This copy was taken from the original letter, and has not hitherto been published in England [at the time the essay was written in 1936]

                                                    June 25th, 1745
My Dear Friend,

I know of no medicine fit to diminish the violent nocturnal inclinations you mention, and if I did, I think I should not communicate it to you. Marriage is the proper remedy.

It is the most natural state of man, and therefore the state in which you are most likely to find solid happiness. Your reasons against entering it at present appear to me not well founded. The circumstantial advantages you have in view of postponing it are not only uncertain, but they are small in comparison with that of the thing itself – the being married and settled.

It is the man and woman united that make the complete human being. Separate, she wants his force of body and strength of reason; he, her softness, sensibility and acute discernment. Together they are most likely to succeed in the world. A single man has not nearly the value he would have in a state of union. He is an incomplete animal; he resembles the odd half of a pair of scissors. If you get a prudent healthy wife, your industry in your profession, with her good economy, will be a fortune sufficient.

But if you will not take this counsel, and persist in thinking a commerce with the sex inevitable, then I repeat my former advice, that in your amours you should prefer OLD WOMEN TO YOUNG ONES. You call this a paradox, and demand reasons. They are these: –

First. Because they have more knowledge of the World, and their minds are better stored with observations; their conversation is more improving and more lastingly agreeable.

Second. Because when women cease to be handsome, they study to be good. To maintain their influence over men, they supply the diminution of beauty by an augmentation of utility. They learn to do a thousand services, small and great, and are the most tender and useful of all friends when you are sick. Thus they continue amiable, and hence there is scarcely such a thing to be found as an old woman who is not a good woman.

Third. Because there is no hazard of children, which, irregularly produced, may be attended with much inconvenience.

Fourth. Because, through more experience, they are more prudent and discreet in conducting an intrigue to prevent suspicion. The commerce with them is therefore safe with regard to your reputation, and with regard to theirs. If the affair should happen to be known, considerate people might be rather inclined to excuse an old woman who would kindly take care of a young man, form his manners by her good counsels, and prevent his ruining his health and fortune among mercenary prostitutes.

Fifth. Because, in every animal that walks upright, the deficiency of the fluid that fills the muscles appears but on the highest part. The face first grows lank and wrinkled, then the neck, then the breast and arms – the lower parts continuing to the last as plump as ever; so that, covering all above with a basket, and regarding only what is below the girdle, it is impossible of two women to know an old from a young one. And as in the dark all cats are grey, the pleasure of corporal enjoyment with an old woman is at least equal and frequently superior; every knack being, by practice, capable of improvement.

Sixth. Because the sin is less. The debauching a virgin may be her ruin and make her life unhappy.

Seventh. Because the compunction is less. The having made a young girl miserable may give you frequent bitter reflections, none of which can attend the making an Old woman Happy.

Eighth and Lastly. They are so grateful.

This much for my paradox, but still I advise you to marry immediately, being sincerely,

Your affectionate friend,

B. FRANKLIN.

"Eighth and lastly" is worthy of the consideration of English lawyers and the English public when a Thompson–Bywaters or Rattenbury-Stoner case is under consideration. Once Stoner had become Mrs Rattenbury's lover, she worshipped him. It was before the consummation of her desire that she was the dominating character, and to that extent she was responsible for the whole tragedy; but to that extent only. She felt this responsibility deeply, and it was remorse as well as love that made her eager and willing to save Stoner even at the cost of her own life. It was, indeed, a terrible responsibility in view of the events. She could not know that Stoner would be wild with jealousy, but she must have known, had she paused to think, that a lad of Stoner's age and antecedents would lose all sense of values when he became the lover of his social superior, who dazzled him with a whole new mode of life. If Stoner's first love-affair had been with a girl of his own class, no ill need have come of it. Nevertheless, another strange assumption was made – that it is somehow harmful for a young man of eighteen to have sexual connexion.

Dr Gillespie, physician for psycho-medicine at Guy's Hospital, a witness for the defence, was asked in cross-examination by Mr

Croom-Johnson, whether "regular sexual intercourse with a member of the opposite sex by a boy of eighteen or onwards would be likely to do him good or harm?" Dr Gillespie replied that it would not do him good "if a moral point of view were meant". Mr Croom-Johnson said that he was not talking from a moral point of view, that he was asking him as a doctor. Still Dr Gillespie wisely refused to commit himself. "Do you think it would likely be good for his constitution – a boy of eighteen – just think what you are saying, Doctor?" "I am not saying that it is good for his constitution, but I am saying that if it were occurring with such frequency . . . as nature would permit, it would not necessarily show the effects in his external appearance." "Take the ordinary case – the ordinary boy, not somebody very strong, talking about the ordinary English youth of eighteen – do you really find yourself in any difficulty in answering the question?" "I find difficulty," replied the Doctor, "in answering the question as I believe you expect it to be answered." Doctors, as a rule, make excellent witnesses, and in this little cross-examination, Dr Gillespie was no exception to the rule – but with what frank, Homeric laughter the question would have been greeted in a Latin country! In England it is apparently impossible to admit the simple truth that a young man of eighteen is an adult who would normally take a mate, were it not that economic conditions render it impossible.

Mrs Rattenbury was a good witness, and in nothing more notably so than in her simple acceptance of the values of life as she knew it. "You have told us that on the Sunday night Stoner came into your bedroom and got into bed with you. Was that something that happened frequently?" asked Mr Croom-Johnson in cross-examination. "Oh, yes," replied Mrs Rattenbury simply. And later on: "Did it occur to you that if you went to Bridport, Mr Rattenbury might want to treat you as his wife?" – "No, if I had thought it was going to happen like that, I would never have suggested going." "It never occurred to you?" – "No." "You know what I mean by saying "treat you as his wife'?" "Yes, exactly," replied Mrs Rattenbury, as though mildly surprised that there could be any mistake about it.

Mrs Rattenbury's vagueness about money matters and her lavish spending came out as clearly in the witness-box as did her attitude towards sensual matters. In answering to a question as to her habit of giving away cigarette-holders, she said: "That is nothing for me. If anyone sees a cigarette-holder and likes it, I always say 'take it'. It is my disposition"; and later: "I am very vague about money." This was certainly true. Mr Croom-Johnson asked her how much money her husband let her have in the course of a year, to which she replied that she "really couldn't say". "Hundreds?" "I suppose so." "About how much a year did he let you have?" "He used to give me regularly £50 a month, and I was regularly overdrawn." "£50 a month would be £600 a year?" "I see," said Mrs Rattenbury; and one received the impression that she had not worked out this fairly simple sum for herself. "In addition to that," went on Mr Croom-Johnson, "about £150 on each of two occasions?" "Yes, I daresay." Later, cross-examining her about the clothes she had lavished on Stoner in London, Mr Croom-Johnson said: "You used the words 'that he required clothes'?" – "Yes, I considered so." "Silk pajamas at sixty shillings a suit?" – "That might seem absurd, but that is my disposition." And certainly it was her disposition.

So, as we have seen, Mr Rattenbury was reserved, kindly, but rather mean in money matters. Mrs Rattenbury was unreserved, also kindly, but in a more indiscriminate fashion than her husband, and her generosity was indiscriminating also. Irene Riggs liked both of them, but her loyalty was naturally for the mistress who had been kinder to her than any human being she had ever met.

Irene Riggs was not as happy after Stoner's arrival as she had been before. When Mrs Rattenbury told her about the liaison, Irene was too fond of her to blame her, but nevertheless felt uneasy about the affair, and sorry that she could not have found happiness with someone more of her own age and class. Though Miss Riggs and Stoner did not like each other, they got on together well enough. He was a very quiet boy; she also was quiet. And she was self-effacing and efficient. She was shocked when Mrs Rattenbury first told her the truth, but human nature quickly adapts itself to knowledge, and she very rightly felt that it was not for her to praise or to blame. She stayed behind when, on 19 March, Mrs Rattenbury arranged to take Stoner with her on a trip to London, because Stoner was very jealous of any third person, and the charm of the little friendly expeditions that had been the highlights in Irene Riggs's life before the coming of Stoner was gone.

In London, Mrs Rattenbury and Stoner stayed at the Royal Palace Hotel, Kensington, and spent their days in shopping and going about town. Mrs Rattenbury explained this trip to her husband by saying that she was going to have an operation (she had had several minor operations in the preceding years), and he gave her the generous sum of £250 for that purpose. Mrs Rattenbury used a large part of the money to pay outstanding housekeeping bills, and the rest she spent wildly upon the London trip and presents for Stoner. The importance of the expedition to London lies in the fact that, for four or five days, Stoner was accepted by the little world about him as Mrs Rattenbury's social equal. He did not go to the Royal Palace Hotel as her chauffeur, but as her brother. They had two rooms opposite each other, and he had free access to his mistress. He was called "Sir" by the servants, and every day Mrs Rattenbury bought him presents which to his simple mind must have appeared equivalent to Danae's golden shower. Crêpe-de-chine pajamas at three guineas a pair and a made-to-measure suit must have seemed to the young man, who was a labourer's son, most exciting luxuries.

The learned Judge referred to the "orgy in London". It is difficult to imagine an orgy at the Royal Palace Hotel at Kensington; I have indeed, never been able to discover of what an "orgy" consists. It is associated, more or less vaguely, in the popular mind with the "historical" productions of Mr C. de Mille; glasses of wine, dancing girls, tiger-skins and cushions are some of its component parts. The private coming together of a pair of lovers and their normal physical ecstasies, however reprehensible these may be morally, do not seem well described by the word "orgy". Even shopping at Harrods does not quite come under this heading. However, in this trial, as in all others of the same nature, the stock phrases were used of which most people are heartily tired. "Adulterous intercourse," "illicit union," "this wretched woman" and the like: they all have a very familiar ring. They are clichés, and come to the lips of those concerned in the administration of the law as inevitably as the adjective "fashionably dressed" is attached to the noun "woman" in any reporter's account of the female spectators at a murder trial. Leaving these clichés, the fact, nevertheless, remains that Stoner's trip to London must have thoroughly unsettled him. He was happy enough at Villa Madeira, where the social régime was easy and pleasant for such as he.

Mrs Rattenbury affected no superiority with anyone in humbler circumstances of life than her own, and Mr Rattenbury had lived for years in the democratic country where Mrs Rattenbury was born. Stoner often played cards with him in the evening, and Mr Rattenbury, Stoner, and Miss Riggs took their meals together.

Therefore, merely to have returned to Villa Madeira, to continue its pleasant, easy life, would not necessarily have upset Stoner. But this was not exactly what happened. The lovers arrived back late on Friday evening. Mr Rattenbury, already having imbibed his night-cap, asked no questions; even next day, according to Mrs Rattenbury, and so far as Irene Riggs's knowledge went, he never enquired about the operation his wife had ostensibly been to London to undergo. The Saturday found him in one of his worst fits of depression. A scheme for building some flats, of which he was to have been the architect, was hanging fire, owing to the financial depression, and Mrs Rattenbury tried to cheer him up in vain.

On the Sunday, he was still more depressed. In the morning Mrs Rattenbury took him for a drive. After lunch he slept. They had tea together, little John with them. He had been reading a book, a novel in which there was a perfect holocaust of suicides, and, according to Mrs Rattenbury, he expressed his admiration for anyone who had the courage to make an end of himself. Mrs Rattenbury suggested that she should ring up their friend, Mr Jenks, at Bridport, and ask whether they could go over on the Monday. She did indeed telephone, and Mr Jenks said he would be pleased to see them, and asked them to spend the night, an invitation which they accepted. The telephone was in Mr Rattenbury's bedroom, which opened off the drawing-room. Mr Rattenbury remained in the drawing-room, but Stoner came into the bedroom, and overheard the arrangements which Mrs Rattenbury was making. He was frightfully angry and threatened her with an air-pistol, which he was carrying in his hand, and which she took to be a revolver. He told her that he would kill her if they went to Bridport. She, nervous lest her husband should overhear the conversation (though, as she said, "He never really took very much notice") urged Stoner into the dining-room, and went there with him.

Once there, he accused her of having had connexion with her husband that afternoon – an accusation entirely baseless – and said that, if the Bridport plan were carried out, he would refuse to drive. Stoner said that at Mr Jenks's house the Rattenburys would have to share a bedroom, but Mrs Rattenbury assured him that that would not be so – and what she said she knew to be the truth, for she and her husband had stayed with Mr Jenks before, and had had two rooms. Stoner, though he appeared to be pacified, continued to brood over the matter, and at about eight o'clock that evening, he went to the house of his grandparents, sat and chatted, apparently normally, with his grandmother for some time, and borrowed a carpenter's mallet, but borrowed it perfectly openly. He went back to Villa Madeira, and Mrs Rattenbury noticed nothing abnormal about him.

That same evening, Mrs Rattenbury sat and played cards with her husband, kissed him good-night, and went upstairs. It was Irene's evening out, and Mrs Rattenbury passed the time by getting together her things for Bridport. She had already put out Mr Rattenbury's clothes in his bedroom downstairs. Irene came in at about 10.15, and went straight to her room. Some ten minutes later, she went downstairs, either to see if all was well or to get something to eat – there seems a slight discrepancy in her evidence here. When she was in the hall, she heard a sound of heavy breathing, and putting her head into Mr Rattenbury's bedroom, she switched on the light. He was not there. The sound of breathing came from the drawing-room, the door between that and the bedroom being open. Miss Riggs concluded that he had, as he so often did, fallen asleep in his chair, and she went back to her bedroom. A few moments later, she went out again to go to the lavatory, and found Stoner leaning over the banisters at the head of the stairs, looking down. She said, "What is the matter?" He replied, "Nothing; I was looking to see if the lights were out."

About a quarter of an hour later, Mrs Rattenbury came to Irene's room and told her about the expedition to Bridport. Mrs Rattenbury then went to her own room, and about ten minutes later Stoner came and slipped into her bed. He seemed very agitated and upset. She said, "What is the matter, darling?" He replied that he was in trouble, but that he could not tell her what it was about. She said that he must tell her, that she was strong enough to bear anything, and he then said, "You won't be going to Bridport to-morrow." He went on to say that he had hurt "Ratz". He said that he had hit him over the head with a mallet, which he had since hidden in the garden. Mrs Rattenbury definitely conveyed the impression from the box that it was possible that the idea in Stoner's head was merely to injure Mr Rattenbury, so that the proposed expedition could not take place. "I thought," she said, "he was frightened at what he had done, because he had hurt Mr Rattenbury . . . I thought he'd just hurt him badly enough to prevent him going to Bridport, and when I said 'I'll go and see him,' he said 'No, you must not; the sight will upset you,' and I thought all I had to do was to fix Ratz up, and that would put him all right.''

It may be that this was the only idea in Stoner's unbalanced and ill-educated mind, but that he found it impossible to stop after the first blow and administered two more. Or it may be that, in his disturbed and jealous state, he would have done anything sooner than allow the Bridport trip to take place. If Stoner had driven the Rattenburys to Bridport, he would have had to do so in his capacity of chauffeur; he would have stayed there in the same capacity, eaten in the servants' hall, not had access to his mistress, and ranked as a domestic with the other domestics. The thought of the expedition to Bridport, coming directly after the "orgy" in London, was unbearable.

It may be argued that, as a motive, this distaste for going to Bridport was very inadequate. But all motives for murder are inadequate. Men have murdered for smaller sums than an embezzler would plot to obtain.

Directly the sense of what Stoner was telling her penetrated to Mrs Rattenbury's mind, she jumped out of bed and ran downstairs as she was, in her pajamas and bare feet. A minute later, Irene Riggs, who had not yet fallen asleep, heard her mistress shrieking for her. Miss Riggs ran downstairs and found Mr Rattenbury leaning back in an armchair, as though he were asleep. There was a large pool of blood on the floor; one of his eyes was very swollen and discoloured, and she thought he had a black eye, but this was, in reality, "contrecoup" – the effect upon his eye of the blows on the back of his head. Mrs Rattenbury asked Irene to telephone for the doctor at once, telling her to hurry and, to use Miss Riggs's own expression, went "raving about the house". "Oh! poor Ratz. Poor Ratz!" she kept repeating, "can't somebody do something?" She drank some whisky; she was violently sick, and drank more whisky. She kept on telling Miss Riggs to wipe up the blood because, she said, little John must not see any blood.

Now, there is no doubt that Mrs Rattenbury knew from the moment she set eyes on her husband that Stoner's talk upstairs had not been a mere attempt to attract her interest and attention. She knew that he had injured her husband in a terrible fashion, and that tragedy, which she could not control, had suddenly taken possession of her life. Her first thought was for her husband, her second for little John. Her third was for Stoner, and this thought persisted, and deepened in intensity, during the hours that followed.

Dr O'Donnell arrived at Villa Madeira at about 11.45. Mrs Rattenbury was, in his opinion, already very drunk. Mr Rooke, the surgeon, arrived at the house about five minutes after midnight, and he also was of the opinion that Mrs Rattenbury was drunk. Dr O'Donnell and Mr Rooke decided that, largely owing to her excited condition, the only proper place for her husband was in a nursing home. They took him there, shaved his head, and discovered three wounds. Dr O'Donnell telephoned the Central Police Station, about ten minutes' walk from the nursing home and two minutes by car, and said: "Dr O'Donnell speaking from Strathallen Nursing Home, Manor Road. Mr Rooke and myself have just taken Mr Rattenbury from 5 Manor Road to the nursing home. On examination, we find three serious wounds on the back of his skull, due to external violence, which will most probably prove fatal." Central Police Station replied: "You want an officer?" Dr O'Donnell said, "Yes, at once." But it was half an hour before a constable arrived. The constable then said he must get an inspector, and at about 3.15 a.m. Inspector Mills, who had already been at Villa Madeira, arrived. At 3.30 Inspector Mills, Mr Rooke, and Dr O'Donnell left the nursing home. Stoner was sleeping peacefully outside in the Rattenbury car, and he drove Dr O'Donnell back to Villa Madeira, following the police car.

When Dr O'Donnell got out of the car, he was struck by the fact that every light in Villa Madeira was on, the door was open, and the radio-gramophone was playing. There were four police officers in the house. Mrs Rattenbury was by now extremely drunk. A constable, who had arrived at 3 o'clock, had observed then that Mrs Rattenbury was under the influence of alcohol, but, as he put it, "to a mild extent". One has, of course, to realise that the police standard of drunkenness is very high; as Mr Justice Humphreys phrased it – "drunk in the police sense seems to mean hopelessly drunk."

At 3.30, according to Dr O'Donnell, Mrs Rattenbury was past knowing what she was thinking or saying. Dr O'Donnell, very shocked, turned off the radio-gramophone, and tried to explain to Mrs Rattenbury the gravity of her husband's condition, but she could not take in what he was saying. Inspector Mills agreed that Mrs Rattenbury was more under the influence of drink than when he had seen her at 2 a.m. He said to her: "Your husband has been seriously injured and is now in the nursing home," and she asked: "Will that be against me?" Inspector Mills then cautioned her, and apparently was satisfied that she understood the meaning of the caution.

Then she made a statement: "I did it. He has lived too long. I will tell you in the morning where the mallet is. Have you told the Coroner yet? I shall make a better job of it next time. Irene does not know. I have made a proper muddle of it. I thought I was strong enough."

Dr O'Donnell, who considered that Mrs Rattenbury was unable to understand what was said to her, or to know what she was saying, pointed out that she was in no fit condition to be asked anything, and took her up to bed. He administered half a grain of morphia – a large dose – and went downstairs again. After a few minutes he went into the sitting-room and found that Mrs Rattenbury had managed to get downstairs again and was again being questioned by the police. Inspector Mills said to her: "Do you suspect anyone?" and she replied: "Yes. I think so. His son."

Dr O'Donnell, who was aware that Mr Rattenbury's son lived abroad, said to the Inspector: "Look at her condition – she is full of whisky, and I have just given her a large dose of morphia. She is in no condition to make any statement." He then took her by the arm and helped her upstairs again. Then (it was by now after 4 a.m.), Dr O'Donnell went home. At 6 a.m. Inspector Carter arrived at the house, where some members of the police had remained all night. He stated in evidence that he went into Mrs Rattenbury's room and she woke up. This was not unnatural, in view of the fact that the police had been in that tiny house all night, perpetually going up and down stairs. Inspector Carter realised that Mrs Rattenbury was ill, and he told Miss Riggs to prepare some coffee. When the coffee came, the saucer shook so in Mrs Rattenbury's hand that she could not hold it. She managed to swallow it, but retched and said that she wanted to be sick. The Inspector telephoned for a police-matron, who arrived and helped Mrs Rattenbury downstairs to her bath and helped her to dress. This matron was not called as witness, but it is reasonable to conclude that she thought Mrs Rattenbury a sick woman. Yet, according to Inspector Carter, Mrs Rattenbury, who had been drinking steadily from about 11 o'clock the night before till 3.30 in the morning (quite undeterred by the police), and who had then been given half a grain of morphia which she had not been allowed to sleep off, was by 8.15 competent to make a statement! The statement which she then made to him, after being duly cautioned, and which he wrote down in his notebook, read as follows:

"About 9 p.m. on 24 March I was playing cards with my husband when he dared me to kill him, as he wanted to die. I picked up a mallet and he then said: 'You have not the guts to do it!' I then hit him with the mallet. I hid the mallet outside. I would have shot him if I had had a gun."

Inspector Carter deposed that Mrs Rattenbury read the statement over aloud and clearly before signing it. He then took her to Bournemouth Police Station, where she was charged. Before she left the house, she had a moment alone with Miss Riggs and said: "You must get Stoner to give me the mallet." This is important; it is quite clear, on reading Mrs Rattenbury's statements all through the night, that, even in her befogged condition, there was one thread of continuity – a desire to help Stoner, and to get hold of the mallet with which he had told her he had hit Mr Rattenbury and then hidden in the garden. At the Police Station, about 8.45, Mrs Rattenbury was formally charged, and said: "That is right. I did it deliberately, and would do it again."

The police did not, at the hearing at Petty Sessions, mention the fact that Mrs Rattenbury had been drunk, and Mr Rooke, noticing this omission, communicated the fact to Mrs Rattenbury's solicitors. Had it not been for Mr Rooke and Dr O'Donnell, the fact that Mrs Rattenbury had been in no fit condition to make a statement, to know what was said to her, or to know what she herself was saying, would not have been given in evidence. At the trial, her counsel, Mr O'Connor, in his cross-examination of Inspector Carter, said: "Dr O'Donnell has told us in his evidence that no reliance can be placed on any statement made by Mrs Rattenbury at 8.15 in the morning." "No," agreed the Inspector. "Do you say she was normal at 8.15?" – "Yes. She was not normal when she first woke up, but I waited till 8.15" "Do you know that the medical officer at Holloway Prison has reported that she was still under the influence of drugs three days later?" – "He has never reported it to me." "Is your evidence to the jury that, from the time you began to take her statement until she left your charge, she did not appear to you to be under the influence of drugs?" – "She did not." "Not at any time?" – "Not at any time." Yet Mrs Rattenbury was, during the whole of the time Inspector Carter had to do with her, *non compos mentis* from morphia!

Later in the trial, Mr Justice Humphreys, turning over the pages of Inspector Carter's notebook, was struck by the fact that there was an entry that had not been put in evidence. This consisted of a statement that Mrs Rattenbury had made directly she woke up at 6 o'clock. Mr O'Connor was handed the notebook, read the entry through to himself, and expressed his gratitude to the Judge. Indeed, Mr Justice Humphreys had made one of the most important points for the defence that were made in the case, as was shown when Inspector Carter was recalled to the box.

By the Judge: "Did Mrs Rattenbury make any statement to you about this alleged crime before 8.15?" – "No statement to me, my lord. Mrs Rattenbury said the words that I have written in that book, while she was lying on the bed, directly she woke up. I did not put them down in statement form. I did not refer to it in my evidence for this reason. When Mrs Rattenbury woke up, I said in my evidence that, in my opinion, she was not then in a normal condition and I did not caution her, and for that reason I made no reference at all to these remarks that I put down in my book that she said. That is why I omitted to say anything at all about it in my evidence-in-chief. I was not entitled, in my opinion, to give anything in evidence if I had not previously administered a caution, and, in my opinion, she was not in a condition normally to make a statement." *By the Judge*: "Then in your opinion she was not in a condition to make a statement at 6.15?" – "At 6.10, no, my lord." *By the Judge*: "Then what was said at that time was something said by a woman who was not in a condition to make a statement that can be acted upon?" – "Not in my opinion, my lord."

There was no doubt that Inspector Carter was actuated by an admirable sense of fair play, and the Judge, in his summing-up, said: "I think there is no ground for complaining of his conduct or saying that he acted improperly here, although, I think, he was mistaken . . . He made a mistake in not informing the Director of Public Prosecutions that that statement had been made by the accused, and that he had it in his notebook. It is not for the police officers to decide . . . what is admissible in evidence and what is not, or what should be given or what not. Their duty is to give all material to the authorities, and let them decide."

Now, the important point about the first entry in Inspector Carter's notebook – the entry he did not put in evidence, that he wrote at 6.15 – and the one which he wrote down after cautioning her at 8.15, is this: the two statements are practically identical. At

6.15 when, according to Inspector Carter, she was not fit to make a statement, she said: "I picked up the mallet and he dared me to hit him. He said, 'You have not guts enough to do it.' I hit him. I hid the mallet. He is not dead, is he? Are you the Coroner?" At 8.15 she said: "He dared me to kill him. He wanted to die. I picked up the mallet, and he said, 'You have not the guts enough to do it.' I hid the mallet outside the house." It will be seen at once that, with the exception of the words, "He is not dead, is he? Are you the Coroner?" the statements are the same, except that at 8.15 she used the word "kill", and at 6.15 the word "hit". To put it concisely: she made the same statement when, according to the Inspector, she was fit to make a statement that she had made two hours earlier, when even he had considered her totally unfit! The importance of this is obvious – Mrs Rattenbury no more knew what she was saying at 8.15 than she did at 6.15, and the second statement was of no more value than the first. At one o'clock of that day, when Dr O'Donnell saw her at the police station, he says that she was supported into the room, that she could not stand without swaying, and that she looked dazed and had contracted pupils as a result of the morphia. Three days later, Dr Morton of Holloway Prison considered that she was still suffering from "confusion of mind, a result of alcohol, and possibly a large dose of morphia. She kept repeating the same sentences over and over again." From 28 March, she was better and appeared to have forgotten what she had said and how she had behaved on the previous days since her reception. It is perfectly obvious that police officers are not fit judges of when a person is under the influence of morphia or not. There is no reason why they should be. But they *are* judges of drunkenness, and Mrs Rattenbury should not have been allowed to go on drinking – or have been questioned during the Sunday night. As the Judge pointed out, Dr O'Donnell knew much more of these matters than the police officer, and much later on Monday, after she had been taken to the Police Court, he declared that it would still be unsafe to attach any importance to anything that Mrs Rattenbury said.

Now, Mrs Rattenbury was not used to drugs, in spite of suggestions made to the contrary; she had, indeed, a horror of drugs, and the only time previously in her life that any had been administered to her was in July 1934, when Dr O'Donnell had administered a quarter of a grain of morphia, as she was ill and excited. On that occasion she was allowed to have her sleep out, and she had indeed slept for some twelve hours. When the stronger dose of half a grain of morphia was given to her on the night of Sunday, 24 March, she had no chance of sleep. It is not suggested for a moment that the police tried to awaken her. But Stoner and the police were up and down and about the house all night long. Now, anyone who has had to have morphia knows that if he is not allowed to sleep off the effects, his condition is far worse than if it had never been administered. This was the case with Mrs Rattenbury, and, according to the experienced Dr Morton, she was still suffering from the effects of the morphia three days later. Many people felt that even if Mrs Rattenbury did not know what she was saying when she was drunk and when she was drugged, what she said came from her subconscious self, and hence was true. This is an error, as any doctor knows. What does come through all her statements, if they are carefully analysed, is her anxiety for Stoner, and her wish to take the blame.

Another strong point for the defence, besides the undoubted one that Mrs Rattenbury was quite unfit to make statements, was the complete blank in her memory when she emerged from her drugged state into ordinary consciousness at Holloway Prison. Mrs Rattenbury remembered nothing from the time when she began to drink after discovering her wounded husband until 28 March at Holloway Prison. Many people, as a result of drinking, "pass out". Mrs Rattenbury did so, and the result of the morphia's effect being thwarted was that she stayed "out" for a very long time. She remembered nothing from when she first became drunk on the Sunday night. So far as her mind was concerned, she knew nothing about the interrogations, nothing about the injection of morphia, nothing about the police-matron having helped to get her up. She did not remember being taken away from Villa Madeira in a car by the police; the only thing that swam up at all in her recollection was Stoner's farewell-kiss in her room, and the face of little John at her door. Mr Croom-Johnson, in cross-examination, asked her: "About conversations, your mind is a complete blank?" – "Absolutely." "About incidents?" – "Yes. It might be somebody else you are talking about." "Is your mind a complete blank about making the statement to Inspector Carter which he wrote down in this little book?" – "I cannot remember that. I have tried and tried and tried yesterday, and last night I tried to remember again." The notebook was handed to her, and Mr Croom-Johnson asked her whether the signature at the bottom of the statement was hers. She

said that it was: "It is my signature, but I do not remember it."
Now, it is natural for the layman to feel that loss of memory is a
convenient form of defence, but Mrs Rattenbury could not have
deceived medical men as highly trained and as astute as Mr Rooke,
Dr O'Donnell, and Dr Morton – the last-named accustomed to all
the tricks of delinquent women.

The prosecution took the unusual step of allowing the defence to
recall one of the Crown witnesses, Mr Rooke, and this courteous
gesture was a great help to Mrs Rattenbury. Mr Rooke deposed
that in his experience patients often talked long and lucidly when
under morphia, but when the effects of the drug had worn off, their
minds were a complete blank regarding anything they had said.
When it is considered that Mrs Rattenbury was not only suffering
from the morphia, but that before the morphia had been administered she had temporarily lost her mind through drink, I think it is
clear that no reliance can be placed on anything that she said.

Mrs Rattenbury was removed to Holloway Prison in London,
and Stoner and Miss Riggs were left in the house at Manor Road.
But Miss Riggs had no intention of being left alone with Stoner.
She knew that Mrs Rattenbury was innocent – not only of striking
the blows, but of complicity in the assault. One of Mrs Rattenbury's most striking characteristics was her horror of cruelty; she
could not have hurt anything. Therefore Irene Riggs thought that
either a burglar had broken in or that Stoner must have been Mr
Rattenbury's assailant.

Irene's mother and brother moved into Villa Madeira and stayed
there with her until Stoner was arrested on Thursday, 28 March.
The story of those days between the commission of the crime and
the arrest of Stoner is a curious one. Dr O'Donnell had been asked
by relations of Mr Rattenbury to keep Villa Madeira under his eye,
and the Doctor accordingly called there on the Monday, Tuesday,
Wednesday and Thursday. On the three first days he tried to see
Miss Riggs alone, but found it impossible as Stoner did not leave
them. On Wednesday Miss Riggs was nearly distracted with
anxiety, and felt she must talk about the case to someone. She
still believed herself to be the custodian of Mrs Rattenbury's secret
love-affair, and she never discussed her even with her relations.
Although not a Catholic, she went to see a priest, because she knew
that what she told a priest would be safe. She came back at about
10.30 that night and her mother opened the door to her. Mrs Riggs
told her that Stoner was very drunk, that he had been going up and

down the road, shouting: "Mrs Rattenbury is in jail, and I've put her there." He had been brought back by two taxi-drivers. Irene Riggs telephoned to the police, and two plain-clothes men arrived. Stoner was in bed and seemed very drunk. This was most unusual for him, for he not only never drank himself, but objected to Mrs Rattenbury drinking, and had a good influence on her in this respect.

On the morning of Thursday, 28 March, Dr O'Donnell called at Villa Madeira. Irene Riggs opened the door. It had always been Stoner who had opened it up to then. Dr O'Donnell asked where Stoner was, and she told him that he had gone to Holloway to see Mrs Rattenbury. Dr O'Donnell then said that Mrs Rattenbury was the best mistress that Miss Riggs had ever had, or that she was ever likely to have, and if there was anything she could tell the police, it was her duty to do so. Poor Miss Riggs, still loyal to her employer, said she could not let Mrs Rattenbury's secret out, but Dr O'Donnell very sensibly said that a secret was nothing when a life was at stake. He pointed out that if she was put in the witness-box, and then had the story of Mrs Rattenbury's liaison dragged out of her, she herself would be implicated for having concealed her knowledge. He asked her whether she thought Mrs Rattenbury had murdered her husband, and Irene Riggs replied: "I know she did not do it." Dr O'Donnell asked her how she knew, and she said that Stoner had confessed it to her: he had told her that there would be no finger-prints on the mallet as he had worn gloves. Dr O'Donnell rang up Bournemouth Police Station, and said that Miss Riggs wished to make a statement; that Stoner had confessed to her. Dr O'Donnell added that Stoner had left for London and that no time should be lost in taking the statement. At 2.30 the police arrived and Irene Riggs told them what she knew. Stoner was arrested at the station on his return to Bournemouth that evening – and this time the charge was murder, for Mr Rattenbury had died.

The very fact that both Stoner and Mrs Rattenbury refused to inculpate each other was a source of great difficulty to their defenders. Stoner further complicated his counsel's task by injecting into his defence the curious suggestion that he was a cocaine addict, which there was no evidence to bear out, and which Mr Justice Humphreys disposed of in no uncertain fashion in his summing-up. The Judge pointed out that there was one human being, and one only, who knew whether Stoner was in the habit of taking cocaine, and whether he took it on the afternoon of Sunday, 24 March, and that was Stoner himself. Stoner was an available witness, and had he wished to prove that he had ever taken cocaine, or was under the influence of cocaine, he could have gone into the box to say so. "What," remarked the Judge, "seems to me in the circumstance of this case a fact of the utmost significance is that Stoner prefers not to give evidence." Stoner had told Mrs Rattenbury a long time before the murder that he took drugs. She was so worried about this that she confided it to Dr O'Donnell, although she was not at all sure – for, in spite of her headlong infatuation, she had a certain shrewdness – that Stoner had not invented the whole thing so as to make himself interesting to her. Dr O'Donnell, at Mrs Rattenbury's request, had interviewed Stoner and asked him what drug he was taking. Stoner had told him that it was cocaine, and that he had found it in his father's house. To anyone who had seen Stoner's father in the witness-box, the suggestion was not only cruel but absurd. Mr Stoner was a self-respecting, honest, hard-working man. It detracts somewhat from what has been called the chivalry of Stoner's conduct that he should have been able to make such a suggestion about his father. Stoner was certainly not a drug-addict. Whether he was a cinema-addict I do not know, but this fantastic story might well have emanated from a cinema-nourished mind. Had he not confused his defence by insisting on this fairy-tale, his counsel would have been able to present a much more sympathetic picture of a boy crazy with love and wild with unreasoning jealously, who had hit without knowing what he did. The cocaine story was too far-fetched. When Stoner was asked to describe what cocaine looked like, he replied that it was brown with black specks in it, evidently describing the only sort of things he knew, such as household pepper or influenza snuff.

During the trial, Stoner sat unmoved in his corner of the dock, with his elbow on the ledge, his cheek on his hand. His eyes were downcast and his face remained immovable. Mrs Rattenbury also was perfectly calm, but it was a frozen, and not an apathetic, calm. Her physical aspect changed, without any movement on her part, in a curious manner. By Friday she looked twenty years older than she had on Monday. On the last day, even her hands changed colour: they were a livid greenish white.

She was an excellent witness. Her voice was low and rich. She gave a great impression of truthfulness, and she was astonishingly self-controlled. Only a nervous tick in the side of her face, which jerked perpetually, betrayed the tension of her mind. Mr R. Lewis-Manning, her solicitor, was impressed throughout all his conversation with her, by her veracity. He, as did Mr O'Connor, felt a terrible responsibility. Mr Lewis-Manning was certain that Mrs Rattenbury was not pretending when for several weeks she insisted that she would not implicate Stoner but preferred to hang rather than that he should come to any harm. Unlike Mrs Thompson, she had immense physical courage. It was the thought of her children, and what a fearful heritage would be theirs if she were found guilty, that eventually made her tell the truth. It is easy to say that all this could have been a pretence on her part, but it would not have been possible for her to make this pretence appear the truth to Mr Lewis-Manning and Mr O'Connor.

The behaviour of a certain section of the press during the course of the trial, had it been made public, which for obvious reasons it was not, would have caused an uneasy feeling in the public mind. Someone engaged in the case was telephoned on the Monday when the case opened, and offered £500 as his "rake-off" if he would get Mrs Rattenbury to write her life-story. Then, as the unexpected angle that the case was assuming became visible, the offer was raised. By Thursday, this gentleman engaged in the case, who was a man of honour, was offered £3500 as his "rake-off," and one paper was foolish enough to put this offer in writing! It is needless to say that none of the offers was considered for a moment, and would not have been if the wealth of the world had been offered.

Mr Casswell was handicapped in his defence of his client Stoner by the fantastic nature of the story which Stoner had told. Mr O'Connor was in no such invidious position; he had a very clear notion of the mentality of his client, and he was able to give full play to his sympathetic interpretation of that mentality. There were cases, Mr O'Connor pointed out, when the accused person had a record and history which might inspire the jury with a revulsion against that person's character. "It is in this case, perhaps," he continued, "that the task of the jury is most difficult of all – the task of separating from their minds the natural revulsion they feel against behaviour which nobody would seek to condone or commend. I am not here to condone, still less to commend, her conduct. I am not here to cast one stone against that wretched boy whose position there in the dock may be due to folly and self-indulgence on her part, to which he fell a victim." Mr O'Connor went on to say that the jury must not imagine that the two defences had been arranged in concert – were connected in any way. Each defence was in its water-tight compartment. "I will say no more," continued Mr O'Connor, "about what is past in Mrs Rattenbury's life. I would only say that if you are tempted to feel that she has sinned, and that her sin has been great and has involved others who would never otherwise have been involved, then you should ask yourselves whether you or anybody of you are prepared first to cast a stone."

Having pleaded one of the greatest of speeches for the defence ever uttered – and the deathless words "cast a stone" sounded through a hushed Court – Mr O'Connor went on to give a very good description of the mentality of Stoner: "Can you doubt seduced; raised out of his sphere; taken away to London; given a very high time there – a lad who was melodramatic and went about with a dagger, violent sometimes, impulsive, jealous, his first love; a lad whose antecedents had been quiet, whose associations had been prosaic; never mixed with girls; flung into the vortex of this illicit love; unbalanced enough, and, in addition to all these things, either endeavouring to sustain his passion with cocaine or already an addict of drugs. You may, as moral men and women, as citizens, condemn her in your souls for the part she has played in raising this position. She will bear to her grave the brand of reprobation, and men and women will know how she has acted. That will be her sorrow and her disgrace so long as she lives. You may think of Mrs Rattenbury as a woman, self-indulgent and wilful, who by her own acts and folly had erected in this poor young man a Frankenstein monster of jealousy which she could not control."

Mr Justice Humphreys's summing-up was a brilliant exposition of the law. There was no judge more capable of weighing evidence, and the right value was given to every piece of evidence that had come before the Court. But the Anglo-Saxon assumption still is that women, whatever their circumstances, want to be married; and Mr Justice Humphreys was no exception in making that assumption. He spoke of the period (the "orgy") which Mrs Rattenbury and Stoner spent in Kensington: "Do you believe that while they were in London, the future was not discussed? What they were going to do when they got back? Could life go on in the same way? Would not something have to be done with – or to – Mr Rattenbury? Would he not ask: 'What about my £250? How much did the operation cost you? Did you have the operation? If so, where? I hope you are better for it.' Or, if he was so callous and disinterested a husband that he would not be expected even to ask about the operation, at least as a mean man would not you expect him, and would not they expect him – that is the point – to make some enquiries about the money? Do you think that these two persons in London imagined that life could go on just the same after their return, after an absence of four days, as before?"

The Judge went on to quote Mrs Rattenbury's account of the events of Saturday – "I think we played cards. I think it was just the same as any other night." – and asked: "Do you believe that? Do you believe that after an absence of four days, Mr Rattenbury never asked a question as to what happened in London?"

Let us consider the history and mentality of these people as we know them through the medium of the trial. Ill-balanced as she was, Mrs Rattenbury was a woman of the world. The last thing she would have wanted was to have married a chauffeur, twenty years younger than herself; she was – again to use a slang expression, but slang fits Mrs Rattenbury's career – "sitting pretty". She had a kind husband who allowed her to live her own life. She had a young and ardent lover who satisfied her emotionally and physically. She had two children to whom she was passionately devoted. She was being supported as extravagantly as she could have hoped for, all the circumstances considered. She was, as she rather pathetically said in evidence, "happy then". For her husband, she had a maternal affection – it must be remembered that in all her loves Mrs Rattenbury was essentially maternal. She spoiled and pro-tected Stoner; she adored her children; she comforted her hus-band; she tried to give Irene Riggs as good a life as possible; she was kind to every stranger who came within her gates. The one thing that would have been impossible to Mrs Rattenbury, amoral, casual, unbalanced, and passionate as she was, would have been to take part in harming another human being. Mrs Rattenbury, both as a humane woman and as a completely amoral woman, did not desire her husband's death, and did not wish to marry her lover; there is no evidence that she had ever desired either of those things.

The unfortunate Stoner, with a much simpler experience of life and with that adolescent urge to heroics which is a hang-over from infantilism, could not see that there was no need for any drama of jealousy at all. The boundary-line between drama and reality was obscure for him, and, living entirely in an unintelligent world of crude emotion, he hit out almost blindly. And this gesture, conceived in an unreal world, materialised in a world of actual facts. Our prisons are, of course, full of sufferers from infantilism: what goes on in their heads bears no relation at all to real life, as it has to be lived, though it could not possibly be said that they are not sane.

The jury were out for forty-seven minutes, and they returned the only possible verdicts to which they had been directed upon the evidence. They found Mrs Rattenbury Not Guilty, and Stoner Guilty, adding a recommendation to mercy. Mrs Rattenbury stood immovable while the verdict of Not Guilty was returned; but when the foreman pronounced the word "Guilty" in respect of Stoner, she gave a little moan and put out her hand. She was led away, and Stoner received his sentence without flinching. He spoke for the first time when asked by the Clerk of the Court whether he had anything to say why the Court should not give him judgment of death according to law. He replied in a low voice: "Nothing at all." He was then taken below, and Mrs Rattenbury was brought back to plead to the accusation of being an accessory after the fact. She could not speak – she could not make any sound at all – her mouth moved a little and that was all. The Clerk of the Court informed the jury that the prisoner at the Bar had pleaded Not Guilty. The prosecution said that they proposed to offer no evidence, and Mr Justice Humphreys instructed the jury to return a verdict of Not Guilty, which they did. Mrs Rattenbury was discharged.

She had had an admirably fair trial. She was not, of course, bullied by the prosecution, as she would have been in France or the United States. In fact, Mr Croom-Johnson could, even within the limits allowed to the Crown, have been more severe than he was. Mr Justice Humphreys told the jury unmistakably that even though they might feel that they could not possibly have any sympathy for the woman, it should not make them any more ready to convict her of the crime: it should, if anything, make them less ready to accept evidence against her. This was admirable, and in the best tradition of the English law.

Unfortunately, there is a custom in the Courts that is not nearly so admirable: to animadvert upon the *moral* qualities, or lack of them, in a person accused of a crime. I am, of course, using the word merely in the only sense that Anglo-Saxons seem to use it, with reference to sexual morality. Though Mrs Rattenbury was a woman at the extreme edge of what it was possible to bear and go on living, she had to listen to the dread voice of the Judge, as he said: "Members of the jury, having heard her learned counsel, having regard to the facts of this case, it may be that you will say that you cannot possibly feel any sympathy for that woman; *you cannot have any feeling except disgust for her*." More could hardly be said of George Joseph Smith, or of a systematic poisoner, or of a baby-farmer.

This may show a very lofty viewpoint, but we are often told that a criminal court is not a court of morals. In this trial apparently it was. And strange as it may seem, there are some of us, though apparently regrettably few, who are so constituted that we cannot see a fellow-human in the extreme of remorse, shame and despair, without feeling pity as well as disgust. Indeed, it is quite possible for the disgust to cease to exist because of the overwhelming nature of the pity. Mrs Rattenbury was in some ways a vulgar and a silly woman, but she was a generous, kindly, lavish creature, capable of great self-sacrifice. She was innocent of the crime of which, entirely on the strength of her own drunken maunderings, she was accused – but, nevertheless, though her life was handed back to her, it was handed back to her in such a shape that it was of no use to her. "People" – that dread judgment-bar of daily life known as "people" – would always say: "Of course, she told him to do it. And, anyway, she was a dreadful woman." For the world has progressed very little since Ezekiel wrote: "And I will judge thee as women that break wedlock and shed blood are judged, and I will give thee blood in fury and jealousy." Such was the judgment of society on Mrs Rattenbury, and she knew it.

Her husband's relatives took her away with them, but the press besieged the flat where they gave her refuge. She was removed to a nursing-home, pursued by newspaper men, one of whom called out to the doctor escorting her: "If you take her to Bournemouth, we'll follow you." A horrible example of what the demands of his newspaper can do to a young man who probably started as a decent human being.

Mrs Rattenbury was by now very ill, physically and mentally. And, in her fear and grief for Stoner, in her misery for her children, in her remorse and shame, she wanted to be alone. She left the nursing-home; and of what she did during the nightmare hours that followed we only know from the tragedy that followed. She must have bought a knife and taken a train down to that part of the world where she had been happy in what was stigmatised as an "adulterous intercourse". And there, beside the placid waters of a little stream, she sat and wrote, feverishly and passionately, on the backs of envelopes and odd bits of paper, the reasons for the terrible deed that she was about to do. She referred to the assumption that she dominated Stoner, and declared that no one could dominate him, and that whatever he wanted to do he always did. She repeated that if she had not been made to tell the truth, she would never have given Stoner away. She complained about the press dogging her footsteps, and she wrote of the scathing attack on her character. How, indeed, was it possible for her ever to make a home for her little boys, to watch them at play, to invite other children to play with them? She must have known that it would be worse for her children if she lived than if she died.

Her writing finished, she thrust the knife six times into her breast. The blade penetrated her heart thrice. She fell forward into the water, dead. When an ancient Roman killed himself, he inserted the tip of the sword between two ribs, and fell upon it; he called it "falling upon his sword". He knew that the shrinking of the flesh was such that it was almost impossible to drive a knife steadily into the breast. Mrs Rattenbury drove it in six times.

The Rattenbury case had revealed a strange and unlovely mode of life; but the woman's last act raised it sharply to higher issues. Most people in England, especially women, seemed easily able to feel superior to Mrs Rattenbury. She had had "adulterous intercourse"; she had taken for her lover a boy young enough to be her son; and the boy was a servant. That out of this unpromising material she had created something that to her was beautiful and made her happy was unforgivable to the people of England. Her life had been given back to her, but the whole world was too small a place, too bare of any sheltering rock, for her to find a refuge.

Stoner lost his appeal, but he was reprieved, and the sentence of death commuted to penal servitude. Blind and muddled humanity had been even more blind and muddled than usual, and everyone concerned had paid a terrible price for the sin of lack of intelligence.

SACCO AND VANZETTI

(Dedham, Mass., 1921)

H. Montgomery Hyde

In America, the case of Sacco and Vanzetti, a pair of anarchist Italian immigrants, began as a simple murder trial but became an international cause célèbre. *Nearly 80 years on, the question remains: did the state of Massachusetts put two innocent men to death because they held radical views? Here, the ordeal of "a good shoemaker and a poor fish pedlar" – Sacco's own estimation – is recounted by the noted British crime historian, H(arford) Montgomery Hyde (1907–89). Known as Monty, he sat as Ulster Unionist MP for North Belfast until 1959 and became one of the most penetrating and prolific writers on crime, publishing nearly 50 titles. He wrote and edited books and articles on a huge range of crime-related topics (including the classic* The Trials of Oscar Wilde *in the* Notable British Trials *series) and produced definitive biographies of leading lawyers including Sir Patrick Hastings, Norman Birkett and Lord Reading. He also wrote on homosexuality, contributed to the* Dictionary of National Biography, *and was an expert on a host of causes* célèbres.

No trial between the two world wars aroused greater controversy both inside and outside the United States than that of two lowly

Italian immigrants named Sacco and Vanzetti, who were twenty-nine and thirty-one years old respectively at the time of their arrest. It was a trial which had strong political overtones, since both its central figures were on their own admission pacifists and anarchists – that is to say, they were opposed to war and to all kinds of organised government which they felt to be evil and against the higher nature of mankind. On 5 May 1920 they were arrested and afterwards charged with murder. They were not brought to trial until just over a year later, at Dedham, a small town in Massachusetts about ten miles from Boston. More than six years were to elapse before they ended their lives in the electric chair at the Massachusetts State Prison.

Public attention was focused on the trial for several reasons, the origins and unorthodox political beliefs of the prisoners, the probative value of the circumstantial evidence adduced, the professional behaviour of the trial judge, and above all the unprecedented delay in carrying out the death sentence. By left-wing elements all the world over, Sacco and Vanzetti were regarded as sacrifices to capitalist tyranny, and even today, nearly half a century after they died, their memory is still honoured in Communist and Socialist demonstrations, particularly in the land of their birth.

Actually there were two trials, and it is the second with which we are mainly concerned here. Since the first was said to have affected the second, it is necessary to give a brief account of the earlier one which solely concerned Vanzetti. But first a few words about the two men themselves.

Nicola Sacco was born on 22 April 1891, the third of seventeen children of a fairly prosperous peasant family in Torremaggiore, an Adriatic village in the foothills of the Appenines. Although the elder Sacco owned olive groves and vineyards and had married the daughter of a well-to-do local wine merchant, he was a Socialist and his son Nicola inherited his political sympathies. At the age of fourteen Nicola left school to work in the fields, where he proved himself a hard worker and a reliable son. Three years later, attracted by the accounts of life in America given by a friend of his father's who had settled in Milford, Mass., Nicola and his elder brother Sabino emigrated. Sabino found life in the New World uncongenial, but Nicola stayed on, working in a road gang and a foundry as an unskilled labourer. He was later employed in a factory where he acquired a certain skill as a shoemaker in the

Milford Shoe Company. Here he met and married Rosina Zambelli, the daughter of another Italian immigrant. He joined the local anarchist club and also an Italian dramatic society with which he and Rosina would put on performances to raise small sums of money for the printing of anarchist pamphlets which he would help to distribute. He was a fond husband and a devoted father to his two children, Dante, his son, born two years after his marriage, and Ines, his daughter, who arrived shortly after his arrest. He had a noticeable charm of manner and was popular in his social circle in Milford where no one ever believed that he was guilty of such a crime as murder. The only offence of which he had been previously convicted was participating as a speaker in a socialist demonstration without a police permit during the First World War, for which he was fined.

Bartolomeo Vanzetti was born on 11 June 1888 in the Piedmontese village of Villafalleto in north-west Italy, where his father, like Sacco's, was a relatively prosperous peasant who owned a small holding where he grew fruit, mostly peaches and grapes. He was a model pupil at school winning among other awards the second prize for religious catechism. But there was no living to be made in the village when he left school, and so his father sent him to work in a city pastry shop where he laboured from seven in the morning until ten at night. He worked in similar jobs in other cities including Turin, then as now a strong socialist centre where he absorbed the teachings of Marx. His mentality was more rigid than Sacco's and he was much more the agitator type. He once told the Massachusetts State Prison psychiatrist that "where he came from in Italy there was a castle above the town and one family living in it had been oppressing the ordinary people in the valley for eight hundred years". The psychiatrist replied that "it wasn't so in America, that a family scarcely lasted three generations here".

Vanzetti arrived in America in June 1908, two months after Sacco. Like him he turned his hand to a variety of jobs, including being a pastry cook, a bricklayer's assistant, a fishpedlar and a loader in the Plymouth Cordage Company, a rope factory where he led a strike and was consequently blacklisted in the other local factories. He first met Sacco in 1916, and in the following year, as the result of the United States coming into the war, he and Sacco fled to Mexico to escape being called up for military service. They returned to Massachusetts after the Armistice, when Sacco went back to shoemaking and Vanzetti to fishpeddling. Vanzetti was unable to obtain any factory employment owing to his reputation as a strike leader, but Sacco's reputation was clean from the point of view of management-labour relations.

The immediate post-war months were a difficult time for left-wing immigrants who were suspected of being "Reds" and were marked down as sympathisers of the Bolshevik Revolution in Russia. A series of outrages in the spring of 1919, culminating in a number of bombs being sent through the mails, resulted in the arrests and deportation of many Communists, anarchists and other "radicals". Several of Sacco's and Vanzetti's friends were caught in the net, and in April 1920 Vanzetti went to New York to make inquiries about them; he was advised to hide his anarchist literature since more police raids were possible.

The following specimen of compromising literature was found in Sacco's possession at the time of his arrest and was later produced at his trial:

> Fellow workers, you have fought all the wars. You have worked for all the capitalists. You have wandered over all the countries. Have you harvested the fruits of your labours, the price of your victories? Does the past comfort you? Does the present smile on you? Does the future promise you anything? Have you found a piece of land where you can live like a human being?
>
> On these questions, on this argument, and on this theme the struggle for existence Bartolomeo Vanzetti will speak. Admission free. Freedom of discussion to all. Take the ladies with you.

On the morning of Christmas Eve 1919, there was an attempted hold-up in the streets of Bridgewater, a manufacturing town some thirty miles south of Boston. A truck carrying the wages of the employees of the White Shoe Company was held up by a car in which sat a party of foreign-looking men, whom several witnesses swore to be Italian. Two of these men fired, one with a shotgun, at the driver of the truck, who being armed returned their fire. The bandits thereupon concluded that their attempt must fail and they accordingly drove off. In the course of their inquiries the Bridge-water police found an Overland car in a local garage which had been brought in for repairs. The police believed that it was owned or was being driven by an Italian named Boda for the purposes of the attempted hold-up and they told Mr and Mrs Johnson, who ran the garage, to let them know immediately if anyone came in for the Overland.

On 15 April 1920, nearly four months after the Bridgewater incident, another hold-up took place in the neighbouring town of South Braintree, this time successfully and with fatal results. Two employees of the Slater and Morrill Shoe Company, a cashier named Parmenter, and a guard named Berardelli, were transferring the weekly pay roll amounting to nearly $16,000 from one factory to another along the main street of South Braintree about three o'clock in the afternoon. They had nearly reached their destination when they were fired upon and killed by two men who had been leaning against a fence. At the same time a car drove up, the two men threw the boxes containing the cash into the car, jumped in themselves and were rapidly driven off, firing at onlookers as they did so and throwing pieces of rubber hose studded with nails into the road so as to puncture the tyres of any car which might pursue them. They succeeded in passing a nearby level-crossing just as it was about to be closed.

Two days later a Buick car was found abandoned in a wood not far away. Leading from it were the tracks of a smaller vehicle, which the police felt might be those of the Overland which had been left in the Johnsons' garage. As for the Buick, this was known to have been stolen in the previous November, while its number plates were also stolen. The police were convinced that it had been used both at Bridgewater and South Braintree.

On the evening of 5 May, Boda called at the garage to collect his car. He was accompanied by Sacco and Vanzetti and a third Italian named Orciani. While Boda was talking to Mr Johnson, Mrs Johnson under the pretext of fetching some milk went into the house of a neighbour and telephoned the police. Her husband pointed out to Boda that the car did not have proper licence plates, and either because of this or because (as was alleged by the prosecution) the men realised that Mrs Johnson was telephoning the police, the Italians left without the Overland, Boda and Orciani on a motor cycle and the other two on foot. Later that evening Sacco and Vanzetti were arrested on a street car and both were found to be armed with revolvers. They were taken to the local police station where they were charged with being in possession of firearms without a permit, to which they pleaded guilty. They were also asked their reason for visiting Bridgewater that evening and about their whereabouts on various other dates. Nothing was said of the two outrages for the time being, though the newspapers began to speculate about their possible participation in them. Boda and Orciano were also picked up, but were allowed to go after questioning, Boda departing hurriedly for Italy and Orciani satisfying the police that he had been at work on the days of both crimes.

While Sacco and Vanzetti were being held in custody, witnesses who had been at Bridgewater and South Braintree were brought in to identify them. Sacco was able to prove that he had been working in his factory on the previous Christmas Eve, so that he could not be charged with the Bridgewater crime. However, unfortunately for him, he had had the day off on 15 April and so he was charged with the South Braintree murders. Vanzetti, being a self-employed fishpedlar at Plymouth, was unable to produce an alibi for either day and so he was charged with both crimes. Since the two crimes had been committed in different counties of Massachusetts – Plymouth and Norfolk – the respective indictments were presented by different grand juries. It was afterwards suggested by the defence that the prosecution deliberately arranged for the Bridgewater case against Vanzetti to be tried first in the hope that he might be convicted and when he came up for the second trial with his co-defendant Sacco the latter might be regarded as under a cloud. However, the prosecution pointed out that the Plymouth grand jury happened to be in session and could indict Vanzetti at once, whereas the Norfolk grand jury was not due to meet before September. Anyhow Vanzetti was indicted without delay and stood trial for the attempted hold-up in Bridgewater before Judge Webster Thayer at Plymouth on 22 June 1920.

Five witnesses called by the prosecution claimed to identify Vanzetti in the unsuccessful hold-up, though the descriptions they first gave the police did not always tally with Vanzetti's actual appearance. One testimony came from a newsboy who had taken refuge behind a telegraph pole during the shooting and from this vantage point had caught a glimpse of the criminal. "I could tell he was a foreigner," said the boy, "I could tell by the way he ran." Under cross-examination this witness admitted that he might have been anything except a Chinaman, a Japanese, an African or an American. Two things told against Vanzetti. One was that when he was arrested he was found to be in possession of gun cartridges similar to those found in the abandoned Buick car. Secondly, he did not give evidence in his own defence, having been advised by his defence counsel that if he took the stand his political views would be elicited with disastrous results. On the other hand, more than twenty people, customers and acquaintances, but all Italian, swore to having seen him in Plymouth on Christmas Eve, and some of them had bought eels from him for the Christmas Eve feasts. Several of these witnesses were discredited in cross-examination, but there was general agreement that Vanzetti always wore a long flowing moustache, whereas some of the prosecution witnesses had deposed that the chief bandit at Bridgewater had a neatly trimmed moustache.

Vanzetti was found guilty and sentenced to imprisonment for ten to fifteen years. A few weeks later he was indicted along with Sacco by the Norfolk grand jury for the South Braintree murders. Their trial opened on 31 May 1921 in the court house at Dedham, Norfolk County, also before Judge Thayer. No mention was made at this trial of Vanzetti's conviction in the other case, but the newspapers drew attention to it in terms which, had it happened in England, would certainly have resulted in their editors being immediately committed to prison for contempt of court.

There was considerable sympathy for the prisoners in liberal circles throughout the United States, concerned over the Government's repressive policy towards radicals, and this resulted in a substantial defence fund being raised which amounted to some $50,000 by the time the trial had ended and which afterwards reached as much as five times that amount. The prisoners could therefore afford the best counsel. In the event Sacco's defence was led by Fred Moore, a prominent "labour lawyer" from California, whom it was hoped would be able to counteract or at least expose the anticipated prejudice of a New England judge and jury from such a conservative community as Dedham. Vanzetti was represented by two outstanding local advocates, the brothers Jeremiah and Thomas MacAnarney, while the prosecution was conducted by the District Attorney, Frederick G. Katzmann, assisted by Harold P. Williams. The latter opened the case for the State on 7 June after some delay caused by the defence challenging all but seven of the five hundred citizens who had been summoned to serve as possible jurors. The remaining five actual jurors were selected from a further panel of two hundred produced by the sheriffs.

The killing of Parmenter and Berardelli was not disputed by the defence. The sole issue to be decided at the trial was the identity of the killers. The prosecution claimed that Sacco did the actual shooting, while Vanzetti was riding in the car and was thus as guilty in law of the murders as Sacco. Mr Williams was afterwards criticised for not referring in his opening speech to what in the American phrase is called "consciousness of guilt" – that is behaviour by the prisoners tending to show that they were guilty of the crime. It is true that such a reference was made by Judge Thayer in his summing up, but the earlier omission to do so explicitly was unfortunate since "consciousness of guilt" was an important link in the chain of circumstantial evidence on which the case rested. According to the prosecution it was evinced by the conduct of the prisoners when they went to the garage for Boda's car, by the revolvers found on their persons and by the lies admittedly told by them to the police when they were arrested.

The trial exhibited a mass of conflicting testimony on the identity question, fifty-nine witnesses going on the witness stand for the prosecution and ninety-nine for the defence. Mrs Johnson, for example, was positive that Sacco was one of the men who called at the garage on the evening of his arrest. Another important prosecution witness was the policeman who arrested the prisoners on the street car. He described how he boarded the car and asked them where they came from.

"I said, 'What was you doing in Bridgewater?' They said, 'We went down to see a friend of mine.' I said, 'Who is your friend?' He said, 'A man by the—they call him Poppy.' 'Well,' I said, 'I want you, you are under arrest'." Then, according to the police witness, Vanzetti put his hand in his hip pocket, and the policeman said, "Keep your hands out on your lap or you will be sorry." At this point, Vanzetti in the dock shouted at the witness, "You are a liar!" As to Sacco, according to this witness, he denied having a gun on him when he and his companion were arrested as "suspicious characters", although in fact they were both armed.

The local police chief testified that Sacco and Vanzetti denied knowing Boda, the owner of the Overland car, or visiting the Johnson garage. He went on to recall his conversation with Sacco at the time about his revolver.

"You had a revolver in your pocket when arrested?"

"Yes," answered Sacco.

"Why did you carry it?"

"To protect myself. Lots of bad men."

"Why did you carry so many cartridges?"

"Well, I go to see my friend. We go into the woods and fire them."

A cap picked up at the scene of the murder was produced by the prosecution and stated to belong to Sacco, who denied owning it. Two firearms experts were also called. One of them stated that in his opinion the fatal bullet had been fired by Sacco's revolver; the other stated that the bullet was "consistent" with having been fired by his revolver. Sacco's employer testified to his good reputation as a steady worker, but he was obliged to admit that Sacco had not been at work on the day of the murders.

For the defence other firearms experts testified that in their view the bullets had not been fired by Sacco's revolver. Otherwise the evidence called by the defence was designed to prove an alibi for both prisoners. In Sacco's case, he swore he had gone to the Italian consulate in Boston on the day of the murders to arrange for a passport to return to Italy, and a deposition in support of this was taken in Italy from a clerk who had formerly worked in the consul's office. Other witnesses, mostly Italian, were called to state that though they had seen the murderers they were not Sacco and Vanzetti. A number of Italians swore alibis, but not always convincingly since their sense of loyalty to their fellow countrymen led them into contradiction and confusion over dates.

Both prisoners testified in their own defence. Vanzetti, who took the stand first, admitted that he had been to the Johnsons' garage on the night of his arrest, although he had previously denied this. Asked why he wanted to use Boda's car, he replied that it was to move a supply of anarchist literature to a safer place than his home and the homes of friends. This was the first mention in the case of his and his co-defendant's political opinions, and was deliberately introduced by the defence in order to provide the most convincing answer to the prosecution's case.

Vanzetti went on to explain why he had lied to the police when he was arrested. "Because in that time there was a deportation," he said, "and the reaction was more vivid than now and more mad than now." Both he and Sacco had lied, he stated, because they would be liable to be deported if it were known that they had fled to Mexico in 1917 in order to evade military service. As for lying about the revolver Vanzetti said that it was not to incriminate his friends, from one of whom he had bought it four years previously in Boston. "It was a very bad time," he said, and he armed himself in self-defence especially because he had to take money, a hundred dollars or more at a time, to Boston to buy fish. "There were many crimes, many hold-ups, many robberies at that time."

Sacco's reason for lying to the police was similar to Vanzetti's. "I know some – most of the friends – Socialists, why they are slackers." Sacco used the term "slacker" to connote the English term "conscientious objector" in wartime. "They got literature in the house. They got papers and everything – Socialist movement. That is why I thought they would do the same way as in New York and Chicago."

On the thirty-seventh day of the trial, Judge Thayer summed up the evidence quite fairly and dispassionately, and it is difficult to fault his directions to the jury, although he was subsequently the target for much abuse from Sacco–Vanzetti partisans. Every prisoner, he said, no matter what his nationality, class, position, education, politics, or religion, was entitled to the same rights, privileges and consideration. "I therefore beseech you," the judge continued, "not to allow the fact that the defendants are Italians to influence or prejudice you in the least degree. They are entitled, under the law, to the same rights and considerations as though their ancestors came over in the *Mayflower*."

On 14 July 1921, the jury found both Sacco and Vanzetti guilty of murder in the first degree. "*Siamo innocenti*," cried Sacco from the dock, raising his hand. "They kill an innocent man. They kill two innocent men." They were not brought up to hear Judge Thayer pronounce the mandatory death sentence until 1 November, a lengthy adjournment necessitated by the appeal procedure. It was the first of a series of delays, which culminated in the death house of Charlestown Prison seven years later. Such a long intervening period between conviction and execution may well seem gruesome and barbaric to English readers who will recall that when the death penalty used to be inflicted for murder in England the maximum time between dismissal of the appeal against conviction and the carrying out of the sentence was three weeks. The inordinately long delay in the Sacco–Vanzetti trial was due to the efforts of their supporters, including their legal advisers, in exhausting every device to save their lives by way of motions for new trials and stays of execution. In deference to public agitation Governor Fuller of Massachusetts appointed an independent committee presided over by President Lowell of Harvard University, but the Lowell Committee found after prolonged investigation that Sacco and Vanzetti were guilty of the South Braintree murders "beyond all reasonable doubt". Meanwhile a young Portuguese gunman Celestino Madeiros confessed to being implicated in the crime and declared that Sacco and Vanzetti were not. However, the Supreme Court of Massachusetts confirmed Judge Thayer's finding that Madeiros's confession fell short of establishing his guilt or in creating reasonable doubt about the guilt of Sacco and Vanzetti. This judgment was handed down on 5 April 1927 and two days later the prisoners were brought up again to hear the death sentence confirmed by Judge Thayer.

"You know I am innocent," declared Sacco from the dock. "That is the same words I pronounced seven years ago. You condemn two innocent men." When it came to Vanzetti's turn to speak, he said: "Never in our full life could we hope to do such work for tolerance, for justice, for man's understanding of man as we now do by accident. Our words – our lives – our pains – nothing! The taking of our lives – lives of a good shoemaker and a poor fish-pedlar – all! That last moment belongs to us – that agony is our triumph."

Still the defence persisted in its efforts. After two Federal judges had refused to issue a writ of Habeas Corpus, Sacco and Vanzetti were made ready for electrocution on the evening of 10 August 1927. Their trousers had already been slit and their hair cut to facilitate the passage of the electric current through their bodies, when news came that Governor Fuller had postponed the execution for twelve days so that the Supreme Court could decide whether or not to issue a writ of error. With that court's refusal to do so, the last hopes of the condemned men vanished.

Also in the death house at this time was Madeiros who had been sentenced for another murder. Shortly after midnight on 22 August, Madeiros, Sacco and Vanzetti were executed in that order, while the jail was surrounded by machine-guns and besieged by a crowd of excited sightseers and partisans. Sacco's last words were, "Long live anarchy!" in Italian and in English: "Farewell my wife and child and all my friends. Farewell, Mother." Vanzetti protested his innocence to the last: "I have never committed any crime but sometimes some sin . . . I am innocent of all crime, not only of this, but all. I am an innocent man. I wish to forgive some people for what they are now doing to me."

Opinions remain sharply divided on the Sacco–Vanzetti trial. My own feeling is that Vanzetti was innocent but that Sacco may well have been guilty. However, on one aspect of the matter there is general agreement. Justice was too long delayed and it would have been better served if the sentence on both prisoners had been commuted to imprisonment. Six years waiting for execution is an ordeal which no prisoner, even if guilty, should have to undergo in any civilised country.[1]

---

1 This is by no means a record. In May 1948, Caryl Chessman was sentenced to death for kidnapping with intent to commit robbery, then a capital offence under Californian state law. He was not executed until twelve years later.

THE SCOPES MONKEY TRIAL

(Dayton, Tennessee, 1925)

John T. Scopes

The Scopes trial dramatized one of the great intellectual struggles of 1920s America: the conflict between religion and science. In the sleepy town of Dayton, Tennessee, John Thomas Scopes, a young teacher at the Central High School, stood trial for breaking a newly minted state statute that outlawed Charles Darwin's theory of evolution. This repudiates the Biblical story of the divine creation of mankind in favour of Darwin's doctrine that we are descendants of apes. Gathered around the soda fountain at Dayton's drugstore, the town's elders decided that a test case would galvanize the local economy. Accordingly John Scopes volunteered to be caught teaching Darwinism to a teenage boy, and was promptly arrested. The newspapers portrayed his trial as a battle between God-fearing religious fundamentalists and new-fangled scientific sceptics. Both sides commanded big hitters: William Jennings Bryan, a former Secretary of State and three-times Presidential candidate, offered his services for the prosecution, while the nation's best-known radical lawyer Clarence Darrow, fresh from the Leopold and Loeb case, appeared for the defence. Pitted together in a case so emotionally charged, bitter clashes between counsel soon erupted. As so eagerly predicted, the trial degenerated into a circus, even before the first day's hearing opened with a prayer and a reading by Judge John T. Raulston of the first chapter of the Book of Genesis. Over a hundred journalists swarmed into town, hot-

dog and lemonade stalls sprouted on the streets, and the Western Union installed twenty-two telegraph operators in a room off a grocery store. In the courtroom itself, reporters, photographers and movie cameramen jostled with grim-faced Tennessee farmers in overalls to record the unfolding drama: "there was a buzz of talk, a shuffle of feet, a ticking of telegraph instruments, an air of suspense like that of a first-night performance at the theatre," recorded F. L. Allen of Harper's Magazine. "Judge, defendant, and counsel were stripped to their shirt sleeves – Bryan in a pongee shirt turned in at the neck, Darrow with lavender suspenders, Judge Raulston with galluses of a more sober judicial hue . . ." The influential journalist H. L. Mencken wrote a series of rasping polemics, guying the townsfolk as "yokels", "buffoons" and "dupes". News of the trial even reached Britain, where some of the newspapers took their cue to inveigh against American stupidity and hypocrisy in general. Amid all the ballyhoo the defendant, John T. Scopes, seemed strangely redundant. Forty years after the trial, he recalled the infamous case that rocked America.

A buzz ran through the crowd as I took my place in the packed courtroom in the little town of Dayton, Tennessee, on that sweltering July day in 1925. Seated near me at the defense table was my chief counsel, the famous criminal lawyer Clarence Darrow. Opposite us, languidly waving a palm-leaf fan, sat the prosecution's star, William Jennings Bryan, the silver-tongued orator, three times the Democratic nominee for President and leader of the fundamentalist movement which had brought about my trial.

A few weeks before, I had been an unknown high-school teacher in a little mountain town. Now I was involved in a trial reported the world over. Seated in the courtroom, ready to testify in my behalf, were a dozen distinguished professors and scientists, led by Professor Kirtley Mather of Harvard. More than a hundred reporters were on hand, and even radio announcers, who for the first time in history were to broadcast a jury trial.

"Don't worry, son, we'll show them a few tricks," Darrow whispered, throwing a reassuring arm around my shoulder as the judge ascended the bench.

The case had erupted around my head not long after I arrived in Dayton to teach science and coach football at the high school. For a number of years a clash had been building up between the fundamentalists and the modernists. The fundamentalists interpreted the Old Testament literally. The modernists, on the other hand, accepted the theory of the nineteenth-century English biologist Charles Darwin – that all animal life, including monkeys and men, had evolved from a common ancestor.

Fundamentalism was strong in Tennessee, and the state legislature had recently passed a law prohibiting the teaching of "any theory that denies the story of creation as taught in the Bible." The new law was aimed squarely at Darwin's theory of evolution. An engineer, George Rappelyea, used to sit around Robinson's drugstore and argue with the local people against the law. During one such argument, Rappelyea said that nobody could teach biology without teaching evolution. Since I had been teaching biology, I was sent for.

"Rappelyea is right," I told them.

"Then you have been violating the law," druggist Robinson said.

"So has every other teacher," I replied. "Evolution is explained in Hunter's *Civic Biology*, and that, of course, is our textbook."

Rappelyea thereupon made a suggestion. "Let's take this thing to court," he said, "and test the legality of it."

When I was indicted on May 7, no one, least of all I, anticipated that my case would snowball into one of the most famous trials in US history. The American Civil Liberties Union announced it would take my case to the US Supreme Court if necessary to "establish that a teacher may tell the truth without being sent to jail." Then Bryan volunteered to assist the state in prosecuting me. Immediately the renowned lawyer Clarence Darrow offered his services to defend me. Ironically, I did not know Darrow before my trial, but I had met Bryan when he addressed my college graduating class. I admired him, although I did not agree with his views.

By the time the trial began on July 10, our town of 1,500 had taken on a circus atmosphere. The buildings along the main street were festooned with banners. The streets near the three-story redbrick courthouse sprouted with rickety stands selling hot dogs, religious books and watermelons. Evangelists set up tents to exhort the passersby. People from the surrounding hills, mostly fundamentalists, arrived to cheer Bryan against the "infidel outsiders". Among them was John W. Butler, the genial state legislator who had drawn up the anti-evolution law. Butler was a forty-nine-year-old farmer who, before his election, had never been out of the county he was born in.

The presiding judge was John T. Raulston, a florid-faced man who announced: "I'm jist a reg'lar mountaineer jedge." At the prosecution table with the aging and paunchy Bryan sat his son, also a lawyer, and Tennessee's brilliant young attorney-general, Tom Stewart. Besides the shrewd sixty-eight-year-old Darrow, my counsel consisted of the handsome and magnetic trial lawyer Dudley Field Malone, forty-three, and Arthur Garfield Hays, quiet, scholarly and steeped in the law. In a trial in which religion played a key role, Darrow was an agnostic, Malone a Catholic and Hays a Jew. My father had come from Kentucky to be with me for the trial.

Judge Raulston called for a local minister to open the session with prayer, and the trial began with the selection of a jury. Of the twelve jurors, three said they had never read any book except the Bible. One admitted he couldn't read. My father growled, "That's one hell of a jury!"

After the preliminary sparring over legalities, Darrow began his opening statement: "My friend the attorney-general says that John Scopes knows what he is here for. I know what he is here for, too. He is here because ignorance and bigotry are rampant, and it is a mighty strong combination."

Bryan sat nibbling on his palm fan as Darrow walked slowly around the baking courtroom. "Today it is the public-school teachers," Darrow continued, "and tomorrow the private. Next, the magazines, the books, the newspapers. After a while, it is the setting of man against man and creed against creed until we are marching backward to the glorious age of the sixteenth century, when bigots lighted faggots to burn the men who dared to bring any intelligence and enlightenment and culture to the human mind."

"That damned infidel," a woman whispered loudly as he finished his address.

The following day the prosecution began calling witnesses against me. Two of my pupils testified, grinning shyly at me, that I had taught them evolution, but added that they had not been contaminated by the experience. Howard Morgan, a bright lad of fourteen, testified that I had taught that man was a mammal like cows, horses, dogs and cats.

"He didn't say a cat was the same as a man?" Darrow asked.

"No, sir," the youngster said. "He said man had reasoning power."

"There is some doubt about that," Darrow snorted.

After testimony was completed, Bryan rose to address the jury. The issue was simple, he declared. "The Christian believes that man came from above. The evolutionist believes he must have come from below." The spectators chuckled and Bryan warmed to his work. In one hand he brandished a biology text as he denounced the scientists who had come to Dayton to testify for the defense.

"The Bible," he thundered in his sonorous organ tones, "is not going to be driven out of this court by experts who come hundreds of miles to testify that they can reconcile evolution, with its ancestors in the jungle, with man made by God in His image and put here for His purpose as part of a divine plan."

As he finished, jaw outthrust, eyes flashing, the audience burst into applause and shouts of "Amen." Yet something was lacking. Gone was the fierce fervor of the days when Bryan had swept the Democratic convention like a prairie fire. The crowd seemed to feel that their champion had not scorched the infidels with the hot breath of his oratory as he should have.

Dudley Field Malone popped up to reply. "Mr Bryan is not the only one who has the right to speak for the Bible," he observed. "There are other people in this country who have given up their whole lives to God and religion. Mr Bryan, with passionate spirit and enthusiasm, has given most of his life to politics." Bryan sipped water as Malone's voice grew in volume. He appealed for intellectual freedom, and accused Bryan of calling for a duel to the death between science and religion. "There is never a duel with the truth," he roared. "The truth always wins – and we are not afraid of it. The truth does not need Mr Bryan. The truth is eternal, immortal and needs no human agency to support it!" When Malone finished there was a momentary hush. Then the courtroom broke into a storm of applause that surpassed that for Bryan. I found myself pounding Malone on the back of his damp jacket. But although Malone had won the oratorical nod over Bryan, Judge Raulston ruled against permitting the scientists to testify for the defense.

When court recessed, we found Dayton's streets swarming with strangers. Pitchmen hawked their wares on every corner. One store announced: "Darwin Is Right – Inside." (This was J. R. Darwin's Everything to Wear Store.) One entrepreneur rented a store window to display an ape. Spectators paid ten cents each to gaze at the simian and ponder whether they might be related. "The poor brute cowered in a corner with his hands over his eyes," Westbrook Pegler noted, "afraid it might be true." H. L. Mencken wrote his sulfurous dispatches sitting in his shorts with a fan blowing on him, and there was talk of riding him out of town on a rail for referring to the local citizenry as yokels. Twenty-two telegraphers were sending out 165,000 words a day on the trial.

Because of the heat and a fear that the old courthouse floor might collapse under the weight of the throng, the trial was resumed outside under the maples. More than two thousand spectators sat on wooden benches or squatted on the grass, perched on the tops of parked cars or gawked from the courthouse windows.

Then came the climax of the trial. Because of the wording of the anti-evolution law, the prosecution was forced to take the position that the Bible must be interpreted literally. Now Darrow sprang his trump card by calling Bryan as a witness for the defense. Judge Raulston looked startled. "We are calling him as an expert on the Bible," Darrow said. "His reputation as an authority on Scripture is recognized throughout the world."

Bryan was suspicious of the wily Darrow, yet he could not refuse the challenge. For years he had lectured and written on the Bible. He had campaigned against Darwinism in Tennessee even before passage of the anti-evolution law. Resolutely he strode to the stand, carrying his palm fan like a sword to repel his enemies.

Under Darrow's quiet questioning he acknowledged believing the Bible literally, and the crowd punctuated his defiant replies with fervent "Amens."

Darrow read from Genesis: "And the morning and the evening were the first day." (This was a slight misreading – the words "evening" and "morning" were switched – but it appears this way in the trial transcript.) Then he asked Bryan if he believed that the sun was created on the fourth day. Bryan said that he did.

"How could there have been a morning and evening without any sun?" Darrow inquired. Bryan mopped his bald dome in silence. There were snickers from the crowd, even among the faithful. Darrow tugged on his lavender galluses and twirled his spectacles as he pursued the questioning. He asked if Bryan believed literally in the story of Eve. Bryan answered in the affirmative.

"And you believe that God punished the serpent by condemning snakes forever after to crawl upon their bellies?"

"I believe that."

"Well, have you any idea how the snake went before that time?"

The crowd laughed, and Bryan turned livid. His voice rose and the fan in his hand shook in anger.

"Your Honor," he said, "I will answer all Mr Darrow's questions at once. I want the world to know that this man who does not believe in God is using a Tennessee court to cast slurs on Him . . ."

"I object to that statement," Darrow shouted. "I am examining you on your fool ideas that no intelligent Christian on earth believes."

Judge Raulston gaveled the hubbub to a halt and adjourned court until next day. Bryan stood forlornly alone. My heart went out to the old warrior as spectators pushed by him to shake Darrow's hand.

The jury got the case at noon the following day. The jurymen retired to a corner of the courthouse lawn and whispered for just nine minutes. The verdict was guilty. Judge Raulston fined me $100 and costs.

Dudley Field Malone called my conviction a "victorious defeat". A few Southern papers, loyal to their faded champion, hailed it as a victory for Bryan. But Bryan, sad and exhausted, died in Dayton two days after the trial.

I was offered my teaching job back but I declined. Some of the professors who testified in my behalf arranged a scholarship at the University of Chicago so I could pursue the study of science. Later I became a geologist for an oil company in South America and Louisiana.

Not long ago I went back to Dayton for the first time since my trial thirty-five years before. The little town looked much the same to me. But now there is a William Jennings Bryan University overlooking the valley.

There were other changes, too. Evolution is taught in Tennessee, though the law under which I was convicted is still on the books. The oratorical storm which Clarence Darrow and Dudley Field Malone blew up in the little courtroom in Dayton swept like a fresh wind through the schools and legislative halls of the country, bringing in its wake a new climate of intellectual and academic freedom that has grown with the passing years.

O. J. SIMPSON

(Los Angeles, 1995)

Brian Masters

From the moment the nation stopped and watched the white Bronco crawling down a California freeway to the reading of the verdict and its far-reaching aftermath, America was held captive by this story. The trial of O. J. Simpson for the murder of his ex-wife Nicole and her friend Ron Goldman riveted and appalled the world. It prompted a debate about American justice and the media; many commentators suggested that the US media had got its priorities wrong by the turning the trial of the black ex-professional football star turned film actor into a Hollywood hoop-la mega-production that, as one British editorial put it, "often bordered on the theatrical and the farcical." Another condemned Simpson's trial as "a sick, dire joke". The jury took less than four hours to reach a unanimous decision to acquit in an extraordinary trial that gripped America for a whole year. Nicole Brown Simpson and Ronald Goldman were stabbed to death outside her Brentwood townhouse in June 1994. Simpson was arrested soon after the killings but insisted from the start he was "absolutely, 100 per cent not guilty". Prosecuting lawyers produced evidence that included a pair of gloves – one found at the crime scene, the other at OJ's apartment – and emphasized his violent relationship with his ex-wife. Simpson's criminal trial was one of the longest in US legal history: the official court transcript was more than 50,000 pages long. Polls suggested most black Americans regarded OJ as a victim of racism while more than half of whites considered him guilty. Orenthal James Simpson's fate became essential television viewing for the American public. Even the journalists covering trial were glamorous. "The crowded press seats are full of exotic creatures reeking of expensive scent and covered in make-up – and they are just the TV anchormen," one British observer reported. "When three of them smile simultaneously, the court is bathed in light." Leading the British charge against the Simpson trial circus, the writer Brian Masters (b. 1939) described it as "an astonishing display of irrelevance". Continuous television coverage "turned what used to be a solemn duty into a frivolous spectacle; moreover, the case had presented serious abuses of justice that would not be permissible under English law." His excoriating appraisal of this Hollywood glamour trial appeared two days before the jury found O. J. Simpson not guilty of murder, a verdict widely interpreted as America's great black hope beating white man's justice.

Whatever the verdict in the O. J. Simpson case, the damage done to American confidence in their criminal justice system is already severe. We have watched an astonishing display of irrelevance for months on end, invented defence strategies, personal jury dramas, and a judge fighting back tears. It has been a long, preposterous entertainment. Simpson himself is of only marginal interest in the long term. but public approval of the way in which his fate has been decided must be an essential foundation of the rule of law. Part of the fault lies in continuous television coverage, which has turned what used to be a solemn duty into a frivolous spectacle, and a lot of senior judges are deeply worried by it. The presiding judge at the Court of Appeal in San Francisco, Anthony Kline, told me, "We thought the OJ trial would be a wonderful opportunity for public education, attracting attention to recondite issues and showing how the system works. Well, it has been a catastrophe. Attitudes towards the system are becoming dangerously contemptuous, and if it ends with a hung jury, that contempt will increase."

Television does not create these problems, it records them. It may well exacerbate them by offering opportunities for ambitious rather than serious lawyers to preen themselves in public and become Hollywood "stars". but in a big trial such as this they will have spent months doing that already. The root of the problem is the American appetite for publicity.

In common law, any comments on the merits of an impending trial, on expected evidence and proposed witnesses, is likely to interfere with the course of justice and is therefore severely discouraged. Had the OJ trial occurred in England, many of the policemen, prosecutors and defence attorneys who planted prejudicial information before it began would be ripe for imprisonment for contempt of court, or at least disbarment for professional misconduct. Not in the United States, where freedom of speech, in effect if not always in law, over-rides the requirement for justice to be impartial. Pre-trial publicity is not the only area of difference between our two systems. There is also the growing menace of the contrived defence, which enables the lawyer to make up virtually anything he likes ("whatever it takes") to get his client acquitted. Americans tend to regard this as normal. At the OJ trial an experienced journalist from the *Chicago Tribune* was astonished that I should react to some of the shoddy nonsense being put forward by his defence team. "Of course it's not justice," she said, eyes aflame, arms aloft, "they're just doing their job." Well, no they're not, actually.

They're undermining it. And some of the public is beginning to notice. Trouble came at the very beginning, when the jury was empanelled. In England and Wales this is a fairly simple matter. The principle is that the selection of a jury should be left as far as possible to chance, on the basis that for twelve ordinary people to represent the community as a whole they must be random and anonymous. The clerk of the court shuffles twenty cards on which twenty names are inscribed, these having been pulled arbitarily from the electoral register, and then reads out the names on the top twelve cards. That is then the jury. If one of the twelve feels he should be disqualified (for instance because he has served time in prison, is acquainted with the defendant, is deaf or has resided in a lunatic asylum), the court relies on him to reveal the fact.

Prosecuting counsel may ask a juror to "stand by", but rarely does, and then only with the agreement of defence counsel; the latter lost his right to peremptory challenge, that is throwing jurors out for no reason, in 1988, and now may only challenge "for cause", that is with reason. This, too, is very rare, and it is up to the judge in such an event to decide whether the challenge is justified. Neither counsel is allowed to engage on a "fishing expedition" by asking questions to discover which jurors they might prefer over others. It would be quite wrong for a defendant to stipulate the kind of jury he wanted to try him. as it would be for the prosecutor to load the jury with people who think the way he wants them to think. So, they are more or less the first twelve people you fall over.

In the United States it could not be more different. Prospective jurors, of whom there might be hundreds, are required to fill in questionnaires which go on for pages, and then will be cross-examined about their life-styles and opinions much as if they were on trial themselves. This process, known as *voirdire* (literally "to see to say", but probably a corruption of *vraidire* "to speak the truth"), may go on for weeks in a case which receives nationwide attention. Judge Kline believes the process is an indication of how much more advanced is the American way. "The law plays a much greater role in the life of our nation than it does in yours", he says. "We have pierced the veil of many a myth that still prevails in England, and one of them is the notion that a jury should be random. Also, in this country we are much more conscious of race and ideology and their effect upon decisionmaking. Our way reflects an acknowledgement that juries are made up of individuals whose predilections cannot be ignored."

In this trial, black jurors may be inclined to credit the absurd defence (unsupported by any evidence) that police officer Mark Fuhrman personally planted a bloody glove to incriminate Simpson. Fuhrman may have a nasty tongue and may brag a bit, but it was not he who was on trial, and the judge fortunately declined to allow more than a fraction of a ten-year-old tape to be played in which the officer talked of "niggers".

On the other hand, the attempt to "appoint" a jury sympathetic to one's cause may misfire. The prosecutors expected that the several black women on the OJ panel would respond with compassion for the dead Mrs Simpson when they heard the frightful tapes of her emergency calls to police when her husband was brutally beating her up. It seems more likely that they simply accept that husbands are wont to behave like that. As OJ himself had said, viewing his wife's black eye and cut lip, "What's the big deal?"

In any case, bias of some kind or other is part of human nature and jurors are expected to confront theirs and leave them out of account in the pursuit of justice; that is mostly what they do. Something mysterious happens to a man or woman when he becomes a juror – he assumes a mantle of responsibility which ennobles and matures him. To make him "prove" himself before he is permitted this responsibility is to humiliate the individual and demean the process. The celebrated author, advocate and law professor Alan Dershowitz told me he would favour taking the first twelve people whose name came up "unless you could show cause why they were unsuitable". Professor Graham Hughes at New York University's School of Law pointed out that the imperative need to select a jury was linked to the extensive publicity which precedes a trial. "You must have a more elaborate method of picking a jury precisely because the amount of exposure they will have have had to the merits of the case needs to be probed. They may have a settled view already. It would not be necessary in England, but here it is crucial". So we come back to the question of publicity. Why are newspapers and radio talkshow cretins allowed to spread highly prejudicial misinformation about a case before a court has heard any of the relevant evidence in it? Because the First Amendment guaranteeing free speech is sacrosanct, and the defendant's right to a fair trial also guaranteed by the Constitution, is less so. "Two hundred years of accretion of doctrine in Supreme Court decisions presents an immoveable boulder," Hughes told me. "The First Amendment is so ingrained in social and legal culture here that any idea of curtailing it would be heretical."

The truth of the matter is that it is already curtailed legally, but that few lawyers pay much heed. In most States the code of practice enjoins legal representatives not to say anything out of court which might reasonably be expected to be disseminated and have prejudicial effect upon eventual court proceedings. This "anything" specifically includes comments about the character, credibility or criminal record of defendant or witnesses, identity of witnesses and predicted testimony of witnesses. The rule is so blatantly and conspicuously disregarded that the public is unaware of its existence. As long ago as 1917 it was established that "membership in the bar is privilege burdened with conditions". Lawyers were subject to greater restrictions on their freedom of speech than were members of the public or newspaper editors because they were privy to information the weight of which ought to be decided by jurors uncontaminated by prior knowledge of the events in question, and whatever the lawyer might say would carry especial authority because of his intimate knowledge of those events. He is not a private citizen, and should therefore shut up.

"An attorney's duties do not begin inside the courtroom door,"

wrote the US Supreme Court in the landmark Gentile ruling of
1991, and his speech is "subject to greater regulation than speech
by others." "The American judicial trial," they went on, "remains
one of the purest, most rational forums for the lawful determination of disputes", but lawyers must not "use their skills and insight
to make untested allegations in the press instead of in the courtroom."

The question, then, is not whether the People have a right to
know, but when they have a right to know it. Ideally, it should be at
or after a trial. The reason lawyers exercise this right on their
behalf prematurely is because, otherwise, prosecutors would have
free rein to present their case in advance of a trial to the detriment
of the defendant. The trouble stems initially from the happy
tongues of state prosecutors who should limit their announcements
to the fact that so-and-so has been accused of such-and-such, but
don't. There are countless examples of individuals being defamed
by prosecutors before any jury has heard a word. Claus von Bulow,
wrongly accused of attempting to murder his wife, was so demo-
nised by leaks to the press that his counsel, Alan Dershowitz, felt
honour-bound to redress the balance. "I had to conduct a major
media campaign because the prosecutors had been so blatant," he
told me. "Defence counsel has an obligation to level the playing-
field when faced with such interference. I would much prefer that
neither prosecution nor defence should talk about a case out of
court. If the prosecution refrains from comment, then so will I."

James Shellow, a lawyer of long experience and high reputation
in Milwaukee, is even more circumspect. "I have a solemn obligation not to contaminate the proceeding," he says. "A lawyer
representing a party can say virtually nothing. I am extraordinarily
cautious; I haven't commented on a case in years."

Others do not see their duty to the court as overriding their duty
to the client in this way. Robert Shapiro, one of the enormous team
defending O. J. Simpson, is a man of great charm and social ease,
much sought as a dinner-guest in Los Angeles. He has written a
paper on how to use the press by developing a rapport with
journalists in order that they should present your case in the
way you want, and by planting opinion. He would not call this
"manipulation", but it comes fairly close. "I think it's grounds for
contempt," said Jim Shellow. Shapiro was very welcoming to me
when I was introduced outside the courtroom – affable and
companionable. He said it was not such a good day at the trial,

as if I had hit upon a poor performance at the Palladium. Simpson's prosecutors have done their share of manipulation, too. Worse still, they conducted some market research to see how well their tactics had worked and whether they should or should not ask for the death penalty in the event of a guilty verdict. Seventeen members of the public were each paid $125 to give their impressions of the case five months before the trial, and were asked their views on capital punishment. The majority said they would not convict OJ if he might face the death penalty. So the state decided to seek life imprisonment instead.

Yet again, this could not happen in England, where the prosecutor's function is to tell the facts, not to suggest an appropriate sentence. The idea that one could "seek" the death penalty (or any other penalty) is incompatible with the impartial application of justice, and smacks more of an arrangement wherein the desire for a "win" is weighed against the likelihood of achieving it. Americans are not offended by such cynical manoeuvring. They expect it. They are also unaware that it is forbidden by statute, because nobody bothers to tell them.

Just as in England, where a famous ruling by Judge Avory in 1916 said that "counsel ought not to struggle for the verdict against the prisoner, but they ought to bear themselves rather in the character of ministers of justice assisting in the administration of justice," so in the United States it is established within the code of conduct that a prosecutor should not regard his purpose in court to win the case at all costs. After a notorious instance of misconduct in 1989, when a US Attorney called Singer against a defendant called Berger, openly talked about the court proceedings as a "game" they were engaged upon, the Supreme Court spelt out very clearly what was the state attorney's genuine function.

"His interest in a criminal prosecution is not that (the state shall win a case), but that justice should be done", they wrote. "He is in a peculiar and very definite sense the servant of the law, the twofold aim of which is that guilt shall not escape or innocence suffer. He may prosecute with earnestness and vigour – indeed, he should do so. But while he may strike hard blows, he is not at liberty to strike foul ones. It is as much his duty to refrain from improper methods calculated to produce a wrongful conviction as it is to use every legitimate means to bring about a just one." It must be said that, apart from their nasty "market" decision not to seek the death penalty for Simpson (had it been a "moral" one it

would not have smelt so awful), the prosecuting team in Los
Angeles – Marcia Clark, Hank Goldberg and the rest – have
conducted the case with scrupulous propriety. They have not
descended to histrionics or showmanship. Mrs Clark was repri-
manded by Judge Ito for wearing a brooch identical to one worn by
members of the deceased woman's family, thereby hinting at an
intimate identification with the victims, which was unprofessional,
but that is all.

They have avoided emotive language, have not presented evidence obtained by deception, and have been absolutely certain that
police evidence was reliable before adducing it, much to the
frustration of Barry Scheck and Peter Neufeld, two of the defence
platoon, who have tried to suggest a police conspiracy worthy of
Hollywood drama. The police and OJ are old friends, and the
proposition is idiotic. Besides which, with the hypnotized gaze of
the world upon them, prosecutors would be mad to try anything
underhand. But when cases are unknown and unreported, neither
the police nor the district attorney's office is incapable of grotesque
behaviour. In the State of Illinois, Girvies Davis was convicted of
eleven crimes even though the county prosecutor admitted that
three of the murders to which he had confessed were committed by
other people. The confessions were handwritten by a man who
could neither read or write and who had not seen them before they
were flourished in court. Davis says the police removed him from
his cell and drove him around for hours, questioning him and
demanding a confession, which he declined to give. Eventually,
they stopped the car, removed his handcuffs, took out their guns
and offered him the choice of signing eleven confessions or trying
to "escape".

The confessions were inadmissible, yet the judge allowed them.
Judges are elected, and must please their electors, or "fans" if they
are to keep their jobs. They are often failed lawyers themselves,
"sometimes of low intellectual quality", says Alan Dershowitz.
James Shellow points out that "it is rare to find an elected judge
who is willing to suffer the criticism of the community by declaring
a mistrial on evidence which is technically inadmissible." In other
words, they are scared. District Attorneys, too, are elected: "their
powers are unfettered and untrammelled", says Graham Hughes.
"They are accountable to nobody, to no higher authority."

Small wonder, then, that corruption is commonplace. George
Kendall, a lawyer with the Legal Defence Fund of the NAACP, is

appalled by the "massive intentional misconduct on the part of prosecutors, who often put on key witnesses who they know are lying. Yet there is not one instance when anyone has been suspended for a single hour." In Florida, the court appointed a real estate lawyer to defend a man charged with murder, despite the fact he had never appeared in a criminal trial in his life. He protested his own incompetence, but was over-ruled and had to appeal to a higher court to be released from the burden. "In the South," says Professor Hughes, "the quality of defence counsel assigned by courts is a national scandal." So, too, is the readiness of elected politicians to smother justice in their zeal for public approval. Everybody told me that I should not imagine for a moment that the O. J. Simpson case was in any way representative of general American justice. Indeed, it isn't. It is about celebrity and television, money and influence, and above all lawyers and their ambition. So I went to Milwaukee to watch an ordinary trial, the State of Wisconsin versus Joseph M. Rucker, black, aged 16, accused of firing a gun at a passing jeep. No injury had been caused; consequently there was no audience in court and not a journalist to be seen.

As an example of style, the trial was utterly riveting. Rucker was prosecuted by the Assistant District Attorney, Marcella De Peters, a lady devoted to the casual approach. Dressed for a students' union coffee-bar (in contrast to the immaculately groomed Marcia Clark in Los Angeles), Miss De Peters slouched, grimaced, yawned, stretched her arms and tapped her feet or fingers throughout the proceedings. Occasionally she would throw back her head and run her fingers through ample long hair while staring at the ceiling, or grin with disdain. All this, I assumed, was to demonstrate her impatience with the points of law raised by defending counsel and her eagerness to get on with the job and convict as soon as possible. But its effect upon a stranger like myself was to suggest a profound lack of respect for the court. She did not even stand up to address the judge, but muttered her objections, which were many, swivelling in her chair, barely even looking up. The judge, Victor Manian, did not rebuke her.

Rucker was defended by James Shellow, whom I have already mentioned. I noticed that he forebore to have a swivel-chair, but sat on an upright one, which rendered a slouch extremely difficult. When he had a point to address to the judge, he stood up and walked over to the bench. His courtesy, manner and precision offered a sharp contrast to his opponent's relaxed style, which served to irritate her all the more. This was no doubt also intended. Shellow is an old hand, who knows how juries respond to a slap-dash presentation. He could have objected to Miss De Peters' manifest eyebrow-raising within feet of the jury, but I suspect he knew he did not have to; they were not favourably impressed.

Shellow's motions to the judge were of crucial importance to the case and deserved close attention. First, an important witness had been shown a photograph of the defendant the day before appear-ing in court, where he was required to identify him formally. No photographs of other young black men had been offered to allow a choice from among several. Second, the prosecution had not disclosed potentially exculpatory evidence to the defence, as they are required to under the so-called Brady rule. Third, the note-books of arresting officers had been withheld. Fourth, a juror had held a damaging conversation with the defendant's mother in the lavatory. Fifth, the bullets allegedly used had been destroyed. Sixth, the defendant had been an asthma sufferer since the age of five and experienced a prolonged attack after arrest; the police had prevented him from using his inhaler until he confessed. Throughout this, prosecuting counsel busily talked with her neighbour or displayed visible lack of interest. She had said that she did not bother much with motions. "She is nonetheless bound by the concepts of the motions she does not read," said Shellow, suggesting, witheringly, that he would not be averse to the court allowing her time to go away and prepare her case. He added a motion that the defendant should receive "a trial untainted by the innuendoes and implications of speaking objections."

Judge Manian did instruct that the police notebooks should be turned over, an instruction with which Miss De Peters complied with a weary sigh. But the motion for a mistrial was not granted. I learnt, by the way, that there is a convention by which the judge can reprimand undignified behaviour from counsel who will not rise from his or her seat by saying, "The court cannot hear you." Mr Manian did not avail himself of this useful device, at least not while I was there.

It is unthinkable that any of our bewigged and polite barristers, with their traditions of referring to opponents as "my learned friend" and to the judge, with meticulous respect, as "my lord" should attempt behaviour of this kind in court. Our courts are much more august and, paradoxically, treat the defendant with much greater civility, involving him in the process. American lawyers would resent active participation from the defendant, for it would deflect attention from their performance. Here, a barrister might not meet the defendant until the day before trial, and has no commitment to him as a person, only a professional commitment to him as the accused. (He may indeed be prosecuting in another case the next day.) In America they become friends, and the lawyer wants to demonstrate he is worth his fee by putting on a robust show. Hence the aggressive battlefield atmosphere of an American court. Bad courtroom behaviour and absurd histrionics are not unusual, as was demonstrated in a much-publicised trial last year, when Leslie Abramson, defending one of the Menendez brothers, flagrantly treated the judge and his court with scorn. In that event, her disgraceful tactics worked with at least part of the jury, which failed to reach a verdict when that verdict should have been obvious to all. More of this later.

In the United States a criminal trial (save for those inadequately handled for an impecunious defendant) can be inordinately long. The judge has it within his power to prevent this. It is not a device, but a duty, and one which has been neglected in the Simpson case. The judge may exclude evidence if it will take up too much time, mislead the jury or confuse the issues. (In California this is enshrined in Rule 352.) Much of the cross-examination of witnesses by Simpson's team has been precisely intended to do all three. Dennis Fung, who collected evidence at the scene of the crime, was questioned for nine days when his testimony need not have taken more than one. The alibi evidence of Mrs Lopez was discredited when she lied on the stand, also after several days, and presumably will now be discarded. We may hear no more of the ridiculous invention that Mrs Simpson and Mr Goldman were murdered by agents of Colombian drug-dealers. The jury, when not bored to oblivion by this endless irrelevance, must have wondered what on earth to think, and out of such confusion a "reasonable doubt" may well emerge. Recently, Judge Ito was showing signs that he wanted to get things moving. He told the egregious Barry Scheck to "sit down" and complained that Peter Neufeld had asked the same question eighteen times. The proper issues – that two nonentities were brutally slain and whether the accused person did the slaying were all but forgotten.

Against OJ are clear indications of motive and opportunity. There are seventy-five minutes of his time on the evening of June 12, precisely when Nicole Brown Simpson and Ronald Goldman were being butchered, that are unaccounted for. There is the bloody glove found in the grounds of his home, and the DNA evidence as to whose blood this was. There is also the attempt to escape, with a gun, a passport, a false beard, and $80,000 (Mr Shapiro told the press OJ had only $60, but everyone in California accepts that a lawyer may not tell the truth if this improves the chances of his client). Why the prosecution did not put this escape before the court is a mystery. Perhaps they reasoned that the whole world knew about it already. The rumour is that OJ and his friend Kato Kaelin bought drugs earlier that evening in the car-park of a hamburger restaurant in Brentwood, and that OJ was high on crystal meth, which would explain the ferocity of the killings (Nicole's head was practically severed from her body.) The dealer, according to this story, is well known in Hollywood, dresses smartly and goes by the name of JR. His look-out dresses like a tramp: it was he who apparently saw OJ snorting in the car. This will never be tested in the court, because there is no worse witness than a drug-dealer, even supposing he would be willing to testify. My own friends out there doubt the story anyway, on the grounds that celebrities never risk getting their drugs in car-parks, but telephone for home delivery! On the other hand the prosecutors have no murder weapon. no confession, no eye-witnesses. The murderer would be not just spattered, but covered in blood, and OJ would have had to clean himself and/or his car. Either he changed clothes between the scene of the crime and the car, in which case there would be a pool of blood at the spot, and no such pool was found; or he changed in the car, in which case it would have been drenched, and only a few spots were found (crucially, of Goldman's and Nicole's blood as well as of OJ's). And where are the clothes?

All of which is germane to the matters in issue. Instead of which we have been treated to a disquisition on the absence of staple holes in a document and a lot of showing-off by lawyers who know the cameras are catching their every trick. Barry Scheck staged a couple of demonstrations similar to those he had no doubt seen on TV when he was a boy, one of which involved getting the witness (Mr Fung) to open an envelope and place a piece of paper in it, then admit the paper was crumpled by the exercise. Fung looked incredulous and bemused, as well he might; the purpose of this charade was not evidentiary, but dramatic. It made for good television.

Scheck had tried to build an edifice of conspiracy upon the paper without staple holes. When his opponents produced the original document, complete with holes, the edifice collapsed, and so did Mr Scheck. He was furious. "Now my credibility is at issue with this jury," he complained, never doubting that his personal credibility should matter. (It is the relevance of the evidence which matters.) That is what happens when lawyers think of themselves not as servants of justice but as "stars", for whom image is a self-evident value. (It might also be important as a passport to further wealth! but that is by-the-by.)

A witness's credibility may be attacked, of course, but whereas in England evidence is not admissible to disprove his denials – in other words his word must be taken as final once the question has been asked and answered – in California counsel may go on and on until he crushes the witness with relentless thunder. Scheck actually accused Fung of changing his testimony to please his masters. The Sixth Amendment to the United States Constitution enshrines the right to confront one's accusers, which is why cross-examination can go on for as long as the judge sees fit. No doubt Mark Fuhrman's refusal to address the question whether he planted the bloody glove was precisely to avoid a couple of weeks' examination into his entire past. Nor, in England, can counsel ask questions which are merely vexatious, or calculated to vilify and annoy. Mr Fung put up with this line of questioning for days on end. Had Scheck stopped in time, he might have made the witness appear as incompetent as he intended, but by asking several questions too many, he enabled Fung to display his resilience and win the admiration of all in court.

One has only to glance at the defence table, dominated by the surly charm of the huge OJ, whom Dominick Dunne has aptly called "magnificent, beyond Othello even", to glean what kind of game is here being played. The lawyers defer to him, humour him, give him eager attention and are too ready to pay court, like people in the presence of fame for the first time (even if they're not). Glance across at Kimberley Goldman, the genuinely grieving sister of Ronald Goldman, slaughtered by pure chance, and you see how offensive is that game. She is there almost every day, silently chiding. David Margolick of the *New York Times* calls her "the conscience of the court", but the galaxy at the defence table never look at her.

There was no such awkward embarrassment at the Menendez

trial, where conscience was banished and image alone triumphed. It is possibly one of the worst examples of how tawdry American justice can become when sacrificed to the need to win, and offers the fairly repellent spectacle of an apparently unprincipled defence lawyer determined to prevail. Let us remind ourselves, first, of what happened. Jose Menendez was a Cuban immigrant who made good. He earned a great deal of money in Hollywood and lived in a mansion in Beverly Hills, one of the three most select suburbs of Los Angeles. He and his wife Kitty had two sons, Lyle and Erik, both handsome, successful in soccer and trophy-winning champions at tennis, both indulged, even spoilt by their doting parents. Kitty went to every match they played. Jose perhaps demanded a lot; like any father, he wanted to be proud of them and was hurt when they failed academic exams and one of them even cheated. They also planned and executed a burglary, which, considering how rich they were, indicated disturbance rather than need. But Jose made everything all right again and the family continued to be happy, if somewhat dull, dining together every evening as families should. It wasn't quite as it seemed, for Jose was an incorrigible womaniser who cheated on his wife. But there was never a bad word said about Kitty. She, if you like, was the silent "conscience" at the subsequent trial of her sons, the equivalent to Kimberley Goldman at O. J. Simpson's. Except that Kitty was dead.

In 1990 Jose and Kitty were murdered as they ate strawberries in front of the television set. Five shotgun blasts to Jose and nine to Kitty rendered them unrecognisable as human beings. The final shot to Kitty had been a "contact" wound, that is with the muzzle of the gun touching her face: her brains lay in her lap and over the wall. Lyle and Erik found the bodies and called the police immediately, with such desperate sobbing that the cops neglected to test their hands for possible residue from shotgun blasts.

After the funeral the brothers went on a spending spree, buying fast cars, Rolex watches and God knows what else. They stood to inherit $14 million. Three years later, having confessed to their psychiatrist Jerome Oziel that they had in fact slaughtered their parents, and had even had to reload outside the house before going back in to despatch their mother, they were arrested. Lester Kuriyama was assigned to prosecute – a decent, scholarly and sober man who would not "struggle" for a verdict but be subservient to the facts. Jill Lansing, also professionally well-mannered, appeared for Lyle Menendez. The style of the trial, and its outcome, were drastically determined, however, by Erik's counsel, Leslie Abramson. The trial has made her famous, which is what she wanted, but it has also demonstrated what an unscrupulous and shameless lawyer, though fine actress, she can be.

The facts presented formidable obstacles to a defence lawyer. Not only had the reloading of the guns indicated the brothers were determined and coldblooded at the time of the offence, but their three-hour drive to San Diego to buy the guns pointed towards planning and premeditation. Further, Lyle Menendez had employed an expert to erase from the hard disk of the family computer a revised will his father may have intended. There was no dispute that the brothers had committed the deed. Nor was there any hope they could claim insanity at the time they committed it. So it was decided they would use a plea of justification, in this case self-defence – that is they murdered their parents because they were in fear for their own lives. The plea of self-defence would normally require the accused to demonstrate that they had to protect themselves against imminent danger. This would be hard indeed. But California has a concept of "imperfect self-defence", which means that even if the fear of immediate danger is irrational and unreasonable, as long as it is honestly held it will be valid. So the trick was now to show that the Menendez brothers, proven liars, could be thoroughly honest when declaring that they were scared of Jose and Kitty.

English law has a similar concept of mistaken belief, which may still, in the words of Lord Devlin in 1949, cause "sudden and temporary loss of self-control" and render the accused "not the master of his mind". For this to happen, there would need to be demonstrated "some act or series of acts done by the dead man to the accused". This was the essence of Leslie Abramson's strategy on behalf of Erik Menendez.

Because Jose Menendez had not done anything to his son except alternately praise him when he did not deserve it and chastise him for not doing better, some ghastly act had to be invented. Three years after their arrest and ten days before trial was due to begin, it was decided that both young men had suffered foul sexual abuse at the hands of their father for a period of twelve years, the last occasion being a matter of days before the murders. Oddly enough, neither had thought it worthwhile to mention this fundamental fact to their psychiatrist, to whom they had nevertheless confessed to brutal murder with no ostensible motive beyond greed. Why?

Because they had not thought of it yet. And why did they think of it now? Because somebody had told them to. They were given books on the sexual abuse of children to read in jail, and it was rumoured they had lessons in how to present this stuff in the witness box, by professional drama teachers.

Erik Menendez gave graphic details of sexual acts told in such textbook order that anyone with the smallest knowledge of the messiness of lustful desire could see through them. Lyle admitted having once played with his brother sexually when they were infants and, weeping, apologised to Erik who, with tormented visage, accepted this public self-abasement with tears in his eyes seventeen years after the event. Leslie Abramson master-minded the performance with skill, referring to the defendants as "the boys" (they were mature adults in their early twenties), mothering Erik with tactile concern and sneering at his detractors. She was on record as calling them both "adorable", though she later reserved her adoration for Erik in the hope all blame could be heaped upon Lyle. Her language was intemperate rather than decorous. She contrived to make the killers victims and the victims invisible. Evidence is relevant if it tends to prove or disprove a fact at issue before the court. The alleged sexual abuse did neither. It is well established in English law that defence counsel must not suggest or invent a more plausible defence or allow himself to be the channel of allegations for which there is no evidence. He must not conjure explanations out of the air. If he does, then the judge must not allow a speculative conjecture to go before the jury, who decide on facts, not theories. "The law will fail to protect the community if it admitted fanciful possibilities to deflect the course of justice," said Mr Justice Denning in 1947.

The United States system is much more lenient in this regard. The accused in a criminal case is entitled to have any theory go before the jury "even though the evidence may be weak, insufficient, inconsistent or of doubtful credibility" (1951). Judge Kline told me that the only restraint on fanciful evidence was its believability, and that even if it was made up, as long as the jury were prepared to believe it, there was nothing amiss. Judge Manian said the same at the unnoticed trial in Milwaukee: "the jury can choose to believe it if they wish to." To this extent, then, Leslie Abramson was not over-zealous within the law as it applied in California.

She is also entitled to have the jury consider the *res gestae* of the case, that is the whole history preceding the events at issue as well as the events themselves. Professor Hughes says it would be a dereliction of duty for counsel not to explore every possible line of defence. "The client might be unsophisticated and need help in seeing what his defence should be." He also says, by the way, that counsel has a duty to enhance his client's testimony, "and if rehearsal of testimony will achieve this, it is not in itself objectionable."

There is, however, even in California, a line to be drawn between encouraging a client to think up his possible defence, and counsel thinking it up for him. It is the line between listening and implanting. The American Bar Association avers that "defence counsel should not intentionally misrepresent matters of fact or law to the court" and should comport himself as "the professional representative of the accused, not the accused's alter ego". We may not learn exactly who concocted the Menendez defence. If Abramson was the active ingredient, it should be grounds for her disbarment. Although few in California would think her unfit to practise because she "wins". But as for being the accused's alter ego, her provocative head-shaking and irritation with the judge as well as her maternal comforting of Erik speak their own language. (She declined my request to see her on the grounds that she was too busy.) In his book *The Abuse Excuse* Professor Dershowitz has written that "a criminal trial should not be a popularity contest." That, alas, is what happens when abuse is thrown into the arena to make the accused appear vulnerable, pitiful, likeable, and therefore (illogically) less responsible for his actions.

Attempts have been made to excuse defendants because they ate junk food (the "Twinkie" defence of Dan White, who murdered gay activist Harvey Milk in San Francisco); because they suffered from premenstrual syndrome (a female surgeon who kicked a breathalyser machine); because they live in a city centre, or were adopted as children.

Many of these have been successful. Even if the Menendez brothers had been abused, their defence, says Dershowitz, "sends the message that a history of abuse is a license to kill. They had cars. They had money. They were adults. They could have left home." If they had not been abused, then the travesty is scandalous. This tendency to concoct a defence strategy, combined with the insuperable American habit of chattering endlessly to the press about impending litigation whether or not the process is set in motion by prosecutors – makes a mockery of the country's pride in both the First and Sixth Amendments. (A really clever defence lawyer might do well to keep his mouth shut even if the prosecutors have prematurely opened theirs, so as to give the jury something new to chew over instead of a repetition of everything they have read.) One sees justice reduced to a contest akin to football. Few seem to mind, however. The experienced James Shellow is not shy of saying that "all criminal trials are passion plays. Some one will be convicted. It is the responsibility of the defence counsel to ensure that it is not the defendant, but some one else, who is convicted." Like Jose and Kitty Menendez. And what have O. J. Simpson's lawyers done? They have tried to convict police officers, DNA experts, scene of crime investigators, anonymous Colombians, video operators, anyone who might help them muddy the waters.

It has all been rather sordid.

After the criminal trial the families of Ronald Goldman and Nicole Brown Simpson filed a civil court case against O. J. Simpson and in 1997 were awarded over $30 million in compensatory damages. The civil jury took six days to reach a verdict and declare O. J. Simpson responsible. Simpson successfully challenged paying the award. He retained custody of his children and moved to Florida.

GEORGE JOSEPH SMITH

(Old Bailey, 1915)

Arthur la Bern

George Joseph Smith, failed property speculator and self-styled estate agent, drowned three bigamous wives in what became known as the Brides in the Bath case. His trial competed for public interest with the Great War, as British justice in all its red-robed majesty deliberated amid the crash of armies over the fate of one worthless individual. Posing as an antiques dealer called Henry Williams, Smith drowned his first bigamous wife, Bessie Mundy, in a bath at Herne Bay in 1912, and turned up in Blackpool where he drowned his new bride Alice Burnham in the bath at their digs. Alice was given the cheapest possible funeral and her body buried in a pauper's grave. Derided for ordering a cheap deal coffin, Smith retorted: "When they are dead they are done with." Alice's estate, willed to Smith, amounted to £600. Just over a year later, Smith, now posing as John Lloyd, drowned wife number three, Margaret Lofty, in a bath at their north London lodgings. Smith was arrested, and the bodies of his three drowned wives exhumed. The young Home Office pathologist Bernard Spilsbury ruled out accident and suicide: all had been murdered. At his Old Bailey trial, the bath in which Alice Burnham died was used to demonstrate Smith's murder method to the jury. In a back room of the court, the bath was filled with water and a nurse, wearing a bathing suit, got in. A detective inspector grasped her feet and pulled the nurse's head under the water. So realistic was this demonstration that the nurse had to be revived by artificial respiration. The jury took just 22 minutes to turn Smith over to the hangman. Arthur La Bern (1909–90) was a writer and journalist. His most successful novel, Goodbye Piccadilly, Farewell Leicester Square, *was the basis of Alfred Hitchcock's last classic movie,* Frenzy. *La Bern claimed to be a Gallic Cockney, having been born in London of French parents. He worked as a journalist for a number of newspapers including the* Daily Mirror *and the* Daily Mail. *During the Second World War he was war correspondent for the* Evening Standard *and flew with the Fleet Air Arm in the Pacific. He was also a crime reporter, and produced biographies of George Joseph Smith, from which this extract is taken, and of Haigh, the Acid Bath murderer, as well as a biographical novel about General Booth,* Hallelujah! *At his trial, Smith was prosecuted by Archibald Bodkin and defended by Edward Marshall Hall KC, already a prestigious silk, who (knowing it was a hopeless case) took it anyway, and for a much-reduced fee. It was the longest murder trial in England for 60 years, featuring a record 264 exhibits (including the bath) and 112 witnesses from more than 40 different towns.*

The band of the Coldstream Guards was playing in the Zoological Gardens and that of the Royal Horse Guards in the Royal Botanical Gardens. The Alexandra Hotel at Hyde Park Corner advertised: "No Germans or Austrians employed." A German spy named Carl Müller was almost lynched by the mob when the taxi taking him to the Tower of London for execution broke down in Upper Thames Street. He was shot at dawn the following day, an event which got three lines in most newspapers, whereas Smith was getting three, four and five columns a day.

For the first few days of the trial at the Old Bailey it was noticed that the Bethnal Green bigamist was more composed than he had been at Bow Street.

"He is dressed as he was at the police court in a sort of yellowish brown tweed suit, soft collar and fancy green waistcoat," wrote a *Weekly Dispatch* reporter: "His sharp features stand out clearly from the dock as he lifts his head, but since he makes copious notes on the evidence for the assistance of his solicitor his face is not often seen.

"His manner is calm and collected. He is surely the most self-possessed prisoner who ever sat in that dock and heard a charge of murder unfolded against him.

"Only once does he show any signs of impatience with the proceedings, and this is when, during the course of a woman witness's evidence, he raises his head and shouts out 'I think this woman is a lunatic'.

"The colouring of the prisoner is sallow, and on the high cheek-bones a patch of red burns, the only outward sign of inward emotion."

On the third day of the trial, Philip de Vere Annesley, a Herne Bay solicitor, gave evidence.

"I recognise the prisoner," he said. "He came to me along with Mrs Williams on 18 June, 1912. I had not seen either of them before to my knowledge. I know the house, 80 the High Street. I had noticed a brass plate on the door of the house."

He then identified the brass plate: H WILLIAMS, ART DEALER, PICTURES, CHINA, CURIOS AND ANTIQUE FURNITURE, &C, BOUGHT.

"Mr Williams brought in two wills which he had roughly drawn up and I informed him they were out of order . . . The chief thing I recollect about the documents is that they were not witnessed. I did not take much notice of them."

He described how the mutual wills were eventually drawn up and engrossed in the presence of himself and his clerk, Mr Frederick Henry Barwood. The latter was cross-examined by Marshall Hall.

"Did you write to the prisoner on a private matter yourself?"

Barwood looked taken aback.

"Did you write to the prisoner yourself on a private matter?"

"No."

"Were you about to purchase a house at that time?"

"No."

"Did you in fact purchase at that time?"

"No."

"Did you never send him a photograph of the house and ask the loan of one thousand pounds to purchase it?"

"No, never."

Barwood was followed by Adolphus Michael Hill, the iron-monger, of William Street, Herne Bay, who described the sale of the bath to Williams.

Marshall Hall: "It was the lady who did the cheapening? She got the half-crown off?"

"Yes," said the ironmonger.

All necks craned forward at this point as the five-foot bath, without taps or other fittings, was brought into the court.

Percy Millgate, the next-door baker, described how he used to see Bessie every day when he delivered the bread: "Oh, very nice – a dark looking woman. She was a tall, medium-sized lady. The last time I saw her alive was on Friday morning, the twelfth, when I was delivering bread. She was in perfectly good health that morning."

When Dr French was describing how he saw the body of Bessie Mundy in the bath the foreman of the jury stood up and said, "My lord, one of the jury has expressed a wish that someone should be in the bath for ocular demonstration."

Mr Justice Scrutton seemed displeased with this and replied: "I can only suggest to you that when you examine these baths in your private room you should put one of yourselves in. Get some one of you who is about the height of five feet nine."

Marshall Hall: "I would ask my friend Mr Bodkin to provide us with someone that height."

Justice Scrutton: "I think it is much better the jury should try for themselves, Mr Hall. There are disadvantages in the French system of reconstructing a crime."

Dr French was then cross-examined by Marshall Hall.

"You knew, did you not, when you gave your evidence before the Coroner that a letter had been received by the Coroner requesting that great care should be exercised in the investigation into this death?"

"Yes."

"And I suppose you would give a carefully considered opinion before expressing it as to the cause of death?"

"I should do so under any circumstances."

"May I take it that having regard to the fact these events took place in 1912, and we are now in 1915, your recollection would be more accurate in 1912 than it is now?" Marshall Hall asked.

"Yes, certainly. I heard Williams give his evidence at the inquest. As far as I could judge, the evidence that he gave tallied with what my own observations had led me to deduce."

(Dr French appears to be more concerned with his own "defence".)

At this point the ladykiller's counsel indulged in his favourite mannerism – polishing his glasses so that the doctor's significant reply could sink in.

"Did you say before the Coroner, 'I believed she had had an epileptic fit and prescribed for that'?"

"Yes."

Marshall Hall again seemed intent on polishing his glasses, taking his time to resume.

"As regards the visit in the middle of the night, did you say this before the Coroner – 'Her hands were moist. It was a very hot night. She said that she felt headachy, which is compatible with the after effects of an epileptic fit.'?"

"Yes, I said that."

More superfluous polishing of the counsel's glasses, followed by the studied holding them up to the light to gauge the effect of his burnishing. There was a feeling in the court that the prisoner's advocate was at last getting somewhere. Could he pull it off again?

After several more questions, Marshall Hall again came back to the doctor's evidence before the Coroner:

"Did you say before the Coroner 'I think she had had an epileptic seizure'?"

"Yes."

"And that was your honest opinion at the time?"

"It was."

"Did you make any examination of the body externally?"

"Yes. There were no marks at all. She was a well-developed woman and of strong health, so far as I could judge from her external appearance."

"There was nothing in her external appearance inconsistent with the opinion that you had formed that she had an epileptic seizure?"

"No."

Marshall Hall sat down. So telling was this piece of cross-examination that Bodkin decided to re-examine. He just could not permit his learned colleague to get away with it.

"My friend has read to you a suggestion quite properly of something you said to the Coroner," he said, "that you thought that she had had an epileptic seizure. Will you tell me your grounds for saying that you thought she had an epileptic seizure?"

"I thought at the time when I was giving evidence before the Coroner that she had had an epileptic seizure."

That really wasn't answering the question at all and gentle-voiced, churchwarden-like Bodkin had to put it again: "Could you throw your mind back to the time and tell us *why* at that time you thought she had had an epileptic seizure?"

Dr Frank Austin French was now getting a bit rattled, realising no doubt that he had been completely "bamboozled" by Mr "Williams" three years previously, but was anxious to justify his professional standing, having the benefit of hindsight.

"Two people walk into my consulting room and tell me a tale that is consistent with epilepsy," he told the hushed court. "At that time I have to put some leading questions, but I have no reason to suppose there is any suspicion attaching to them. However, I get the information, and the information leads me to suppose that it sounds like epilepsy that this woman is suffering from. It is not wonderful that I do not see her in a fit, because in nine cases out of ten when you are first consulted about an epileptic attack you do not see the patient in a fit. I am called in a day and a half afterwards, and again I do not see her in a fit, but her condition is not inconsistent with that of a person who has had a fit recently.

"The following day I am called in and I find her drowned in a bath. Again I have no suspicion; I have no suspicion that there is any foul play.

"The woman is grasping a piece of soap in her hand, and, as Mr Marshall Hall has said, people when they are seized by the legs, or something else like that, would put out their hands to grasp the bath. I cannot understand to this day how it was that she was grasping the soap. I did not examine the soap at all; I simply released it from her grasp."

Marshall Hall holds his spectacles up to the light again. Bodkin's re-examination has come unstuck.

Mrs Frances Stone, of High Street, Herne Bay, told the court: "I recognise the prisoner. He came to my house on 13th July for a week, to sleep there, and he had his meals at the Millgates'. During the week he had a bedroom at my house he had a latch-key. He was always late when he came in at night, except on one occasion when he came in about eleven o'clock, and I gave him a candle.

"After I gave him his candle he came down again and said 'It's no use; if I went to bed I could not sleep; I must go out again.'

"He looked very hot and frightened. He went out and I do not know when he came back again."

Again there is one of the tantalising gaps in the life of this acrimonious hypocrite, this murdering Cockney Casanova. What did he do after midnight in Herne Bay, when the rest of that little seaside town was asleep? What midnight prowlings did he get up to? Or did he have an assignation in another brass-knobbed bedstead?

Mrs Frances Stone was followed by Mrs Alice Minter in the witness box at the Old Bailey.

"I am the wife of Laurence Minter, carpenter, and I live at 9 North Street, Herne Bay. I remember going to 80 the High Street, Herne Bay, about 4 pm on 13th July, 1912, in consequence of a message from Dr French's dispenser. Mr Williams, the prisoner, opened the door and asked me, 'Are you the nurse that has come to lay my wife out?' and I said, 'Yes'.

"He took me upstairs to the middle bedroom. When I got into the bedroom I saw the lady lying on the floor behind the door. I asked Mr Williams for the usual things for laying her out – a nightdress, brush and comb, bath sponge, and a towel, and I then prepared the body for burial.

"I noticed that the deceased woman's hair was done up in curling pins, and that there were curdles of soap all intermixed with it. The hair was dry then, but the soap suds were left. I noticed foam on her mouth. I was paid five shillings by the prisoner and I then went away."

Yet another seaside landlady, Mrs Ellen Millgate, takes the place in the witness box to provide another macabre little facet of the drama enacted in Herne Bay during the high summer of 1912, when the promenade was speckled with the contents of thousands of bags of confetti.

This good neighbour asked the ginger-whiskered honourable Christian gentleman, art dealer and figure artist, whether he had had any dinner.

"He said 'No' and I handed him some food over the garden fence. In the evening he came and asked me if I knew where he could get a bedroom. As my house was full of summer visitors I sent him next door to Mrs Stone's, at number 78, where he got a bedroom. He took his meals at my house for a fortnight and slept at my house for one week.

"The first night he came to sleep at my house he asked me about a lamp being put in his room, as he said he could not sleep without a light. I put a lamp in his room and he asked me to light it before I retired for the night and turn it low, which I did.

"I gave him a latch-key. I do not know at what time he used to come in as I never heard him once. When he left me he told me he was going to Margate."

The poor man who was afraid to sleep in the dark wrote her a letter from Margate on the back of a telegram to save the cost of note-paper, but went to the expense of registering it. He asks Mrs Millgate to forward carriage paid "all the washing belonging to me; shall be glad if you will pay for it your end as I shall not be in when it arrives".

A few days later this foxy-eyed, penny-pinching philanderer sends a letter-card to the woman who has befriended him:

> Dear Madam, I have sold all the washing you have of mine, therefore I trust you will be good enough to forward same without delay as you promised to do. Referring to the payment for washing, you had the blinds and other things for the payment of same. I can say no more at present.

Obviously, he had told Mrs Millgate she could have the blinds in the house he had just vacated, having sold everything saleable. Now he regards this "gift" as payment for washing, which also includes Bessie's laundry.

The very next day Mrs Millgate got another letter-card from her ex-lodger, the man who couldn't sleep without a lamp in the room.

> Dear Mrs Millgate, the goods have not arrived. The person who paid me the money for them expects to have them today. Please send them to me as promised, and prevent further unpleasantness.

It is in the evidence of landladies and the like, rather than in the depositions of doctors and detectives, that the truly squalid character of this man emerges.

When she does send the washing he does condescend to write and thank her ("I have not forgot your kindness to me in the time of need") but he omits to pay her. Bessie's clothes he sells.

The parade of landladies in the witness box at the Old Bailey, gay in summer bonnets, was followed by a regiment of sober-suited bank managers, insurance inspectors, solicitors and others, giving details of how Smith cashed in every last penny of his deceased wives' resources.

On the sixth day, Monday, 28 July, the jury again had to retire while a legal argument took place in their absence. Marshall Hall was objecting to Drs Bernard Spilsbury and William Willcox being called for the Crown.

Hall knew that once Spilsbury and Willcox got in the box any lingering doubts in the jurymen's minds as to whether or not Bessie Mundy did die as the result of having an epileptic seizure in the bath would soon be demolished. Mr Justice Scrutton overruled Marshall Hall once again and Spilsbury was called.

"I am a Bachelor of Medicine and a Bachelor of Surgery at Oxford," he told the jury, as if to leave them in no doubts as to his qualifications. "I am a pathologist at St Mary's Hospital. I have had a very extensive experience not only in making post-mortem examinations, but in dealing with a variety of conditions of the human body.

"On or about 19th February this year I went to Herne Bay and saw a coffin which had been recently exhumed. The plate bore the name of: Constance Annie Williams, died 13th of July, aged thirty-five years . . .

"The body was in an advanced state of decomposition . . .

"The body was well covered with fat. About the thighs and abdomen there was a condition of the skin known as goose skin. That condition occurs in some cases of sudden death, and perhaps more frequently in sudden death from drowning . . .

"On 10th February I was at Blackpool and there I saw a coffin taken from the ground with the name on its plate: Alice Smith, died December 12th, 1913, aged twenty-five years. That body was in an even more advanced state of decomposition.

"She appeared to me to be a very well-nourished woman, a fat woman with large breasts and buttocks. Over the breasts there was three inches of fat. The buttocks were large in proportion . . .

"She was big-bodied from the shoulders and round the hips, and the hips were tightly wedged in the coffin . . .

"On 4th February this year I went to the mortuary at Finchley and there I saw a coffin recently exhumed with a plate on it stating: Margaret Elizabeth Lloyd, died 19th December, 1914, aged thirty-eight years . . .

"She was a well-nourished spare woman. There was a bruise on the back of the left elbow which was visible on the surface and I found two other bruises close to that one on the back of the left arm which was not visible on the surface . . ."

After he had given further evidence about decomposition of

various organs which must have given the jury and some of the public "goose pimples" if not "goose flesh", Spilsbury was asked about the various positions in which the ill-fated brides might have taken a bath, and then died by suddenly collapsing.

"It is highly improbable and I think, in two of these baths, almost certainly impossible, if not quite so, for the head to become so submerged as to cause death by drowning."

Spilsbury was still giving evidence when the court adjourned. He continued his evidence the following morning.

Mr Bodkin: "I was asking you last night about the positions of the women – the three positions – standing, kneeling, and sitting while facing the narrow end of the bath with her back to the sloping end."

Mr Justice Scrutton intervened here, asking: "Does that exhaust the possible positions? Have you ever heard of a person lying in a hot bath and soaking? Had you not better deal with that also?"

Mr Bodkin: "I was going to put that; but that was in another connection."

Mr Justice Scrutton: "As long as you bear in mind that the three positions, kneeling, standing and sitting do not exhaust the possibilities."

"No," said Mr Bodkin gravely. "I am much obliged to your Lordship."

He turned to the confident, almost cocksure Spilsbury again.

"May we take the three positions? Taking it the other way round – facing the sloping end?"

"Yes."

"Supposing she was standing facing the sloping end and some sudden collapse occurred, pointing, you say, to falling into the water in that position?"

Spilsbury: "If she fell face downwards she would probably drown."

Bodkin: "And kneeling?"

Spilsbury: "The same would probably occur – more probably occur."

Bodkin: "Sitting?"

Spilsbury: "Sitting she would probably fall backwards, but I do not think the nose and mouth would be submerged."

Bodkin: "You have seen these three baths, have you not?"

Spilsbury: "Yes, I have."

Bodkin: "And appreciate the depth of the baths?"

Spilsbury: "Yes."

Bodkin: "How is it you say you do not think she would become submerged if while sitting she became collapsed?"

Spilsbury: "If she were facing the sloping end she would be sitting near the lower end, and in falling back her back would be supported by the lower or foot end of the bath."

Bodkin: "Now, applying those answers to Miss Mundy, whose height was five feet seven and a half inches, and to the particular bath in Herne Bay, in view of the size of the bath, and the stature of the woman, do you qualify any of your answers?"

Spilsbury: "No, I do not."

Bodkin: "Have you anything to add?"

Spilsbury: "No."

Mr Justice Scrutton again interposed with a question: "Is there any average height from the top of the body of the head to the bottom of the spine, or does it vary so enormously that you cannot measure it?"

Dr Bernard Spilsbury framed the question a little more adroitly for his lordship.

"The ratio of height from the top to the bottom of the body?" he asked.

"Yes," said the judge.

"It varies to some extent," said Spilsbury. "The fair average would be somewhere about half of the height."

Mr Justice Scrutton: "From the top of the head to the bottom of the spine would be about half?"

Spilsbury: "Yes, only roughly. From the bottom of the spine to the heel would be about half."

(If the jury was trying to keep track of this involved and somewhat tortuous line of questioning and wondering what it was leading up to, it is difficult not to believe that some of them were not uncertain whether they were themselves on their heads or heels!)

The judge having had his little spot of elucidation, Mr Bodkin resumed the examination: "It is better to mention it now, my Lord. Take the fourth, and I think the only other possible, position, that of a person lying soaking in a bath.

"Dealing with the particular case of Miss Mundy in that particular bath, if she was lying at full length in it, her legs would be, on that assumption, along the bottom?"

Spilsbury: "Yes, in the usual position if she was sitting facing the foot end."

The Santa-Claus judge tugged his short beard, held up a finger and came across with another deeply forensic observation: "She would be very unlikely to lie the other way?"

Spilsbury: "I should think so."

Mr Justice Scrutton: "It would certainly be most uncomfortable?"

Spilsbury: "Yes, it would."

Mr Bodkin resumed his examination: "The narrow end is at right angles to the bottom of the bath?"

"Yes."

"The other way, with her back towards the sloping or narrow end, if she was lying at full length, bearing the measurements of the body in mind, where would her head be?"

(One cannot help wondering what was going on in the heads of the twelve good jurymen as they tried to follow this somewhat Gilbertian discussion on female positions while taking a bath, conducted entirely by gentlemen.)

"Her head would be resting on the sloping end of the bath. May I add to that that usually a lady taking a bath of that sort would have the head completely out of water; they do not usually wet their hair when they are having a bath."

Bodkin: "So have you considered at all whereabouts on the sloping end, in view of her length and the length of the bath, her head would come?"

Spilsbury: "It would depend, of course, upon the amount of water in the bath; and if you are assuming the amount of water mentioned—"

Here the prosecutor cut the pathologist short.

"I am leaving out the water," said Bodkin. "Whereabouts on the sloping end do you think her head would come, in view of the length of the bath?"

"You see, lying with the legs extended, the head would be very near to the top of the sloping end; in fact, I do not think she could lie fully extended."

"Because?"

"Because her total length is greater than the total length of the bath."

"Now, supposing in any one of those four positions there came on an epileptic seizure to that woman. I think you describe the first stage as a stiffening of the whole body?"

"Yes."

"And does the body remain stiff for a time?"

"For a few seconds."

"And when stiff in the first stages of an epileptic seizure, is the body straight?"

"Yes."

"Is it straight, or is it stiff in any bent position?"

"It would be stiff and the legs would be extended – the arms and the legs . . ."

"In such a bath as that at Herne Bay, do you think it possible that Miss Mundy could have been submerged?"

"I think it highly improbable."

"In any one of those four positions?"

"In a sitting position I think it is very improbable she would be submerged, but not absolutely impossible. In the lying position, lying at full length, the same applies – I think it highly improbable, but possible. In the standing or kneeling positions, if she fell face downwards in the water she would probably drown, owing to her unconscious condition."

"Now, we have heard described by Dr French here that the woman was with her back towards the sloping end, and resting wholly or partially against it – the back of her head resting on the sloping part, and her legs straight out from the hips, resting up against the narrow end of the bath?"

"Yes."

"Can you give us any help at all as to how a woman could get into that position who has suffered from an epileptic fit?"

"No, I cannot."

"Is it possible?"

"I do not see how the feet could be raised to that position in the bath."

Spilsbury went on to give similar evidence in the cases of Alice Burnham and Peggy Lofty. Marshall Hall did his best to make some dent in Spilsbury's armour.

Marshall Hall: "You have had the advantage of seeing the doctor in all three cases?"

Spilsbury: "Yes."

"Dr French, Dr Billing and Dr Bates?"

"Yes, I have . . ."

"May I take it that, as a result of your interviews with Dr French and those two medical men, you have come to the conclusion that they are not only competent but honourable members of their profession?"

"Oh, they certainly are."

"With a view to saving time, do I understand you to say . . . that in the Herne Bay case accidental death was so improbable as to amount in your mind to impossibility?"

Spillesbury: "Almost."

Marshall Hall: "Almost – I will accept your candid admission. You say almost?"

Spilsbury: "Yes."

Marshall Hall: "The soap is a very difficult problem?"

Spilsbury: "Yes."

Marshall Hall: "There is no theory under which you can deal with the clutching of the soap satisfactorily with the theory of a violent death – no absolute theory; you have to make some qualification?"

Spilsbury: "I think one would assume a violent death in order to account for the soap being there."

Marshall Hall: "I mean a violent death from an outside agency, that is to say, from a person deliberately murdering her?"

Spilsbury: "Yes."

Marshall Hall: "It is very difficult, because assuming the attack was a hostile one, that is to say by what my learned friend suggested, pulling up the feet – coming into the room with the woman in the bath sitting or prone, I do not care which, and pulling up the feet – one of two things must happen.

"Either she puts out her hands, in which case her arms would go over the side of the bath?"

"Yes."

"Either she puts her arms out of the sides of the bath in which case the soap would drop outside, or, if in the case of a struggle, she would loosen her hold on the soap in order to try to save herself?"

"Yes."

"The clutching of the soap does lend some probability to the theory of epilepsy?"

"It is not impossible. It is not very likely."

Both Hall and Spilsbury were extremely good-looking and it would not have been difficult to imagine that their duel was really taking place, not in the Old Bailey, but in one of those colourful replicas of it that the Melville brothers used to have built for the old Lyceum.

Marshall Hall: "Can you account for this? I ask you – I do not know what the answer is – could you possibly force a piece of soap into a person's hand in simulation of its having been clutched in the act of death – could it be done?"

Spilsbury: "I do not think it could."

Marshall Hall: "I thought that would be your answer, although it was a dangerous one to put. My learned friend has acceded to the suggestion I made, he has not asked you for a possible theory, and therefore I have not had an opportunity of objecting to it. I take it that if this woman had filled the bath herself by a repeated number of journeys from the ground floor to the first floor that would have produced a certain amount of exhaustion if it had been done in the morning by about twelve or thirteen journeys?"

Spilsbury: "I do not know the number of journeys it would have required."

Marshall Hall was a great advocate, a wily one, a theatrical one, a persuasive, smiling, silver-toned one, but Bernard Spilsbury wasn't going to allow himself to be browbeaten either by his blandishments or by his ingeniousness.

Marshall Hall: "I think we have been given it, although it is very difficult to get it exactly, because, of course, the quantity of water is not known; but it is said to have been three-quarters full with the body in it, and the doctor has marked it. The displacement of a body of that size would be considerable, would it not?"

"Yes, it would."

"I do not accept the exact measure, but there would be a considerable number of journeys to fill that bath with a bucket?"

"There would."

"The temperature of this bucket being so nearly cold that the doctor thinks it was slightly raised – he will not undertake to say it was raised above the temperature of the surrounding atmosphere – would that strike cold to a person coming out of bed – you follow me – on a hot night like this?"

"Yes, it probably would, if it were the same temperature when the person took the bath . . ."

"If a woman whose temperature has been raised by a night in bed like that, the bath having been prepared over night, suddenly gets into a cold bath, there would be a considerable shock?"

Spilsbury wouldn't even yield on that point.

"There might be," he said. "It is partly a matter of surprise."

Marshall Hall, himself a doctor's son, tried another line, a feasible one.

"Have you ever known of a case – in your experience have you

ever had the misfortune of getting into a bath and as you were
sitting down – slipping up?"

"Yes, I have."

Deviously, Hall came back to the question of a woman defending
herself when in the bath from sudden attack:

"The moment she sees anybody – this man – clutching hold of
her feet to pull them up suddenly she has only to drop the soap, if
she had it in her hands, and seize hold of each side of the bath, and
he could not pull her up?"

"Yes, I quite follow that."

"Do you now see that that is a serious difficulty in the way of the
theory of drowning in the way suggested?"

"It is all a question of surprise. If it is done sufficiently quickly
there would not be time to do that."

"But surely she would be alarmed when she saw a man coming
down to catch hold of her feet, and the first upward movement of
her would lead her to instinctively move her arm, and the result
would be to pull her side under?"

"By the time that process is commenced, the whole thing would
be done."

"Do you really say that the effect would be so immediate that she
would be precluded from struggling?"

"Yes, I think she would, and even from crying out in some
cases."

HARRY K. THAW

(New York, 1907–8)

Rupert Furneaux

Almost a century before O. J. Simpson of Brentwood, California, there was Harry K. Thaw of Pittsburgh. Born to a wealthy family in 1871, Thaw was an idle spendthrift best known for his bizarre sexual appetite and his marriage to Evelyn Nesbit, a beautiful chorus girl who had once been the lover of the distinguished architect Stanford White. This fact came to obsess Thaw, and on 25 June 1906, during a musical revue at Madison Square Garden – which White himself had designed – Thaw shot the architect dead in front of hundreds of witnesses. "He ruined my wife," he later explained to police. The story had everything – a beautiful woman, fame, the titillating sex lives of the jaded and wealthy – and people all over the country found themselves warming to Thaw after it became clear that White himself was something of a cad. His subsequent trial was a sensation attended by thousands of fascinated onlookers. "One evening his adoring crowd offered to rush the jail to rescue him," according to one account, "but Harry appeared on the second-floor balcony and spoke to them, calming their fears for his safety." In fact there were two trials. At the first, the jury was deadlocked: at the second, Thaw again defended himself on the grounds of "dementia Americana", a condition supposedly unique to American men that caused Thaw to develop an uncontrollable desire to kill White after he learned of his rival's earlier affair with Evelyn Nesbit. This time, the jury was convinced,

*and found him not guilty by reason of insanity. Thaw died in 1948, but
he took at least one secret to the grave with him, the only real mystery
surrounding the murder he committed: how had so many law-abiding
people become so fanatically devoted to a man the social chronicler
Cleveland Amory described as a "sadistic pervert", a man whose only
distinguishing act was to murder one of the country's greatest archi-
tects? Together with the Lindbergh baby trial and the Sacco–Vanzetti
affair, the Thaw–White case ranks high in the crime annals of
twentieth-century America. Here it's recalled by a very English
writer, Rupert Furneaux (1909–81). Furneaux visited the United
States frequently, writing, directing and producing several documentary films. He wrote more than 25 books on murder cases, historical
mysteries, New Testament studies and "battle-pieces". He was also a
formidable golfer, playing off a handicap of two. Furneaux was a
prolific true-crime miniaturist, who condensed complex cases to render
them reader-friendly.*

1

Harry Thaw's nine-year battle to beat the courts could have
happened only in the City of New York, and only in the early
1900s, still the epoch of the "Gay Nineties", the halcyon days
of New-World flamboyance and unabashed, uninhibited
wealth: the squandering by the second generation of the for-
tunes amassed by the Robber Barons, and the men who sold
whisky to the Indians, rigged the stock-market, and criss-
crossed the American continent with railroads. Their daughters married the impoverished aristocrats of Europe and their
sons dallied with the ladies of the Broadway Chorus at Del-
monico's, Maxim's, Rectors', and Sherrys'. It was the exuber-
ant day of Flo Zeigfeld, the Floradora Chorus, Abe Hummel,
and Harry Thaw.

The son of a Pittsburg railroad magnate, "Mad Harry", as he
soon became known from his ridiculous pranks, was a millionaire
at twenty-one. He followed in the great tradition of the sons of the
nouveau riche; he gave a dinner to a hundred actresses, costing
$25,000, with a gift of jewellery by every plate; he rode his horse up
the steps of his Fifth Avenue club, he fought with policemen, and
he indulged in less savoury episodes. He grew up to believe that
money could buy anything, love and even justice, and he lived to

prove the Broadway saying "You Can't Convict a Million Dollars", for it cost him just that to escape the electric chair.

Early in his career of doing nothing in an expensive way, Thaw became obsessed with hatred against another millionaire, the world-famous architect, Stanford White, the "Great Voluptuary" of the period, the wholesale ravisher of pure American maidens, according to Thaw. He made it his self-appointed task to expose White. For years he pursued him, trailing him with detectives and setting the notorious New York Society for the Suppression of Vice on his track. Then on 25 June he shot White. He claimed he acted as an Instrument of Providence. His motives were of the highest. White had seduced, when she was barely sixteen years old, the girl who became Mrs Thaw.

The extraordinary story of Thaw's obsession was unfolded at two long trials, the most famous in New York's criminal history. He claimed the protection of the Unwritten Law and temporary insanity. He suffered, his attorney declared, from *Dementia Americana*, the unchallenged right of the white American male to take the law into his own hands in protection of his women-folk. But the plea fell rather flat for Thaw had waited for four years to wreak vengeance on his wife's ravisher.

Evelyn Nesbit, the sixteen-year-old member of the Floradora Chorus, who became notorious as the "Girl on the Red Velvet Swing" is the pivot of the story. Stanford White and Harry Thaw both made her acquaintance in 1901, and White seduced her. Thaw sent American Beauty roses to her, back-stage, around which was entwined a fifty-dollar bill. In 1903 Evelyn had an operation and she and her mother accompanied Thaw on a trip to Europe in which the mother was left behind in London. All the while Evelyn was receiving money from White. In Paris Thaw proposed marriage. Evelyn refused him. She was unworthy to become his bride, she said. She revealed the story of her seduction by White. Thaw carried her off to a remote castle in Austria where he proceeded to flog her to secure a statement incriminating White. Unsuccessful, he packed Evelyn back to New York where she revived her friendship with Stanford White. White took her to his attorney, Abe Hummel, the notorious shyster lawyer of Broadway, in an attempt to secure an affidavit accusing Thaw of unspeakable cruelty and sadism.

Then on 4 April 1905, in the presence of his family, Evelyn married Harry Thaw. But Thaw was not satisfied with his conquest. His hatred of White preyed on his mind. "The Beast", the "blaggard", he called him. It became his mission in life to destroy Stanford White.

On the night of 25 June 1906, Harry and Evelyn, accompanied by two male guests, attended the opening night of a new show at Madison Square Roof Garden, a theatre in which the spectators dined as they watched the stage. At another table sat Stanford White alone. The Thaws rose to leave, Harry following his wife. As he passed White's table he stopped, drew a revolver and shot White twice through the head, putting a third bullet into his body. White slumped to the floor. Thaw stood still, slowly raising his smoking revolver in the air, holding it by the muzzle, to show that he was finished. Then he walked to his wife who ran towards him crying, "My God, Harry, what have you done? What have you done?" "I have probably saved your life, dearie," he replied. "Harry, I'll stick by you," declared Evelyn, "my, you are in an awful mess," a sentiment soon shared by everyone in New York except Thaw, who told reporters he had shot White because he had ruined his wife. He was charged with murder in the first degree, a crime for which the penalty was death.

The Thaw family rallied to Harry's aid. His mother heard the news as she docked at Liverpool on a visit to her daughter, the Countess of Yarmouth. She took the next ship back. The Thaw millions were mobilized to save Harry's life. The most experienced and expensive lawyers were retained – all those who could be briefed, though they even proved to be too many for they quarrelled at once about Thaw's defence. William Olcott, a personal friend, wished to prove that Harry had always been insane. He sent a psychiatrist to examine him in prison. It was a put-up job to keep him quiet, declared Thaw, to prevent a trial at which White's debaucheries would be exposed. Olcott was thrown out. Another attorney, John Gleason, inclined to the view that Harry's act could be excused by temporary insanity at the time of the shooting. But he was now sane. If this view prevailed Harry might get off scot-free. The Californian spell-binder, Delphin Delmas, called in to lead the defence, declared that the proper line to adopt was the Unwritten Law, the right to kill, given sufficient provocation. Thus divided, the defence attorneys prepared for Thaw's trial. To support the latter plea, Press agents were engaged and the Thaw family sponsored the Broadway production of a play featuring the Unwritten Law.

The trial of Harry Thaw started on 23 January 1907, before Judge Fitzgerald. The District Attorney, the famous William Jerome, a cousin of Sir Winston Churchill, came himself to prosecute to prove that justice could not be bought by the Thaw millions. Officially the defence claimed that Thaw was insane and they sought a verdict of guilty but insane, a plea which, as in England, it was up to the defence to prove to the satisfaction of the twelve men of New York called as the jury. Excited crowds besieged the courthouse and packed its corridors. Thaw sat with his family, beside him the star witness, Evelyn Thaw, whose revelations were expected to rock society. The greatest *cause célèbre* of New York City was under weigh.

Legal insanity was defined by Section 20 of the New York Penal Code as follows:

> An act which is done by a prisoner who is an idiot, imbecile, lunatic, or insane, is not a crime. A prisoner cannot be tried, sentenced to any punishment, or punished for a crime, while he is in a state of idiocy, imbecility, lunacy, or insanity, so as to be incapable of understanding the proceedings or making his defence.

Section 21 provided:

> A prisoner is not excused from criminal liability as an idiot, imbecile, lunatic, or insane person or of unsound mind, except upon proof that, at the time of committing the alleged criminal act, he was labouring under such a defect of reason as either: (1) not to know the nature and quality of the act he was doing, or (2) not to know that the act was wrong.

But Section 23 of the Code also laid down that:

> A morbid propensity to commit prohibited acts, existing in the mind of a person who is not shown to have been incapable of knowing the wrongfulness of such acts, forms no defence to a prosecution therefore.

The question for the court to decide was therefore, as in England, could Thaw satisfy the jury that he did not know that what he did was wrong and against the law? If he failed to do that, however, there was the second line of defence, that he had acted under extreme provocation such as to justify his act.

2

Assistant District Attorney Garvan opened the case for the State of New York. The killing of Stanford White was a premeditated murder from jealousy, he declared, telling the jury:

"The defendant walked about the theatre. The defendant saw Mr White. He returned to his wife and friends, and in the middle of the second act started to leave the theatre with them. As he went out, he let the rest of his party go ahead, and he fell back. When he got opposite Mr White he turned round and wheeled in front of him and deliberately shot him through the brain, the bullet entering the left eye. Mr White was dead. For fear he had not completely done his work, the defendant shot him again. This time the bullet went through the mouth and through Mr White's brain. Still not content, he shot him again, this time in the left shoulder.

"Mr White, or rather the body of Mr White, tumbled to the floor. The defendant turned round and faced the audience. He turned the pistol upside-down in his hand, holding it by the muzzle, and faced the audience in that way. The audience understood that his act was complete, what he had intended to do had been done, and the audience understood him and there was no panic. He walked towards the door and a fireman threw his arms around him and took the gun away. He was placed under arrest.

"The People claim that it was a cruel, deliberate, malicious, premeditated taking of human life. After proving that fact to you, we will ask you to find the defendant Guilty of the crime of murder in the first degree."

Unprovoked and without legal excuse, Thaw had killed Stanford White. The State took only two hours to prove his act. An eyewitness described the shooting. "Mr White was sitting at the table. A moment or two before the shot was fired, I saw him, with one elbow on the table. The other was thrown carelessly over and it was twisted round the next table. I heard the shot, glanced immediately and saw Thaw standing at the table, probably about a foot from it, with the revolver pointing down. My eye got on to him in time to see the other two shots." Asked how long a time elapsed between the two shots, the witness said there was about a second between each shot. He testified that after the shooting Thaw said to him, "I did it because he ruined my wife." There was no cross-examination. The defence did not dispute the facts.

John Gleason opened the case for Thaw. He told the court that the circumstances of the case had caught public attention to an extraordinary degree. Never before in a capital case, he said, had such ingenuity been expended on theories as to what the defence would be. "It is important therefore, Gentlemen," he emphasized, "at the outset that your minds should be absolutely disabused of any idea or impression that the defendant comes before you to defend himself except by the law." The jury could dismiss from their minds the idea that Harry Thaw was making any appeal to the higher law. He declared, "The defence will rely upon all defences which we may be able to prove under the plea of 'Not Guilty'; upon all circumstances tending to show that the defendant acted without malice and without premeditation and in the belief of self-defence, induced by the threats of Mr White to kill the defendant. But the greater part of our evidence will be to prove to you that the defendant killed Stanford White under the delusion that it was an act of Providence, that he was the agent of Providence to kill Stanford White."

Mr Gleason told the jury: "The defendant for three years has been suffering from a disease of the brain which culminated in the killing of Stanford White and which left its effect clearly observable after the homicide. When examined, he was not aware of his mental condition and insisted he was sane and that the act was an act of Providence. Now, Gentlemen, we have here then, the principal defence which we will present to you. The defendant killed Stanford White because he did not know that that act was wrong, because he was suffering from a disease of the brain which induced that condition of mind under the expansive operations of which he believed that it was right to kill Stanford White, acting under the influence of his insanity."

Gleason stated that Thaw's mental condition was the result of hereditary insanity in the family. Under the acts of Stanford White his mind finally gave way. What had made Harry Thaw insane? asked Mr Gleason. The answer, two influences, heredity and stress. The defence would prove, he said, that Harry Thaw was born with a psychopathic temperament, one liable to a mind diseased, and insane heredity. He fell in love with Evelyn Nesbit. He loved her with an honourable love. She refused him marriage.

Evelyn herself would tell the jury why, the attorney stated. The character of Harry Thaw became changed. He suffered delusions, culminating in the final idea that it was right for him to kill Stanford White. He was also under the delusion that his own life was in danger. On the fatal night he believed that White was glaring at him.

Gleason concluded his opening address with these words:

"And acting under the belief that it was an act of Providence for him to kill Stanford White, and that that act was right and not wrong, Harry Thaw turned and went calmly down as a gentleman might walk down to speak to a friend, and shot that man. He did not have any idea of evading any consequences of his act, he did not regard the act as wrong, but he regarded himself as the agent of Providence to carry out this act. He acted entirely and directly under the domination of an insane impulse and compulsion that the killing of Stanford White was an act of God's Providence and was not wrong.

"Now, Gentlemen, I say to you that we will show the reason why this man was killed. We will show to you the evidence that overturned his mind and led to this calamity, the evidence of this disaster in his mind and the cause of it, both before and immediately after the homicide. And, Gentlemen, we say that upon that evidence it will be impossible for you, upon your oaths, to say that this man at the time he shot Stanford White was sane beyond a reasonable doubt."

A number of doctors were called to back up Mr Gleason's insanity plea. In cross-examination District Attorney Jerome tore their testimony to shreds. "Do you consider that everybody who is actuated by jealousy is of unsound mind?" he asked one, who would only say that Thaw's remark to his wife immediately after the shots, "I have probably saved your life," showed that he was acting under a delusion. Three family doctors stated that Harry had been a nervous child and had suffered from St Vitus's Dance.

The ineptness of Gleason's handling of his witnesses led Delphin Delmas to declare that he would withdraw from the case unless he was given full charge of the defence. Gleason gave way and Delmas took over, succeeding in the face of bitter prosecution protests in calling as a witness, the stage-door keeper of the Madison Square Theatre, who testified that Stanford White had made threats against the life of Harry Thaw. At Christmas 1903, he had called to see Evelyn Nesbit, and on hearing that she had left with Thaw, he drew a revolver and, his face black with anger, shouted, "I will kill him before daylight."

Triumphantly, Delmas called Evelyn Thaw to take the stand. Under his expert guidance she made an excellent witness, radiantly beautiful, demure, her voice trembling with emotion. She started to tell her story. At once the District Attorney objected. Her story of her relations with Stanford White was not admissible as evidence, he declared. It had nothing to do with White's death. But Delmas was ready for the thrust. What Evelyn had *told* her husband, the story, true or untrue, which had affected Thaw's mind, was admissible, he asserted, and he was allowed to proceed with his examination of the witness on that basis. By this adroit manoeuvre Evelyn's story could be unfolded to the jury. But only what she had actually told Harry Thaw could be related.

Evelyn told the sympathetic court of her father's early death, of her mother's struggles to make ends meet, how she became an artist's model at fifteen, and a member of the Floradora Chorus in New York. In Paris, she said, Thaw had proposed marriage. "What was said?" asked Delmas, leaning forward expectantly. In the hushed courtroom Mrs Thaw answered:

"Mr Thaw was sitting down opposite to me and he suddenly said he loved me and wanted to marry me. I stared at him for a moment and then he said, 'Don't you care for me? Don't you care anything about me?' I said, 'Yes,' and he said, 'What is the matter?' I said, 'Nothing at all.' He said, 'Why won't you marry me?' and I said, 'Because.' Then he said, 'Well, tell me, why won't you, for what reason, why won't you marry me?' Then he leaned over me and put his hands on my shoulders and said, 'Is it because of Stanford White?' And I said, 'Yes.'

"He was very kind and nice but he looked at me straight. Then he sat down and told me he cared more for me than he had for anyone else, that he never could love any other woman, and if I would not marry him, he would never marry anyone else. He told me that he loved me and always would take care of me, and he wouldn't think any the less of me if I told him what had happened. So I began by telling him how and why I had first met Stanford White."

The moment for which the whole of New York's society had been waiting for over six months had come. Evelyn was about to tell the terrible story of her seduction. Swaying on the witness-stand, Evelyn described how a girl at the theatre had asked her to go to dinner with some friends of hers. Her mother did not want her to go but she agreed at last that she could go to a lunch-party with the girl. Evelyn continued:

"This young lady came for me one day in a hansom cab. My mother dressed me and I went with her. We turned into West 24th Street and stopped in front of a little dingy door. This was in August 1901, and I was sixteen years and some months old.

"The door opened without anybody opening it. We went in and up some stairs and another door opened the same way. Then we went up some more steps. A man's voice called down. That man was Stanford White. We went into a room in which was a table set for four people. The furnishings of the room were velvet and very fine, but I thought the man big and ugly. He asked us to take off our hats. Another gentleman was there and they teased me because my hair was down my back and I wore short dresses. This other gentleman went away, and we went up two more flights of stairs into another room. There was a red velvet swing. Mr White put us on this swing and we would swing up to the ceiling. There was a big Japanese umbrella on the ceiling, so, when we pushed up very high, our feet went through it."

But nothing happened on that occasion. Evelyn said that she went again to lunch with Mr White at the same place. After that he sent her some new dresses and invited her to a surprise party. He sent a carriage for her which drove her to the Madison Square Theatre, and she was taken up to the tower of the apartment by the elevator. Another young lady and another man were present. She said that this party was perfectly proper and she had a very nice time. Mr White would not let her drink more than one glass of champagne and told her that she must not stay up late and he sent her home to her mother. After this Mr White came to call on her mother several times and arranged for Mrs Nesbit to visit Pittsburg. Next day Mr White sent a carriage for her at ten o'clock in the morning, which took her to his studio. A photographer would be there to make studies of her, he told her. Mr White gave her lunch, but again, he would allow her to drink not more than one glass of champagne, and he put her in a carriage and sent her home.

The next night Mr White's carriage called for her again. When she got to the studio he was there but no one else. When Evelyn asked if anybody else was coming he said, "What do you think? They have turned us down. They have probably gone off somewhere else and forgotten about us." "Had I better go home?"

asked Evelyn. "No, no, we will sit down and have some food, anyhow, in spite of them," replied White. After they had supper, Mr White took her over the studio, which had three floors. He took her upstairs into a strange room she hadn't seen before. In it was a piano, there were paintings on the walls, and it was filled with very interesting cabinets.

Evelyn went on, "Mr White asked me to come to see the back room and we went through some curtains. It was a bedroom. I sat down at a table on which was a bottle of champagne and one glass. Mr White picked up the bottle and poured a glassful of champagne. I paid no attention to him because I was looking at the picture on the mantel. Then he told me that he had decorated this room himself, and he showed me all the things about. It was very small. He came to me and told me to finish my champagne. I said I didn't care much for it. He insisted. I don't know whether it was a minute or two after, but a pounding began in my ear, a something and pounding, then the whole room seemed to go round. Everything got very black.

"When I awoke I was lying in a room whose walls and ceiling were covered with many mirrors. As consciousness returned, I screamed repeatedly. Mr White came in and tried to quieten me. He got down on his knees beside me and picked up the ends of my dress and kissed it. I do not know how I got home. Next day he came to see me. I was quiet and sat staring out of the window. After a while he said, 'Why don't you look at me, child?' I said, 'Because I can't.' Then he began to talk to me. He said I had the most beautiful hair he had ever seen. He would do many things for me. Then he told me that only very young girls were nice, and the thinner they were, the prettier they were, that nothing was so loathsome as fat, and that I must never get fat. He said the great thing in this world was not to be found out. He said that all women did this kind of thing, but the wise ones were not found out. He made me swear that I would not say one word to mother of what had happened, and that I must not tell anyone about it. Some girls at the theatre were foolish and got talked about. They ought to follow the example of society women, and not be found out. He spoke of several who, he said, were very clever about it.

"I asked him about my stupor, and he begged me not to ask him anything about it. He had not hurt me a bit, and I must not worry about it."

Evelyn sobbed incoherently. After a pause Delmas solicitously inquired, "What was the effect of this statement of yours upon Mr Thaw?"

Evelyn replied:

"He would get up and walk up and down the room a minute, and then come and bite his nails and say, 'Oh God. Oh God,' and he kept sobbing. It was not like crying, it was a deep sob, and he kept saying, 'Go on, go on, tell me the whole thing, all about it.' We sat up all night. He asked me a great many questions and tried to find out if my mother knew about it. I said she did not. She thought that Mr White was very noble and a kind-hearted man. Then Mr Thaw said that she had been a very foolish woman and she should not have allowed her daughter to go out with an old, married man. He told me that any decent person who heard my story would say it was not my fault, that I was a poor, unfortunate girl, and he did not think any the less of me. Two months after he told me he had made up his mind that I was not to be blamed for what had happened, and that he was going to marry me, in spite of it. I told him that, if I married him, friends of Stanford White would laugh at him and make fun of him and it would not be right for us to get married. We had several quarrels. He said that there were lots of decent women in the world. I said that I had been to a great many apartments with Stanford White and I did not think it would be right for us to marry. He kept on saying that he could not care for anybody else and could not love anybody else, and that his whole life was ruined."

To Mr Delmas's urgings, Evelyn told of her early life and how she met Harry Thaw. She said he visited her mother and herself and came to see her at the school in New Jersey to which Stanford White had sent her. When she was taken ill he came to see her. When she recovered from her operation in May 1903, Mr Thaw arranged to take her and her mother to Europe, because the doctor recommended a sea voyage.

Continuing with her story, Evelyn related how, after her return to New York from Europe, Stanford White had taken her to see his attorney, Abe Hummel, by whom she had been shown documents relating to a breach-of-promise suit which was being brought against Thaw by a girl. She was also told that Thaw was in the habit of taking morphine and that he beat girls. When she told Thaw about this, he shook his head sadly and said, "Poor little Evelyn. I see that they have been making a fool of you." It was a case of blackmail, he declared. She told him the story she had heard of how he had put a girl in a bath and poured scalding water over her. The man who had told her, she said, lived in a hotel and he heard screams and shrieks and burst into a room and there was Harry Thaw beating a girl with a horse whip. Thaw told her that she had no business to believe these stories. They were spread by friends of Stanford White. Evelyn told the court that when she was taken to see Abe Hummel, the attorney drew up a statement of her alleged allegations against Thaw but she refused to sign it.

Harry Thaw, in his turn, Evelyn said, had made similar allegations against Stanford White. When Delmas asked her if she had discussed with Thaw the fate of other girls who had been seduced by Stanford White, William Jerome protested, "Stanford White is dead. The law does not permit us to controvert a single one of these allegations. Are there no limits to the condemnations which may be thrown on the dead?" But Delmas refused to be baulked. He declared that Thaw's insanity could have been made worse by such a discussion with his wife. It did not matter whether the stories Thaw might have heard were true or false; it mattered only if they could have affected his mind and increased his animosity against Stanford White. The judge ruled that such statements were admissible as evidence. In consequence Delmas was able to pose the question, "Did Mr Thaw at any time mention a fate similar to yours having befallen other young girls at the hands of Stanford White?" To that Evelyn replied, "Yes." Delmas left it at that saying, "I desire to utter no word against the memory of Stanford White but the duties which I owe to the living compel me to utter, but, defending here as we are doing, we would be derelict in our duty if we omitted to supply every atom of proof which we conceive will aid this defendant in arriving at a correct conclusion of his mental attitude."

Carrying on with her story, of her relations with Harry Thaw, and what she had told him, Evelyn said that he constantly referred to her affair with Stanford White. He would awaken in the middle of the night, or she would be awakened by his sobs, and he would ask questions about it. That would happen several times in one night. Her husband, Evelyn said, was determined to bring Stanford White to punishment. But he did not seem to have much success. He met with a great deal of opposition, for Stanford White had many influential friends. Her husband had pressed her to discover any stories she could against Stanford White. She told him of one she had heard, of a girl from the Knickerbocker

Theatre, who was only fifteen years old. Stanford White had given
a supper party and on the table was a great big pie. When the pie
was cut this little girl rose and stood up in the middle, wearing only
a little gauze dress. Stanford White had told her of it himself and
said it was the best thing of the kind he had ever done but
afterwards he had a terrible time over it, for the newspapers got
hold if it and he had the greatest difficulty stopping publication.
One newspaper insisted on printing the story, and Stanford White
had to go on his knees to the owner and entreat him not to print it.
Thaw, Evelyn said, had followed this story up, and he told her that
he found out that the girl had died in want and Stanford White had
not done anything for her. He said that White ought to be in the
penitentiary and he would do what he could to put him there.

That concluded Evelyn Thaw's examination in chief. The District Attorney postponed his cross-examination while the defence
concluded its case.

3

Against bitter objections, the defence was allowed to put Harry
Thaw's will into evidence. The clause which Delmas particularly
wished the jury to hear read:

> In case I die other than a natural death, or upon my death
> there shall be any suspicion surrounding the cause of my
> death, or in case I should be made away with in any suspi-
> cious way, without full knowledge of the circumstances of my
> end being known, I direct that my executors immediately set
> apart the sum of $50,000 to be used in all or in part in
> discovering the circumstances relating thereto, and should
> any person or persons be suspected of guilt in connexion
> therewith, the said sum to be used in bringing to justice such
> suspected person or persons with the utmost diligence.

A special codicil provided a trust-fund which was authorized to be
used to prosecute suits by young women against Stanford White.
The trust was to be administered by Anthony Comstock, the
secretary of the New York Society for the Suppression of Vice.

Next came a succession of psychiatrists, called by the defence to
prove Harry Thaw's insanity. Dr Charles Wagner, having listened

to a long and involved hypothetical question posed by Mr Delmas, gave his opinion that Harry at the time of the shooting of Stanford White was labouring under such a defect of reason as not to know that his act was wrong. Dr Britton Evans, who said he had visited Thaw in prison, stated, "As a result of my observations I was then and I am now firmly of the opinion that Harry Thaw is of unsound mind, because of the diseased condition of his brain. At each of my successive visits this mental condition was impaired, though it improved somewhat over the condition I found at first. His condition showed a gradual improvement." The defence were delighted. This testimony supported their contention that Thaw was insane at the time of the murder, but he was now becoming sane and could be, it was implied, released with safety. Thaw had told him, Dr Evans said, that Stanford White's friends were trying to railroad him to an asylum. They wanted to have him declared insane. They didn't want him to undergo a trial at which he might be vindicated and at which so much might be said that would blacken Stanford White's character. They had conspired, Thaw declared, with the District Attorney to keep the matter from the public and to prevent his vindication.

Dr Evans told the court of Thaw's attitude towards Stanford White. Thaw told him, "I never wanted to shoot that man. I never wanted to kill him. I never had any desire to kill him but I wanted through legal means to bring him to trial. I wanted him to be brought to justice and to suffer for what he had done. Providence took charge of the situation. Had it been my judgement, I would have preferred for him to suffer the humiliation and all that comes from laying bare this matter of his doings before the public." Thaw told him, Dr Evans said, that he had been to Mr Comstock, to Mr Jerome the District Attorney, to detective agencies, and they all advised him to let the matter drop; there was nothing to it. Thaw told him that he had been advised to carry a pistol because Stanford White had hired thugs to kick him to death or mutilate him. But he never had any intention of shooting Stanford White, he assured the doctor.

Finally Mrs Thaw, Harry's mother, testified. She said that towards the end of 1903 her son's manner became very strange and she discovered that he was suffering anxiety over Evelyn Nesbit. "He told me he thought that she had the most beautiful mind of any person he had ever known, that she had been neglected, that, if she had a mother or someone to look after

her, there was still a chance for her to be all that she should be."
Her son, she said, asked her whether she would be willing that he
should marry Evelyn and bring her to their home, and she gave her
consent, if Evelyn's past could be a sealed book. When Thaw's
mother started to say something about "the hereditary" Delmas
shut her up politely. It was not the defence policy at this stage to
prove that Harry Thaw always had been and always would be
insane. They hoped that the jury would find that he had suffered
from a purely temporary insanity at the time of the killing, that he
was insane enough to be excused from legal responsibility, but not
so insane that he could not be released.

4

The high-spot of the trial, now in its seventh week, came with the
cross-examination of Evelyn Thaw by District Attorney Jerome,
which took three days during which she was forced to admit several
damaging facts. It was only because of the insanity plea, Jerome
said, that it became a stern necessity to take this unfortunate young
woman through her story. The defence forced him to submit her to
this ordeal, he said. He made Evelyn admit that Stanford White
had paid her twenty-five dollars a week, and that she had been
cited as co-respondent in a divorce case in 1904. She agreed, too,
that while she was a member of the Floradora Chorus she had been
friendly with a married man named Garland, but Jerome's question as to whether she had been cited in that particular divorce suit
was disallowed. But he was permitted to ask Evelyn whether she
had spent most of her Sundays on Mr Garland's yacht and had
dined with him at various restaurants. She said she had, but her
mother had always been present. Jerome's questions came quick
fire.

"Did you think that Stanford White told you the truth when he
told you that all women were bad?" – "I did."
    "And you were then sixteen and three-quarters years old?" – "I
was past sixteen."
    "When did you first begin to doubt that proposition?" – "When
I went abroad in 1903."
    "Have you read the Bible?" – "Slightly."
    "Have you been to Church?" – "Slightly."

"Have you been to Sunday School?" – "Slightly."

"Why, if you thought all women were bad, did you think yourself unworthy to accept Thaw's offer of marriage? Did you think you were worse than other women?" – "I thought perhaps in a few ways I was."

What was the date of her seduction by Stanford White? queried the District Attorney. Evelyn was forced to admit that she did not remember, either the day of the month or whether it was in September or October. Nor could she recollect what the weather was like, or what sort of dress she wore. Jerome probed relentlessly.

"Did you feel intensely bitter against Stanford White?" – "No."

"After Thaw proposed to you, your feeling of hostility and enmity to Stanford White had not abated?" – "I would not call it enmity. I was hostile about this one thing, I am thinking of Stanford White's extraordinary personality."

Evelyn admitted that after her betrayal by Stanford White she went with him for a long time. She had visited him again and again. Under Jerome's merciless questioning she broke down and sobbed. She agreed she had had various operations. Jerome asked, "And these operations, were not some of them of a nature not countenanced by all surgeons?" "I don't know. I know that one was not," admitted Evelyn.

But she insisted on standing up for Stanford White. He was kind and considerate. He did many kind things for her family. He was a very grand man. She said his friends were always unwilling to believe the things that were said against him until they actually found out that they were true and even then they found it hard to understand them. When she told Harry Thaw what she thought of White, he said that made him all the more dangerous.

The District Attorney now produced the affidavit which it was declared that Evelyn (though she denied this) had signed at the instigation of Abe Hummel after her return to New York from her trip through Europe with Harry Thaw. In it she was alleged to have described how she travelled throughout Europe with Thaw, as his wife, how he took her to a castle in Austria, and what happened on the first morning there.

After breakfast Thaw said he wished to tell me something and asked me to step into my bedroom. I entered the room, when Thaw, without any provocation, grasped me by the throat, and tore the bath-robe from my body. I saw by his face that he was in a terrific excited condition and I was terrorized. His eyes were glaring and he had in his right hand a cowhide whip. He seized hold of me and threw me on the bed. I was powerless and attempted to scream, but he placed his fingers in my mouth and tried to choke me. He then, without any provocation, and without the slightest reason, began to inflict on me several severe and violent blows with the cowhide whip. So brutally did he assault me that my skin was cut and bruised. I besought him to desist, but he refused. I was so excited that I shouted and cried. He stopped every minute or so to rest, and then renewed his attack upon me, which he continued for about seven minutes. He acted like a demented man. I was absolutely in fear of my life.

Mr Jerome read further, in which Evelyn was alleged to have stated that Thaw attacked her again on the following morning giving her an unmerciful beating with the whip. He then took her to Switzerland, where he beat her over the leg with a rattan whip. Reaching Paris, she found herself watched by Thaw's hirelings, including his coachman and valet. She was attacked again by him suffering many severe blows on the body, as the result of which she fainted. In Paris she learned that Thaw took morphine. He constantly mistreated her.

To Jerome's question, Evelyn denied absolutely that she had ever made such an affidavit or signed it. Shown the signature she said that it looked like hers.

The District Attorney called Abe Hummel to the stand. Notorious as Broadway's most unscrupulous lawyer, Hummel had recently been prosecuted by Mr Jerome himself for perjury. He had been sentenced to a year's imprisonment for persuading a witness in a divorce case to tell lies, and he had been disbarred from his profession. At once Delmas objected to Hummel's evidence on the ground that it was immaterial and irrelevant. This led to a bitter wrangle with the District Attorney, who pointed out that, to prove justifiable homicide, the defence had put Evelyn Thaw on the stand to show that her husband's mind was so affected by her revelations that it became unbalanced, thus causing insanity which led him to kill Stanford White. The truth or falsity as to whether Stanford White had done the acts alleged was, he agreed, immaterial, but the issue was, he declared, "Did Harry Thaw's mind become unhinged by what was told him by Evelyn?" The question therefore whether or not these revelations were ever made to Thaw was surely most important. It was the very root of the case. If the jury believed that Evelyn told Thaw in Paris this awful story of wrong and outrage, that might weigh seriously with them in determining the question of whether or not his reason was unseated at the time of the killing. "But," Jerome emphasized, "if, on the other hand, I can say that Mrs Thaw did not tell Thaw in Paris in 1903 that White had drugged her, and, when drugged, wronged her, if I can show the jury that there is very grave reason to doubt the truth of Evelyn Nesbit's story, will not that be a matter for this jury seriously to weigh in determining whether this man was of unsound mind?"

"If I can show that Evelyn Nesbit, under the solemnity of an oath, swore absolutely that she denied to Thaw that she had been drugged by White, that Thaw tried to induce her to swear to papers setting forth those very assertions that she had been drugged, and that she resisted Thaw's solicitations, and repelled them, and he was so set and determined in his enmity to Stanford White that he actually beat this girl, actually stripped her and beat her with a whip, to induce her to sign these papers, and that she resisted and refused to sign these papers, telling him that what he desired her to swear to was not true. And she made this sublime renunciation, and I characterize it as sublime in no spirit of sarcasm or of insincerity, because if her story of that is true, I know nothing in history that succeeds in sublimity the sacrifice she made in rejecting Thaw in Paris. If she went to the office of Mr Hummel with a man who she has sworn had drugged her and had done it more than once, plying her with wine and taking advantage of her and then and there she said to Mr Hummel, 'He beat me, he stripped me nude, and lashed me with a whip; he did it to make me swear to a paper to put Stanford White in the penitentiary, and I stood his beatings and lashings and refused to do it, because it was not so. Stanford White did not drug and wrong me; Stanford White never maltreated me.' And if I can show that all that was embodied in a written document, signed and sworn to, I say that laying these facts before an intelligent jury will go very far in determining the question at issue, whether or not Evelyn Thaw did or did not tell Harry Thaw in Paris that Stanford White had wronged her. She has sworn that she did. Whether she did or not affects her credibility; it is a question of the most vital importance in determining whether or not this man's mind was swept from its moorings."

This was the crux of the case. Had Evelyn testified truthfully as to what she had told Harry Thaw in Paris? Or did the affidavit, it was said she had made to Abe Hummel, represent the truth? It was vital for the defence to get Hummel's evidence excluded. Delmas declared that Evelyn's relationship with Hummel was that of counsel and client, and therefore privileged. After a long argument, it was agreed between prosecution and defence that Hummel must be asked whether or not she had told Thaw it was not true that Stanford White had drugged and wronged her. "She certainly did," declared Hummel. When Delmas claimed that the defence should have the right of recalling Evelyn to deny what Hummel had said, she was allowed to return to the witness-stand. Evelyn agreed that she had been taken by Stanford White to consult Abe Hummel in a professional capacity, but she declared that she had signed no statement whatsoever.

Her version of the meeting was hotly denied by Abe Hummel when he resumed the witness-stand. He declared that Evelyn had sworn to him that Thaw had begged her time and time again to swear to written documents which he, Thaw, had prepared against Stanford White, charging him with having drugged and wronged her when she was fifteen. She swore that she had told Thaw that this was not so and that he had beaten her because she would not sign these documents. He dictated a statement to that effect, for Evelyn's signature. At the conclusion of his examination of Hummel, Jerome produced a photographic print of the final page of the affidavit on which appeared the name Evelyn Nesbit. Hummel was forced to agree that Evelyn Nesbit had twice called at his office, demanding that he give her the original affidavit but he refused to do so as he had given it to Mr White who was his client, for whom he was acting. He considered it Stanford White's property.

Thus, although Evelyn denied that she had signed any such statement, the State had gone far to establish its contention that she had never told Thaw that she had been drugged and seduced by Stanford White. As well as that, Jerome had done something to discredit the picture the defence was trying to build up of the innocent child betrayed by the great debauchee. Although only sixteen when she met Stanford White, Jerome had suggested that she was something quite different from the innocent child she had portrayed herself. She was a chorus girl, going about with men. She had admitted to an operation, one "not countenanced by all surgeons".

The State had done much to damage the defence contention that Thaw had been insane when he shot Stanford White.

5

In rebuttal the State called no less than six psychiatrists, or alienists as they were called in those far-off days. Dr Austin Flint, an internationally regarded mental expert, in answer to Mr Jerome's long and involved hypothetical question, stated his opinion that Thaw knew the nature and quality of his act. Dr William Hirsch of Cornell University Medical School declared that Thaw did not labour under such a defect of reason as not to know the nature and quality of his act. The other doctors agreed with them. On the conclusion of this testimony, the defence were allowed to call a further five doctors, all of whom stated their opinion that Thaw lacked criminal responsibility at the time of the shooting.

The testimony of the last of these defence doctors, Dr Alan Hamilton, who had been called by the defence to examine Thaw directly after the shooting, led to an extraordinary situation. He completely shattered the defence case, which was that Thaw was temporarily insane at the time of the shooting only. To the consternation of Thaw's attorneys Dr Hamilton stated that Thaw had always been insane, was now insane, and always would be insane. "If that is true, I have no right to be trying this case," announced the District Attorney, for Thaw would then be incapable of instructing counsel and preparing his defence. Jerome asserted that the defence counsel had known this from Dr Hamilton's report and they should not have allowed Thaw to plead. They had concealed vital evidence from the court. Thaw, insisted Mr Jerome, whether he was now sane or insane, knew the nature and the quality of his act, the test laid down by the British House of Lords in 1842 in the M'Naghten case. The District Attorney told the court that he had information of insanity in Thaw's family. This was exactly what the defence did not want brought up. The defence contended that Thaw was now sane and that he had been temporarily insane at the time of the shooting. If this could be proved to the satisfaction of the jury, the worst that could happen to him was that he might be confined in an asylum for a short time and then released. But if on the other hand the jury came to the conclusion that he was an imbecile, he might be locked up for life.

Gleason tried to rectify the position by questioning Dr Hamilton. He only made it worse. The questions and answers posed suggest that Gleason had either been misled or that he had completely misunderstood Dr Hamilton's original report.

"Dr Hamilton, I desire to ask you whether, in your opinion, this defendant at the present moment is incapable of instructing his counsel?" – "I think he is."

"Have you made any such statement to his counsel?" – "I have."

"At what time did you make that statement?" – "Several months ago."

"Did you ever make any such statement to me?" – "I did."

"Did you not state to me, sir, that, in your opinion, the defendant, as a result of your inquiry, was probably able to instruct counsel and that you would so testify?" – "I made no such remark."

"Did you not state to me, sir, that you would testify that the form of insanity which you regard the defendant was suffering from was one which, according to recent authorities, the defendant might recover from?" – "I did not. I told you that two per cent of them might recover."

The situation was now this: the court had to consider this evidence that Thaw was incapable of understanding the charge and of instructing his counsel. In other words whether or not he was an imbecile. Judge Fitzgerald appointed a Lunacy Commission to consider and report, consisting of Mr David McClure, a lawyer, Mr Peter Olney, an ex-District Attorney, and Dr Leopold Putzel, a mental expert. The Commission examined Thaw and a number of doctors and officials of the Tombs Prison in which he had been confined. When Thaw's own counsel insisted on testifying that they had found him capable of instructing his defence, Mr Jerome threw up his hands in horror. The case was costing $800 a day in experts' fees alone, he said. Surely these experts were more capable than lawyers of discerning the truth, he declared. The defence psychiatrists told the Commission that Thaw was capable of instructing counsel, the prosecution experts said he wasn't. The "middle man", Dr Hamilton, further confused the issue by stating that Thaw was suffering from a delusion that the opposing attorneys were conspiring to put him into an asylum to silence his disclosures about Stanford White. The Commission found that Thaw was now sane and capable of instructing counsel, and the trial was allowed to proceed. It remained only for counsel to make their closing speeches and for the judge to sum up.

Delphin Delmas regaled the jury with an impassioned emotional appeal. Thaw was a chivalrous knight seeking only to protect American womanhood. His act was justified by the Unwritten Law. Delmas talked at length about Evelyn Nesbit; what had happened to her at the hands of Stanford White was all her mother's fault, he insisted. Mrs Nesbit had been paid $300 a year by Stanford White. He referred to the unnatural mother who destroyed her little girl "to receive the wages of her downfall and to dress herself in finery and in diamonds and in jewels as the price of her daughter's dishonour." Delmas piled it on:

"Oh, most unnatural mother. I have seen the poor little quail, when I was out hunting, with a brood of her young ones, huddled in the sand. I have seen the pointer dog come running down upon her, and I have seen the little mother bird, not as big as your fist, her feathers bristling, flying at the dog, fighting for the protection of her young. Oh, shame, shame, that she, not content with what she had done, would seek to destroy the life of the one human being who was sent by God to her daughter, who came like an angel to her and said, 'Whatever you may be in the eyes of the world, whatever your life has been I know that your soul is pure. I know that it was not your fault. Come to me and I will protect you. I will fight the fight of life with you by my side. I want you. I will throw my strong arms around you. In the eyes of others you may be stained; in my eyes you are an angel. In my eyes you are the embodiment of all that is pure and all that is good. You are fairer than Rachel, fairer than Ruth amidst the fields of corn.'"

Delmas struck at Abe Hummel and the faked affidavit, the falsehood that Thaw had "beaten like a hound the woman he adored". Hummel, he declared, had committed perjury, as he had done before, for which he had been convicted and disbarred from his profession. On the testimony of such a man, the jury were asked to convict Harry Thaw of murder, Delmas charged. Then he turned to Thaw's thoughts on the night of the shooting.

"What condition of mind, Gentlemen, was Mr Thaw in, when he walked down that aisle and suddenly saw before him the form of the man who had caused him so much of suffering and so much sorrow? . . . In the form that sat there, Gentlemen, Thaw saw, in the flash of lightning, the whole panorama of his past life. He saw it in the form of a pretended friend and protector, when he had insidiously introduced himself into this family where dwelt this beautiful child.

"And then he heard his own voice in protestations of love that he had made to her, the proposal of honourable marriage which he had made to her. He heard her refusal and heard once more the agonizing story that she had told him, he pacing back and forth during the whole of that terrible night.

"He knew not, he reasoned not, but struck as the tigress strikes the invader who comes to rob her of her young. He struck for the purity of the home, for the purity of American womanhood, for the purity of American wives and daughters, and he believed on that occasion that he was the instrument of Divine Providence. Who shall say he was in error? . . ."

Delmas wound himself up for his final appeal. The type of insanity under which Harry Thaw was suffering at the time of the murder had not, he declared, been specified. But, although it might be unknown to the learned psychiatrists, it was perfectly familiar to every man who had a family and to the history of jurisprudence in the United States, Delmas emphasized. "If you desire to give it a name I will ask you to label it *Dementia Americana*," he cried explaining, "It is that species of insanity which makes every home sacred. It is that species of insanity which makes a man believe that the honour of his wife is sacred, it is that species of insanity which makes him believe that whoever invades the sanctity of that home, whoever brings pollution upon that daughter, whoever stains the virtue of that wife, has forfeited the protection of human laws and must look to the eternal justice and mercy of God."

Delmas invoked the aid of the Almighty. He went on: "On that night he had raised his eyes to God, and God at last answered the cry of the poor fatherless child, as He had promised thousands of years ago to the children of Israel that He would hear and that He would answer that cry. And God redeemed the promise that He had made, that those who afflicted the fatherless child, He would smite and kill them with the sword."

And leaning across the jury-box Delmas fairly shouted his last words, "Would you send this young man to his death for what he did, goaded to frenzy by the persecution he had suffered, when he turned, even as the worm turns against his tormentor? And I say to you, shall Jonathan die for working this great salvation in Israel? God forbid. No hair of his head shall fall to the ground, for on that day he wrought with God. Gentlemen, I will now leave in your hands the fate of Harry Thaw."

William Jerome spoke for three and a half hours. "The issues here cannot be determined by quotations from the ancient scriptures," he declared.

Jerome told the jury that it was not a question of vindicating or blackening the memory of Stanford White whose lips were now sealed. They were not trying that here. Nor were the jury determining whether Evelyn Nesbit had been wronged by Stanford White. The issue between the people of the State of New York and Harry Thaw was whether he was, in law, justified or excused, or whether he should be punished for taking the life of Stanford White. "Justifiable homicide does not mean *Dementia Americana*," he explained. "Justifiable means self-defence, and when a man sits with his head in his hand, quietly looking at a play, and is shot down by an enemy with a revolver, even the wildest stretch of imagination will hardly picture that to a jury east of the Mississippi River as a case of self-defence. That it was excusable is equally absurd."

The jury could find one of four verdicts, Jerome told them: "Murder in the first degree, because there was a design to kill, and that design was premeditated and deliberate; murder in the second degree, because the premeditation and deliberation were absent, but there was a design to kill; manslaughter in the first degree because, while there was no design to kill, it was in the heat of passion with a dangerous weapon; or not guilty on the ground of insanity."

Jerome emphasized, "An effort to inflame your passions and to turn the real issue aside to the trial of another, is not, as we conceive it on the Atlantic sea-board, the professional manner of presenting a case to a jury. Your oath binds you, but the oath of a counsellor of the Supreme Court binds him, or it should. And the appeal to you to do or not to do because of the sympathies of your passions is a broad and wide departure from the duties of an attorney."

Jerome described the act of killing as an act of sanity. Thaw had nursed an enmity against Stanford White for three years. And now, declared Jerome, he comes to the jury pleading *Dementia Americana*. His had been a premeditated and deliberate design to take the life of the man he hated. Who were the three people in this drama? asked Jerome. Let me deal first with the man who is dead, he said. He was a man with a wife and a family, a man of genius. According to the counsel for the defence he had come into the life of Evelyn Nesbit insidiously. The District Attorney pointed out: "But, up to that awful night, if there ever was such a night, does he make a single insidious advance towards this girl, does he give her a single rich gift? Did he try to dazzle her childish imagination by rich gifts? Did he try to see whether she would yield to drink and so yield to these terrible desires that he is pictured as having conceived? No. If the girl tells the truth, day after day, night after night, party after party, he said, 'You must have but one glass of champagne, no more.'"

What of Evelyn Nesbit Thaw? asked Jerome. Was she "the angel child that Mr Delmas would paint her to be, reared chastely and purely, as she herself tells you, drugged and despoiled? What nonsense to come here and tell twelve men. She of the Floradora Chorus. She dragged into this den of vice and drugged. And drugged with what, pray? And drugged on a night, the date of which she could not fix within three months. And the State had proved that there was no drug known to science which could produce insensibility in two minutes, and the person recover from it so as to be around next day." Mr Jerome waxed sarcastic, "And yet the next morning apparently this despoiler of virtue could go and teach that girl that all women were unchaste, only some were more clever than others in concealing. Does that appeal to your sense? And yet what does she do? She meets him again and again and again, this human ogre that had drugged her. She goes to his apartment, eight or ten times she goes to his studio. Surely, surely, surely an extraordinary condition."

The lips of Stanford White were sealed in death, stressed Jerome. Who would deny that he had his faults and that his faults were gross? But, declared Jerome, there was a difference between unchastity and brutality. There was a difference between the man who erred and the man who brutally despoiled. It was a marvellous

Jekyll and Hyde theory. But Evelyn's own words had ruined that theory. If what she said had occurred at Stanford White's studio had happened, could Evelyn Nesbit now look back on her despoiler and describe him in the way she had? Jerome asked.

Jerome was not done with Stanford White and Evelyn Nesbit. He continued, "As I have said before, a wealthy man, finding enjoyments, God knows how or why, in this class of people, sees this young child blown into his circle. She who was told when she applied for a position in the Floradora Company they were not running a baby-farm or kindergarten. That a wealthy man in these circumstances should have tried to help her, that he should, when she was out of work, have given her twenty-five dollars a week, that he should not have given her gifts except those administered to her comfort, all these are perfectly consistent with his conduct. It is consistent with his conduct that there never was any relation sustained between this girl and Stanford White except those that were pure."

The defence, charged Jerome, had transformed Stanford White into a horrible monster.

And what of the third party to this tragedy? asked Jerome. The man described by his attorney as paying honourable court. "The man we find wrapping fifty-dollar bills around the stems of American Beauty roses, and sending them to a girl on the stage whom he did not know. We find him meeting her at a dinner to which she was invited by another girl. We find him offering the weak mother a competence to interfere and help him to gain the girl. Is that honourable court? Why are men of wealth and station seeking by honourable court young women such as live in the chorus? Is that your notion of honourable court?" Thaw, Jerome declared, had taken Evelyn from her mother and flaunted her through every capital of Europe as his mistress. Yet the Defence Attorney dubbed him "Sir Galahad". And Mr Delmas, he said, had had the effrontery to claim that Thaw suffered from *Dementia Americana*, the higher and Unwritten Law. Pointing to Thaw as he sat by his attorneys, Jerome cried, "This is your protector of the home. This is the man who has struck for the virtue of the American woman." Raising his voice, the District Attorney declared, "Why, Gentlemen, every element in this case is simple. It is simply a mere vulgar, everyday Broadway homicide. That is what it is, and you know it."

A low, sordid murder, emphasized Jerome. The case of a

married man getting the girl from the unmarried one and the unmarried man taking the girl and living with her and marrying her. He was fearful that the married man would take her from him. Between them, like a tiger egging them on, lay the girl. Thaw told her she had been wronged by White; White reminded her she had been lashed by Thaw.

"Why," declared Jerome, "the same old elements that existed before the foundation of the world, and, because the girl has a childish face, she comes here to tell a pack of lies to persuade the jury to acquit a cold-blooded, cowardly murderer on the ground of *Dementia Americana*."

If that was to be the result, shouted the District Attorney, "we are going to get in this community pretty close to who has the first brain storm, if he has any enemies about. I have heard strange opinions voiced in courts of law. But surely the strangest is this, that the defendant could be sane in 1903; that he could be insane the night when he brutally and cowardly shot down his enemy, who he hated and then suddenly his insanity departs and he can sit here and his multitudinous learned counsel can take his fees. That murder can be a cure for insanity is a new thing in this jurisdiction until it was introduced by my learned friend Mr Delmas, with his *Dementia Americana*."

Judge Fitzgerald explained the law in relation to a plea of insanity, telling the jury, "An irresistible impulse to commit a crime, where the offender has the ability to discover his legal and moral duty in respect to it, has no place in the law. If there existed in the mind of the defendant an insane delusion with reference to the conduct and attitude of the deceased, it will not excuse the homicide, unless the delusion was of such a character that, if it had been true, it would have rendered the act excusable or justifiable."

The judge emphasized: "The settled law of this State is that the test of responsibility for criminal acts, where unsoundness of mind is put up as a defence, is the capacity of the defendant to distinguish between right and wrong at the time of the act."

The judge advised the jury that the legal presumption was that the defendant was sane when he committed the act and it was not necessary for the prosecution to offer evidence to show that he was sane. The burden of overthrowing the presumption of sanity lay on the defence. If the defendant knew the nature and quality of the act he was doing and knew it was wrong, he had committed a crime.

The jury might either convict him of one of several degrees of murder or acquit him on the ground of insanity.

The jury retired. After deliberating for forty-seven hours they reported they had failed to agree. Seven had voted for a verdict of murder in the first degree, five for guilty but insane. The trial had lasted for fifty-nine days and had cost the State of New York $100,000, and the Thaw family $250,000. Now it had to be gone through all over again.

6

Thaw's second trial for the murder of Stanford White started on 6 January 1908, before Judge Victor J. Dowling. Mr Jerome again prosecuted, but the defence was now conducted by Mr Martin W. Littleton, Delphin Delmas having retired from the scene. With his disappearance there was no further talk of the Unwritten Law, of *Dementia Americana*, and the defence now concentrated on the straight and pure issue of insanity. But there was another great difference from the first trial. The defence no longer hoped to satisfy the jury that Thaw had been insane only at the time of the shooting. They were now prepared to admit that his insanity was of long duration, and that it still continued. The only hope of saving Thaw from the death sentence was to prove that he was completely insane, which, as a result, could lead to his committal to a criminal lunatic asylum for life. Otherwise the second trial followed much the same course as the first. Evelyn Thaw sat by her husband's side; but the public excitement about her evidence was gone, for all New York now knew the story of her seduction. As in the first trial, over three hundred potential jurymen were examined before the jury was chosen.

The tone of the defence was immediately set by Littleton in his opening address. He informed the jury that he would tell them of Harry Thaw's life from the cradle. He would not bring to the jury, he said, the story of a man who was strong and virile and active, and who suddenly, under the power and acuteness of a passion, was overthrown, and then suddenly restored to health again. He would bring them a story, he declared, which he would willingly forego the telling for the sake of that delicacy of feeling which might affect those who were the next and closest to the defendant, a story which he would prefer not to have to unfold. It was not a pleasant matter, he emphasized, to pull aside the curtain that shuts out the past of a family. He warned the jury, "It is therefore in the light of science and enlightenment that we must approach the understanding of this particular question, not in shame, not in humiliation, not in mortification, but in earnest inquiry, for those who have suffered have been those who have been on the border-line of genius instead of on the border-line of imbecility." He told the jury that there had been what was called convergent heredity upon Thaw's father's side. His aunt had been insane from the age of seven years. A cousin had died of melancholia. A half-sister of his father's was suffering from insanity and confined in a mental hospital. A cousin had died from a form of delusions of insanity. Thaw, he stated, had inherited a nervous temperament from his father's family. On his mother's side Thaw had inherited instability. One uncle was nervous, over-wrought, and infirm, another was insane or feeble-minded. A first cousin of the defendant's had gone insane at an early age. It was necessary, insisted Littleton, that the court look back into the defendant's past in order to understand the despotism of his destiny which had been decreed, before he was born, the tyranny against which no man could rebel: the tyranny established over him by his ancestors.

Numerous witnesses were called to testify to Thaw's abnormality in childhood, and in youth. Harry's mother told that when he was an infant he had a remarkable condition of sleeplessness that enabled him to sleep only one-third as much as a healthy child should. When he returned to visit his home in 1903, she was shocked by his appearance. When she asked, "Harry, what is the matter?" he would reply only, "I cannot tell you, I can never tell you." Night after night, she heard him groaning and prowling about his room. One night she found him weeping bitterly and she pressed him to confide in her. He told her that he was in trouble about some young girl in whom he was interested and who had been injured by a man in New York. She had been wronged by one of the wickedest men in New York, and she was not the only one. He could not overcome his affection for her, although she had been so wronged; she was the only girl in the world for him. Then, to her entreaties, her son Harry mentioned the name of Stanford White. He had told her that this man had wronged a mere child. Old Mrs Thaw frankly admitted to the court that various members of her family, and those of her husband's, had been subject to epilepsy and some of them had been confined in asylums. This, pointed out Mr Jerome, was something quite different from what she had said the year before. Mrs Thaw, he reminded the court, had then said that there were no secrets, no family skeletons to be guarded or hidden from the court.

Other witnesses testified to Thaw's oddities. The court learned that he had been asked to quit Harvard University at sudden notice, the implication being that he had been expelled for moral misbehaviours. A London doctor, brought to New York to testify, stated that he had been called to see Harry Thaw at Claridge's Hotel in July 1899. He found him talking disjointedly and he made arrangements to put him in a nursing-home. Thaw became highly excited and rushed about the room using blasphemous and obscene language. At the nursing-home nothing was right for him; the large room in which he was placed was not big enough, and he could not breathe. He insisted that the doctor should have the walls torn down, and Thaw assured him that while this operation was taking place he would shelter under the bed-clothes so that he could not come to any harm. He insisted also that tons of ice should be packed in the bed around him, and he demanded that twenty nurses should be in constant attendance on him, under a captain who would drill them in his room each morning. The doctor found that he was suffering from mania. A French doctor testified that while in Paris Thaw had tried to commit suicide. But this evidence did little more than to show that Thaw had always been thoroughly irresponsible, the spoilt son of rich parents, allowed to run wild from his earliest youth.

Evelyn Thaw told her story again. Why, she was asked, had she not told the jury at the first trial that Thaw had tried to commit suicide after hearing of her seduction by Stanford White? She did not, she replied, because Mr Delmas had said it would make him out too crazy. Mr Jerome suggested that when she had gone off on her tour of Europe with Thaw she had left her mother stranded in London so that she had been forced to take a job as a chambermaid. Mrs Thaw denied this, declaring that her mother had been left in charge of her husband's valet. But she could not controvert the fact that her mother had gone to the American Embassy in London, charging Thaw with having kidnapped her teenage daughter. From the witness, Mr Jerome extracted the important information that, on the first occasion he had seen Evelyn Nesbit, Harry Thaw had been told that she belonged to Stanford White.

The notorious Anthony Comstock, who was reputed to use his Society for the Suppression of Vice for the blackmailing of the wealthy and prominent, stated that Thaw had come to him, complaining that a number of wealthy men were maintaining establishments to which they lured and ruined young women. He asked him to keep a particular watch on Stanford White. But one important witness was lacking. Abe Hummel was now in prison for his perjury in the Morse divorce case, and he was reported to have collapsed and to be too ill to appear. The evidence he had given at the former trial was read in his absence.

In his final speech Mr Littleton challenged the District Attorney to produce one doctor who could state on oath that Harry Thaw was now sane. All Mr Jerome had succeeded in doing, Mr Littleton declared, was in brow-beating the wretched Mrs Thaw, and making insinuations and innuendos against her character. Harry Thaw, at the time of his act, was rational and sane, declared Jerome. All his acts immediately prior to and after the killing proved it, he insisted. There was not, he declared, one scintilla of evidence supporting a defence of brainstorm, of manic-depressive insanity, or insanity in general. He suffered from nothing more than thirty-six years of dissipation.

Coming to the crux of the case, the story which Evelyn Thaw had or had not told her husband, Jerome said:

"Thaw's mind is supposed to have been swept from its moorings by that story, but, remember, he had already heard three years before that she was Stanford White's property. There is no doubt, however, that in its essential details, the story she told was true. I did not believe so once, but I do now, all but the drugging. Whatever her past may have been, this woman was grossly wronged. She told Thaw her story in Paris, but do we find in his condition anything analogous to the brain-storm theory? The girl herself said that his conduct was not that of an insane man. And when the woman in the case told this story, she no doubt tried to make Thaw believe she refused his offer of marriage because she loved him. If she did it was an unparalleled renunciation. In the face of it, this miserable man here paraded her through the capitals of Europe. Was he insane then? What is there to show that, at that time, he was not as sane as he sits there now, as sane as the night he slew the man into whose past he had put himself? There was no insanity about it. It was a fight over a poor little waif."

Jerome pointed out that if Thaw had taken White's life then and there, when he had just been told Evelyn's story, he might not have justified himself in the forum of the law, but he might have done so in a higher court. But he waited one, two, three years and then shot the man in the back when he was defenceless. Jerome asked the jury to think of this: "What kind of a man is that, who twice allows the story of his wife's shame to be spread on the records of a court, to save his own miserable life? . . . He could have been forgiven if he had killed quick," he ended.

In his summing-up Judge Dowling advised the jury on the matter of uncontrollable impulse. He said, "You will recollect that mere impulse, impelling a person to commit a crime, is no defence. Indulgence in evil passions weakens the restraining power of the will and conscience, and a rule recognizing a controlling passion would be the cover for the commission of crime and its justification. The doctrine that a criminal act may be excused upon the notion of an irresistible impulse to commit it, when the offender has the ability to discover his moral and legal duty in respect to it, has no place in the law. But it is a defence if his mind is in such an unsound state that reason and judgement are overwhelmed, and he acted from uncontrollable impulse and as an involuntary agent. A man must have sufficient control of his mental faculties to form a criminal intent, before he can be held responsible. But partial or incipient insanity is not sufficient to excuse from responsibility for a crime, if there is still the ability to form a correct perception of the legal quality of the act, and to know that it is wrong. Heat of passion and feeling produced by motives of anger, hatred, or revenge, is not insanity. The law holds the doer of the act under such conditions responsible for the crime, because a large share of homicides committed are occasioned by just such motives as these."

The second jury required only twenty-four hours to reach their verdict. "We find the defendant Not Guilty," they declared, "on the ground of his insanity *at the time of the commission of the act*." But Thaw was not to get away with it. The judge ordered that in the interests of public safety he should be detained in safe custody at the Mattewan State Hospital for the Criminally Insane, and he was to be kept there until discharged by due process of law. Thaw was furious. Through his influential friends, Stanford White had reached out from the grave to railroad him to an asylum. It was all grossly unfair, for, he declared, he was quite as sane as the next man and he should be immediately set at liberty. The State of New York would not succeed in incarcerating him, he said.

Thaw stood a chance of freedom. Application was immediately made to various judges of the New York Supreme Court for writs of habeas corpus, to secure his release. Thaw's first application was heard by Judge Morschauser in May 1908. Dismissing the application, the judge stated, "I do not deem it proper to allow Thaw his freedom, suffering as he is from some form of insanity, with the possible recurrence of an attack similar to that which the jury believed he was suffering from when he killed Stanford White. The safety of the public is better insured by his remaining in custody and under observation until he has recovered, until such time as it shall be reasonably certain that there is no danger of a recurring attack of the delusion, or whatever it may be."

Thaw's lawyers now tried another trick. He was declared bankrupt in the State of Pennsylvania and application was made for his appearance before the State courts. If this had been allowed, he would have been taken out of the jurisdiction of the State of New York, which would have had no method of compelling his return, for there could be no extradition from one State to another purely on the charge of being an escaped lunatic. Not unnaturally the State of New York refused to let him out of their jurisdiction. So Thaw conceived another idea, to escape from Mattewan and reach another State where he might be secure. But the time for such a drastic move had not yet been reached. There were millions of dollars to be spent and every legitimate means of securing his freedom needed to be tried first. Anyhow he was very comfortably housed in the asylum, where his dollars secured the most favoured treatment. He was comfortably lodged in rooms in the Superintendent's house, and allowed meals from a local hotel and all the drink he wanted. Meanwhile a rift had broken out between Mother Thaw and Evelyn. Evelyn wanted control of Harry's fortune, but Mrs Thaw refused to allow her more than $6,000 a year. "It is absurd," declared Evelyn. "How can I live on that in New York?"

Old Mrs Thaw started a campaign against William Jerome, who she looked upon as her son's chief enemy. Seventeen doctors, she declared, had stated that her son "was and is sane". It was only Mr Jerome who prevented his discharge to the custody of his mother, who would care for him and protect him. Not surprisingly, Mr Jerome pointed out that Harry Thaw was either a lunatic or a murderer. In either case it was in the interests of the public that he should be kept under control. Jerome opposed each hearing made to procure a declaration that Thaw was now sane and fit to be released. At one of these hearings the District Attorney was supported by Mr Hartridge, Thaw's earliest counsel who, it appeared, was now claiming $73,000 for his fees and expenses, which had not been paid to him. His evidence did Harry Thaw little good, especially when he produced in court a bundle which he said had been entrusted to him by Harry Thaw, which contained morphia needles and whips, those which Thaw had used to beat young girls. One of Thaw's many applications for release brought forth the testimony of a New York brothel keeper, who, at the time of his trial, had been safely removed by the defence from the State of New York. Now back in residence, and presumably in business, she had been found by the District Attorney's office. This lady, Mrs Susan Merrill, testified that, when she operated a house in New York, Thaw had rented three rooms under the name of Professor Reed. He advertised for young girls to train for the stage and many between fifteen and sixteen years old called to see him. He kept two whips in the room and one night she heard screams and on going into the room she found a young girl, only partially dressed, her arms and limbs covered with weals. On other occasions she found girls screaming and writhing from his beatings. One night she burst in while he was actually striking a girl. His eyes, she said, were protruding from his head and he looked mad. Finally she got rid of the girls and of Thaw. After Thaw's arrest, she stated, a number of these girls had been paid to keep silent. An amount of $40,000 had been divided amongst 233 girls. In an affidavit, Thaw declared that he had used Mrs Merrill's rooms only to secure evidence against Stanford White. When Evelyn Thaw heard Mrs Merrill's testimony, she screamed at her husband, "Here I have sacrificed myself and utterly ruined my reputation for you, and you have turned out to be a degenerate scoundrel." Up to that time she had supported her husband throughout his trials; now she refused to help him any longer. She appealed to the judge not to release Harry, for, she said, he had threatened that when he got out of the asylum he would kill her. The judge recommitted him to the asylum.

Thaw appealed again under a writ of habeas corpus in July 1912.

Jerome was there again to oppose him, although he was no longer District Attorney of New York County. The chief psychiatrist at the asylum testified that Thaw was now entirely rational. But he was forced to agree in cross-examination that Thaw was capable of being provoked to an act of violence, under the influence of liquor. Dr Flint reappeared to testify that Thaw was still dangerous. "He is a true paranoiac," he said, "and they never recover. They are dangerous at all times when at large." The Superintendent of the Mattewan Asylum stated that in his opinion Thaw was still dangerous, and if released might commit another murder. Dr Alan Hamilton reappeared to repeat his former evidence that Thaw was hopelessly insane, an opinion which was perhaps slightly tinged by his admission that he was in the course of suing Thaw for the balance of the fee promised him for his testimony at the first trial. When the District Attorney called Mrs Merrill for examination, she could not be found. She had been smuggled out of the State but detectives managed to find her and bring her to the court. She had been kidnapped, she declared, by four detectives paid by Thaw and held in Jersey City. She stated that she had been offered $10,000 by the Thaw family to keep out of the State of New York. Evelyn Thaw was now a hostile witness. "I want it understood right here," she stated, "that Harry Thaw hid behind my skirts through two dirty trials, and I won't stand for it again. I won't let him throw any more mud at me. We might as well understand each other now. I am not going through all this revolting story again and I absolutely decline to answer questions." Evelyn declared that she felt no resentment against Harry Thaw, and she had been induced to give evidence at the previous hearing only by his threats that he would kill her when he got out of the asylum. She only wanted her marriage annulled, as she wished to get out of the whole dreadful business.

On this occasion Thaw testified himself. He now appeared quite a different man from what he had shown himself during the trial proceedings in New York. He gave the appearance of a sane man, anxious to answer questions intelligently and truthfully. When he thought some of Jerome's questions were unfair, he quietly appealed to the judge for guidance. His only show of indignation came when he was asked to describe the conditions under which he was held at the Mattewan asylum. He complained of the general inefficiency of the institution and the "vagaries" of the Superintendent. He declared that many sane people were held there deliberately. The chief invective came from the opposing counsel. Clarence Shearn, for Thaw, described William Jerome as a "human hyena, befouling and bespattering with irrelevant filth", who had pursued Thaw for six years. But the judge refused to help Thaw. He pointed out, "My whole duty is to decide the single question of fact presented for decision, namely, is Harry Thaw at present sane or insane, and would his release be dangerous to the public peace and safety?" In dismissing Thaw's application, the judge stated his opinion that he was still insane, and that his discharge would be dangerous. Thaw was remanded back to the custody of the Superintendent of the State asylum.

There was still another avenue for Thaw to pursue. If he could escape from the jurisdiction of the court of New York to another American State, or to Canada, he could there resist all attempts at extradition, for the law did not provide for the extradition of a person deemed to be insane. Thaw's escape from Mattewan was carefully planned. On the morning of Sunday, 17 August 1913, a motor-car loitered near the asylum. As the warder opened the main gate to admit a milk cart, Thaw slipped out and was hurried into the waiting car. Pursuit was blocked by a second car. Within a few hours he had crossed the border into Canada. The excitement in the State of New York was tremendous. A homicidal maniac was at large. It was believed that Thaw had escaped with one intention in mind, to kill Evelyn. She was at once given police protection. American detectives traced Thaw, and the members of a notorious New York gang who had effected his escape, to the town of Coaticook, a few miles inside the Canadian border. Application was at once made to the Canadian authorities for his extradition. Hosts of officials, lawyers, and reporters descended upon the little town. Thaw appeared pleased to see them all. "That was a neat piece of work done at Mattewan, eh?" he told them. He declared that he was a sane man, as sane as anyone else, and that he had escaped from Mattewan because he was not given a fair deal in the State of New York. "I felt I needed a little vacation," he remarked. With some justification he said, "If I had stayed in Mattewan, with all those raving lunatics around me, I might not have kept a balanced mind."

The battle for Thaw's freedom was transferred to Ottawa. The New York officials claimed that the Canadian authorities should expel Thaw both because he was a certified lunatic and because he had entered Canada irregularly. William Jerome arrived in the

Canadian capital as a special commissioner for the Attorney
General of the State of New York. Ten attorneys, representing
Thaw, clamoured at the door of the Canadian Immigration
Department. In Canada there were strong feelings of sympathy
for Thaw. When he appeared in court on a habeas corpus
application to prevent his removal to the United States, the
spectators demonstrated in his favour. The medical officer at
the prison at which he was temporarily held as an illegal immigrant gave his opinion that Thaw was a sane man. Canadian
animosity turned against William Jerome, Thaw's persecutor.
Thaw's sympathizers swore out a warrant for Jerome's arrest as a
common gambler, declaring they had seen him engaged in a game
of poker with newspaper reporters. In dismissing the case, the
magistrate expressed his regret at the indignity placed upon the
representative of the sovereign State of New York. When the
American authorities applied for a writ for Thaw's extradition,
the Attorney General for Canada ordered his release on the
ground that he had been illegally detained. He was at once
rearrested by the Canadian Immigration Department as an un-
desirable alien. This was done partly for his own protection, for
local rumours stated that the unspeakable Mr Jerome had a
powerful motor-car standing by with asylum attendants ready
to kidnap Thaw and carry him back to New York. At the
proceedings for Thaw's deportation, his attorneys declared that
he was merely a tourist passing through Canada, and therefore
not subject to deportation. A special board of inquiry ruled that
Thaw should be deported, because he had entered Canada by
stealth. Thaw's counsel blocked this move by declaring again that
he was not an immigrant and could not therefore be dealt with by
the Immigration Department.

By this time everyone in Canada was getting heartily sick of
Thaw. The Minister of Justice issued an order that he should be
taken forcibly back to the United States. When officials came to
deport him Thaw picked up a bottle to defend himself, shouting,
"They are kidnapping me, they are kidnapping me." He was
thrown into a motor-car and driven across the Canadian border
into the State of Vermont. There the Canadian officials dumped
him. He wandered about the countryside for some hours before
reporters from various New York newspapers discovered him and
carried him into the State of New Hampshire. Immediately another long legal struggle commenced to secure his extradition to

New York. This was countered by Thaw's lawyers who applied for a writ of habeas corpus in the courts of New Hampshire, which led to the appointment of a Sanity Commission to inquire into Thaw's mind. Mr Jerome, at last exhausted by his pursuit of Thaw, did not appear. Thaw's application was unopposed, and on 11 January 1914 the court found "Whatever may have been the mental condition of Harry Thaw at the time of the homicide, upon which question we express no opinion, he is not now suffering from any of the forms of mental diseases alleged by the prosecution at the time of the trials or subsequently thereto. In our opinion, it is reasonably probable that his liberty under bail would not be dangerous or a menace to the public peace and safety." But Thaw was extradited to New York on the charge of conspiring to defeat the ends of justice. New York had at last got its man, but the jury selected to try the charge found him Not Guilty.

Thaw now applied to the Supreme Court of New York for a declaration of his sanity. Once again Harry Thaw supplied the people of New York with a great popular spectacle. Much of the old evidence was repeated. The same accusations were made against Stanford White, and the prosecuting attorney found it necessary to defend the dead man. "It is a shame and a disgrace to the honesty and decency of the American people to continue to make a beast out of Stanford White, when the only evidence is the testimony of Evelyn Nesbit Thaw, which was produced so that Thaw might hide behind her skirts," he asserted. Thaw's counsel told the court that he was now a sober, chastened man, very different from the man of convivial habits of 1906. Prison doctors, officials, newspaper reporters, and countless other witnesses, were called to testify to Thaw's sane behaviour since the end of his trials. The defence psychiatrists declared now that Thaw had always been sane and that he killed Stanford White in a fit of ungovernable rage due to the story which Evelyn Nesbit had poured into his ears. But that story had been told him four years before, and Thaw's rage had had time to cool, rejoined the prosecution. Evelyn Thaw did not give evidence. A process server sent to find her was given a medical certificate that she was too ill to appear. Mrs Susan Merrill, brought to court, was forced to admit that the story she had told at the second trial was grossly exaggerated as regards the number of young women Thaw had supposedly beaten and the amount of hush-money paid to them. Thaw himself gave evidence. Asked to give his own story of the murder of Stanford White he stated, "I saw Stanford White sitting there and he glared at me. I went twenty or twenty-five feet from where I was standing and then turned round and looked at him. When he saw me his hand dropped from his head and it seemed that he was reaching towards his pocket. I didn't know what he intended. I am simply telling the fact. He glared at me and I walked up and shot him." Asked why he had allowed nearly four years to elapse from the time Evelyn had told him of her seduction before he shot Stanford White, Thaw replied, "There is no answer to that question. I cannot give you one. There was no reason." The famous Dr Flint reappeared to reiterate his opinion that Thaw was insane and incurable, but he was unable to advance any reasons for his opinion other than what he called Thaw's incoherence and slowness of utterance. Dr Flint was forced to admit in cross-examination that he did not think that Thaw was now suffering from manic-depressive insanity, or from his original delusion that he was being railroaded to an asylum. The failure of Dr Flint to substantiate his opinions brought the case to an end. The jury declared that Thaw was now sane, and he was released, being given a vociferous welcome by the vast crowds which thronged the courthouse. Outside, Thaw was photographed as he was shaking the jurymen who had freed him by the hands. Thaw returned to his mother's home at Pittsburg, and he lived there with his family until his death in 1948. It had cost him a million dollars and nine years of his life to get away finally with the shooting of Stanford White. The Thaw millions had triumphed over the law.

Thaw divorced Evelyn and she married her dancing partner. When he deserted her she worked as a hostess in night-clubs and honky-tonks, moving finally to live unknown and forgotten in California. But fame came to her again in 1955 with the filming of the story of Harry Thaw and Stanford White under the title of *The Girl in the Red Velvet Swing*. She came to New York for its première, revisiting the scenes of her Broadway triumphs. But the old Madison Square Theatre had been pulled down; Harry Thaw was dead, Stanford White forgotten, the uproarious days of the Floradora Chorus a thing of the past. And it didn't matter any more if a girl did get found out.

7

It is difficult to comment adequately on the Thaw case. It is too unreal, almost beyond our imagination. It is an American period piece. It cannot be judged by British standards for there is nothing like it in British criminal annals. In England or Scotland in 1907 Thaw would have received short shrift. He could not have satisfied the legal test of insanity for he clearly knew that what he was doing was wrong and against the law, and there could be no excuse for what he did. Yet, clearly, his mind was unbalanced; he was a lunatic. In Britain he would certainly have been convicted of murder and then, possibly, reprieved on the ground of insanity. Like Ronald True in 1922, his execution would have been stayed, for it is the law that a person found to be insane after conviction cannot be executed. Nor could his crime have been reduced to manslaughter by provocation, for such provocation as he believed he had received occurred four years before he shot his wife's alleged seducer. Sufficient time had elapsed for his temper to cool, and a spouse, and a spouse only, is justified in killing if he or she actually catches the matrimonial partner in adultery. A mere confession is not sufficient to excuse, and the admitted unfaithfulness of a mistress or lover does not count. In any case, there was considerable doubt over what Evelyn had told Thaw four years before, and whether or not she had actually been "betrayed" by White.

Thaw's wealth and social position, which did so much to aid and to hinder his defence, would have availed him nothing in Britain. The courts of England and Scotland have not shown themselves sympathetic to the peccadilloes of the wealthy for at least a hundred years, and the antics of Thaw's defence could not have occurred in Britain's more sober climate.

Nor, in all fairness, could the Thaw case be repeated in the United States today. The lavish days of American plutocracy have given way to the more sober deeds of the men in the grey-flannel suits. Thaw's *Dementia Americana* belongs to the day when the American frontier was still a living memory. When, if you were rich enough, you could shoot the other fellow and get away with it. It was just a matter of who shot first.

Thaw's enmity for Stanford White was obsessional. When he visited Domrémy on his tour of France, he surreptitiously wrote in the visitors' book: "Jean d'Arc would not have been a virgin long if

Stanford White had been around." Thaw was jealous of White's conquests; the "Great Ravisher" of pure American womanhood was a role which Thaw had cast for himself. So White had to die. Perhaps it was just as simple as that.

Evelyn Nesbit died in 1966 in a nursing home in Santa Monica, California, aged 81. In her later years, she taught ceramics and served as a technical consultant to a 1955 movie about the White shooting, The Girl in the Red Velvet Swing, *in which she was played by Joan Collins. She was also portrayed by Elizabeth McGovern in the movie* Ragtime.

ROBERT THOMPSON AND JON VENABLES

(Preston, 1993)

Blake Morrison

The Bulger trial became a bleak metaphor for its time. Seldom has a trial aroused such passions and public feelings of hate towards the defendants. On 12 February 1993, in the Liverpool suburb of Bootle, Robert Thompson and Jon Venables murdered James Bulger. The killers were ten years old, their helpless victim had not turned three. Seizing the child in the Strand Shopping Centre, Thompson and Venables led him on a long, exhausting walk along nearby streets, past the reservoir and the job centre to the railway line. There, they splashed him with sky blue paint, then battered him with bricks and an iron bar. They placed him, not yet dead, on the tracks and built a little shrine of bricks around his head. Later, a train cut James's body in half. This sordid, senseless murder plunged Britain into an orgy of soul-searching and finger-pointing; the whole world took notice of a crime that seemed to mean something about the way we live now, though no one knew what it was. Thompson and Venables were tried as adults. To allow them to see above the railings, a special raised platform was built on which the two boys would sit during the trial. (It would later be argued that this extraordinary "displaying" of the defendants constituted an unfair trial.) Carpenters bolted down the chairs in the public gallery so that no one could throw them. The

*judge, Mr Justice Morland, set the hours of the trial to approximate
the school day, with a late start and an early finish. He ruled that the
boys be known as Child A and Child B (Robert Thompson and Jon
Venables, respectively). Some spectators were convinced that porky,
unemotional Robert was the instigator of James Bulger's murder. Jon,
on the other hand, seemed more contrite, anxious, constantly looking
back at his mother for her support. The prosecution, led by Richard
Henriques QC, contended that both boys took part in James Bulger's
death. Because both defendants were under the age of fourteen, the
prosecution had to prove they knew that their actions were severely
wrong. As the jury received files, which included photos of the crime,
they were visibly moved. Jon's mother also began to cry and Jon leaned
over the rail to see if she was all right. One by one, the witnesses
confirmed the boys' route to the murder spot. Many were clearly
racked by guilt that they had failed to stop the deadly march. But who
could have known that the little boy was going to be killed by the older
children holding his hands as they walked? Neither defendant took
part in the trial; they did not give evidence and the judge rarely
addressed them. But the evidence clearly indicated their guilt: the
Strand security videos, blood-splattered bricks, stones, clothing, a tin
of blue paint, and a heavy bar. Did the boys know the difference
between right and wrong? This was an important issue for the
prosecution. The Victorians established the concept of* doli incapax
*to protect innocent (and ignorant) children from corporal punishment.
It meant that children were incapable of wrongdoing because they
cannot grasp the consequences of their actions. But psychiatrists
testified that both Thompson and Venables knew the severity of their
crime. The court heard the recorded police interviews, which also
revealed their understanding of the charges. Jon's hysterical, high-
pitched crying affected many who heard it. The writer and poet Blake
Morrison (b. 1953) covered the four-week trial for an American
magazine. He found the case harrowing, but thought he'd be able to
forget it. He was wrong. "The world moved on," he reported, "but I
didn't. I was still stuck in Preston . . . It was as if something important
had happened there that still hadn't been faced or explained." Three
years later, in an award-winning book, Blake Morrison described the
air of expectancy as the prosecution finished its case, and it was the
turn of the defence.*

For days we've been wondering what the boys' defence will be. There are admissions of guilt. There are blood stains and paint stains. There are expert testimonies that T & V knew right from wrong. Some witnesses have been inconsistent, but that's excusable, given their distress about the crime, and may even have endeared them to the jury. It's all gone the way of the Crown.

For David Turner, Robert Thompson's barrister, the experience has been frustrating. His private view is that the trial is "bloody medieval". The kids shouldn't be paraded like circus animals. He can't pretend to warm to Robert, even less so to his mother, but that's beside the point. He's doing the best he can. At the start he thought his side had the better chance, Jon having coughed "I did kill him". But Robert hasn't made a good impression. He's hard to get through to. If he'd been more mature, he might have seen the point of pleading immaturity – of exploiting *doli incapax*. But he's continued to lie even to his helpers. The only other defence line would have been the videos: to have used *Child's Play 3* against Jon. But that route was lurid and sensationalist, with the risk it might rebound. Which left only a damage-limitation exercise – avoid a murder verdict. Now even that looks optimistic.

Frustration, too, in the Venables camp. Any sympathy going in court is all for Jon, but how to exploit it? An offer to the Crown to plead guilty to manslaughter was rejected before the trial began. An argument that Jon has a mental age of less than ten, and shouldn't stand trial, was not firmly enough supported by the psychiatric reports. There's the defence that Jon was coerced by Robert: a killer under duress. It's what his parents believe. But Jon needs to say it himself. Since the police interviews he's not talked about the killing at all.

Might he now, in the stand? Mary Bell spoke, in her case, a quarter of a century ago; so did her accomplice, Norma. Gitta Sereny, in her book, describes it well: the simple, bewildered Norma, the younger but cleverer Mary in her yellow cotton dress, the long hours in the stand. The two of them had killed two little boys, but Norma was cleared and Mary found guilty only of manslaughter. It seems to have helped their case that they took the stand; it certainly didn't do them any harm. But T & V are suffering from post-traumatic stress disorder (which had no name at the time of Mary Bell). To call them might be cruel and counterproductive: Jon would look furtive, Robert cheeky. Questions might bring out further lies, and there have been lies enough already. Every lie is a victory for the Crown, evidence that the boys are trying to exculpate themselves and thus understand right from wrong. The risk is that by speaking they'd weaken an already flimsy case.

On the other hand, if they stay silent, or are heard only as voices on a tape, they may seem more sinister than they are. To take the stand might move the jury. Never mind the words they speak, there'll also be the words they fail to speak. To stammer, to break down, to show their vulnerability: it might feel bad but do them good. Help the rest of us, too: differences between them would emerge, traits to help us allocate responsibility.

Some thought's been given to this: not in Jon's camp (he bangs the wall hysterically whenever James's killing is even mentioned), but in Robert's. When [his mother] Ann, on advice, told him he'd have to speak, he said OK – he was frightened, but OK. They had a dry run, in private. Robert did all right at first, holding eye contact with David Turner and sticking to the story he'd told the police – everything had been done by Jon. But the story had obvious flaws: he was lying, as if by reflex, and began to panic at the questions. "If they put him in that box, they'll bury him," said Ann, backing down. "I'm not going in that box," said Robert, reusing her coffin image. That established, he became cocky again, accusing Turner of asking silly questions and declaring that the shoes in court, with D rings, exhibits 45 and 46, key evidence against him, must belong to someone else. Afterwards, all agreed: it was not in Robert's interest to be called.

That's why, today, it's over in a flash, two men standing up then sitting down again. "We call no defence," says David Turner for Robert. "We call no defence," says Brian Walsh for Jon.

"No defence." But that doesn't mean no answers. I try to set down some of my own:

- Because Jon was disturbed, having grown up in a tense, unhappy home
- Because Robert was brutalized, having grown up in a violent one
- Because of the chemistry: they spurred each other on
- Because of a dare, an incredible plan they never expected to work
- Because no adult they met listened to their appeals to intervene

- Because James became a surrogate for their loathing of their siblings
- Because they didn't know where illusion ended and reality began
- Because they didn't understand death's irrevocability
- Because they were scared of getting into trouble, and silencing James looked like the best way to avoid it.

Tomorrow the prosecution will sum up. The day after, the defence will. The day after that: the judge.

No one doubts T & V killed James Bulger. But there are different kinds of verdict, and now the jury's moment is coming near. What are they like, the jury? They sit to the side, in pews, nine men, three women, middle-aged mostly, middle-class too by the look of it, a dozen earnest burghers, grey, stolid, grave as the dead judges on the wall. From time to time I've felt a pang for them, turning up for jury service perhaps not knowing this was one of the cases and then, sweet Jesus, being chosen for it: four weeks of torment instead of a quickly over GBH in the next court. The more nervous jurors have looked to be on trial themselves, so much expected of them. One woman, taking her oath, stumbled over her words, like a bride forgetting who she was marrying. There aren't many things in life so serious you have to swear on the Bible. This is one.

Twelve honest citizens determined to be serious. But who can say what they'll decide? It only takes an oddball, a dissenter, a charismatic radical. Maybe they'll be moved by Jon's daily tears. Maybe they'll believe that Robert, one shoe-print aside, was a mere spectator. Maybe they'll choose manslaughter. The dead judges look down from their frames. The door screams at the back of the gallery. The hacks are back, in spades. At last, adrenalin, suspense.

It's getting to the boys, too. What happened to Robert's self-possession? Captain of his own soul, he's hardly flinched for three weeks. When one barrister used the trope of a "broad brush", Robert mouthed to his social worker: "What's a broad brush?" But self-possession (the passage to remorse sealed up) isn't a great asset when you're accused of killing. And I see Robert differently now. I notice how tense he is, and fidgety. I understand, despite his cropped hair, how he might have once been teased for being a girl. "Those who have been dry-eyed may also be feeling pain and misery," says his barrister, David Turner, summing up. Yesterday and today Robert has expressed that misery. "Thratching" my mother would call it, and though some would claim it's behaviour typical of a child who has been sexually abused, I see it as unhappiness and nerves. He rubs a wet finger around his upper lip, pulls out his lower lip (I remember James's injury), strokes his tongue, massages his chin, twiddles his fingers, sucks his clasped hands, chews his neck chain, mock-types on the wooden rail in front of him, rotates the ring on his little finger, nervously dabs his mouth with blue tissue paper, silently coughs into it, folds and refolds the tissue, puts a finger in an ear, screws up his eyes, gazes at the ceiling, fits his fingertips against his teeth, wipes his wet hands on his trousers, licks his fingers one by one. He sucks his thumb, too, not having been warned, as thumb-suckers used to be, that a red-legged scissor man will come and cut it off. And he tears the paper tissue to confetti, bit by shredded bit.

Maybe it's the prosecution summary that upsets him – hearing himself described as the greater and more cunning liar. But he seems just as upset by his own counsel. When David Turner speaks of the terrible sorrow felt for the Bulgers ("The city of Liverpool missed a heartbeat, and the country was shrouded in grief"), and of "a tragedy for three families, not one", Jon starts to blub, and then Robert, too, just a little. There's an awkward moment when Turner discusses the matter of the marks on James's cheek. The Crown has shown conclusively that these marks, looking like staples and horse-hooves, must have come from Robert's shoes: black brogues, traditional uppers coarsely stitched, the laces criss-crossing through D-rings. But doesn't scientific evidence also suggest, Turner asks the jury, quoting from the standard work, *Footwear Impression Evidence*, that bruises like those left on James come from blows of light impact? Could it be that James's cheek, that is to say, impacted on Robert's shoe, not vice versa? That he fell on the shoe, rather than was kicked by it? So it runs. A desperate line of defence. Awkward for all of us. But what is Turner to do? The footprint is the main evidence against his client, who has instructed him to plead not guilty. He has to fight as best he can. His job is to make bricks from straw, or *vice versa*. It doesn't mean he's unfeeling, uninvolved, cab-rank impartial. He has walked from Bootle to Walton with two of his own children, incredulous at the distance. He has been attacked in the papers for upsetting witnesses (particularly female witnesses) with his abrasive questions, and been caricatured as a Georgy-Porgy making them cry. But he can't help his defence sounding desperate – it *is* desperate. Robert knows this. Robert's not stupid. He tears at his tissue. He knows the verdict's coming near.

Maybe it's his mother Robert is worrying about, more than himself. Ann's here every day now, in a brighter, stripier dress, not the sackcloth and ashes she first came in. It hasn't been easy: the other day one of the Bulger relations, passing her in the corridor, called her a twat. She put that down partly to the five-pointed Orange Lodge star she wore on her neck, the denominational jewellery. Typical of Ann to shift the blame from the more obvious source of the Bulgers' anger: her being Robert Thompson's mum. But she does have a point. Liverpool is a sectarian city, and the killing of James had its religious element, its whiff of an ancient feud – like the medieval legend of the Christian boy murdered by Jews, as narrated by Chaucer's Prioress. Tribalism, and the shedding of innocent blood: perhaps Ann is right to feel that, to the Bulgers, Robert and Jon were two Prods (Walton being a strongly Protestant area) slaughtering a little Catholic.

Ann fidgets in her seat as Turner sticks up for Robert. People are staring at her – as if what happened were her fault. I stared at her this way myself at first and loathed the big-eyed self-pitying. But separation, poverty, too many sons to look after and now this – no wonder she feels sorry for herself; I feel sorry for her too. Still in denial, she can't believe Robert guilty of killing. He's too soft for that – the kind of boy who likes to suck his thumb and sit in his mother's lap. She knows when he tells lies and believes him when he says it was Jon. If Robert had planned the killing, why walk back to Walton, where neighbours would recognize him, and why choose the railway, where every kid in the area likes to play? Her boys are always getting the blame. They've been arrested so often, she even asked at Walton Lane for a job, joking she spent more time down the police station than the police did. You have to laugh or you'd kill yourself, as she tried to, with an overdose, after her third child. She'd hoped once for two boys and a girl in the middle (the two boys to protect the girl), and has gone on trying for a girl, without success. Sometimes it feels – here in court especially – that nothing's gone right for her from the beginning, and she'll be struggling still when she goes to her grave.

The counsellors stroke and pet Ann. At the front of the court, David Turner winds up, reminding the jury of the "petulant" Jon's deceitfulness (that "magical mystery tour" he took the police on for five interviews) and of his own client's denial of the offence. He steps down. We break for coffee. On the pew-rail in front of Robert, like a guinea pig's nest, there's a little mound of paper bits.

Jon's defence takes much longer than Robert's – 160 minutes, rather than 75. It starts before lunch and goes on past knocking-off time. It's not just that Brian Walsh is more fond of peroration, but that he feels he has a better case. He follows much the same line as Turner: the killing of James was a mischievous prank that went horribly wrong when the boys had to rid themselves of their burden. But it's a cut-throat defence, and Walsh's is the sharper blade – a blade he has to bury in Robert. Jon's tears and diffidence, Walsh argues, set him apart: a "brave and truthful little boy", he is "obviously genuine" in his remorse. Any talk of getting a kid lost had been bravado, one of those "dreadfully silly things children say to make themselves look big". Unlike Robert – calm, cunning, arrogant, sophisticated, brazen – Jon was no schemer. He intended to take James to the police station. His lesser part on the railway was "shameful behaviour but not murder". Later, he co-operated with the police. He hadn't tried to absolve himself. He'd come clean. He'd stopped lying. He was *good*.

The jury sit stony-faced. I'd guess Walsh doesn't wash with them. His tone is *de haut en bas*. And there's a fundamental flaw in his defence: Jon may be brave and truthful, but admitting "I did kill him" highlights his active part. [His parents] Neil and Susan bury their heads. For three weeks they've been icons of ordinariness, guarantors of their offspring's decency. But it's too late for this to have effect any more, if ever it did. They won't have to wait much longer. Walsh winds up. Now only the judge.

How can you tell what a judge thinks? For most of the trial he just sits there, wrapped like a pharaoh and almost as dumb. But what he says at the end can sway the jury. He can steer them gently, or lead them by the nose. He can distil the essence of the case or pour away the lot in favour of a brew of his own. Is this judge, Michael Morland, a distiller or a homebrewer? How will he turn out?

He's been kindly up till now: solicitous towards the jury, patient with witnesses, affable, impeccably liberal, a good egg. But he hasn't looked at T & V much, hasn't been heard to ask: "Do you understand?" It doesn't bode well for them. Nor does his reca-pitulation of evidence. What the jury has to decide, he says, is not who struck the fatal blow but "were they in it together?" – he makes the analogy of the burglar who nicks a television and his mate who drives the getaway car, both under the law equally guilty. What the jury has to decide is not what T & V planned to do with James along the route, but "were the blows they struck on the railway intended to cause death or serious injury?" What the jury must also decide is whether the boys told lies out of panic, stupidity, confusion and fear – or because they knew what they'd done was wrong and were trying to hide it. Through a long day he goes over what happened, circuitous but also circumspect: "You may think", "It is for you to decide if . . .", "It is a matter for you to . . ." "You may think . . ." They may think. It's up to them to think. He isn't paid to do their thinking for them. Except that he is doing, by thinking aloud himself.

He follows the same line with the taped interviews: by taking them one by one, even-handedly, he implies an equal complicity. I wish I had a tape for his own performance, but tape-recorders are forbidden in court. He repeats the boys' words and mimics their accents: "on me own", "yeah", "cos", "yeah", "If you want, like", "yeah", "God's honest truth", "yeah", "yeah", "yeah". In another context, it might be funny: an impeccably RP judge trying to do Scouse but sounding stage-Cockney instead. The context here is murder, though, and the impersonations, if not malicious, have a sniff of distaste. Middle-class children wouldn't be mimicked like this. T & V are being treated as street urchins (the phrase has occurred more than once during the trial), their dress and accents held against them. There's enough to hold against them without having to refer to their scruffiness and Scouse.

But I don't suppose anyone notices. There's too much else to notice: the pain inflicted on the railway, the pain inflicted still. When the judge recites James's injuries again, Ann Thompson starts crying (she's not heard the kicks and bricks in detail before), and soon Jon and Neil are crying, too; as usual, Susan and Robert are the tougher ones, the non-weepers, though they too have shed tears. This trial is as salt-smeared as the sea.

At 11.45, the jury prepare to go out. T and V face three charges – murder and abduction of James, attempted abduction of another child – and each must be judged on each. It's a lot to think about, all at once. The verdict must be unanimous, the jury is told, "the verdict of each and all of you". It only takes one to be awkward, and, even if all are agreed, after three and half weeks' slow torture it would be indecent to hurry now. Twelve beds have been reserved at a nearby hotel. We expect them to be slept in.

The jury out, a barrister for the Mirror Group is petitioning to be allowed to name names. The *Mirror* owns an exclusive on Child X, the child (allegedly) almost abducted before James, and believes that the public has a right to be informed exactly who this four-year-old is. A barrister for Associated Newspapers is making a similar appeal: he, too, talks of "public interest" – if Boy A and Boy B can become Robert Thompson and Jon Venables, the world will be a safer, better place. The arguments have been poorly prepared (there's mention of the precedent of Mary Bell "and her sister" Norma, a schoolboy howler), and I can't imagine them succeeding. We've grown used to the sound of Boy A and Boy B. To name them now will make their eventual rehabilitation more difficult. No public interest is served by naming a child who was *nearly* abducted. To print the names (and photographs) of T & V is mere gawping – and will wreck the lives of their parents and siblings. This is what the defence lawyers are arguing, and I go along with them. T & V should remain initials. I'd want my children to remain initials. I'd want anyone's children to remain initials. Offenders under sixteen are never normally named in public: why should these two be? But there are counter-arguments. That fair, accurate and open reporting is better than sneaky imputation. That disclosing T & V's names and backgrounds will be a deterrent to other potential child child-killers. That murderers shouldn't be granted the privilege of anonymity when it's been denied to the murderee. The debates run on. The judge says he'll announce his decision after the verdicts. But he hints at what it will be: the "bizarre and terrible circumstances" of the killing are an argument for names to be in the public domain; only detailed and open investigation of the boys' backgrounds can help explain the crime.

Later a clerk hands out a hastily typed sheet, "varying the orders". The embargo will be lifted. I look at the judge suspiciously: has he a streak of vindictiveness towards the boys and their parents? Or is he acting from humane and reformist motives, as if he were Dr Barnardo stumbling on the squalor of children's lives and exposing it to public gaze? Either way, it's a confession of failure. The trial has brought us no nearer to understanding the reason that James was killed. It has failed to give us the Why. The *Sun* and *Star* and *Mirror* will have to do the job instead.

As if.

I sit in the corridor, just outside court, afraid to leave in case the jury reach a verdict. To pass the time, I'm reading Liam Hudson's *Contrary Imaginations*, subtitled "A Psychological Study of the English Schoolboy", which cites intelligence tests performed on teenage boys. The boys were asked to write down as many different uses they could think of for certain objects. These were among their answers.

1: The Brick: To throw at someone. To smash my sister's head in. To tie to cats and drown them in ponds. For hitting and killing people. As a weight to remove a pistol after committing suicide.

2: The Barrel. To put spikes round the inside and shove someone in and roll along the ground. For stuffing headless bodies in. To close the lid on someone and roll over a cliff. To put a cat in when half full. To tar and feather in. To fill with stones and roll down a hill and squash somebody.

3: The Paper Clip. As a thumbscrew. To jab an enemy with. For pinching skin. For hurting someone's finger.

4: The Tin of Boot Polish. For suffocating insects. To make people sick with by putting small quantities in their food. To slap in someone's face.

5: The Blanket. To smother my mother. To remove from my baby sister's bed in winter while she's asleep. For suffocating a person to death. To wrap a dead wife in so blood does not stain the car seat when the body's being dumped.

These answers seem as shocking as anything we've heard in court – and shocking for the same reason. There's a peach-glow and vulnerability about children that seems incompatible with their having violent thoughts, or performing violent deeds. We imagine them as milk-white and pure. We imagine them as old words from the *Golden Treasury*: blossom, gossamer, foam flowers, sea-down, dewy eyes. We imagine them as imagining only good. *As if.*

Just after five, there's a rumour the jury is returning. We take our seats. The boys take their seats. The Bulgers take their seats;

heavily pregnant, Denise is here for the first time, to see what her
son's killers look like. Susan and Neil Venables are here, too, but
not Ann Thompson, who has been left below court, downstairs.
The jury comes in. Word is, the foreman's going to say they need
longer. The bearded, Scottish, rumbling-voiced clerk asks: "On
the first count of attempted abduction, have you reached a verdict
yet?" "No", says the foreman, brusque, blunt, in broad Lancas-
trian. As you were. As we thought. Relax.

"On count 2, have you reached a verdict on which you are all
agreed?"

"Yes."

Guilty of the abduction of James Bulger, both of them.

"On count 3, have you reached a verdict on which you are all
agreed?"

"Yes."

"Do you find the defendant Robert Thompson guilty or not
guilty of the murder of James Bulger?"

"Guilty."

"Do you find the defendant Jon Venables guilty or not guilty of
the murder of James Bulger?"

"Guilty."

"And is that the verdict of you all?"

"It is."

"Yes," someone shouts from the public gallery, a Bulger relation
punching the air. Jon cries. His parents cry. Albert Kirby walks to
the gallery, leans over, kisses Denise. Robert doesn't cry but is
taking deep breaths, traumatized, hyperventilating. Down below,
Ann, asthmatic, her legs buckling under her, hasn't been able to
climb the stairs in time for the verdict. Now she's been told and is
crying. When Robert's brought down he hugs her and cries too.

Some minutes later the judge calls everyone back to pass
sentence on the boys: "The killing of James Bulger was an act
of unparalleled evil and barbarity . . . The sentence that I pass
upon you is that you shall be detained during Her Majesty's
Pleasure, in such a place and under such conditions as the Secretary of State may direct, and that means that you will be securely
detained for very, very many years, until the Home Secretary is
satisfied that you have matured and are fully rehabilitated and are
no longer a danger to others." Her Majesty's Pleasure. HMP, as T
& V have already learned to call it. They hang their heads and try
not to cry too freely. Her Majesty would not take pleasure in the

sight of them now. The Bulgers aside, no one could. The judge says: "Let them be taken down."

The boys are taken down. "How do you feel now, you little bastards?" shouts Ray Matthews, Denise's brother, as they go. The words will look much worse in tomorrow's headlines than they sound here. In Scouse, "little bastards" is how you might address two kids who've kicked a football through your window, not affectionate exactly, but acknowledging that this is what kids are like. Even "evil" has this level of acceptance: you wouldn't have to murder to be called it; you'd only have, occasionally, to be bad.

With the boys out of the way, the judge addresses the court, adult to adult, just as it's been all along. "It is not for me to pass judgement on their upbringing, but I suspect that exposure to violent video films may in part be an explanation. In fairness to Mrs Thompson and Mr and Mrs Venables, it is very much to their credit that during the police interviews they used every effort to get their sons to tell the truth. The people of Bootle and Walton and all involved in this tragic case will never forget the tragic circumstances of James Bulger's murder. The Bulger family have the sympathy of us all, and everyone in court will especially wish Mrs Bulger well in the months ahead and hope that her new baby will bring her peace and happiness. I hope that all closely involved in this case, whether as witnesses or otherwise, will find peace at Christmas time."

We file out a last time from the chamber of dead judges. No sign of Christmas stars overhead, but I see what the judge means, to invoke a message of hope and healing, of good will to all men. His earlier words are hard to fit with this. "Unparalleled evil and barbarity"? Horrendously cruel, certainly, but "unparalleled evil"? For nearly a month, Michael Morland has seemed kindly, liberal. Now the wolf hiding under his robe has bared its teeth. But it could be that he is coming on strong to keep the tabloids happy, and to appease the relatives of James Bulger. Only the sentence he recommends will show him for what he is. How long does he intend "very very many years" to be?

Robert Thompson and Jon Venables were released in June 2001, having served less than eight years of their sentences. Both were promised lifelong anonymity.

WILLIAM HERBERT WALLACE

(Liverpool, 1931)

W. H. Wallace

In the days of capital punishment, few lived to tell the story of their own murder trial. William Herbert Wallace, an unprepossessing insurance agent accused of murdering his wife, was convicted by a sleepy Liverpool jury against the weight of the evidence. From the condemned cell, he was whisked to London and the appeal court, where his conviction was quashed. This was the first time that this had happened in a murder trial. Indeed the Wallace case was remarkable in many ways: it was a baffling murder, in the view of the trial judge Mr Justice Wright, "almost unexampled in the annals of crime". Crime writer Raymond Chandler called it the "impossible murder", and declared the case "unbeatable". More than seventy years on, the killing of Julia Wallace, with its cat's cradle of alibis, possibilities, times and places, remains as impenetrable as ever, a haunting mystery that transcends the tragic ordinariness of domestic murder. This is partly because the story has a riveting symmetry (a set of agreed facts that can logically support two mutually exclusive solutions) and partly because of the strange personality of Wallace himself. A bookish adherent of Stoicism, he claimed to have been lured on a wild goose chase across Liverpool by a caller who'd telephoned his chess club the night before, giving the name of R. M. Qualtrough. Qualtrough had left a message asking Wallace to call on him at 25 Menlove Gardens East to discuss some insurance business. Wallace set out to keep the appointment, but found that although there were Menlove Gardens North, South and West, there was no East. He returned home to find his wife battered to death on the parlour rug. The case became a public obsession, with opinion split between those who believed Wallace had been duped by a cunning but unknown killer masquerading as Qualtrough, and those who believed that Wallace himself had murdered his wife, devising a split-second plan to give himself just enough time to beat out his wife's brains before setting out on the fool's errand to Menlove Gardens that would furnish an alibi. The police arrested him after a blundering investigation and, after a four-day trial, Wallace was convicted and sentenced to death. No convincing motive was adduced. The packed court greeted the verdict with astonishment, the press was swamped with protest letters, and the Bishop of Liverpool ordered a special prayer to be said for Wallace's deliverance. In the event, he was freed on appeal, the first occasion on which the appeal court judges had overturned a jury verdict in a murder case. Although Wallace (b. 1879) was an inveterate diarist, he appears to have left it to others to chronicle his story for publication. This unique account of his trial and subsequent appeal was almost certainly the work of a Fleet Street "ghost".

It is difficult for me to describe the feelings of an innocent man about to be put on trial for his life. There can be no position in human experience so terrible. Not to be able to convince one's fellows of the truth is a desperate sensation. What does it count if one has been a truthful man all one's life? No torture of the Inquisition could have rivalled this appalling sensation of a rat in a trap.

The assizes opened on the Monday. I was brought down from Walton Jail along with other prisoners to the Court in that gruesome "Black Maria" and placed in a cell below. At half past ten all the prisoners were taken up and stood by some stairs near the prisoners' entrance to the court, there to await the decision of the Grand Jury. It was an anxious time for me for there was some considerable opinion that my "bill" would be thrown out. But it was not until after five o'clock in the afternoon that my solicitor came to me and informed me that the Grand Jury had returned a "True Bill" and that the hearing of the case had been fixed for the following Wednesday week. This meant a return to Walton Jail and a resumption of the old dreary waiting for yet another ten days. Fate seem to be conspiring against me.

The actual day arrived and once more I was taken to the court in readiness for the opening. I hadn't the slightest idea how an assize trial was conducted and in spite of the ordeal before me I was interested to see what it was like. Two warders – I believe they much prefer to be called "officers"! – stood with me at the foot of some steps leading to the dock and from this position I could hear the jury being sworn in. I could see nothing except the ceiling of the court but part of the oath administered to each juryman came to my ears distinctly and because of its reiteration has fixed itself in my memory. "And true deliverance make before our Sovereign Lord the King." The words "true deliverance" rang in my ears with a soothing sound. That is what I wanted. The truth – a true deliverance out of this hell . . . And then came the words of the clerk of the court – or so I judged him to be.

"Put up Wallace!"

Immediately I was ushered up those steps and took my stand in a sort of wooden pen surrounded by an iron rail. The judge and his retinue had not yet come into court.

The clerk asked me if I had objection to make to any of the jury. I spoke to my solicitor who sat just below me and queried if there *was* any objection I should make but he told me none.

"Silence!" rang out in stentorian tones and the crowded court stood up to attention. A door opened behind the bench and a little procession entered. It struck me as slightly theatrical for first came a man bearing a white wand, then the sheriff and his chaplain, followed by the judge himself, Mr Justice Wright, in his scarlet trappings and goat-hair wig.

It is given to very few to describe what one sees from the dock. It is a position or point of view no one should envy but it has advantages. Facing me, on a level with my eyes, was the bench, his Lordship being directly opposite. On the left in two pews boxed in were the twelve good men and true (two as a matter of fact were women), and I should like to put on record here and now that never in my life had I ever imagined any jury of my fellow men could appear so utterly stupid. Twelve blank, unintelligent, and, as it proved, unfriendly faces. I have since been told that spectators in court described them as "twelve morons" and "not an ounce of real intelligence or sense amongst the lot of them." It is an Englishman's privilege to be tried by his peers, i.e. his equals;

if those people were classed as my equals, mentally at least. I feel that all my studies and thinking have gone for nothing. How juries are chosen I do not know; that they are chosen with little regard to their mentality was to me painfully obvious.

Behind me I was conscious of a packed court. The public interest in my case was very great. I have since heard that a queue formed outside the court in the early hours every morning!

It is strange how my eyes did not single out individuals. My brother, who had come all the way from the Malay States to be with me through this ordeal, sat in the well of the court below me side by side with my solicitors and his was, probably, the only face I particularised. The press box situated above the jury box was packed with reporters. Looking at their keen faces I could have wished that those two boxes had been transposed!

With a rustle of his stuff gown, the Clerk of the Assize rose.

"William Herbert Wallace, you stand charged upon the Indictment for that you on the 20th day of January in the present year at Liverpool in this county murdered Julia Wallace. Are you guilty or not guilty?"

"Not guilty."

I meant to make my reply as emphatic as possible. If it were only possible to make the truth sound true! People talk glibly about "words ringing true". But do they?

I had determined that nothing should cause me to show emotion; that this vile and unjust charge should be met with all the dignity I could command.

The jurors' names were then called over and they were sworn in. I fancy that the formula which I imagined I had heard while waiting below the dock was the one now made. But that phrase "true deliverance make before our Sovereign Lord the King" has so stuck in my mind that now I am not sure at what moment of my trial they were uttered.

The Clerk of the Assize then turned to the jury.

"Gentlemen of the Jury, the prisoner at the Bar, William Herbert Wallace, stands charged upon the Indictment for that he on the 20th day of January in the present year at Liverpool in this county murdered Julia Wallace. To this Indictment he has pleaded not guilty. Your duty is to say whether he be guilty or not and to hearken to the evidence."

These archaic forms gave me an odd sense of amusement. It seemed so ridiculous that they should be said over me.

The counsel for the prosecution was on his feet. Mr Hemmerde K C began to outline the case against me. It all sounded so futile, so absurd, so much waste of time. The very idea that I could have ever raised my hand to any women, and particularly my wife, was monstrous. The main contention of the police was that *I* had sent the telephone message to myself at the Chess Club so as to set up an alibi the following night. That, without the shadow of any conceivable motive, I had murdered my wife, using an iron bar or poker which couldn't be found.

The question of time put the police in a quandary for it was proved positively by the police themselves that my wife had been seen alive at half past six and that I had left the house no later than a quarter to seven. There being no bloodstains found on my clothes, boots, or person, no finger-prints anywhere, and no bloodstains or smears anywhere in the house except in the sitting-room where my poor wife had been done to death, taxed their ingenuity to suggest how I had actually committed the crime. It was necessary for them to make some reconstruction of the crime and Mr Hemmerde made an extraordinary and fantastic suggestion which to any intelligent mind was not only most improbable but humanly impossible. The suggestion was that *I had been stark naked, attired only in my mackintosh, and that before leaving the house I must have had a bath and put on my clothes*. But this ingenious theory hardly fitted in with the condition of the bathroom which, on their own showing, showed no signs of having been used. Even the towel was quite dry and, as stated before, no trace of blood was found. (It is quite evident to me that the murderer did not go upstairs at all.) Later in the evidence the time named, viz, fifteen minutes, in which I had to do all these things was still further reduced to *ten minutes* or even less and accepted by the judge. I leave it to all men with any thinking capacity at all whether any human being could have committed an atrocious crime, arranged a "faked" burglary, taken a bath, put on a full suit of clothes, socks, and boots, got rid of an incriminating weapon, and been out of the house without leaving so much as a trace *in ten minutes*. In addition, would a premeditating murderer, having arranged an elaborate alibi, leave himself a bare ten minutes in which to commit the crime? But the jury apparently thought that they themselves could have managed this most marvellous feat!

Another puzzle was the fact that my mackintosh was found under the shoulders of my wife, badly burnt at the bottom and heavily blood-stained. The front of my wife's skirt was also burnt and the prosecution saw no way out than that my wife, being struck, had fallen on the gas fire. But if the murderer had been wearing the mackintosh how had it become burnt also? I was as much surprised as anyone and could not agree to the suggestion of my own counsel that my wife had thrown the mackintosh over her shoulders to go to the door to admit – whoever she did admit. It was a thing I had never known her to do and I could not imagine her doing it. But I confess that my poor brain could invent no other possible alternative to that theory. I can't imagine what the murderer was doing with it or how it came to be burnt, unless it had been worn in some way by my wife. An odd and most amazing point was pressed by the police. I had told four people, three of them being policemen, that the mackintosh was mine; on being asked a fifth time by other detectives and replying "If it has two patches it is mine," I was supposed to be hesitating, hedging, or something equally futile. Why or for what purpose, the learned counsel under pressure was forced to admit he didn't know. Even the judge wondered what it was supposed to prove or disprove. (Later, in the Court of Criminal Appeal, the three judges swept it aside as irrelevant.)

This was an example of the stupid points out of which the police tried to pin this abominable and dastardly crime on me. They endeavoured to twist every little fact to fit their preconceived theory. Mountains were deliberately manufactured out of mole-hills, my simplest action was invested with sinister significance, coloured and exaggerated to an almost amusing extent. Wiping my eyes in broad daylight in the street at least *four* hours before the crime could possibly have been committed was solemnly put forward as the most damning evidence – I suppose of remorse *before* commission of the deed! (The prosecution had to drop this later!) And yet these points appear to have been swallowed by the jury, hook, line, and sinker.

And there I had to sit in that dock and listen to this weaving of coincidences, suggestions, theories, perhaps, ifs, and might be's, none of which had the slightest weight as evidence, without being able to reply in any way or protest. A hundred times I wanted to shout out a refutation of some vile suggestion. It seemed to me then and it still is a firm conviction that the prosecution was vindictive and was pressing every conceivable and inconceivable point with "malevolence" – a word used by my counsel in the Court of

Appeal. And all this desperate struggle to saddle me with a foul murder after the prosecution had been forced to admit, reluctantly I am certain, that my relationship with my wife had been blissfully happy for the whole time of my married life, *seventeen* years, that there was an entire lack of motive – my bank balance being satisfactory, no life insurance on my wife except one for £20, no other woman in the background, and my business affairs in strict and correct order . . . And *every* point in what was called evidence against *me* fitted the alternative theory of the crime having been committed by some other man whose motive was, obviously, that of robbery.

The examination and cross-examination of the witnesses for the prosecution who were, with the exception of the police officials, all entirely in my favour, took the whole of two days. Each night I was taken back to Walton Jail but on these occasions the routine in the reception-room was omitted.

The third day was occupied by the examination and cross-examination of myself in the witness-box and other witnesses called for the defence. I had been led to believe that cross-examination was an ordeal to be dreaded but I should like to affirm that any witness telling the truth need not have the slightest fear. Far from being an ordeal to me, I welcomed the opportunity of reiterating the truth. No truthful person need fear the questions of an examining counsel, be he ever so clever.

Nothing at all transpired to uphold or strengthen that amazing theory of the police. The opinion of everyone in court with the exception of the jury who were, all too obviously, a class mentally apart from the normal run of humanity and prejudiced by unfounded rumours long before ever they were called upon to serve, was that there was no evidence to go before a jury and that the case should have been dismissed forthwith. However, my counsel, who concluded that the judge would direct the jury (which in effect he did!), did not claim that there was no case; and, having called witnesses in addition to his client, myself, had by law to address the jury first. He, too, was conscious of a certain hostility when speaking. This was on the morning of Saturday, the fourth day of hearing. Mr Hemmerde followed for the prosecution and reiterated in the strongest language and with the utmost force at his command the totally unsupported theory of the police.

Mr Justice Wright then summed up and, without definitely instructing the jury to acquit, made it perfectly evident that the crime on the evidence before them could not be brought home to *anyone*. He said with meaning: "Was it possible that Mr Wallace could have done all that the police say he had to do in the limited time of ten minutes? Was it possible?" He also touched on the telephone call on which the police based their case. They had affirmed that whoever sent that message was the murderer. The judge suggested that it had not been proved that I had sent it and if I had not "there was an end of the case". Mr Beattie, the member of the Chess Club who had taken the message and had held a comparatively long conversation with the speaker, the man who called himself Qualtrough, had stated that by no stretch of imagination could the voice be said to be that of Mr Wallace.

No summing-up, to my mind, could have been fairer or more indicative of the judge's personal view. I should like to put on record that I have no fault whatever to find in Mr Justice Wright's able conduct of the case or of his summing-up. Short of actually instructing the jury to acquit, he was all that I could have wished my judge to be.

The jury retired, and I was taken down the steps to the corridor below the court. Then began a distressing period of nerve-strain. As the minutes dragged by and I was not called up I began to wonder what the jury were discussing. It seemed to be impossible that any human beings could hesitate for a single moment. One of my warders suggested that they were having a meal! After all, it was close upon two o'clock when they retired.

My solicitor came down and I told him that I did not feel any great confidence as the whole attitude of the jury had appeared to me distinctly hostile. In fact, one of the jurymen during Mr Roland Oliver's final speech had interjected a remark definitely antagonistic to my counsel's argument. And the fact that they were remaining out of court for so prolonged a period was surely against my interests and boded ill for me. My anticipations proved to be all too correct.

Forty minutes crept slowly on leaden feet and then the summons came. Once more I stood within that railed dock. The judge and his retinue entered.

How can I describe my feelings then? One idea was dominant in my brain – to retain my dignity whatever the verdict might be. The injustice of the charge against me had made me bitter and my soul seemed to have coagulated to hard steel. I could feel emotion no more. Never again should I be able to trust my fellow men. This was a world of evil into which by some strange chance I had wandered. I was a stranger here; I did not belong.

The court was tense and deathly silent as the Clerk of Assize turned to the jury.

"Gentlemen of the Jury, are you agreed upon your verdict?"

"We are."

"Do you find the prisoner at the bar, William Herbert Wallace, guilty or not guilty?"

A terrible pause – a blank nothingness – in which all the world stood still.

"*Guilty*!"

Even at that awful moment I could hear a tone of grim satisfaction, almost of pride in that foreman's voice; a note of jubilance . . . Then throughout the court, before and behind me, rushed one great gasp of absolute amazement. Even the Clerk of Assize looked dumbfounded. I have since learnt that all those sitting on the bench, sheriff, chaplain, clerks, and even the judge, were shocked at the unexpected verdict.

If I had any feelings they were those which one might imagine a fly would have, caught in a web and unable to break loose. Fate had been physically unkind to me all my life. This was only one more knock.

Then, after what seemed an age of suspended animation, the Clerk of Assize turned towards me.

"William Herbert Wallace, you stand convicted of wilful murder. Have you anything to say why judgment of death should not be pronounced upon you according to law?"

What could I say? I am told that what I actually said was –

"*I am innocent; I can say no more.*"

But to this moment I do not know what I said. I was looking into a blank space. I did not see the judge's clerk place a square of black silk on the crown of his Lordship's wig or the chaplain rise and move towards the judge's right hand.

Mr Justice Wright made not the slightest comment but in a slow and rather low voice pronounced sentence of death. This came to my ears from far away though his tones must have impinged on my brain since I can now recall every word.

"The sentence of the Court upon you is that you be taken from this place to a lawful prison, and then to a place of execution, and that you be hanged by the neck until you be dead, and that your body be afterwards buried within the precincts of the prison wherein you shall have been last confined before your execution. And may the Lord have mercy upon your soul.''

The chaplain's "Amen!" came in the faintest whisper.

Without giving me time to pause. I was hustled down the steps and into a cell below where my dinner was brought to me. I could not even look at it. My whole being was sick with despair. The shadow of the gallows was black and very close. Already I could feel the rasp of a rope about my neck.

In about an hour's time I was rushed back to Walton Jail and this time taken direct to the cell reserved for those prisoners condemned to death. I was surrounded by officials and compelled to change into the grey convict uniform prescribed by law. The broad arrow so familiar with fiction readers and habitues of cinemas has long since been done away with. This brought home to me with savage grimness the hopelessness of my position and for the first time since my committal I broke down completely and wept.

I found I was to be under the constant eye of two officers, day and night, who would live with me in the cell . . . until a certain morning at eight o'clock. These death watchmen kept guard in pair and in eight-hour stretches.

The chief officer and the governor of the prison came in shortly and asked if there was anything they could do for me, but all I wanted was to be left alone in my misery and despair.

The size of the main cell was some thirteen feet by ten or eleven. A small adjoining cell contained a bath, lavatory, and wash-basin, and a gas-ring on which to boil a kettle. The main cell contained a bed, a fair sized table, and three "easy" armchairs. The floor was of stone tiles covered with a carpet which had obviously seen service in an ordinary room some otherwhere. The walls were white distempered. From this cell a door led into another and smaller cell where I was allowed to see visitors. "To see visitors" is a literal expression since no one was permitted to come within arm's length of a prisoner condemned to death. The reason, of course, is obvious. A weapon or poison might be smuggled to the prisoner – and the law is ever jealous of its prey! The visitor sat in another cell. A glass window surrounded by close-meshed double wire gauze through which conversation was perfectly audible was let into the wall between. The two warders always sat with me and the visitor had one attendant officer.

During the long night I tossed and turned on my bed but could not sleep. There were the two grim sentinels of death – sitting in easy chairs reading. The light came from outside the cell through thick glass let into slots in the walls. Novels were brought in from the library. Friends sent scientific books for me to read and I had a number of my own brought in later. The literary taste of the prison officials did not apparently rise beyond the level of the ordinary novel, although one or two were of superior education.

There was a complete change in diet and the restrictions under which I had previously suffered. The medical officer now permitted me to have all I might reasonably desire in the way of varied food. And to my astonishment I was now permitted to smoke a daily allowance of ten cigarettes. Smoking was absolutely forbidden in every other part of the prison by prisoners. To have a single cigarette, even a shred of tobacco, on one's person was a heinous offence for which one might suffer the most drastic penalties. But to a man with only three clear Sundays to live, most restrictions are cancelled.

I could write as many letters as I pleased, subject to the usual censorship regulations. A chessboard and men were brought in and I taught one warder the rudiments of the game. Ring board and quoits were two games I played with my lawful guardians in the cell.

From Saturday when I was sentenced to death until midday on Monday, I lived in a state of extreme nervous strain. I was frightfully agitated mentally. The most appalling shock of all came when the governor visited me and announced that the date for my execution had been officially fixed for Tuesday, 12 May . . . From that moment I was dazed. It struck me that although one heard so much of "the law's delay", in my case the law had lost no time. It seemed as if the law was eager and panting for my blood.

Hope sprang to life again when my solicitors brought me the news that an appeal was to be formulated and sent in. There is no anodyne in all the science of narcotics quite so satisfying as hope; it gave me at least much peace and quietness of mind. It seemed to be totally impossible that three great wise judges, learned in the law, with only the bare facts of the case before them, and free from any trace of rancour, prejudice, or evil rumour, could do otherwise than set me free.

The routine of a condemned man's last days of life begins with breakfast at about 7 a.m. In my case this consisted of porridge and milk, bacon and eggs, tea and bread and butter. I made my own bed. I am not sure if I was compelled to do this but having done it for so long in the hospital dormitory I continued the labour. Then would follow a friendly chat with the changed guard who had relieved the other two watchers at half past six. Sometimes we talked about books, about my case, and I realised that they believed I was an innocent man. Of course, the regulations did not permit them to express any opinion but it would be a poor psychologist who could not read what was in their minds. This friendly attitude was a great solace to me and I could not have desired a better set of jailers. I am certain that only the most inhuman type of man could find any pleasure in such an occupation.

About eight o'clock one of the chief officers would look in and just voice the inquiry: "Everything all right?" At nine-thirty the medical officer would come along with a similar query: "Everything all right? Anything I can do? Anything you want?" After his visit we were left alone for about an hour and usually the two warders and I had a little competition with the ring-board game, and I may state – with a certain amount of justifiable pride – that I was never beaten in that death cell.

Between ten-thirty and eleven o'clock, the governor of the jail accompanied by one of the chief officers would come into the cell and make a kindly inquiry: "Anything you want? Sure you're quite all right? Anything I can do for you?"

From that time until twelve o'clock we might settle down to reading. Midday brought dinner which might be boiled mutton, cabbage, potatoes. Here I might mention that I was not allowed the use of a knife or fork; every thing was cut up for me and I was only permitted the use of a spoon . . . How jealous the law is of its prey! . . . A good-sized rice pudding completed the meal. Another day it might be beef or minced meat or a stew, and the vegetables, too, would be varied. But *always* rice pudding!

After dinner, half an hour's walk in some quiet portion of the grounds usually alongside what is known as the Ropery. On this walk there was a long narrow garden built up against the wall and here were planted lupins, hollyhocks, irises, delphiniums, and other flowers. The irises during my last walk there were just about to burst into flower and I used to wonder if I should see them in full bloom and if they would be the last flowers I should ever see on this earth.

Back to the cell; more reading and a change of guard at half past two. When I took a bath the warders would stand just without the open door of the little cell, making themselves as unobtrusive as the regulations permitted. Indeed, in every way, they were as courteous as I could desire.

About three my visitors usually arrived and I was allowed a half hour's interview each day. The result of such kindly visits was an uplift of my spirits. Confidence in my innocence expressed by their presence and work progressing towards my appeal built up my hopes again and again.

Tea came along at four o'clock – incidentally this meal is libellously called supper in prison! – and consisted of a plate of bread and butter, a boiled egg, a small portion of jam (I preferred Damson – and Damson it was!) and a quart of tea in a large jug. The crockery necessary for all meals was kept in the main cell and I myself did the washing-up. The warders, who brought their meals with them, often joined me, and very often handed me pieces of cake. As the quantity of food supplied was generally more than plenty, I frequently saved some to eat at a later hour, making use of the kettle to reheat the tea or brew some fresh from the officers' private store.

Weather permitting, another walk of an hour's duration followed this afternoon "supper". I might mention here that before leaving my cell every precaution was taken to see that all other prisoners were safe in their cells, and no one with the exception of the uniformed staff ever succeeded in catching a glimpse of me. The authorities were most particular in this matter. A second visit from the governor and the doctor followed.

On returning to my cell at approximately six to half past. I might play a game of chess or ring quoits, or we might all sit quietly reading until any time after eight o'clock. At that time we usually had a cup of tea together with whatever I had reserved from tea-time. Many topics were discussed between us. The officers would recount to me many interesting episodes of the life in the service, but carefully avoided anything which might in any way hurt my feelings or intensify the dreadful prospect in front of me.

At half past ten another change of guard took place, the last for the day. In the death cell a prisoner is permitted to retire to bed just when he likes, and being by custom somewhat of a late bird I availed myself of the privilege. In moments of despondency which would persist in recurring, I felt my days were growing short and endeavoured to make each individual one as long as possible.

This, then, was the general routine of each and every day, though very often I had a prolonged spell of letter-writing or reading.

My appeal was formally handed in to the governor of the prison on the tenth day after my conviction, this being the last day permissible. My solicitors had brought the appeal first to me to read and for my signature to be appended.

A fortnight elapsed, during which time I received an official notification from the Clerk of the Court of Criminal Appeal that my appeal had been lodged. This information, of course, came to me through the governor. Later I learnt that the date of hearing was fixed for Monday 18 May. Two or three days prior to this date I was notified that I should be taken to Pentonville Jail, London. I dreaded the ordeal of that journey for I knew that I should have to travel all the way in handcuffs, and I had a natural dislike amounting to horror of being gaped upon by the curious and morbid public.

I travelled to Pentonville on the sixteenth of May, attired in my own clothes, with two uniformed officers. I was taken in a taxi to the railway station and into a compartment reserved for the purpose. A few station officials and a mere handful of the public had got wind of my prospective movements and had no difficulty in catching sight of me as I was hurried across the platform.

Arriving at Euston, by a similar process I was carried to Pentonville. The prison loomed grim and grey before me as I entered it. The very name sent a shudder through me. Here I was taken to the customary reception office. On the floor in front of me was spread a large, coarse white sheet. On this stood a small deal chair. I was ordered to strip myself completely. I knew there was no alternative. Silently I discarded my clothing, article by article, feeling utterly dejected and depressed. Nothing lowers a man's pride and dignity as this enforced disrobing. In front of me stood the official whose duty it was to search me, together with the chief officer and the deputy-governor of the prison.

Once stripped, a revolting and degrading search of my person was made. My hair was combed thoroughly, hands passed over my ears, under my armpits, down my legs, under the soles of my feet, and even between my toes. Let it be remembered that I had just arrived from another prison where I had been under the strictest observation for three weeks, handcuffed and in the presence of two warders all the way from Liverpool, and then ask what on earth they expected to find I had or could possibly have secreted about my person.

However, the ordeal was soon over and then a blue suit of clothes was more or less pitched at me. I dressed as well as I could. The clothes were the same old, ill-fitting, rough, degrading garments I had worn at Walton Jail, the only difference being that now the colour was blue instead of grey. All this in utter silence on my part.

I was then marched off to the condemned cell which was to all intents and purposes a replica of the one I had left at Walton. I thought that this cell must be haunted with the ghosts of other poor fellows who had passed through the same tragic and terrifying ordeal. Something of their mortal agony seemed to cling to the very walls. The atmosphere was pregnant with their tears and heartache. Actually in the very next cell was a case similar to my own. A much younger man, indeed a mere boy, was awaiting his appeal which was to take place on the same day as my own. I know since that his case, poor unfortunate fellow, was dismissed, and in these days of my own freedom I can realise as no other man can what he must have suffered during those last days on earth.

Again I had the same routine day as at Walton. Close observation by night and day, similar food; but there was a difference for I knew I had no more than two or three days to remain in Pentonville.

All through that weekend I was in a state of distressful anxiety and the nearer the time came the more apprehensive I became. It was actually a *relief* when preparations were made to take me down to the Court of Criminal Appeal. I cannot recall what my sensations were when I was ushered in to that final court of all. I knew it was to be all – or nothing.

There was a great difference in the atmosphere of this court and that of the assize court in Liverpool. What I did feel was that here, if nowhere else, my case would be fairly tried, without prejudice, without conflicting rumours, without the dramatic witness-box or the forensic melodrama of the prosecuting counsel. I knew that the evidence for and against me would be weighed with studied accuracy and impartiality on the scales of justice . . . And with thoughts like these I entered my railed-off gallery, tense and expectant.

To the right of me – the three supreme judges of the land, attired in their robes of scarlet and hoods of silk. Below me, the court official solicitors and barristers. Behind these, my many friends who had come up from Liverpool to support me with their presence and their confidence in my innocence. Beyond – the public gallery packed to suffocation with, as I have since learned, much of the light and learning of the City of London. Literary celebrities, actors, and other cultivated people were there, feeling, no doubt, that this was a case which might very well make history.

Mr Roland Oliver K C, my counsel, opened up the grounds on which my appeal was based. In a masterly speech of over five hours' duration, he outlined the whole of the evidence from the first word to the last. It was a complete analysis of the salient points. It was evident to me as well as to everyone in court that the three judges were conversant with the whole case from beginning to end. They were never at a loss as to which page of the transcription of the notes certain evidence appeared. This impressed me with the care and study these three great judges must have exercised in reviewing the case. What few questions they put – and each spoke as the point occurred to him – seemed to me to touch the very core of the facts presented.

At the close of my counsel's speech, the court adjourned until the next morning, when Mr Hemmerde K C opened the case for the prosecution. From the first it was evident that he was floundering in very deep waters. Here was no jury of "morons" to be swayed by rhetoric or histrionic display. The brandishing of an assumed model of the weapon used by the murderer would have left the eminence of jurisdiction completely cold. Here, crystal clear logic and proved fact alone told. The evidence was so obviously strained, bolstered up, and essentially feeble, that many times the judges pulled the counsel up in his stride, demanding to know just exactly what he was trying to prove. The telephone call and the mackintosh, and my own very natural behaviour, with which he had made such play at the assize court and on which, mainly, the police had based their case, were almost contemptuously brushed aside by one or other of the judges.

For something like four hours Mr Hemmerde battled with his feeble arguments – they were all broken reeds – and then he sat down.

The three judges bent over towards each other and conversed for a few moments. At length, the Lord Chief Justice announced that they would retire for a short while – and I was taken out of the court into the corridor behind. I learned then that this retirement was almost unprecedented. Again the same strain of waiting, the anxiety, the mental torture, but this time I felt that the delay was all in my favour, in striking contrast to my feeling when the jury retired at the Liverpool assizes.

Five and forty minutes I waited, pacing that bare corridor in grim suspense. Then came the summons.

The court was hushed to an almost uncanny silence. No one coughed. No one moved. Not a paper rustled. The very breathing of all there seemed suspended.

The three supreme judges came in, with slow dignity. Their faces were as grave and grey as tombstones. The Sphinx in the desert was not more solemn and immobile.

Again that determination swept over me to maintain my composure in the face of the public. It had become an obsession. I would not show emotion of any kind, least of all fear. I did not – of that I have been assured.

With what seemed callous deliberation, the Lord Chief Justice of England began to speak. I know now that every sentence had to be taken down for the purpose of reference in future cases. The judgment of that Court of Appeal may be quoted a century from now. But at the time, the careful weighing of words and sentences, the long pauses, the unemotion of that even voice, the almost icy mechanism of his diction, kept all hearers strained and tense. To almost his Lordship's last word, the issue seemed to be in doubt.

My brain refused to register that voice any longer. Only disjointed fragments penetrated my consciousness. I could not see. The same blankness rose up before me. And then . . . what was he saying?

"We are not concerned with theories however ingenious or with suspicions however strong . . . We do not find that the evidence . . . was sufficient. Therefore . . . this appeal . . . must be . . . upheld . . . and the conviction . . . quashed!"

I have been asked so many times just what I felt at that supreme moment. I cannot attempt to define them. I could not if I would. The weight of the whole universe which had been pressing the life out of me was magically lifted. My ears heard the song of birds and I saw a kaleidoscope of glorious colours.

I was free! Free to go out into the world, free to breathe the wild winds of the heavens, free to walk the streets that seemed in my imagination as soft and fragrant as the fields.

Of all the riotous excitement of my friends I cannot adequately write. They are my friends; through all my long ordeal they proved that fact. The know how much I think of them.

This case, I am given to understand, is now the only one on record in which a jury's verdict in a murder trial has been reversed on point of fact. I am, too, I believe, the only man condemned to death for whom prayers have been offered in an English Cathedral. So perhaps my sufferings have somehow been worth while. At least, I have made history!

What remains? I am free to live, to take up – if it were possible – the thread of my life. But there is a brutal murderer at large. Who is he? Where is he? Who was that man of mystery in the telephone box? Who was this masquerader, Qualtrough? Who was the man of blood whose face must have been familiar to my poor wife and whose voice would have been recognised by me? Who was it who knew the routine of my business and exactly where I kept my weekly collections of cash? Who plotted this vile crime and was content to let an innocent man go to the gallows in his stead? There is an old saying that "murder will out" . . . Time alone will show.

Wallace died less than two years later, in 1933, of chronic kidney disease. No one was ever brought to book for his wife's murder. Wallace's own theory was that a young man called Gordon Parry had killed Julia in the course of a bungled robbery. But Parry was fireproof: he was well-connected in Liverpool circles and his girlfriend, Lily Lloyd, told police he was with her at the time of the murder. Shortly after Wallace's death, when Parry jilted her, she offered to swear an affidavit repudiating the alibi, but nothing came of it. Gordon Parry himself died in 1980.

CAROLYN WARMUS

(White Plains, NY, 1991–2)

Albert Borowitz

The trials of Carolyn Warmus are a chilling illustration of how a woman can be gripped by a deadly and destructive obsession in her determination to have the man she craved at any price. At her first trial, the prosecutor declared that Warmus was driven by a "consuming passion to possess", echoing newspaper comment that likened the case to the recent hit film Fatal Attraction. *The Warmus trials are treated here by Albert Borowitz (b. 1930), undoubtedly America's finest historian of true crime. A practising attorney in Cleveland, Ohio, for more than forty years, Borowitz in retirement has continued to build on his pre-eminent reputation as an artful analyst of crime literature. His characteristic literary genre is the true-crime essay, a form that links his writings to those of classic authors such as Thomas de Quincey. Borowitz suffuses his crime writings with literary allusions while keeping a firm grasp on trial tactics and a rigorous regard for the evidence.*

Even before the facts were known in detail, journalists as well as the police had decided that the case of Carolyn Warmus showed that Nature was up to her old trick of imitating Art. Within days of Warmus's indictment in February 1990 for the murder of her lover's wife, Betty Jeanne Solomon, a year before, the press labeled the prosecution a real-life "Fatal Attraction" case, identifying the defendant with the character played frighteningly by Glenn Close in the popular 1987 movie that happened to have been filmed in Westchester County, to the north of New York City, where Mrs Solomon was killed. In the view of *New York Times* film critic Caryn James, it was "safe to guess that Glenn Close made Carolyn Warmus the celebrity she is today."

The parallel that reporters drew between the murder of Betty Jeanne Solomon and the *Fatal Attraction* film was hard to resist, because the police and the prosecution shaped the image of blonde Carolyn Warmus as a woman obsessed with her former lover, Paul Solomon, who had wanted the freedom to move on to other infidelities. The police investigators released stories that Warmus had, since her college years, established a pattern of pursuing married or unavailable men.

The daughter of a wealthy insurance executive, Warmus grew up in suburban Detroit and received her undergraduate degree in psychology from the University of Michigan. Her classmates recalled that she took her dates with Paul Laven, a pre-med teaching assistant, so seriously that she became a convert to his religion, Judaism. When, however, Laven broke off the relationship and became engaged to another woman, Warmus undertook a relentless campaign to win him back. She called the couple and left long messages on their answering machine, annoyed their friends, and deluged them with notes. One message, left on the windshield of Laven's car, falsely claimed that Carolyn was pregnant and begged him to call her. Another, sent to Laven's fiancée and filled with misspellings to disguise Warmus's authorship, insisted that the woman stood no chance of competing with Carolyn's more voluptuous figure and newly-acquired tan. Finally, the couple were forced to obtain a restraining order against their persecutor in a Michigan court to ensure that she would not attempt to ruin their wedding.

After her college graduation, Carolyn Warmus moved to New York City, where she earned a master's degree in education from Teacher's College at Columbia University and went on to serve as a substitute in school districts of Westchester County for teachers who were on maternity leaves. In the New York area the skein of romantic fixations that had begun back home in Michigan continued to lengthen. She hired a private detective, Vincent Parco, to trail a married New Jersey bartender whose affection for her had slackened. Together, she and Parco devised the idea of superimposing photographs of Warmus in sexy poses upon pictures of the bartender, apparently with the intention of mailing the resulting montages to his wife. Parco was just the man for such a deception, since he taught a Learning Annex course to aspiring snoops, entitled "How to Get Anything on Anybody". Inculcating the priceless lessons of his craft in classes held on the premises of Manhattan's swanky Birch Wathen School, Parco taught his students how to hide a video camera in a purse or a looseleaf notebook, and how to obtain unlisted telephone numbers by consulting reverse directories or examining registration records at the Board of Elections.

The collaboration of Warmus with Parco was a blending of kindred spirits, because the young teacher was herself adept in fraud and forgery. She successfully carried off her first swindle after graduation from college, when she was working as a waitress at the Jukebox, a popular 1950s-style dance club in Royal Oak, Michigan. The club manager, Debbie Mullins, explained to a *Newsday* reporter how Warmus's scheme was accomplished:

> Warmus was accused of running credit cards through an imprinting machine two or three times, using one imprint for the credit card customer and the others for customers who would pay in cash. Warmus . . . would then pocket the cash she collected rather than put it into the till. Federal agents were brought in to investigate, but they could not find enough evidence to bring charges against her.

Several years later, Carolyn again had recourse to forgery, this time to establish an alibi as a defense to a damage claim. In 1987, a woman identifying herself as Carolyn Warmus was involved in an automobile accident. Subsequently, Warmus wrote to the other driver involved, stating that she had been chaperoning a school trip in Washington on the day of the accident and offering as proof a letter signed by a school official, Dr Richard Sprague. Later Sprague denied both that he had written the letter and that Warmus had attended the class trip to which she had referred.

In September 1987 Carolyn Warmus, then twenty-three, met Paul Solomon, who was thirty-eight, when she began teaching at the Greenville School in the Edgemont School District in Greenburgh, Westchester County; she later moved on to the Byram Hills School District in nearby Armonk, where she taught computer science, but Solomon remained at the Greenville School. Betty Jeanne Solomon, Paul's wife, was an account executive with the Continental Credit Corporation in Harrison, New York, and she and her husband lived with their daughter Kristan (thirteen years old in 1987) in a condominium on South Central Avenue in Greenburgh. The marriage bond between the Solomons was apparently not very strong; Paul admits to having had two brief affairs before meeting Carolyn Warmus, and he suspected Betty Jeanne of carrying on a relationship of several years with her former boss.

Some months after their first meeting, Carolyn Warmus and Paul Solomon embarked on an affair which featured sexual encounters in her apartment above the comedy club "Catch a Rising Star" on Manhattan's east side, as well as in hotel rooms and Warmus's car. Doing her best to keep the liaison a secret, Warmus took on the role of a friend of the whole Solomon family, showering Kristan with gifts and taking her on a skiing trip. It was on this excursion that Warmus confessed to the teenager a fear that Betty Jeanne Solomon did not like her very much. Kristan tried to persuade her to the contrary, but "deep down" she knew that Warmus's concern was well-founded. In August 1988, when Paul Solomon had briefly stopped seeing her, Warmus confided to a college friend, Ryan Attenson, of Southfield Michigan, that her relationship was not "progressing in a manner with which she was comfortable"; she spoke of her desire to engage a private investigator to prove to her errant lover that his wife was cheating on him.

Shortly before midnight on Sunday evening, 15 January 1989, police in Greenburgh received a call from Paul Solomon, who had returned home to find his wife murdered. Betty Jeanne was lying on the living-room floor; she had been pistol-whipped about the head and had nine bullet wounds in her back and legs. None of the neighbors had heard the shots, there was no sign of forced entry, and the only indication of a struggle was a disconnected telephone; police photographed a black woollen glove near the corpse.

At first, the investigation focused on Paul Solomon. After initially telling Greenburgh detectives that he had spent the evening bowling near his home, he admitted that he had stopped only briefly at the bowling alley and had spent the evening with

Carolyn Warmus at the Holiday Inn in Yonkers, New York. After drinks in the motel's Treetops Lounge, followed by hamburgers, french fries and some oysters, the couple had repaired to Warmus's red Hyundai car, in which, as she later told the police, they performed a sex act; Carolyn specified in her statement that during their lovemaking she occupied the driver's seat. Witnesses came forward to confirm that they had seen Solomon at the bowling alley and later in Warmus's company at the Holiday Inn.

After some months, police suspicions shifted from Solomon to Warmus. One of the reasons for heightened interest in Carolyn was evidence of her relentless pursuit of Paul Solomon after the murder. In June 1989, after Solomon broke off his relations with Warmus, she followed him to Puerto Rico, where he was vacationing with a new girlfriend, Barbara Ballor. Posing as a police officer, she called Ballor's family from the island, urging them to end the romance. An even more startling development in the investigation was receipt of a tip that in early January 1989, shortly before the murder, Carolyn had purchased from private-eye Vincent Parco a handgun equipped with a silencer.

On 2 February 1989 Carolyn Warmus was indicted for second-degree murder and the possession of an unregistered firearm. Six months later, however, the indictment was dismissed by Judge John Carey, on the ground that the state had not disclosed to the grand jury the fact that Vincent Parco had been granted immunity from prosecution in exchange for his agreement to testify about his sale of the pistol to Warmus. The prosecutors promptly obtained a fresh indictment, and the widely heralded "Fatal Attraction" trial of Carolyn Warmus opened on Thursday, 14 February 1991, in Westchester County Courthouse, where headmistress Jean S. Harris of Madeira School had been convicted of murdering Dr Herman Tarnower a decade earlier. The prosecution team was headed by thirty-eight-year-old Assistant District Attorney James A. McCarty, and David L. Lewis defended Carolyn Warmus. Lewis was president of the New York Association of Criminal Defense Lawyers and a director of the National Association of Criminal Lawyers; he had acted as a trial lawyer for the former Panamanian dictator, General Manuel Noriega, and was accustomed to trying cases in the limelight. Judge John Carey presided; and a jury of eight women and four men was selected. The jurors scanned with understandable interest the features of the celebrated defendant, whose appearance was described by the *Newsday* reporter with a mixture of attentive observation and prurient imaginings:

> Her thick blonde hair is cut in a neat, chin-length chop. Just enough makeup coats her milky-white skin to hide a large crop of freckles. It is easy to imagine her long legs, hidden by a modest black skirt, in the gym shorts and sneakers of her athletic, teenage years. But then the smile is oddly cut short by a hard blink of her eyes and a quick, convulsive grimace. It is a startling, spasmodic reaction, almost a nervous tic – and it periodically breaks on the smooth planes of Carolyn Warmus's face. Her apparent confidence is gone for an instant, and in its place one sees a flash of the troubled history that has been so widely reported in the media since she was indicted a year ago.

In his opening statement, prosecutor McCarty told the jury that Warmus was driven by a "consuming desire to possess" Paul Solomon. The evidence was circumstantial but, "like pieces of a puzzle . . . would reveal a clear picture of the killer of Betty Jeanne Solomon: the defendant, Carolyn Warmus." The proof would include testimony from private investigator Parco, who had sold Warmus a gun and silencer, as well as telephone company records of a call on the day of the slaying made from the defendant's apartment to a gunshop where she later bought bullets, using as false identification a driver's licence that had stolen from a secretary in an office where Warmus worked in the summer of 1988. The Solomons' marriage had had its ups and downs over the years, McCarty admitted; both husband and wife were having affairs, but they were "not ready to call it quits." In the summer of 1988, after Solomon temporarily ended his relationship with Carolyn Warmus, she wrote him notes, gave his daughter Kristan extravagant gifts, and told her college friend Ryan Attenson that Paul Solomon was the perfect person for her. The only obstacle was Betty Jeanne Solomon, and the defendant had made it clear to Attenson that she would do anything to get her out of the picture so that she could take her place in the household.

David L. Lewis responded for the defense by arguing that the case was not about the impropriety of Warmus's adulterous affair, and that her love for Paul Solomon did not demonstrate her guilt. There was no physical evidence, he emphasized, to show that

Warmus was in the Solomon's home on the night of the killing. Charging that the prosecution was hampered by sloppy police work, Lewis strongly suggested that Paul Solomon and private detective Vincent Parco were responsible for the murder and for faking evidence to incriminate Carolyn Warmus. When the defense counsel took his seat at the end of his address, the jury was left to wonder how he would support his conspiracy allegations.

Early in the prosecution's case, two Greenburgh police officers related their impressions of Paul Solomon's mental state when they questioned him at the murder scene. Patrol officer Michael Cotter described Paul as shaken: "He said he rolled her over and saw all the blood and started crying; he cried again when he looked at the blood on his hands." In cross-examining the two officers, David Lewis attacked the police for losing possible traces of evidence that might have pointed to other suspects. One of the trial reporters agreed, comparing the Greenburgh police to the Keystone Kops; Paul Solomon had been allowed to wash his hands, and the black glove that was pictured in a police photograph had subsequently vanished and could not be located at the time of the trial.

Lewis had limited success in his efforts to weaken the testimony of Carolyn Warmus's friend Ryan Attenson, to whom she had spoken of the setback in her relationship with Paul Solomon in August 1988. In a telephone conversation, she had asserted that "with her money and Paul's family" (by which Attenson assumed she was referring to the Solomons' teenage daughter Kristan) "they would have a perfect life together." She said that she would take it upon herself to make sure that she ended up with her lover. Several months after the killing but before her arrest, Warmus had spoken to Attenson again; on this occasion she informed him that Solomon and she were going to end up together and that everything had been taken care of – the other woman was no longer an obstacle. Under cross-examination, Attenson conceded that he did not remember Warmus's exact words but was relating the essence of what she had told him.

Kristan Solomon held the courtroom spellbound with her account of Warmus's campaign to win her goodwill. Paul Solomon had introduced Kristan, an athlete who competed in several sports, to Warmus when he was coaching his daughter and her teammates during an after-school basketball practice. During the next few months she had chatted with Warmus in her classroom, seen her at basketball games, and gone to a Christmas show in Manhattan with her father, Warmus and another teacher. It was in early 1988, when she and her parents had gone out to dinner with Carolyn Warmus, that the defendant had offered to take her skiing during the winter break. Kristan also told the jury about the birthday gifts that she had received from the defendant. On the girl's fifteenth birthday in August 1988, when the prosecutors asserted that Solomon had temporarily broken off their affair, Warmus had unexpectedly arrived at the Solomons' condominium with two outfits and a bracelet for Kristan. "I was in shock," Kristan testified. "I was not frightened but hesitant, because I knew my Mom didn't enjoy her in the house, and I was worried there would be words." After Betty Jeanne's death, Warmus had left notes on the door of the Solomon's condominium but had not seen Kristan; however, two weeks before the girl's sixteenth birthday, she had arrived home to discover a pale blue Tiffany's box at her doorstep containing diamond stud-earrings and a note from Warmus signed, "Love always, Carolyn."

Prosecution lawyers began their efforts to tie Warmus to the murder weapon with the testimony of a private investigator, James A. Russo, who swore that the defendant had consulted him a few months before the slaying to seek protection from a woman named "Jean or Betty Jean," who was trying to hurt her family. When Russo had suggested a bodyguard, Warmus had stated her preference for a "machine gun and silencer." On three earlier occasions in the late summer and early fall of 1988, Warmus had consulted Russo about other fears. During one of her interviews she had claimed that her father's jet had been sabotaged in Michigan and that a "woman was seen in the vicinity in the hangar"; during her next visit, Warmus had told Russo that the same woman had struck her sister's car in Washington in a hit-and-run. In his cross-examination, Lewis tried to discredit Russo by portraying him as a sleazy detective who would do anything for money. At his prodding, the witness recounted his recent work for a landlord who suspected a prostitution ring in his upper eastside apartment building; the witness said he had "gone undercover" and paid a prostitute $400 in exchange for sex.

Dramatic evidence of the murder night was provided by an operator of the New York Telephone Company. Since a direct police emergency network was not established in Westchester County, customers who dialed 911 were answered by a private operator who then referred messages to the local police. Shortly before 7:12 on the night of the killing, the witness, Linda Viana Newcombe, had received a call from a screaming woman whose only decipherable words sounded like "trying to kill me." The call was quickly disconnected and the operator, now thoroughly rattled, had transposed the digits of the number of the telephone on which the incoming call had been made; because of this mistake she had reported the emergency to the Scarsdale police, who had then rerouted the message to the Greenburgh station. David Lewis attempted without success to have the witness specify whether the caller had said " '*he*' is trying to kill me" or " '*she*' is trying to kill me."

On 8 February Paul Solomon, who had been granted immunity from prosecution, took the stand to tell the jury about his strained marriage of nineteen years, his feelings of guilt over the affair with Carolyn Warmus, and his actions on the murder night, culminating in the discovery of his wife's body. He had not had sex with Carolyn Warmus in the summer of 1988, but in the fall they had resumed relations despite his conflicting feelings. When they had met for drinks at the Holiday Inn in Yonkers, Paul told the jury, he had encouraged Warmus to seek her happiness elsewhere:

> She said it was difficult finding good people to date. I said, "I'd be so happy to dance at your wedding and see you happy." She said, "What about *your* happiness, Paul? Don't *you* deserve to be happy?" And I said, "If anything happens to Betty Jeanne and me, I'd never get married anyway."

Despite this exercise in dissuasion, he had then accompanied her to her car to have sexual relations.

For months after his wife's death, Solomon had not seen Warmus and had begun dating a new girlfriend. After playing basketball in Manhattan in July 1989, he stopped by Warmus's eastside apartment. At a nearby bar he had asked her whether she had had anything to do with Betty Jeanne's death. She replied that she was pleased he felt "comfortable enough" to ask her that, but said she had had no involvement. Solomon had asked her again later and she repeated her denial; he told the jury that he had "absolutely believed her." Prosecutor McCarty elicited Solomon's story of how Warmus had followed him and his new girlfriend to Puerto Rico eight months after the murder, even though he had never told her of his vacation plans. He had become so "frightened" when she appeared on the scene that he notified hotel security, called the Greenburgh police, and left that night.

At the start of his cross-examination, Warmus's lawyer David Lewis held up a card that Solomon had given the defendant early in their affair. Its passionate terms contrasted with Warmus's banal messages about school and community events. The note read:

> If you're smart you'll do one of two things. Turn away and never see me again and save yourself from the pain and hurt, or keep loving me and take the risk of you and I having something together forever.

A lot of people write cards, Solomon stated defensively under Lewis's questioning, and sometimes "people put down things that others put more into." The witness's constant reliance on qualifications cannot have strengthened his testimony in the jury's minds. Asked at one point whether he spoke Russian, Solomon replied, "Not that I'm aware of."

On the fifth and final day of the cross-examination on 21 February, Solomon burst into a rage when David Lewis bluntly suggested that he was involved in the killing. Calling the insinuation "obscene", the witness charged the defense counsel with an inclination to "twist and turn words, manipulate facts or half-truths, and incomplete reports, to make them what they aren't."

Following Solomon to the stand was investigator Vincent Parco, who had also been granted immunity in exchange for his testimony. Parco stated that Warmus had badgered him for months to provide her with a gun to protect her against burglars who were ravaging her eastside neighborhood. Succumbing at last to her insistence, in the first week of January 1989 he sold her an unregistered black Beretta .25 caliber pistol, a homemade silencer and a dozen bullets for $2,500 in cash delivered in three separate envelopes. It was Parco's suggestion that he have the silencer made – so that she could "practice in the woods, the house, in relative obscurity." The detective was able to locate a Brooklyn machine-tool company operator, George Peters, who had agreed to mill the silencer in accordance with diagrams in a book, *How to Make a Silencer*, which Parco had obtained from his friend Rocco. Parco, ever the perfectionist, was dissatisfied with the performance of

Peters's silencer (which he had tested by firing into a tree in lower Manhattan) and had insisted on alterations.

The day after the murder, Carolyn had called to tell Parco that some teacher had been "stabbed or bludgeoned eight or nine times"; the police had come to question her, and she had hidden the gun inside one of the posts of her brass bed. Parco offered to pick up the gun the next day, but Warmus had told him that the weapon was gone; she had thrown it off a parkway.

Judge John Carey excluded as prejudicial any testimony relating to Warmus's engagement of Parco to aid her persecution of the New Jersey bartender, or any other evidence indicating that she had obsessively pursued men prior to her affair with Solomon. However, Parco admitted that he had become infatuated with his attractive client – although he stoutly insisted that he had rejected her sexual advances. Parco also stated that in August 1989 Carolyn Warmus asked him to check out a license plate and a telephone number. The phone number belonged to a woman Solomon had started dating, while the license was for her father's car. During the summer of 1989 Warmus had denied any relationship with Paul Solomon and had told Parco she was out bowling with a "bunch of teachers" on the night of the murder.

Defense attorney Lewis subjected Parco to a daylong cross-examination, eliciting admissions that as a private investigator he often used disguises and false names, and, in order to obtain information, engaged in deceptive practices known in the trade as "gags". In a surprising show of modesty, though, Parco refused to rate himself an expert in assuming an "acting role" in his undercover work.

On 5 March a *Newsday* reporter, who regarded the prosecution's evidence to that point as flimsy, disclosed that Paul Solomon stood to gain $120,000, more than twice his annual salary, if a movie was made about the case. A week later the case took a turn in the prosecution's favor with the testimony of Patricia January, a nurse at the Bedford Road Elementary School in Pleasantville, New York, who swore that a week before the killing of Betty Jeanne Solomon, Warmus, after completing a telephone call from the school, had told her that she was "terrified" to live alone and had a gun. According to the nurse, Warmus had added that "of course" she would never kill anyone, and didn't have ammunition; she had also mentioned that the gun was "specially made" by a private detective. Defense attorney Lewis told Judge Carey that he was surprised by the testimony and obtained an adjournment. In two hours of cross-examination when the court reconvened, Lewis focused on why Patricia January had waited so long to tell authorities of her conversation. The nurse had two answers: she had thought it was common knowledge that Carolyn owned the gun and, besides, she had "wanted someone to open the door" for her to talk about the incident.

After Patricia January was excused from the stand, the opposing legal teams girded themselves for the principal evidentiary battle of the trial, a clash between inconsistent telephone records for 15 January 1989, the day of the murder. A microfiche, obtained by the prosecution from the MCI telephone service that Warmus used, showed a call from her apartment at 3:02 p.m. to Ray's Sport Shop, where bullets were purchased later that afternoon. In response, David Lewis, bringing to the fore at last his principal evidence of a conspiracy to incriminate his client, offered a document that he claimed to be the original MCI bill received by Warmus for January 1989. This document, printed in an MCI bill format and bearing the company's logo, lacked the call to Ray's Sport Shop on 15 January but included a direct-dial call at 6.44 p.m. on the same day that brought the total telephone charge to the same figure shown in the MCI record. Lewis told the judge that the 6:44 call "made it all but impossible for [Warmus] to have been in Westchester at 7:15 to commit the murder." The prosecution mounted a devastating attack on the authenticity of the "bill" offered by the defense, showing that the MCI record it had introduced was consistent with the company's computer tapes and that the paper on which the defense version of the bill was prepared lacked a slogan that was imprinted on all MCI customer statements in January 1989. Ultimately Judge Carey permitted both versions of the disputed telephone bill to be submitted to the jury.

In the days that followed, the prosecution completed its chain of evidence. Lisa Kattai, a secretary for a telecommunications company, identified Warmus as a temporary office employee who had worked with her in August 1988, when Kattai had noticed that her New York State driver's license was missing. According to Kattai, Warmus resembled the witness's photograph taken for her driver's license at a time that she had shorter, "frosted" blonde hair. It was the prosecution's theory that Warmus had posed as Kattai when she purchased ammunition at the gunshop on the afternoon before the murder. Subsequently, Detective Joseph Reich of the Westchester County Police testified that he had compared six shell casings found at the murder scene with a seventh picked up eleven months later in the Brooklyn machine shop of George Peters, who had admitted milling a silencer at Parco's request; all seven bullets had been fired from the same gun.

The testimony for the defense began with trucker Anthony Gambino, who supported Lewis's conspiracy theory by stating that Parco had asked him to commit a murder in the summer of 1988; he had virtuously declined the request. Another witness implicating Parco in the crime was Joseph Lisella, who stated that from a stall in the men's room of a bowling alley where he had stopped between 7:30 and 8:30 p.m. on 15 January 1989, he had heard two men exchange $20,000 and talk about having thrown a gun in the "deepest part of the river." He had not seen the men's faces, but they had called each other Vinnie and Paul, the first names of Parco and Solomon. The conspiracy theme was pursued with the testimony of Thomas A. Warmus, the defendant's father, who stated that Parco had tried to shake him down for a substantial sum of money in the summer of 1989; Mr Warmus left the courtroom without having looked at his daughter. On 10 April, the defense rested after Lewis had shown the jury a news videotape of Parco making threatening remarks about Gambino after the trucker's testimony.

In the closing arguments, the prosecution claimed that it had established a persuasive chain of circumstantial evidence, while Lewis, pounding home his conspiracy theory, invoked the Salem witchcraft trials as a parallel to the unjust persecution of his client.

The jurors deliberated for twelve days, a record in Westchester County, and ultimately deadlocked, with eight reportedly in favor of conviction and four holding out for acquittal; Judge Carey regretfully declared a mistrial. Interviews with the jury revealed that the minority of the jurors who favored acquittal were disturbed by the circumstantial nature of the evidence and could not believe that a woman could have brutally pistol-whipped Betty Jeanne as the murderer had done. All of the jurors agreed that the defense telephone bill was a fake, but the minority faction thought that the forgery might have been an act of desperation on the part of someone being framed for murder. One juror could not credit the possibility that Carolyn Warmus, given her inexperience with guns, could have hit a moving target with all nine bullets, even at close range.

When the second trial began in January 1992 (after an unsuccessful attempt by the state to have Judge Carey replaced on the ground that he was biased in favor of Warmus), the prosecution trial team and strategy remained intact, but the defense had been thoroughly overhauled. Warmus had hired a new lawyer, William I. Aronwald, whose low-key style was in stark contrast with the theatrical and bellicose manner of the defendant's original counsel, David Lewis. It was Aronwald's intention to cast suspicion on Paul Solomon and Vincent Parco, as Lewis had done, but the "frame-up" theme would be subordinated to a broader plan to create reasonable doubt on a number of issues. Aronwald's less melodramatic approach was mandated by the first jury's obvious rejection of the principal evidence that Lewis had offered to show that the case against Warmus was pure fabrication. Even jurors who had held out for acquittal were persuaded that the telephone invoice introduced by the defense at the first trial was a fake and that two key defense witnesses, trucker Anthony Gambino and men's room eavesdropper Joseph Lisella, were not worthy of belief. After the first trial ended, the state indicted Warmus for forgery of the telephone bill; subsequently Judge Carey ruled that the prosecution could not introduce the alleged forgery into evidence at the second murder trial as proof of Warmus's consciousness of guilt, since she might have been unaware of the fabrication of the document.

The prosecution case appeared to be following its expected course until 4 March, when Westchester Assistant District Attorney James McCarty made a stunning announcement. He told the court that the black glove that had been photographed at the murder scene and later vanished had now been rediscovered. In January the prosecution had asked Paul Solomon to search again for evidence for the new trial, and he had delivered the glove, which he said he had found in a box in his bedroom closet. Forensic tests had turned up barely visible finger-shaped human bloodstains on top of the glove.

Unprepared for this turn of events, defense counsel Aronwald accused prosecutor McCarty of "trial by ambush," and Judge Carey initially ruled the glove inadmissible. He, was, however, promptly induced to rethink his stand when McCarty told him that he had procured credit-card and store records revealing that on 9

November 1987 Carolyn Warmus had purchased a pair of gloves at Filene's Basement in Greenburgh matching the glove found in the Solomon residence. Faced with this offer of proof, Judge Carey ruled that the glove could be admitted if the prosecution was able to show that Warmus had bought gloves "having similar intrinsic characteristics" of color, material, size and style.

The Filene's sales slip did not specify the color of the gloves purchased but permitted their identification as Shalimar Vanity Glove Inc.'s style 6781, a $10 one-size-fits-all wool glove manufactured by a Chinese state-owned cooperative. The Solomons' daughter, Kristan, testified that Warmus had worn black gloves, and a forensic expert, Dr Peter DeForest, testified that, after comparing the fibers found in the victim's hand during the original murder investigation with the fibers of the glove, he had found the two sets to be "indistinguishable."

Satisfied that sufficient evidence had been established to link the glove to the murder and to the defendant, Judge Carey ruled that it could be admitted, but excluded any reference to the tests revealing that spatters on the glove might be human blood. To the bafflement of observers, defense counsel Aronwald himself highlighted the evidence of the apparent bloodstains by contending that Solomon might have placed the stains on the glove recently in an attempt to incriminate Carolyn Warmus.

The prosecution rested its case on 5 May and the defense, shuffling the order of its witnesses to meet the menace posed by the black glove, called to the stand William Bohus, president of Shalimar Vanity Glove Inc., the importer of the gloves identified in the Filene's sales slip as purchased by Warmus. Bohus testified that his company had sold some 36,000 pairs of the gloves since 1986, a quarter of which were black. Carolyn Warmus's stepmother, Nancy K. Dailey, also gave evidence intended to minimize the impact of the prosecution's newly rediscovered glove. She showed the jurors a black and gold ski suit, with its own matching black gloves, that she had bought for Carolyn long before the murder. Mrs Dailey's testimony seemed to prove only that Carolyn Warmus might have owned more than one pair of black gloves, and the prosecution was quick to emphasize this fashion note. The ski suit was almost all black, prosecutor McCarty's assistant Douglas FrizMorris observed. Was black one of Ms Warmus's favorite colors? . . . Might she not have liked the color so much that she had bought a second pair? . . . According to the

New York Times reporter: "for a minute every eye shifted to the young woman at the defense table in the flowing black skirt and the black boots." Carolyn's stepmother stood firm, however; black, she maintained, was not among Carolyn's favorite shades. "She looks very good in bright colors."

After the last echoes of the glove controversy died down, the balance fo the defense's evidence seemed humdrum by comparison. A firearms expert, Jerold Steinberg, asserted that the silencer that machinist George Peters had supposedly made for Vincent Parco would not have functioned well enough for use in a shooting. Aronwald called a Bedford school secretary in a final effort to refute nurse January's belated recollection that, after finishing a conversation on the school's telephone, Carolyn Warmus had told the nurse that she had purchased a gun. The secretary described a telephone log in which teachers were asked to write down any private calls for later billing. There were no listings of any calls by Carolyn Warmus on the date of the conversation reported by nurse January. Aronwald suggested that this detail was a sufficient ground for the jurors to conclude that the nurse had made up the entire story.

Since Warmus's questionable telephone bill could not be introduced in evidence, the defense was compelled to take a fresh approach to the disputed call from Warmus's apartment to the gun shop. Aronwald summoned to the stand a private investigator, who said that it was possible for someone to have "tapped" into Warmus's apartment line and made the call without her knowledge.

In his closing argument on May 19, Aronwald argued that the victim, Betty Jeanne Solomon, was "unwanted baggage" to her husband Paul and that he, not Carolyn Warmus, had the motive and the opportunity to kill his wife to clear the way for a series of love affairs. Aronwald strongly urged the jury to reject the wondrously materializing woolen glove. This was the evidence, he argued, that the prosecution hoped would swing the second jury in its favor. It was no accident, in Aronwald's view, that Solomon claimed to have discovered in his apartment the glove that the police had photographed next to his dead wife's body in January 1989 and then had lost. That glove, he reminded the jurors, was tested at the time and did not appear to have blood on it just after the murder. It was no accident either that now, according to prosecution witnesses, the glove was bloodstained, for it was

Mr Solomon himself who had placed the blood there to try to link Carolyn Warmus to the murder scene.

Replying for the state, Assistant District Attorney McCarty urged that there was too much evidence tying Carolyn Warmus to the shooting to be explained away. "These aren't a series of coincidences, ladies and gentlemen," he said. "Sooner or later the picture should become clear to you: you can see Carolyn Warmus doing this." He argued that Paul Solomon had nothing to gain from the death of his wife and that only Warmus could have killed the woman she had come to view as an obstacle. Warmus's telephone bill showed that, on the day of the murder, she had called Solomon and talked to him for 55 minutes. During that call, she had learned that the Solomons' daughter was away for the weekend and that Betty Jeanne would be alone. When Solomon told her that he had accompanied his wife to a bar mitzvah the day before, it was brought home to Warmus once again that she was on the "bad side of a lovers' triangle." In the course of the conversation she had made plans to meet Solomon at 7:30 that night at the Holiday Inn, and thirty minutes after the conversation ended, her phone bill showed the call to the New Jersey gunshop. The police placed Mrs Solomon's death at around 7:15 that night; the prosecutor reminded jurors that one witness at the Holiday Inn restaurant said that Solomon had arrived there at 7:30 and Warmus only later. In greeting Solomon, the prosecutor said, Carolyn had explained that she had been caught in traffic. "Traffic," McCarty repeated to the jurors with an expression of disbelief, "on a Sunday night?"

After seven days of deliberations, the jury found Warmus guilty of second degree murder and illegal gun possession. Among the jurors, the black glove was the most frequently cited reason for the verdict. William Aronwald said: "I have no doubt in my mind that without the glove the prosecution would not have hoped anything better than a hung jury. It really derailed our defense." David Lewis, defense lawyer at the first trial, was not reluctant to second-guess his successor, suggesting that Aronwald might have been hurt by moving away from a strategy of claiming more centrally that Warmus had been framed by Solomon and Parco:

> I think what we did in the first trial was to address the issue of
> a frame-up from the first meeting with the jury. That is, as

far as I'm concerned, the major difference between the two trials.

In a decision announced on 26 June 1992, Judge Carey passed sentence on Carolyn Warmus. Belying the prosecution's persistent charges that he had a soft heart for the defense, Carey doubted neither the justice of the jury's verdict nor the gravity of the risk that Warmus might repeat the criminal acts of which she had been convicted. Characterizing Warmus as a woman who "unhesitatingly took another's life for no apparent purpose but that of having the victim's husband to herself," the judge considered that the assurance of a long incarceration was necessary for the benefit of anyone who might anger her in the future as well as for those persons she might consider to have contributed to her conviction or to have harmed her in some other fashion. Operating under statutory sentencing guidelines, Carey defined his task as prolonging the time within which Warmus's adversaries, such as Paul Solomon and Vincent Parco, could "sleep somewhat more soundly." Any speculation, however, that the defendant might threaten a broader circle of the public "would fly in the face of her non-violent career up to the time she brought herself under the evil influence of Vincent Parco, whose respect for the law is minimal." Weighing these considerations, Judge Carey imposed a murder sentence of imprisonment for a term of not less than twenty-five years and a concurrent sentence under the gun possession count of confinement for not less than five years nor more than fifteen.

Even before the jury returned in her second trial, Carolyn Warmus had condemned herself to a more durable penance. In a courtroom conversation with a *Newsday* reporter, she vowed that she was finished with married men for all time.

Afterword

On 15 March 1993, Carolyn Warmus's attorney filed a motion for a new trial, claiming that two pieces of key evidence had been withheld by the prosecution. Aronwald asserted that the prosecution knew that Paul Solomon had been having an affair with another woman, Barbara Ballor, three months *before* his wife was killed, and not four months *after* the murder, as he had testified. Moreover, the defense counsel asserted, the prosecution had not disclosed to the jury the existence of a *second* glove, apparently found outside the Greenburgh apartment building; Aronwald contended that the prosecution had used the first glove to link Warmus to the slaying, but that the second would have acquitted her. Unimpressed with these arguments, Judge Carey denied a retrial.

ROSEMARY WEST

(Winchester, 1995)

A. N. Wilson

The case of Rosemary West, a 41-year-old prostitute from Gloucester convicted of murdering ten young women (including one of her own daughters), is unparalleled in modern criminal history. When her trial opened at Winchester in October 1995, the evidence disclosed a harrowing story of sexual abuse, torture and degradation that transcended even the uglier excesses of the Moors Murders thirty years before. The story traumatized Britain because of its brutal and brutalizing details. Mrs West and her husband Fred preyed on countless children and young women (some of them their own flesh and blood) over a 15-year period, subjecting them to terrifying, cruel and degrading sexual assaults before murdering them, butchering their bodies and burying them under their house at 25 Cromwell Street. It is hard to conceive of the domestic regime instituted by the Wests. The family and its routine were motivated, driven and directed almost exclusively by the couple's bizarre, insatiable sexual urges that shaped not only their world but that of their growing family. Sexual abuse of the grossest kind was visited upon most (if not all) of the West children at an early age, as though it were a rite of passage. During wild orgies at Cromwell Street, the children were tied naked to table legs for the pleasure of their mother's clients. Her son Stephen's nightmarish recollections included being forced to sleep in the cellar, a freezing dungeon which flooded in wet weather and where he would wake to find a tide of filthy water threatening to engulf him and his sleeping sisters. At the age of eleven Stephen's sister Anne Marie was forced to have sex with her mother's clients, including some of Fred West's workmates. Lodgers mingled with Rose West's clients; some slept with other lodgers, or with Fred or Rose, or both. "It was a free-for-all," Stephen recalled. "If you wanted a bed, there was a bed. If you wanted a woman, there was Mum. Dad just provided the entertainment. And that was either a porn video, or Mum." The first of the Wests' murder victims was Charmaine, Fred's daughter by his first wife, who vanished in 1971. She was followed by a series of Cromwell Street lodgers, hitch-hikers and runaways who were murdered, decapitated and dismembered before being buried under the house or in the back garden. The tenth and final victim was Fred and Rose's daughter Heather, murdered (according to Stephen) because she was about to blow the whistle about what was happening at Cromwell Street. Fred West reportedly told Stephen that he'd strangled Heather, cut her up, put her remains into a black bin bag and buried her under the patio. It was Heather's disappearance that finally brought the police calling at Cromwell Street in February 1994. Both Fred and Rose West were arrested but, before their case came to trial, Fred hanged himself in his prison cell. It was Rosemary West, alone, who faced a jury of eight men and four women at Winchester crown court. At the end of the seven-week trial, the verdicts came in stages; initially the jury returned verdicts of guilty on three counts of murder, but they took two more days to agree on the other seven. Rosemary West, impassive in the dock, was sentenced to life imprisonment. "If attention is paid to what I think," the judge told her, "you will never be released." The trial deeply affected everyone who attended it, myself included. As the author Brian Masters put it, there was contagion in the air. The historian and novelist A. N. Wilson (b. 1950) also covered the trial and captured the sense of defilement that tainted not just the spectators in court but everyone who read or listened to the evidence.

They say that after the first verdict came through, she was creating a scene down in the cells. Her defence counsel, Mr Richard Ferguson QC and his junior Miss Sasha Wass, paced the corridors outside the courtroom during the long hours while we awaited the final verdicts. "She's in a terrible state down there," said Mr Ferguson. "Surely the jury could put her out of her misery."

You wanted to ask: "Her misery? What about the misery of all her victims?" But it was a strong example – the last, one hopes and prays – of Rosemary Pauline West's capacity to exert power over another human being. We are often cynical about barristers. There could be no doubt, however, that her counsel in court were defending Rose West not because they felt they had to but because they had come to believe in her. And in her grief and her concealed sorrow she was in a paradoxical way more powerful than the lawyers who would pack up their wigs and gowns and return to London while she went off to prison.

By the time she returned to court to hear the next lot of verdicts, Rosemary West had recovered her equilibrium. Her eyes were red. Who can guess what had been passing through her mind? Who can know whether she has not in some perverted and terrible way managed to blot out the memory of the crimes she has committed and whether she has not actually come to believe in her own innocence? When she was first arrested by the police she railed at them, "f-ing and blinding" freely.

Her behaviour in Winchester, both in the cells and in court, has been to all appearances much calmer. Her demeanour in court has, indeed been of increasing fascination for those of us who sat, day after day, and observed her. As the catalogue of horror unfolded, the jury had to look at this plump, bespectacled woman with dyed hair and ask themselves: "Is it really possible that *this* person did *these* things?" When we heard the worst of the evidence – unspeakable things done to children and young women with vibrators, milk bottles, whips, binding tape, knives – Mrs West seemed truly sinister.

Seated between two uniformed female officers, she seemed as though she might herself be in uniform. Her dark coat might have been the battledress of some female Gestapo officer. One imagined her as the prison guard in a Nazi concentration camp, using her victims – as Brian Leveson QC, counsel for the prosecution claimed in his cross-examinations – "for pleasure".

But on occasion, one saw her in a different light. One of the miscellaneous teenage lodgers from 25 Cromwell Street, now entered upon a raffish middle age, remembered a woman who was not just a sex maniac, but who could be companionable, jolly, even kind. We heard from those who had drunk coffee with her, or paid their rent to her, and liked her. "Your besetting vice is to think the best of women," my wife warned me at this stage of the trial; she was right – on the first day that Rosie gave evidence, I could imagine almost liking her.

Then we could think of a different Rose as we looked at the figure in the dock; a more imaginable domestic person who hung washing on the line – albeit sometimes the clothes of women her husband had murdered, or took the children to school – albeit the children she had abused. Could any of this horrible story be true? Only the figure before us really knew, and in her mind the past was shielded not just by a desire to lie but by the much more persuasive blanket of forgetfulness. "I don't recall, sir." "I don't remember, sir." We were to hear her little voice say it over and over again.

Many of the reports which we have read in the papers have suggested that she was calm but this was not how she struck me. The very first prosecution witness to be summoned was Rosemary's mother, Daisy Letts. Her evidence made Rosemary weep, and one suspected from the first that beneath a placid exterior there lurked a tormented soul, carrying memories which were intolerable.

Whether they were – as the prosecution alleged – memories of murders for which she was responsible was something the jury would have to decide on hunch more than reason. No one had witnessed any of the murders, all the evidence was circumstantial and that was why the appearance and demeanour of Rosemary in court was of such vital importance. Her tongue was never still. As the hideous memories of witness after witness were drawn forth, that tongue snaked in and out of her lips.

And there is something very strange about the upper part of her face – the eyes and the brow. Although she is a pale woman, with soft, rather beautiful skin, when you try to call the face to mind, you remember a darkness, a shadow over the top part of her face. It is not just that she has currant-dark eyes and large glasses and a dark fringe. The shadow, remembered, seems almost spectral.

Rumour had it that her counsel advised her against taking the witness stand herself. Whether or not that was true, on the afternoon of Monday 30 October, after four weeks of watching her sit in that vast dock (designed for a terrorist trial) we watched her walk across to the witness stand. It was a managerial, school matron sort of march, her right hand swinging mannishly. And we could hear her voice, which veered, as she gave evidence for three solid days, between baby-softness and an indignant vigour. It seemed for the first time possible to reconstruct what Caroline Owens and Miss A and the others claimed to have heard – the voice which half the time was gentle and cooing and half so furious and cruel.

It was disconcerting, somehow, that she called both the counsel for the defence and for the prosecution, "Sir". Her mother had been the last witness to do this. In a woman of Rosemary's age it seemed anachronistic, as though she were someone playing the part of a rustic housemaid in amateur dramatics. The contention of the defence was that Mrs West might have been a lesbian, she might have been a prostitute, she might have presided over a disorderly house and she might have abused her children, but this did not make her into a murderer. Mr Ferguson elicited her sad childhood story – the violence of her father, the fact that she had been raped twice before she was 15 and the notion that she was, from the moment of their first meeting, in Fred West's thrall.

She denied all knowledge of her husband's murderous nature and said that now she knew of what he had done, she hated him. He was "a figure of walking evil. It may seem daft – I saw him with horns and complete with a satanic grin . . ."

Stupidly, perhaps, this denunciation of Fred made me sad. The prosecution's case was that Fred and Rosemary did everything together and they produced letters, written as recently as 1992, which revealed a passionate love between the two. There would have been something evil, but magnificently evil, in her continuing to protest that love. In her wilting verbal betrayals of her husband, there seemed something tawdry, evil as he might have been. He died in part to protect her and to give her a plausible chance of acquittal.

While Mr Ferguson examined his client, she frequently wept – in particular when she was recalling the disappearance of her daughter Heather. She had feared that Heather was turning into a lesbian and a Welsh lesbian at that; Heather only had eyes for her father; it was Fred who persuaded Rosemary that the girl had left home. Even in this account, given to her own defence counsel, there seemed a degree of confusion.

Some witnesses claimed to have heard Rosemary say that she had spoken to Heather on the telephone; or that she had seen the girl getting into a Mini to drive to Wales; or, in another story, to Devon with a friend. None of it quite seemed to add up. In parts of her evidence, one felt she was giving rehearsed answers and that sometimes the rehearsed answers were blurted forth in response to the wrong questions.

"It was unfortunate that my statement made to the police in 1972" – the case of Caroline Owens – "has been lost." "I was in shock." "All that was consensual sex, sir, as I should like to emphasise." These were phrases which would have seemed more natural on the lips of a lawyer than of a woman who is – among many other odd things – a bumpkin. Richard Ferguson did his best for her. She had told him she was innocent and it was his job to put the best case of which he was capable. His learned junior, Miss Wass, a beautiful, intelligent-eyed, crop-haired woman, had conducted Rose's defence at the committal proceedings in the magistrate's court. She is said to have a passionate belief in Rosie's innocence. God send Miss Wass to my defence if ever I am prosecuted!

In the courtroom drama which unfolded during the three days when Rosie took the stand there were many human paradoxes. Mr Ferguson is a former Ulster Unionist MP with a resonant voice and a manner with witnesses which is, to put it mildly, abrasive.

The prosecutor, Mr Leveson, is by contrast slight of build and quietly spoken with a slight Liverpool accent. There were times when one felt he was going to lose the case simply by giving out such distaste for the material under discussion that he left important questions unasked or crucial areas of evidence only partially explored.

There were times when the judge intervened, urging him to be bolder and to ask a few leading questions. "Mr Leveson, the jury will think we are completely mad!" "You could ask the witness, Mr Leveson, whether the screams he heard were those of a man or a woman", etc. But this was all in the early days of the trial. As a cross-examiner of Rosemary West, the mouse began to roar. Mr Leveson's questions, which went on for three days, were relentless, and Rosie did not have a convincing answer to any of them.

Sometimes he left her lies, her transparent lies, floating in the air. (The claim, for example that while living in Midland Road, she could not have hit Charmaine with a wooden spoon because this cigarette-smoking woman whose husband owned a van "couldn't afford a wooden spoon".) Sometimes Mr Leveson pounced and accused her, in a strong and righteously angry voice, of abusing, maiming, torturing and killing children and young women. By the end of his cross-examination, it did not look to me as if there was one member of the jury who believed a word she said.

But this being the case, how had she managed to persuade her lawyers that it was worth defending her? If her lies were as transparent as Mr Leveson made them seem, why had Miss Wass and Mr Ferguson not urged her to plead guilty? The answer, I think, was touched upon in one of Mr Leveson's questions when he accused her of suppressing the memory of these hateful deeds in her own mind.

She wanted them all to have been only a bad dream. She desperately did not want them to have happened. So she cut them out, persuaded herself they had not happened. It was certainly astonishing, the amount she appeared to have forgotten under cross-examination – almost the whole of the Caroline Owens incident, for example, even though she had kept the cutting from the Gloucester newspaper which described her own 1972 court appearance.

When Heather, whose remains were found in the garden of Cromwell Street, was mentioned, her mother wept. In all the other tears, there was an element of theatricality. She would produce the handkerchief and then weep ostentatiously as if she had taken out an onion and decided that she should appear vulnerable to the jury. But in the case of Heather, there could be no doubt that the tears were genuine. As I listened to her, I veered between thinking that she could not possibly have murdered her own daughter, and realising, sadly, that the stories she span about the girl's disappearance simply failed to make sense.

So what happened? Was Fred alone responsible for the killing of this, their first-born child, in order to stop her blabbing their sordid secrets to the police? Did Rosemary half-fear that she knew what had happened to Heather and was she so unable to face the truth that she told herself that Heather had "gone away" without leaving a forwarding address?

Or did she actively participate in Heather's murder just as she had killed her step-daughter, little Charmaine, in Midland Road and hurled her down the coalhole? Just as she had killed the pregnant Shirley Robinson – pregnant by Fred?

It was the murder of Heather which created the doubt in my mind. Of all the other deaths, one believed Rosemary West to have been capable. But of this?

*　　*　　*

Something very strange happened while Rosemary West was in the dock. She did not come over as a sympathetic figure; one did not find her loveable, still less did one find her crimes forgiveable. But one saw glimpses of her world which were "normal" – Rosie having coffee with friends, Rosie laughing in a pub, Rosie shopping, smoking, meeting neighbours. These fleeting vignettes were as far removed from the horror stories as the rigidly divided rooms in 25 Cromwell Street were separated from the cellar.

Beneath the jaunty kitchen with its Marilyn Monroe wallpaper – "I'm afraid I wasn't a very serious person, sir" – there was a torture pit which might have turned the stomach of the Marquis de Sade. By the same token, beneath the "ordinary" surface of this middle-aged Gloucestershire housewife who several times told us how much she prided herself on keeping the house "nice" and "clean" and the children "nice" and well-behaved – there lurked a maniacal destroyer of lives.

She did not "do herself any good" by appearing in the dock – if by that one means ingratiating herself with a jury who were clearly appalled by her lifestyle as well as by her crimes. But she gave us a few little glimpses into what it was like to be her. She will spend the rest of her life being her and I suspect that won't be much fun.

In many ways, and one does not mean this to be a bad taste remark, one can envisage her enjoying prison life – the ordered discipline, the hatchet-faced female guards. One suspects that this self-confessedly "not very serious person" has not been cursed with the gift of intelligent introspection.

But when the memories flickered across the mind which fought to keep them out and betrayed themselves on the face in the dock of Court Number Three, we saw a shadow of something like Hell.

The village of Much Marcle in Herefordshire presents to the visitor an aspect of picture-postcard prettiness. Its redstone church and its half-timbered cottages nestle in rolling country. Beyond may be glimpsed the blue Clee Hills. To stand, as I did earlier this year, in Fingerpost Field and gaze towards the village, is to see England at its most idyllic; or, if you are a reader of Conan Doyle, it is to be reminded of that striking moment in "The Copper Beeches" where Sherlock Holmes makes the pronouncement: "It is my belief, Watson, that the lowest and vilest alleys in London do not present a more dreadful record of sin than does the smiling and beautiful countryside."

Just over the brow of the hill in Fingerpost Field, barely a hundred yards from the road, the traveller finds a faded bouquet of flowers, put there to commemorate the fact that this was the spot where, in March 1994, the police disinterred the mortal remains of two women, Rena Costello and her friend Anne McFall. No one had ever reported these two as "missing". They had been dead for more than 20 years; and in all likelihood their murders would never have been discovered had not the police already begun to excavate in the back garden of a house in Gloucester – 25 Cromwell Street.

Rena Costello was the first Mrs Frederick West. Anne McFall was her friend. Frederick West buried them on the edge of the village where he was born and grew up and where his father and brothers worked as farm labourers. He buried them in a field which his old Dad had often ploughed. From his earliest days, Fred West knew the truth of what Sherlock Holmes told Doctor Watson. In the depths of the countryside, you can very easily get away with murder.

Holmes's reasoning is practical. "The pressure of public opinion can do in the town what the law cannot accomplish. There is no lane so vile that the scream of a tortured child, or the thud of a drunkard's blow, does not beget sympathy and indignation among the neighbours and then the whole machinery of justice is ever so close that a word of complaint can set it going and there is but a step between the crime and the dock."

The truly astonishing thing about the career of Frederick West and his monstrous accomplice Rose is that they were living dis-proofs of this. You would have thought that to conceal one murder, and to bury the body in your kitchen or your cellar was to take the most extraordinary risk. This is a case of multiple murder, and torture, which apparently went undiscovered. The excavations in Midland Road, Gloucester and Cromwell Street have revealed that you can get away with murder in the middle of a town.

Charmaine – the daughter of Rena Costello – lay buried under the kitchen floor of Midland Road for more than 20 years and it was only when the police dug up the body of Heather West in Cromwell Street that they came looking for Charmaine. Although a neighbour had seen Mrs West threatening violence to the child, who had her hands bound behind her back and was standing on a kitchen chair, no very searching questions were asked when Charmaine disappeared. She had gone to stay with Rena in Glasgow, apparently. And that was that.

It is little wonder, having murdered several people with complete impunity, that Frederick West should have developed the sense that he could do so again and again without being found out. Witnesses during the trial of Rosemary West spoke of Frederick West's passion for DIY, and of the fact that there was continuous building work in progress at Gloucester's most notorious address.

The population of young people who drifted in and out of the house as lodgers was what might be termed "floating". Fred was forever hammering and digging and banging in the cellar. The sexual ethics of the household would have been deemed easy-going by alleycats. Only hindsight can make us wise to the perils which those young women faced when, for one reason or another, they came to spend a night or two at Number 25, and ended up, having been tortured and mutilated, buried in the cellar.

Frederick and Rosemary West appeared before the Gloucester magistrates on 12 January 1973, charged with the abduction and sexual molestation of a 17-year-old girl, one Caroline Raines. Her ordeal has been rehearsed so many times that there is no need to repeat it. Suffice it to say that this was a girl who gave evidence to the police about Mr and Mrs West which has never been disputed until Mr Richard Ferguson, QC, chose to cast doubt on some of it during the trial at Winchester.

At the time, Mr and Mrs West pleaded guilty to abducting Caroline and to subjecting her to a series of sexual tortures of quite unspeakable horror. No one who watched Caroline repeat the story of her ordeal during the Winchester trial could doubt the truth of what she said. She also told us that in addition to the many degradations to which both the Wests subjected her, she had been raped by Mr West, but that the police had told her that if she persisted with this charge she would have to give all the grisly evidence in court. So the rape charge was dropped. The rest, however, was not.

The bench of magistrates heard that in the very middle of Gloucester, a stone's throw from the Cathedral and the little shop which Beatrix Potter sketched for her immortal tale, there were a pair of sadistic sex maniacs prepared to perform on young girls such rites as would have made the Gestapo seem tame. The Gloucester newspaper, *The Citizen*, reported the next day that the chairman of the Bench of Magistrates said that he was bound to "take a very serious view of offences of this description". He fined the Wests £50 apiece, adding: "We do not think sending you to prison will do any good".

On the same page of *The Citizen* we read that a man has been fined £10 for stealing a book from W.H. Smith and that a drunken man from Coney Hill has been fined £15 plus £10 in costs for pulling his wife's hair during a brawl. In the 20 years which elapsed after this case was heard by the Gloucester magistrates, a succession of girls went missing; but it would seem that no one considered it worth investigating 25 Cromwell Street, even though the Drug Squad made frequent raids on the place in search of lodgers committing the heinous sin of smoking marijuana.

During the testimony of these pot-loving lodgers, one had time to reflect on the nature of a society which asked its police force to perform such "drug raids". One is not attaching any blame to the officers involved in this story. On the contrary, we must all feel immense sympathy for those officers who have had to interview victims' families, and to interview the Wests themselves. Those who did not find bodies in the Seventies or Eighties when they visited the house are to be pitied, as are those in the Nineties who did make such gruesome discoveries. A strange combination of fantastic luck and low peasant cunning allowed the Wests to get away with it for so long.

Since most of the bodies found buried in 25 Cromwell Street had been similarly gagged with masking tape just as Caroline Raines was during her ordeal, it is a reasonable inference that these young women suffered in a manner comparable to Miss Raines. We can only infer, however. And it is this which makes the fates of the victims so chilling. One cannot imagine what their families suffered at the time, nor what they have been made to suffer since all this hideous history was made public.

I think of Mrs June Gough, the mother of Lynda, who gave her testimony in such a bright, brave voice on 11 October 1995 at Winchester Crown Court. She last saw her 19-year-old daughter alive on 19 April 1973. She came home from work and found a note: "Dear Mum and Dad. Please do not worry about me. I have got a flat and I will come and see you sometime. Love, Lin".

When a fortnight passed and the Goughs had heard nothing of their daughter, Mrs Gough made inquiries at the Co-op where Lynda had worked as a seamstress. A series of questions from different sources eventually led her to 25 Cromwell Street – where, as we learned from a subsequent witness, Lynda Gough had formed an attachment to one of the male lodgers.

When Mrs Gough rang the doorbell of 25 Cromwell Street it was opened by a "dark-haired lady. I immediately recognised that she was the same woman who had called for Lynda to take her out for a drink a fortnight earlier. The dark-haired woman was joined at the door by her husband. I said that I had come to see Lynda and they said she wasn't there, that she had left and gone to Weston-super-Mare. Then I noticed suddenly that this woman was wearing Lynda's slippers and some other items of clothing – a blouse or a cardigan."

Mrs Gough also recognised other items of Lynda's clothing flapping on the washing-line at the back of 25 Cromwell Street. But in spite of getting in touch with the police, and the Salvation Army, Lynda Gough's parents were to wait 20 years before they learned what had happened to Lynda. It was particularly heart-rending to hear how these parents, on the heartless tip-off from the Wests, had gone to Weston-super-Mare and tried, in vain, to persuade the DHSS offices to tell them whether a girl answering Lynda's description had been applying for work in the area.

All that survives of Lynda now is that note – "Dear Mum and Dad". To see it produced in court in its plastic container – an exhibit – was one of the first moments in the trial when the sensational newspaper story became a haunting individual tragedy. One had heard and read so much about the bloody Wests. Here at last, tremulous and tiny, was a whisper from one of their victims.

The very fragmentary nature of the "evidence" – the fact that in strict terms none of it was evidence at all – added to the poignancy of this trial. One did not imagine that Lynda Gough's slippers were of a kind so exclusive that they might not have been bought in British Home Stores or Marks and Spencer. A callous defence lawyer could have pointed this out to her mother, but it would not have done him or his client any good. Everyone who heard the testimony knew it was true. Those slippers were Lynda's.

In the case of most of the victims, there was even less material on which to work. Lucy Partington, a student at Exeter University, said goodnight to her disabled friend, with whom she had spent the evening discussing her chances of getting into the Courtauld Institute to do an MA in Medieval Art. She walked to the bus stop and was never seen again. Therese Siegenthaler, a Swiss girl hitchhiking from London to Ireland vanished in comparably mysterious circumstances. Neither of these young women came, as some of the others did, from broken sub-working-class homes; they were not nameless waifs whom the system had rejected; they were much-cherished daughters and friends. But this did not make it any easier for the police or the authorities to have any idea what had happened to them. As a result of the brave testimony of those who got away, we can now reconstruct the sort of thing which is likely to have happened to them, and perhaps their families would have been happier to remain in ignorance. This trial has painted some scenes which in all honesty one would prefer not to have fixed as images in the mind.

The trial is now over. Many of those who attended it, either as witnesses, or as lawyers, or as journalists, will have looked across the court at the figure in the dock and tried to ask a number of questions which pain and muddle could not quite articulate. One of the young women tortured by Mr and Mrs West, and subjected to the most unpleasant sexual degradation, bravely told the court that at the back of her mind during the ordeal, there was this question: "Why, why, why?"

Such questions are unanswerable, except in the most spurious terms. We know, for example, that Mrs West's father was a violent man. We know that both the Wests had unhappy family backgrounds, but this neither explains nor excuses the dreadful tale which has unfolded of the murders which took place at 25 Cromwell Street. There are so many ways of living a life, filling a day – even in a place like Cromwell Street. Why did this woman, whose face we have come to know so well, choose to spend so much of her time inflicting pain on other people?

The question itself is absurd; since what has emerged is that Mrs West, like all erotomaniacs, was living in a miasma of insatiable sexual frenzy. She said in the hearing of one of the witnesses that she wished to spend her retirement doing nothing except indulge in sex. The only thing which was remarkable about this statement was that it somehow implies that Mrs West had been doing anything else except this before her "retirement", which, fortunately for the young women of Gloucestershire, has come rather earlier than perhaps she had planned.

The ghastly picture given by more than one witness of the Wests pleasuring themselves over the squirming, screaming bodies of their victims; of prying fingers, straying so violently that one witness feared that they might be about to perform one of their much-bragged-of pieces of amateur surgery; of Rosie murmuring: "Enjoy, enjoy!" to her husband as the young women and barely-pubescent girls whimpered and wept – all this builds up a picture of a woman in the grip of an addiction quite as strong as any narcotic.

It was perfectly believable when the counsel for the defence said his client had no recollection of meeting some of the witnesses who were quite unable to forget Mr and Mrs West. For Rosie, pre-sumably, many of the girls have blended into one.

Having trussed them with binding tape and tormented them and killed them, these human beings must have seemed about as distinctive to the Wests as a row of carcasses does to the butcher when he suspends them from hooks in his shop window.

The trial had a number of purposes, but one of these purposes was, surely, to perform a secular requiem over those girls who died. There is absolutely no doubt that there are others, and in the coming weeks and months and years we might hear their names; some however will be nameless for evermore. The assembly in Winchester was saying, among other things: "We the British people and our judiciary and legal system – consider each individual to be of infinite importance and worth. We can not bring them back to life – Lynda Gough, Carol Cooper (Caz), Lucy Partington, Therese Siegenthaler, Shirley Hubbard, Juanita Mott, or Alison Chambers – but we, can treat their disappearance and death as something which is quite as im-portant now as when it first happened; and we shall want the jury, our representatives, to see that justice is done for those girls".

The point was affectingly made by Caroline Raines, now Mrs Owens – one of the bravest women I ever saw – who had to brave Mr Ferguson's cross-examination and the implication that she had made up her story to titillate readers of the *Sun*. Having described the indignities which she suffered at the hands of Rosie and Fred West, she exclaimed: "I want to get justice for the girls who didn't make it. I feel it is my fault."

Shortly before this trial began, the crime writer P. D. James irritated various of her fellow crime-writers with the assertion that it would be difficult to set an old-fashioned detective story in a modern "inner city" where murders and crimes of violence were commonplace. There was much ridiculous over-reaction to Lady

James's comments; it was almost as if she was saying that those in inner cities did not have consciences or had a different moral standard from those lucky enough to live in suburbs.

This was not what she meant, of course. She was making a literary point: namely that the old-fashioned detective story is, essentially, one in which a deed of darkness occurs in an apparently harmless or even idyllic world: a country house, an olde worlde village, a rectory. When the body is found in the library or by the swimming pool in such a story, it is almost as if, in a trivial way, we are replaying the ancient myth of the serpent who has found his way into the Garden of Eden. The harmony of this world is destroyed by the murder, until the detective – often an amateur such as Poirot or Miss Marple rather than a professional policeman – restores order by identifying the murderer.

It is impossible to imagine Miss Marple, or P. D. James come to that, turning up at 25 Cromwell Street, or even being much use if they did.

From an early stage it must have been pretty obvious to the police who was responsible and as we have already asserted, the persistent "Why, why, why?" which rings in our heads – how much more it must have rung in the heads of those who disinterred the corpses – is a question which could drive us mad, since it will never be answered.

This is not an old-fashioned murder mystery, and, now it has been "solved", we cannot feel any of the cleansing or the sense of completion which must always accompany Poirot's final summing up to the circle of suspects as they sit in the library listening to his logical conclusions. Yet many of us must have feared, as the trial approached, that Cromwell Street had been a place not merely where a detective story could never be written, but one where the human values held dear by the rest of us were indeed non-existent. Were we going to enter the world of the urchin seen in Auden's *Shield of Achilles*:

> *That girls were raped, that two boys knife a third,*
> *Were axioms to him, who'd never heard*
> *Of any world where promises were kept.*
> *Or one could weep because another wept.*

But that has not been the case at all. The reason that this trial has been such a harrowing experience for everyone who has taken part is the discovery that we can all weep because another weeps. The tears which have flown from Cromwell Street continue to stream down the faces of those who remember what went on there.

Miss A sat in the witness box all day, inarticulate with sorrow, and weeping continuously. That day must have been the most painful thing that many of us have ever experienced. Miss A's life was so desperately sad. Mum and Dad separated. Dad abused her. Brother abused her. She was taken into care. From hanging around in the adventure playground in Gloucester, Miss A met a friend. "Can you remember her name?" "Not at all," said the whimpering, quiet voice of Miss A. This kind friend introduced her to the reassuring atmosphere of 25 Cromwell Street, where Rosie was the elder sister Miss A never had, the Mum in whom she could confide her worries about life, and about sex.

A complete innocent – looking at Miss A's poor face, one thought what a cruel burden innocence is, and that guilt was the kindest gift ever bestowed on Adam and Eve – Miss A found nothing strange about the fact that Rosie West fondled her and made love to her. She believed, as Rosie's own step-daughter Anne-Marie was taught to believe, that this was how "normal" people behaved.

And then, Miss A was led one stage further, to the room where other naked and barely-pubescent victims awaited their "turn" – as she phrased it – with the masking tape, the sex toys, the milk bottle. Nothing in this world can redeem the sorrow of Miss A's life. On a purely selfish level one regrets having heard it. It is unforgettable, and one would like to be able to forget it.

But the trial has done something. It has been the most telling demonstration of what the law is able to do better than anything. Justice is different from redemption. By the painful and often absurd rituals of the court – the self-satisfied little exchanges between judge and counsel, the ludicrous poring over Archbold – "Help me, Mr Leveson." "We are looking at page 629, my lord." – they attempted merely to establish Mrs West's guilt, or innocence, under the law. The very narrowness of the task – the conscious lack of emotionalism with which it was conducted from the first – these things have been in themselves cleansing.

There will have been those at the end of the great ritual of a murder trial who feel that it is a little lame that the judge should merely have committed Mrs West to life imprisonment. Surely

this was an occasion which called for something more dramatic –
the donning of the black cap, and the imprecation: "May the Lord
have mercy on your soul". It is not so much a question of revenge
and certainly not of deterrence, so much as a ritual need for
sacrifice after such a catalogue of horror.

Certainly if there is a case for hanging anyone, there would be a
case for hanging Mrs West. But after hearing of so much torture
and so many bodies being hung up, strapped, taped, tortured and
dismembered, the public would perhaps, in the end, have sickened
at the prospect of yet another bondage session, albeit one performed judicially and in the name of Her Majesty.

The pornographic and ghoulish interest which the case will inevitably generate, and which has already led to Fred West's
memoirs being sold for more than £1 million, is, if anything,
more stomach-churning and more distasteful than the sight of a
public hanging. Every one of us who has written about the case,
whether for the newspapers or in book form, must bear part of the
responsibility for that. But it would have been completely wrong,
of course, if this case had been hushed up on the grounds of good
taste; or if, horrified by the idea of an unsavoury interest, the
newspapers had been silent. We cannot see multiple murder on an
unprecedented scale and say nothing at all.

I think it perfectly possible that the great majority of missing
young women in the Gloucester area between 1970 and 1994 were
murdered by Frederick West, with or without the assistance of his
Lady Macbeth. That is a very distinct likelihood, and since it is so,
it it is only right that we should know it.

But the case reminds us of other things, all of which are rather
remarkable. It is embarrassing to write about these things, and it
sounds as if one is concluding a newspaper article with words
which would be more fitting to a secular sermon. But there is
something within us which rebels against evil, which cherishes and
values human life and which reverences the human body, dead or
alive.

The girls whom Fred and Rosemary West picked up in their
nocturnal trawls can have had no more reality for the murderers
than dolls. Having been brutally played with, for sexual gratification, the time came when they had to be destroyed, dismembered,
hidden. It would seem likely from the forensic evidence that before
or after death these bodies were mutilated.

Our need to reverence the dead is a profound one. Much of our greatest literature is full of this need – as for example a glance at Sophocles's *Antigone* would show. The manner in which the Wests disposed of their victims is horrible beyond words – first the dismemberment, and then the wedging of the corpses, head first, into the inadequate, jerry-dug little holes in their cellar and garden of No 25.

Those murderers who leave their victims hidden under a pile of leaves, or try to throw them into water, at least have displayed some residual sense of reverence for what an awesome thing they have done by depriving another human being of life. Many of us take more trouble with the disposal of our weekly rubbish bags than Fred and Rosie West did with these poor girls. Again, as in the case of their deaths, so in the case of their burials. Nothing can redeem the callousness, the ugliness, the sheer foulness of it all, unless it is the recognition that most of us – the overwhelming majority of those who read the story, but also the overwhelming majority who were, as neighbours or family members involved in the story – are disgusted: a flickering sign in the midst of so much horror that the concept of decency itself is not dead.

Religious people have tried, from time to time, to envisage what hell would be like – a place or condition of eternal punishment. My sceptical, late twentieth-century turn of mind has usually found such speculation distasteful even when drawn by the pens of the greatest poets such as Milton or Dante. During the last few weeks in Winchester, however, I am sure that I have not been alone in sensing something truly infernal about 25 Cromwell Street, its late master and its gruesome chatelaine.

At the height of his bloody crimes, Macbeth exclaims: "I have supp'd full with horrors!" Until this trial I had never understood how well this phrase conveys the satiety and heaviness brought on by contemplating repeated murderous acts. As one witness after another came forward to describe Mr and Mrs West's predilections, one felt a sensation which was not blasé enough to be boredom but which had the weight of boredom, the nausea of the full stomach. "Not again! Not another!" Always the same old hateful routines. And – in the forensic evidence – the same old telltale signs, the binding tape, the mutilated bones.

Hell must be an endless replay of evil done, forever bored and yet forever hungry with its destructive appetites. This is what one felt when looking at the figure in the dock, with her cruel, twitching mouth and, when she was led away at the end of each session, her alarming, bossy, school matron walk. It is not for us to know the state of her soul – for which judges no longer pray. But now that the trial is over and justice has been done, we can feel nothing but relief. Let others read, or write, more of this horrid affair. I shall not be among them. Enough!

OSCAR WILDE

(Old Bailey, 1895)

Edward Marjoribanks

In the spring of 1895, the homosexual playwright and wit Oscar Wilde found himself at the centre of no fewer than three criminal trials. First, in what became a notorious cause célèbre, *the most celebrated aesthete of the age tried to sue the oafish and eccentric Marquess of Queensberry for criminal libel. Queensberry was the outraged father of Wilde's younger lover Lord Alfred Douglas, known as "Bosie". The previous summer, Queensberry had acquired some passionate letters from Wilde to Bosie, despite Wilde's efforts to pay blackmail and get them back. Told that the letters themselves would not support a charge of sodomy, Queensberry trimmed his allegation against Wilde to one of posing as a sodomite, which didn't necessarily involve committing the offence itself. Accordingly, Queensberry left a card at Wilde's club, furiously addressed to "Oscar Wilde posing as a somdomite [sic]". Despite advice to the contrary, the litigious Wilde swore out a warrant for Queensberry's arrest, and the Marquess was duly brought to court on a charge of publishing a libel against Wilde. Queensberry's counsel was Edward Carson, an Irishman (like Wilde) and his contemporary at Trinity College, Dublin, in the 1870s. "I'm going to be cross-examined by old Ned Carson," Wilde announced. "No doubt he will perform his task with the added bitterness of an old friend." In fact Carson had hesitated to take the brief, believing the case to be weak. But when police uncovered a male brothel patronized by Wilde,*

Carson changed his view. Wilde's friends pleaded with him to drop the case. "You are sure to lose it," warned Frank Harris, "you haven't a dog's chance." He was right. As the case proceeded it seemed that Wilde himself, rather than Queensberry, was on trial. Carson cross-questioned Wilde to such deadly effect that the judge himself commented on it, describing their encounter as the most searching cross-examination he had ever heard. Here Wilde's libel action against Queensberry is recalled by Carson's biographer Edward Marjoribanks (1900–32), a brilliant young barrister who died before completing his task.

The case was heard on the 2nd April in the original Old Bailey, that terrible old Court of Tragedies. Judges and counsel had for generations denounced its sordid aspect inside and outside, together with its miserable proportions, and continued to do so till it was pulled down at the beginning of this century and succeeded by the present fine edifice: everyone who entered the place was influenced by a sense of tragedy and gloom, and even by a feeling of imprisonment. For the Court was tiny; its air was fœtid; the roomiest place was the dock itself, where thirty prisoners could be seated. And now it was crowded with fashionable people. There was not a seat or corner to be had. Somebody made a jest about "The Importance of Being Early," and there was a laugh. When the Court was already packed, the tall figure of Oscar Wilde was seen squeezing his way through the crowd accompanied by Lord Alfred Douglas: he was elaborately dressed in a long Melton overcoat, and carried a strange, very tall, but conical-shaped silk hat: he was not wearing his white flower, but the entrance of this extraordinary person introduced an atmosphere of Gilbert and Sullivan. Somewhere in Court was the prisoner, who was on bail, but his squat little pugnacious figure could not yet be identified. Wilde seemed to be in high spirits; he chatted and laughed to his friends, and settled down into a seat at the solicitors' table.

Behind him sat the counsel; for Wilde, Sir Edward Clarke, Charles Mathews, and Mr Travers Humphreys, now a Judge: for the defendant, Carson, Charlie Gill, one of the greatest of criminal advocates, and his brother Arthur, now a police magistrate. Oscar turned round and smiled at Carson, who looked coldly past him.

There was a pause; the Judge was a little late: then were heard the usher's three knocks at the door. Everybody rose, and Mr Justice Collins entered in his scarlet and ermine robes, followed by the High Sheriff of London, carrying a sword and wearing court dress. The gentlemen of the Bar bow to the Judge, and the Judge to the gentlemen of the Bar. The Judge sits down, takes up the bouquet of beautiful flowers supplied for his use by old custom as a disinfectant against the plague; the Marquess of Queensberry steps into the dock; the charge is read to him; he turns an implacable look towards Oscar Wilde, and pleads in a clear voice that he is not guilty; that the words were true and published in the public interest.

Then Sir Edward, a short, stout man but of a great dignity, looking rather like an eighteenth-century parson, rises and opens the case for the prosecution. He soon shows that he is a master of words. The form is perfect. Carson afterwards said to a friend in the House of Commons, "I never heard anything to equal it in all my life." But which line was he choosing? Two courses lay open; one a course of extreme moderation; the other to anticipate attack by attack, and introduce the whole story of the Queensberry family, the Marquess's neglect and cruelty, and the bitter feud arising therefrom, in which his unfortunate client had been involved, and by reason of which Lord Queensberry was really pursuing him, as a friend of his divorced wife and estranged children. It would have been safe to prophesy that an advocate like Marshall Hall would have taken this course: he would have given battle over the whole front, and in every corner of the field. The Judge would have rebuked him and pulled him up again and again, but he would have succeeded in introducing such an atmosphere of prejudice against Lord Queensberry into the minds of the jury that some would have taken Lord Queensberry's side and some that of Lord Alfred and his mother, and Oscar Wilde's part in the story might have become quite a secondary issue. The terribly relevant and penetrating mind of Edward Carson might, perhaps would, have brought the jury back to the central issue of the trial, but it appears to the writer that a Marshall Hall at his best, flinging himself into the fray, with all his strength, might easily at least have secured a long consideration and a disagreement.

But Sir Edward Clarke had decided otherwise: relying absolutely on Wilde's protestation of innocence, he was out for a conviction on the single issue, and was determined to avoid all irrelevancies. He considered that his client would suffer and not gain from a wide and bitter discussion of the Queensberry family history. The jury might then condemn Wilde for no sin of his own, but visit the sins of the Douglas children on Wilde's innocent head: such irrelevancies would widen and expose the front for attack by the angry Queensberry and his clever counsel. No doubt there were wrongs on both sides, and the more completely his client was kept clear of all this, the better for him. Besides, for such a plan of attack Lord Alfred Douglas was an indispensable witness; no jury would like to see a young son attacking his father in a criminal trial before his father had said a word in his defence. Lord Alfred was headstrong, eloquent, and full of bitterness against the Marquess; besides, the whole case arose out of the friendship between Wilde and Douglas, and it would be folly to subject a young nobleman to cross-examination as to this. Who knew what materials Queensberry had concocted or imagined and given to Carson? Sir Edward did not know that Carson was determined not, under any circumstances, to use such material in this trial.

It was a difficult decision, and it is easy to be wise after the event; it is always the golden rule for the prosecution to pursue a course of studied moderation; but this was no ordinary prosecution; here the real prosecutor stood in the dock, while the real defendant was to stand in the witness-box, exposed to the widest and bitterest attack on his life, on his works, on his very thoughts and ideas; but, had Clarke known all the information concerning Wilde on other charges which Carson had at his disposal, and the deadly use to which he would put it, and had continued to hold his brief, without much doubt he should, for the sake of his client, have taken the other course.

From the moment that Clarke opened the case on these lines, perfect as his quiet argument was, Oscar's fate was really sealed. Though his counsel did not know it, he was really defending, not an innocent man who would be prejudiced by his friends' faults, but a guilty man, whose only chance of escape depended on the exposure of his enemy's malice and wickedness.

But, of course, Sir Edward held the close interest and sympathy of everyone: there was this great literary man, this acknowledged genius – and he was only thirty-eight years old – not indeed accused of any offence, but of whom a certain word with an obvious reservation had been used by an old nobleman so eccentric that he could hardly be held responsible for his actions. Nevertheless, Oscar Wilde could not let such an expression pass in connection with his name, although there had been no accusation of any offence. He had had trouble of this sort before. A man named Wood had found some letters in a pocket of a coat given him by Lord Alfred Douglas, and had come, when in great need, to Mr Wilde, asking for money. Mr Wilde had given him the money, but Wood had retained the most important letter for subsequent use. This letter had been used by two men named Allan and Clyborn to ask Wilde for more money; in the end they had given the letter to Mr Wilde. This was the first intimation the Court heard that Wilde had been the victim of low blackmailers. One reflects that, had Wilde prosecuted those men for blackmail instead of Queensberry for libel, they would have undoubtedly been convicted, and Wilde would have enjoyed the protection which the Court always gives to blackmailed persons with the courage to come forward; thus all his troubles might have been averted.

As for this letter, of which the defence would make so much, there was really nothing in it: Sir Edward observed that it was a sort of "prose sonnet" which had indeed been translated into a French sonnet. "The words of this letter may appear extravagant to those who are in the habit of writing commercial correspondence" (the British jury laughed), "or those ordinary things which the necessities of life force upon us every day; but the jury need place no hateful construction upon it." Sir Edward then read the famous and amazing letter addressed to Lord Alfred Douglas by Wilde, "My own boy, – Your sonnet is quite lovely, and it is a marvel that those red rose-leaf lips of yours should have been made no less for the music of song than for the madness of kisses. Your slim gilt soul walks between passion and poetry. I know Hyacinthus, whom Apollo loved so madly, was you in Greek days. Why are you alone in London, and when do you go to Salisbury? Do go there to cool your hands in the grey twilight of Gothic things, and come here whenever you like. It is a lovely place – it only lacks you; but go to Salisbury first. – Always with undying love, Yours Oscar."

Mr Wilde, said Sir Edward, would satisfy the jury that there was nothing to be ashamed of in this letter. He looked up as if for reassurance at the jury, but they were far from satisfied. The foreman asked ominously, "What is the date of that letter?" Sir Edward said the letter was undated, and passed on, having left, like the good advocate he was, the best to the last, to much surer ground. According to the plea in justification, Oscar Wilde was being attacked for something which he had never written; nay, more, the publication of which his influence had prevented. He had been invited to subscribe an article for an Oxford under-graduate paper called *The Chameleon*. He had obligingly sent them an article entitled "Phrases and Philosophies for the Use of the Young." They were brilliant and effective epigrams, and "even wisdom in a witty form." Perhaps some of the jury had thoroughly enjoyed such things in *The Woman of No Importance*, and Sir Edward smiled at the jury as one who shared with them the appreciation of good things. In the same magazine, however, there also appeared a disgraceful and indefensible short story, called "The Priest and the Acolyte." This was not written by Wilde, and, when he read a proof copy, he instantly wrote to the editor, who withdrew the magazine. How could this be urged in justification of this terrible charge? Nor was this the measure of unfairness: his client was to be assailed on moral grounds for his especial mas-terpieces, for his *Picture of Dorian Gray*. Could anything be more absurd? "It can be bought on any bookstall in London. It has Mr Wilde's name on the title-page: it has been published five years. The story is that of a young man of good birth, great wealth, and great personal beauty, whose friend paints a picture of him. Dorian Gray expresses the wish that he shall remain as in the picture, while the picture ages with the years. His wish is granted, and he soon knows that upon the picture, and not upon his own face, the scars of trouble and bad conduct are falling. In the end he stabs the picture and falls dead, and the picture is restored to its pristine beauty, while his friends find upon the floor the body of a hideous old man." "I shall be surprised," concluded Sir Edward with a side-glance at Carson, "if my learned friend can pick upon one passage in that book which does more than describe, as novelists and dramatists may – nay, *must* – describe the passions and fashions of life."

Sir Edward had finished his opening address: the conclusion had been made with consummate skill, which Wilde himself must have admired, in an absolutely just attack on the unfairness, ignorance, and confused logic of the plea in justification; nevertheless, the speech had failed of its full effect. There was no hint of apology or admission that Wilde had been indiscreet, weak, or foolish. He had not even excused Wilde's letter to Douglas. It left the defence to open its full assault without a foreboding. Throughout, Clarke, with studied moderation, was putting Wilde on a high pedestal, whereas he should have placed him in the arena, and stigmatised with ridicule and disdain the almost blasphemous assaults made on him, without in any way discrediting the assailants. He was putting his case altogether too high, and scorning in Olympian fashion to hit back. If Sir Edward Clarke had been defending William Shakespeare for stealing a deer, it would have been as well for him to have noticed the particulars of the charge, the poverty of his client, and the incidence of the game laws.

After the porter of the Albemarle Club, whom Carson did not cross-examine, had been called to prove the publication of the libel, Oscar Wilde went into the witness-box and kissed the book. Turning to Sir Edward Clarke, he adopted an attitude which seemed urbane and candid. He gave his age as thirty-nine, at which his old classmate, Carson, looked steadily at him and took a note. He went modestly through all the story of his good birth, academic distinction, and literary achievements. The first amusing incident in his evidence appeared when he described his interview with the blackmailer Allan on the subject of his letter to Lord Alfred Douglas. The man had said, "A very curious construction could be put on that letter." Whereon Oscar said that he replied, "Art is rarely intelligible to the criminal classes." The man persisted, "A man has offered me £60 for it." Oscar blandly retorted, "If you take my advice you will go to that man and sell it to him for £60. I myself have never received so large a sum for any prose work of that length, but I am glad to find that there is someone in England who considers a letter of mine worth £60." This was a touch of the real Oscar Wilde, and the Court rose to it: he was really a very engaging person. Nevertheless, Wilde admitted twice having paid blackmail on his letters. Even then, however, he had not been too proud to lavish his wit on the blackmailer. "I am afraid you are leading a wonderfully wicked life." The man replied, "There is good and bad in every one of us." "You are a born philosopher," Oscar flung at his retreating figure. Oscar was making a good impression. The man who could pay blackmail and laugh at the blackmailer at the same time was a very rare creature. His letter to Alfred Douglas was a work of art; the translation of it into French had been done by a French poet of great distinction, writing as "Pierre Louys." The "Priest and the Acolyte" was bad and indecent: he had nothing to do with the writing of it, and had stopped its publication. "It was bad and indecent, and I thoroughly disapproved of it." Then, as a final question from Sir Edward Clarke:

"Your attention has been called to the plea and to the names of persons with whom your conduct has been impugned. Is there *any* truth in these allegations?" "There is no truth in any of them."

Now the real contest began: Carson rose to cross-examine. It was a painful and embarrassing moment as they faced each other. Many memories must have occurred to each of them, but Wilde smiled in a friendly way, as if inviting him to begin. Carson had now to ask his first question in cross-examination, which he always considered was the crucial moment in a case. He had puzzled long as to this first question. He knew how clever Wilde was, and how he could turn into ridicule the most serious and honourable matters. Up to the actual commencement of Wilde's evidence, he had not known how to begin. His plan was first to examine him on his literature and his views of morals as shown in his books, which was the weakest part of the plea, and then pass to specific accusations which the information before him warranted. If he could obtain admissions from Wilde as to his writings, this would make the other dreadful evidence more credible to the jury. This, however, meant embarking on a literary enquiry on unequal terms with the cleverest writer in London, and on this ground it was an unequal contest. "Impar congressus Achilli." Then Wilde quite unconsciously gave him his cue. He said he was thirty-nine: Carson knew that he and Wilde were almost exactly of an age, and he was forty-one. He had before him a copy of Wilde's birth certificate. Wilde, out of pure foolish vanity, had "posed" as to his age. Wilde had put the first question into his adversary's hand.

"You stated that your age was thirty-nine. I think you are over forty. You were born on the 16th October, 1854? Did you wish to *pose* as being young?" "No."

"That makes you more than forty?"

Wilde recovered himself; he made a gesture, and gave a long-drawn "Ah," as if he were congratulating Carson on his clever mathematics, and at the same time comically mourning his lost youth.

It was a small point, but nevertheless Wilde had told a vain and stupid lie in answer to the very first question put to him. But the age had a significance and a context. Carson passed on to ask Wilde the age of Alfred Douglas: he was now twenty-four, and Wilde had known him for three years. Wilde's answers showed that the two of them had stayed together in many places at home and abroad. Carson then passed on to cross-examine him on the literary side of the plea. He began with *The Chameleon*; it was true that Wilde had not written the "Priest and the Acolyte", but the magazine began with Wilde's "Phrases and Philosophies for the Use of the Young" and ended with "The Priest and the Acolyte", written by a young man. It was an Oxford magazine; Wilde had been frequently at Oxford. Although Wilde had nothing to do with the writing of the tale, was not it attributable directly to his corrupting influence? Carson was tempted into this field; it was unfair to make the witness responsible for what he had not written, and Wilde scored again and again: Carson invited discussion of the whole inexhaustible subject of moral purpose in literature.

"You are of opinion there is no such thing as an immoral book?" "Yes."

"May I take it that you think 'The Priest and the Acolyte' was not immoral?" "It was worse – it was badly written."

Everybody laughed; the jury were as delighted with their places as if they had been given free seats for *The Importance of Being Earnest*.

Carson put to Wilde the prurient details of the story: Wilde shrugged his shoulders, as if imputing prurience to the counsel who studied such things with care; really, he could not remember. "I have only read it once, in last November, and nothing will induce me to read it again."

Counsel pressed him as to whether the story was not blasphemous: Wilde answered that it violated every canon of artistic beauty: the story was "disgusting", "horrible", but not "blasphemous." Then he leant forward and said earnestly, "I do not believe that any book or work of art ever had any effect on morality whatever." This obviously seemed a surprising paradox to Carson: the man who said it could surely not be sincere.

Carson had again and again used the word "pose" with ironic emphasis: he did so again. "So far as your work is concerned, you *pose* as not being concerned about morality or immorality?" "I do not know whether you use the word 'pose' in any particular sense."

"It is a favourite word of your own?" "Is it? I have no pose in this matter," answered Wilde, almost apologetically, dropping altogether his flippant air. "In writing a play, or a book, or anything, I am certainly concerned with literature – that is, with art. I aim, not at doing good or evil, but in trying to make a thing that will have some quality of beauty." This, though Carson had no sympathy with the point of view, was Wilde at his best and most sincere. Whether in the melodrama of *Dorian Gray* or *The Ideal Husband*, or the exquisite *Fairy Tales*, or in the sweet triolet, *Do you remember Sicily?* all that was sincere in Wilde was preoccupied with the search for beauty, and its expression in the English language. He did not seek to teach; he sought to reveal.

By a strange paradox, in denying the cause of morality in literature, Wilde had almost become morally earnest. But Carson's questions led him back again to flippancy. Wilde said there was no moral purpose in his work. Why then had he written his "Phrases and Philosophies for the Use of the Young"? One by one they were put to Wilde. As spoken by Carson they sounded shallow and even pernicious, but Wilde's retorts again and again blunted the edge of Carson's construction and irony, and showed the epigrams as something exquisite and delightful. Was not all this quite harmless, and, in Clarke's phrase, "wisdom in a witty form"? Never was Wilde more entertaining in any of his comedies. Carson was like a knight in full armour attacking a dancer. He never faltered in his answers; nor were these always superficial. He passed easily from axiom to epigram.

"Listen, sir; here is one of the 'Phrases and Philosophies for the Use of the Young': 'Wickedness is a myth invented by good people to account for the curious attractiveness of others.' You think that is true?" "I rarely think anything I write is true."

" 'Religions die when they are proved to be true.' Is that true?" "Yes, I hold that. It is a suggestion towards a philosophy of the absorption of religions by science, but surely it is too big a question for you to go into now."

"Do you think that was a safe axiom to put forward for the philosophy of the young?" "Most stimulating."

" 'If one tells the truth one is sure, sooner or later, to be found out'?" "This is a pleasing paradox, but I do not set very high store on it as an axiom."

"Is it good for the young?" "Anything is good that stimulates thought, in whatever age."

" 'Pleasure is the only thing in life one should live for'?" This was surely only a restatement of what both Carson and Wilde had read in many philosophies down to the heyday of Herbert Spencer. The gloss was better than the epigram. "I think that the realisation of oneself is the prime aim of life, and to realise oneself through pleasure is finer than to do so through pain. I am on that point entirely on the side of the Greeks."

Carson next turned to *Dorian Gray*, and said that a decadent construction could be put on that work. "Only by brutes and illiterates," retorted Wilde.

"But an illiterate person reading *Dorian Gray* might consider it such a novel?" "The views of illiterates on art are unaccountable."

Carson put further questions of the views of ordinary individuals upon *Dorian Gray*. "I have no knowledge of the views of ordinary individuals."

"You did not prevent the ordinary individual from buying your book?" "I have never discouraged him."

Carson then went on to put to Wilde views expressed by the characters in *Dorian Gray*, and referred to one character who had adored another man "madly". Had Wilde ever entertained such an adoration? "I have never given adoration to anybody except myself." There was loud laughter at this, but Carson treated it with cold scorn.

He put another passage: "I have adored you extravagantly."

"Do you mean financially?" Wilde asked.

Carson was angry now. "Oh, yes," he said, with deep irony. "Financially. Do you think we are talking about finance?" "I don't know what you are talking about," replied Wilde in mock despair.

"Don't you?" said Carson, reserved and cold again. "Well, I hope I shall make myself very plain before I have done."

Then came a cruel analysis of Wilde's strange letter to Alfred Douglas, which had already made such a bad impression on the jury. Wilde defended it on the highest grounds. "I think it is a beautiful letter," said Wilde. "It is a poem. You might as well cross-examine me as to whether a sonnet of Shakespeare was proper."

"Apart from art," persisted Carson sternly.

"I cannot answer apart from art," said Wilde.

"Suppose a man who was not an artist had written this letter, would you say it was a proper letter?" asked Carson.

"A man who was not an artist could not have written that letter." The laughter which greeted the sustained wit of this dialogue was now mixed with a low murmur of approval.

Carson's Dublin brogue had contrasted strongly, throughout the duel, with the classical accent of the most practised dialectician, and the best conversationalist except perhaps Whistler, in London.

"Can I suggest, for the sake of your reputation, that there is nothing very wonderful in this 'red rose lips' of yours?"

"A great deal depends," retorted Wilde, with an air of politeness, and with obvious reference to Carson's Irish accent, "on the way it is read."

" 'Your slim gilt soul walks between passion and poetry.' Is that a beautiful phrase?"

"Not as *you* read it." The taunt was now flung openly.

"I don't profess to be an artist," replied Carson hotly, "and when I hear you give evidence I am glad I am not."

Carson took another of Wilde's extravagant letters to Douglas. "Is *that* an ordinary letter?" he asked. "Everything I write is extraordinary," was the witness's disarming reply. "I do not *pose* as being ordinary."

So far the honours had all been with the prosecutor, except for the first few questions. It is true to say that Oscar Wilde had scored immensely. He had favourably impressed, not only the people in Court, but the contemporary Press. There had been something sincere in his talk about beauty and the Greek ideal. Very few people could have parried every powerful blow of Carson's by so skilful and light, and withal so good-humoured a blade. The evening newspapers commented in a not unfriendly way on the strange attitude of this "lover of the beautiful" who thought books could not be immoral, who was not concerned to do good or evil, but merely to create beauty: the "wonderful intellectual force and flow of perfect language with which he had defended his positions" was praised, although some doubt was expressed as to what the very workaday British jury had thought of Wilde's views on the "ordinary individual". As in his plays, his wit had delighted the many: but to the few, to some who believed in Oscar's innocence and could not understand Carson's bitterness, the duel began to assume a symbolic form – the struggle of art against philistinism in its most intolerant and British form; to others who knew the truth, another antagonism presented itself; it seemed as if hypocrisy was about to baffle justice.

Carson had done his best: he had prepared his cross-examination with the same thoroughness and care as he had done in the case of Havelock Wilson, and he had failed. No tears this time; not once had he really pierced the joints of his armour. Well, for once he had failed: let him pass on. It was late in the afternoon, and the shadows of evening began to darken the old Court of Tragedies, and with the changing light Carson left the field of literature and he began to question Wilde on a lower and more specific plane, where the Poet of the Beautiful joined company with valets and grooms and blackmailers in dim-lit, curtained, perfumed rooms. But even here Wilde was making a case for himself. He had a great contempt for social distinctions. Why should his characters all come from the drawing-room? He was a student and lover of life and youth. He dismissed the half-sovereign given to the blackmailer with a scornful gesture. "I gave it out of contempt." "Then your way to show your contempt is by paying ten shillings?" asked Carson. "Yes, very often," replied Wilde drily, and regained the sympathy of the Court.

Wilde had asked another young man, employed in a publisher's office, to an expensive dinner at a hotel.

"Was that for the purpose of having an intellectual treat?" asked the advocate.

"Well, for him, yes," answered Wilde. Once more the jury laughed at the man's wit, but it was almost the last kindly laugh that the case aroused in any of the audience. The Court adjourned, and Oscar Wilde had undoubtedly scored a great intellectual triumph over the barrister; his evidence had been a sort of *tour de force*. But it was seen that Carson had many more pages to his brief, and his threat was remembered: "I shall make myself very plain before I have done."

Next day Wilde appeared at about ten minutes past ten: he began to talk and laugh with his second counsel, Charles Mathews, about the reports in the newspapers. Yet he did not look so well or so gay as on the day before. At half-past ten he was already in the box, again smilingly inviting Carson to begin. Today the questioning was far more serious: there was more about those darkened, perfumed rooms; of an old public school man named Taylor, who introduced Wilde to young men in humble situations of life; of specific dates and interviews; of champagne dinners attended by these two men, and young boys of no education or culture to whom Wilde gave presents of jewellery. Wilde must have been amazed at Carson's knowledge of his movements over a period of years.

"Did you know that one was a gentleman's valet, and the other a gentleman's groom?" asked Carson. "I did not know it, and, if I had, I should not have cared," replied Wilde.

"What enjoyment was it to you to be entertaining grooms and

coachmen?" "The pleasure of being with those who are young, bright, happy, careless and original."

Carson: "Had they plenty of champagne?"

Wilde: "What *gentleman* would stint his guests?"

The Court laughed for the very last time – with Wilde.

Carson: "What *gentleman* would stint the valet and the groom!"

Name after name was mentioned; Sir Edward Clarke looked nervously at a letter of one of these people which Carson was handling. Surely it was hardly possible that Carson could be calling these young men to admit terrible charges against themselves. He said really his lordship had better see a very ordinary respectful letter which Wilde had himself produced from one of the persons named.

"Never mind that," said Carson grimly. "Parker himself will be in the box, and the jury will see what he is like."

A whisper of excitement went round the Court. So Carson had the evidence to prove his allegations after all!

Name after name was mentioned: throughout this terrible ordeal Wilde had behaved with quiet dignity and restraint. No matter how wounding had been Carson's suggestions, this arrogant man had never faltered. His evidence yesterday had not been forgotten. The Press had been generous in praising his fine work. There was much that seemed fine about the man himself under this severe cross-examination by his own contemporary at college. If the case was not exactly the butterfly on the wheel, it seemed at any rate to be the man of genius on the rack; would the inexorable lawyer never leave the poet alone?

Wilde had never faltered up till now: Carson mentioned the name of a young servant at Oxford almost casually.

"Did you ever kiss him?" asked Carson with sudden emphasis.

Wilde made a gesture of disgust. "He was a particularly plain boy. He was unfortunately very ugly. I pitied him for it."

It was a deadly question and a fatal reply. That one question told the jury more than all the previous two days of questioning. Carson had almost finished his cross-examination, and this question had been a mere bow drawn at a venture. Both witness and counsel knew the truth was out. The former struggled to escape, but Carson would not let him pass from it. He fastened on to Wilde's answer like a hawk. Why had he given that reason? Why? Why? Wilde strove to explain. Several of his answers began inarticulately: some were broken off unfinished: all were excited and indignant. But Carson was relentless. Why had he mentioned the boy's ugliness? Wilde was almost in tears now, on the point of a breakdown like that of Havelock Wilson. Finally he pulled himself together, and gave the reason. "You stung me by your insolence, sir. You are trying to unnerve me," he cried out pitifully. This was a very different Oscar Wilde from the man who could not answer "apart from art," and who had said, "Not as you read it, Mr Carson."

For he was broken: a further name, more suggestions. Wilde's recovered self-possession disappeared almost at once. Had he done this, and that? "No, it has never occurred – never, *never, never.*" But Carson still pursued him with further questions. The witness, who had almost lolled in the witness-box, recoiled backwards, as if to shield himself: gestures of repudiation, disdain, disgust.

Finally came the words which must have been heard with relief by Oscar Wilde. Only one question more: would he know again a certain waiter at a Paris hotel? The witness winced again. Yes, he thought that he would.

It was the end of the most sensational cross-examination of those times, quiet but not without menace. Sir Edward Clarke rose to re-examine. Carson's attack had been so effective that he realised he must now reluctantly use the letters of Lord Queensberry to his son. These letters revealed the greatest malice towards his wife and children, especially to Alfred Douglas, whose legitimacy he questioned: no one, however august, who had been on close terms with his wife or children was spared from his attacks, not even the Prime Minister, Lord Rosebery, whose private secretary his eldest son had been, and Mr Gladstone, who had made him a peer. But these letters were of little avail now to obscure the prejudice which had gathered round Wilde; they might have been more useful at the beginning. Moreover, the introduction of entirely new documents gave Carson the right to cross-examine Wilde again, and so enjoy the last word.

Before this occurred the Court adjourned till the afternoon. After the interval the Judge came back, and the whole Court waited for the prosecutor. The rumour started, and ran round the Court, that he had abandoned the case and left the country rather than face Carson again. The rumour soon proved a *canard*, for he appeared and apologised to the Judge on the grounds that the clock in his restaurant had been wrong. Carson then destroyed much of the effect of the Queensberry letters by reading a letter to

Wilde written by Alfred Douglas to his father, which was full of hatred and bitterness. Then at last Wilde withdrew from the witness-box. Everybody then expected Clarke to call Lord Alfred Douglas, whose friendship with Wilde was the prime cause of the whole case. Lord Alfred, who afterwards got the better of Marshall Hall, F. E. Smith, and Douglas Hogg in the witness-box in various trials, fully expected it himself. He had been at Wilde's side all through the trial, and was more than anxious to give evidence. There was great surprise when Clarke closed his case "reserving to himself the power to claim to call evidence to rebut anything that may be sprung upon him." All who had followed the case were amazed at Clarke's decision. The last letters had been Alfred Douglas' correspondence, not Wilde's. The strikingly handsome youth had sat beside Wilde all through the trial, coming to the Court and leaving with him in his brougham. Why was Clarke not calling him? Was he afraid of the effect of his evidence or of Carson's terrible questions? It was most peculiar. Probably only lawyers realised that Clarke was pursuing the policy again of keeping Lord Alfred in reserve. While he still had not given evidence, there was still something which might restrain Lord Queensberry and his advisers from making certain allegations against his son. But, after the letters had been read, a reply from Queensberry in any event was almost certain of rebuttal, and, on ordinary rules of advocacy, an obvious refusal to call a relevant witness, who was visible to all in Court, was calculated to do as much harm as any deadly cross-examination of that witness.

Carson now rose to open the case for the defence. Lord Queensberry, he said, withdrew nothing that he had said or written. He had done everything with premeditation and a determination at all risks and hazards to save his son. That was his client's one object. He was glad that the letter containing the Prime Minister's name had been mentioned, which showed that he was in no way connected with the facts of this case. Lord Queensberry's grievance here was purely political. Lord Drumlanrig had been given a seat in the House of Lords which was denied to his father, that was all. Carson then cleverly contrasted the artist and the man in Wilde, which the trial had shown. There was a great contrast between his books, which were for the select and not for the ordinary individual, and the way he chose his friends. Then his excuse was no longer that he was dwelling in regions of art, but that he had such a noble, such a democratic soul – Carson paused, while the Court laughed loudly against Wilde, who had confessed to "no knowledge of the ordinary individual" – such a democratic soul, that he drew no social distinctions, and that it was "quite as much pleasure to have the sweeping-boy from the streets to lunch or dine with him as the greatest litterateur or artist."

"I consider the position absolutely irreconcilable. On Mr Wilde's literature alone, Lord Queensberry's action was justified. A more thinly veiled attempt to cover the real nature of the letter to Lord Alfred, called a sonnet, has never been made in a Court of Justice. My learned friend has said that Wood had stolen the letters from Lord Alfred Douglas. But who was Wood? He too was Alfred, the friend of Wilde, the friend of Taylor. *One of the lot* . . . Taylor, the old public school boy, might have given a little useful information. He was Wilde's bosom friend. Wilde has said he was in close conversation with him only on Tuesday last. *Why has he not been called?*" Carson was now talking very slowly. "Why did Wilde give Wood £16? The one thing that he was anxious for was that Wood should leave the country; so he paid his passage, and, after a farewell luncheon, he shipped him away to New York, and, I suppose, hoped that he would never see him again." There was a pause. "But," said Carson dramatically, "he is here, and will be examined."

At this point there was a great sensation in Court. The Court had once more been growing darker all through this powerful and menacing speech. The atmosphere of comic opera and of high comedy which Wilde had introduced at the beginning of the trial had completely vanished. The evening shadows seemed only symbolic of the darkening shadows of the case itself. Everybody in Court seemed conscious that they were assisting at a great tragedy, the fame of which was indeed already ringing through the world. The climax of the drama had not been reached, but it now seemed to all certain and foredoomed. Even the cultured Judge, who had been obviously impressed, amused, and delighted with Oscar Wilde on the previous day, sat with his head buried in his hands. It was noticeable to everyone that throughout the speech no attack and little mention had been made of Lord Alfred Douglas, except as the son of the defendant. The attack had been concentrated on Wilde. But at the very end Carson used his name. "In view of these disgusting letters from Wilde to Lord Alfred Douglas, I wish to know, are you going to send Lord Queensberry to gaol? I ask you to bear in mind that Lord Queensberry's son is so dominated by Wilde that he threatened to shoot his own father. Lord Queensberry did what he has done most deliberately, and he is not afraid to abide by the issue in this Court."

The Court adjourned at this point. Wilde's hopes had now fallen to the dust. His counsel was dumbfounded by Carson's advocacy, and what it had revealed. It had convinced Sir Edward Clarke that his confident assumption of Wilde's innocence, derived from the most solemn assurance from the man himself, was wrong. He was overcome by a sense of responsibility. If the case proceeded, and Carson, whom he was sure now was not bluffing, were allowed to call that terrible evidence, in the event of an adverse verdict Wilde must be arrested on leaving the Court. The Judge would impound the papers for the use of the Public Prosecutor. This was not the only evil. Lord Alfred Douglas was insistent on being called in rebuttal of evidence given, and, indeed, upon his evidence the only hope now rested. But how could he, a young man of impulsive mind, longing for vengeance on his own father, succeed where Wilde had been brought so low? Might not he too be involved in the tragedy? His duty as counsel too was far from clear. From a consultation with Wilde he was now convinced and certain of Wilde's guilt; how could he go on with the case? His junior, Charlie Mathews, was not in agreement with him. They had no right, as counsel, to assume anything against their client: their duty was to fight the case to a finish: with Carson's many witnesses, the case could be indefinitely prolonged. The witnesses were themselves accomplices and criminals, and little reliance could be placed upon their testimony. The case was far from lost. In the meanwhile, Wilde would have plenty of time to escape if Hamilton Cuffe, the Public Prosecutor, was contemplating arrest. Meanwhile he could hardly prejudice the course of a criminal trial by taking any steps against Wilde till the Queensberry case was over. If they withdrew the prosecution, the authorities would be free to act at once. Both men were actuated by high motives. In the mind of one, professional honour was perhaps foremost; in that of the other, the safety of his client. Oscar Wilde was like a man in a dream. He had lost all power of decision. He did not know which was best; a certain sense of pride and honour prevented him from leaving the country that night. On the other hand, he did not wish to involve Alfred Douglas in further trouble by allowing him to give evidence. He could not make up his mind either to withdraw the prosecution or to go on with it. The fact that Carson had Wood and the others in Court to give evidence against him had taken him completely by surprise. He could not make up his mind: he must try and get a little sleep.

Next morning the Old Bailey presented the same scene, but to-day there was a large crowd waiting outside the Court to see the main figures of the trial arrive. Public interest was intense and extremely hostile to Wilde. Inside the Court the same scene presented itself. There still were the fashionable crowds. There was the Judge and his bouquet; Carson, on his feet ready to begin; and Sir Edward Clarke, looking very white and miserable, sitting by his side. Everyone was present except the principal character, Oscar Wilde, although a pile of letters addressed to the Old Bailey awaited him. The last act was beginning without him. It was, however, noticed that Wilde was not in Court when Carson resumed his speech. Counsel said that he had done with the literary aspect of the case, and with the relationship of Wilde and Alfred Douglas. "I now, unfortunately, approach a more powerful part of the case. I have to bring before you these young men, one after the other, to tell their tales – for an advocate a most distasteful task. One word I will say. These young men are more sinned against than sinning. Let those who would blame them remember that." Carson looked mournfully at the jury; with his sad dignity, he seemed to be like a recording angel. There was, he said, a startling similarity with all those other friendships of Wilde. They were neither his equals in age, in education, nor in social position. "It may be a very noble and generous instinct in some people to wish to level down all social barriers . . . But if Wilde had wanted to assist them, was it a benefit for boys in their class of society for a great man of letters to take them to a magnificent dinner and prime them with the best champagne? . . . After you hear the evidence you will wonder, not that the gossip reached Lord Queensberry's ears, but that the man Wilde has been tolerated for years in Society as he has."

At the beginning of his speech Sir Edward Clarke had gone out, but he had now returned. He touched Carson's sleeve, and they began to consult together in whispers. Everyone guessed something dramatic was about to happen. Had Wilde run away and left his counsel in the lurch?

Carson sat down, and Sir Edward Clarke rose: he began to speak with obvious embarrassment. He put the best face upon the matter that he could. But he relied with some ingenuity for his excuse on the part of the case on which the defence had manifestly failed. He said that it had become clear during the case to Mr Wilde's advisers that the jury might well excuse Lord Queensberry *as a father*, having regard to the passages relied on by the defence, for the expression which he had used. Mr Carson was about to make the most terrible allegations. Since, in his opinion, the jury might well return a verdict of "not guilty" merely on the literary side, it would be manifestly dangerous and contrary to his duty to Mr Wilde to allow the prosecution to continue. For a verdict of "not guilty" for Lord Queensberry, as a result of the literary evidence, would carry an implication of "guilty" on his client on the whole of the allegations in the plea for justification, whatever view the jury might hold as to the terrible charges to be advanced by his learned friend. "I am prepared to submit to a verdict of 'not guilty,' having reference to that part of the particulars which is connected with the publication of *Dorian Gray* and with the publication of *The Chameleon*. I trust, my lord, that that may make an end of the case."

The device was transparent: Sir Edward Clarke was admitting a lesser charge, which had not been made out, in order to avoid far graver and more specific charges which he dared not face.

Mr Carson rose, and pointed out with terse and telling courtesy that a verdict of "not guilty" would mean a verdict of justification on the whole plea. The Judge concurred.

"Then," said Carson, "the verdict will be that complete justification is proved, and that the publication was for the public benefit."

Again the Judge assented, and so charged the jury. Once again, as in the Havelock Wilson case, Carson had succeeded without calling evidence for the defence. Once more he had broken down the witness; once more the complaining party had proved the case for the defence.

There remained only the formalities. "Do you find the complete justification proved or not?" asked the clerk of arraigns. "Yes," replied the foreman of the jury.

"Do you find a verdict of 'not guilty'?" "Yes," replied the foreman.

"And that is the verdict of you all?" "Yes," replied the foreman, "and we also find that the publication was for the public benefit."

There was loud applause heard in Court, which was taken up by a great crowd below. But the ribald demeanour and exultation of this crowd did little credit to the British public opinion, or to the gravity of the occasion. As Carson and Sir Edward Clarke left the Old Bailey together, both exhausted and miserable, they passed through the cheering crowds, and saw loose women dancing wildly in the streets. "What a filthy business!" said Clarke. "I shall not feel clean for weeks."

Oscar Wilde had come to the Old Bailey, but he had not come into Court. He had driven down rather late, and Clarke had gone into Court without further instructions. Clarke had been called into a small consultation-room, and with his approval and advice Wilde had decided to abandon the case. Charles Mathews' strong advice was to continue. He issued at once an explanation to the Press: "It would have been impossible for me to have proved my case without putting Lord Alfred Douglas in the box against his father. Lord Alfred Douglas was extremely anxious to go into the box, but I would not let him do so. Rather than put him in so painful a position, I determined to retire from the case and to bear on my own shoulders whatever ignominy and shame might result from my prosecuting Lord Queensberry. – Oscar Wilde."

After scribbling these words, and while Sir Edward Clarke was making his statement, he hurriedly left the Old Bailey with Lord Alfred Douglas in his brougham; he was observed to drive to the offices of Sir George Lewis in Ely Place.

As soon as Lord Queensberry had been discharged, another letter was written on behalf of the defence:

37 Norfolk Street, Strand.

Hon. Hamilton Cuffe,
    Director of Public Prosecutions,
        Whitehall.
            re Oscar Wilde.
DEAR SIR,
    In order that there may be no miscarriage of justice, I think it my duty to send at once to you a copy of all our witnesses' statements, together with a copy of the shorthand notes of the trial.

Yours faithfully,
CHARLES RUSSELL.

Wilde's interview with Sir George Lewis was not reassuring. "What is the use of coming to me now?" he said. "All this trouble was perfectly unnecessary."

Wilde and Douglas then went to a private room at the Holborn Viaduct Hotel. His carriage remained outside. George Wyndham, MP, Lord Alfred's cousin, came to see them. He was to warn Wilde to escape abroad, as a warrant might be issued for his arrest at any moment. But Wilde would not see him. After luncheon, he drove from the Viaduct Hotel to the Cadogan Hotel, where Alfred Douglas was staying. He passed through Fleet Street, where he had worked and written, along the Embankment, past the Savoy Hotel, where he had dined so often, through the Mall and Birdcage Walk, past the early flowers and green lawns of St. James's and the Green Parks, till he reached his destination. On his way he stopped at a bank, where he drew a considerable sum of money by a cheque payable to self. It is impossible to withhold pity from this man of genius, but yesterday so arrogant and proud, now driving for the last time through the scenes he knew and loved so well. What terrible reflections and apprehensions must have been his as he drove along, past the familiar places, his "wonderful life" wrecked for ever. Did he know, as he sat huddled in a corner, that another carriage was following him?

He reached the Cadogan Hotel. He had decided to go abroad that night. A friend and neighbour of his was walking up Tite Street at about 6.45, and saw a cab piled high with luggage outside Wilde's house; he noticed that his mother, Lady Wilde, the distinguished Irish poetess, was superintending the loading of the cab. Alas! too late; a newspaper boy was coming up the street, shouting at the top of his voice, "Arrest of Oscar Wilde."

Shortly after six, Inspector Richards and Sergeant Allan of Scotland Yard found Wilde at the Cadogan Hotel. They had a warrant for his arrest. "Really," said Wilde, and he stumbled out of the hotel into a waiting cab. He was seen to be very drunk. He was taken to Scotland Yard and then to Bow Street, and charged. He spent the night in prison; he could not eat, and all night paced and paced his cell in deep and black despair. The Poet of the Beautiful. Poor Wilde, he was to see nothing of beauty again for more than two years, except what suffering could reveal from the depths.

Almost at the same time as that of Wilde's arrest, Edward Carson walked slowly into the precincts of the Palace of Westminster. A crowd of members and correspondents were waiting for him in the Lobby. Bitter political opponents like Tim Healy and Swift McNeill, his countrymen and Wilde's, patted him on the back. "Well, done," they said. Carson shrugged his shoulders. It had been a filthy business: he was tired and exhausted. Whatever else, it was certainly no cause for congratulation. "Did you ever compete against Wilde at Trinity?" asked a Lobby correspondent. "I was never an infant prodigy," said Carson, and moodily walked off to the library to be by himself. "He does not seem to be in a hurry, even now," said the correspondent.

Nevertheless, it was felt that justice had been done, according to Lord Halsbury's prophecy, and that Carson had rid England of a pest, at whatever cost to her fair name in the world; and the cost was great, perhaps not yet fully paid. Hundreds of congratulatory letters reached him, of which he kept only two:

Central Criminal Court,
City of London, E.C.,
5th April, 1895.

DEAR CARSON, – I never heard a more powerful speech, or a more searching cross-exam.

I congratulate you on having escaped most of the filth.

Yours ever,
R. HENN COLLINS.

Another tribute came from a distinguished firm of American lawyers, far away in New York State:

First National Bank Building,
Carlton, N.Y., *Ap. 9th, 1895.*

Hale and Bowers,
    Counsellors at Law.

SIR, – I judge from newspaper reports that your cross-examination of Oscar Wilde is one of the finest examples of the art of cross-examination in recent times. If you have a verbatim copy in pamphlet form I would esteem it a great favor to receive one. Or if you cannot supply it, will you kindly inform me where I can procure it.

Very respectfully yours,
J. P. HALE.

But his career was only beginning, and the future lay before him: for him was waiting a great cause, the love of a whole people, fame, and, despite bitter political disappointment and private griefs, as much personal happiness as falls to the lot of most mortals. While for Wilde, whose name, by an ignoble compromise, was then being removed from the St James's and Haymarket Theatres, where his plays, *The Importance of Being Earnest* and *An Ideal Husband*, were being performed, there remained overwhelming obloquy, imprisonment, poverty, a short-lived repentance, mental and physical decay, and an agonising death. The fact that his sufferings secured for his writings, which might otherwise have had a short-lived popularity limited to his own countrymen, after his death a world-wide and lasting fame, probably did not occur and certainly would have been no comfort to this child of his own time and of this world, who was, as Mr A. C. Benson has said, "so gifted, so brittle, and withal so lovable."

He was tried on a criminal charge, but Carson would have nothing to do with it: a prosecution was a different matter. The jury disagreed, and the Judge, Mr Justice Charles, it was said, would only have sentenced him to a six-months' term. Carson then went to his friend Sir Frank Lockwood, the Solicitor-General, who was to prosecute. "Cannot you let up on the fellow now?" he said. "He has suffered a great deal."

"I would," said Lockwood, "but we cannot: we dare not: it would at once be said, both in England and abroad, that owing to the names mentioned in Queensberry's letters we were forced to abandon it." So Wilde was tried again, this time immediately after the man Taylor, whose conviction was certain and his guilt obvious; the immediately preceding conviction of a man known to be his associate was certain to prejudice him. This time a law officer, Sir Frank Lockwood himself, led for the prosecution: in the previous trial Mr Charles Gill had led. It was thus that his conviction was secured. He was punished with two years' imprisonment, with hard labour – a savage sentence; and, had the Court of Criminal Appeal existed then, it is possible that either the conviction, owing to the circumstances of the trial and uncorroborated evidence of the accomplices, or the sentence, which was a heavy one, would not have stood.

He was defended passionately on both occasions by Sir Edward Clarke, who charged no fee. In the interval between the two trials he was granted bail in thousands of pounds. One of the sureties was Lord Douglas of Hawick, Lord Alfred's eldest surviving brother. Such, however, was the obloquy into which the name of the once popular poet had fallen, that no other friend would stand bail for him. It was left to a stranger, a young English clergyman, to come forward to offer the risk of a heavy fine if Wilde escaped, to whom, as he said, Wilde "had shown Beauty on a high hill." During the interval Wilde was given the means of escape, and perhaps the authorities would have welcomed it; Wilde would not do it and leave his sureties in the lurch. Frank Harris, in his *Life of Wilde*, uses this as evidence of Wilde's weakness and lack of resolution. Should it not be credited to him for honour? That the verdict was just, there can be no doubt. He confessed to Harris before the second trial, who was genuinely surprised. But, even so, to a lawyer at least, or to anyone interested in the administration of justice, it does not dispose of the question of whether or no he was unfairly convicted.

There remains only to be recorded a circumstance as strange and terrible as the culminating scene in *Dorian Gray*. Some years afterwards, Edward Carson was walking by himself in Paris on a wet day in the early months of the year. He was about to cross the street when the driver of a *fiacre*, with Parisian recklessness, almost ran him down, and splashed his clothes with mud. He stepped back quickly on to the pavement, and knocked someone down. Turning round to apologise, he saw a man lying in the gutter, and recognised the haggard, painted features of Oscar Wilde! Like a flash, his mind went back to that occasion eight years before, in London, when Wilde's fine carriage had almost overrun him. The eyes of the two men met, and they recognised each other. Carson turned round and said, "I beg your pardon." Wilde, under the name of Sebastian Melmoth, was living in Paris, dying of a terrible disease, "beyond his means," as he observed with the wit which never deserted him, preying on the generosity of his friends: in a week or two he was dead.

ACKNOWLEDGMENTS
AND SOURCES

Once again, the editor wishes to express his gratitude to Jonathan Goodman and Wilf Gregg for allowing him the run of their encyclopaedic collections of true-crime books containing many of the cases featured.

He would also like to thank the following for their kind permission to reprint the extracts indicated:

Sybille Bedford for an extract from the Bodkin Adams trial in *The Best We Can Do* (Collins, London 1958);

Rogers, Coleridge & White Ltd for an extract from *The Age of Illusion* by Ronald Blythe (Hamish Hamilton, London 1963) © Ronald Blythe 1963;

Albert I. Borowitz for *The 'Fatal Attraction' Murder* in *Crimes Gone By: Collected Essays of Albert Borowitz 1966–2005* (*The Legal Studies Forum* vol XXIX, no 2, University of West Virginia, Morgantown, WV, 2005) © Albert Borowitz 1994;

The Estate of Joan Colenbrander for F. Tennyson Jesse, Introduction to *The Trial of Rattenbury and Stoner* (Hodge, Edinburgh 1935);

Constable & Robinson for H. Montgomery Hyde, *The Good Shoemaker and the Poor Fishpedlar* from *Crime Has Its Heroes* (Constable, London 1976);

Malcolm Gaskill and Felicity Bryan Literary Agency for an extract from *Hellish Nell : Last of Britain's Witches* (Fourth Estate, London 2001) © Malcolm Gaskill 2001;

Hodder Headline for an extract from *The Robbers' Tale* by Peta Fordham (Hodder and Stoughton, London 1965), reproduced by permission of Hodder and Stoughton Ltd.;

Liverpool Post for its abridgment of William Cooper, *Shall We Ever Know?* (Hutchinson, London 1971);

His Honour Alan King-Hamilton for Janie Jones from *And Nothing But The Truth* (Weidenfeld & Nicolson, London 1982) © Alan King-Hamilton 2006;

The Trustees of the Estate of the late Edgar Lustgarten for *Modern Suite for Strings* (the case of Elvira Barney) from *Defender's Triumph* (Allan Wingate, London 1951) © Edgar Lustgarten 1951;

Solo Syndication for Brian Masters on the O. J. Simpson trial from the *Mail on Sunday* (1 October 1995);

Blake Morrison, Granta Books and Peters Fraser & Dunlop Group for an extract from *As If* (Granta Books, London 1997) © Blake Morrison 1997;

Robin Odell for an extract from *Exhumation of a Murder: The Life and Trial of Major Armstrong* (Harrap, London 1975, © Robin Odell 2006);

Penguin Group for Truman Capote, extract from *In Cold Blood* (Hamish Hamilton, London 1966) © Truman Capote 1965 and renewed 1993 by Alan U. Shwartz. Used by permission of Random House, Inc.;

The extract from William Herbert Wallace's *Life Story* is from a typescript in the editor's collection, © Roger Wilkes 2006;

Rebecca West, extract from *William Joyce and Some Others* in *The Meaning of Treason* (Macmillan, London 1949) Copyright © Estate of Rebecca West 1947, by permission of PFD on behalf of the Estate of Rebecca West;

Solo Syndication for A. N. Wilson on the Rosemary West trial in the London *Evening Standard* (23 November 1995).

Every effort has been made to trace the original copyright holders of the following, without success; the editor and publishers would be pleased to hear from any claimants to legal copyright of :

Arthur La Bern, extract from the trial of G. J. Smith in *The Life and Death of a Ladykiller* (Leslie Frewin, London 1967);

George Bishop, extract from *Witness to Evil: The Inside Story of the Tate/LaBianca Murder Trial* (Nash Publishing, Los Angeles 1971);

William Bolitho, extract from *The Poetry of Desire Landru* in *Murder for Profit* (Dennis Dobson, London 1953);

Tom Cullen, extract from *Crippen: The Mild Murderer* (Bodley Head, London 1977);

Rupert Furneaux, *Harry Thaw* from *Courtroom USA 1* (Penguin Books, 1962);

Nina Warner Hooke and Gil Thomas, extract from the Fahmy case in *Marshall Hall : a biography* (Arthur Barker Ltd., London 1966);

Pamela Hansford Johnson, extract from the trial of Brady and Hindley in *On Inquity* (Macmillan, 1967);

Edward Marjoribanks, extract from *The Oscar Wilde Case* in *The Life of Lord Carson* (Gollancz, London 1932);

Ronald Maxwell, *The Christie Case* (R. S. Gray 1954);

Damon Runyon on the Capone trial in the New York *American* (1930);

John T. Scopes, *The Trial That Rocked the Nation* in *Great True Stories of Crime, Mystery and Detection* (Reader's Digest, Sydney 1965);

George Waller, extract from the trial of Bruno Hauptmann in *Kidnap* (Hamish Hamilton, London 1961).